modern chess.

move by move

Colin Crouch

EVERYMAN CHESS

www.everymanchess.com

First published in 2009 by Gloucester Publishers plc (formerly Everyman Publishers plc),
Northburgh House, 10 Northburgh Street, London EC1V 0AT

First published 2009 by Gloucester Publishers plc

British Library Cataloguing-in-Publication Data
A catalogue record for this book is available from the British Library.

ISBN 978 185744 599 2

Distributed in North America by The Globe Pequot Press, P.O Box 480,
246 Goose Lane, Guilford, CT 06437-0480.

All other sales enquiries should be directed to Everyman Chess, Northburgh House,
10 Northburgh Street, London EC1V 0AT
tel: 020 7253 7887 fax: 020 7490 3708
email: info@everymanchess.com
website: www.everymanchess.com

EVERYMAN CHESS SERIES (formerly Cadogan Chess)
Chief advisor: Byron Jacobs
Commissioning editor: John Emms
Assistant editor: Richard Palliser

Typesetting and editing by First Rank Publishing, Brighton.
Cover design by Horatio Monteverde.
Printed and bound in America by Versa Press.

Contents

Preface

This is by far the most ambitious of the various chess books and articles I have written. To have analysed in detail a win by 33 different 2700+ grandmasters against 2600+ strength opposition is a big effort. It is fair to say that no writer could even have considered such a task fifteen years ago. One reason is that only Kasparov and Karpov had reached this chess stratospheric level, although a few others were pressing hard. Chess has changed considerably during the age of the computer, and players have had the opportunity of improving their play and understanding considerably.

Without the computer, I myself would only be able to scratch the surface in analysing the games, and would not be able to say with confidence whether such a move is good or a mistake. It is good not to have to guess. Of course, in some positions the play is so complicated, or so subtle, or both, that even the computers and the strongest players would find it beyond themselves to understand everything. Quite often it is a major task of the top players to try to understand what is going on in such difficult lines, on the basis that if the top player has been able to analyse the position in depth at home, and is capable of outplaying the opponent over the board, there is an excellent chance to win. A 2600 grandmaster is still a very strong grandmaster, but a 2700+ grandmaster will take his opponent out of their comfort zone. We must not forget that ultra-sophisticated positional play can also work.

The main dedication I give is to the players who have dedicated themselves to such high levels of chess. Without them, there would have been no book.

The games themselves were at the time completely fresh to me. After a serious brain seizure in 2004, I was fortunate that I was able to play chess, or even see the board. I feel grateful in having the opportunity, with this book, to catch up with so many marvellous games, and even participate in discussing them.

It turned out that it has taken almost a whole year to write up such an effort. The world outside has changed considerably in terms of chess, and the world in general. At some stage, I will no doubt want to catch up with the world of chess from Easter 2008 onwards. Outside chess, there has been a year of financial and economic crisis. It seems a long, long time since I wrote a PhD on the economics of recession and unemployment in Britain in the early 1980s, and I would like to think that the argument I made at the time still has merit. The question was always not whether there would be another serious recession, but when. Naturally there has always been the dominant opposite argument, among politicians, economists, journalists and others, that the economy is stable, that there is no such thing as unemployment, that the banks have stabilized growth, and that politicians have ended the problems of boom and bust. It will be of interest to see how the orthodox thinkers will now empirically justify such a point of view.

Colin Crouch
Harrow
July 2009

Introduction

This book is based on games by contemporary players at the very highest level. The idea is based around a move-by-move approach to annotation, with the hope that players from all levels will be able to appreciate something of top-level chess.

Do not be excessively deterred at what might seem a long-winded approach, a dozen or more detailed pages over a single game. Chess is complicated. While writing up this book, I played through Sergey Shipov's annotations of Shirov-Aronian, Moscow 2006 (Game 16), in *New in Chess Magazine* (2006, vol. 8, pp. 23-35). Shipov went through the first 22 moves at great speed, and commented that the players have reached 'another deep-water tabiya. The best analysts in the world began their analysis in positions which simple chess amateurs are not even capable of reaching.' Which is, of course, absolutely believable. The problem for the reader is that Shipov gives no analysis. This is understandable enough, since space is precious, and there is no room to go through moves which are already established and analysed. Where does this leave the reader, though? Half the content of the game has been dropped in the annotations, and the simple chess amateur has no chance of trying to understand what is going on. One of the main aims in this book is to try to bridge the gap in understanding between the amateur and the top players, which I suppose means I must regard myself as somewhere midpoint in this gap. It is up to the reader to decide how deeply, or how briefly, he or she would want to explore the opening. There is no obligation to try to plough through every variation.

There is also another reason, beyond the opening part of the game, why the analysis might seem long-winded. The point is that a top-level grandmaster when writing up games will tend to concentrate only on the most difficult positions, and will tend to ignore writing down what is seen as 'obvious'. The obvious points are, though, absolutely fundamental to good chess, and no top grandmaster will ignore them while playing a competitive game. A player may note that there is a simple back-row checkmate if he snatches a piece, and he will avoid this. It would seem hardly worthwhile to mention this elementary tactic while annotating, but the tactic is central to the game, and needs if possible to be mentioned.

Inevitably there will need to be some juggling when trying to annotate games which will be satisfactory both for stronger players and for the less-experienced player. My hope is that everyone will be able to gain something.

As time goes on in chess, analysis tends to become more complicated. The use of the computer means that an author is these days expected to cover long strings of analysis. There is no longer any excuse. Nowadays it will be easy enough for the reader to check, with the help of the computer, whether the author might be dodging critical lines. In the old days an author might give a one-move line in a complicated position, saying that 'White is better' or 'Black has compensation for the pawn', or whatever, and not much is gained. Perhaps before the computer, it would have taken a whole afternoon for the writer to try to work out what is going on, in even a relatively uncomplicated position, and it is often better to be more economical with the time. With the help of the computer, it is now possible to delve into any position or variation. This makes things both easier and more complicated. One can jump much higher, but the bar is also much higher. There is also the standard warning that the computer can make mistakes in interpreting a position. The best analysis is through the combination of the computer and human assessment. If pushed, I would argue that a conscientious human analyst without the use of the computer would still be preferable to the routine use of the computer.

It would be flattering if 2700+ players were to be interested in this book, but no doubt they will be able to show that I have misinterpreted parts of the game. Such is life. As the reader will be able to verify, there are 33 games in this book in which a 2600+ player has done something wrong, and lost. I cannot pretend that I too will not have made some extra errors, maybe serious. The hope of the annotator is always that new and good ideas will outweigh the introduction of extra errors. Of course, the audience would be extremely small if I were trying to write for the top 33 players. What guidance might there be for the much wider chess public?

Good and interesting chess games are always complicated. There is no way of avoiding this. The most complicated positions may take up two pages of analysis, to decide whether the grandmaster has in fact found the best move, or whether a mistake has been made. The cardinal rule of scientific chess theory is that if a player loses a game, he must have made a mistake somewhere. The conscientious chess writer is always extremely interested in trying to untangle where the decisive mistake has been made, and will also be worried about the possibility that a question mark is given, maybe by the author himself, maybe by other commentators, when the supposed error is in fact sound.

Much of the analysis in a game will concentrate on the technical point of whether any move is correct, or a mistake. This might seem boring and technical, but it is not. There is only such a small gap between a mistake and a brilliant move that it is a wonder that so few mistakes are made at higher levels. In a really complicated position, two amateur players may make half a dozen slips each, and one of them eventually wins, and the other player loses. It will still be a good and entertaining game, but a really top grandmaster will be able to guide his way through even the most mind-blowing positions, and will often be able to find a win after even the slightest of the opponent's mistakes. This is great chess, and vastly entertaining chess, at the highest level.

When playing though these games, it is probably best to skim through the games first time around. Gain the general features of the game, and then look at the position more closely next time. Take note of the careful thought behind the modern opening in chess, take note of the mistakes of the loser in each game, and also enjoy the creativity of chess.

Some Points on the Chess Rating System

We start with the final official tournament event of Garry Kasparov, Linares 2005. It is, of course, quite possible that he may decide that he will try a tournament or match at some subsequent event, but on the other hand, why bother? He has already made his mark in history, and this will never be forgotten for as long as chess is played. He now has other interests.

If we go back to the match when Kasparov beat Karpov to become World Champion in 1985, Kasparov's rating was 2700, and Karpov's 2720. These days, there are now more than 30 players who have reached 2700. There has been considerable speculation as to whether the ratings have been inflated to some extent. Certainly from playing through the current games, one feels the 2700 player is not quite as strong as Kasparov in 1985. This, however, is a relatively small gap. A guesstimate would be that Kasparov's 2700 at the beginning of the match would equate to about 2725 these days, and Karpov's 2720 would have been the equivalent to 2745 nowadays. Going through other players, Timman would probably have been equivalent of around 2700 at that time, but no-one else. We provide this merely as a base-mark.

Kasparov continued to improve considerably since 1985, and it was clear at the time that he was not yet at his peak. In Belgrade 1989 he won, three points ahead of Timman and Ehlvest, and rather more points ahead of other 2600+ opposition. His reward was to reach 2800 for the first time, for himself or for anyone.

Kasparov's rating dropped slightly, at various times during the 1990s, but then between 1997 and his retirement in 2005, his play was consistently over 2800. Other players, such as Anand, Kramnik and Topalov, have reached 2800, but have since dropped down again at some point. In early 2004, for example, both Anand and Kramnik had a frustrating 2799 rating score, while Topalov was 2780, although the Bulgarian is now back over 2800.

No player as yet has emulated Kasparov's achievement in keeping his rating over 2800 for a consistent length of time. We have many players now who would like to aspire to this challenge, but who will fully emulate it? Maybe one of the younger players? Who knows?

The Games

I wanted to write up games from 2004 onwards, for strong personal reasons. As a result of a stroke, a 'brain attack', and a loss of much of my eyesight, I had missed seeing many top-level encounters. It was time to rectify this gap, and to try to study the game properly.

How could I decide which games to use in this book? There soon turned out to be an obvious and natural answer. Garry Kasparov retired at the beginning of 2005. My aim was to select a game from Linares 2005, and then to give a win by any players who were over 2700 at any stage since the beginning of that Linares. What I had not appreciated at the time was that this involved 33 players. This involved roughly twice as many players to study, and twice as many games, than I had originally anticipated.

A Summary of the Outcome of the Game

In each of these 33 games, one of the players wins, and consequently the opposing player must have made a mistake. It is quite possible that both players may have made a mistake. If neither player makes a mistake, the game necessarily ends up as a draw.

In only one game, the Jakovenko one, have I deliberately chosen in advance a game in which the winner made a serious mistake, but then recovered. In many other games, when I made my selection, I felt that in many lines the win seems so paradoxical that this must immediately be chosen as of great interest. Sometimes such a game will, under closer examination, prove to be a flawless brilliancy. More often alas, it will prove to be interesting but almost certainly unsound.

It is hoped that none of the chosen games is boring, too one-sided, or contains too many amateur mistakes.

After having attempted to analyse in detail over thirty games, it is of some interest to give an assessment of how many of these wins prove to be flawless, or perhaps only with minor flaws (for example, a slight hesitancy on move 39), and how many of these wins prove, on closer examination, to contain mistakes made on both sides. It often is the case that the ultimate winner tried too hard to win early on, and overpressed, but that the opponent felt under pressure, and also made mistakes.

We can jot up the preliminary results.

1) Clean wins

Dreev, Game 2; Adams, Game 3; Bacrot, Game 5; Anand, Game 6; Svidler, Game 7; Nisipeanu, Game 8; Leko, Game 9; Ivanchuk, Game 10; Bareev, Game 12; Kramnik, Game 13; Navara, Game 14; Aronian, Game 16; Grischuk, Game 18; Radjabov, Game 19; Eljanov, Game 21; Carlsen, Game 23; Wang Yue, Game 26; Ponomariov, Game 28; Bu Xiangzhi, Game 29; Gelfand, Game 30; Mamedyarov, Game 31; and Karjakin, Game 33.

Thus two-thirds of the games may be regarded as clean games, which does not necessarily imply that the winner played a 'textbook' win, clearly refuting the opponent's play in classic style, although some such games are included. This seems an impressively high proportion. In my previous book, *Great Attackers*, based on games by the young Kasparov, Tal and Stein, there is a far fewer proportion of clean wins, certainly so if one excludes textbook games when the loser makes an unnecessary mistake early on, and the winner makes an attractive exhibition. Play seems to have tightened up since a generation ago. One obvious tendency is that with the help of the computer, strong players have been able to analyse much deeper, and cut out so many plausible slips. In many of the most complicated lines in this book, both players will have been able to examine the position at home, and will have avoided mistakes in the first twenty moves, even in the most complicated lines. Yet wins still happen!

2) Not so clean wins

Kasparov*, Game 1; Topalov*, Game 4; Akopian, Game 11; Polgar, Game 15; Shirov, Game 17; Jakovenko, Game 20; Alekseev, Game 21; Kamsky*, Game 24; Morozevich, Game 25; Cheparinov, Game 27*; and Ni Hua, Game 32.

An asterisk indicates that the doubt is according to whether the opening is completely accurate, and that the rest of the game seems clean. In most of the other games, the problem is one of over-exuberance.

A simple list of statistics is useful, but also only the start of our analysis. We need to move further.

Many of the doubly-flawed games given above are of such extreme complexity that even the strongest of strongest grandmasters, such as Topalov, Anand and Shirov will make serious mistakes, but usually through excessive imagination, rather than lack of understanding.

One of the most interesting encounters is Game 17, **Shirov**-Illescas. This illustrates the great dilemma in attacking chess. On the one hand, the choice is to go for the imaginative and dangerous attack, with the full knowledge that he will be unable to calculate everything through to the end, and that he could easily miss a vital resource. On the other hand, he could play solidly. Illescas's resource would have been extremely difficult to find over the board, and indeed he later missed it, and lost. Shirov could have played objectively quieter, still with good results. But what a game!

An even more extravagant encounter is Game 4, **Topalov**-Anand, where Topalov sacrificed a knight in the opening, almost out of thin air. Anand's king was slightly exposed, but could it really work? It turned out that Black's light-squared weaknesses were just about serious enough to give White interesting attacking chances, so long as White did not mind sacrificing the exchange as well. This was amazing play, but Anand had a couple of good opportunities to improve his play, and rather less complicated than Illescas's slip. Topalov too made a slip later.

A third flawed win is Game 20, Ni Hua-**Jakovenko.** Here Jakovenko was caught by his opponent's opening preparation, and was soon in deep trouble with his king, fastened down by his opponent's queen and bishop. It was startling for the author to find that he was able to win. There was indeed a win, but Ni Hua missed a tactic. Under the microscope, there were other slips by either side beforehand, so it was not quite the perfect defence after a serious mistake.

The wins by Polgar, Alekseev and Morozevich all demonstrated considerable enterprise, but perhaps excessively so. In Game 21, **Alekseev**-Tkachiev, White's idea, of ♗c1-g5-c1, just to provoke an ...f6 pawn push, is wonderfully original; a new idea in a recently explored opening, but sadly one cannot fully believe it.

As so often in battles between attack and defence, Game 15, Sokolov-**Polgar**, saw the eventual winner play more consistently aggressive chess than her opponent, and won, but objectively the win seems to be not quite convincing. In the end, Polgar reached victory with a string of sacrifices in front of the opposing king.

This previous game was relatively finely balanced. Morozevich's win, Game 25, was, it has to be admitted, much more of a sophisticated hack, but with an excellent tactical finish. See the comments on the discussion on symmetrical openings.

Game 27, **Cheparinov**-Nepomniachtchi led to an extremely sharp sacrificial gambit from the opening. Many of the other games in this collection are just as sharp, but in the end seem to be sound. In the Cheparinov game, momentarily Black had the chance of a serious edge, but Nepomniachtchi recaptured a pawn at the wrong time. It was to Nepomniachtchi's credit that he found probably the best line in the opening battle, when many players would have folded much earlier. Sometimes, when tactical play dominates, there is only a small gap between safety and a quick loss.

Game 32, Inarkiev-**Ni Hua**, was another gambit line, this time, one suspects, the product of improvisation rather than close analysis. Black had positional pressure, and there were plenty of tactical opportunities throughout, making it difficult for the defender. Ni Hua won, but the gambit was unnecessary, as he could easily have gained equality without risk.

Attack on the King

We have noted the slightly suspect attacking wins, and we have already suggested that there is often a strong degree of risk when playing for an attack. It is more remarkable, perhaps, quite how many of these attacks prove to be sound, in often incredibly sharp games. The ultimate winner not only senses that the apparently risky attack proves to be sound, but also avoids making any serious mistakes in the subsequent play. This is quite an achievement.

If neither attacker nor defender avoids mistakes, the end result should be a draw, however wild the position is. An extremely sharp sacrifice could end up as a draw by perpetual check. This is not accidental, but absolutely central to the theory of positional chess. The attacker cannot force checkmate, as he has not got enough pieces. The defender's king cannot reach complete safety, however, and he cannot take full advantage with the extra material. Play through many of the sidelines in these games, and you will find many examples of perpetual checks.

The impression still remains, though, that in practical terms it is more likely for the attacker to win than the defender in a tense position.

Winning Opening Innovations

A new idea in the opening can often be just as devastating in the era of the computer, as under the chess of old. Consider Game 31, **Mamedyarov**-Nepomniachtchi. Quite clearly, Mamedyarov has thought long and hard about the Semi-Slav, and has found something sharp and original, even from an early stage. This is quite an achievement. Nepomniachtchi found himself off-balance, and had to improvise. He found a plausible way of counter-attacking by threatening a knight with a check, but Mamedyarov simply carried on his pawn storm, with the help of tactics based on discovered checks.

This game was played in April 2008. As a matter of policy, I have made a cut-off point of analysis in all games in this book, not considering any games played after then. There are probably some extremely relevant games in the year beyond. I do not as yet know. All I have is my own thoughts, which might be good or not so good. Others will no doubt take the chance of analysing these new ideas.

Strangely enough, the other great quick theoretical win, Game 6, Karjakin-**Anand** is now very much a side-line, not so much because the line of the loser was abandoned, but rather because the line of the winner was abandoned. What happened is that both players were studying a newly fashionable position, and both players were considering a particular position, which at first sight looked good for White, and Karjakin played it, having analysed it. Anand anticipated this, playing effectively a second-string option in order allow his opponent to fall for a brilliant double-piece attack.

In contrast, in Game 28, Eljanov-**Ponomariov**, Eljanov decided to try some offbeat theory, and quickly lost. The idea was far from senseless, and indeed there may well have been an improvement for White, with chances of a slight edge. Eljanov developed his pieces actively, but his king was slightly exposed, if somehow Ponomariov could get at the king. A well-reasoned pawn sacrifice, to open up lines against the king, cut back Eljanov's attempts, and he soon made a tactical oversight, losing quickly.

More Attacking Games...

Not all attacking games are won so quickly, of course.

Sometimes games may become remarkably intense, bolstered by the possibility that both White and Black have studied the opening in great detail, perhaps twenty moves or so deep. There will still be unexplored complications over the next twenty moves, and quite often some extremely complicated lines may arise. Game 19, Van Wely-**Radjabov**, was a sequel to a long theoretical battle between the two participants. Not even such players of the positional resourcefulness as Radjabov and Van Wely could have played such intensive and accurate chess without the help of home analysis. This must surely be regarded as a great tactical game, with both players having to find great ingenuity. Even the apparent slight slips around move 27, by both players, while writing up their games for publication, will have their reason. Sometimes if you have to play the same opening again, it is best not to give away all one's secrets.

For this writer, the ideal game of chess would involve sharp theoretical thinking, good and accurate play by both sides, outstandingly wild tactics, plenty of paradox on both sides, and if at all possible, interesting endgame play. In the Van Wely-Radjabov game, we did not have the endgame battle, but with 27 ♗b3!? that would have followed. White's queen and two bishops would have been strangely ineffective in an endgame against queen, knight and pawn.

Advocates of the King's Indian will often argue that this opening is the most interesting of all openings. We have just discussed a win by Black, but White too may come on top. Our next example, Game 29, **Bu Xiangzhi**-Zvjaginsev, is a complete all-out attack in a Sämisch, White rushing through the g- and h-pawns, and being prepared to abandon a few pawns, and giving up pieces as well. All depends on forcing the black king into the open, by chopping off a few black pawns, and eliminating the dark-squared bishop in front of Black's king. My initial assumption was that White's attack was probably unsound. I am pleased to say that Bu Xiangzhi's play seems to holds water. If so, this is an excellent result for the attack.

In a different opening, the Ruy Lopez, Game 14, **Navara**-Socko, caused considerable theoretical interest. Navara sacrificed a knight on g5 for two pawns, to pin Black's knight against the queen. The main motif in the game was the struggle against the knight. Nevertheless, the slightest lapse by Black on the kingside would soon lead to a mating attack.

Game 2, **Dreev**-Dominguez, was an entertaining attacking game, with sacrifices in front of the black king. White had previously given up both f- and g-pawns to open up lines for the rook, and Black's knight was stuck on the edge on h3, unable to return to help defend. Dreev's initial pawn sacrifice seemed sound, but there is the possibility that he overpressed later on. Dominguez, however, did not find the best move, and lost.

Winning the Endgame

So ends the theme of tactics against the king. This is an important part of chess, but by no means the whole of chess. If Black defends fully accurately, White cannot force a win by a direct mating attack.

One might argue that any other type of win could be regarded as a 'positional', unless there is a gross attack by the loser. Sometimes the last part of a win is through tactics, although throughout the preliminaries the battle has been mainly positional. Jumping ahead, Game 30, Gelfand's win in this book is very much of this kind.

Before this, we consider endgame wins.

Pure Endgame Strategy

It is a remarkable achievement in chess to create a pure endgame win, where the player keeps a microscopic edge, and holds it, keeping a slight advantage through to the endgame without any distraction of tactical complications. Then at the end of the game, one wonders how on earth the loser made a mistake, all his moves ending up so natural, and yet leading to a zero.

There are also games in which it is clearly level at the start of the endgame, and yet one of the players makes a microscopic slip, and his position deteriorates, and continues to deteriorate. Endgames win games.

Kramnik is perhaps the greatest exponent of the microscopic edge in current chess. Our next example, Game 13, **Kramnik**-Leko, is already a modern classic. There is a flurry of tactics in the opening, but this is a very well-known line, where the queens soon get exchanged, and many games at high level soon end up as quick draws. Kramnik wonders, though, whether he can still play for a win, with the comfortable option of taking the draw at any time. It works. The pawn structure is almost symmetrical, but Kramnik has slightly the better bishop in an opposite-coloured bishop ending, and his knight is more forceful than Black's. Kramnik scored the full point.

Then there is another bishop and opposite-coloured endgame, this time with a couple of extra rooks on either side. Game 23, **Carlsen**-Tiviakov, looked as though it had been heading for a draw for a long time, but Carlsen fixed on a slight opportunity for his bishops, with his own bishop on d4 being protected by a pawn on e3, while Black's bishop had no coverage to protect the pawn on d5. Before too long, Tiviakov was close to zugzwang.

In Game 22, Stellwagen-**Eljanov**, Black puts in a lot of hard work in a Berlin Variation, Ruy Lopez, but it is difficult to try for an edge, his c-pawns being doubled, and White having an extra kingside pawn. Eljanov sets up a thematic pawn sacrifice to double his opponent's pawns, but even here this does not seem to force a win. Stellwagen blunders, presumably short of time, exchanging his bishop for knight, with a losing pawn endgame. Remarkably, it would seem that the knight could have been left on the board, allowing the loss of a couple of pawns, but with a likely draw.

Clear-cut Positional Chess

There are many more examples on the endgame to be considered, but these tend to lead to complicated mixtures of middlegame and endgame themes. We will consider these later. For the time being, we concentrate on clear-cut positional chess in the middlegame. The attack on the king in such games is only a subsidiary feature. If, furthermore, the player with an edge cannot force an extra pawn, or another material edge, then what happens next? The answer is to try to take control of weak squares. There is no point in playing for a quick attack, but maybe twenty moves later, the player on top starts to think about playing for checkmate.

Perhaps my favourite example is Game 3, **Adams**-Yusupov. It is pure positional chess, and Adams plays the middlegame very accurately. He also plays it highly imaginatively. The ♕h1 idea, hiding behind the king and pawns, does not actually get played, but as so often the most interesting moves are found in the analysis, rather than in the game. Yusupov accepts an isolated d-pawn, quite a common strategy in the French and various other openings. The pawn is slightly weak, and there is a slight weakness in front of the pawn, but this will hardly be enough to win the game. Adams needs to find some extra little weakness, and his queen rushes around with great agility, trying to attack several of the opponent's pieces, prodding the occasional pawn to advance, and then buzzing away, maybe to attack something else. The queen is the star piece here, both in the early stages, and in mopping up later.

Black also suffers a slight weakness on the d-file in the Pelikan/Sveshnikov Variation. Black's pawn on d6 is backward, and there is a hole on d5. The games of Sveshnikov and others suggest that while the pawn structure looks ugly, Black also has serious compensation on the other files. Leko has been a strong advocate of Black in this opening, but on the other side of the board in Game 9, **Leko**-Radjabov, he shows great understanding of the problems he can set up as White. The star idea in this game is 19 ♘e3-f5! g6 20 ♘e3, giving away a couple of tempo to provoke Black into advancing a pawn. This pawn advance later led to serious weaknesses.

In this context, there is also the extraordinarily extravagant line White chose in Game 21, **Alekseev**-Tkachiev. Alekseev has already gambited a pawn in a recently fashionable line, and then he 'gambits' a couple of tempi with 10 ♗c1-g5 h6 11 ♗c1. All he has is that Black's pawn structure is slightly weakened, and during the rest of the game he prods the kingside pawns just a little further, and in the end breaks through against the king. It would have been the positional game of the century if it not only worked, but was fully sound. Sadly Tkachiev had several possible improvements, which he avoided, and so the game is merely interesting.

Symmetrical Pawn Structures

We have already noted the outstanding win by Kramnik against Leko. Game 33, **Karjakin**-Inarkiev, leads to a broadly similar pawn structure, but with queens remaining on the board, rather than Kramnik's earlier queen exchange. Karjakin knew exactly what he was doing, and set up the better bishop-pair in the symmetrical pawn structure. A good positional win.

Game 24, **Kamsky**-Carlsen leads to another symmetrical pawn structure, with the player with the more active pieces improving his position, and later winning. Kamsky was able to force his opponent on to the defensive when he was starting to press for a weak pawn. In the earlier part of the game, however, Kamsky's play was inaccurate, and Carlsen could have taken his chances.

There was an attempt for White to blast through with a kingside attack in a symmetrical opening, in Game 25, **Morozevich**-Sakaev. He succeeded, but it should not really have worked. Sakaev himself overpressed, when the position started to favour him, and Morozevich in reply set up some sacrificial pawn breaks. The tactics were memorable, but the positional play was not at its highest level.

More Space in the Centre

Strong players will take care with the centre, and will not give way there unnecessarily. There are relatively few examples in this collection of players playing much too quietly, and just waiting for the opponent to take a big advantage. Books of this type a few decades ago might well have given illustrative games, analysed in depth, of masters beating amateurs, but such games are now relatively rare in top grandmaster encounters. There might occasionally be games in which a player is slow on the uptake in a sharp tactical opening, the Mamedyarov win (Game 31) being an obvious example, but usually the top grandmasters will not play passively and make unnecessary moves.

The only real example, perhaps, is Game 8, Sargissian-**Nisipeanu,** after an early ...b5 thrust in the Benoni, here a Blumenfeld Counter-Gambit rather than a Benko or one of the lines of the King's Indian. Black's ...b5 worked, and he was able to break open his opponent's queenside pawns, and create a central piece advantage for himself. These days, players need to be aware of these ...b5 thrusts.

Black was able to keep an advantage in the centre in Game 11, Karpov-**Akopian**, but this was against the run of earlier play. Karpov developed well, and kept a slight edge, but somehow he found himself tied up with an unnecessary and wasteful knight manoeuvre. Then Akopian started to take over the initiative.

Not really covering the basic theme, but still well worth noting is Game 5, **Bacrot**-Rublevsky, where White kept slightly the better pawn structure. The unusual feature was that as White, Bacrot was able to stick his bishop on h6, preventing Black from castling kingside, and keeping a slight edge through to the endgame.

Pressure in the centre often coincides with countervailing pressure on other parts of the board. Game 30, **Gelfand**-Alekseev, allowed White pawn control in the centre, with pawns on d4 and e4, while Black kept an extra pawn battalion on the queenside. Black castled queenside, and his pawns looked sturdy. Gradually, however, Gelfand was able to exchange a couple of queenside pawns, and then a central break allowed him to set up an attack against the king.

Unusual Piece and Pawn Battles
Finally we have a few unusual battles with an imbalance of pieces and pawns. My instincts would not regard these games as gambit lines. In none of the games is the player speculating any material in return for the possibility of a strong attack against the king. Rather, both players are trying to calculate what degree of compensation there is, in positional terms, for any slight degree of material imbalance.

There are two outstanding games of this type, both ending up in an endgame, so neither winner was aiming for mate. By coincidence both games end up as a rook sacrifice in the endgame.

Game 16, Shirov-**Aronian**, is classified as the Marshall Gambit, and hence a gambit. It is now almost a century since Frank Marshall introduced his big idea, and the line has now been highly analysed, and the immediate shock effect has gone. There are lines where White can go wrong quickly, falling for a mating attack, but by now the Marshall Gambit is a highly respectable 'positional gambit', or perhaps, if one prefers, a positional sacrifice. In fact, it is Shirov as White who gives up rook for bishop, to neutralize Black's kingside pressure. Shirov also keeps a couple of extra pawns, so material is arithmetically level (3+1+1=5). Both players will need to consider what impact an extra rook would have for Black, and what impact each of the bishop and two pawns would have for White. In addition, there are clear weak squares on either side, but what impact would each of these pawns give to the game? We are dealing with immense positional complexity, and it is far from surprising that both players make slight slips at some stages. Shirov finds himself close to zugzwang before the time control, but he counterattacks with sudden tactics. The finish is memorable.

Game 7, **Svidler**-Topalov, is another titanic struggle, the more so in that Topalov, like Shirov in the game before, was keeping an eye of the possibility of aiming for a win. In a queenless middlegame, Svidler bravely gave away a central pawn, and indeed gave away a central square in order to press forward with a pawn on the kingside. He was not aiming for checkmate, nor even to create a passed pawn, but rather to make it difficult for Black to coordinate his pieces. Svidler was taking note that Black's extra pawn on the queenside was doubled, and so Topalov could not take any real active advantage of the extra pawn. White had the better kingside pressure with his pawns, but with no extra pawn on that side. It was a long, hard struggle, and eventually Svidler, like Aronian, found a spectacular endgame finish.

Game 10, **Ivanchuk**-Aronian, is one of the most interesting material imbalances of all, with Ivanchuk accepting three minor pieces in return for a queen. Games with rook, minor piece and pawn against queen are relatively common, with perhaps a piece dropping along the way. Three pieces against the queen is unlikely to happen unless there has already been a sharp sacrificial attack against the king, and the exposure of the king is likely to dominate the questions of strategy. In the Ivanchuk-Aronian game, both kings are relatively secure, with an unusual struggle. The usual rule of thumb in lines with queen versus assorted material is that if the various lesser pieces are secure, without serious pawn weaknesses, the player with the lesser pieces will tend to dominate. The queen cannot make much impact against the opponent, if the opponent's pieces are firmly defending all attacks. In Ivanchuk's game, it looks at first as though his position is insecure, but with original and accurate play, he gradually takes control.

Another much more common imbalance is the exchange sacrifice. In Game 1, Kasimdzhanov-**Kasparov**, Black's exchange sacrifice is delicately balanced, and the suspicion is that at one stage after the exchange sacrifice, Kasparov may have been slightly worse. This though would need practical testing. Kasimdzhanov would undoubtedly have been under considerable psychological pressure, and was unable to find the best lines. Kasparov, throughout his very early days, and up to his final top grandmaster tournament, excelled in taking his play very close to the edge, giving the opponent the chance to play for an edge if he were to play with 100% accuracy, but giving himself the opportunity of playing for a win after the slightest inaccuracy by his opponent.

Game 26, **Wang Yue**-Movsesian, is another exchange sacrifice from the opening, based on an idea by Topalov. In Kasparov's win, he obtains more active pieces and pawns for himself, without directly attacking anything. Here, Wang Yue is aiming to keep his opponent's pieces behind in development for as long as possible. The position remained unbalanced, until Movsesian made a strange and un-explained piece sacrifice leading to a clear loss.

Now for some battles of the minor pieces. There are plenty of examples of the 'minor exchange sacrifice', accepting bishop and knight or, less commonly, the two knights, against the bishop-pair. There are several examples of this theme, which is highly relevant to the Berlin Variation of the Ruy Lopez, the Nimzo-Indian, and various other openings. For another example, in the Scotch, consider Game 18, Rublevsky-**Grischuk**. White finds no advantage with the bishop-pair, and Black has the more active bishop, and as time goes on, his knight becomes even more dominating. We have not catalogued all the bishop and knight struggles in this book, but the reader is recommended to pay considerable attention to this strategic battle.

The bishop-pair takes its revenge though in Game 12, **Bareev**-Efimenko, a Nimzo-Indian. Bareev has carefully worked out that while Black's queen and bishop on the long diagonal look threatening, White can cover the attack against his king, and his bishop-pair work better than the bishop and knight. The main basic difference between this game and the Grischuk win for the bishop and knight is that in Bareev's game his pawn structure is far more fluid, with the bishops being able to attack, and the opposing knight is unable to be firmly established.

The Best of the Best

This last classification gives us a useful opportunity to give a few suggestions of the best of the great games in the early post-Kasparov years. It needs to be emphasized that this selection of 33 games was a personal selection, and that I had not analysed in depth in advance any of the other candidate games. I have given, for example, only one win by Topalov, but there are genuine doubts as to whether his win was sound. It would seem more than likely that there are several Topalov startling wins which are totally sound and brilliant, and may well be very high up in a top five list.

Of the imperfect sieving from the best games since Kasparov's retirement in early 2005 to April 2008, we have several excellent and outstanding games to consider. Which is the best of the best? Everyone would have different points of view. My short-list would perhaps be the wins by Svidler, Aronian, Adams, and Radjabov among the longer games, and among the opening shock wins, Mamedyarov, Anand and Bu Xiangzhi. These all come quickly to my mind, but there are many other possibilities.

Out of this suggested short-list, I leave it to the reader to decide which he or she thinks of as best. Quite possibly players of different strengths would give different values over the idea of which game is best, and everyone will have different opinions.

Other Players in the Hall of Fame

We have given wins by all those players who passed 2700 level between the time of Kasparov's retirement, and April 2008. Quite a few players have since reached

2700. Quite a few other players have passed 2700, and then dropped down again. Also, there was no international Elo rating system before the 1970s. Retrospective calculations have suggested that many World Champions will have reached something between 2670 and 2690, with Fischer going beyond 2700. There has been, as noted earlier, a degree of inflation since these calculations have been made, and it is reasonable enough to suggest that all modern World Champions can be regarded as 2700 level. This would include Lasker, a superb exponent of the middlegame. Had he somehow been transported into 21st Century play, he would undoubtedly have been able to catch up with opening ideas, and would have done well. With Steinitz, the assessment is not so clear. He was a great thinker of his time, but to modern players, there are many obvious weaknesses in his play.

We include in the Hall of Fame:

1) World Champions from Lasker to just before Kasparov's reign
Emanuel Lasker, Jose Capablanca, Alexander Alekhine, Max Euwe, Mikhail Botvinnik, Vassily Smyslov, Mikhail Tal, Tigran Petrosian, Boris Spassky, Bobby Fischer, and Anatoly Karpov. Also David Bronstein, and Viktor Korchnoi.

2) Players who have passed 2700, but have since dropped down again
Valery Salov, Alexander Beliavsky, Loek Van Wely, Rustam Kasimdzhanov, Alexander Khalifman, Zurab Azmaiparashvili, Nigel Short (he has very recently passed 2700 again), Michal Krasenkow, Ivan Sokolov, and Ilia Smirin.

3) The 33 current players given in this book
There has been a minor technicality in this book, in that players of exactly 2700 are not included, and that only players of 2701 or more are included. There is a practical reason. Three players in the period covered in this book have reached exactly 2700, but not gone beyond. This would make the book several pages longer. We add these three players to the Hall of Honour, though: Viktor Bologan, Krishnan Sasikiran, and Sergei Tiviakov. Also Vladimir Malakhov, who reached 2700 at the start of 2004, but a few months later dropped back.

4) The players who have passed 2700 since April 2008.
Vadim Milov, Lenier Dominguez Perez, Vugar Gashimov, Hikaru Nakamura, Maxime Vachier-Lagrave, Francisco Vallejo Pons, Sergei Rublevsky, Sergei Movsesian, and Alexander Motylev.

We may feel reasonably confident of assessing the players up to the 1960s. During the Fischer era, it was clear that so many strong grandmasters were so far behind Fischer that they could not be regarded as 2700+ players. There were too many 6-0 results during this era.

There are many statistical problems to encounter between the ratings of the 1970s and 1980s, and the current rating performances. We may feel reasonably confident that in their best years, Jan Timman and Leonid Stein would have reached 'hall of fame' level. Are we to say definitely that Timman is a lesser player than both Euwe and Van Wely? Presumably not. Stein's record, with three USSR Championship wins, and his consistent plus score results against world champions, must surely be regarded on the highest level.

Such highly conscientious analysts as Lev Polugaevsky and Lajos Portisch achieved ratings well over 2600 in the 1970s, before the most recent slight inflation. It is possible to argue that they could be regarded as scoring very slightly less than the 2700 level much of the time, but that had they had the access of computer technology, they would have passed the current 2700 level.

But before we get too enthralled with the statistics, it is the chess that matters.

Game 1
R.Kasimdzhanov-G.Kasparov
Linares 2005
Semi-Slav Defence D48

1 d4 d5

Solid symmetrical play to start with. The positional imbalances start off later.

2 c4

The Queen's Gambit.

2 ♘f3 is an accepted developing move, and much of the time White later transposes into a Queen's Gambit.

2...c6

Black usually strongpoints the pawn on d5 with this or 2...e6. He wants to ensure that he is firm on at least one of the four central squares.

2...dxc4 is possible. Usually White re-captures the pawn without too much difficulty with e3 (or e4) and ♗xc4, so it is not really a proper gambit. If, for example, 3 ♘f3 ♘f6 4 e3 b5?! (better 4...♗g4 or 4...e6) 5 a4 c6 6 axb5 cxb5 7 b3, and White keeps a pleasant slight advantage. One of the points of the Slav Defence with 2...c6 is that Black could seriously consider ...dxc4, either trying to keep the pawn or, as in the game, to set up counterplay with ...b5 after a ♗xc4 recapture.

3 ♘c3

The one slight practical defect of the Slav Defence for Black, particularly if White is much lower rated (much lower rated that is than the gap between Kasimdzhanov and Kasparov) is that White could simply play for drawish chess with 3 cxd5 cxd5, hoping for a steady equality. Usually this doesn't happen between strong players. It is generally better to play one's normal game as White, hoping for a continued slight advantage and forcing Black to work out how to equalize and hold the position.

3...♘f6

Black could accept the gambit offer with 3...dxc4 4 e4 b5 (or even 4...♗e6). Then it is best to take immediate action to regain the pawn with 5 a4 b4 (5...a6? 6 axb5 cxb5 7 ♘xb5, and the pawn is pinned) 6 ♘a2. In G.Kasparov-P.Svidler, Russian Championship, Moscow 2004, White eventually won the queenless middlegame, and later endgame, after 6...♘f6 7 e5 ♘d5 8 ♗xc4 e6 9 ♘f3 ♗e7 10 ♗d2 a5 11 ♘c2 ♘d7 12 ♘b3 h6 13 0-0 ♕b6 14 ♕e2 ♗a6 15 ♖fc1 0-0 16 ♗xa6 ♕xa6 17 ♕xa6 ♖xa6 18 ♔f1. Here Black has not quite equalized, his queenside pawns being open to attack.

4 e3

Kasimdzhanov moves from the more traditional Slav, with 4 ♘f3 dxc4 5 a4, later recapturing the pawn with e3, into a Semi-Slav.

For the Exchange Variation with 4 cxd5, see Game 25, Morozevich-Sakaev.

4...e6

And Kasparov agrees to the Semi-Slav.

4...a6!? is a credible option, and is now common. A basic idea is that even after Black plays ...b5, White's edge is only slight in an exchange variation, such as 5 e3 b5 6 cxd5 cxd5. Naturally either side could play more adventurously; see, for example, Game 32, Inarkiev-Ni Hua, where White tried 6 c5.

5 ♘f3

A good and natural move. The classic plan of development in chess is to bring a couple of pawns out into the centre, maybe also the c-pawn, and then bring the knights into play early, moving each knight just once at the beginning. Later, each player decides the best way to bring the bishops into play, and where to castle. The queen and the other rook usually wait until it is clearer where these pieces are best placed. The first thought in opening strategy is to start to bring a few pieces into play, and this includes finding open lines for the bishops. The second consideration is to try to develop flexibly, for attack with White and for defence with Black. It is usually a bad idea to attack in the first half dozen moves. One must develop first.

Opening theory these days can be incredibly deep and complicated; as we shall see Kasparov has prepared an un-

expected exchange sacrifice well in advance. Even so, the top players, however deeply they analyse, still concentrate on the basic ideas of opening strategy, and can usually find their way even when they have not previously studied a particular position in advance.

5...♘bd7

To the uninitiated, the initial impression would be that Black's pieces seem unnecessarily cramped, his light-squared bishop in particular being stuck behind a closed fortress of pawns, and the knight on a passive square adding to further cramping. This would be deceptive. Black has a plan of attack, with the idea of ...dxc4; ♗xc4 b5 followed by ...♗b7, and then it is only a matter of time before a pawn break with ...c5. Then the smothered bishop escapes on to a good open diagonal. We will see this plan emerging during the next few moves.

6 ♗d3

This is the most direct line, but it also gives up a tempo when compared with, say, 6 ♕c2 dxc4?! 7 ♗xc4.

The 'battle of the tempo' is quite a common theme in several Queen's Gambit lines, in which White is delaying ♗d3 for as long as feasible, and Black is delaying ...dxc4, again for as long as he can. Dao Thien Hai, for example, tried 6 ♕c2 ♗d6 7 a3 0-0 8 b4 ♕e7 several times in the early 1990s, but without any special success. Indeed, quite often one of the players decides that there is no good way for any further quiet moves, and instead simply plays the natural move.

6 ♕c2 ♗d6 7 g4!? is an extremely sharp alternative, aiming for a direct attack against the king – see Game 2, Dreev-L.Dominguez. We slightly alter the chronological order of this book (the Dreev game was played a day before the Kasparov game), in honour of the retiring outstanding former World Champion. Garry Kasparov remains the only player who has consistently reached 2800+ chess levels.

6...dxc4

6...♗d6 is a simple enough reply. If then 7 0-0 0-0 8 e4 dxe4 9 ♘xe4 ♘xe4 10 ♗xe4,

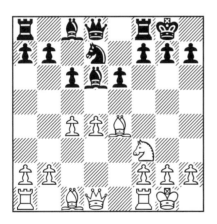

the safest reply is probably 10...♕c7 11 ♖e1 c5 with only a small edge for White. Instead 10...e5?! 11 dxe5 ♘xe5 12 ♘xe5 ♗xe5 13 ♗xh7+ ♔xh7 14 ♕h5+ ♔g8 15 ♕xe5 gives White an ex-

tra pawn. There was a time when occasionally players with Black would deliberately steer through this line, on the basis that bishops of opposite colour should lead to a draw, even a pawn down. These days players with the extra pawn are happy to grind for as long as it takes to try to prove the win. Here the natural 10...♘f6?! is in fact a positional slip-up, and after 11 ♗c2 the databases show clear plus scores for White. Unfortunately Black's knight move, apparently gaining time, ends up weakening his squares on c5 and e5, making it difficult to achieve counterplay.

7 ♗xc4 b5

It is this move that makes the line interesting for Black. After ...♗b7, the bishop soon becomes a very active piece once Black has made a ...c5 pawn push.

Black now has active play, but this does not necessarily mean that Black is better or fully equal. If White plays accurately, then he will still be better or equal. Black cannot be better unless White has made a mistake. If though Black plays actively and aggressively, he is making every chance of inducing his opponent to make an error. Kasparov was always superb at exploiting such opportunities, and plays for a win with Black from move 1. He is, of course, even more dangerous with the extra move as White.

8 ♗d3

The most active retreat.

8 ♗e2 is safe enough, and indeed on a couple of occasions Kramnik played this against the sharp tactician Topalov in his 2006 World Championship match. Most high-level games have ended up as steady draws, but in the Kramnik-Topalov games there were wins for both sides.

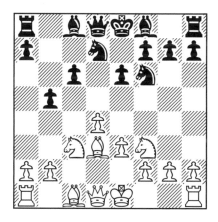

8...♗b7

'Of course!' one might think, since the bishop is aiming for the long diagonal, but there are a couple of alternatives:

a) 8...b4 (the Wade Defence) 9 ♘e4 ♘xe4 10 ♗xe4 ♗b7 is certainly playable, and keeps up the tempo on Black's development, but also slightly loosens the queenside pawn structure. A slower build-up on the queenside, before aiming to break open lines there, is more dangerous.

b) 8...a6!? is the more traditional main line of the Meran Defence, over-

protecting the pawn on b5, and thus allowing quick counterplay with ...c5. White's most active line is 9 e4 c5

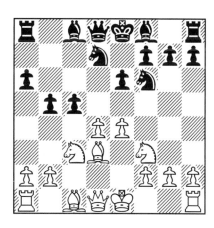

10 d5 c4 11 ♗c2 ♕c7 12 dxe6 fxe6, with a possible transposition to Kasimdzhanov-Kasparov. White can also try 10 e5!? cxd4 (10...♘d5?! 11 ♘xd5 exd5 12 0-0 strongly favours White, it being difficult for Black to castle kingside safely) 11 ♘e4 ♘d5 12 0-0 h6 (the g5-square is dangerous) 13 a4!? b4 14 ♗c4 with unclear play. With a slightly different move order in this line, starting with 8...♗b7 9 0-0, the e4-e5 idea is much less effective for White, Black's bishop adding protection to the knight on d5. See the note to White's 11th.

We are covering in this book only brief summaries of complicated theory. There is little attempt to cover the latest details in critical side-variations from the game actually played. It is up to the reader to study for himself or herself and to examine alternatives. There are, of course, plenty of books or articles on opening theory to consider.

9 0-0

For 9 e4, see Game 31, Mamedyarov-Nepomniachtchi.

9...a6

Black will soon play ...c5, opening the long diagonal for the bishop, and setting up an active queenside pawn majority. This sounds good, but White can still keep active play in the centre.

9...b4 10 ♘e4 is possible, but loses some of the queenside flexibility and so White has chances of a slight edge.

10 e4

10 a4 b4 11 ♘b1 (or 11 ♘e4, likely to transpose) 11...c5 12 ♘bd2 has been tried a few times at top levels, but seems only to be equal.

10...c5

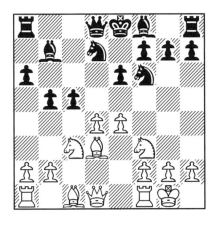

The counterattack begins.

11 d5

This has superseded 11 e5 ♘d5 when Black has good control of the light squares, and should equalize.

11...♕c7

11...exd5 12 exd5 is deeply unfashionable for Black, his king being wide open on the kingside.

After 12...♗e7 13 ♗xb5 axb5 14 d6 ♘e5 15 ♘xe5 ♕xd6 16 ♕xd6 ♗xd6 17 ♖e1 in I.Farago-E.Sveshnikov, Sochi 1980, the renowned theorist Sveshnikov found himself a pawn down, and eventually lost. Any takers in this line for 14...b4 15 dxe7 ♕b6 16 ♘b1 ♘g8 (he has to take

the passed pawn somehow)? Entertaining, but it is unlikely that Black will have many supporters.

11...e5 is the old-fashioned way of handling this line of the Meran. Black accepts that White has a strong passed pawn, but is arguing that everything else is solid. White generally tries 12 b3.

12 dxe6

Isolating Black's pawn, but 12 ♕e2!? is worth considering.

12...fxe6 13 ♗c2

13 ♘g5 is premature. Black defends with 13...♕c6, and it is not quite clear what White is doing with the knight.

13 ♕e2 c4 14 ♗c2 is natural play for White, but with the text White tries to squeeze alternative play with ♗c2 first.

13...c4

13...b4 14 e5 ♘xe5 15 ♘xe5 ♕xe5 16 ♖e1 ♕c7 17 ♖xe6+ appears yet to have been tried. Black faces carnage after 17...♔f7? 18 ♖xf6+ gxf6 19 ♕h5+ ♔e7 20 ♗f4 ♕xf4 21 ♘d5+ ♗xd5 22 ♕xd5 ♕e5 23 ♕xa8. Thus 17...♗e7 is better, but White remains ahead after 18 ♘d4 0-0 19 ♘xf6+ ♗xf6 20 ♕d3. Such lines explain why players have tried 13 ♗c2, instead of keeping the e-pawn protected with 13 ♕e2.

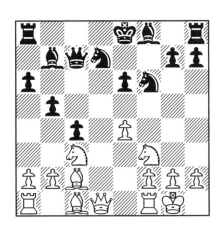

We now reach the classic pawn structure of the modern Meran. Black has an excellent queenside pawn majority, well advanced, and he has good diagonals for the bishops and queen. There is no doubt that Black has excellent attacking chances.

White too has his options, otherwise this variation would have become obsolete a long time ago. The main point is that in compensation for Black's pawn advantage on the queenside, White has a good extra pawn on the kingside, with slight damage to Black's kingside pawns. White is not so much trying to create a passed pawn, but rather to put pressure on Black's isolated e-pawn, and thereby on the squares around it.

This is a popular opening for both sides, with the thought that both sides will have to play with great accuracy, and who plays better, wins.

14 ♘d4

This is not a bad move in itself. It centralizes, puts pressure on Black's e-pawn, and helps open up lines for his kingside. Even so, White's next few moves look far too elaborate, taking three knight moves instead of one in bringing the knight from f3 to g5. White may well be happy in inducing the ...e5 response, but is it all worth the effort?

14 ♕e2 and 14 ♘g5 are more traditional approaches, but maybe fashion will swing?

14...♘c5

The knight too aims for an active square.

15 ♗e3

Kasparov as White tried, several years ago, 15 ♕e2, but he had to work hard to keep equality after 15...♗d6 16 f4 e5 17

♘f5 0-0 18 ♘xd6 (a recent attempt at improvement, H.Koneru-D.Stellwagen, Wijk aan Zee 2008, varied with 18 ♖d1!?, ending up with equality after 18...♘d3 19 ♘xd6 ♕xd6 20 ♗xd3 cxd3 21 ♖xd3 ♕c7 22 f5 b4 23 ♘d5 ♘xd5 24 exd5 ♖xf5, and later a draw) 18...♕xd6 19 fxe5 ♕xe5 20 ♖f5 ♕c7 21 ♗g5 ♘fxe4 22 ♖xf8+ ♖xf8 23 ♘xe4 ♕e5 24 ♘f6+ gxf6 25 ♗xh7+ ♔xh7 26 ♕h5+ ♔g8 27 ♕g6+, and a draw by perpetual, G.Kasparov-V.Akopian, Yerevan Olympiad 1996.

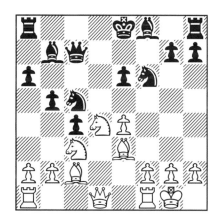

15...e5

15...0-0-0 has also been tried, by Akopian and others. Bringing the rook to the d-file is aggressive, but castling queenside is not as safe for the king as castling kingside. After 16 ♕e2, White has achieved a plus score.

16 ♘f3

After 16 ♘f5 Black can snatch the e-pawn with 16...♘cxe4 17 ♘xe4 ♘xe4, and White has shown various ways of achieving some compensation, nothing decisive but still workable. More recently Anand has tried 16...g6!?. Then Marin annotating for ChessBase gives 17 ♗g5!? ♘xe4 18 ♗xe4 ♘xe4 19 ♘xe4 ♗xe4 20 ♗f6 gxf5 21 ♗xh8 ♗d3, and

Black can be happy with this. He has a pawn in return for the exchange sacrifice, two good bishops, and White's bishop will need some work in disentangling. The stem game saw, however, 17 ♘h6, which may well be better, and after 17...♗g7 18 ♕f3 ♘e6 19 ♕h3 ♗c8 20 ♕h4 (Marin prefers 20 ♕g3) 20...♕e7 21 ♖fe1 ♘d5 22 ♕xe7+ ♘xe7 23 ♘d5 ♗b7 Black was already slightly better in A.Morozevich-V.Anand, Mexico City World Championship 2007.

16...♗e7

16...♘cxe4 17 ♘xe4 ♘xe4 18 ♖e1 ♗d6 19 ♗xe4 ♗xe4 20 ♘g5 ♗d3 21 ♕f3 led to a slight advantage for White in B.Gelfand-E.Bareev, Novgorod 1997. Once White's pawn on e4 had vanished, he was able to compensate by making use of both the long diagonal through the e4-square, and the e-file with the rook. He even had the possibility of using the knight on e4 as well, although in the end this did not quite happen.

17 ♘g5

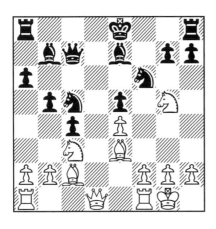

17...0-0!?

Kasparov, like Tal, was always ready to sacrifice, if appropriate, given a reasonable opportunity. Another former World Champion, Tigran V. Petrosian (there is now a strong young namesake, hence the middle initial) was also famed for his positional sacrifices, but with a particular speciality. Petrosian scored many boa-like wins by sacrificing the exchange, giving up a rook for bishop or knight, and showing that in the right type of position he could squeeze all counterplay. Here Kasparov's sacrifice was probably more in the mould of Petrosian, rather than of Tal.

There is also an additional point, which Petrosian would not have had the opportunity to deal with, namely that Kasparov had experience of playing high-level computer opposition. As anyone who has tried using computer help will be aware, computer engines are not necessarily secure of their assessments when sacrifices as concerned. They are far more secure in their evaluation when material is level. In Lutz's commentary for ChessBase, he noted that Kasparov had already considered the diagram position, when preparing for his 2003 match against the computer, *Deep Junior*. The exchange sacrifice would have been 'psychologically' excellent against computer opposition, but would it necessarily have been so good against human opposition?

Alternatively, 17...h6!? is unclear, but without sacrifices, so perhaps would not have been so effective against a computer. In Y.Kruppa-D.Collas, Cappelle la Grande 2001, play continued 18 ♗xc5 hxg5 19 ♗e3 g4 20 ♕e2 0-0-0 21 a4 b4 22 ♘d5 ♘xd5 23 exd5 ♗xd5 24 ♕xg4+, and was possibly about level. There are, of course, several deviations from this line. An attractive alternative for Black would seem to be 22...♗xd5 23 exd5 e4 24 g3 ♖xd5 with apparently strong pressure. The computer engine likes this for a little, and then quickly notes that 25 ♗b3! ♖dh5 26 h4 gxh3 (26...♖xh4 27 gxh4 ♖xh4 28 ♕xc4 stops the sacrificial attack) 27 ♗xc4 h2+ 28 ♔h1 proves to be strong for White, Black's king being by now the more exposed of the two.

With many hidden reefs like this, it is understandable that Kasparov chose 17...0-0. He did not have the opportunity of making this particular sacrifice against the computer, and so in the end it was Kasimdzhanov who was the 'victim'.

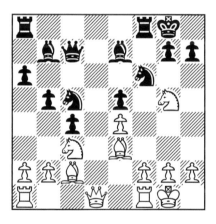

18 ♗xc5

If White does not want to accept the challenge of the exchange sacrifice, Kasparov notes that 18 b4 is acceptable: for example, 18...cxb3 (or 18...h6 19 ♗xc5 hxg5 20 ♗xe7 ♕xe7 21 a3, also unclear, maybe level) 19 ♗xb3+ ♘xb3 20 ♕xb3+ ♕c4 21 ♕xc4+ bxc4 22 ♖ab1 ♗c6, which is unclear, but maybe level.

18...♗xc5

The bishop takes over an excellent diagonal.

19 ♘e6

With a knight fork.

19...♕b6

So that bishop and queen create pressure on the f2-pawn, and then, Black hopes, on the king.

20 ♘xf8

There is no sensible way back. 20 ♘xc5 ♕xc5 still gives pressure on White's kingside, but without involving material sacrifice.

20...♖xf8

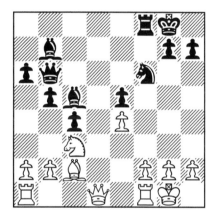

The end of the sacrificial phase. Now Kasparov will have to prove that his minor pieces create a positional impact.

21 ♘d5!?

This has been criticized by Lutz and others, but it would seem that it is valid. White's mistake comes later.

The intention for White is to simplify by a minor piece exchange, so keeping the rook versus bishop advantage without giving away excessive attacking chances. The exchange on d5 also opens up the b1-h7 diagonal, although this may be obscured by Black's ...e4 pawn push. Kasimdzhanov's move is not minimal defence, though, as it gives away material. The maximalist defensive idea, giving away absolutely nothing, is 21 ♕e2!, which covers, at least temporarily, the e4- and f2-weaknesses. Then Kasparov suggests in *Informator* 21...♕e6, with the idea of adding pressure with ...♘g4. However, 22 ♘d1!, not given in Kasparov's notes, seems an improvement for White, quietly restructuring:

a) If 22...♗d4 then 23 ♖b1!, again cementing the barricades, and a possible idea for counterplay would be a later b3 c3; b4!, using the long diagonal from a2 to g8.

b) Black could try 22...♕f7 23 a4 b4, but again the tight position holds after 24 ♖c1 ♗d4 25 ♗b1 ♖c8 26 ♗a2!? b3 27 ♗b1.

In either case, White is not relying on permanent passive defence, but is aiming for pawn counterplay on the queenside to allow the pieces back into play. Thus the suspicion is that Black has not reached full equality after this exchange sacrifice.

21...♗xd5!

Black needs the knight, rather than the light-squared bishop, to attack the dark squares. Indeed, 21...♘xd5 22 exd5 ♖xf2 23 ♖xf2 ♗xf2+ 24 ♔h1 ♗d4 25 ♕f3 leaves White better; a good indication of what Kasimdzhanov was hoping for with his exchange on d5.

22 exd5 ♗xf2+

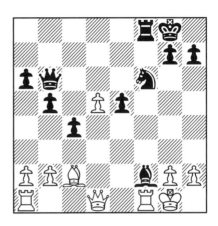

Kasparov has reasonable compensation for the exchange sacrifice. He has four active pieces, pushing at the king, and a central passed pawn, more effective than White's. What holds for White, or rather what should have held, is that White has good control of the light-coloured squares.

23 ♔h1

23 ♖xf2?? ♘g4 loses quickly.

23...e4

Black's passed pawn is likely to be more troublesome than White's. In attacking terms, it is not quite as effective as it looks, though, since Black is relying heavily on defending with the pawn on the b1-h7 diagonal, and if the pawn moves for an attack, then White may resume play on the light-coloured squares.

24 ♕e2

This is criticized by Kasparov and by others, but it seems okay. Trying to consolidate on the dark squares usually helps defend on the light squares as well. It is the next move which is questionable.

Kasparov suggests 24 d6 e3 25 ♗f5 g6 26 ♗h3 ♔g7 27 d7 when White has coordinated his queen and bishop to a certain extent, and his pawn is safe on the seventh, but Black is in a better situation to improve his pieces further. White's bishop, for example, protects the passed pawn, but cannot attack anything, while Black's bishop and knight have good attacking chances. Kasparov suggests 27...♘e4 28 ♕d5 ♘d2 29 ♖fd1 ♕f6 30 ♗g4 h5 31 ♗e2 ♖d8 32 a4 ♕xb2 33 axb5 ♕xb5 34 ♕d4+ ♔h7 35 ♕f6 with advantage to Black, but even this is less than clear after 35...♖xd7 36 ♖xa6 ♖g7 37 ♖a8. However, 27...♘h5, a suggested alternative by Kasparov, looks promising for Black, with ideas of ...♘f4 and ...♘d3.

Instead 24 a4!? looks good, and Kasparov analyses play to a perpetual after 24...♗d4 25 axb5 axb5 26 ♕e2 ♗xb2 27 ♖ad1 ♗d4 28 ♗xe4 ♖e8 29 ♖xf6 ♕xf6 30 ♗xh7+ ♔f8 31 ♗e4 ♕e5 32 ♕f3+ ♔g8 33 ♖f1 ♕xe4 34 ♕f7+.

24...e3

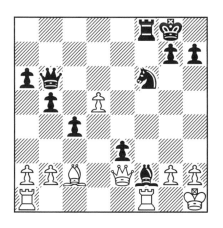

And Black's pawn push, although getting closer to promotion, weakens his light squares.

The position is delicately balanced.

Even the slightest inaccuracy by either side would turn the position to being worse, and any further inaccuracy would slide the position to a clear loss. The author's own assumption in his earlier assessment was that Kasimdzhanov was slightly better at this point, but further consideration suggests that Kasparov's position, as Black, was already slightly better.

25 ♖fd1?

This is generally recognized by the commentators as a mistake, weakening the kingside. They, including Kasparov himself, have suggested 25 ♖ad1 as an improvement, keeping open the return exchange sacrifice on f2. If, for example, 25 ♖ad1 ♕d6 26 ♗f5 ♔h8 27 ♖xf2 exf2 28 ♕xf2 ♖e8, and White has stopped the direct attack against the king with level material. Look more closely though, and White cannot improve his pieces, while his d-pawn is well covered by the defender. Black keeps a slight edge.

Can White improve on this? The obvious thought is to open up a different file for the rook, with 25 a4! and then:

a) 25...♘xd5 26 ♗xh7+ ♔xh7 (26...♔h8 27 ♗e4 ♘f4 28 ♕f3 is good for White) 27 ♕h5+ ♔g8 28 ♕xd5+ ♖f7 29 axb5! e2 30 ♖fc1 ♕xb5 (30...♕e3? 31 bxa6 e1♕+ 32 ♖xe1 ♗xe1 33 a7 wins for White; Black's rook is pinned!) 31 ♕e6 e1♕+ 32 ♖xe1 ♗xe1 33 ♖xe1, and we end up with a queen and rook each, but Black having the more scattered pawns. White is better.

b) It is not immediately clear how Black can improve his pieces. If, for example, 25...♖d8 26 axb5 axb5 27 b3 c5 28 ♖fd1, then White has found two good files for his two rooks. He seems better after 29 ♗f5, and then ♗e6+, although play is still unclear.

c) The less than obvious 25...g6! improves. Play might continue with 26 axb4 axb4 when 27 ♖fd1? ♕d6 transposes into game, in which White quickly faced great tactical dangers. However, the rook move is unnecessary, and wastes time. Instead 27 b3! sets up queenside counterplay just in time:

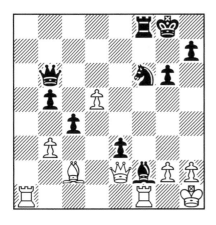

c1) 27...c3 28 d6 ♕xd6 29 ♕xb5, and White has freed his position. Note that 29...♘g4?? 30 ♕xc4+ would merely lose a piece.

c2) 27...♕d6 28 bxc4 ♘h5 (28...bxc4 29 ♕xc4 is good for White) 29 cxb5 ♘g3+ 30 hxg3 ♕xg3 31 ♖a4! opens up the rank and file for White, and keeps the win.

c3) 27...♘xd5 is the best and most natural reply: 28 bxc4 ♘c3 (probably slightly more accurate than 28...♘f4 29 ♕f3) 29 ♕d3 e2 30 ♕xc3 exf1♕+ 31 ♖xf1, and we are heading for a draw.

25...♕d6

White's passed pawn is now securely blockaded, and Black can think about attacking the king. Observe how Black's queen is very difficult to attack, while White will have problems on h2 and g3.

Also, as we shall soon see, there is a knight threat to f4.

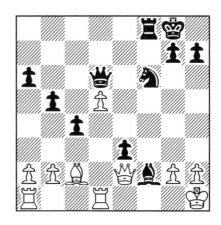

Of course, the story is of pawns as well as bishops. Black's passed pawn is much more dangerous than his opponent's, not least because it is much closer to promotion. If White's queen were somehow to abandon the e2-square, Black would quickly play ...e2, threatening to take the rook with check, and presumably winning. However if Black's queen were to move away, perhaps with the idea of a quick mating attack, White's d-pawn would require three advances before queening.

26 a4

Slightly delayed, and also White has mishandled his rooks. However, on 26 b3 Kasparov gives a strong attack for Black after 26...c3 27 ♗f5 g6 28 ♗e6+ ♔g7 29 ♖ac1 ♘e4.

26...g6!

Not immediately obvious, but strong. Black covers both the h5- and f5-squares with the pawn, and prevents White's bishop or queen cutting out these squares. The next stage will be ...♘h5, and if White does nothing to respond, there will be a threat of ...♘g3+; hxg3 ♕xg3 and a winning ...♕h4 mate.

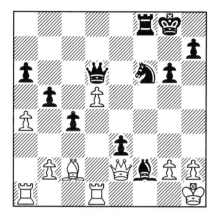

27 axb5

Continuing his plan of opening up lines for the rooks, but again, this should have been tried earlier.

27...axb5 28 g3

28 b3 is too late to equalize: 28...♘h5 29 bxc4 ♘f4 (29...♘g3+? 30 hxg3 ♕xg3 31 ♖d4!) 30 ♕f3 e2! 31 ♖dc1 (31 ♕xf2 exd1♕+ 32 ♖xd1 ♘h3! winning) 31...e1♕+ 32 ♖xe1 ♗xe1 33 ♖xe1 bxc4 will lead to the fall of the d-pawn, since if 34 ♖d1? ♘d3!, and Black wins the exchange. A better defensive plan is 34 ♕c3 ♕xd5 35 ♗e4 ♕f7 when it will take a long grinding struggle for Black to take full advantage of the extra pawn, but one suspects that he would succeed.

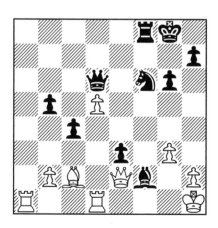

28...♘h5!

Kasparov still needs to play with great accuracy, and he intends to sacrifice a piece, remaining a rook down, in order to force White's king to be exposed to the elements. There will be ways for White to avoid any quick checkmate, through return sacrifices, but even in any endgame, Black will be on top.

Kasparov notes the alternative try, 28...♕e5!?, so that if for some reason, either tactical or positional, White moves his queen, Black has ...e2. Play might continue with 29 d6 ♘h5 30 d7 ♘xg3+ 31 hxg3 ♕xg3, with, one might assume, a quick checkmate. Except that the players will have noted a saving tactical response with 32 ♗f5!!. If then 32...gxf5? Black's queen is pinned, and after 33 ♖g1 White wins, but with 32...♕h4+ 33 ♔g2 ♕g3+ there is a perpetual.

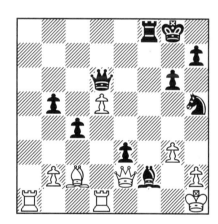

29 ♕g4

Otherwise 29...♘xg3+ 30 hxg3 ♕xg3 crashes through, and there was little chance of salvation with 29 ♖xg1 ♗xg1 30 ♔xg1 ♕e5.

29...♗xg3!?

Kasparov looks for the clincher.

29...♖e8 is the alternative: 30 ♔g2 e2 31 ♔xf2 exd1♕ 32 ♖xd1 ♘f6 33 ♕f3 ♖e5 34 ♔g1 ♖xd5 35 ♖xd5 ♘xd5 36 ♗e4 leaves Black a pawn up in an endgame, but there will be a lot of hard work before he can force a win.

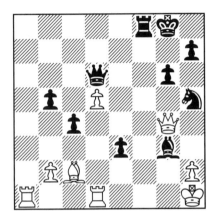

30 hxg3

This loses quickly, probably under time pressure, and misses one of the points of Black's tactics.

Instead 30 ♕e6+ ♕xe6 31 dxe6 keeps play alive for a while. Kasparov gives 30...e2 32 hxg3 ♘xg3+ 33 ♔g2 exd1♕ 34 ♖xd1 ♘h5 as a clear win for Black, who has two extra pawns. Kasparov also gives 30 ♖g1 ♗f2! 31 ♕xh5 ♗xg1 32 ♖xg1, which at first looks fine for White, but Black has a winning resource in 32...♖f1!. Play might continue 33 ♕g4 ♖f2 34 ♖g2 e2, soon queening a pawn.

30...♘xg3+

Aiming for mate.

31 ♔g2

Or 31 ♔g1 e2 32 ♖e1 ♕c5+ 33 ♔h2 ♕f2+ 34 ♔h3 ♘h5 35 ♕e6+ ♔g7, winning for Black.

31...♖f2+

Queen, rook, knight and pawn, working together, against king, queen

and sundry other defenders, make a formidable attacking combination, and even a quick glance will suggest that Black should be winning. He has to be careful though, as he is still a rook down.

32 ♔h3

32 ♔g1? ♘e2+ allows Black to checkmate next move.

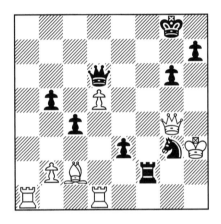

32...♘f5!

Sometimes a quiet move, admittedly with the help of a direct threat, may be more effective than a loud check. Black is now threatening mate on h2.

32...♖h2+?, which Kasimdzhanov was no doubt hoping for in time trouble, does not work. After 33 ♔xh2 ♘f1+ 34 ♔g2! (the only move; anything else loses) 34...♕h2+ 35 ♔f3 ♕f2+ 36 ♔e4 White is two rooks up, and his king is about to escape: 36...e2 37 ♕e6+ ♔g7 38 ♕e5+ ♔h6 39 ♕f4+ soon wraps things up.

33 ♖h1

33 ♖a8+ ♔g7 34 ♖a7+ ♔f6! makes no real difference. Black still wins after 35 ♖h1 h5!.

33...h5!

An attractive finish as White's kingside pieces are surrounded.

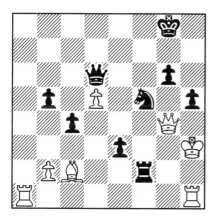

34 ♕xg6+

A nice try, but White is now material down. Instead 34 ♕g1 ♖f3+ 35 ♔g2 ♕g3 mate is a memorable final position. White's rook on h1 obstructs the king, but it needed to go there to defend the earlier mate threat on h2.

34...♕xg6 35 ♖hg1 ♕xg1

It is time for simple play. 35...♖f3+? 36 ♔h2 ♖g3 37 ♗xf5! ♕xf5 38 ♖xg3+ would force Black to start all over again.

36 ♖xg1+ ♔f7 0-1

White's position is hopeless.

Kasparov's tournament chess career is over, as far as we can see, but who is next in line? There is no obvious answer. Some players have reached 2800 occasionally, but only Kasparov has reached that level for any length of time. Kramnik, Anand and Topalov are all great players, but could it be that some of the younger players, such as Karjakin or Carlsen, could reach that level, and maybe go beyond? Or what about various other super-grand-masters?

Game 2
A.Dreev-L.Dominguez
Poikovsky 2005
Semi-Slav Defence D45

1 d4 d5 2 c4 c6 3 ♘c3 ♘f6 4 e3 e6 5 ♘f3 ♘bd7 6 ♕c2

For 6 ♗d3, see both Game 1, Kasimdzhanov-Kasparov, and Game 30, Mamedyarov-Nepomniachtchi.

6...♗d6

6...dxc4 7 ♗xc4 is a loss of tempo in comparison with the 6 ♗d3 dxc4 7 ♗xc4, and White should have an edge.

7 g4!?

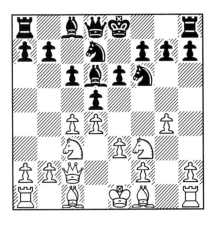

Shabalov's move, and a relentlessly aggressive gambit idea, a traditional thought in a new setting. White is going to attack with the g-pawn, pushing the knight to a worse square, but Black can, of course, take the pawn. White then gains some time for an attack, and this sets up genuine pressure. Gambit play on both sides tends to be difficult to handle, requiring good judgement, good calculating ability, and cool nerves.

One is reminded of a much earlier gambit, giving up the b-pawn. This was the Evans Gambit, 1 e4 e5 2 ♘f3 ♘c6 3 ♗c4 ♗c5 4 b4!? ♗xb4 5 c3 followed by d4, which dates from the 1820s, and has still occasionally been tried by Kasparov, including a win against Anand.

What plans might follow over the next few moves in the Shabalov Gambit? White is unlikely to castle on the kingside, and so will castle queenside with ideas of attacking on the kingside if Black castles on that side. But, of course, Black has not castled yet, which makes the g-pawn thrust all the more surprising. Does it work? This remains to be seen.

There are several non-sacrificial alternatives. 7 b3 or 7 ♗d2 are possibilities, as are 7 ♗e2 and 7 ♗d3, met by 7...dxc4. Finally, 7 e4 dxe4 8 ♘xe4 ♘xe4 9 ♕xe4 e5!? 10 dxe5 0-0 11 exd6 ♖e8 12 ♕xe8+ ♕xe8+ 13 ♗e3, with rook, bishop and passed pawn for the queen, is unclear. This was explored a lot in the early 1980s, but interest died down somewhat when it was apparent that White could not establish a clear edge.

7...dxc4

Black could consider snatching the g-pawn with 7...♘xg4 8 ♖g1. After 8...♘xh2 9 ♘xh2 ♗xh2 10 ♖xg7 experience favours White. If instead 8...h5 9 h3 ♘h6, White treats this as a gambit line: 10 e4 (rather than 10 ♖xg7?!) 10

dxe4 11 ♘xe4 ♗b4+ 12 ♗d2 ♗xd2+ 13 ♕xd2 with pressure, such as after 13...♘f6 14 ♘c3 ♘f5 15 0-0-0 ♔f8 16 ♗d3 ♗d7 17 ♘e5, White later winning the game in A.Shirov-V.Akopian, Oakham 1992. This was one of the very early examples of this line.

After the earlier attempts at refuting the pawn sacrifice by snatching it, many have played more quietly, arguing that opening up a kingside pawn creates weaknesses for White, rather than Black, on the kingside. 7...h6 and 7...♗b4 have therefore been tried.

8 ♗xc4

8 g5 ♘d5 9 ♗xc4 is also to be considered, but White is not required to push the pawn, and he can keep more options without pushing it immediately.

8...e5

8...♘xg4 9 ♖g1 is even more dangerous now.

9 ♗d2

A recent innovation. Older games concentrating on 9 g5 ♘d5, and now 10 ♘e4 or 10 ♗d2. White has not tried 10 ♗xd5 cxd5 11 ♘xd5, snatching a pawn. It is worth considering, at least in analysis, but too many of White's pieces

seem too open.

9...0-0!?

It is very brave to castle in front of White's pawns. Still, we should not hastily give a question mark just yet. Dominguez has clearly examined this position in advance, and decided that it is interesting and playable. Now Dreev has to take up the challenge.

Dominguez has also tried 9...exd4 10 ♘xd4 ♘e5 11 ♗e2 ♘fxg4 12 ♘e4 ♗e7 13 0-0-0 0-0 14 ♗c3 (Lutz prefers 14 f4 in his analysis) 14...♕c7 15 ♖dg1 f5 16 h3 with complicated play, favouring Black, in B.Gelfand-L.Dominguez, Calvia Olympiad 2004. It ended up in perpetual check, although Black was at one stage winning.

Evidently Dominguez must have decided that this was not fully satisfactory for Black. White has a few promising attacking ideas after 14 f4 ♘g6 15 f5 ♘6e5, such as starting off with Lutz's suggestion of 16 ♗xg4 ♘xg4 17 ♖hg1 c5 18 ♘c6 bxc6 19 ♗c3, with unclear play.

There are other possibilities to be considered too, and it is noticeable that since 2004 after 9 ♗d2, Shirov has won both as White and as Black against strong opposition. This variation is complicated; there are few options of a quick draw.

10 0-0-0!?

Dreev has played this line on both sides, and is therefore fully aware of what the most dangerous lines are, and also what the safest lines are. As White here he aims for a wild kingside attack, castling queenside first.

In V.Dobrov-A.Dreev, Internet 2004, White played more quietly with 10 g5 ♘d5 (actually reached by transposition after 9 g5 ♘d5 10 ♗d2 0-0), and after 11 0-0-0 (11 ♘e4 or 11 ♘xd5 are to be considered) 11...exd4 12 exd4 ♘b4 13 ♕e4 ♘b6 14 ♗b3 ♖e8 Black was comfortable, and later won.

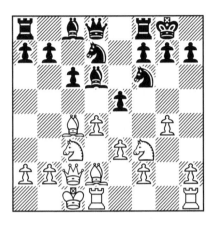

10...exd4

10...♘b6!? is a possibility, White replying with 11 dxe5:

a) After 11...♘xc4?! 12 exf6 ♕xf6 13 ♘e4 ♕xf3 14 ♘g5 ♗f5 (the only move) 15 gxf5 White is clearly better.

b) 11...♗g4! is better, with unclear play after 12 exf6 ♗xf3 13 fxg7 ♖e8 14 ♕f5 ♘xc4 15 ♕xf3 ♕b6 16 b3 ♖ad8 17 ♘e4 ♗e5.

11 ♘xd4

Much more active than 11 exd4.

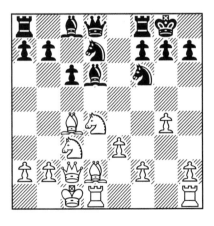

11...♘e5

11...♘b6 seems dangerously decentralizing. Maybe then 12 ♗d3 ♗xg4 13 f3.

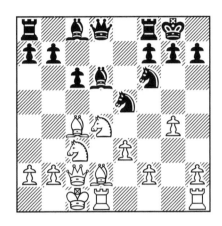

12 ♗e2

Offering a pawn.

12 g5 ♘xc4 13 gxf6 ♕xf6 14 ♘e4 ♕e7 15 ♘xc6 bxc6 16 ♕xc4 ♗a6 17 ♕xa6 ♕xe4 18 ♗c3 ♖fd8 19 ♖hd1 ♗f8 ends up level.

12...♘exg4

Otherwise, 12...♘fxg4?! 13 ♘e4 gives White a strong attack, and 12...♗xg4 13 f4! ♗xe2 14 ♘cxe2 ♘g6 15 e4, as given by Dreev, offers excellent compensation for the sacrificed pawn. White has the better pawn structure, and the abandoned g-pawn allows him to attack on the g-file. Here Dreev also gives 13...♘g6 14 ♗xg4 ♘xg4 15 ♘f5 without comment, but implying that White is doing well. After 15...♘f2 16 ♘e4 ♘xd1 17 ♖xd1 ♗e7 18 ♗c3 ♕c8 19 ♘xe7+ (not 19 ♘xg7? ♕xh3) 19...♘xe7 20 ♖g1 ♘g6 21 f5 White wins the knight. The computer gives this as equal, but queen, rook, bishop and knight versus queen and two rooks gives the attacker a good variety of attack: 21...♕c7 22 fxg6 fxg6 23 ♘g5 ♕e7 24 ♔b1 is promising for White.

13 ♖hg1

By now he is obliged to give up both pawns, otherwise the initiative will fade.

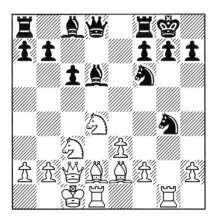

13...♘xf2

A difficult decision to make. Black takes the second pawn, but his opponent will have a dangerous attack. Is the attack sound, or not? Or should Black quietly defend, relying on a single extra pawn? Ultimately, no player over the board will be able to calculate to the end which plan is better, and it will end up as a matter of judgement. A player who has previously analysed the position at home will have a significant advantage, not necessarily because he has a better position, but rather because his opponent has to make a critical decision without assistance.

The move that Dominguez played, taking the f-pawn, is quite clearly better than taking the h-pawn, which gives White a clear attack on the g- and h-files. In practical terms, there is no need to analyse further.

What is more interesting is whether Black should develop quietly with 13...♖e8!?:

a) The natural line is 14 ♖g2 ♘e5 15 f4 ♘g6 16 ♖db1, but then Black has 16...♗h3! with some tactics.

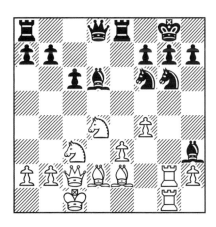

If then 17 ♖f2, Black has an unexpected bishop pin with 17...♘xf4! 18 exf4 ♗c5. Thus play might continue instead with 17 ♖g3 ♕d7 18 f5 ♗xg3 19 ♖xg3, apparently trapping the bishop, but Black again has 19...♘f4! 20 exf4 (20 ♗c4 ♗g4) 20...♕xd4 21 ♖xh3 ♖ad8 with advantage. He has set up considerable pressure on the d- and e-files, and White's minor pieces are ineffective.

b) This leaves 14 ♘f5!? ♗xf5 15 ♕xf5 with standard gambit play. It is always difficult to establish whether the active pieces have more impact than the extra pawn. Here White might have the edge. He has pressure on the g-file, and if he can set up advancing pawns on the e- and f-files, his bishops become dangerous. A computer suggestion is 15...♖e5 16 ♕f3 ♖g5 17 e4 ♘xh2 18 ♕h3 ♖xg1 19 ♖xg1, but Black is under pressure.

Overall, Black has to work hard to equalize, and this is the purpose of the opponent's gambit play.

14 ♖df1

The only move, but good. Two rooks

on half-open files against the king will provide excellent attacking chances.

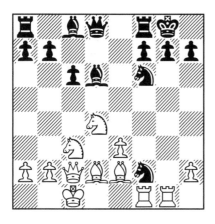

14...♘h3

Black could go the full monty with 14...♗xh2 15 ♖g2 ♘2g4 16 ♖h1. Again, the computer prefers the three pawns, but human players will tend to want the pieces. Black's pawns are only of decisive significance if he can force the exchange of queens, or if he is able to try to promote.

It may well be that Black's position is playable after 16...h5 17 ♖gxh2 ♖xh2 18 ♖xh2 ♕d6 19 ♖h1, but who is better? This is the usual difficult question of gambit play. Possibly at some stage someone will analyse this over the board.

15 ♖g2

The only move. White has no other safe moves on the g-file.

This would seem to be a highly acceptable gambit line. White's pieces are more active, and he has particular pressure on the f- and g-files, and on the various diagonals leading to the king's fortress. There is also the problem for Black that his knight on h3 is out on a limb. Certainly it stops White from doubling rooks on the f- or g-files, but

otherwise it is a weakness, especially if the light-squared bishop is going to be exchanged.

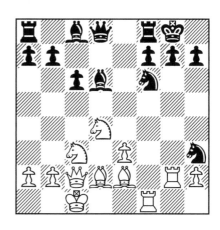

15...♗e5

Regarded by Dreev as a mistake at the time, although the question mark was dropped by the time he wrote up this game in *Informator*. There Dreev gave as his main line 15...g6 16 ♗c4 ♔h8 17 ♘e4!? ♘xe4 18 ♕xe4 ♕e7 19 ♕xe7 ♗xe7 20 ♗c3 ♔g8 21 ♘f5 ♗xf5 22 ♖xf5 b5 23 ♗b3 ♖ae8 24 ♔d2 c5 25 a3! c4 26 ♗c2 ♖b8 27 ♖h5 ♘f2 28 ♖e5 (28 ♖xf2? ♖fd8+, and then ...gxh5) 28...♘h4 29 ♖h5 ♗e7 with a draw by perpetual.

This is, of course, just one line in a whole string of variations. Black forces the exchange of queens, not really what White wants, but White's rooks and bishops are so powerful that Black only just finds a way for equality. One cannot help feeling that the trend of play favours White, in the sense that any slight improvements are more likely from White, rather than from Black. One possibility is 16 ♗d3!?, with ideas of a sacrifice on g6, and also adding pressure with ♘f5:

a) If then 16...♗e5 17 ♘f3 ♕e7, and

we have transposed into Dreev-Dominguez, which is fully satisfactory for White.

b) 16...♖e8 17 ♘f5!? ♗f8 18 ♖f3 ♔h8 19 ♖xh3 gxf5 20 ♗xf5 gives White ample pressure for the pawn; Black's king is in danger.

c) 16...♘d5 17 ♘xd5 cxd5

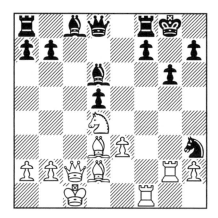

looks as though the position is ripe for a sacrifice, but this does not quite seem to work. Slower play with 18 ♗c3 ♕e7 19 ♔b1 keeps Black under pressure, facing problems over attacks on the king, and finding a way to keep the knight safe. If, for example, 19...a6 (preventing ♘b5) 20 ♘f5 ♗xf5 21 ♖xf5 ♕xe3 22 ♖xd5, and White is ready to sacrifice on g6. Black has to react quickly with 22...♘f4 23 ♖xd6 ♘xg2 24 ♕xg2 ♖fd8 25 ♖xd8+ ♖xd8 26 ♗c2. It is difficult to assess what is going on with two bishops versus rook and two pawns, but here White's unopposed bishop-pair appears to have the more impact.

16 ♘f3

There is no obvious follow-up after 16 ♘f5 g6 15 ♖f3 ♔h8!, and if 18 e4 gxf5 19 exf5 ♖g8. Dreev prefers to gain a tempo.

16...♕e7

Or simply 16...♗c7. There are so many different possibilities for White to try to prove an edge, but everything seems inconclusive:

a) Dreev himself gives 17 ♗d3 ♔h8 18 ♗f5 h6 as 'unclear'. The computer suggests that Black is winning, but usually the human player will be sceptical about such pronouncements. Nevertheless, there is an onus for White to prove he can show equality at least.

b) The author prefers 17 ♘h4!?, which at least gives no winning for Black score on the computer. The program gives Black two extra pawns, while White has at least a pawns-worth of piece activity, and the human might feel rather more. It will take many pages to analyse in detail, and there are many complicated lines that remain to be given in this game, so we leave it to the reader to decide what is going on. A starting point for analysis might well be 17...♔h8:

b1) Then 18 e4 ♕e7 19 ♘f5 ♗xf5 20 exf5 (now Black's knight is in trouble) 20...h6 21 ♖f3 ♘g5 22 ♗xg5 hxg5 23 ♖xg5 ♕b4! keeps sufficient defensive possibilities for Black.

b2) Possibly 18 ♘f5, and if 18...g6 19 ♘h6 when the unusual symmetry of the knights prevents Black's knight on h3 escaping into active play. Here 18...h6, giving an escape square, would be provocative. White would seem to have good prospects for the exchange sacrifice after 19 ♖xg7!? ♗xf5 20 ♕xf5 ♔xg7 21 ♕xf3 followed by e4, for example: 21...♘h7 22 e4 ♘g5 23 ♕h5 ♕d6 (threatening ...♕xh2) 24 h4 ♘h7 25 ♖g1+ ♔h8 26 ♗xh6 ♖g8 27 ♖f1 ♖g6 28 ♗g5. Here Black can hold out with a draw by perpetual after 28...♕e6! 29 ♗g4 ♕c4 30 ♗e2 ♕e6.

17 ♗d3

White delays taking the bishop. There is no need to hurry, as the bishop won't run away. If 17 ♘xe5 ♕xe5 18 ♗d3, Dreev gives 18...♖d8! 19 ♗f5 h6 (adding an escape square on g5 for the knight) 20 e4 ♔f8, and Black is consolidating.

17...g6

If 17...♗c7 Dreev's plan is to swallow up Black's exposed knight on h3 with 18 ♗f5 followed by exchanging the bishops, and then ♕f5.

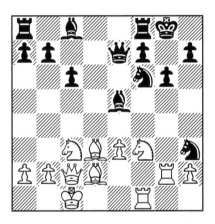

18 ♗c4?!

White makes a change of approach, and perhaps most importantly sets up threats of ♖xg6+.

Dreev was clearly already tempted by 18 ♘xe5 ♕xe5 19 ♗xg6 hxg6 20 ♖xg6+, but it is only a draw after 20...hxg6 21 ♕xg6+ ♔h8 21 ♕xg6+ ♔h8 22 ♕h6+ ♔g8. Black could even play more ambitiously with 20...♔h8, but Dreev notes another draw after 21 ♖h6 ♘g5 (21...♕e7 22 ♘d1! followed by ♗c3 is painful) 22 ♕g6 ♗g4 23 ♖xf6 ♖xf6 24 ♕xf6+.

This could in fact be the correct fin-

ish, with best play on both sides. Dreev is starting to overpress, despite his subsequent quick win.

18...♘g4?

Black underestimates how quickly the f6-square will collapse. There may be three pieces covering that square, but in three moves time it is White who controls this critical square.

Dreev suggests that Black should play 18...♗c7 when there are several options for White. One possibility is the rook sacrifice with 19 ♖xg6+ hxg6 20 ♕xg6+ ♔h8 21 ♕h6+ ♘h7 22 ♗d3 f6 23 ♘h4 (23 ♗xh7 ♕g7!) 23...♕g7 24 ♘g6+ ♔g8 25 ♗c4+ ♖f7 26 ♘e7+ ♔f8 27 ♘g6+ ♔e8!? (27...♔g8 leads to perpetual) 28 ♕h5 ♘3g5 29 ♘f4,

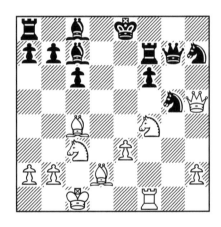

which is given as unclear by Dreev. White is a rook down, but he can regain the exchange without problem, and attacking with h4 will threaten the remaining piece. But is White's position encouraging? Probably not. Black can, for example, try 29...b5, and wait to see whether White can show sufficient compensation.

White does not have to sacrifice the rook, but quieter moves would not be as threatening as he would like. If 19 e4?! (instead of the violent sacrifice on g6), then 19...♗e6, and if 19 ♘e2, then 19...♔h8. White is not making any progress. Instead White could consider 19 ♘d4!?, and if 19...♗e5, then 20 ♘f3, repeating. Quite often this is a fair enough response after sharp play.

Could Black try for more, though? 19...♔h8 is possible, and if 20 ♖f3 ♘g4! 21 ♖xh3 ♘e5 with advantage to Black. Here 20 e4 gives reasonable, if slightly vague compensation for the extra sacrificed pawns, but one must beware counterplay. Black can, for example, try 20...♖d8 21 ♗e3 ♗f4! with advantage.

The general impression is that White is struggling after 18...♗c7!, and that objectively White's 18 ♗c4 was an error. Sometimes, though, a slight error, followed by a bigger error from the opponent, turns out much better than totally accurate play often ending up in a draw.

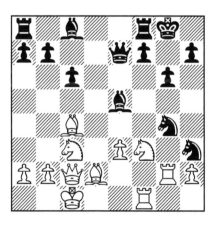

19 ♘xe5

The bishop must not escape this time.

19...♘xe5

Dominguez must have relied a lot on this centralizing move, but White too can take up the middle squares.

20 ♘e4!

The knight is about to arrive on f6 without Black having the chance of playing ...f5.

20...♔h8

There are other moves, but in each of these cases White will reply with ♘f6+, and Black replies with ...♔h8 anyway.

21 ♘f6!

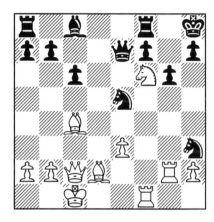

The impossible square for the knight! Compare this diagram with that after 17...g6, and one can see how much progress Dreev has made over the last few moves.

Both players have entrenched their knights on the sixth rank, but what a difference of prospects they have! White's knight is on an extremely dangerous attacking square, with ideas of checkmate, while Black's knight does little. Indeed, the worry for Black is how to recover the horse into play. Covering the squares on g1 and f2 from the knight is useful for Black, but in the broader context of play, it doesn't do all that much.

21...b5

If 21...♕c5, White even allows the exchange of queens with 22 ♗e2 ♕xc2+ 23 ♔xc2 ♘d7 24 ♘e4, which

Dreev gives as a win for White. There is no immediate checkmating attack when the queens are off, but Black's h3-knight is likely to fold: for example, 24...f6 25 ♗c3 ♔g7 26 ♘d6 ♘e5 27 ♗xe5 fxe5 28 ♖xf8+ ♔xf8 29 ♘xc8 ♖xc8 30 ♗g4, and the horse end up in the knackers' yard.

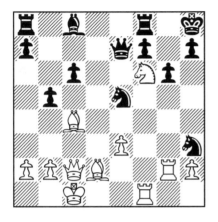

22 ♗e2

Thinking about hitting the knight, rather than trying to keep up much less effective pressure on f7.

22...♘d7

On quiet moves, such as 22...b4, White continues with 23 ♕e4 followed by ♕h4.

23 ♗c3

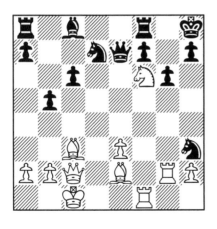

A decisive scissors attack.

23...♕xe3+

Gaining a pawn with tempo, but not altering the basics. Black is about to lose.

24 ♔b1

To a safe square, and keeping the queen and bishop on strong attacking squares.

24...♘xf6

After this White sacrifices and checkmates, but if 24...♘e5 25 ♕e4 ♕xe4 26 ♘xe4 ♖e8 27 ♘d6 ♖e7 28 ♗xe5+ then White wins too.

25 ♖xf6

With an enormous threat of discovered attack.

25...♔g8

Which Black avoids.

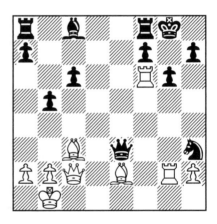

26 ♖gxg6+

The usual reason for a sacrifice in front of the opponent's king – to destroy the pawn cover, and thereby to bring the king into the open.

Here 26 ♖fxg6+ also works.

26...fxg6

26...hxg6 loses immediately after 27 ♖xg6+ ♔h7 (or 27...fxg6 28 ♕xg6 mate) 28 ♖g7+.

27 ♖xg6+

27 ♕b3+? ♗e6! 28 ♖xe6 ♕g1+ 29 ♔c2 ♖f7! would be careless.

27...♔f7

Obviously, 27...hxg6?? 28 ♕xg6 is mate.

28 ♖g7+

Forcing the king further out.

28...♔e6

28...♔e8 29 ♗h5+ wins.

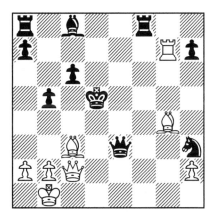

30 ♕d1+

Back to square one.

30...♔e4

30...♔c5 31 b4+ isn't quite check-mating for White, but he picks up the queen with a winning position after 31...♔b6 32 ♗d4+ ♕xd4 33 ♕xd4+, or 31...♔c4 32 ♕b3+ ♔d3 33 ♕c2+ ♔c4 34 ♗d2+.

31 ♖e7+

This too wins the queen.

31...♔f4 32 ♖xe3 ♗xg4

Since if 32...♔xe3 33 ♕d4 mate.

No further comment is needed now. It is just a case of check, check, check, then checkmate, with queen and rook slicing open the king. There must have been a massive time scramble here, otherwise Black would have resigned.

33 ♕d4+ ♔g5 34 ♕g7+ ♔h5 35 ♕xh7+ ♔g5 36 ♖e5+ ♖f5 37 ♗d2+ 1-0

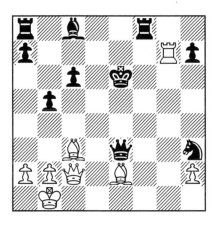

29 ♗g4+

Another piece to help the mating attack, with gain of tempo. Indeed, extra pieces work!

29 ♕b3+? allows Black to slip out with 29...♔f5 30 ♗g4+ ♔f4 31 ♗e5+ ♔e4! 32 ♕b4+ ♔d3, and while it is clear that White can force a perpetual easily enough, it is much more difficult to find a win.

29...♔d5

29...♔d6 leads to the same result.

Game 3
M.Adams-A.Yusupov
French League 2005
French Defence C09

1 e4

The first example in this book of the initial e4-pawn advance. Naturally White would like to be able to play both e4 and d4 without opposition, but Black has counter-plans against the double pawn advance.

1...e6

The French Defence, and by coincidence this game was played in France. Black allows White to play both e4 and d4, but immediately sets up counterplay with ...d5. 1...c6 has similar ideas, again with ...d5, but without blocking the light-squared bishop.

2 d4

The obvious reply. Two advanced d- and e-pawns together are useful.

2...d5

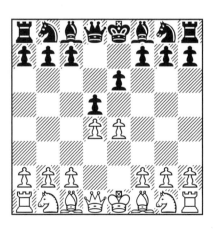

Black too advances in the four central squares.

3 ②d2

The Tarrasch Variation of the French Defence. To the uninitiated, this might look strange, blocking the knight from the bishop, but it allows White to play c3 if required to bolster d4. Otherwise:

a) 3 ②c3 is common, but allows complicated play in the Winawer Variation with 3...②b4.

b) 3 ②d3 is ineffective, since 3...dxe4 4 ②xe4 ②f6 forces White to lose time or to give up bishop for knight.

c) 3 e5 is strategically direct, but in the end does not give White so many chances of an edge after good defence.

d) Then there is the Exchange Variation with 3 exd5 exd5. Boring? Or still with chances of an edge?

3...c5

Black offers, in the main line, to allow an isolated d-pawn.

3...②f6 4 e5 ②fd7 is the alternative, with two different types of play after 5 f4 c5 6 c3 ②c6 7 ②df3, and 5 ②d3 c5 6 c3 ②c6 7 ②e2 cxd4 8 cxd4 f6!? 9 exf6 ②xf6.

Black could also exchange with 3...dxe4 4 ②xe4, and this would also be effective after 3 ②c3 instead. After the central exchange, Black can try 4...②d7 or even 4...②d7 followed by ...②c6, and an exchange on e4. In either case, pawn structures are similar to the Caro-Kann (1...c6) or the Scandinavian (1...d5). Not, however, the immediate 4...②f6?!, since 5 ②xf6+! ②xf6 6 ②f3 allows White to gain time by threatening the queen with ♗g5.

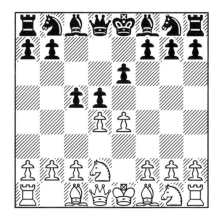

4 exd5

Adams has also played 4 ♘gf3 with success. Then 4...cxd4 5 exd5 ♕xd5 inter-transposes usually into the next variation.

4...exd5

4...♕xd5 leads to sharper, more tactical play, after, for example, 5 ♘gf3 cxd4 6 ♗c4 ♕d6 7 0-0 ♘f6 8 ♘b3, winning back the pawn on d4.

5 ♘gf3

Developing.

5...♘c6

Black develops too.

6 ♗b5

Using the pin to add to the pressure on the centre.

6 dxc5 ♗xc5 is possible, but White usually prefers to wait until Black has played ...♗d6, thereby losing a tempo. H.Nakamura-D.Sadvakasov, Miami 2007, continued 7 ♗d3 ♕e7+ 8 ♕e2 ♘f6 9 ♕xe7+ ♔xe7 10 0-0 with White attempting to make an edge from Black's isolated d-pawn. Nakamura kept a slight edge after 10...h6 11 a3 followed by b4, but the game was later drawn. The obvious reply would have

been 10...♘b4 11 ♘b3 ♘xd3 12 cxd3, but sometimes knights can be better than bishops even in an open position.

6...♗d6

Standard play, certainly at top level. Instead 6...♕e7+ 7 ♕e2 helps White, Black's pawn structure having been weakened.

6...a6 7 ♗xc6+ bxc6 is possible, but usually regarded as a slight loss of tempo.

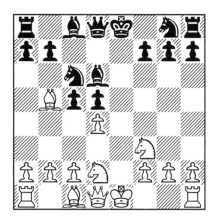

7 dxc5

Forcing Black to take on an isolated d-pawn. This is a slight technical weakness, but if Black can keep his pieces active, he has good chances of holding. Certainly White would have to play extremely accurately to take an edge against strong opposition.

7...♗xc5 8 0-0

8 ♘b3 ♗d6 might well transpose.

8...♘ge7

A flexible square for the knight, avoiding, for example, later pins with ♗g5.

9 ♘b3

The knight aims for d4.

9...♗d6

The best move for the bishop. 9...♗b6 has been tried many times, but White has the choice of making use of the h2-b8 diagonal or offering an exchange of bishops with ♗e3, normally after ♖e1.

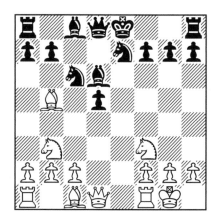

10 ♖e1

This natural developing move, bringing the rook to an open file, has usually been associated with ♗g5, but as we shall soon see, White has a newer idea with ♗d3.

At some stage, it needs to be noted that 10 c3 leads to well-known play. This is likely to be reached via the 2 c3 Sicilian, after 1...c5 2 c3 e6 3 d4 d5 4 exd5 exd5 5 ♘f3, and returning to the French. Via the French move order, however, c3 is not necessary, and White has extra options. It is better to develop White's pieces, such as with the text or one of 10 ♗g5, 10 ♘bd2 and 10 ♗e3.

10...0-0

Black breaks the two pins, again all very natural.

10...♗g4 is also possible, and is relatively unexplored. Black adds to the pinning himself. In Zhang Pengxiang-S.Lputian, Fuegen 2006, Black gradually equalized after 11 h3 ♗h5 12 ♗e2 0-0 13 ♘fd4 ♗g6 14 ♗d3 ♘e5 15 ♗xg6 ♘7xg6 16 ♘b5 ♖e8 17 ♘xd6 ♕xd6. Here 11 ♕xd5?? ♗xh2+ is, of course, a

blunder, and 11 ♕d4?! ♗xf3 12 ♕xg7? is a slightly more sophisticated slip-up. After 12...♔d7! White would lose the queen on 13 gxf3? ♖g8, but 13 ♕xf7 ♗e4 gives White no real attacking chances in return for the piece sacrifice. Maybe 11 ♗g5 is best with a likely slight edge.

11 ♗d3!?

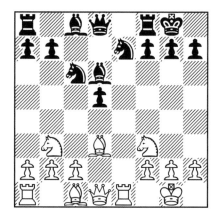

This is a relatively new idea. White gives up a tempo, in return for adding pressure on Black's kingside.

11 ♗g5 is the more traditional line.

11...h6

The first impression might well be that this is unnecessary, but in practice piece moves have favoured White, making use either of the bishop or the knight on g5. If, for example, 11...♘g6?!, Psakhis for ChessBase quotes a line with 12 ♗g5! ♕d7 13 c3 ♘f4 14 ♗f1 ♕f5 15 ♗h4 ♕h5 16 ♗g3 ♗g4 17 ♕d2 ♕h6 18 ♘fd4, and White is better, V.Akopian-E.Vladimirov, Moscow 1990; the manoeuvre of White's dark-squared bishop has proved to be useful.

12 h3

White in turn prevents the pressure with ...♗g4.

12...♘f5

The natural and most popular move. Black's pieces start to move into play.

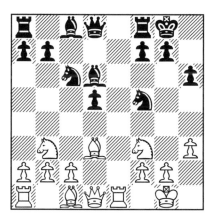

13 c3

It is difficult to find any good piece moves, so White provides coverage of d4.

There are many openings in which White may be slightly better, but with no realistic possibilities of immediate attack, while Black cannot claim clear equality either. Both players have to tack around, maybe little pawn moves (h3 or ...h6 for Black), or maybe aiming for any tiny weaknesses after the opponent has moved a piece to a new square from its original square. In terms of bishop manoeuvres, for example, here White's bishop has already moved to b5, and then halfway through the diagonal to d3, without any direct provocation. There are many more strange little manoeuvres by either side, and White's queen shifting over the next few moves is deeply impressive.

In the end, the strategic point in such a position is not to find a clear way that White can attack a defined weakness, but rather it is a case of finding a way, move by move, of keeping

some sort of slight edge to make the opponent's position difficult.

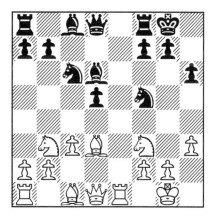

13...♕f6!?

The natural developing move, and the most popular.

13...♗c7 14 ♗c2 ♕d6 15 ♕d3 (threatening g4) 15...g6 has also been tried. Then a few years ago, Motylev tried a reverse tack with 16 ♕d1!?, threatening to exchange the bishop for knight on f5, then taking on h6. If Black tries 16...♔g7, there is another quiet queen move with 17 ♕d2! ♖d8 18 ♖d1, and with every move that Black makes, his king is further out of position. In the stem game, A.Motylev-A.Roghani, Yerevan 2001, play continued with 16...h5 17 ♗g5 ♗d7 18 ♕d2 ♖ae8 19 ♖ad1 ♖xe1+ (19...f6!? also, according to Psakhis, gives White a slight edge) 20 ♖xe1 f6 21 ♗xf5 ♗xf5 22 ♗h4, and White had provoked Black's three castled kingside pawns into being weaker than White's. Motylev later won.

So the underlying positional idea with the queen over Adams's next few moves has been seen before, but with a slightly different setting. The most impressive idea by Adams is yet to come.

14 ♗c2

White, as before, aims for ♕d3 followed by g4.

14...♖d8

White keeps a slight edge after 14...♗e6 15 ♕d3 g6 16 ♗d2.

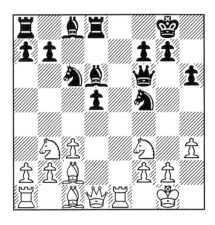

15 ♕d3

So far the attention in the four central squares has been concentrating, directly or indirectly, on the d4-square. If White has unambiguous control of d4, and has no worries about any active counterplay from Black, then he can expect to be at least slightly better.

15 ♘bd4 is premature, unless of course your sole ambition as White is to aim for an equal endgame with level and symmetrical play after 15...♘fxd4 16 ♘xd4 ♘xd4 17 ♕xd4 ♕xd4 18 cxd4. The records on ChessBase show that a young player achieved this draw as White with a highly-experienced Grandmaster. He gained several Elo points, and later became a GM himself.

White is clearly not able to take full control with a piece on d4. He needs to think about other squares, and lines. Here Adams focuses on the b1-h7 diagonal as a possible weak spot. Clearly there is a direct threat of g4, as a result of White's manoeuvring on the diagonal, and as soon as Black covers this threat, White immediately starts setting up a weakness on another square. Then, who knows, a second weakness may turn into a third weakness.

15...g6

Black is understandably concerned about the diagonal.

15...♗f8?! has also been tried, but is unconvincing. Black's idea is that after 16 g4 ♕g6 his position holds. White can improve with 16 ♗f4, and Black had to try 16...g6 anyway, losing coordination after 17 ♗c7!? ♖d7 18 ♗h2 ♖d8 19 ♖ad1 ♗e6 20 ♘e5 in S.Zagrebelny-W.Uhlmann, Schwerin 1999. It would seem better for Black to keep some control of the b8-h2 diagonal.

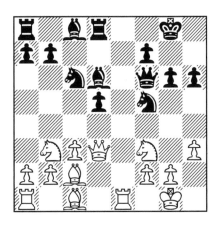

16 ♕d2!

Backwards and forwards with the queen, and there is more to follow! White's main aim is to poke Black's h-pawn, with the threat of ♗xf5.

16 ♗d2 a5 17 ♗e3 ♘xe3 18 ♖xe3 was equal in M.Carlsen-A.Yusupov, Amsterdam 2006. This, of course, has the implication that Yusupov had sorted out his opening since his game against Adams in 2005.

16...♗f8

16...h5?! seriously weakens the h4-d8 and c1-h6 diagonals. Any reasonable queen move would give an edge.

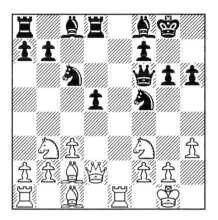

17 ♕f4!

Notice the way in which the queen immediately takes over the square of which the opponent relinquished its defensive cover. The queen manoeuvring continues, not just for attack (ideas of g4), but also for getting the bishop into play. At some stage White would like to develop the queenside rook, given the chance.

White has to be careful not to be over-elaborate with his play. After 17 ♘h2 (if 17 ♕e2, Psakhis gives 17...♘d6 as a good reply, presumably about equal) 17...♕g7 18 ♘g4 d4! 19 ♕e2 (Psakhis gives 19 ♗xf5 gxf5 20 ♘xh6+ ♔h7 as winning for Black, but this needs to be proven; 21 ♕g5 ♕g6 22 ♕xg6+ ♔xg6 23 ♘g8 ♗d6 24 ♘h6 ♗f8 ends up only as a perpetual) 19...h5 20 ♗xf5 hxg4 21 ♗xg4 dxc3 22 bxc3 ♕xc3 23 ♗g5 ♗xg4 24 ♕xg4 play is about equal, with chances for both sides, J.Ivanov-J.Ulko, Moscow 1998.

17...♗g7

17...♗d6 18 ♕a4! still allows the queen to run around, and Black is not making any progress with his pieces or pawns:

a) 18...♗d7 19 ♗xf5! with advantage. Then, for example, continuing the theme of the queen wandering, if 19...♕xf5 20 ♕h4!? h5 21 ♘bd2, and White is in control, or 19...gxf5 20 ♕h4.

b) If 18...g5 19 ♕b5 (yes, another queen move!) 19...a6 20 ♕d3, and the traveller returns. In comparison with White's 15th move, White has moved his queen from d3-d2-f4-a4-b5-d3. Black meanwhile has moved the bishop from d6 to f8 and back to d6, while his a-pawn has moved to a6, which is genuinely useful, and his g-pawn has moved twice to get from g7 to g5, which is a weakening. Black now has kingside difficulties.

Such complicated positional manoeuvring is characteristic usually of the endgame rather than the middlegame, and is rare indeed to see this in the late opening phase. In the endgame, such play can be complicated with maybe two or three pieces (including king) on either side, and every pawn push has to be handled with great care. Here we have such themes with almost a full board of pieces and pawns. Enjoy it!

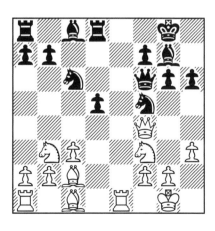

18 ♗d2!!

Adams plays a star move, and an improvement on previous play. At first, this is only a routine developing move, and anyone could play it. Look more closely, however, and the bishop is covering the queen's best escape square, and horrors, the queen may even get stuck on the nightmare square of h1. Most strong players who have reached this would presumably have rejected the text move, just on this basis. Adams has seen further, and seen that the queen will return.

Adams had in fact reached this position before with 18 h4 (18 ♕c7? led to a loss after 18...♘d6 19 ♘c5 ♗xh3 20 gxh3 ♕xf3 21 ♖e3 ♕h5 in K.Asrian-S.Lputian, Yerevan 1995; the queen is allowed a few lives, but should not take things too far) 18...♕d6 19 ♗d2 ♗e6 20 ♖ad1 ♕xf4 21 ♗xf4 d4 22 ♗xf5 ♗xb3 23 axb3 gxf5 24 ♘xd4 ♘xd4 25 cxd4 ♗xd4 26 ♗xh6 ♗xb2 27 ♖xd8+ ♖xd8 28 ♖e7 ♖d1+ 29 ♔h2 ♗d4, uncomfortable for Black, but leading to a draw before too long in M.Adams-S.Lputian, Moscow 2004. He clearly wanted to find improvements.

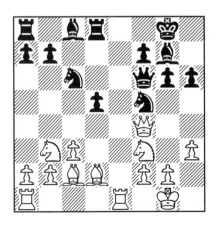

18...g5

Otherwise White is safe, and better.

19 ♕h2

The queen finds another square. Note that 19 ♕a4? ♘d6, threatening ...♗xh3, leaves White's queen under pressure, for example, 20 ♘bd4 ♗d7 21.♘xc6 bxc6.

19...b6?!

Psakhis notes that this move looks a little strange, as the bishop is unable to find any good squares on the a6-f1 diagonal. He suggests that 19...♗f8!? would have been better. It is difficult to know what Adams would have intended here, there being no single clearly best move, and a few possible ideas for maybe a slight edge.

The most visually paradoxical suggestion, though, is 20 ♖ad1!?, good standard development, and then 20...♗d6 21 ♕h1!!, the only move, but wow! This is well worth a diagram.

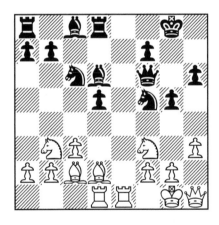

The game A.Nimzowitsch-A.Rubinstein, Dresden 1926, and Nimzowitsch's famed 18 ♘h1! is, in comparison, just so early 20th Century. The knight goes back to h1, but then it manoeuvres to f2 and h3, so what is the problem? These days we need greater entertainment. Adams's queen is stuck like a horror story, king and pawns, plus the opposing dark-squared bishop, burying any escape, but if White keeps the option of g4, the queen has breathing space, with chances of attack on the long diagonal.

Here 21...♘h4!? is a sensible reply, with the idea that if 22 ♘xh4 gxh4 there are en passant problems after 23 g4? hxg3. White could still continue with the exchange of knights with 23 ♗e3 ♗e6 24 ♖d2, with *Fritz* suggesting a substantial edge, but the human eye being worried about the lack of space for White's queen. Or, simpler, White could, and probably would, try 22 ♘fd4 ♘xd4 23 ♘xd4, and if 23...♘f5 24 ♗xf5 ♗xf5 25 ♘xf5 ♕xf5 26 g4! with stabilization and a positional edge for White.

The line actually played by Yusupov is, of course, worth studying, but one cannot help feeling that it was a loss that we did not see the ♕h1 idea in genuine match-play.

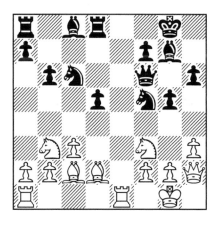

20 ♖ad1

Adams can now enjoy the luxury of a simple and straightforward developing move. His position is comfortable.

20...♗a6

Black is at least being consistent, but

his bishop is not that well placed here.

Psakhis gives 20...♗f8 21 ♘e5 ♗d6 22 f4 with advantage to White; Black's ...b6 in this line is of course a loss of tempo.

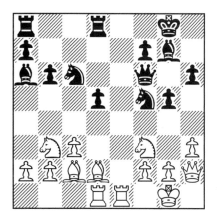

21 ♗xf5!

The end of the shadowboxing. Adams now uses the standard idea against the Tarrasch Defence of exchanging the knight that covers the outpost on d4.

21...♕xf5 22 ♗e3

Now with two knights, a bishop, a rook and a pawn all covering d4, White keeps an edge. He can use d4 as a transit station for attacks against other pieces and squares. So often in Isolated Queen's Pawn positions, the critical square is not so much the isolated pawn itself, but rather the square in front of it.

22...♗c4

22...♖ac8 23 ♘bd4 ♕g6 24 ♘xc6 ♕xc6 25 ♗d4, for example, gives White an advantage.

23 ♘bd4

Consistent play.

23...♗xd4

Just about playable, but with queens and rooks onboard, it is often best for the defender with a few weaknesses to avoid the bishops of opposite colour.

Psakhis suggests that Black should have tried 23...♘xd4! 24 ♗xd4 f6, and White will have to work hard to try to force a win.

24 ♘xd4 ♘xd4 25 ♗xd4

On the light squares, Black can attack the pawn on a2, but this is hardly of significance. Much more importantly White is pressing hard on the dark squares, making piece outposts maybe on e5 or e7, and setting up pawn attacks, supported by the bishop, on g5 and h6.

25...♖e8

There are several ways of handling 25...♗xa2. Maybe the simplest is to double on the e-file with 26 ♖e5 ♕g6 27 ♖de1. He has no need to hurry, and Black can do nothing with the extra pawn. White can set up a pawn-spike with f4 or h4 at the right time.

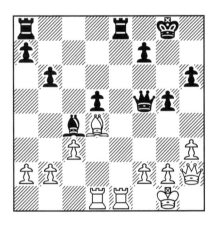

26 ♕c7?!

White even finds weak squares on the queenside. It's an attractive move, but 26 ♕d6! seems even better. Then 26...♖e6 27 ♖xe6 ♕xe6 28 ♕xe6 fxe6 29 b3 ♗a6 30 f3 leaves White better in the endgame, but it is going to be a long

struggle. White has the better pawn structure, with two islands of three pawns against three islands of two pawns, and there are definite weaknesses on each of Black's pawn islands. White could, most obviously, try to break up Black's g- and h-pawns with a well timed h4, or he could try to drill open the queenside pawns with a4 and a5, or, of course, he could combine both options.

If 26 h4 instead, then 26...♗e2! 27 ♖c1 ♖e6 could easily lead to deadlock. Black will need to double the rooks, and keep the bishop on e2, otherwise his position will start to fold, but it is not so clear that White can play for an advantage.

26...♗xa2?

Missing the one real chance of trying to hold the position.

26...♗e2! 27 ♖c1 ♕c8 28 ♕g3 ♕b8! traps the queen, forcing an endgame with only slight chances.

White can try 28 ♕d6 ♕e6 29 ♕g3 in this line, but he must be careful of counterplay after 29...♖e4.

27 ♕c6

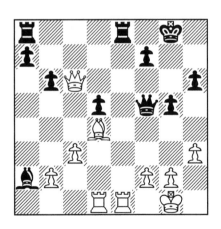

White is on target again.

27...♖f8

If 27...♖xe1+ 28 ♖xe1 ♖f8 29 ♖e8 (threatening ♕xh6) 29...f6 30 ♖xf8+ ♔xf8 31 ♕a8+, and White wins a piece.

28 ♕xh6

Now it is simple mopping up.

28...f6

Otherwise there is checkmate on the dark squares, and 28...♕h7 29 ♕xg5+ ♕g6 30 ♕h4 is miserable.

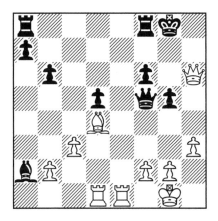

29 ♖e7

The rook joins in on the seventh rank, now that Black's pawn has moved out of the way.

29...♖f7

The only way to delay checkmate. Remember that Black's pawns and pieces are level, so it is not yet time for Black to give up.

30 ♖de1

This however gives a very clear message. White is threatening checkmate with 31 ♖e8+, and if Black tries to exchange with 30...♖xe7 31 ♖xe7, the other rook checkmates on the seventh. There are other moves, but this is the

quickest and cleanest.

30...♖af8

Trying to set up some barriers.

31 ♖xf7

Again, quickest and simplest.

31...♔xf7

And 31...♖xf7? 32 ♖e8+ is quicker.

32 g4!

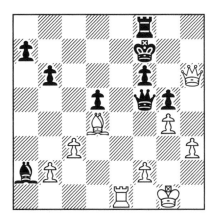

We have seen this pawn move before, though previously White's queen may have started off from the extremely unlikely square of h1 or h2. Here the queen is out in the open, and quickly wins.

Black's queen has no good square, in view of White's pressure on f6 and h7. If 32...♕g6, White wins material with 33 ♖e7+ ♔xe7 34 ♕xg6. So:

1-0

One of the most interesting games in this book. The only real regret, from the point of view of the reader, is that Yusupov did not find the way to force Adams into a rook and opposite-coloured bishop endgame.

Game 4
V.Topalov-V.Anand
Sofia 2005
Queen's Indian Defence E15

1 d4 ♘f6

Initiating the Indian Openings. Why 'Indian'? The basic point would seem to be that after 1...♘f6, Black makes only one-pawn advances in such openings (for example ...b6, ...e6 and ...g6), instead of the 'European' double pawn-advance with ...d5. Chess has evolved over the many centuries, with different innovations in the structure of the game in both east and west. But that is another story.

Black's 1...♘f6 prevents White from setting two central passed pawns on d4 and e4, a good start.

For 1...d5, see Game 1, Kasimdzhanov-Kasparov 2005, and comments thereafter.

2 c4

White wants to make it difficult for Black to play ...d5. 2 ♘c3 d5 is possible, but White cannot quickly put pressure on the d5-pawn with c4.

2 ♘f3 is more mainstream, and usually transposes (as in Game 8, Sargissian-Nisipeanu) into one of the Indian Systems, or perhaps the Queen's Gambit. There are extra independent possibilities if White tries 3 ♗g5 after 2...e6 or 2...g6.

2...e6

2...d5?! would be mistimed. After 3 cxd5 ♘xd5 4 e4 (or maybe 4 ♘f3 followed by e4), the knight will have to

wander. Better ...d5 on move 1, or move 3 or beyond.

2...g6 is the King's Indian Defence. Black castles as quickly as possible, without attempting to gain pawn space in the centre, and waits to hit back if and when White tries to set up a large pawn centre. Play can become highly complicated. Kasparov favoured this opening, and earlier Tal and Fischer. See the comments to Game 19, Van Wely-Radjabov; an example of how unbelievably complicated such lines may become.

3 ♘f3

3 ♘c3 will tend to end up into the Nimzo-Indian with 3...♗b4, although 3...d5 would lead into a main line Queen's Gambit. For further comments on the Nimzo-Indian, see Game 12, Bareev-Efimenko.

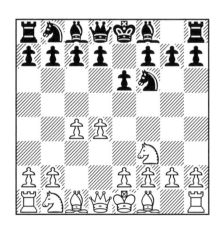

3...b6

Instead 3...d5 would be an Orthodox Queen's Gambit.

Anand here played the Queen's Indian Defence. In many countries, the King's Indian would be described as the East Indian, while the Queen's Indian would be called the West Indian. Back in the 1980s, when the Caribbean countries were dominant in the game of cricket, a booklet gave the intriguing possibility of an idea of the fianchetto system versus the West Indians! It remains unclear whether the fianchetto is a weapon for batsmen or bowlers.

4 g3

And here we have the anti-West-Indian fianchetto, in chess at least.

A standard opening plan, fianchettoing the bishop, quietly castling kingside, and settling down perhaps for a slight positional edge, or steady equality. That would be the normal course of events, but it so happens that White does not manage to complete the fianchetto.

4 ♘c3, 4 a3, 4 e3 and 4 ♗g5 are possible too, but not necessarily dangerous after good play.

4...♗a6

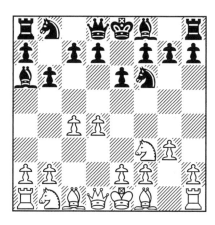

Black disrupts, but only slightly, the natural development plans, forcing White to protect the c4-pawn.

For the standard alternative 4...♗b7, see Game 23, Carlsen-Tiviakov.

5 b3

For 5 ♕c2, see Game 21, Alekseev-Tkachiev.

5...♗b4+

Black ensures that White cannot create simple and harmonious development with ♘c3 and ♗b2.

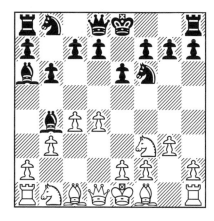

6 ♗d2

White would already be under pressure after 6 ♘db2? ♗c3 7 ♖b1 ♗b7, with threats of ...♗xd4 and ...♗e4.

6...♗e7

This is maybe a difficult point to understand for the less-experienced player. After all, we are taught about developing as quickly and efficiently as possible, in order to bring the pieces into play without delay, and ...♗b4+ followed by ...♗e7 would seem to be a loss of time. Try to look through things from White's point of view, though. His dark-squared bishop ideally belongs on the long diagonal, there is not all that much to be done on g5, f4, or indeed even d2. If the bishop arrives on c3, that is on a useful diagonal, but the bishop also gets in the way of the knight. If White were to set up the natural queenside diagonal – with ♘c3, ♗c1 and ♗b2; or ♗c3, ♗b2, ♘c3 – he would be losing a tempo as a result of Black's bishop check, rather than gaining it. In consequence, White will need to find a different approach.

6...♕e7 7 ♗g2 is possible, but White should have a slight edge. Black's pieces are not fully coordinated.

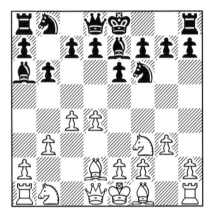

7 ♘c3

7 ♗g2 is, of course, also possible with 7...d5 or 7...♗b7 being the main responses. As we shall soon see, Topalov has in mind something more ambitious.

7...c6

Black wants to add the security of a recapture with the c-pawn on d5, after ...d5; cxd5. If immediately 7...d5 8 cxd5 exd5 9 ♗g2, the 'minority pawn attack' on the queenside tends here to be in favour of White. He attacks hard against the pawn on d5, and eventually forces Black to play ...c6. Then White puts pressure on the half-open c-file, and eventually tries to attack the c6-pawn with b4-b5. Any exchange of

Black's c-pawn will then leave Black with an isolated pawn on d5, and White will eventually try to win that pawn. This is a well-established plan of attack, and usually Black will want to avoid it. The problem is often even worse with ...b6 than with the pawn still on b7, since Black has further weakened the light-squared pawn chain.

8 e4

Three good central pawns, and indeed why not? Black needs to start central counterplay immediately.

8 ♗g2 d5 9 cxd5 cxd5 is, of course, possible, but is realistically only a drawing attempt.

8...d5

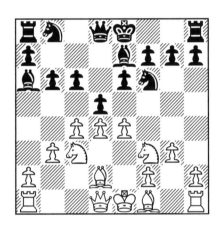

Finally, the clash of centres opens up after much hedging around. Neither side is fully developed yet, but there is an immediate pawn clash. This often means a particularly violent sequence of play, as the attacker wants to take advantage of the opponent's lack of development. This sometimes means sacrifices, to break through before his opponent develops. On the other hand, everything might well fizzle out as equality, if both players complete their development, and the pawn structures could end up as level. With Topalov playing as White, what do you think will happen?

9 ♕c2

White keeps the balance in the centre, for the time being. 9 e5 ♘e4 has been tried several times, but it is only about equal.

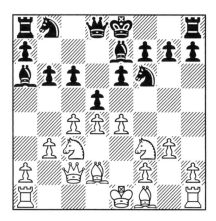

9...dxe4

Nothing out of the ordinary, one might think. The only peculiarity about this opening is that White's g3 has weakened the long diagonal, and this if anything might be in favour of Black.

10 ♘xe4 ♝b7!?

As a result of the outcome of this game, Anand gives this as a question mark. It was certainly dangerous, but maybe it was not objectively wrong.

So what else? Since this game, most top-level encounters have continued with 10...c5, and only then ...♝b7, with good equalizing chances. If, for example, 11 dxc5?! ♝b7!, taking advantage of the exposed long diagonal. After 12 ♝d3 bxc5? 13 ♝c3 ♕b6 14 0-0-0 White has a slight edge, and later won in B.Gelfand-A.Grischuk, Khanty-Mansiysk 2005; Black never getting the chance to castle after further inaccuracies. How-

ever, Gelfand suggests that Black could have improved with 12...♘bd7!, so that if 13 cxb6? ♘c5 14 ♘xc5 ♝xf3, and Black wins material.

11 ♘eg5?!

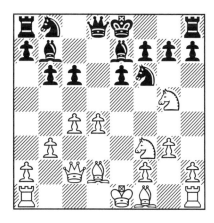

This is marvellous chess, absolutely brilliant, but if Black has an advantage at a later stage, then White must have made a mistake. In the end, the exchange sacrifice was not quite sound, but if it was good enough to beat Anand, then it would have been good enough to beat anyone.

11...c5

Topalov would, of course, have analysed this position in depth at home. There will inevitably be hidden depths, including sacrifices and unexpected manoeuvres, making it extremely difficult for Anand to steer a way through to safety over the board.

Black's move is certainly logical and natural, opening up the long diagonal, and continuing his earlier development plan. Is it good or not? We wait and see. However, could Black have tried to refute or undermine White's attacking plans?

11...h6?! looks rather too drastic. White is clearly intending to sacrifice, so we try 12 ♘xf7! (better than 12 ♘xe6) 12...♔xf7 13 ♘e5+:

a) If then 13...♔f8, Anand gives 14 ♗h3 ♕xd4 15 ♘g6+ ♔e8 16 0-0 ♕e4 (any tame rook move would give White excellent compensation for the piece) 17 ♕xe4 ♘xe4.

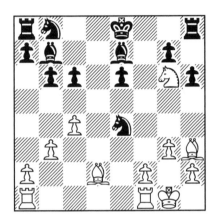

Now White has to continue the attack, and has no time to snatch a rook with 18 ♘xh8? ♘xd2.

Therefore 18 ♖fe1!, and if 18...♘xd2 19 ♖xe6, and White will clearly win back the bishop on e7, and will win even more material, ending up ahead. Anand continues the analysis with 18...c5 19 ♗g2 ♗f6 20 ♖xe4!!. Material is level now, and all four rooks are under attack, directly or indirectly, by minor pieces; an unusual situation. After 20...♗xe4 21 ♗xe4 ♗xa1 22 ♘xh8 g5 23 h4 ♗xh8 25 hxg5 hxg5 26 ♗xg5, White will end up a pawn ahead in a minor piece endgame. Anand gives too 20...♔d7, and then demonstrates that White can set up another desperado sacrifice with 21 ♖xe6 ♗xg2 22 ♖xf6 gxf6 23 ♘xh8, and eventually win, a pawn ahead.

b) Alternatively, Anand analyses 13...♔g8 14 ♗h3 ♕xd4 15 ♗xe6+ ♔f8

16 ♘g6+ ♔e8 17 0-0-0! ♕a1+ 18 ♕b1 ♗a3+ 19 ♔c2 ♕xb1+ 20 ♔xb1, with advantage to White. Here Tyomkin suggests 14...♗c8 15 0-0, with pressure and excellent compensation for the sacrificed knight. Carrying on with possible moves by Black, play could continue with 15...♗d6 16 ♘g6 ♖h7 (Black needs his extra compensation) 17 ♖fe1 ♘a6 18 ♗xe6 ♗xe6 19 ♖xe6.

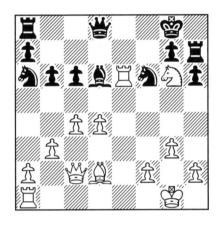

White now has a second pawn in compensation for his knight, and still can put on the pressure. Here 19...♘c7 20 ♖e3 ♕d7 21 ♖ae1 ♖d8 22 ♘e7+ ♔f8 (better than 22...♔h8 23 ♕g6) gives White a perpetual, but it is not so clear that he has more: 23 ♖f3 ♗xe7 24 ♕xh7 ♘e6 25 ♗e3!? (25 ♗xh6 gxh6 26 ♕xh6+ draws) 25...♘xd4 26 ♗xd4 ♕xd4 27 ♕h8+ ♔g7 28 ♖xe7 ♔xe7 29 ♕xg7+ ♔e6 30 ♖e3+ ♔f5 31 h3 h5 32 ♖f3+ ♔e3 33 ♖e3+ is a perpetual. Naturally, this is only one line of several possibilities, but it provides a useful indicator that first, Black's position is not about to collapse, and, second, that White's sacrifice on f7 seems sound.

Black should also consider 11...0-0, but White could start attacking with 12 0-0-0 h6 13 h4, and if 13...c5 14 d5 exd5

15 cxd5 with ideas of attack, as in the game, but without forcing White to sacrifice the knight.

Black might just as well try for extra material.

12 d5!

The d4-d5 pawn push, famed by Kasparov in his youthful years, and with several new twists by Topalov and by others. It is a specialty of the Queen's Indian, but there are also similar d5-pawn pushes in the Grünfeld.

On any other move, Black is better.

12...exd5

And Black must take up the challenge.

13 cxd5

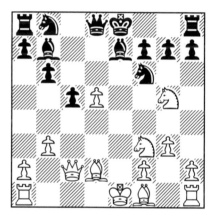

The sacrifice is familiar and dangerous, but there is an unusual peculiarity following White's opening set-up, with his pawn being on g3 rather than the more natural g2, and his other pawn being on b3 rather than b2. One might expect that Black could set up counterplay on either of the long diagonals, and certainly there are threats along these lines, but White, maybe unexpectedly, can parry these threats and set up his own. This is the sort of position where no player could try such a gambit purely by instinct over the board. Topalov would clearly have looked at this at home, and decided it was good, or at the very least promising.

13...h6

And Black has to make another extremely difficult decision. He has three different ways to take the pawn on d5, could attack the knight (13...h6), or could castle. Five tempting moves, and even if further analysis suggests that, say, two of these moves may be rejected quickly as unsound, it is possible that only one of the remaining moves might prove to be good, or at least clearly better than anything else.

On such assumptions, there may only be a 30 to 40 percent chance of finding a good move. Then after that the defender has to find a string of further correct moves to defend against the attack. Over several moves, the chances of playing ten accurate moves against a strong attacking player may end up to be very slight. All great attackers rely on this arithmetic.

Let us try to whittle down some of the weaker moves just here:

a) 13...♕xd5? 14 ♗c4 leaves Black with no good moves. After 14...♕c6 15 ♗xf7+ ♔f8 16 ♗c4 White is clearly better. In this line, take notice of the way in which the queen and four minor pieces cover so many squares. Coordination is an important part of attack.

b) 13...♗xd5 14 0-0-0 leaves Black's pieces looking rather frayed on the d-file. Anand gives 14...h6 15 ♗c3 hxg5 16 ♗xf6 gxf6 17 ♗c4 with a big plus for White. Play this on for a few moves, and it becomes decisive after 17...♗xf3 18 ♖xd8+ ♗xd8 19 ♖e1+ ♔f8 20 ♕d3 ♘a6 21 ♕d7.

c) 13...♘xd5 14 ♗b5+ allows two ways to block the check with the knight:

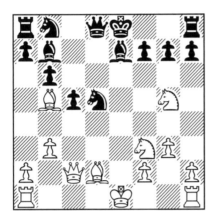

c1) 14...♘d7 allows White to play the simple tactic 15 ♘xf7?! ♚xf7 16 ♗xd7, with the idea 16...♕xd7?? 17 ♘e5+, but Black can be more sophisticated: after 16...♗f6!, he has taken the edge. Here 15 0-0-0! is much better, making full use of the various open lines. If, for example, 15...♘c7 16 ♗c4 ♗xf3 17 ♕f5 f6 18 ♘xf3, and Black's play will be uncomfortable.

c2) The other try for Black is 14...♘c6. If 15 ♘xf7? ♚xf7 16 ♗xc6, Black has 16...♗f6! 17 ♗xb7 ♕e7+ with an edge. 15 ♘e5?! also lacks subtlety, and after 15...♗xg5 16 ♘xc6 ♗xd2+ 17 ♕xd2 ♕f6 Black is again very comfortable. Sometimes it is wisest to complete one's development, here with 15 0-0-0 followed by ♖he1, with highly promising gambit play.

d) Finally, 13...0-0 14 0-0-0 g6 15 h4 gives White excellent attacking chances: for example, 15...♗xd5 16 ♗c3 ♘bd7 17 h5, and Black's position is horrible.

Ultimately there is no safe and simple way for Black to try to refute Topalov's play, or even to equalize with any

sort of ease. Technically, Anand's 13...h6 is almost certainly best. Sometimes the defender has to ride the storm.

14 ♘xf7!?

The art of sacrifice is still alive! Often sacrificial play has been enhanced, rather than diminished, by modern opening theory.

Topalov does not allow Anand the luxury of a quiet equal endgame after 14 ♗b5+ ♘bd7 15 ♘e6 fxe6 16 ♕g6+ (16 dxe6? 0-0 wins for Black) 16...♚f8 17 dxe6 ♕e8 18 ♕xe8+ ♘xe8 19 exd7 ♗xf3 20 dxe8♕+ ♖xe8 21 ♗xe8 ♗xh1. Rather he forces his opponent to work harder.

14...♚xf7

15 0-0-0!

Sacrifices can sometimes be almost routine. Not so much, though, when a player is not ahead in development, and castles quietly without a direct attack. White is relying not so much on his own pieces' strength, but rather Black's weaknesses in front of the king.

15 ♘e5+ ♚g8 16 d6 is the obvious attacking idea. Black can then take the rook: 16...♗xh1 17 ♗c4+ ♗d5 18 ♗xd5+ ♘xd5 19 ♕g6 ♕xd6 20 ♕f7+ ♚h7 21 ♕f5+ ♚g8 (not 21...g6?? 22 ♕f7 mate)

with a perpetual. In this line, 17...♔f8 18 ♘g6+ ♔e8 19 ♘xh8 ♗xd6 20 ♕g6+ ♔d7 21 0-0-0 would be extremely risky for Black: 21...♗e4 seems the best way of keeping the position under control, with 22 ♕xg7+ ♕e7 23 ♗xh6 ♕xg7 24 ♗xg7 ♘e8 25 ♗c3 leading to complicated endgame play, with three connected passed pawns versus knight and another pawn.

After the text, the attack is strong, and very few people would be able to find a way to safety for Black.

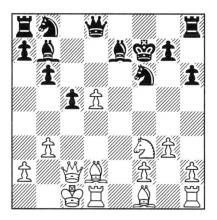

15...♗d6!?

Anand displays tough defensive chess, manoeuvring his bishops to the b8-h2 and c8-h3 diagonals. It is fair to say that the vast majority of players would have fallen quickly against Topalov's onslaught. As we shall see later, even Anand gave way at a critical moment.

The simple pawn capture, 15...♗xd5?, has to be regarded with suspicion. Black may have the long diagonal for the bishop, but he has also weakened the d-file and the c4-g8 diagonal, and the pins will soon intensify. After 16 ♗c3 ♘bd7 (16...♘c6 17 ♗xf6 ♗xf6 18 ♖xd5 quickly regains all the

material, and the attack continues) 17 ♖xd5 ♘xd5 18 ♕f5+ ♘7f6 19 ♘e5+ ♔f8 20 ♘g6+ ♔g8 21 ♗xf6 ♗xf6 22 ♗c4, sure enough, White wins by the pin.

A more interesting battle emerges after the line 15...♘bd7 16 ♘h4 ♘f8 17 d6:

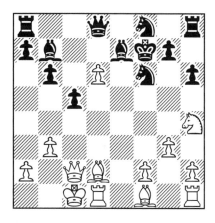

a) After 17...♕xd6 18 ♗c4+ ♘e6 19 ♕g6+ ♔f8 20 ♖he1 ♕d4 21 ♗xe6 ♕a1+ 22 ♕b1 ♕xb1+ 23 ♔xb1 Black has succeeded in exchanging the queens, but not much else. Material is equal, but White has clearly a winning piece advantage.

b) 17...♗xd6 similarly does not slow down the attack much: 18 ♗c4+ ♗d5 19 ♗xh6!? ♖xh6 20 ♖xd5 ♘xd5 (20...♘e6 21 ♖dd1 gives White massive compensation for the knight) 21 ♗xd5+ ♘e6 22 ♕f5+ ♖f6 23 ♗xd6+ with a winning attack.

c) Black might just as well take the rook, 17...♗xh1!, and hope for the best. Tyomkin, no doubt pressed by deadlines, suggests only that after 18 dxe7 ♕xe7 19 f3 the bad bishop on h1 drops, White is only the exchange down, and still has an attack. If, however, one of the players is still a whole rook down, it is useful to look further:

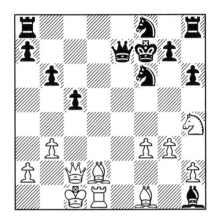

c1) 19...♕e5 is a possibility, and White must be careful not to allow ...♕a1+. Maybe then 20 ♗c3 ♕e3+ 21 ♔b2 ♘e6 22 ♗xf6! gxf6 (22...♔g8 23 ♕g6 ♖d7 24 ♗d3 wins, as does 22...♔xf6 23 ♕g6+ ♔e7 24 ♘f5+) 23 ♕g6+ ♔f8 24 ♖d7 with a mating attack.

c2) 19...♘e6 looks reasonably solid at first, but Black still has problems with developing his pieces. After 20 ♕g6+ ♔g8 21 ♗c4 ♕f7 22 ♖xh1 ♖e8 23 ♖e1 Black cannot unravel his pieces, and White should win. Here 20...♔f8 escapes the dangerous diagonal. There is complicated play after 21 ♕f5 ♘d4 22 ♘g6+ ♔e8 23 ♗b5+ ♔d8 24 ♗f4!, but White's queen and bishop pair remain dominant: for example, 24...♕b7 25 ♘xh8 ♗xf3 26 ♕e6 ♗h5 27 ♕d6+ ♘d7 28 ♖e1, and White wins, or 24...♕d6 25 ♘xh8 ♘xf5 26 ♘f7+ ♔c8 27 ♘xd6+ ♘xd6 28 ♖xd8, which does not provide real safety.

c3) 19...♗xf3!? 20 ♘xf3 g5 returns the bishop quickly, but diverts the knight from covering g6. However, White retains excellent compensation for the exchange and pawn sacrifice, his minor pieces being formidable, while Black's knights have no good

squares. Play would continue with 21 ♖e1 followed by ♗c4+.

So it seems that Anand's assessment is absolutely correct in preferring 19...♗d6.

16 ♘h4!

On the edge, but hitting hard on the light squares, with ideas of ♕g6+ and ♘f5.

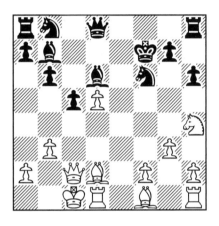

16...♗c8!

Steady defence. Alternatively:

a) 16...♗xd5? opens up the position too quickly. After 17 ♗c3 ♗xh1 18 ♗c4+ White is, of course, winning, and Tyomkin signs off here. The stubborn computer gives 18...♔e7 19 ♘f5+ ♔f8 20 ♖xd6 ♘bd7 21 ♘h4 ♗e4, but then a queen sacrifice 22 ♕xe4 ♘xe4 23 ♘g6+ ♔e8 23 ♖e6+ ♔f7 24 ♖f6+ wins.

b) 16...♖e8 17 ♕g6+ ♔g8 18 ♘f5 is highly threatening, and helps explain why Anand chose 16...♗c8 instead. Tyomkin gives 18...♕c7 19 ♗xh6 ♗f8 20 ♗xg7! ♗xg7 21 ♗b5! with far too many threats.

c) Anand himself gives 16...♘a6 17 ♗h3 in *Informator*, but probably without much expectation that Black would survive. At least though Black is starting to develop his queenside. One possibility is 17...♗xd5 18 ♖he1 ♘c7 19 ♗c3. The practical player over the board would not have to analyse hard to conclude that White, although a knight down, is almost certainly winning. He has excellent diagonals for his queen and bishops, and strong open lines for his rooks, while Black has several weaknesses. Play might continue 19...♔g8 20 ♗xf6 ♕xf6 21 ♖xd5 ♕a1+ 22 ♔d2 ♕xe1+ 23 ♔xe1 ♖e8+ 24 ♔d1 ♘xd5 25 ♕c4 ♖e5 26 ♗g2, winning material.

17 ♖e1!

Just as White's attack appears to be slowing down, Topalov throws a log on to the fire with ♖e6, sacrificing the exchange to regain control with ♘f5.

17 ♕g6+ ♔g8 18 ♗c3 a5!? would have given nothing.

17...♘a6

To develop the minor pieces, or to contest the open file – which is better?

After 17...♖e8 18 ♗b5 ♖e7 Anand, looking from the defender's point of view, recommends 19 ♗c3!. Clearly the idea is to eliminate the f6-knight. The sort of line that Anand would have been thinking of is presumably something like 19...a6 (trying to gain a tempo, and helping to defend with ...♖a7) 20 ♕g6+ ♔g8 21 ♗xf6 ♖xe1+ 22 ♖xe1 ♕xf6 23 ♖e8+ ♗f8 24 ♗d3 ♕a1+ 25 ♔d2 ♕b2+ 26 ♔e1 ♕a1+ 27 ♔e2 ♕b4+ 25 ♔f3, and Black is running out of checks, while White continues his powerful attack. Here too 19 ♗xh6 would have been a possibility, demolishing a pawn, and if 19...♖xe1+? 20 ♖xe1 gxh6 21 ♕xg6+ ♔g8 22 ♕xh6+ ♔g8 23 ♕g5+ ♔f7 (or 23...♔f8 24 ♖e8+!) 24 ♗e8+!, making attractive use of the pin. However, Black could decline the sacrifice, and 19...♔g8! is probably playable for White, but not better for him.

18 ♖e6!

The promised sacrifice. Or at least a breakthrough on the light squares, rather than a genuine sacrifice.

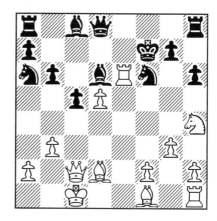

18...♘b4?

Of course, Black cannot take, as if 18...♗xe6? then 19 fxe6+ ♔g8 20 ♗xa6, so really it is a pseudo-sacrifice, for the moment at least.

With the move played, Anand forces Topalov to exchange his dark-squared bishop for the knight, but as play moves on, it becomes increasingly clear that it is the pressure on the light squares that becomes more important.

Instead 18...♘c7! is critical. The knight stays on a good square, attacking and/or defending the e6-, d5- and e8-squares. Inevitably play will be sharp.

a) The most direct reply is 19 ♕g6+ ♔g8:

a1) Then 20 ♖xd6 ♕xd6 21 ♗f4 ♕d7 22 ♗xc7 ♕xc7 23 d6 ♕f7 24 ♗c4 ♗e6 25 ♗xe6 ♕xe6 26 ♘f5 ♖h7 does not quite work for White.

a2) Therefore the critical line is 20 ♘f5 ♗f8 21 ♗c4 with counterplay with

21...b5. Now 22 ♗c3 ♘xe6 23 dxe6 bxc4 24 e7 ♕e8 holds fine for Black. Tyomkin therefore recommends 22 ♘e7+ ♗xe7 23 ♖xe7 with a further divide:

a21) 23...♖h7 24 ♗c3 ♕f8 25 ♖he1 leads to obvious zugzwang potential. Carrying on with this, White wins after 25...bxc4 26 ♗xf6 ♘xd5 27 ♖f7 ♕xf7 28 ♖e8+ ♕f8 29 ♖xf8+ ♔xf8 30 ♗e5.

a22) Black therefore has to jettison material with 23...♕xe7! 24 d6+ bxc4 25 dxe7 ♗e6 26 bxc4 ♗xc4 27 ♗f4 ♗f7.

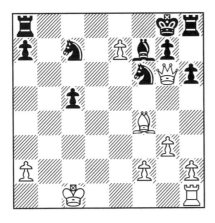

Having reached this position in his analysis, Tyomkin comments that 'the outcome here is completely unclear'. This is no cop-out. The position is genuinely difficult. White has queen and two pawns for the rook and two minor pieces, about level according to positional theory, but of course such a position is likely to be unbalanced. One of White's extra pawns is passed on the seventh, which is useful, but it cannot win material, and merely ties down Black's pieces. If Black can gradually bring his pieces into better squares, he will be on top. Probably the position favours Black: for example, 28 ♕f5 ♘cd5 29 ♗d6 g6!? (there are several alternatives, but this seems among the

most direct) 30 ♕e5 ♔h7 31 ♖d1 ♖ac8 32 h4 ♘d7 33 ♕b2 ♖he8, and while Black's pawn structure has been slightly compromised by his ...g6 pawn push, his pieces have been quickly activated, and are strong.

b) Anand himself, who after all has tried over the board to defend this position as Black, concentrated on a different line, 19 ♗c4 b5 20 ♗c3 (20 ♕g6+ ♔g8 21 ♘f5 ♗f8 transposes to variation 'a2') seeing this as a dangerous:

b1) If 20...bxc4?, Black's position collapses after 21 ♕g6+ ♔f8 22 ♗xf6.

b2) Black's position also folds after 20...♘xe6? 21 dxe6+ ♗xe6 22 ♕g6+ ♔f8 23 ♗xe6 ♕c7 24 ♕f5 threatening ♘g6+.

b3) 20...♘fe8!, avoiding the capture on f6, is the most secure.

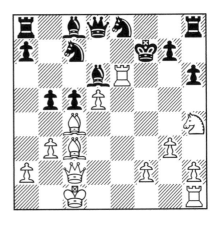

If then 21 ♗xg7?? ♕g5+ with a quick win. The same resource is found after 21 ♕g6+ ♔g8 22 ♗xg7? ♕g5+! 23 ♕xg5 hxg5, and White, already a piece down, has four more pieces under attack. Instead the superior 22 ♖xe8+ ♘xe8 23 ♗xb5 ♕g5+! is highly thematic, and gives Black a substantial edge after 24 ♕xg5 hxg5 25 ♘g6 ♘c7 27 ♗c6 ♖h6.

There is also plenty of entertainment value in 18...♔g8!? 19 ♗c3 ♘xd5 20

♕g6 ♕g5+ 21 ♕xg5+ hxg5 22 ♖xd6 ♘xc3 23 ♗c4+ ♔h7 24 ♗d3+ g6, which probably ends up as a draw. The author looked at this in depth, but there seems to be little reason to publish the line when 18...♘c7! is almost certainly better, with advantage to Black.

Should we say that objectively Topalov's play was unsound? Or should we congratulate him on winning? There is no clear answer, and there are two opposing views on this point. Broadly, the tactical player will tend to argue that he will win by playing better than his opponent, and if there is a mistake on the way, then so be it, no player will be expected to play absolutely perfect chess in a genuinely complicated game. The positional player, in contrast, will want to keep the position under control, arguing that if he makes no mistakes, then he will not lose, and if his opponent makes a mistake, he will lose. Topalov is clearly one of the tacticians.

19 ♗xb4

19 ♕g6+ ♔g8 20 ♘f5 ♗f8 does not achieve much: 21 ♘xh6+ ♗xh6 22 ♗xh6 ♗xe6 23 dxe6 ♕d4 and Black takes over.

19...cxb4 20 ♗c4

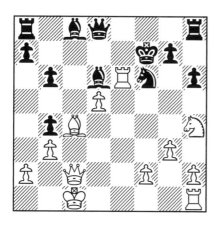

Ultimately, however great the complications may be, the positional strategy is consistent and clear. White must control as many light squares as possible of those covering Black's king. The only justification of White's early sacrifices was to fracture Black's light squares, making the king open to attack. White needs to be consistent, making further sacrifices if necessary. Strangely the bishop has not been needed just yet, but now needs to pile in. The e6-square is critical, whether for rook or pawn, and that square needs to be bolstered.

20...b5!

And Black needs to divert the bishop. Anand gives 20...♔g8 21 ♘f5 ♗xe6 (21....♗f8 22 d6) 22 dxe6 ♗e7 23 ♖d1 ♕f8 (or 23...♕c7 24 ♖d7) 24 ♖d7 ♖e8 25 ♘h4 ♘h7 26 ♕g6 ♘g5 27 f4 b5 28 ♗xb5 as winning for White. Indeed, it is positional strangulation.

21 ♗xb5

There's not much else. If 21 ♘f5 ♗f8, and Black is safe and solid.

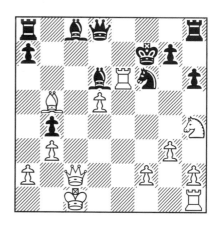

21...♗e7?

Even Anand slips after Topalov's fierce attack.

21...♗xe6? loses quickly after 22

dxe6+ ♔g8 23 e7! ♗xe7 24 ♗c4+ ♘d5 25 ♖d1 ♗xh4 26 ♖xd5. Grandmaster commentators such as Anand and Tyomkin may have regarded this too elementary to be worth publishing, but of course the players would need to have analysed this during the game.

The view given at the time was 21...♔g8! with 22 ♗c4 regarded as the best reply, and if 22...♖b8 (22...♗xe6 23 dxe6 is still too dangerous) 23 ♘f5 ♖b6 'and Black manages to survive' (Tyomkin). However, it is not so clear that White should continue to concentrate on the diagonal. 22 ♕e2!, based on active play on the central files, looks more effective. Of course, if 22...♗xe6?? 23 ♕xe6+ White immediately wins. This ensures that for the moment at least White controls the light squares. If, though, 22...♗b7, White should not try the same trick: 23 ♖e8+?, hoping for 23...♘xe8?? 24 ♕e6+, as Black instead gives up the queen with fully adequate compensation after 23...♕xe8! 24 ♗xe8 ♖xe8, and White runs out of attack. Here 23 ♖d1! is better, with good centralization:

a) 23...♕c7+? 24 ♗c4 ♖d8 25 ♘f5 ♔h7 26 ♘xd6 ♖xd6 27 ♖e7 is inadequate for Black.

b) 23...♖c8+ looks best. Then 24 ♗c4 is a self-pin, and White makes no progress after, for example, 24...♖c5. However, 24 ♔b2! is better. Then if 24...♕c7, White invades a further light square with 25 ♗c6!, obtaining a clear advantage after 25...♗xc6?! 26 dxc6 ♕xc6 27 ♖exd6. Better is 25...♗f8 when there would be no more than equality after the obvious exchange sacrifice 26 ♖xf6? gxf6 27 ♕e6+ ♔h7, but 26 ♗xb7! ♕xb7 27 ♘g6 wins the battle of the light

squares, most convincingly after 27...♖h7?! 28 ♖e7 ♕b6 (28...♗xe7 29 ♕e6 mate) 29 d6.

It is, of course, more than possible that somewhere along the many variations Black could avoid being close to losing, but the general run of play would suggest that White is still better. The judgement is that after Anand's mistake, Black is worse, not 'unclear' as in early assessments.

22 ♘g6

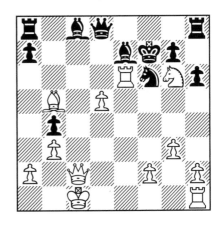

Now Black has too many pieces under attack.

It is quite possible that Anand had missed that after 22...♗xe6 23 dxe6+ ♔g8 24 ♖d1 a queen move was no longer defending the bishop. Or, more likely, that after 24...♘d5 25 ♖xd5 ♗g5+, he overlooked the winning 26 f4!, instead of the drawing line 26 ♖xg5? ♕xg5+ 27 f4 ♕xb5 28 ♘e7+ ♔f8 29 ♘g6+ ♔g8.

To put this in context, Anand's 'elementary' blunder is about seven moves deep, much deeper than most club players would be able to calculate.

22...♘xd5

Anand changes tack, and hopes for the best.

23 ♖xe7+?!

Now Topalov makes a much simpler mistake himself, but one which did not change the end result. One would assume that under the great complexity of the game, both players must already have been in deep time trouble.

There was a simpler win after 23 ♖e5! ♗b7 24 ♕f5+ (24 ♘xh8+ also wins) 24...♔g8 25 ♗c4 with a highly thematic pin against the knight on d5.

23...♘xe7

Black does not have to resign yet.

24 ♗c4+

And White continues the attack.

24...♔f6!

Maybe Topalov had thought that this was hopeless, the king being well out in the open. Instead 24...♗e6 25 ♗xe6+ ♔xe6 26 ♖e1+ ♔f6 27 ♘xe7 ♖c8 28 ♘xc8 ♕xc8 29 ♖e4 leads to a winning rook and pawn ending for White.

25 ♘xh8

Now White is a pawn up.

25...♕d4!

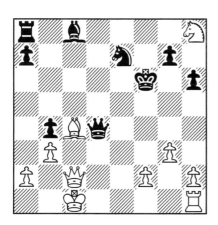

There have been slip-ups in the game, understandably given the complexity of play. Anand has shown great presence of mind, however. He is able to keep the position alive, even when his king is stuck on f6, and so many of White's pieces are hovering.

25...♕xh8? would have won a piece, but lost the king: for instance, 26 ♖d1 ♘f5 27 ♕e4 ♖b8 28 ♕c6+ ♔g5 29 f4+, and mate in a few moves.

26 ♖d1

The king slips round to the other side of the rook. It is the only winning attempt, indeed the only way for White to get out of trouble.

26...♕a1+

The only way to keep the initiative.

27 ♔d2

27 ♕b1?? ♕xb1+ 28 ♔xb1 ♗f5+ is, of course, a blunder.

27...♕d4+

27...♕c3+ 28 ♕xc3 bxc3+ 29 ♔xc3 keeps White two pawns up in a safe position. The knight cannot be trapped: for example, 29...♗e6 30 ♖d6, winning easily.

28 ♔e1

He goes for a win, whereas 28 ♔c1?! repeats.

28...♕e5+

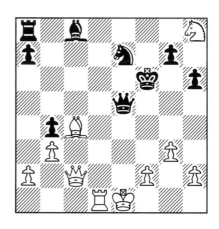

The checks must continue.

29 ♕e2!

The only good move:

a) 29 ♔f1? ♗h3+ loses a piece instantly.

b) 29 ♔d2? is too late to offer a draw; 29...♗e6 again wins a piece.

c) 29 ♗e2?! sets a vicious trap. After 29...♗g4? 30 f4 ♕xe2+ 31 ♕xe2 ♗xe2 32 ♖d6+ ♔f5 33 ♔xe2 if Black finally takes the knight with 33...♖xh8?, he gets mated. White plays 34 ♔f3! h5 35 h3, and mates with g4. An attractive finish, and many players would fall for it, but Black improves with 29...♗e6! 30 f4 ♕c3+, and this time he can win the knight safely.

29...♕xe2+ 30 ♔xe2

After all the complications, we have now reached a semi-endgame with Topalov a pawn up. A good result, but presumably he would have liked to have done better.

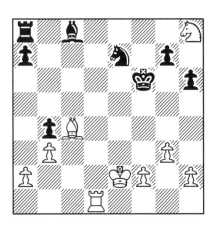

31...♘f5

Unfortunately Black cannot regain his pawn: 30...♗g4+ 31 f3 ♗xf3+ 32 ♔xf3 ♖xh8 33 ♖d6+ ♔g5 34 h4+ ♔h5 35 ♗g7+ g6 36 ♖e6 and mate soon follows.

31 ♘f7

After the recent setback, Topalov is presumably not too interested in playing for combinations, and relies on keeping the extra pawn.

31 ♖d8!? was a possibility, and after 31...♘xg3+ 32 ♔e1 (32 hxg3?? ♗g4+) 32...♘f5 33 ♖f8+ ♔g5 34 ♘f7+ ♔h4 35 ♗d5 ♖b8 36 ♗e4 Black is seriously tied up. It would take time to calculate and verify all this, though, and when time is short, it is usually best when the position is already favourable to play simply.

31...a5?!

This makes life easier for White, allowing the chance to coordinate his pieces.

After 31...♗e6, the straightforward 32 ♘d6 would have been good to reach the time control, and 32 ♗xe6 ♔xe6 33 ♘d8+ also seems good.

32 g4

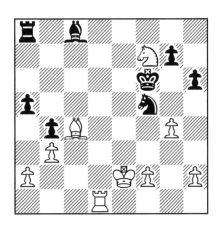

Pushing away the knight from a strong square.

32...♘h4

Forced to the edge.

33 h3

Keeping the g-pawn.

33...♖a7

Somehow he needs to bring the rook into play.

34 ♖d6+

Forcing the king to a worse square.

34...♔e7 35 ♖b6

Now White's pieces are working together, and he has an extra pawn. 'The rest is a matter of technique', as they say.

35...♖c7

Still looking to develop the rook.

36 ♘e5

But even the knight is on a safe square.

26...♘g2

The knight was not doing anything on h4. Anand makes a last-ditch try, giving up two pieces for a rook, and hoping to pick up the pawn on a2, which may eventually allow Black to set up a passed pawn.

37 ♘g6+

Blocking Black's knight.

37...♔d8 38 ♔f1 ♗b7 39 ♖xb7

This still seems best and the most direct, and makes it to move 40 without White having to think.

39...♖xb7 40 ♔xg2 ♖d7

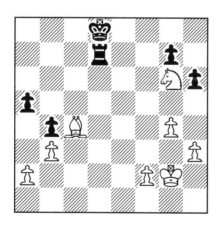

White now is clearly ahead in material. The only chance for Black to hold is to win White's a-pawn, then create a passed pawn, and then try to pick up a minor piece in return for the advanced passed pawn. However, with reasonable care, White should win.

41 ♘f8

White plays with the knight actively.

41...♖d2

Black too must get moving. There is no point in holding on to the g-pawn with 41...♖a7 42 ♘e6+, which would leave several alternative winning plans for White.

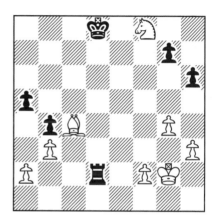

42 ♘e6+

Continuing his plan.

42 a4?? bxa3, taking en passant, is a common type of blunder for less experienced players. See further comments to the ending of Game 16, Shirov-Aronian.

42...♔e7

The king needs to rush to the kingside in view of White's 3-1 pawn majority, and 42...♔d7 43 ♘xg7 ♖xa2 44 ♘f5 a4 45 bxa4 ♖xa4?? 46 ♗b5+ does not help.

43 ♘xg7

Now just a few pawns go, mostly Black's.

43...♖xa2 44 ♘f5+ ♔f6 45 ♘xh6 ♖c2

A last-ditch attempt to create a passed pawn, supported by the rook, and to force White to sacrifice the bishop.

45...a4 46 bxa4 ♖xa4 47 f4 is ineffective for Black: 47...b3 48 g5+ ♔g6 29

71

♗f7+ ♚g7 50 ♗xb3 ♜xf4 51 ♚g2, and White has too much material for Black to cope.

46 ♗f7

Naturally White must avoid the sacrifice on c4. After the move played, the bishop and knight at first look fragile, but White's pawns save the day.

46...♜c3

If 46...♚g7 47 g5, and White will be able to cover the pawn with h4 or f4, while 46...♚g5 47 ♘f5 is simple; the knight returns to queenside play via e3 or d4.

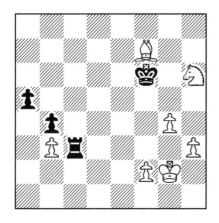

47 f4!

Black was threatening 47...a4, and White can do nothing about this, at least in terms of pure defence.

White will want to push his three passed pawns as quickly as possible, aiming for ultimate promotion, but also taking up a few squares for the minor pieces.

47...a4

The only try.

48 bxa4 b3 49 g5+

The pawns push through.

49...♚g7

This will end up in checkmate, but if instead 49...♚e7 50 f5 b2 51 f6+ ♚d7 52 ♗g6 ♜b1 53 ♗f5+ ♚d8, then using White's two passed pawns, with the help of the piece, wins: 54 g6 b1♕ 55 ♗xb1 ♜xb1 56 g7.

50 f5 b2

He can queen, but he cannot save the king.

51 f6+

Connected passed pawns must be pushed.

51...♚h7

He is also checkmated after 51...♚f8 52 g6 b2Q 53 g7.

52 ♘f5 1-0

52...b1♕ 53 g6+ ♚h8 54 g7 ♚g7 55 g8♕ is mate, while Black runs out of checks after 52...♜c2+ 53 ♚f3 ♜c3+ 54 ♚g2 ♜c4+ 55 ♚h5 (but not 55 ♗xc4? b1♕).

Game 5
E.Bacrot-S.Rublevsky
Khanty-Mansiysk 2005
Sicilian Defence B46

1 e4 c5

The first example of a Sicilian. Black covers the d4-square with a pawn away from the centre. The idea that if White later plays d4, then an exchange of pawns will give Black theoretically the better pawn structure, with an extra pawn in the centre. White in return has quicker development with his pieces, and more squares for his pieces.

Play can often become extremely complicated, as we shall see in later games. The usual rule of thumb is that White scores well in short games, with the help of rapid attacking chances, while Black tends to do well in the long positional games, once he has covered White's attack, then making use of his better pawn structure. There are, of course, many exceptions.

2 ♘f3

White generally plays for an Open Sicilian, with ♘f3 followed by ♘xd4, at least at top levels. The problem for White, at anything below professional level, is that Black has so many different possibilities, often ending up in vastly different, yet still complicated opening structures, that it takes enormous time and effort for White to understand in detail what is going on in the Sicilian.

A quieter way of playing the Sicilian is 2 c3, keeping a pawn in the centre with d4. At the moment, Tiviakov is the main advocate of this at top level. Play tends to end up with a high proportion of draws, which can be frustrating for Black if he is aiming for a win.

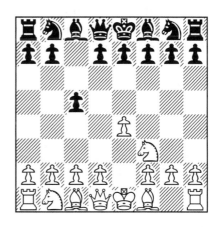

2...e6

There are various possibilities, often involving inter-transpositions later on.

2...d6 can lead to the late Bobby Fischer's favourite, the Najdorf Sicilian after 3 d4 cxd4 4 ♘xd4 ♘f6 5 ♘c3 a6. See Game 6, Karjakin-Anand, an outstanding win for Anand. Depending on how White plays, Black may consider either ...e5, as in Anand's game, or ...e6. Here 5...g6, with a bishop fianchetto, is a popular line, although not included in this book. This is the Dragon Variation. Black has a splendid diagonal for his bishop, but he has lost some pawn control in the centre.

2...♘c6 3 d4 cxd4 4 ♘xd4 ♘f6 5 ♘c3 e5 6 ♘db5 d6 would have looked extremely anti-positional a couple of generations earlier, leaving the hole on d5, a weakness, and also the backward pawn on d6. The Pelikan Variation is popular, though, and Black argues that if White's knight reaches b5, then no problem, Black can force it away with ...a6. Difficult play follows for both sides, as in Game 9, Leko-Radjabov.

2...e6 has the merit of avoiding the most complicated attacking lines, while still keeping positional tension.

3 d4

3 c3 would still return to the quiet 2 c3 line, and indeed this is Rublevsky's favoured line for White, including a good win against Topalov in 2004.

3...cxd4 4 ♘xd4

The natural replies on each side.

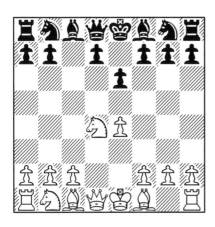

4...♘c6

4...a6 could easily transpose into the game after 5 ♘c3 ♘c6, but Black could also consider 5...b5, or 5...♕c7, and White could consider, a move earlier, 5 ♗d3 or 5 c4.

4...♘f6 5 ♘c3 d6 leads to the Scheveningen, a trusted defensive measure by Kasparov over many years.

5 ♘c3

5 ♘b5 d6 6 c4 (or maybe 6 ♗f4 e5 7

♗e3) is also possible, but tends to be drawish.

5 ♘xc6 is too early. White should at least wait until Black has lost a move with ...a6.

Similarly, White would want to delay c4 until Black has played either ...a6 or ...d6. Just here, it is not worth playing cat-and-mouse. Simple development has its virtues.

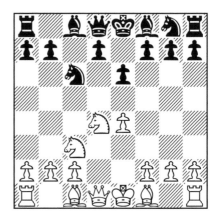

5...a6

With designs of a Paulsen Variation, with an early ...♕c7, or perhaps a Scheveningen, setting up the barricades with ...e6 and ...d6.

Black does not activate his development with ...a6, but it is a good waiting move, forcing White to decide what he is going to do next. In most lines, the ...a6 move is in any case useful.

For 5...♕c7, see Game 20, Ni Hua-Jakovenko, which leads to a more classic Paulsen/Scheveningen structure.

6 ♘xc6!?

White deviates, and so finds the one way in which ...a6 is something of an irrelevance. White is hoping for a slight plus, but the exchange of knights suggests that he has no real ambitions of a forcing attack.

6 ♗e2, as in Game 17, Shirov-Illescas, leads to a Scheveningen structure, with the twist that Black then delays ...♗e7, and unusual complications result.

6 ♗e3 and 6 g3 are alternatives.

6...bxc6

6...dxc6?! 7 ♕xd8+ ♚xd8 8 ♗e3 gives White an edge. Black's problem is not so much that the king has been moved, usually only a slight irritation when the queens have been exchanged, but rather that he has weakened his dark squares, as a result of his early ...a6.

7 ♗d3

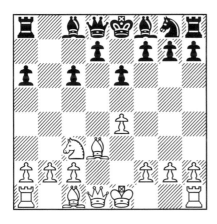

Quiet development.

7 e5 ♕c7 8 f4 is playable, but is perhaps premature. After 8...d5 9 exd6 ♗xd6, White has induced a slight structural weakness on Black's isolated a- and c- pawns, but White also has weaknesses on the kingside and in the centre.

7...d5

Black could also set up a more defensive formation with 7...d6 8 0-0 ♘f6.

8 0-0

8 exd5?! cxd5 allows Black too easy equality. White's pawn on e4 is more effective in the centre than Black's

pawn on c6, so why should White exchange?

8...♘f6

Natural development.

Black has occasionally experimented with 8...♗d6 9 ♖e1 ♘e7, but White has chances of an edge, and good kingside freedom, after 10 ♕h5.

9 ♖e1

Still keeping the light-square tension in the centre.

9 ♕e2 ♗e7, and then maybe 10 b3, is an alternative.

9...♗e7

9...d4 10 ♘b1! e5 11 ♘d2 weakens any chance of influence by Black on c4.

9...♗b7 is also possible, with the point being that if 10 e5 ♘d7, Black still has the g7-square guarded by the bishop, so that 11 ♕g4?! is pointless. The strongest grandmasters tend to prefer instead 11 ♗f4.

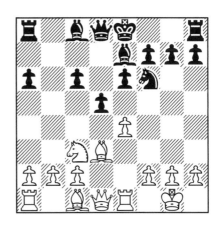

10 e5

Now it is time for White to take over the initiative.

10...♘d7

The only sensible square.

11 ♕g4

11 ♘a4 ♘b6 12 ♘xb6 ♕xb6 13 c4 has been tried a couple of times re-

cently, and arguably White's queen might be better centralized than on g4. However, Black can play more directly with 11...0-0! 12 c4 a5 (aiming for ....♗a6) 13 ♕c2 g6 14 ♗h6 ♖e8, and in comparison with the Bacrot-Rublevsky game, the king and the rook are at least the right way round. In V.Bologan-S.Rublevsky, Poikovsky 2006, Black set up a favourable bishop exchange after 15 cxd5 cxd5 16 ♗b5 ♖b8 17 ♕e2 ♗g5! 18 ♗xg5 ♕xg5, which was equal, with Black later winning.

11...g6

Black cannot castle safely, as if 11...0-0? 12 ♗h6 g6 13 ♗xf8, and White wins the exchange.

This is of course an elementary tactic, but sometimes such small points may influence the positional outcome of a whole game.

12 ♘a4

At the moment, as a result of Bacrot's win in this game, this knight move has become the centre of attention among top-level players. At first sight, it looks strange. The knight is stuck on the edge, and cannot attack anything. It covers defensive squares on b6 and c5 though, and arguably Black would like to use those squares himself. Perhaps more importantly, White is opening up a nibble with c4, starting to undermine Black's central pawn structure.

In slightly earlier games, White tried 12 ♗h6. J.Polgar-V.Anand, Sofia 2005, continued 12...♖b8 13 ♕h3 ♖b4 14 ♗g7 ♖g8!? (sacrificing the exchange; 14...♖h4 has previously been tried) 15 ♕xh7 ♖xg7 17 ♕xg7 ♗f8 18 ♕g8 ♕g5!, leaving White's queen in great peril. Polgar baled out, trying for a draw with

18 g3 ♘xe5 19 f4 ♘f3+ 20 ♔f2 ♕h5 21 ♗xg6 fxg6 22 ♖xe6+ ♗xe6 23 ♕xe6+ ♗e7 24 ♕xc6+ ♔f8 25 ♕a8+ ♔g7 26 ♕xd5 ♘xh2 27 ♕xh5 gxh5. Black maybe had an edge, but it was later drawn. Some sharp tactics.

12...♕a5

12...c5 is possible, but weakens his pawn structure. 13 c4 0-0 (or 13...♕a5 14 ♕d1! and Black too will have to retreat his queen before long) 14 ♗h6 ♖e8 15 ♖ad1 ♖b8 16 b3 d4 17 f4 ♕c7 18 h4, and White has good chances on the kingside. White later won in G.Sax-G.Franzoni, Thessaloniki 1984. Black has a visually impressive passed pawn on d4, but he has not got much purchase on the other dark squares.

13 ♗h6

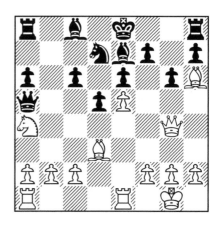

Obviously the bishop was going to have to move, as White's rook on e1 was under attack. Clearly the bishop is also an irritation on Black's kingside, stopping Black from castling that side. What is slightly unusual is that more than 20 moves later, Black's rook found itself unable to enter into open play, and his king unable to castle. The bishop proved to be more than an irritation, it strategically dominated the whole game.

In an earlier game, Black soon equalized and later drew after 13 c3 c5 14 ♗c2 ♗b7 15 ♗h6 ♗c6, A.Eismont-O.Romanishin, Biel 1995.

13...♕b4

Clearly Eismont wanted to avoid this queen exchange, but Bacrot was able to show that White is able to attack Black's various slight weaknesses without needing the queens.

13...♖b8 14 g3 ♖b4? 15 ♕e2 went seriously wrong for Black in J.Benjamin-L.Piasetsky, Thessaloniki 1988. It is as if he had forgotten the white bishop can return to d2. Black sacrificed the exchange with 15...♖xa4 16 bxa4 ♗b4 17 ♖ed1 ♗c3, but it was clear this would be insufficient after 18 ♗d2.

13...c5!? is an attempt at counterattack, rather than merely holding the position. After 14 b3 c4 15 ♗f1 ♗b7, it would seem that White is under pressure. In M.Carlsen-S.Mamedyarov, Moscow 2006, Carlsen had to throw everything into his attack on f7 with 16 ♖e3 ♗c6 17 ♕f4 ♗xa4 18 ♖f3.

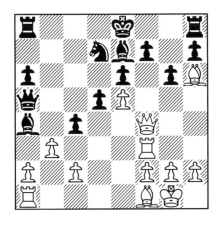

Here there are plenty of dangerous tactics, mainly favouring White, after

18...f6 (or 18...f5 19 exf6, transposing) 19 exf6 ♗xf6 20 ♕d6!:

a) 20...0-0-0 21 ♖xf6 ♘xf6 22 ♕xe6+ will give excellent compensation, and an attack, for the exchange.

b) After 20...♗xa1 21 ♗g5 Black cannot castle kingside, but then 21...♗f6 22 ♖xf6? would allow Black to castle safely after 22...0-0-0!.

c) Another option for Black is 20...♗e5 21 ♕xe6+ ♔d8 22 bxa4 ♗xa1 23 ♗g5+, and while it is easy to see that White, a rook down, has perpetual, the question is whether he can play for more:

c1) 23...♔c7 24 ♗f4+ ♔e8 25 ♕c6! proves to be impossible for Black to hold. After 25...♖c8 26 ♗g5+ ♗f6 27 ♗xf6+ ♘xf6 28 ♕xf6+ ♔c7 29 ♕e5+ White wins.

c2) 23...♔c8 24 ♕c6+ ♔b8 25 ♕xd7 ♗e5 26 ♖f7 ♗xc7 27 ♗f4 ♖a7 28 g3!? leads to good zugzwang possibilities for White.

Mamedyarov avoided these extremely dangerous tactics, showing that sharp attackers are also sharp defenders. Play was still on the edge after 18...0-0-0 19 ♕xf7 ♖he8 20 bxa4 ♗c5 (20...♗f8 21 ♕xh7 ♖e7 22 ♖f7!, and White is pressing) 21 ♖b1 ♕xa4 22 ♗g5 ♕c6 23 ♗xd8 ♘xe5 24 ♖b8+ ♔xb8 25 ♗c7+ ♕xc7 26 ♕xe8+ ♕c8 27 ♕xc8+ ♔xc8 28 ♖h3 ♘g4 29 ♖f3 ♘e5 30 ♖h3 ♘g4 31 ♖f3, and drawn. All very complicated, and one can be sure that there are hidden resources for both sides.

14 ♕xb4

The simplest. There is no need to allow doubled pawns with 14 h3 ♕xg4 15 hxg4.

14...♗xb4 15 c3

Again the simplest, with gain of

tempo, although possibly White might be worried that the knight is unable to run away if it were to be attacked (rather than exchanged). Black cannot get there though, and White's pieces and pawns are safe.

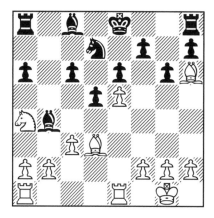

15...♗a5

Black aims to keep some pressure on the pawn on e5.

Black has also tried simplifying, aiming to getting rid of the annoying bishop with 15...♗f8 16 ♗xf8 ♖xf8 in M.Carlsen-G.Vescovi, Wijk aan Zee 2006, but remains under pressure. After 17 c4 ♔e7 18 cxd5 cxd5 19 ♖ac1 ♖a7 20 b4 White's pieces are clearly more active. In terms of pawns, Black has a passed d-pawn, certainly, but this is no serious advantage, especially if White can blockade with king or, as happened, knight on d4. In compensation for the passed d-pawn, White has an extra outside pawn on the queenside, and Black is stuck in the game with a weakened isolated pawn. Also, White was able to create pressure on the kingside. Carlsen duly won.

15...♗e7 does not quite seem to equalize. After 16 b4! a5 17 a3 ♗a6 18 ♗c2 White keeps pressure with his pieces.

16 b4

Mainly to prevent Black from gaining space with ...c5.

16...♗c7 17 f4

Covering the advanced pawn.

17 ♗c2!? is also to be considered, so that if 17...♗xe5? 18 ♖xe5 ♘xe5 19 ♗g7 White gains material. The tactic is obvious, but the positional point is that if White can avoid or delay the f4 push, he keeps the option of swinging the bishop from h6 to the queenside. Here 17...a5 18 a3 ♘b6 gives White a slight edge, but nothing special.

17...a5

Somehow Black must loosen his pieces.

18 b5

18 a3 is still possible, but White is aiming for a more active breakthrough.

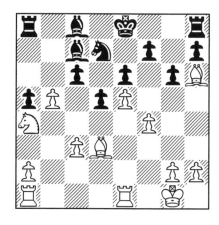

18...♘b6?!

This was at one stage seen as a drawing line, but Bacrot can play for an edge.

18...c5! seems better. Then after 19 ♖ab1 c4 20 ♗c2 ♖b8 White has a good passed pawn. It is, however, difficult to see how White could improve the rest of his pieces or pawns, with the three minor pieces remaining ineffective. After 21...♗d8 and a few quiet moves, Black should be able to consolidate for equality quite comfortably.

19 ♘xb6!

An innovation, strangely enough. Sometimes a new move is played in a blaze of glory, but sometimes, as here, it is just the obvious follow-up, but a new interpretation to the follow-up.

In L.Hazai-O.Romanishin, Sochi 1982, the players agreed a draw by repetition after 19 ♘c5 ♘d7. Unexciting, but as David Bronstein used to say, twenty years later players will find improvements. Or five years, or ten years, or a day.

19...♗xb6+ 20 ♔f1

White has lost a tempo as a result of the check, but does that really matter? The king is moving towards a more centralized square, which is going to be a help for the endgame. In the meantime, Black has to prove that he genuinely has equality. In the subsequent games that resulted, it was clear that there were unexpected difficulties.

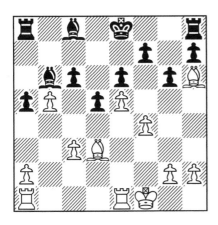

20...cxb5?!

Black is hoping for some simplifica-

tion, but it does not quite work out. White gains some time.

Ftacnik suggested 20...c5 21 c4 ♗b7 22 ♖ad1 a4 23 a3 ♖d8 24 ♗b5 ♖d7 25 ♔e2 with a slight edge for White. This has not resolved Black's basic problem, that he has not been able to castle kingside, and his rooks therefore remain unconnected. Here the obvious solution is to castle queenside with 22...0-0-0!?. Black keeps the tension of whether to exchange pawns on c4, whether to create a passed pawn with ...d4, or whether to delay until the time is right. In view of this, maybe White could put the other rook on the d-file with 22 ♖ed1!?, placing rooks on the c-file and the d-file, keeping some tension himself.

21 ♗xb5+ ♗d7

22...♔d8 23 c4 keeps an edge for White.

22 ♖ab1

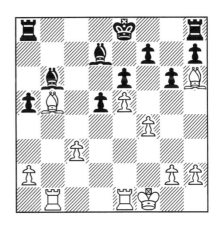

Is this really the sort of position that a player would want to try as Black a second time? Rublevsky wanted to prove that his defence was sound.

22...♖b8

Rublevsky questioned this move in his annotations in *Informator*, and suggested that 22...♗xb5+ 23 ♖xb5 ♗c7! led to equality. Unfortunately his analysis was not quite watertight, and Ponomariov, an excellent grinder in the endgame, was able to show that White still had chances of playing for an advantage.

Rublevsky's analysis continued with 24 c4 (he gives 24 ♖d1 ♔d7 25 c4 ♔c6 26 a4 dxc4 27 ♖d4 ♖hb8 28 ♖xc4+ ♔d7 as equal) 24...dxc4 25 ♖c5 0-0-0 26 ♖xc4 ♖d7 27 ♗g5 ♔b7, and now 28 ♗f6 ♖b8 with level play. It is not so clear what White has gained with his ♗f6 move, which merely forces the rook to a better defensive square. Ponomariov no doubt had the opportunity in his preparation to sort out weaknesses in his opponent's analysis, even as late as move 28, and found a possible improvement.

In R.Ponomariov-S.Rublevsky, Poikovsky 2006, play went on with 28 ♖b1+ ♗b6 29 f5!? (Ftacnik suggests that the quieter 29 ♔e2! was even better) 29...♔a7? 30 ♖c6! and White was winning material with a decisive attack, only three moves away from Rublevsky's analysis.

Ftacnik points out that Black has good chances of holding after 29...♖c7! 30 ♖d4 ♖b8 31 ♖d6 ♖c6 32 ♗e3 ♔c7 33 fxe6 fxe6 34 ♔e2 ♗a7, the point for the defence being that after 35 ♖xc6+ ♔xc6 36 ♖c1+ ♔b7 37 ♗xa7 ♔xa7 38 ♖c7+ ♖b7 39 ♖xb7+ ♔xb7 the king and pawn endgame is only a draw. Black oscillates with the king between b6 and c6, and the h-pawn can play ...h6 to cover any kingside weaknesses.

Unfortunately, not Rublevsky's finest day.

23 c4

Aiming to exchange White's isolated pawn for Black's best pawn.

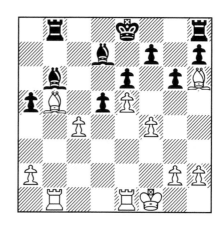

23...♗a7

If 23...dxc4 24 ♗xc4 Black is close to zugzwang:

a) His position does not fold immediately, but after, for example, 24...♗c7 25 ♖xb8+ ♗xb8 26 ♖b1 ♗c7 27 ♗g7 ♖g8 28 ♗f6 White has a long and leisurely squeeze.

b) Rublevsky gives 24...♗a4 25 ♖e4!? as a possibility, with the idea that if 25...♗c2 26 ♖d4 ♗xb1 27 ♗b5+, and checkmate after 27...♔e7 28 ♖d7+ ♔e8 29 ♖a7+ ♔d8 30 ♗g5+ ♔c8 31 ♗d7. Here Black would be able to force the opponent to work much harder with 25...♔d7 26 ♗xe6+ ♔xe6 27 ♖xa4 ♖hc8 when White has won a pawn, but Black's pieces are by now the more active.

However, 23...d4? loses a pawn without compensation after 24 ♗a6 ♗c6 25 c5 ♗a7 26 ♖xb8+ ♗xb8 27 ♖d1.

24 ♗a6

Quite a symmetry of the White bishops, on a6 and h6. Of course, they threaten nothing, but they cut out important defensive squares. Even now, Black cannot castle.

24 ♖ec1?! allows Black to escape for equality with 24...♗xb5 25 cxb5 ♔d7 26

a4 (26 ♖c6 ♖hc8!) 26...♖hc8 27 ♔e2 ♗c5, as Rublevsky notes. An advanced passed pawn is useful, but if the pawn cannot queen, and the other forces give nothing, the end result is a likely draw.

24...♗c6

Rublevsky gives 24...dxc4? 25 ♖xb8+ ♗xb8 26 ♖b1 ♗c7 27 ♖b7 ♗d8 28 ♗xc4 as a zugzwang for White. Perhaps this is not quite clear just yet, as after 28...♗c6 29 ♖b8?! ♔d7 Black will be able to disentangle the back row. However, a quieter approach is 29 ♖a7 a4 30 g3 ♗e7 31 ♖c7 ♗d7 32 ♗g7 ♖g8 33 ♗f6 ♗xf6 34 exf6 ♔d8 35 ♖a7 with a winning bind.

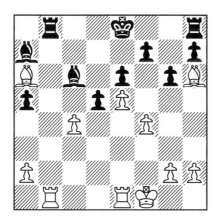

25 cxd5

This is the sort of position where it is easy enough to say that White is slightly better, but very difficult to find a clear way of improving his position. Given the chance of ...♔d7, Black would have excellent chances of consolidating for equality. After, for example, 25 ♖xb8+ ♗xb8 26 ♗g7 ♖g8 27 ♗f6 ♔d7 28 ♖b1 ♗c7 29 cxd5 exd5 30 ♗h4 ♖b8 31 ♖xb8 ♗xb8 32 g4 White's edge is slight. White can, of course, attempt to play for a win, as he has a slightly better pawn structure.

It is equally understandable that Bacrot would wish for more, and he finds an inspired pawn breakthrough. The trouble is that the breakthrough weakens his own pawn structure, as well as his opponent's. Black has to play very carefully, avoiding a couple of traps, to hold the position.

Instead 25 f5 gxf5 26 ♗e3 ♖xb1 27 ♖xb1 ♔d7 (27...♖xe3? 28 ♖b8+) 28 ♗xa7 ♖a8 29 cxd5 exd5 (29...♗xd5?? 30 ♗b5+) 30 ♗d3 transposes into the notes to Black's 27th, below, where Black has chances of holding.

25...exd5

25...♗xd5? 26 ♖xb8+ ♗xb8 27 ♖c1! cuts through on the back rank. If 27...♔d7 28 ♗b5+, the bishops help as well.

26 f5!?

Given an exclamation mark elsewhere, but while it seems good it is not the most accurate.

Instead 26 ♖xb8+ ♗xb8 27 ♖c1! ♔d7 28 ♗e2!! is a highly subtle try, with zugzwang ideas.

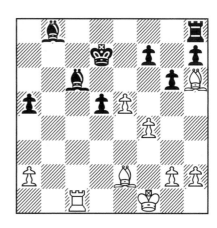

If 28...♗c7?? or 28...♖c8??, then White has immediate wins with 29 ♗g4+ (and, for beginners, don't forget the en passant after 29...f5 30 exf6+).

Tactically this is elementary, but positionally this is significant, as it eliminates two of Black's best chances of bringing his pieces into play.

28...♗a7 activates the bishop, but can no longer put pressure on the e5-pawn, so White has 29 f5! If 29...♖e8, White has a pawn breakthrough close to the queening square with 30 e6+ exf6 31 f6, winning. Alternatively, Black has 29...gxf5 30 ♗d3, and we now reach the winning line in the game, but bypassing an improvement for Black on move 27.

Black could also have tried developing the rook with 28...♖e8, but even here the rook hits a mine. After 29 ♖c5! a4 (29...♗c7? 30 ♗g4+) 31 ♗g4+ ♔c7 32 ♗d1 White wins at least a pawn, as if 32...♔b6 33 ♖xc6+ ♔xc6 34 ♗xa4+, skewering the rook.

A blemish for White, perhaps, but it is difficult to imagine how a player would be able to calculate over the board why 26 f5 is less accurate than 26 ♖xb8+.

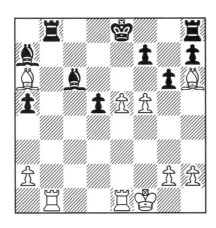

26...♖xb1

If 26...gxf5 27 ♗e3! ♖xb1 28 ♖xb1 ♗xd3 29 ♖b8+, winning the exchange. A simple but attractive combination,

using the whole range of the board.

27 ♖xb1

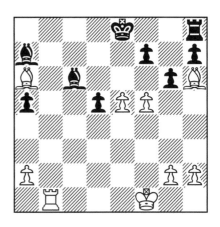

27...♔d7?

Black has at long last brought his king into play, no doubt with some relief, but the timing still seems to be incorrect.

Rublevsky suggests 27...gxf5 28 ♗e3 ♔d7! (28...♗xe3? 29 ♖b8+) 29 ♗xa7 ♖a8 30 ♗d3 ♖xa7 31 ♗xf5+ ♔e7 32 ♖b6 (32 ♗xh7 ♔e6 33 ♖e1 ♖b7 is level) 32...♖c7 33 ♔e2 with an edge to White. However, Ribli gives it as a substantial edge. Black's pawns are all isolated, and White's pieces are active, with the king threatening to end up on d4.

Can we have any clear indication that White is winning, or is close to winning? Or can we show that Black's position is tenable? Quieter moves for Black tend to lead to an uncomfortable defence, but 33...f6!? is more challenging:

(see following diagram)

a) If 34 exf6+ ♔xf6 35 ♗xh7 ♖xh7 36 ♖xc6+ ♔e5 37 h3 ♖b7!, and Black has excellent counterplay in return for White's extra pawn. White will need to cover Black's advanced passed d-pawn, and so he will not have any opportunity of pushing his g- and h-pawns. In rook and pawn endgames, active pieces make all the difference.

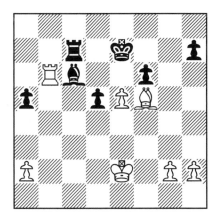

b) 34 e6 looks dangerous, but with accurate play by Black, it is difficult for White to set up a check on the seventh rank. Then 34...d4! brings the bishop into play. If 35 ♔d3 ♗xg2 36 ♔xd4 ♗f1!, and Black can use the c4-square with rook or bishop (after 37 ♗xh7 ♗c4), just about holding the balance, and 35 g4 ♗d5 36 ♔d3 (36 a3? ♖c3 with strong counterplay) 36...♗xa2 37 ♔xd4 a4 also holds the balance.

This is the deep defensive resource that White could have avoided by playing 26 ♖xb8+ ♗xb8 27 ♖c1! ♔d7 28 ♗e2! ♗a7 29 f5 earlier, instead of 26 f5.

28 ♖c1!

And this is an easily missed quiet rook move, the tactics shifting from the b-file to the c-file. White is now thinking of threatening e6+, and almost any active Black move makes things worse.

28 e6+ fxe6 29 f6 e5 30 f7 ♗c5 would have been more aggressive, but offers no clear way of taking advantage of the seventh rank pawn. 31 ♗b5 ♗xb5 32

♖xb5 ♗f8 33 ♗xf8 (33 ♖b8? ♔e7) 33...♖xf8 34 ♖xd5+ ♔e6 35 ♖xa5 ♖xf7+ is, for example, a draw.

28...gxf5

Black makes the most straightforward reply.

28...♗a4 29 ♗c8+! (29 e6+ fxe6 30 f6 ♗b8!) 29...♖xc8 30 e6+ fxe6 31 fxe6+ ♔xe6 32 ♖xc8, as Rublevsky notes, favours White, possibly decisively.

29 ♗d3

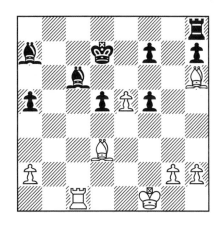

We have seen this position before. See the notes to move 26.

Even without White's advanced f-pawn, he still has generated considerable attacking chances, with just rook and two bishops versus Black's more passive rook and two bishops. Black has not yet fully completed his development, even though we are at the early stages of the endgame. Had the rook been on a better square, he would have been able to equalize comfortably, but just at the moment he lacks the coordination of his pieces.

29...♖e8

Alternatively:

a) If 29...♗a4?, White has a mating attack after 30 ♗xf5 ♔e7 31 ♗g5+ ♔f8 32 ♖c8+ ♗e8 33 ♗f6.

b) If 29...♗d4? 30 ♗g7!, then 31 e6+, and the underdevelopment of the rook again causes a problem.

c) 29...♖b8 30 ♗xf5+ ♔c7 31 e6! followed by ♗f4+ picks up the rook on another diagonal.

d) 29...♗b6 avoids immediate trouble, but after 30 ♗f4 ♗b7 31 ♗xf5+ ♔e8, Black has still been unable to bring the rook into play.

Rublevsky decides to try to complete his development.

30 ♗f4

30 ♗xf5+ ♔c7 31 ♗f4 ♔b7 32 ♖b1+ ♔a8 33 ♗xh7 is no doubt also strong, but Bacrot prefers to keep a hit against the king in the centre.

30...♗d4

In their notes, Ribli and Rublevsky both suggest that 30...♖e7 31 ♗xf5+ ♔c7 32 e6 ♔b7 33 ♖b1+ ♔a8 34 ♗d6 ♖xe6 35 ♗xe6 fxe6 36 ♔e2 gives more resistance, but it is difficult to see any chances for Black to hold. White's 2-1 kingside pawn structure seem decisive, not least because of the danger that Black could lose his final h-pawn.

31 ♗xf5+

This wins even more comfortably.

31...♔c7

Otherwise he loses material.

32 e6+

The pawn is pushed. Had this not been close to the time scramble, when sometimes strange accidents happen, Black would probably have resigned shortly.

32...♔b6 33 ♖b1+!

Bacrot is unlikely to fall for 33 exf7?? ♗b5+ when Black wins. Others might.

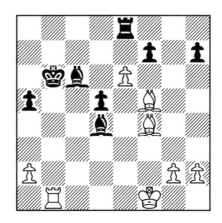

33...♔c5

33...♗b5+ 34 ♗d3 wins for White. Black's bishop is pinned.

34 exf7 ♖f8 35 ♖c1+ ♔b6 36 ♗e6

He safely keeps the pawn on f7, and Black has no more than a couple of inconclusive checks.

36...♗c5 37 ♗h6 ♗b5+ 38 ♔e1 ♗b4+ 39 ♔f2 ♖d8 40 ♖c8 1-0

Game 6
S.Karjakin-V.Anand
Wijk aan Zee 2006
Sicilian Defence B90

1 e4 c5 2 ♘f3 d6 3 d4

A possible disadvantage for Black, in attempting to keep play tense with 2...d6, would be the quiet 3 ♗b5+. Without attempting to provide detailed analysis of this line, Timofeev has made an impressive plus score as Black after 3...♗d7 4 ♗xd7+ ♘bxd7!? (instead of the standard 4...♕xd7) against 2600+ opposition.

3...cxd4 4 ♘xd4 ♘f6 5 ♘c3

Standard play on both sides. The only likely deviation on these moves is 4 ♕xd4, with Black choosing either 4...♘c6 5 ♗b5 ♗d7 or 4...a6.

5...a6

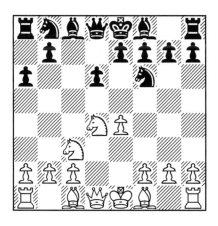

The Najdorf Variation. This pawn move is useful for Black anyway, and he might just as well play it early. He is waiting to see exactly what White plays next move, before deciding whether to try ...e5 or ...e6.

The approximate frequency of play in this position in high-level games would be, first, 5...a6, the Najdorf; then second, 5...♘c6, the Classical Variation; then third, 5...e6, the Scheveningen; then fourth, 5...g6. the Dragon. Thus Bobby Fischer's great favourite still retains its popularity.

6 ♗e3

There are many lines here, the most direct line being 6 ♗g5 e6 7 f4. Fischer in many games tried to grab the pawn with 7...♕b6 8 ♕d2 ♕xb2, while Polugaevsky concentrated instead on 7...b5 8 e5 dxe5 9 fxe5 ♕c7 with great complications. These two leading grandmasters were great pioneers during the sixties, seventies and beyond of detailed and sharp opening analysis. There are many later top grandmasters, including Kasparov, and later Anand, who have carried this process through. The use of computer analysis, predicted at an early stage by Polugaevsky, has led to a major jump in chess understanding at the top.

It has to be recognized that the computer does not automatically provide a detailed list of significant improvements, which players can copy and win. More it is a case of the computer setting up a framework of interesting ideas for the player to examine, and then finding out which moves are worth examining in much greater depth. A recent theme in top-level chess is working out possible ways to find in advance attempted improvements by the opponent, and then trumping these improvements with deeper counter-improvements. This game gives an excellent and attractive example.

Without attempting any deep theoretical analysis of this position, the approximate order of popularity is 6 ♗e3, 6 ♗e2, 6 ♗g5, then jointly 6 ♗c4 and 6 g3 (two radically different approaches), and finally 6 f4. In the days of Fischer, 6 ♗e3 was still a rarity. It was later popularized by English grandmasters in the 1980s.

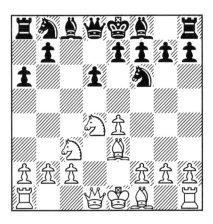

6...e5

The obvious point is that 6...♘g4 hits the bishop, although it is not quite so clear that this is such an obvious advantage for Black after 7 ♗g5. There is, of course, by now considerable theory after 7...h6 8 ♗h4 g5 9 ♗g3 ♗g7 10 h3 ♘e5. Black has gained some time, but has also weakened his kingside pawn structure.

6...e6 sets up a Scheveningen approach, and a direct transposition is of course possible. There are many possible alternatives by White.

7 ♘b3

An advantage of the Najdorf, when compared with the Sveshnikov, is that White cannot create pressure with ♘db5.

7...♗e6

The main line, keeping the option of developing the knight to d7 quickly without obstructing the bishop. There are also questions as to whether Black can play ...d5 sensibly, not just yet but maybe later. Most of the time it doesn't quite work, but both players need to be alert.

8 f3

Keeping the pawn centre solid.

8 ♕d2 ♗e7 9 f3 is a harmless transposition. Not though 8...d5? 9 exd5 ♘xd5 10 0-0-0 and White wins a piece.

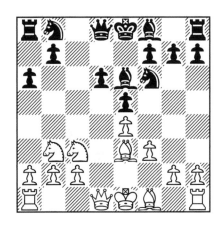

8...♗e7

8...d5?! is too early. After 9 exd5 ♘xd5 10 ♘xd5 ♕xd5 11 ♕xd5 ♗xd5 12 0-0-0 White gains the bishop-pair with either 12...♗xb3 13 axb3 or 12...♗e6 13 ♘c5 ♗xc5 14 ♗xc5. White has then made a healthy plus score.

9 ♕d2

9 g4?! for once allows the thematic breakthrough after 9...d5! 10 g5 d4 11 gxf6 ♗xf6 with advantage to Black.

9 ♘d5 ♘xd5 10 exd5 ♗f5 is equal.

9...0-0

9...d5?! 10 exd5 ♘xd5 11 ♘xd5 ♕xd5 12 ♕xd5 ♗xd5 13 0-0-0 gains a tempo for Black, when compared with the 9...d5 line, but White is still clearly better.

9...♘bd7 is possible, and could transpose into the main line after 10 0-0-0 0-0, but White has the extra option of 10 g4!? when 10...d5? is not playable.

10 0-0-0

White continues to keep pressure on the d5-square.

10 g4?! d5 11 g5 d4 12 gxf6 ♗xf6 is, as we have already seen, a good line for Black.

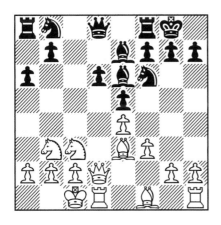

10...♘bd7

The usual move, developing.

10...b5, via a slight transposition, leads into V.Topalov-L.Van Wely, Wijk aan Zee 2007. After 11 ♘d5 ♗xd5 12 exd5 ♕c7 13 g4 ♖c8 14 ♔b1 b4 15 g5, Van Wely was able to show why he wanted to delay ...♘bd7. He was able to try 15...♘fd7. Play continued 16 h4 a5 17 ♗h3 a4 18 ♘c1 with unclear play:

a) Van Wely continued 18...♘a6 19 h5 ♖cb8 20 g6 ♗f6 21 gxf7+ ♔xf7 22 ♗e6+ with perhaps a slight edge to

White, Topalov later winning.

b) 18...a3 19 b3 ♖a5 20 ♖h2 ♘a6 21 h5 ♕c3 22 ♕xc3 ♖xc3 was tried a couple of times by Maenhoet at Istanbul 2005, but White still looks slightly better.

11 g4

We are still on the highway of theory. White charges through with the pawns on the kingside, while Black pushes hard on the other side.

11...b5

Prioritizing the pawn push.

11...♕c7 is playable, although it is noticeable that in games between top grandmasters, White has a significant plus score.

12 g5

The most direct move, and the most popular.

12 ♖g1!? has been tried, and indeed was introduced by Anand in a couple of Melody Amber events. The idea was that if Black pushed the pawn, 12...b4, White has 13 ♘d5, and if 13...♘xd5??, the bishop gets trapped by 14 exd5. Here 13...♗xd5 is of course playable, probably equal, and also, a move earlier, 12...♘b6!?. Anand has experimented on both sides with these lines.

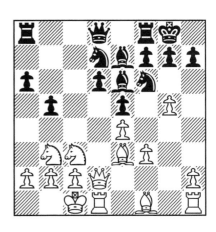

12...b4

Attack and counterattack. Black does not want to concede a tempo.

12...♘h5 has also been tried, occasionally after a slightly different move order, but it seems less effective. There has been a recent improvement for White in P.Svidler-R.Ponomariov, Sofia 2007. After 13 ♘d5 ♗xd5 14 exd5 f5 15 gxf6 ♗xf6 16 ♘a5 ♘f4 17 ♘c6 ♕c7 18 c4!? (before Black can quietly play ...♘b6) 16...♘b8 (18...♘b6?! 19 ♕a5 is uncomfortable) 19 ♕a5 ♖c8 (Ftacnik suggests 19...♕b7) 20 ♔b1 bxc4 21 ♕xc7 ♖xc7 22 ♗xc4 ♔f8 23 ♘a5! Black fell into difficulties on the queenside, and lost.

13 ♘e2

There have been no takers for 13 gxf6?! bxc3 14 ♕xc3 ♘xf6, and if 15 ♖g1, then maybe 15...♔h8. Black has two semi-open files against White's king, and can add to the pressure with ...a6-a5-a4. White has only one semi-open file to attack against Black's kingside, and no obvious pawn push. Black should be comfortable.

13...♘e8

Black keeps the king out of the way, which is the most popular line.

After 13...♘h5, Topalov had a smooth win in his younger days in V.Topalov-N.De Firmian, Polanica Zdroj 1995. Play continued 14 ♘g3 ♘f4 (14...♘xg3? 15 hxg3 and Black is in trouble on the h-file) 15 h4 a5 16 ♔b1 a4 17 ♘d4 exd4 18 ♗xf4 ♕a5 19 ♘f5 ♗xf5 20 exf5 ♕xf5 21 ♕xd4 b3 22 ♗d3 bxa2+ 23 ♔a1 ♕c5 (23...♕e6 24 ♖he1 ♘e5 25 ♗xe5 dxe5 26 ♖xd5 would not have lasted much longer) 24 ♕e4 g6 25 ♗e3 (Topalov decided against 25 ♕xe7 a3) 25...♕e5 26 ♗d4 ♕xe4 2 ♗xe4 and

White had a dominating bishop-pair. Naturally there must be improvements for Black, maybe on move 18.

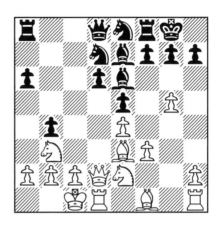

14 f4

After 14 h4, Anand has shown a significant innovation as Black in this line, again at Wijk aan Zee, but a year later. And yet again, the victim was Karjakin. The preliminaries went 14...a5 15 ♔b1 ♘b6 16 ♘g3 a4 17 ♘c1 d5 18 ♗xb6 ♕xb6 19 exd5 ♖d8 20 ♗c4 ♘c7 21 dxe6!? (21 ♕e2 was quickly drawn in Z.Almasi-K.Sakaev, German League 2004) 21...♖xd2 22 exf7+ ♔h8 23 ♖xd2.

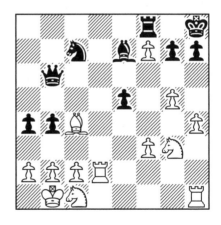

In P.Leko-S.Karjakin, Wijk aan Zee 2006, play continued 23...♕c6 24 b3 ♘b5 25 ♗xb5 ♕xb5 26 bxa4 ♕xa4 27

♖hd1 ♖xf7 28 ♖d7 ♔g8 29 ♘e4, and a draw was agreed. This looks normal enough, if complicated, but there have been improvements for both sides. Morozevich found an improvement for White with 26 ♘f5! (instead of the pawn exchange on a4) 26...♖xf7 27 ♘xe7 ♖xe7 28 ♖d8+ ♖e8 29 ♖hd1 g6?! (Black could have exchanged on b3) 30 ♖1d5 ♕c6 31 ♖5d6 ♕b5, and now a tactic with 32 ♖b6! ♕xb6 33 ♖xe8+ ♔g7 34 bxa4, and White was eventually able to take advantage of the queenside pawns in A.Morozevich-A.Volokitin, Biel 2006.

Anand meanwhile made his own assessment, and found a way of gaining a tempo a few moves earlier with 23...♘b5! (instead of 23...♕c6). After 24 ♗xb5 ♕xb5 the position was much as in the earlier games, except that this time Black had not provoked the b3-pawn push. Play through the second Karjakin-Anand game, and we see that after 25 ♘f5 ♖xf7 26 ♘xe7 ♖xe7 27 ♖d8+ ♖e8 28 ♖hd1 ♖g8, White found nothing more he could do than play 29 b3, as he was starting to be in sight zugzwang.

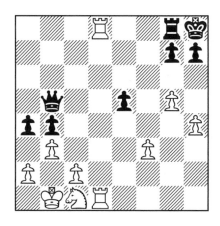

We could have reached this position in the Morozevich-Volokitin game at move 29, if Volokitin had tried 29...♖g8 instead of 29...g6, except for a small but critical distinction. In Anand's game, it was Black's move!

Anand avoided the exchange of pawns on a4, or indeed on b3, and gained space with 29...a3. After 30 ♖1d5 ♕f1 31 ♖xg8+ ♔xg8 32 ♖xe5 ♕xf3 Anand had reached an endgame with queen versus rook, knight and pawn, level in material, but of course White's knight was heavily constrained, and, even more important, the king in serious danger of being mated on b2. The remainder of S.Karjakin-V.Anand, Wijk aan Zee 2007, is of interest, and can easily be accessed by computer.

These Karjakin-Anand games form a spectacular double against an extremely strong opponent, and show why Anand is the most dangerous of all opening theorists. Also an indication of how extremely deeply Anand has analysed in his specialty lines. It is not just a single innovation in a critical line, it is a whole string of innovations against many of the World's leading grandmasters.

14...a5

An obvious move, but there is also an obvious alternative in 14...exd4 15 ♗xd4 ♘c5. This has hardly been played though.

15 f5

White too makes the most direct and aggressive line.

The quieter 15 ♔b1 is playable, making an escape square for the knight. Then 15...a4 16 ♘bc1 exf4 17 ♘xf4 ♗xg5 18 ♘xe6 ♗xe3 19 ♘xd8 ♗xd2 20 ♖xd2 ♖xd8 21 ♖d4 ♘ef6 22 ♖xb4 ♘c5 23 ♗g2 ♖fe8 24 ♘d3 ♘fxe4 25 ♘xc5 ♘xc5 26 ♗c6 ♖e5 ended up as perhaps slightly the better of a draw in Z.Almasi-V.Anand, Turin Olympiad 2006.

15...a4

The most consequential.

15...♗xb3 16 cxb3 a4 17 bxa4 ♖xa4 18 b3 should give an edge to White, who can look forward to taking over the a2-g8 diagonal.

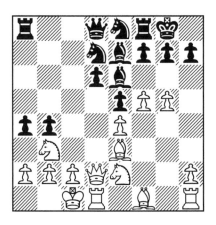

16 ♘bd4!?

Not so much a genuine capture, more an invitation to take the knight on a different square.

16 fxe6 axb3 17 exf7+ (but not 17 exd7?? bxa2) 17...♖xf7 18 ♔b1 (18 axb3?? ♖a1 mate) has been tried and then abandoned, although maybe there could be a later revival:

a) One of the basic strategic points is that after 18...bxa2+ 19 ♔a1, or 18...♕a5 19 ♘c1 bxa2+ 20 ♔a1, the extra pawn on a2 is a liability rather than an asset, and prevents Black from setting up any checkmates on the a-file.

b) Black therefore tries 18...bxc2+ 19 ♔xc2 (19 ♕xc2? ♗xg5). In V.Topalov-F.Vallejo Pons, Linares 2005, play continued 19...♘b6 20 ♘c1 d5 21 exd5 ♘d6 22 ♔b1 with a slight edge for White. Black's play was not helped by trying

the unnecessary 22...♖f3?! 23 h4 ♘a4 24 ♕e2, and a later White win. Moreover, it was not clear that the 20...d5 pawn sacrifice was required.

16...exd4

16...b3 17 ♔b1 exd4 soon transposes.

17 ♘xd4

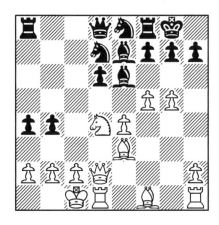

White's knight sacrifice is only temporary.

17...b3

If 17...♗xa2?! 18 ♘c6, and the more important bishop goes.

18 ♔b1

Again, White must not allow a pawn promotion with ...bxa2.

18 cxb3 axb3 19 a3 ♖c8+ 20 ♔b1 ♗c4 21 f6 ♘exf6 22 gxf6 ♗xf6 23 ♗xc4 ♖xc4 24 ♘xb3 ♖xe4 was clearly better for Black in M.Borriss-J.Gallagher, German League 2003.

18...bxc2+

The idea is to force White to take the bishop with a pawn on b3, thereby allowing Black to make a pawn recapture, and open up an attack on the a-file.

18...bxa2+ 19 ♔a1 a3 20 b4 is worth considering, and the computer gives this as good for Black. This seems slightly to overestimate Black's doubled a-pawns, but maybe the debate will continue. Then, for example, 20...♗xf5 21 exf5 ♘e5 22 ♖g1 ♔h8 23 ♖g3 leads to unclear play.

19 ♘xc2

19 ♕xc2 ♗xa2+ 20 ♔xa2 ♗xg5 21 ♘c6 ♕f6 22 ♗d4 ♘e5 is good for Black.

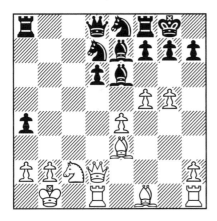

19...♗b3

The desperado theme. The piece decides where it needs to be sacrificed, and not where the opponent wants to take it.

19...♗xa2+ 20 ♔xa2 ♘e5 is also to be considered, and Black would seem to be at least equal. In A.Motylev-Bu Xiangzhi, Khanty-Mansiysk 2007, play continued 21 ♘b4 ♕b8 22 ♕c3 ♘c7 23 ♗f4 ♖c8 24 ♗xe5 ♘b5 (24...dxe5? 25 ♘c6 ♕b3+ 26 ♕xb3 axb3+ 27 ♔xb3 ♗xg5 28 ♗c4 with a clear advantage to White) 25 ♕d3 dxe5 26 ♕xb5 ♗xb4 27 ♕xb8 ♖axb8, soon drawn.

20 axb3 axb3

The a-file has now been successfully opened.

21 ♘a3

And closed again.

21...♘e5

A few months later, Karjakin with

the black pieces did not follow the Karjakin-Anand encounter, but instead demonstrated a forced quick draw: 21...d5? (unsound) 22 ♕xd5 ♗xa3 23 ♕xd7 ♕a5 24 ♕b5?! ♕c7 25 ♕c4 ♕a5 26 ♕b5 and the double-queen tango soon ended as a draw in P.Harikrishna-S.Karjakin, Foros 2006.

Harikrishna then did his homework, and found that 26 ♕xb3! keeps good winning chances for White:

a) In P.Harikrishna-A.Volokitin, Cap d'Agde (rapid) 2006, Volokitin was pressed for time (this was a quickplay), and could not find the best line. After 26...♗xb2?! 27 ♕xb2 ♕c7 28 ♗b5 ♖b8 29 ♖d5 Harikrishna consolidated and won.

b) 26...♕e5 27 ♗c1 ♕xe4+ 28 ♗d3 ♕b4 29 ♗c2 still keeps Black under severe pressure.

One gets the feeling that quite possibly Anand had seen all this in advance, such is his mastery, or supergrandmastery, of the opening in chess. Karjakin, himself a superb grandmaster, lost all three theoretical battles in this line, and was fortunate that he did not lose against Harikrishna, as well as twice against Anand.

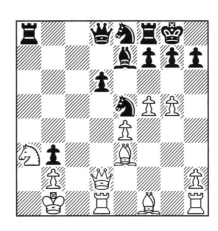

22 h4

Unexpectedly this ends up as a fatal flaw several moves later, in that White needed a check on h4 with the queen, after sharp combinative play, but the pawn is in the way. In the text line, although the pawn is useful, it does not actually do anything. Could White improve with an incredibly subtle improvement following the Karjakin-Anand idea, but keeping the chance of a critical queen check? In the end, this is likely to end up as engaging fantasy. If White were to play slightly differently, all other intervening points, whether as White or Black, could also be amended.

22 ℤc1!? looks a reasonable try, and if Black tries the tactic 22...♗xb5?, the knight would be trapped after 23 ♗xb5 ♘f3 24 ♕d3! ♘g5 25 h4. There are, however, probably a few ways of equalizing: for example, 22...ℤa4 23 ♗g2 d5 24 ♕xd5 ♕xd5 25 exd5 ♘d6.

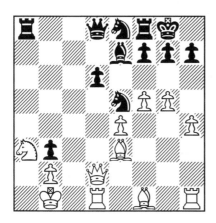

22...ℤa5

The one very slight flaw in what might otherwise have been a perfect game of chess is that there is no totally logical reason why 22...ℤa5 should be better than 22...ℤa4. Indeed in later games Black has preferred 22...ℤa4 instead of 22...ℤa5.

What is happening here is an extraordinarily deep trap, which Karjakin fell into. Once this trap becomes known, other players will not fall into it, and there is no point for Black in trying this again if other moves provide fractionally better alternatives.

We should consider Black's possible theoretical improvement, 22...ℤa4. This makes logical sense, threatening the pawn on e4, rather than the rook being awkwardly placed on a5. Then the most popular try has been 23 ♕g2 ♕a8 24 f6 ♗d8 25 ♗d4 ♘c7, which is sharp but maybe equal. An unusual plan of kingside defence was seen in A.Shirov-L.Van Wely, Wijk aan Zee 2007 (yes, another Dutch encounter here!): 26 fxg7 ♔xg7 27 h5 ♘e6 28 g6?! (Ftacnik preferred an intervening 28 ♗xe5 dxe5 29 g6 ♗g5 with equality) 28...ℤxd4! (again the rook was more active on a4 rather than on a5) 29 ℤxd4 ♘xd4 30 h6+ ♔f6! 31 g7 ℤe8 32 ♕f2+ ♘df3, and Black had swamped the position with central defenders, later winning.

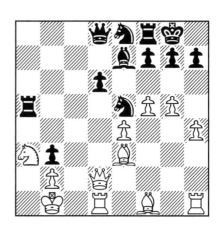

23 ♕c3?

23 ♕e2 had been tried before. In P.Leko-F.Vallejo, Monaco (rapid) 2005,

Black broke open the centre with 23...d5 (23...♛a8 might be better) 24 ♖xd5 ♖xd5 25 exd5 ♝xa3 26 bxa3 ♞d6. This ended up as a tense draw after 27 ♝c5, but possibly 27 ♝f4 would have kept an edge.

The next stage of analysis is to try to set up improvements for White, and a natural idea would be to try to chew up the pawn on b3 with 23 ♛c3. It looks good, and no doubt Anand in his analysis was asking why this straightforward move is not good for White. The next stage is to set up the ideal trap, a move which looks to be good for the opponent, but falls into an unexpected reply. These days, 'unexpected' would mean 'not seen by the computer'.

Another try would be 23 ♛b4!?, covering White's pawn on e4, as well as Black's pawn on b3.

If 23...d5 24 ♛xb3 (24 ♝b6 ♝xb4 25 ♝xd8 soon ends up as equal) 24...♝xa3 25 bxa3 ♛a8 26 ♚a2 ♞d6 27 ♖xd5 ♞xe4 28 ♖xa5 ♛xa5, and the bishop-pair will outweigh the knight-pair. In E.Najer-V.Popov, Moscow 2006, Black tried instead 23...♛a8 24 ♝b6 ♖a4 25 ♛xb3 ♛xe4+ 26 ♞c2 ♖a8 27 ♛d5 ♛xd5 28 ♖xd5. The white bishop-pair, plus an outside passed pawn, seems attractive, while the computer prefers Black, but the third result happened, a draw.

23...♛a8

Doubling the a-file. There may be the occasional threat on a3, but Karjakin was probably still feeling in control.

24 ♝g2

Otherwise the e4-pawn drops.

Anand gives 24 ♖d4 d5 with advantage to Black. If, for example, 25 exd5 ♝xa3 26 bxa3 ♖xa3, and it is difficult

for White to cover his pieces before Black has time to play ...♞d6 and ...♖c8, or other winning plans. One possibility is 27 ♝c1 ♖a4 28 ♝b2 ♖xd4 29 ♛xd4 ♞f3 30 ♛c5 ♞d6 30 ♛a3 ♞d2+ 32 ♚c1 ♖c8+ 33 ♚xd2 ♛xd5+, and the king is out in the open.

After the text, White looks safe enough, and his pieces are developed, while Black has yet to find a way to bring the knight and the castled rook into play.

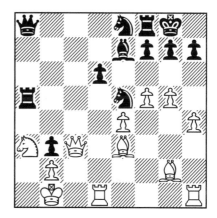

24...♞c7!!

Anand has seen this idea.

24...♖a4 would have been level.

25 ♛xc7

The one good reason for White to have tried 23 ♛c3 is to stop the knight playing to c7. So for better or worse, he might just as well take the knight,

25 ♝b6 ♖xa3 26 bxa3 ♞b5 27 ♛xb3 ♞xa3+ wins for Black. All his pieces are suddenly on good squares.

25...♖c8!

It is the second sacrifice which sets up the winning attack. 25...♖xa3? 26 bxa3 ♛xa3 27 ♛a7 easily covers Black's mate threat.

Trying this idea on the computer, this is only about tenth in the line of suggested ideas, each of these being apparently losing moves. It is human imagination which brings about the brilliancy here, and not the machine.

26 ♕xe7

He might just as well take the second piece.

The retreat with 26 ♕b6 ♘c4 27 ♕xb3 ♘xa3+ 28 bxa3 ♖xa3 29 ♕b2 ♖b8 30 ♗b6 ♖a6 31 e5 ♖a1+! 32 ♕xa1 ♖xb6+ 33 ♔c2 ♕xg2+ 34 ♔c3 dxe5 gives a likely quick checkmate. This is the line given by Ftacnik, although there are undoubtedly good alternatives.

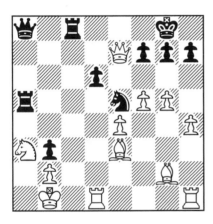

So what next? Black has successfully diverted the queen away from White's defensive squares, but he has lost two pieces, and must make his attack work.

26...♘c4!

It is only this move that justifies the combination. While the knight move is aggressive, it is not even a violent attacking move, in the sense that there is this no immediate threat of 'take, check, then check and wins'. Black is instead 'threatening to threaten' with 27...♘xa3+ 28 bxa3 ♖xa3, and then threatening a check on a1. This gives White two tempi before he can be

checkmated, and he is two pieces ahead. Normally such an attack for Black would not work. Here, amazingly, Black is just in time, even though with White's first tempo he is able to attack against the black kingside.

The computer (at least my computer) suggests that Black's position is losing, and after a trip to summer gardening and later return, the computer still says that White is winning. Quite clearly, the fact that Black wins is not the result of routine electronic suggestions, but instead the result of human endeavour. Anand is probably the greatest opening analyst of all.

Incidentally, 26...♖xa3?? 27 bxa3 ♕xc3 28 ♕a7 refutes the immediate attack.

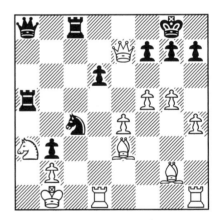

27 g6

Karjakin aims for an immediate counterattack, with the hope that his own play arrives first. The problem for the white defender is that his queen cannot help defend the king, and so what else can he do?

27 ♘xc4?? ♖a1 mate is of course elementary, but on such elementary considerations deeper tactical ideas may be built. The knight on a3 cannot

be moved, and may be cracked open.

27 ♖xd6?! may also be regarded as elementary. After 27...♖xa3 28 bxa3 ♘xa3+ 29 ♔b2 ♘c4+ 30 ♔c3 ♘xd6+ any experienced player will conclude immediately that Black is heading for a win. 31 ♔d4 ♕a4+ 32 ♔e5 ♖e8 33 ♕xe8+ ♘xe8 may hold out for a while, but perhaps not for very long.

This leaves bishop moves:

a) 27 ♗c1 ♘xa3+ 28 bxa3 ♖xa3 29 ♗xa3 ♕xa3 30 ♖d2 ♖a8 is not difficult to calculate, even though Black has now, in total, sacrificed a rook and bishop.

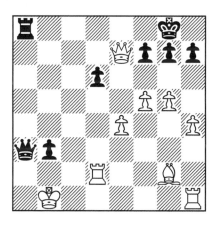

There is no way for White to avoid checkmate, except the temporary reprieve of a queen sacrifice with 31 ♕e8+ ♖xe8 32 e5 (preventing ...♖a8), but Black is now material ahead after 32...♖xe5 33 ♖c1 h6 34 g6 fxg6 35 fxg6 ♔f8. Earlier, 27...♕c6! wins more cleanly, without allowing White the queen sacrifice.

b) If 27 ♗d4, Anand gives 27...♖xa3 28 bxa3 ♘xa3+ 29 ♔b2 ♘c4+ 30 ♔c3 ♕a2! 31 ♗c5 ♕c2+ 32 ♔d4 dxc5+ 33 ♔d5 ♘e3+ 34 ♔d6 ♘xd1. At least White's king and queen have been reunited, but now Black is material

ahead, and is about to queen.

c) Finally, Anand gives 27 ♗c5!?. White's idea is to slow down one of Black's pieces by distracting them with the bishop:

c1) If, for example, 27...♖axc5?! 28 ♖xd6! 29 ♘xd6 (29...♘xa3 30 bxa3 ♕xc3?? 31 ♖d8+) 29 ♕xd6 and White is better.

c2) 27...♖cxc5?! 28 e5! again with ideas of a back-row mate.

c3) 25...dxc5?! 26 ♖d7, and White now has mating threats himself.

c4) However, Anand shows there is still a winning attack with 27...♖xa3!. He is not to be distracted, and White has now used up one of his precious tempo moves. After 38 bxa3 ♖xc5 29 a4 ♘a3+ 30 ♔b2 ♖c2+ 31 ♔xa3 ♕b8! wins, since if 32 ♖a1 b2 33 ♖a2 ♖c3 mate.

Karjakin's line looks the more natural. He tries to get in his retaliation in first.

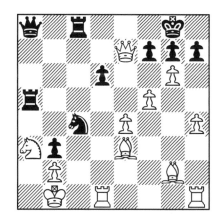

27...hxg6

Anand needs to create an escape square for the king.

28 fxg6

And Karjakin needs to restore his threat. A glance at the computer might suggest that there are several ways for

White to set up an advantage, but these all turn out to be rejected choices from move 27.

28...♞xa3+

28...♜xa3 also wins, and if 29 gxf7+ ♔h7 30 f8♞+, then 30...♜xf8, much as in the main line. If instead 30 bxa3, Black soon checkmates after 30...♞xa3+ 31 ♔b2 ♜c2+ 32 ♔xb3 ♛b8+.

The one line in which Black needs to be careful, to avoid a trap, is 29 ♛xf7+ ♔h8 30 bxa3 ♞xa3+ 31 ♔b2, and if now 31...♜xc2+?? 32 ♔xb3 ♛b8+ 33 ♔xa3, and unexpectedly Black is running out of checks, while White is vastly ahead in material. The queen on f7 covers so many squares, particularly the hoped-for checking squares on a2, b3 and c4. If 33...♜c3+ 34 ♔a4 ♛a8+ 35 ♗a7, covering another square with the help of the queen, and then 35...♛c6+ 36 ♔b4, and Black runs out of checks. So Black has to be careful here with 31...♞c4+ 32 ♔c3 (32 ♛xc4 ♛a2+) 32...♞e5+ 33 ♔xb3 ♞xf7, and he still wins.

29 bxa3 ♜xa3

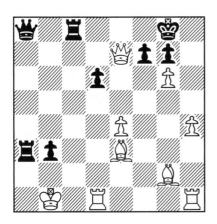

This is a highly delicate position, meaning not so much that the position is equal (it isn't), but rather that even the smallest nuance in the position

could result either as a win for White, or a win for Black, or even a draw. The position itself is relatively straightforward for Black by now, but evaluating this position several moves in advance would be incredibly difficult over the board.

Look at that pawn on h4, apparently an insignificant pawn making up the numbers. Unfortunately the pawn is in the way. Had the pawn been on h2, White would be winning with 30 gxf7+ ♔h7 31 ♛h4+. An unpredictable outcome after White's confident pawn push on move 22, but if White had played something different just then, the whole outcome would have been different, for better or worse. Sometimes even the tiniest details have global significance.

30 gxf7+

The only move. 30 ♛xf7+? ♔h8 runs out of checks, and White will lose. Then 31 ♗d4 does not help: 31...♜a1+ 32 ♗xa1 ♛a2 mate.

30...♔h7

30...♔h8?! 31 f8♛+ ♜xf8 32 ♛xf8+ ♛xf8 33 ♗d4 is far less clear.

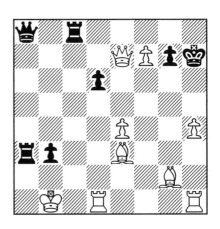

31 f8♞+

It has to be with check. 31 f8♛? ♜a1+ loses instantly.

31...♖xf8

Anand is interested in far more than perpetual check after 31...♔h8?! 32 ♘g6+ ♔h7 33 ♘f8+.

32 ♕xf8

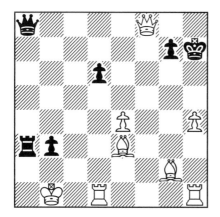

If 32 ♕xd6 ♖a1+ (32...♖c8? 33 ♕e5! allows White to coordinate his pieces) 33 ♔b2 ♖a2+ 34 ♔b1 ♖c2!, and Anand notes that Black wins. The desperation sacrifice with 35 ♕h6+ gxh6 36 ♖d7+ ♔g8 37 ♖a7 ♕c6 38 ♖g1 ♕c3 does not quite work.

32...♖a1+

Anand is not interested in taking the queen with 32...♕xf8? 33 ♖d2. Maybe Black still has an edge after 33...♖a4!, but one of the first lessons we are taught in chess is that queen and rook in an open position can checkmate against king.

33 ♔b2 ♖a2+

Black must not overdo the mating

ideas though. After 33...♕a3+? 34 ♔c3 the only safe way is a draw after 34...♕a5+ 35 ♔b2.

34 ♔c3

If 34 ♔b1, Black has gained a valuable tempo with his rook checks, and can win comfortably after 34...♕xf8 35 ♗h3 ♕a8 36 ♗f5+ ♔h8. If then 37 ♖c1, Anand gives 37...♖a1+ 38 ♔b2 ♕a3+ 39 ♔c3 b2+.

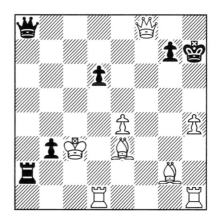

34...♕a5+

Check, check, check, and...checkmate.

35 ♔d3

35 ♔xb3 ♖a3+ mates in a couple of moves.

35...♕b5+ 36 ♔d4 ♖a4+ 37 ♔c3 ♕c4+ 0-1

38 ♔d2 ♖a2+ 39 ♔e1 ♕e2 is mate.

A superb example of accurate combinational attacking play, and also a superb example of detailed opening innovative play.

Game 7
P.Svidler-V.Topalov
Morelia 2006
Ruy Lopez C67

1 e4 e5

The first example in this book of a symmetrical kingside opening.

2 ♘f3

These days the King's Gambit with 2 f4!? exf4, and then 3 ♘f3 or 3 ♗c4, has long been highly unfashionable. White gives away a pawn and exposes his king, without even bringing his pieces into play. This does not sound so promising, but White keeps two pawns in the centre, on e4 and d4, with excellent attacking chances, and this line is dangerous. If Black falters, his position, even now, can end up in collapse.

Curiously a list of top-level games from 2004 to early 2008 shows that White has a big plus score, with no losses, with a 100% score in blitz games and quickplays. In standard play, V.Zvjaginsev-E.Tomashevsky, Serpukhov 2007, led to a win for White that 19th Century players would surely have appreciated. After 3 ♘f3 d6 4 d4 g5 5 ♘c3 ♘c6 6 g3 g4 7 ♘h4 f3 8 ♗e3 Black had an impressive advanced passed pawn, but White has excellent piece development and good central pawns. Zvjaginsev later scored a miniature win (25 moves or fewer), with Black's king being fully exposed in the centre.

2...♘c6

For 2...♘f6, see Game 24, Kamsky-Carlsen.

2...d6, the Philidor Defence is playable, but has the disadvantage of blocking the dark-squared bishop.

3 ♗b5

This has been played about three-quarters of the time here, putting pressure on the knight, and thereby putting pressure on the e5-pawn.

3 d4, the Scotch Opening, is examined in Game 18, Rublevsky-Grischuk. See the comments there for other third move alternatives.

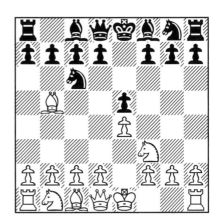

The text reaches the Ruy Lopez, now even more fashionable in the 21st century than in the 16th. White does not aim for the natural attack on the f7-pawn with 3 ♗c4, but pressurizes the e5-pawn by attacking the defending knight on c6.

3...♘f6

The Berlin Defence, but the main line remains 3...a6 4 ♗a4 ♘f6. See Game 10, Ivanchuk-Aronian.

4 0-0

4 ♘c3 leads to the 'boring' Four Knights, with Rubinstein's 4...♘d4 removing much of the interest from White's point of view.

4 d3 is more flexible for White, without necessarily achieving much of an advantage. James Mortimer achieved his moment of fame in London 1883, with the trap he set with 4...♘e7!?, with the idea that if 5 ♘xe5? c6! Black wins a piece after either 6 ♗c4 ♕a5+ or 6 ♘c4 ♘g6! (but not 6...cxb5?? 7 ♘d6 mate) 7 ♗a4 b5. Mortimer's three opponents in that tournament avoided the little trap, and were much stronger than Mortimer, and so won easily each time. The move itself is playable, and the idea of ...c6 and ...♘g6 is sensible.

4...♘xe4

4...♗c5 has been described as the 'Berlin Classical', a mixture of the Berlin and Classical (3...♗c5) defences. The bishop move is playable, but less solid than the Berlin Defence proper. White can aim at a hit with d4 against an early ...♗c5.

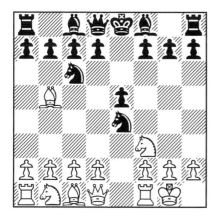

5 d4

This has been tried many times in recent years and for the most part it has proven to be difficult for White to break down Black's position. The present game does not give White a clear or decisive edge, despite the final result.

The older 5 ♖e1 ♘d6 6 ♘xe5 ♗e7 (or maybe immediately 6...♘xe5) was tried several times in the 1886 World Championship, with Steinitz as White against Zukertort. Steinitz achieved a good plus score, but these days it is seen basically as a drawing line with symmetrical pawn structures, and a gradual equalization by Black.

The knight on d6 gets in the way. Could Black have considered 5...♘f6 instead? After 6 ♘xe5, White is slightly ahead in development, and it is not quite as easy as it looks to develop Black's pieces: 6...♗e7 7 d4 0-0 8 ♘c3 keeps a slight edge.

5...♘d6

5...♗e7, the traditional way, keeps a slight edge for White after 6 ♕e2 ♘d6 7 ♗xc6 bxc6 8 exd5 ♘b7. A year previously, Black tried 7...dxc6, which is much sharper, and then 8 dxe5 ♘f5 9 ♖d1 ♗d7 10 e6 fxe6 11 ♘e5 ♗d6 in P.Svidler-A.Morozevich, Wijk aan Zee 2005. Play continued 12 ♕h5+ g6 13 ♘xg6 ♘g7 (the knight goes to the other fianchetto square) 14 ♕h6 ♘f3 15 ♕h3 (declining the repetition) 15...♖g6 16 ♕xh7 ♖g7 17 ♕h5 ♕f6 18 ♘e5+ ♔e7 19 ♘g4.

This dates back over a century, and in Taubenhaus-Pollock, New York 1893, Black continued with 19...♕h4?! 20 ♕xh4 ♘xh4 21 h3 e5 22 f3, and White later consolidated with his extra pawn. Morozevich preferred keeping his pieces better centralized with 19...♕g6 20 ♕xg6 ♖xg6 21 h3 e5 22 ♘d2 ♘d4 23

c3 ②c2 24 ‡b1 ⌐xg4 25 hxg4 ‡xg4.
Pawns are level, and Black has the more
active pieces, except that the knight on
c2 looks overextended. However, the
knight is irritatingly difficult to attack,
with, for example, b4 and ‡b2 giving
an escape square on a3, and a knight
move followed by ‡d2 giving an escape
square on e1. Play eventually ended up
in a typically tense late queenless middlegame, and a later draw.

There is also the question why Black
has not really bothered with 5...exd4.
After 6 ‡e1 d5 7 ②xd4 ⌐d6 8 ②xc6
⌐xh2+

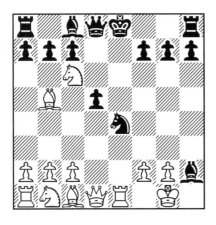

9 ⌦h1 (to avoid perpetual) 9...♕h4
10 ‡xe4+ dxe4 11 ♕d8+ ♕xd8 12
②xd8+ ⌦xd8 13 ⌦xh2 we have reached
a position which can also come about
with ...a6 and ‡a4 included. Here with
White's bishop still on b5, Black has the
more constructive pawn attack with
...c6.

This line has only occasionally been
played, with a win for Black after unclear play in M.Djurdjevic-M. Trajkovic,
Novi Sad 1989. Play continued with
13...h6 14 ②c3 c6 15 ‡c4 f5 16 ‡e3
⌦e7 17 ‡d1 b6 18 ‡d4 ‡e6 19 ‡xe6
⌦xe6 20 ‡xg7 ‡hd8. Although White

had regained one of Black's pawns,
Black by now had a dangerous d-file.

Another try for White is 7 ♕xd4!?,
given by Fine, quoted in *ECO*, which
might be a deterrent, with 7...♕d7 8
‡xc6 ♕xc6 9 c4 giving an edge for
White. Computer analysis suggests the
possibility of 7...‡e6 8 ♕a4 ♕d6, with a
possible perpetual after 9 ‡f4 ♕c5 10
‡e3 ♕d6 11 ‡f4. White can of course
try for more with 11 ②e5 ‡e7!? 12
②xc6 bxc6 13 ‡xc6+ ‡d7 14 ‡xd7+
♕xd7 15 ♕xd7+ ⌦xd7, and White has
slightly the better pawn structure as
the endgame approaches, which might
or might not prove significant.

We now return to 5...②d6:

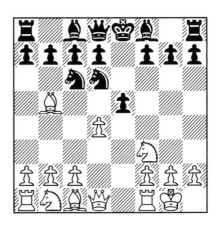

6 ‡xc6

Obvious? Maybe. The only sensible
move? No.

6 dxe5 ②xb5 7 a4 traps the knight,
and immediately recovers the minor
piece. There is some sharp gambit play
after 7...②d6 8 ‡g5! f6 (8...‡e7 9 ‡xe7
♕xe7 10 fxd6 cxd6 11 ②c3 leaves
Black's extra pawn a liability rather
than an asset) 9 ‡e1!. A simpler and
safer option is 7...d6 8 axb5 ②xe5 9 ‡e1
‡e7 10 ②xe5 dxe5 11 ♕xd8+ ⌦xd8 12
‡xe5 ‡d6 with equality. Yet again, we

reach the familiar pattern in open games of many tactics early on, subsiding to a queenless late middlegame.

6...dxc6

6...bxc6 7 dxe5 ♘b7 is playable, but not enticing for Black. *Fritz* gives this as equal, after, for example, 8 ♗g5 ♗e7 9 ♗xe7 ♕xe7 10 ♘c3 0-0 11 ♖e1, but White, with his better development and centralized pieces, should have chances to play for more than that.

7 dxe5

7 ♘xe5 has no realistic hope of an advantage. White is attacking nothing, and so Black can quietly complete his development, and eventually try to take advantage of the bishop-pair.

7...♘f5

7...♘e4 is playable, but the knight loses some flexibility. If Black wanted to manoeuvre his knight via c5 and e6, putting a little pressure on the d4-square, he would take three moves to cover the d4-square, whereas ...♘f5 does it in one.

8 ♕xd8+

The only try for a win. If 8 ♕e2 ♘d4, Black is comfortably equal.

8...♔xd8

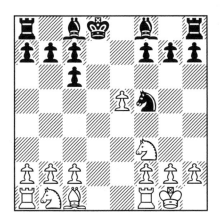

After the preliminaries, the battle starts here. White has the better pawn structure, while Black's set-up is solid, and he keeps the bishop-pair. There are no sharp attacks against the king, but the position is difficult for both sides.

The Berlin Defence is quite a significant challenge for the Ruy Lopez. If White cannot find an advantage in this position, then he might well decide that it is time to give up the Ruy. Kasparov, many years ago, found no effective way of breaking up the Berlin Defence against Kramnik. Since this 2000 match, players with White have tried hard to find something here. See too the comments to Game 22, Stellwagen-Eljanov.

9 ♘c3

As one can imagine, there is a wide choice of moves. Black is not making any direct threats, and there are various developing ideas, including the move played, and checks such as 9 ♗g5+ and 9 ♖d1+. Also 9 b3 and ♗b2, providing back-up to White's kingside pawn advantage.

9 ♘c3 is the most popular, on the basis of the principle of 'knights before bishops'. The player will generally have a good idea of where the knight should go, but it is less clear where the bishop wants to go, and it is useful to delay for a move, while developing the knight, to see what the opponent will try. Flexibility is an important part of modern chess.

9...♘e7!?

For 9...♗d7, see Game 22.

The knight move is a relatively recent idea, pioneered by Zoltan Almasi in the late 1990s. Of course, all this is now a decade ago, but in the decades before Black did not think of trying it.

The reason for this neglect is presumably that Black has already taken four moves with his knight, ...♘g8-f6xe4-d6-f5, to end up on a good square, and it seems extravagant for Black to make two extra knight moves when neither his bishops nor his rooks have moved. Why should Black spend another couple of tempi with ...♘e7-g6? The obvious answer is that Black is attacking something, the pawn on e5, and this provides the possibility of a counterattack.

10 h3

The main line. White wants, at some stage, to stop ...♗g4.

10...♘g6

And this is the logically consistent main line for Black. 10...h6 has been tried a few times, on the basis that if White has the luxury of playing a quiet line, Black too should have the luxury of playing another quiet line in return, and waits to see what the opponent does next.

11 ♗g5+

Postny suggests, in annotations for ChessBase, that White's intention is to force his opponent's king to the kingside, to stop Black's plan of ...♗e6 and ...♔c8. This seems an over-elaborate

interpretation. A much simpler point is that White is gaining a tempo with check, bringing the undeveloped rook into play quickly.

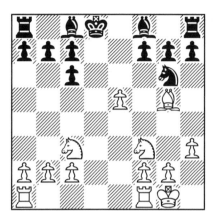

11...♔e8

Perhaps it is time to mention, much more specifically, the central strategic battle of the Berlin Defence. White has given up bishop for knight, in return for doubling Black's c-pawns. White now has much the better pawn structure. He has a good 4-3 pawn advantage on the kingside, and if there is quiet play on both sides, White will have excellent chances of setting up a kingside pawn-roller. On the queenside, Black too has the extra 4-3 pawn majority, but the pawns block each other, and do not create the chance of setting up a passed pawn. The problem for Black is not so much that his doubled pawns are weak, as it is easy to defend them. The real problem is rather that Black's queenside pawns are less effective, in terms of active play, than White's kingside passed pawns.

Black has compensation, though, with his bishop being traditionally slightly stronger than the knight. Usually bishops work in pairs for maximum effect. In the Berlin Defence, it is important for Black's bishops to stay together for as long as possible to offset the negative impact of the doubled pawns.

11...♗e7 is playable, but it makes concessions. 12 ♖ad1+ ♔e8 13 ♗xe7 ♔xe7 14 ♘d4?! has been tried a few times. Black has avoided grabbing the hot pawn with 14...♘xe5!? 15 ♖fe1 ♔f6, but there is no obvious refutation. Possibly White needs to play safely, but then any edge for White is minimal, the knight on g6 making it difficult for him to establish his pawn roller with f4.

12 ♖ad1

White wants to keep control of the d-file.

12...♗d7

Or 12...♗e6 13 ♘d4 ♗c4 14 ♖fe1 ♗b4 15 ♘f5 ♗xc3 16 bxc3 ♖g8 17 a3 h6 18 ♗c1 ♗e6, equal and later drawn in P.Leko-V.Kramnik, Dortmund 2004. Can White find a slight edge in this?

Topalov tries to leave the bishop less exposed.

ter ...♘xe5-c4. In P.Svidler-V.Kramnik, Dortmund 2004, White was a pawn down, but was able to draw after 14 ♖fd1 ♗e7 15 ♘e2 ♘xe5 16 ♘xe5 ♗xg5 17 f4 ♗e7 18 ♘d4. Maybe better is 14 ♘d4 h6 15 ♘xe6 fxe6 16 ♗e3 ♘xe5 17 ♖e1 ♘c4 18 ♖d4 ♘xe3 19 ♖xe3 ♗c5 20 ♖xe6+ ♔f7 21 ♖de4 ♖he8 with a likely draw.

Another high-level try has been 13 a3 h6 14 ♗c1 ♖d8 15 ♖fe1 ♗e7 16 ♘e4 ♗e6 17 ♖xd8+ ♔xd8 18 ♘d4 ♗d7 19 f4 ♘h4 20 ♔f2 h5, ending up as drawn in V.Topalov-F.Vallejo Pons, Benidorm 2003.

One gains the feeling from the Berlin Defence that play is generally theoretically about equal, in a late queenless middlegame, but that either player could easily go seriously wrong positionally. Among top players, competitors are expected to handle all types of position, but many amateur players might find such openings uncomfortable to handle, especially against even slightly stronger opposition.

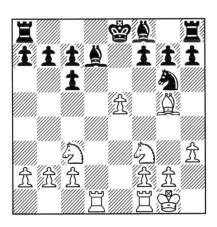

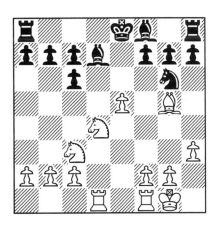

13 ♘d4

On 13 ♖d2, Kramnik has tried 13...♗e6!?, on the basis presumably that White's rook is slightly more exposed on d2 rather than d1, such as af-

13...h6

13...♘xe5?! 14 ♖fe1 f6 15 ♘f3 ♗d6 16 ♗f4 definitely favours White, with the more active pieces and the better pawn structure.

14 ♗e3

14 ♗c1!? is to be considered, keeping the bishop out of the way of the e-file. If 14...♗c5 15 ♖de1 with maybe a slight edge. Here too 14...♗b4 15 ♖d3 ♖d8 16 ♖fd1 ♗e7 17 f4 led to a slight edge in V.Kotronias-P.Eljanov, German League 2008.

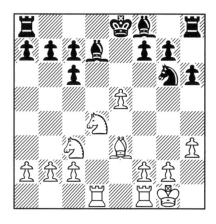

14...h5

A new move, with the idea of pushing the pawn further to h4, and trying to cramp White's kingside pawn majority.

An earlier try was 14...♗b4 15 f4 ♗xc3 16 bxc3 c5 17 ♘e2 b6 18 ♘g3 h5 19 f5 ♘xe5 20 ♗f4 f6 21 ♖fe1 ♗a4, agreed drawn in A.Shirov-Z.Almasi, Monaco (rapid) 2002. Here Svidler notes that if 15 ♘e4 c5 16 ♘e2 ♗b5 17 ♘4g3 ♘xe5 18 c3 ♗a5 19 ♗xc5 f6 play is equal. He notes too that the exchange sacrifices after 16 ♘f3 ♗b5 17 c3 ♗xf1 18 ♔xf1 ♗a5 and 16 ♘b3 ♗b5 17 c3 ♗xf1 18 ♔xf1 c4 are unconvincing.

15 f4

The most aggressive, although 15 ♗g5 and 15 ♖e1 also seem to give White chances of a slight plus.

15...h4

If 15...♗c5, White has several alter-natives, including perhaps 16 ♖d2 or 16 ♖fe1. Svidler gives instead 16 ♘e4 ♗xd4 17 ♖xd4 ♗f5 18 ♘g3 ♘e7, which he feels is unclear, but maybe 19 ♖d2 still keeps an edge.

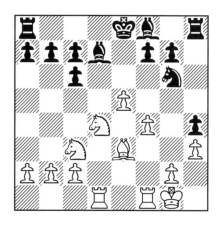

16 f5!?

Postny gives this a double-exclamation mark, describing Svidler's pawn sacrifice as 'very deep and sound'. Svidler, he says, seizes the initiative. Svidler himself is more cautious. Neither player will have been able to calculate whether the pawn sacrifice is fully sound, although undoubtedly Svidler would have believed in his play. As further analysis shows, there are possible ways in which Black could have improved, and there are a few questions as to whether White was better throughout.

This is in effect gambit play, but also highly sophisticated gambit play. White is not charging through with an attack on the king, hoping that somewhere along the way, Black may make a tactical mistake, giving White a brilliancy and a point. It is more a case of setting the opponent a challenge. Black has an extra pawn, but has a few structural defects, and his pieces are under pressure. Can Black hold the balance, or even take over the initiative? The only answer, for player and reader, is to wait and see.

Postny also gave as equal 16 ♖d3 ♗c5 17 ♖fd1 ♗xd4 18 ♖xd4 ♗f5. I doubt this interpretation. After 19 ♖4d2 White has the more active pieces, keeps the open d-file, and still has the better pawn structure. White's knight could also make its presence felt after ♘e2 and ♘d4.

There are many other ways for White to aim for a slight edge: for example, 16 ♘e4 c5 17 ♘e2 b6 18 ♘2c3 ♗f5 19 ♖f2 ♗e7 20 ♖fd2 ♖d8 21 ♖xd8+ ♗xd8 22 ♔f2. Probably any edge here is very slight.

White keeps a slight edge in most lines, and is in no danger of being worse, but does he feel he has realistic chances of playing for a win? Or has he got better chances by sacrificing?

In the end, this is as much a question of chess psychology as of analysis.

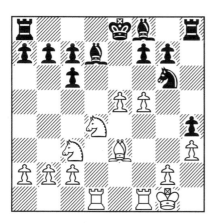

16...♘xe5

Naturally he must take the pawn.

17 f6

And White must go through with the sacrifice. 17 ♗f4 f6 18 ♖fe1 ♔f7 19

♗xe5 dxe5 19 ♖xe5 ♗d6 leaves Black with comfortable play.

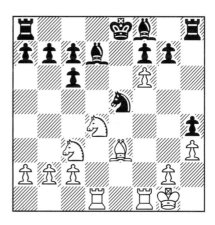

17...♖h5

Topalov, with his new 2800+ rating, is a formidably imaginative player, and he has the ability of playing for an attack out of seemingly nothing. One senses that Svidler was deliberately trying to provoke his opponent, and perhaps it worked, as he won the game.

Svidler's notes in *Informator* suggest a draw after 17...gxf6 18 ♘e4 ♗e7 19 ♘xf6+ ♗xf6 20 ♖xf6 ♖h5 21 ♘f3 ♘xf3+ 22 ♖xf3 ♗e6 23 ♖f4 ♖d8 24 ♖xd8+ ♔xf8 25 a3. White will soon recapture the pawn, winning the one on h4, and Black should hold the draw.

A draw with a 2765-rated opponent will be more than satisfactory for most players, but Topalov, with a valuable but fragile 2801 rating, would not want to give away half an Elo point so readily. He would try to put his opponent under some pressure.

As for whether Topalov's combative alternative is good, bad or equal, we need to analyse what happens later.

18 ♘e4

Now Black cannot take the pawn, which remains an irritation. Moreover,

White's knights remain excellently centralized.

A reminder for the reader. Black's position is not as good as it looks, as he cannot castle, and the king is therefore under pressure in the centre.

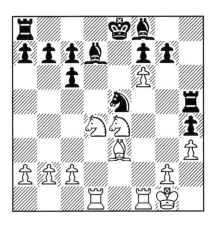

18...g6

Again one senses that Topalov is aiming for a win.

Svidler gives 18...c5!? 19 fxg7 ♗xg7 20 ♘xc5 ♘c4 21 ♘xd7 ♘xe3 22 ♖fe1 ♔xd7 23 ♖xe3 ♖d5 24 ♖ed3 ♗f6 25 c3, and White has slightly the better pawn structure, thanks to the exchange of Black's g-pawn. Topalov prefers to keep the pawns united.

19 ♗f4

White wants to keep the f-pawn as firmly protected as possible. 19 ♖fe1 loosens, and after 19...♗d6! 20 ♗f4 ♔f8 21 ♘xd6 cxd6 White has no advantage.

19...c5?!

If 19...♗d6 20 g4! hxg3 21 ♘xg3 ♖xh3 22 ♖de1 ♔f8 23 ♖xe5 ♗xe5 24 ♗xe5 with, according to Svidler, a clear advantage for White. Is this so clear? Black would want to defend the pawn on c7 with 24...♖c8, and either equality or a slight edge for White. This would have been an interesting struggle, one

problem for White being that there is no cover with the pawns to set up any outposts for the knights on the kingside. This seems better than the move actually played.

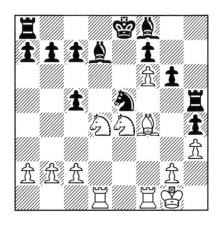

20 ♘f3?

This is a very difficult position to understand, even with the help of the computer, and plenty of leisure. In the constraints of tournament chess, all the players can do is to find moves, and hope for the best. Often what is remarkable in top-level chess is not so much that mistakes can be made, but rather that so often players find good or reasonable moves.

Maybe there is a positional argument to be made in that Black's knight is vulnerable, and that White should not consider exchanging the knights with such ease. Svidler would presumably not have wanted to slow the tempo of play with a knight retreat, and so forces the exchange of knights. But maybe he should have kept the knights.

White's basic idea after 20 ♘e2! would be to play g4, kicking the rook away, and then kicking again with ♘2g3, and winning the knight on e5:

a) Black can try to get the knight out of the way with 20...♘c4, but White has a clear positional edge after 21 ♖fe1 ♔d8 22 ♘g5 ♔c8 23 b3.

b) Svidler gives as the main line 20...♖f5! 21 ♖de1! (improving on 21 g4 hxg3 22 ♘2xg3 ♖xf4! 23 ♖xf4 ♗h6, regaining the exchange after 24 ♖ff1 ♗xh3) 21...♔d8 (avoiding the pins, semi-pins, and discovered attacks; in other lines, White plays g4 again) 22 g4! hxg4 23 ♘2xg3 ♖xf4 24 ♖xf4 ♗h6 25 ♖f2, and White is probably winning with the extra exchange. This g4 idea in such a setting is highly unusual, and can easily be missed.

20...♘xf3+

Half-forced, but a piece exchange would be something of a relief for Black anyway.

21 ♖xf3

White's advantage has now been considerably been trimmed down. He is a pawn down, but he still keeps his initiative.

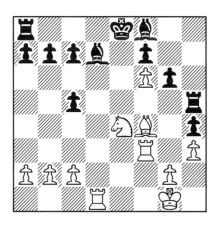

21...♗e6

Topalov decides he must activate his pieces.

21...c4 22 ♗xc7 leaves White clearly better.

21...♖f5?! 22 ♖e3! would please the spectators after 22...♖xf4 23 ♘d6+ ♔d8 24 ♖e8+! ♗xe8 25 ♘xf7+ ♔c8 26 ♖d8 mate. Instead 22...♗e6 23 ♗xc7 c4 24 ♖e2! ♖c8 25 ♖ed2 ♖d5 26 ♖xd5 ♗xd5 27 ♖xd5 ♖xc7 28 ♔f2 (Postny) leaves White better in the endgame. Black's king is still caught in the middle, White's pieces are better, and Black's h-pawn is weak.

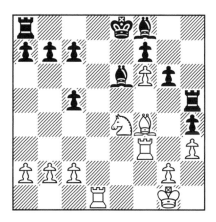

22 ♖fd3?!

He wants to play for a win, and so cut out ...♖d8. This aim is commendable, and indeed Svidler scores the full point, but he is in danger of overpressing.

22 ♘g5 ♖d8 23 ♖e1 c4 24 ♘xe6 fxe6 25 ♖xe6+ ♔f7 26 ♖e4 ♗c5+ 27 ♔f1 ♖d4 is about level, with perhaps some minimal pressure in favour of Black.

22...c4

Gaining some space for the dark-squared bishop.

23 ♖3d2

The only sensible move.

23...c6

Black must put something on the d-file, quickly.

24 ♘g5

And White squeezes out Black's rook.

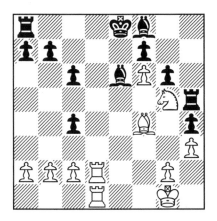
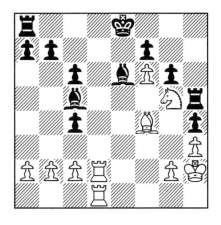

24...♗c5+

With gain of tempo, but it is going to be difficult for Black to coordinate his pieces further.

25 ♔h2

Over the board it would be impossible to *calculate* whether this or 25 ♔h1 would be better, given that 25...♗d5 or 25...c3 would have different ramifications according to whether the king is on h2 or h1. The best that one can say is that occasionally Black might have a useful checking resource on the b8-h2 diagonal, but that also in some lines the king is more active on h2 than on h1.

Trying to sort this one out is more like chess sudoku rather than normal chess. My instinct, for what it is worth, would probably be to prefer to avoid any checks on the dark squares with 25 ♔h1, but Svidler sees a different approach, setting up ideas of g4, and if ...hxg3+ then ♔xg3.

Neither Postny nor Svidler makes any comment or analysis on this move. This could mean either that Svidler's move is so obvious and hardly worth considering, or, more likely, that the position is so obscure that it is hardly worth dealing with.

25...♗d5?

But this is far less difficult to evaluate. There is here a choice between setting up some sharp tactical play, or, as Topalov ends up choosing, trying to keep the balance.

Postny gives this as the critical slip, suggesting 25...c3! 26 bxc3 ♗xa2 when both sides have obvious problems and opportunities. He gives as the main line 27 ♖d7 b6 28 ♖b7 ♗d5 29 ♖e1+ ♔f8 30 c4 (to divert the bishop; not immediately 30 ♖ee7? ♗xe7 31 fxe7+ ♔e8, and the bishop stops the knight from reaching e4) 30...♗xc4 31 ♖ee7 a5 32 ♖xf7+ ♗xf7 33 ♖xf7+ ♔e8 34 ♖g7 a4 35 f7+ ♔e7 36 f8♕+ ♔xf8 37 ♘e6+ ♔e8 38 ♘c7+ ♔f8 39 ♘e6+ ♔e8, and a perpetual.

Just a steady draw? It turns out that White has been indeed taking too many risks. Instead of 34...a4?, which is premature, Black improves with 34...♗f8! 35 ♖b7 ♖xg5 36 f7+ (36 ♗g5 ♔d8 37 f7+ transposes) 36...♔d8 37 ♗g5 ♔c8 38 ♖xb6 ♔d7 39 ♗xh4 a4, and it is Black who has the more effective passed pawn. After 40 ♖b1 a3 41 ♖f1 ♗g7 White is in trouble.

Can White even equalize? It is difficult. Postny gives an alternative for White, 29 c4!? ♗xc4 30 ♘e4 ♖d5 31 ♖e1 ♔f8 32 ♘xc5 bxc5 33 ♖ee7 ♖f5 34 ♖xa7 ♖xa7 35 ♗h6+ (setting up a mate threat) 35...♔g8 36 ♖e8+ ♔h7 37 ♗g7 ♖xf6! (37...g5? 36 ♖h8+ ♔g6 37 ♖h6 mate) 38 ♗xf6 g5, and with care White should hold the draw after 39 ♖e5 ♗d5 40 ♖xg5 ♖a2 41 c3.

26 ♖e2+

To keep the pressure on the king.

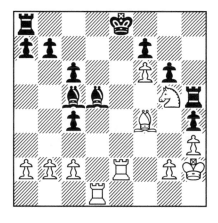

26...♔f8

Svidler gave this a question mark, while Postny passes it without comment.

Certainly there is a problem now that Black's kingside pieces are tied up, but Topalov is still hoping that Black has good compensatory activity on the queenside, with a powerful bishop-pair and an extra pawn on that side. The position is still finely balanced, but it is unclear as yet which way the balance will fall.

After 26...♔d7!? White has the obvious and natural 27 ♘xf7, and then Svidler gives 27...♖f8 28 ♘e5+ ♔c8 29 ♘g4 ♖f5, which he gives as unclear. The likelihood is that at some stage Black will give up the exchange in return for

the passed pawn, and keep the bishop pair as active and excellent defenders. So, for example, 30 ♗h6 ♖f7 31 ♗e3 ♗d6+ 32 ♔h1 b5 33 ♘h6 ♖5xf6 34 ♘xf7 ♖xf7 35 ♖f2 ♖d7, and Black's position is extremely difficult to break down. Here 27 ♖de1 ♖f8 28 ♖e7+ ♗xe7 29 ♖xe7+ ♔c8 30 ♖c7+ ♔d8 31 ♖xb7 ♖e8 32 ♖b8+ ♔d7 33 ♖b7+ is a draw, since Svidler notes that 32 ♘xf7+ ♗xf7 33 ♖xf7 ♖f5 34 ♗h6 ♖e1 presses too hard. Earlier, 28 b4?! ♗xb4 29 ♖b1 a5 30 c3 ♗d6 31 ♖xb7+ ♔c8 32 ♗xd6 ♔xb7 33 ♗xf8 ♖xg5 is over-elaborate, and White would need to press hard for a draw.

27 ♖de1

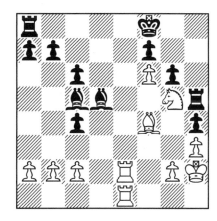

Certainly White is putting his opponent under pressure, but it is difficult to see how he can win material.

27...b5

If 27...c3, then simply 28 b3, and Black's advanced pawn is weak rather than strong.

28 c3

White wants to try to stabilize his queenside pawn structure.

28...a5

While Black wants to push his pawns further.

29 a3

More consolidation.

29...Rc8

If 29...b4?! 30 a4!, and Black can make no real progress on the queen-side, but has broken up his own pawns.

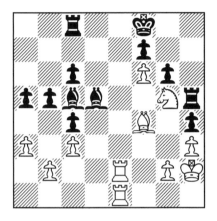

30 g4

A slight error, according to Svidler.

30 Re5! is, remarkably, close to zugzwang, and if Black were to play quietly, with for example 30...a4 or 30...Ra8, White has gained a small tempo with 31 g4.

Of the bishop moves, 30...Bd6?? 31 Bd6+ is a blunder. We shall see this idea again.

However, 30...Bb6 is possible, and if 31 R5e2 Bc5, the position is repeated. There is tactical entertainment after 31 Re8+ Rxe8 32 Bd6+ Re7 (32...Kg8?? 33 Re8+) 33 Rxe7 Rg5 34 Re5+ Kg8 35 Rxg5 Be3! 36 Rg4 Bc1 37 Rxh4 Bxb2 38 Bf8 g5! (38...Bxc3?? 39 Bg7 and mate) 39 Rh5 Be4 40 Re7 Bc1, and remarkably it is White's rook, rather than Black's, which gets stuck in the blind corner on h5. White will have to return the exchange with 41 h4 Bg6 42 Rxg5 Bxg5 43 hxg5 b4 44 axb4 a4 45 b5 cxb5, leading to a draw.

30...hxg3+

The natural response, but White still has to demonstrate a win after 30...Rh8. He should be able to squeeze through after, for example, 31 Re5 a4 32 R1e2 Ra8 33 Ne4 Bxe4 34 R2xe4 Bb6 35 Re7 Rc8 36 Rd7 Rd8 37 Rxd8+ Bxd8 38 Bd6+ Kg8 39 g5 when White will win the h-pawn, then work out what to do next.

31 Kxg3

White has gained a little more space for the king after the pawn exchange.

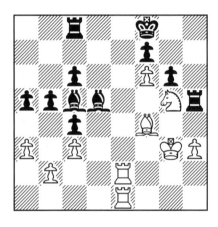

31...Be6

Postny poses the question of how White could be able to improve his position after 31...Ra8!?, just waiting. There is no obvious answer. 32 h4, certainly, then 32...Rc8, with a deadlocking of play. Black would have to be careful not to exchange the bishops, but White cannot force an exchange.

32 h4!

Squeezing the rook out of active play, and allowing his bishop to move freely.

32 Nxe6+ fxe6 33 Rxe6 Kf7 seems safe for Black: for example, 34 Bd6 Rg5+! 35 Kf3 Rf5+ 36 Kg4 Bxd6 37 Rxd6 Rc7, suggested by Postny, and if

anything, Black seems better.

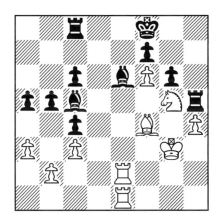

32...♚g8

A divergence of opinion here, with Postny suggesting that this move was too eager, and changed the course of events, while Svidler implied it was just a normal move, and gave an exclamation mark for Black on the next move. On the whole, the current writer tend to agree with Postny's interpretation, but this is on the basis of examination of what was happening after move 40, and whether, after close analysis, Black could have held the position. Black can try to make a 'positional' assessment on move 32, and this of course is what the player is forced to do over the board. Chess is complicated.

Or maybe it can be quite simple. After 32...♗d5!?, the commentators have suggested no clear edge for White. One continuation might be 33 ♖e5 ♖a8 (not 33...♗d6?? 34 ♖e8+) 34 ♖1e2 ♖c8 35 ♖e1, and a draw.

Chess sporting psychology seems important here. Black is a pawn up, and he has a good bishop-pair. Topalov is also a 2800+ player, and he, more than anyone, has obligations to try to play for a win if given a chance. Why should he be trying for a draw?

The normal situation when reaching for an unbalanced position with chances for both sides is to play for a win for as long as possible, while trying to take care of an escape route, a draw option, if something is going wrong. Sometimes unfortunately the escape route is not there. This seems to be what happened to Topalov.

33 ♖e5

Emphasizing the way in which Black's rook is being squeezed out.

33 ♘xe6 fxe6 34 ♖xe6 is possible, and indeed the computer likes it, but after 34...♚f7!?, Black's rooks are suddenly more active than White's.

Svidler also considered the exchange sacrifice with 33 ♖xe6 fxe6 34 ♖xe6, but there is no breakthrough after the counter-sacrifice with 34...♖xg5+! 35 hxg5 ♚f7 36 ♖e1 ♖e8 37 ♖h1 ♚g8!. The point is that after 38 ♖h6?! ♗f8 39 ♖xg6+? ♚f7 the rook is trapped. Naturally, White could still carry on to try for a win in other ways, but the best chance has disappeared.

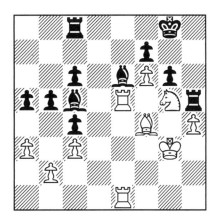

33...♗f8

Svidler has been trying to lure the bishop to d6, but Topalov is not interested. After 33...♗d6 34 ♖xe6! ♗xf4+ 35 ♔xf4 fxe6 36 ♔g4 White's knight is clearly stronger than Black's rook, and with no possibility of Black setting up defences by returning the exchange, it is difficult to equalize. Black's best move is 36...♔f8, and now White has to play it accurately:

a) 37 ♖xe6 ♖c7 38 ♖d6 ♔e8 39 ♘e6 ♖ch7! 40 ♘g7+ ♔f7 41 ♘xh5 ♖xh5 42 ♖xc6 a4, for example, is only a draw, as Svidler notes.

b) 37 ♖d1! ♔e8 38 ♖d6 is much better when none of Black's pieces coordinate. Svidler gives 38...e5 (there is nothing much else to do) 39 ♖e6+ (39 f7+ ♔e8 40 ♖xg6 ♖xg5+! draws) 39...♔d7 40 ♖e7+ ♔d6 41 ♖g7:

b1) Here he continues with 41...♖ch8 42 ♘f7+ ♔e6 43 ♘xh8 ♖xh8 44 ♔g5 ♖h5+ 45 ♔xg6 ♖xh4 46 ♖e7+ ♔d6 47 ♖e8, and a narrow but convincing line by White. It eventually depends on a zugzwang after 47...♖g4+ 48 ♔h6 ♖f4 49 ♔g7 ♖g4+ 50 ♔f8 e4 51 f7 ♔d7 52 ♖e5 ♔d8 53 ♖e7 a4 54 ♖e6 ♔d7 55 ♖e8. Black now has to give way. If the rook moves on the g-file, White takes the e-pawn, and then, depending how Black defends with the rook, White plays the rook to the g-file or checks on the d-file.

b2) Even so, it is not clear that White is winning after 41...♔d5!, trying to activate his pieces and pawns. After 42 ♖d7+ ♔c5 43 ♘e6+ ♔b6 44 f7 ♖f5 45 ♖e7 ♖h8! 46 ♖e8 (or 46 h5 ♖f6! 47 ♔g5 ♖xf7 48 ♖xf7 ♖xf5+ 49 ♔xg6 ♖h2, with level play) 46...♖xh4+ 47 ♔xh4 ♖xf7, White is not winning. Neither though is he not pressing.

So possibly Black is still holding after 33...♗d6, but the position is extremely difficult.

34 ♘xe6

Svidler notes that the exchange sacrifice is only a draw after 34 ♖xe6 fxe6 35 ♖d1 ♗h6! 36 f7+ ♔g7 37 ♗e5+ ♔f8 38 ♗d6+ ♔g7 39 ♖f1 (39 ♗e5+ is of course a perpetual) 39...♗xg5 40 f8♕+ ♖xf8 41 ♗xf8+ ♔g8 42 hxg5 ♖xg5+. The only way to escape perpetual on the g- and h-files is 43 ♔g4??, but this is mined. After 43...♖f5! Black wins a piece, and keeps several extra pawns.

34...fxe6

The only way. 34...♖xe5 35 ♗xe5 fxe5 36 ♖d1 breaks through.

35 ♖d1!

Aiming for the d-file. 35 ♖xe6 ♖d5 is only equal, or at best a very small edge for White.

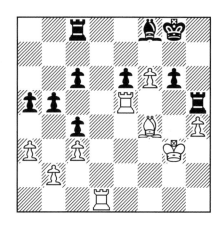

35...♖h7

Given an exclamation mark by Svidler, without comment, and implied as best by Postny. This assessment seems slightly puzzling. After 35...♔f7 36 ♗g5 ♖c7 37 a4 ♖b7 the position is deadlocked. White can do nothing actively and can patrol with the rook between d5, d7 and d8, while Black can do nothing much. 38 ♖d2 ♖h7 39 ♔g4 ♖h8 40 ♖d8 ♖h5 41 ♖d2, and a draw is looming.

One suspects that the exclamation mark is given to the general idea, defending on the second rank, which is important for defence and counterplay, rather than the specific move. The way that Topalov plays it, his rook move is more 'active', but the loss of the e6-pawn is a defect.

36 ♖xe6

The pawn count is now level. Sometimes it has been easy to forget that White was a pawn down, given his strong passed pawn and active pieces.

36...♖b7

This was Topalov's idea, aiming to set up counterplay with both rooks. It remains to be seen whether this was better, worse, or about the same, as the passive defence on move 35. Postny commented on Topalov's strong preference for active defence rather than trying to hold the position. That was at an earlier stage of the game. Topalov is at least consistent here!

37 ♖e4

A choice of moves with the rook. He wanted to prevent Black from playing ...b4.

37...♔f7

The king finally comes back into play.

38 ♗g5

And White, of course, defends the pawn.

38...♖e8

Black does not want to allow White to control two open files for the rooks.

39 ♖xe8

39 ♔f3 or 39 ♔f4 could also be considered.

39...♔xe8 40 ♔g4

But he was thinking of the king to go this way. The main idea with h5 is not so much to exchange the pawns, but rather to enter with the king on f5.

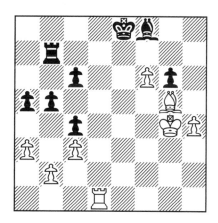

40...♖h7?!

Move 40, and as so often in chess, this is the critical mistake after a tense and exhausting game. The rook finds itself out of position.

There is an even more painful blunder with 40...♖d7?? 41 f7+ ♖xf7 42 ♖d8 mate.

Svidler suggests, however, that 40...♔f7! is the correct way of handling the position, and holds the draw. The king is the best piece for blockading an advanced passed pawn, and the rook can help guard the checks on the second rank. The rook is far less effective in guarding the pawn itself. The king covers all eight adjoining squares, while the rook covers only four, and is open to attack from the next-door diagonals.

After 41 ♖d8 b4 42 axb4 axb4 43 ♖d4 bxc3 44 bxc3 ♖b5, so far as given by Svidler, and if 45 ♖xc4?! ♖c5, Black escapes with a draw. White can try harder, though, through controlling the seventh rank, rather than trying to snatch a doubled isolated pawn, and 45 ♖d7+! causes trouble:

a) After 45...♔g8 46 h5 gxh5+ 47

♔xh5 Black's pieces are totally passive.

b) Therefore he has to try 45...♔e6, but is in serious trouble after 46 ♖c7: for example, 46...♖b6 47 ♔f3 ♖b3 48 ♖xc6+ ♔d5 49 ♖c8 ♖xc3+ 50 ♔e2 ♗a3 51 f7, or 46...♖c5 47 f7 ♗d6 48 ♗h6 ♖f5 49 ♖xc6 ♖xf7 50 ♖xc4, and the onus is very much on Black to prove he can hold the position. Once the best block-ading piece, the king, has been pushed away, life becomes much easier for the player with the passed pawn.

Black, it seems, made two identifi-able errors over the last few moves, and presumably in time trouble. On move 35, his position went from tenable to worse, and then at move 40 it went from worse to losing.

White's play is still far from straight-forward, and Svidler has to show some imaginative and well thought-out ideas to secure the win.

41 ♖e1+

Aiming to forcing Black to block the rook.

41...♔d7

If 41...♔f7, Svidler gives 42 a4! ♗d6 43 ♖a1 ♗c7 44 ♖d1 ♔e6 45 ♖e1+ ♔d7 (45...♔f7 46 ♖e7+ ♔g8 47 ♖e6, and the rook breaks through) 46 ♗c1!, and the king joins the passed pawn with ♔g5 and ♔xg6. Some agile manoeuvring from the rook, and Black's pieces lose their balance.

Svidler does not give 41...♔d8 in his notes, implying that there are several strong alternatives.

The natural 42 f7+ ♔d7 43 ♖f1 ap-pears at first to be a dead end, but there are zugzwang possibilities with ♖f6 and king manoeuvres. This seems overcomplicated.

The pawn on f6 is a strong asset, and

the pawn on f7 is potentially weak. Maybe Svidler would have tried some-thing like 42 ♗f4, followed by ♔g5. If Black tries 42...♖h5, only then 43 f7 ♖h8 (43...♖f5? 44 ♖e8+) 44 ♖e8+.

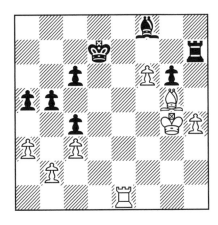

42 a4!

It is generally best to attack two weaknesses, rather than one. This pawn push starts to attack on the queenside. If Black ignores the pawns, White will exchange on b5, and then attack the pawns with ♖e5.

42...bxa4

After 42...♗d6, to cover ♖e5, Svidler gives 43 ♖a1 ♗c7 44 ♖d1+ ♔e6 45 ♖e1+ ♔d7 46 ♗c1, transposing into the win-ning line he gives with 41...♔f7. Again, note the way in which the switching around with the rook, adding pressure on several different files, makes it diffi-cult for Black to defend.

42...b4? 43 ♖e4 wins a pawn for White without difficulty.

43 ♖e5

When picking up pawns, he needs to keep the rook behind Black's pawns. 43 ♖e4? a3 is only equal.

43...c5

43...a3? 44 bxa3 ♗xa3? 45 ♖xa5 ♗d6 46 ♖a7+ ♗c7 47 ♗f4 is a White win.

44 ♗f4!

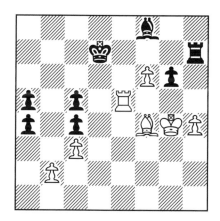

Svidler is setting up a zugzwang.

44...♖h8

The bishop cannot move. If 44...♗d6?? 45 ♖d5, while if 44...♖h6 45 ♗xh6 ♖xh6 46 ♖xc5, and White chews up all Black's queenside pawns. Otherwise:

a) 44...♔d8 (other king moves allow ♖e8) 45 ♔g5 ♗h6+ 46 ♔xg6 ♗xf4 47 ♔xh7 ♗xe5 48 f7 ♗d6 49 ♔g8, and the h-pawn eventually decides.

b) 44...♖f7 45 ♔g5, winning the g-pawn, and again promoting his h-pawn.

c) 44...♖h5 45 ♖xh5 gxh5 46 ♔xh5 ♔e6 47 ♔g6, again winning.

d) 44...a3 45 bxa3 drops a pawn for nothing, so the text move is the only way to try to hold.

45 ♗g3!

Again keeping the zugzwang squeeze, since 45 ♔g5? ♗h6+ is too early.

45...♗h6

If 45...♖h7, then White takes a more direct approach with 46 ♔g5 ♗d6 47 f7 ♖xf7 and White has a simple king and pawn win after 48 ♖d5 ♖f5+ 49 ♖xf5 gxf5 50 ♗xd6 ♔xd6 51 ♔xf5.

Or 47...♗xe5 48 f8♕ ♗xg3 49 ♔xg6 ♖xh4 50 ♕f5+, and Black will lose the rook or bishop: for example, 50...♔d6 51 ♕g5 ♗e1 52 ♕d8+ ♔c6 53 ♕e8+.

46 ♖e7+

46 ♖xc5 also looks good, the tactical idea being that after 46...♗c1 47 ♖c7+ ♔e6 48 ♖e7+ ♔xf6 49 ♖e1 ♗d2 50 ♗e5+ ♔e6 51 ♖e2 White wins a piece. There are, however, a few loose ends after 46...♖f8, and Svidler, after much calculation, finds a clearer win.

46...♔c6

46...♔d8 47 ♗c7+ ♔c8 48 ♗xa5 continues the winning squeeze.

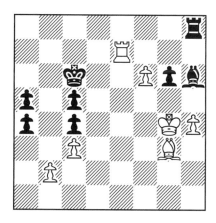

47 ♗f4!

With a study-like win. While enjoying the finish, do not overlook the way in which White has made a reverse manoeuvre with ♗g5-f4-g3, just before the next bishop return.

This move involves a rook sacrifice by White. The more natural alternative, with 47 f7?, forces the win of Black's rook, but this turns out to be only a draw. Svidler gives 47...♖f8 48 ♗e5 ♔d5 49 h5 gxh5+ 50 ♔xh5 ♗c1 51 ♗g7 ♖xf7 52 ♖xf7 ♗xb2 53 ♖a7 a3 54 ♖xa5 ♔e4. Black can hold this, White's king being so far away from the battle on the queenside. Then if 55 ♗f8 ♔d3 56 ♗xc5 ♔xf3 57 ♗xa3 (otherwise ♔b3) 57...♖xa3 58 ♖xa3 ♔b2, and Black is in ample time to hold the draw, or 55 ♔g4 ♔d3 56 ♔f3 ♔c2 57 ♔e4 ♔b3 58 ♔d5 a2 58 ♖xa2 ♔xa2 59 ♔xc4, and again it is a draw.

47...♗xf4

47...♗f8 48 ♖e8 ♔d7 49 f7 wins for White.

48 ♔xf4 ♖h5

The sharpest defence. After 48...♖xh4+ Svidler gives 49 ♔e5 (49 ♔g5 is also good) 49...♖h5+ 50 ♔e6 ♖h2 51 f7 ♖e2+ (51...♖xb2 52 ♖c7+! ♔xc7 53 f8♕) 52 ♔f6 ♖xb2 53 ♔g7 ♖b8 (53...♖f2 54 ♖e6+ followed by ♖f6 wins a queen) 54 ♔xg6 ♖f8 55 ♖e2!:

a) If 55...a3, White wins after 56 ♖a2 ♔d6 57 ♖xa3 ♔e6 58 ♖xa5 ♖xf7 59 ♖a6+.

b) If 55...♔b5 56 ♖a2, and Black's king and pawns advance no further.

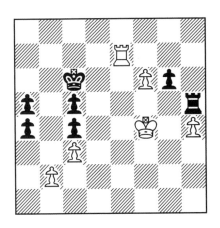

49 ♖e5!!

The star move, whereas 49 f7?! ♖f5+ only draws.

49...♖xh4+

49...♖xe5 50 ♔xe5 ♔d7 51 ♔d5 wins for White.

50 ♔g5

Of course, this is an old winning idea, but it is attractive to see it in new and realistic settings.

50...♖h5+

He might just as well.

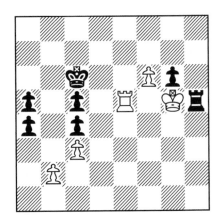

51 ♔xg6!

Giving up the rook, but Black cannot prevent the pawn from queening.

51...♖xe5 52 f7

Black has covered both the f5 and e8 defending squares.

52...♖e6+

Starting the Saavedra manoeuvre. The Spanish priest has been remembered for only one thing in chess, a long time ago, but it was a classic:

He gave 1 c7 ♖d5+ 2 ♔b4! ♖d4+ 3

♔b3! ♖d3+ 4 ♔c2! and White queens the pawn and wins. Except, though, that two readers of a local journalist pointed out first that Black can escape with stalemate after 4...♖d4! 5 c8♕ ♖c4+! 6 ♕xc4, and, second, that 5 c8R!! is a win. White is threatening checkmate on the a-file, and if 5...♖a4, he wins with 6 ♔b3!!.

Svidler pays his tribute to the classics.

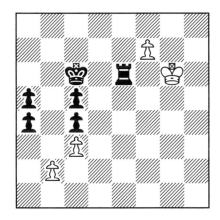

53 ♔g5

He needs to cover the f6-square. Not 53 ♔g7?? ♖e7, pinning the pawn when Black wins the king and pawn ending.

53...♖e5+

He must give checks.

54 ♔g4

54 ♔g6?! ♖e6+ repeats.

Not though 54 ♔f6?? ♖f2 55 f8♕ ♖f2+. The f-file has been mined.

54...♖e4+

Again, the check.

55 ♔g3!

More accurate than 55 ♔f3?, when White still has to prove he can win after 55...♖e1 56 ♔f2 ♖b1 57 f8♕ ♖xb2+ and ...a3!.

55...♖e3+

He gives another check.

55...a3 56 f8♕ axb2? is the right idea, but the tactics are wrong. White wins instantly with 57 ♕a8+. Here 56...a2! sets up a crafty drawing trap, as Svidler points out, with 57 ♕a8+? ♔b5 58 ♕b7+ ♔a4 59 ♕xe4, a queen up, and now not 59...a1♕?? 60 ♕xf4 mate, but rather 59...♔b3!! 60 ♕e1 ♔xb2, and it's only a draw.

So how is White going to win? He needs to be able to manoeuvre the queen to a4, and the only way of doing this is to check with the queen on d7. That being established, Svidler's idea is 57 ♕c8! ♔b6 58 ♕d8+ ♔b5 (58...♔a6 59 ♕d6+ followed by ♕d7+) 59 ♕d7+ ♔b6 60 ♕a4, job done.

56 ♔f2

Time for the king to enter the f-file.

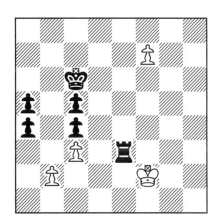

56...a3!

Black's last chance.

57 f8♕!

57 bxa3? ♖xc3 58 f8♕ ♖xa3 allows Black to hold the draw.

57...axb2

If 57...a2, then 58 ♕c8+! wins after 58...♔b5 59 ♕d7+ followed by ♕a4, or the queen manoeuvring to a4, as in the notes to 55...a3. Here too there is a fiendish drawing trap that White could fall into: 58 ♕h6+? (or 58 ♕a8+? transposing) 58...♔b5 59 ♕h1 ♖h3! 60 ♕a1 a4 61 ♕xa2 ♖h1!, and the queen cannot enter active play. Therefore a draw.

58 ♕c8+

58 ♕a8+ ♔c7 is not as quick.

58...♔b5

Topalov sets up a final stalemate trap.

59 ♕b7+

59 ♔xe3 ♔a4 60 ♕b8 ♔a3 transposes.

59...♔a4 60 ♔xe3

60 ♕xb2?? ♖f3+, with an instant draw, is not difficult to see.

60...♔a3

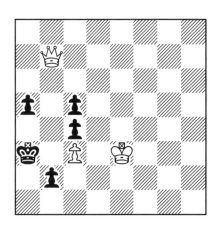

61 ♕b5!

61 ♕b6!, hitting the c5-pawn, also works, but not 61 ♔d2?? a4!! 62 ♔c2 b1♕+ with stalemate.

61...a4

If 61...♔a2 62 ♕a4+ ♔b1, White has the choice between immediate stalemate with 63 ♔d2??, or an almost immediate checkmate with 63 ♔e2 ♔c1 64 ♕d1 mate. Here 62 ♕xa5+ also wins, but there is another stalemate try in

62...b3!? 63 ♕xc5 b1♕ 64 ♕b5+?? ♔xc3! 65 ♕xb1, draw. Instead the careful 64 ♕b4+ ♔c2 65 ♕xb1+ ♔xb1 66 ♔d4 wins.

62 ♕xc5+

It's almost over now. If White has avoided the stalemate traps in the last few moves, he is unlikely to fall for any traps now, such as 62 ♔d2?? b1♕.

62...♔b3 63 ♕b4+ ♔c2 64 ♕xa4+

64...♔xc3

If 64...♔c1, then the simplest of many simple lines is 65 ♕xc4 b1♕ 66 ♕f1+.

65 ♕a5+

He makes a final check.

If 65 ♕d1?? b1♕ 66 ♕xb1, stalemate.

65...♔c2

65...♔b3 66 ♕b5+ ♔c3 67 ♔e2 avoids the stalemate.

66 ♕f5+

He must keep checking, otherwise the pawn queens.

66...♔c1 67 ♕f1+ 1-0

After 67...♔c2 38 ♕xc4+, it is time for Black to resign.

Game 8
G.Sargissian-L.Nisipeanu
German League 2006
Blumenfeld Counter-Gambit E10

1 d4 ♘f6 2 ♘f3

Quite often, as here, this transposes into c4 lines, after 2...e6, 2...g6, 2...d5 or 2...b6. There are a few independent possibilities, however, with, for example, 2...g6 3 ♗g5, or 2...e6 3 ♗g5, or various possibilities with a quick g3.

Usually White prefers 2 c4, but with 2 ♘f3 he can avoid the Benko Gambit, with 2 c4 c5 3 d5 b5!?, and if 4 cxb5 a6, a line which has often been tried by Magnus Carlsen.

2...e6

2...c5 is nevertheless still possible, and indeed can transpose into the Blumenfeld main line after 3 d5 e6 4 c4 b5. However, White could also try 4 ♘c3, with the normal slight edge after 4...exd5 5 ♘xd5 ♘xd5 6 ♕xe5 ♗e7 7 e4. Earlier, 3...b5 is still a possibility, ending up with a Declined Benko Gambit after 4 c4, although White has also tried 4

♗g5.

There has been much exploration in the various Benoni systems, lines with an early ...c5 after d4, but there is still much to be uncovered.

3 c4

Keeping to the standard main lines. As noted earlier, 3 ♗g5 or 3 g3 are good independent systems, but maybe they have less punch in aiming for an edge. Two pawns in the centre, d4 and c4, covering Black's d5 and e5 squares, still constitutes very much traditional main line.

3...c5

So we have reached a Benoni System. Black prods the white pawn on d4, and plans to put pressure on the advanced pawn, if the pawn doesn't advance.

Any exchange with Black's c-pawn of White's d-pawn gives Black a slightly better pawn structure, although of course the pieces need to be considered as well. Comparisons are to be made with the Sicilian, but in the Benoni without d5 White does not even have the pawn push with e4. White therefore usually pushes the d-pawn.

For other more standard lines, the Queen's Indian, 3...b6, was introduced in Game 4, Topalov-Anand, 3...d5 will soon transpose into one of the main lines of the Queen's Indian, and 3...♗b4+ is a Bogo-Indian.

4 d5

Natural enough, but now White has weakened his dark squares. In compensation, he has gained space on the light squares. There is every reason to believe that White keeps the first move advantage, but the position is unbalanced, and with any slight slip by White, Black has the chance to take over.

Otherwise:

a) 4 ♘c3 cxd4 5 ♘xd4 ♗b4 6 g3 ♘e4!? transposes into, and from, a line from the Nimzo-Indian. Black's play is satisfactory.

b) 4 e3 is solid enough, but not particularly aggressive. Two obvious transpositional replies would be 4...d5, the Semi-Tarrasch Queen's Gambit, or 4...b6, a line of the Queen's Indian. Also, 4...cxd4 5 exd4 ♗b4+, and if 6 ♘c3, then another Nimzo-Indian.

4...b5

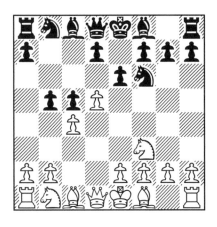

Side-tracking from the Modern Benoni, or should one say that the Modern Benoni is side-tracking from this? Black is aggressively attacking both pawns in the centre, and intends to sacrifice a pawn in return for having extra pawns in the centre.

There are a few similarities with the Benko Gambit (1 d4 ♘f6 2 c4 c5 3 d5 b5), but there are also clear differences in the basic strategy of the pawn sacrifice. In the Benko, Black in most lines after the pawn sacrifice does not attempt any hand-to-hand pawn attack in the centre, but instead fianchettoes with ...g6 ...♗g7, and, after a pawn exchange with ...axb5 or bxa6, Black adds pressure with rooks on the a- and b-files. White's a- and b-pawns, far away from the centre, are under severe attack, and if the extra pawn drops, White is under severe pressure.

5 ♗g5

Quite often White does not even bother to accept the Blumenfeld Gambit, Black's attacking chances having been reckoned as being quite strong. The classic example is S.Tarrasch-A.Alekhine, Bad Pistyan 1922: 1 d4 ♘f6 2 c4 e6 3 ♘f3 c5 4 d5 b5 5 dxe6 fxe6 6 cxb5 d5 7 e3 ♗d6 8 ♘c3 0-0 9 ♗e2 ♗b7 10 b3 ♘bd7 11 ♗b2 ♕e7 12 0-0 ♖ad8 13 ♕c2 e5 14 ♖fe1 e4 15 ♘d2 ♘e5 16 ♘d1 ♘fg4 17 ♗xg4 ♘xg4 18 ♘f1 ♕g5, and Black ground through to victory, with the help of a passed d-pawn reaching the seventh, and an attack against the king.

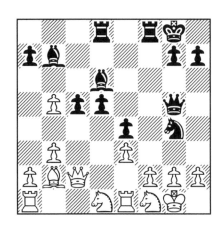

White's 7 e3 move was passive. 7 g3, making use of the fianchetto, makes it more difficult for Black, after ...d5, to press forward with either of the central pawns. A recent example is 7...a6 8 bxa6 ♗d6 9 ♗g2 0-0 10 0-0 ♘c6 11 b3 ♗xa6 12 ♗b2 ♕e8 13 ♘bd2 ♖d8 14 ♖e1 ♘g4!? (aiming for a second sacrifice) 15 h3 ♘xf2 16 ♔xf2 ♘d4 17 g4 (naturally, there are complicated alternatives) 17...h5 18 g5 ♕f7 19 e3? (Nisipeanu suggests that 19 ♔g1! would have held) 19...♘xf3 20 ♘xf3 ♗h2!!, and White's king was now stuck in the open, and Black won with a king hunt in K.Georgiev-L.Nisipeanu, Fuegen 2006.

5...exd5

Not the only approach:

a) 5...bxc4!? leads to relatively unexplored territory after, for example, 6 e4 ♕b6 7 ♕e2.

b) 5...h6 6 ♗xf6 ♕xf6 7 ♘c3 b4 8 ♘b5 ♔d8 leads to unclear play. The computer suggestion, 9...dxe6!? fxe6 10 ♖b1, and if 10...e5 11 ♕d5 ♘c6 12 ♖d1, remains unexplored.

c) 5...b4 is another possibility: 6 a3 h6 7 ♗h4 a5 7 ♗h4 a5 8 axb4 cxb4 9 ♘d4 be7 10 ♘b5 d6 11 c5 0-0 12 dxe6 dxc5 13 exf7+ ♔xf7 14 ♘d2 ♔g8 15 e3 led to a heavily unbalanced pawn structure in V.Ivanchuk-L.Nisipeanu, Khanty-Mansiysk 2007. Quite probably Black should just continue developing with, for example, 15...♘c6. Instead Nisipeanu spent time offering the exchange of dark-squared bishops with 15...♘g4?! 16 ♗g3 ♗h4, and Black soon lost his c-pawn after 17 ♘e4.

One starts to develop the impression that the Blumenfeld is going to become more fashionable. It can easily be a win-or-lose battle.

6 cxd5

6 ♗xf6? ♕xf6 7 ♕xd5 ♕xb2 8 ♕xa8?? ♕c1 mate, and 6 ♕xd5?? ♘xd5 7 ♗xd8 ♘b4, winning a piece, have both surfaced in my database.

6...d6

In an earlier round of the same league season, Nisipeanu had tried 6...h6 7 ♗xf6 ♕xf6, hoping to take advantage of the bishop-pair, but after 8 ♕c2 c4 9 a4 ♗b4+ 10 ♘c3 bxa4 11 ♖xa4 a5 12 e3 0-0 13 ♗xc4 White was slightly better in E.Postny-L.Nisipeanu, German League 2006.

7 e4

With a small detail. White wants to play a4, but he wants to induce Black to defend with ...a6 first. Therefore, he delays 7 a4 b4 8 e4.

7...a6

7...♘bd7? tactically does not work. White plays 8 ♗xb5 ♕a5+ 9 ♘c3 ♘xe4 10 ♕e2 f5 11 0-0 with a likely win for him.

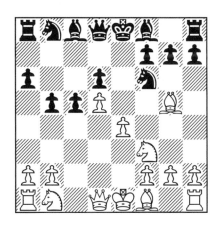

8 a4?!

An obvious and natural move, breaking open Black's queenside pawn structure, but over the next few moves, Nisipeanu smoothly sets up good play for Black. The Blumenfeld Gambit is commonly regarded as interesting but slightly suspect, but here it starts to seem very effective. Is the Blumenfeld so good? Or is there an improvement for White?

In a later game, Ivanchuk carefully delayed a4, concentrating first on piece development. He could still play a4 later. 8 ♘bd2! ♗e7 9 ♗f4 0-0 10 a4 (avoiding Black's tactic in Sargissian-Nisipeanu) 10...bxa4 11 ♗d3 ♗e7 12 0-0 ♗b5 13 ♕e2 ♘bd7 14 ♗xb5 axb5 15 ♕xb5 ♖b8 16 ♕d3! ♖b4 17 ♘c4 gave White a slight advantage in V.Ivanchuk-L.Nisipeanu, Khanty-Mansiysk 2007. Nisipeanu was later able to hold a position a pawn down in a rook ending. Indeed, Nisipeanu eventually beat Ivanchuk in this knockout match at the FIDE World Cup, but later lost to Karjakin.

8...♗e7!

Setting up some tactics on the d8-h4 diagonal.

8...b4?! allows a big hole on c4, which ♘bd2-c4 might exploit. Similarly 8...bxa4?!.

9 ♘bd2

9 axb5 ♘xe4 10 ♗f4!? (or 9 ♗f4 ♘xe4 10 axb5) is about equal. If 11 ♗d3, then simply 11...♘f6.

9 ♗xf6 ♗xf6 10 axb5 ♗xb2 11 ♖a2 ♗f6 is also comfortable for Black. The long dark-squared diagonal, plus the protected passed c-pawn, suggest that Black has good prospects.

So has White got any advantage whatsoever?

9...♘xd5!

With at least equality.

10 ♗xe7

10 exd5?! ♗xg5 leaves White with a weak pawn on d5.

10...♕xe7

10...♘xe7 is also fully playable.

11 axb5

White regains the pawn. His pawn structure is, however, not good.

11...0-0

There is no point in delaying this.

12 ♗c4

12 ♗e2?! ♘f4 leaves White under pressure: for example, after 13 0-0 d5 14 ♖e1 d4.

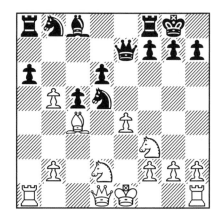

12...♘f4!?

A theoretical novelty, apparently, although sometimes the only question to be asked is why this didn't happen much earlier. The older moves, 12...♘b4 and 12...♘b6, direct Black's pieces to the queenside. This is safe enough perhaps, but it is easier for Black to attack on the kingside. He has queen, knight and bishop already ready to attack, and other pieces are on their way.

13 0-0

13 g3 d5! 14 gxf4 dxc4 15 ♕c2 ♗b7 may allow White to win a pawn, but his pieces will be open, leaving many open squares behind the pawns. It will be difficult for White to decide whether the king should be on the kingside, the queenside, or the middle. Play might continue 15 ♕c2 ♗b7 16 bxa6 ♘xa6 17

♕xc4 ♘b4 18 ♖xa8 ♖xa8 19 0-0 ♖d8 (but not the hasty 19...♗a6?! 20 ♖a1), with good attacking chances in return for the pawn.

13...♗b7

The most natural move, developing the bishop to a good long diagonal. There may perhaps be a temptation to keep the bishop at home, and so keep the option of ...♗g4, playing for example 13...♖d8, but this seems slightly slow and indirect.

14 ♖e1

White does not want to give an extra tempo with 14 bxa6 ♘xa6 with Black being slightly better.

14...axb5

Black could delay this with, for example, 14...♕f6 or 14...♖d8, but there is no real point just now. With the immediate exchange, he takes over the initiative, an improvement on quiet manoeuvring.

15 ♖xa8

15 ♗xb5 ♖xa1 16 ♕xa1 leaves the queen off-centre.

15...♗xa8 16 ♗xb5 ♘c6

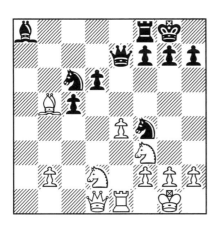

Now Black has more or less completed his development, his pieces have ended up on good squares, and he has the better pawn structure. White's isolated pawn on b2 is a real problem. The pawn is open to attack, and if the pawn falls, Black would have an excellent passed c-pawn. If White has to defend his b-pawn, his pieces will become severely constrained.

17 ♗f1

White also has problems with his other knight's pawn, g2. 17 ♘c4 is visually more active, perhaps, but 17...♖d8 is comfortable for Black. How does White retreat the bishop for defence?

17...♕f6

Developing, and attacking the weak pawn on b2. If that is not enough for White to deal with, Black is also thinking about an attack on the kingside.

18 ♘c4

White has to set up some piece activity, otherwise his position is in danger of folding.

18...♖d8

A sturdy reply.

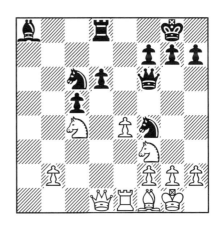

19 ♕d2?

Black has done well, with good pawn control on the central dark squares, but White's position should not collapse. Sargissian seems to have misjudged the tactics here.

19 g3!, renewing the idea of a fianchetto, still holds the balance, just about. After 19...d5 20 exd5 ♘xd5 21 ♕e2?! h6 22 ♗g2 ♘bd4 Black keeps a slight edge, all his minor pieces being more active than White's. However, here 21 ♘fd2! keeps the balance.

19...♘g6 or 19...♘e6 are sensible alternatives, again aiming for slight pressure. For example, 19...♘g6 20 ♗g2 ♘b4 21 ♕e2 h6 22 ♖d1 ♕e6, and White cannot attack any weaknesses in Black's position, but Black has chances to grind away.

19...♘h3+

Now Black is significantly better.

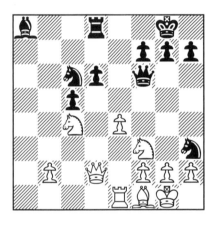

20 ♔h1?!

20 gxh3 ♕xf3 21 ♗g2 may be ugly, but at least White keeps going. Then 21...♘d4?! 22 ♕xd4 ♕xg2+ 23 ♔xg2 cxd4 24 ♘b6 gives White good chances of holding, but 21...♕f6! keeps an edge. White will have permanent problems with his d4-square.

20...♘d4!

Had Sargissian underestimated this?

21 ♖e3

21 ♘xd4 ♘xf2+ 22 ♔g1 ♘xe4 23 ♖xe4 ♗xe4 is only a slight material edge for Black, but the d-pawn rolls

through dangerously.

21...d5!

And the d-pawn again makes its presence, even if this is merely a pawn exchange. Black's minor pieces soon work together very well.

22 exd5

22 e5 ♕f4 23 ♘b6 ♘xf3 24 gxf3 d4 25 ♘xa8 ♘xf2+! 26 ♕xf2 dxe3 is another way for Black to break through.

22...♗xd5

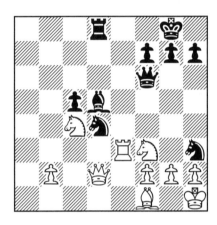

A slight pause in Black's attack, but he is of course very much in control. White's central pawns have disappeared, and Black has two excellent minor pieces occupying the four central squares. Black's Benoni pawn on c5 is still there, the start of attacking options in the centre early on, and still guarding the knight on an advanced square. If one can add to all this the irritation caused by Black's knight on h3, White has serious problems.

23 ♘ce5

Or 23 ♘xd4 ♘xf2+ 24 ♔g1 cxd4, and Black wins a big pawn.

23...♘xf3

23...h5!, cutting out back-row checkmates, is also good, indeed sharper. 24 ♘xd4 ♘xd2+ 24 ♔g1 cxd4 25 ♕xd4

25 ♕xd4 ♘g4 wins a piece.

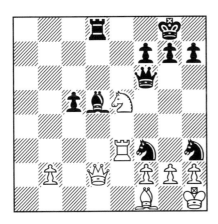

24 gxf3?!

Were we hitting a time scramble?

24 ♘xf3 ♗xf3 25 ♕e1 (with a back rank check) 25...♗c6 26 ♖xh3 ♕xb2 leaves Black an extra passed pawn, but it is isolated. Probably Black should be able to win this, but there is much technical work to be done. How confident, for example, would Black be in reaching an extra isolated pawn in a bishop endgame just before the time control? Or could Black break through with queen, rook and bishop still on the board?

24...♘f4

Not 24...♗xf3+?? 25 ♘xf3 with a back-row cheapo. Black sees that comfortably, and again the knight keeps control.

25 ♕c3

If 25 ♕e1, then maybe 25...h6!?, opening up a hole. Black is in no great hurry, since White is close to zugzwang.

25...♕h4

With a direct threat.

26 ♕e1

26 ♕xc5 ♕xf2 27 ♕c1 f6 is a Black win.

26...♖e8

Nearing zugzwang.

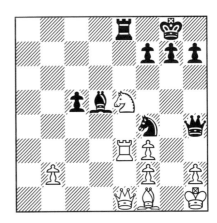

27 ♗c4

If 27 ♗g2 ♘xg2 28 ♔xg2 ♖xe5! 29 ♖xe5 ♕g4+ 30 ♔f1 ♗c4+ 31 ♖e2 ♕xf3, and Black ties White up and wins.

27...♖xe5

Another sacrifice on e5.

28 ♗xd5

28 ♖xe5 ♗xf3+ 29 ♔g1 ♕g4+ and mate next move.

28...♕g5

Also 28...♕h3 with another mate threat on g2.

29 ♕g1 ♕xg1+ 0-1

Black wins a piece after 30 ♔xg1 ♖xe3.

A good advertisement of why Benoni positions are well worth considering for Black, especially if wanting to play for a win. There is often only a small gap between White having an edge and Black having the upper hand.

Game 9
P.Leko-T.Radjabov
Morelia 2006
Sicilian Defence B33

1 e4 c5 2 ♘f3 ♘c6 3 d4

3 ♗b5 is a quieter 'more positional' alternative, doubling the pawns after 3...g6 4 ♗xc6 dxc6 5 d3. It is noticeable that Leko, when playing as White against Van Wely, has chosen this line twice, with a draw at the Melody Amber Rapidplay 2005, and a powerful win at Dortmund 2005. Many other players have tried to avoid Van Wely's deep theoretical analysis.

It is perhaps equally noteworthy that Leko has faced problems with Black in this line, in Shirov-Leko, Monaco (rapid) 2005, Svidler-Leko, Dortmund 2005, and Ivanchuk-Leko, Mukachevo (rapid) 2007; three straight wins against Leko. This suggests that the 'Sicilian Lopez' still provides significant dangers for Black.

3...cxd4 4 ♘xd4

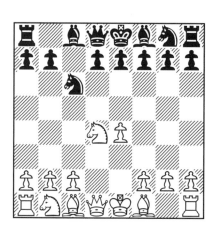

Best, and natural play on both sides.

4...♘f6

There are, of course, many different ways of handling this position. One of the older ideas is the Löwenthal Variation, 4...e5 5 ♘b5 a6 6 ♘d6+ ♗xd6 7 ♕xd6 ♕f6, and then various possible queen retreats by White, which should keep a slight edge. This is very much a mid-19th Century rendering of the Sicilian, with no hedgehog style set-ups with ...d6 and ...e6, but instead moving the pawn quickly in the centre and bringing the pieces into play just as quickly. There is a slight loss of subtlety in Black's play.

5 ♘c3

The natural reply. 5 ♘xc6 bxc6 is only equal.

5...e5

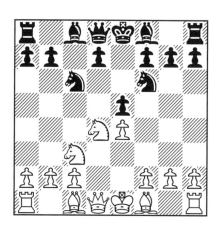

An improved Löwenthal Variation, the Pelikan. Jorge Pelikan was one of many European players (he was originally Czech) who played at the Buenos Aires Olympiad in 1939, and stayed in Argentina after the announcement of the War. He experimented with this line in the mid-1950s, but it was regarded as slightly suspicious in view of the weakness of the light squares. The line was revitalized in the mid-1970s by Evgeny Sveshnikov, who showed that there were considerable tactical and positional complexities, which force White to take care. An old idea becomes modern.

6 ♘db5

Alternatively:

a) 6 ♘xc6 bxc6 is only equal. Black keeps a solid pawn structure.

b) 6 ♘f5!? is worth considering, avoiding much of the complicated main line. White wants to try ♘d6+ and also ♘e3, covering rather more efficiently the pressure on d5. Black should probably try 6...d5 7 exd5 ♗xf5 8 dxc6, when the queen exchange after 8...♕xd1+ 9 ♘xd1 bxc6 10 ♘e3 gives White a slight edge in view of Black's isolated pawns. There are many who would very happily grind away for White in such an opening. Thus 8...bxc6 9 ♕f3 (9 ♕xd8+ ♖xd8 is less impressive this time, Black being ahead in development) 9...♕d7 10 ♗g5 has been tried, maybe with a slight edge for White, but seems under-researched. Something to be tried for the adventurous? Or even for the less adventurous?

6...d6

6...a6 7 ♘d6+ ♗xd6 8 ♕xd6 is now far less effective than the Löwenthal Variation, as Black no longer has ...♕f6: 8...♕e7 9 ♕xe7+ followed by ♗g5 leaves White positionally better, the weaknesses on d6 and d5 again being a concern.

7 ♗g5

The main line these days, although Pelikan's opponents in the 1950s did not like the idea of White being stuck with knights on a3 and c3, when Black can retaliate with ...b5. Therefore 7 a4 was a natural reply. Play might continue with 7...a6 8 ♘a3 ♗e6 9 ♗g5 ♖c8, with strategies not too different from the main line, but it is not all that clear that a4 gains that much.

7 ♘d5 is very direct. After 7...♘xd5 8 cxd5 ♘b8!, White has no more than the usual slight edge. The knight retreat looks paradoxical, but 8...♘e7 gets in the way of the bishop, and would not give Black the opportunity of manoeuvring the knight to c5.

7...a6

Time to push the knight away, before White has the chance of playing ♘d5 followed by ♘bc3.

8 ♘a3

8 ♗xf6 gxf6 9 ♘a3 used to be popular, but allows counterplay with 9...f5.

8...b5

8...♗e6 has been tried many times, but after 9 ♘c4 ♘d4 10 ♗xf6 ♗xf6 11 ♘d5 White's d5-knight is more secure than Black's corresponding d4-knight, and White should have a slight edge. There are no recent examples in top-level games.

9 ♘d5

Varying from a game they played at Linares two years earlier. There have been man recent tries with 9 ♗xf6 gxf6 10 ♘d5 ♗g7 11 ♗d3 ♘e7 12 ♘xe7 ♕xe7 13 0-0 f5 14 c4 0-0 15 ♕f3, and now a startling pawn breakthrough with 15...d5!.

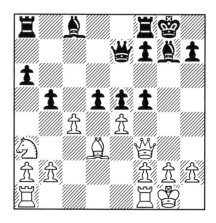

Much of the theory of the Pelikan depends on whether or not Black can squash the light squares on d5 and f5, and here Black takes the radical suggestion of making pawn breakthroughs on both of these squares. White cannot hold the pawn on e4, and if Black can push with ...e4 himself, then he will have excellent attacking diagonals on the dark squares, h8-a1 and f8-a3.

The main line continues with 16 cxd5 fxe4 17 ♗xe4, and now 17...♖b8, escaping from White's h1-a8 diagonal. White has then tried various rook moves. We continue with the Leko line after 18 ♖ad1 ♖d6. Then 19 ♕d3 ♕d7 20 g3 f5 21 ♗g2 ♖h6 22 f4 exf4 23 gxf4, drawn before too long in P.Leko-T.Radjabov, Linares 2004. But surely, one might think, there is a simple pawn snatch earlier? After 20 ♗xh7+? ♔h8 21 ♕e3 ♖h6 22 ♗c3 ♕d6 White's position collapsed with remarkable speed on 23 g3 ♗h3 24 ♖fe1 f5 25 f4? (speeding the crash) 25...exf4 26 ♕e7 ♕b6+ 0-1, P.Smirnov-T.Radjabov, FIDE World Championship, Tripoli 2004. One may feel reasonably certain that Radjabov had analysed this well in advance.

9...♗e7

9...♕a5+ 10 ♗d2 ♕d8 is an implicit draw offer, which White does not have to accept. Apart from 11 ♗g5, there is the complicated line with 11 c4 ♘xe4 12 cxb5, or the quieter 11 ♘xf6+ ♕xf6 12 ♗d3.

10 ♗xf6

This gives White a dominating d5-square for the knight, making Black's position look dubious, at least according to much earlier theory. That view existed until Sveshnikov, in the second half of the 1970s, showed that Black had compensation for the d5-gap. Black has, of course, gained the bishop-pair.

Otherwise:

a) 10 ♘xf6+ gxf6! followed by ...f5 is comfortable for Black.

b) 10 ♘xe7 ♘xe7 11 ♗d3 ♗b7 12

♕e2 ♘d7 13 c4 b4 14 ♗e2 c5 15 0-0 ♘c5 16 f3 ♕c7 with a small edge for White, later drawn, in A.Morozevich-T.Radjabov, Kemer 2007. Possibly better is 12...♘g6!? 13 c4 h6 14 ♗d2 0-0 15 0-0 ♖b8 16 ♖fd1 bxc4 17 ♘xc4 d5 18 dxe5 ♕xd5 19 f3 e4, equal, later drawn, in K.Georgiev-P.Eljanov, Sochi 2007.

10...♗xf6

10...gxf6 is possible, but usually Black prefers to bring the bishop back into play via g5.

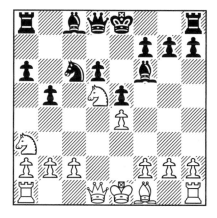

11 c3

The knight has to re-emerge, and if it can arrive on e3, it can be strong.

11 c4 b4 12 ♘f2 is a possibility, but the general preference is to keep the c4-square open, with the help of a later a4 push, rather than to block c4 with a pawn. Morozevich is the main current advocate of this line: for example, 12...♖b8 13 b3 ♗g5 14 g3 0-0 15 h4 ♗h6 16 ♗e3 ♗e6 17 ♔f1 a5 16 ♔g2 with a slight edge for White, later drawn, in Morozevich-Leko, FIDE World Championship, San Luis 2005. There are some obvious similarities in development patterns with the Leko-Radjabov game, but also a substantial contrast. The Leko game as White leaves the light squares on the queenside open, and able for use by the pieces, whereas the Leko game as Black ends up with a closed queenside.

11...0-0

Here 11...f5 12 ♘c2 0-0 often transposes, although Black could also experiment with delaying castling, with, for example, 12...♖b8.

Independently 11...♘e7 12 ♘xf6+ gxf6 breaks off White's knight dominance on d5, but Black's pawns are still slightly weakened. White usually tries 13 ♗d3 or 13 ♕f3. Black has a slightly weakened pawn structure. If, for example, ...f5 followed by a pawn exchange on d4, Black has three pawn islands (a+b; c+d+e; h), whereas White has two bigger and safe islands (a+b+c; f+g+h).

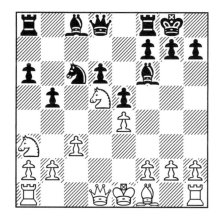

12 ♘c2

Preferring the knight-pair, rather than the bishop-pair. Also, White is planning to break up Black's queenside pawns with a4.

12 ♘xf6+ ♕xf6 is only equal. Then 13 ♗e2 or 13 ♗d3 are rare. We shall see why on move 15, when White makes a bishop jump to c4 in one go, instead of using up a tempo with ♗f1-e2-c4. Another example of the theme, 'knights

before bishops'.

12...♗g5

Black wants to keep his bishop-pair.

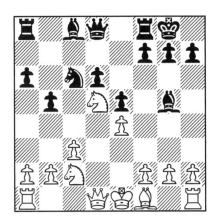

13 a4

In the pre-Sveshnikov days of the Pelikan, White tried 13 h4 ♗h6 14 g4 ♗f4 15 ♕f3, but Black's play was comfortable after 15...♗e6 16 ♘xf4 ♕f6 17 g5 ♕xf4 18 ♕xf4 exf4 19 ♗h3 ♘e5 20 ♗xe6 fxe6, eventually winning in D.Minic-K.Langeweg, Budva 1963. If White could split Black's queenside first, then maybe the h4 idea would seem more promising, as in the Leko-Radjabov game.

13...bxa4

13...♖b8? 14 h4 ♗h6 15 axb5 axb5 allows White a clear open a-file, and after 16 g4 ♗f4 17 ♕f3 ♗e6 18 ♘xf4 ♕f6 19 ♖a6 White wins a pawn.

14 ♖xa4

The exchange has improved White's pawn structure, two good queenside pawns versus one isolated pawn. It is not just a case of trying to win a pawn. White now has useful outpost squares on c4 and a4. He is aiming for control of the light squares.

14...a5

If 14...f5 15 exf5 ♗xf5, White happily

plays 16 ♗xa6. Black instead wants to secure his pawn, and makes it more difficult for White to try ♘cb4.

15 ♗c4

Finally the bishop emerges, in just one go. 15 b4 ♗b7 16 b5 ♘e7 does not do that much for White.

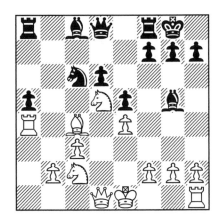

15...♖b8

Later Radjabov was to prefer 15...♗d7!?. For example, in V.Anand-T.Radjabov, Wijk aan Zee 2007, play carried on with 16 0-0 ♖b8 17 ♖a2 ♔h8 18 ♘ce3 g6 19 ♕d3 f5 20 b3 ♗h6, and Black was far more active than in the Leko game. One main point is that Black does not want to allow the rook to stay on a4 when the position is opened.

16 b3

White continues to build up his pawns.

16 ♖a2 ♔h8 17 ♘ce3 ♗xe3 18 ♘xe3 ♘e7 has been tried, and is equal. Leko prefers to keep the rook active a little longer.

16...♔h8

16...♗e6 was of considerable theoretical and historical interest in A.Karpov-E.Sveshnikov, USSR Championship, Moscow 1973. After 17 ♕a1 g6 18 0-0 ♕d7 19 ♖d1 f5 20 exf5 gxf5 21

b4 axb4 22 cxb4 ♔h8 23 b5 ♗xd5 24
♖xd5 ♘e7 25 ♕xe5+ dxe5 26 ♖xd7 ♘c8,
the knight threat on b6 led to equality.

This line, with 16...♗e6, quickly died
out. Quite a few non-theoreticians tried
17 0-0, which at the very least cuts
down the Leko-Radjabov line, but there
is no reason at all for Black to avoid this.

So why has the Karpov-Sveshnikov
line been abandoned? Maybe there is
nothing seriously wrong with
Sveshnikov's move in the position; it is
quite simply that 16...♔g8 is more flexible, allowing Black to think of ...f5, and
deciding later where the bishop should
go.

Sveshnikov himself showed the way
in E.Geller-E.Sveshnikov, USSR Championship, Tbilisi 1978, with 16...♔h8 17 0-
0 f5 18 exf5 ♗xf5 19 ♕d2 ♕d7
(19...♗g6 is nowadays more usual) 20
♘ce3 ♗e6 21 ♖d1 ♗d8, equal, but
Sveshnikov later demonstrated a spectacular sacrificial kingside winning attack.

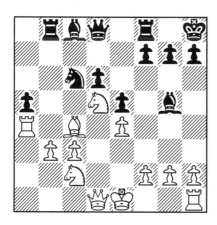

17 ♘ce3

17 ♕e2 is the chief alternative at top
level. Black has made various replies
(17...♗d7!?, 17...f5!?), with reasonable
chances of equality.

For 17 0-0, see the previous note on
Geller-Sveshnikov.

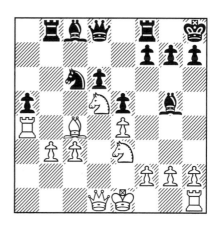

17...♗e6

A natural developing move, but
there is also an argument to be made
that by this stage of the game, it is
more important to concentrate on attack, defence, counterattack, and useful
exchanges, rather than just bringing
the bishop out.

Leko has reached this position both
as White and as Black. A year earlier he
tried 17...g6, the reply being 18 h4!
♗xh4 19 g3 ♗g5 20 f4 exf4 21 gxf4
♗h4+. This had been known before, but
after 22 ♔f1?! f5 23 ♖a2 fxe4 24 ♖ah2
g5 25 ♘g2 ♖b7 Black had covered his
weaknesses, and White's kingside had
been opened up a little, in M.Stanga-
S.Kindermann, Altensteig 1987.

In V.Topalov-P.Leko, Linares 2005,
White brought his king to the other
side with 22 ♔d2!? ♘e7 23 ♔c1 ♘xd5
24 ♘xd5 ♗e6 25 ♕d4+ ♔g8 26 ♖a2
(there have also been experiments with
26 ♔b1, avoiding any checks from c3)
26...♗xd5 27 ♕xd5 ♕f6 28 ♕d2 ♗g3 29
♖f1 with complicated play. This ended
up with a draw, but with queen, rook
and opposite-coloured bishops, there

were perhaps not surprisingly some slip-ups.

Radjabov, in a later encounter against Leko, tried to keep play simple with 17...♗xe3 18 ♘xe3 ♘e7 19 0-0 f5 20 exf5 ♗xf5, P.Leko-T.Radjabov, Morelia/Linares 2008. Leko showed, yet again, his great understanding on both sides of the board in the Sveshnikov system, and found a way of setting up serious pressure on d6 after 21 ♖a2 ♗e4 22 ♖d2 ♖b6 23 ♖e1 ♕b8 24 ♕a1 ♕c7 25 ♖ed1 h6 26 h3 ♗b7 27 ♕a3 ♖d8 28 ♗e6! ♕xc3 29 ♖xd6, and Black's d-file soon collapsed.

Two wins by Leko in the same line against the same top-rated opponent. A result!

18 h4!?

Leko would, of course, have remembered his game as Black against Topalov with 17...g6 18 h4, and would have recognized this as being at least promising after 18...♗e6.

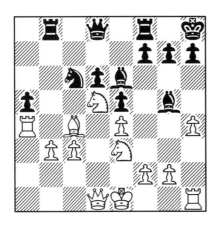

18...♗f4?

Missing an extremely deep idea.

18...♗h6? 19 ♘g4 is also strong for White.

The simplest line, exchanging, is 18...♗xe3 19 ♘xe3 ♘e7!. It is far from

clear that White has an edge, his king not yet being safely developed. If, for example, 20 ♗xe6?! (doubling the pawns, but opening up the f-file for Black) 20...fxe6 21 ♘c4 d5 22 exd5 exd5 23 ♘xe5 ♕c7 24 ♕d4 ♖xb3 and Black wins a pawn. There are of course safer options, such as 20 0-0 ♘c8 21 ♗xe6 fxe6 22 h5, but it remains to be proven that White has an edge.

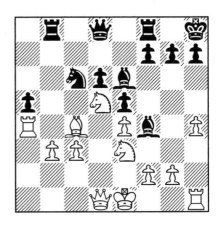

19 ♘f5!

A natural enough move, taking advantage of Black's dark-squared bishop not having been exchanged. White has two knights on light squares, and it is very difficult for Black to exchange the light-squared bishop for one of the knights, since then the other knight dominates.

Radjabov's idea had been that if White had played 19 g3 ♗xe3 20 ♘xe3 ♗xc4 21 ♘xc4 f5, Black is comfortable, White having weakened his kingside pawn structure. Also 19 ♘xf4 exf4 20 ♘d5 ♘e5 21 ♘xf4 ♗xc4 22 bxc4 ♖e8 is comfortable for Black.

Leko had foreseen his opponent's innovation, and found a bigger counter-innovation. Such things happen in top level chess.

19...g6

Radjabov was, of course, relying on this. Anything else, and White is comfortable, making full use of his light squares.

20 ♘fe3!

A sensational idea, giving away two tempi with the knight, just so that Black has to weaken his pawn structure, slightly but significantly.

Leko's move makes a great impression, but sadly from the purely technical point of view, there is also an equally good alternative: 20 ♘xf4! ♗xf5 (20...exf4? 21 ♘xd6) 21 exf5 exf4. Leko gives this as unclear, but after 22 ♗d5!? (there are other promising moves), White has better control in the centre, despite initial appearances. Once Black has tried ...♘e5, he would of course have excellent use of the e5-square, but White would have the remaining three central squares. Play might continue with 22...♖e8+ (22...♕f6 23 ♖h3! makes good use of the ranks, as well as the files) 23 ♔f1 ♘e5 23 fxg6 fxg6 25 ♖xf4 ♕c7 26 ♖h3, and again White uses the files effectively.

Black quite simply has too many pawn weaknesses.

20...♔g7

It proves to be difficult for Black to equalize. The pawn weakness on g6 is a severe problem. Black could, of course, try 20...h5, to prevent White playing h5 himself, but extra pawn pushes to try to conceal other pawn weaknesses tend to have a tendency to create even further weaknesses.

20...♗xe3!? 21 ♘xe3 ♗xc4 22 ♖xc4 ♘e7 23 h5 g5, and if 24 0-0 f5, might keep White down to a slight edge, but Black is not yet equalizing. This seems a

much smaller edge than in the lines starting with 20 ♘xf4, so with regrets, the impression is that Leko's line is not totally the best. It is still good, though, and refreshingly paradoxical.

21 g3

Or maybe 21 h5 immediately, also with active play.

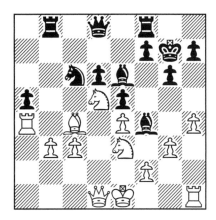

21...♗h6?!

Radjabov wants to keep the tension with the bishop, but it soon turns out that it is White who is keeping the tension on the bishop, and in the end White can force the exchange for knight against bishop on a much more uncomfortable square.

21...♗xe3 22 ♘xe3 looks better, but White has a definite slight edge. Black has weaknesses on the d-file, and has to pay attention to possible h5-pushes. Here 22...♕b6 keeps White down to a slight edge, as if 23 ♕xd6?! ♖fd8 24 ♕a3 ♗xc4 25 ♖xc4 ♕xb3, and Black is now slightly better.

22 ♘g4!

Superb flexibility by the knight, before Black can cut out this knight option with ...f5.

Even if Black goes just slightly wrong in the Sveshnikov Variation, White can have excellent opportunities of exploiting light-squared manoeuvring.

22...f5

Black finds a way of activating his pawns, but his king is soon stuck on h6, and Leko plays vigorously.

22...♗xg4 23 ♕xg4 ♕c8 24 ♕xc8 ♖fxc8 cuts out any weaknesses against the king, but Black's pawns and minor pieces are under severe pressure. After, for example, 25 g4 (squashing the idea of ...f5) 25...♗f4 26 ♔e2, Black's bishop can attack nothing on the dark squares, and of course has absolutely no influence on the light squares.

23 ♘xh6

The bishop-pair is worth getting rid of. One bishop gone means that the defender cannot cover the remaining squares.

23...♔xh6

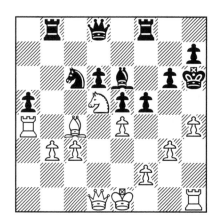

Radjabov's position would be comfortable had his king been on h8 or g7, rather than the unusual h6-square. Leko must move quickly before his opponent may consolidate.

24 h5!

Leko notes that 24 ♘e3 is also possible, with slight edges after either 24...♗xc4 or 24...f4. The move that Leko

chooses is more direct. If the opponent's king is on a strange square, he might just as well take advantage of it.

24...g5

Ugly, but Radjabov is uncomfortable about the thought of opening the h-file: 24...♔g7 25 hxg6 hxg6 26 exf5 ♗xf5 27 ♗e2 (or 27 ♗f1!? – Korotylev) 27...♖h8 28 ♖xh8 ♕xh8 29 ♖h4 ♕f8 30 ♗c4 with advantage. White has successfully opened and closed the valve on the fourth rank, and with much more space, White's second rook takes over the attack on the fourth rank, while Black's second rook cannot defend so successfully.

25 exf5

Breaking open Black's kingside pawns.

25...♗xf5

25...♖xf5? 26 ♘e3 ♖f6? 27 ♗xe6 ♖xe6 28 ♘f5 mate is a quick finish.

26 ♘e3

Another punchy move by the knight.

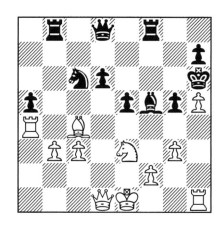

26...♗c8

26...♗e4!? is more active, with perhaps the implication that it is not so good in defence. Black would ideally like to keep some control on the c8-h3 diagonal:

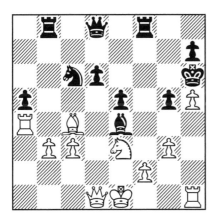
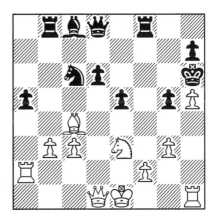

a) 27 ♗f7?! ♘b4! (or 27...♖xf7 28 ♖xe4 with a slight edge for White) 28 ♕f3?! is spectacular, but not quite sound. Instead of 28...♗xf3?? 29 ♘f5 mate, Black has 28...♘c2+ 29 ♔d2 ♘xe3 30 ♖xe4 ♘d5, and he is better.

b) 27 0-0 ♗f3 28 ♗e2 ♗xe2 29 ♕xe2 is Leko's suggestion as White's best, with a clear advantage. Rogozenko puts this even stronger by suggesting that 'Black is strategically lost'. *Fritz* in contrast gives this as equal, but is the computer always to be trusted?

Further examination suggests that after 29...♔g7 30 ♕c4, Black still has problems. He faces the standard pawn weaknesses with the a- and d-pawns in this opening, and his kingside light-coloured squares have been opened up rather more than is comfortable.

A line might be 30...♖c8 31 ♕e6 ♕f6 32 ♕d7+ ♔h8 33 ♘d5 ♕h6 34 ♖c4 ♖fd8 35 ♕b7 ♕g7 36 ♕a6, and White continues to keep pressure on. Alternatively, 30...♕d7 31 ♖d1, or 30...♘e7 31 ♖fa1 d5 32 ♕g4 ♘c6 33 ♕e6 ♕f6 34 ♕xf6+ ♖xf6 35 ♘xd5 ♖d6 36 ♘e3, and White keeps the extra pawn. So White keeps an edge.

27 ♖a2!

We have already seen this rook retreat, in the other Leko-Radjabov game (note to Black's 17th). White is ready to defend on f2, and to attack from d2, while still keeping in touch with the attack on Black's a-pawn.

27...♘e7

Leko in *Informator* gives 27...♔g7 28 ♖d2 ♖f6 29 h6+ ♔h8 30 ♕h5 as winning for White. It is comfortable for him, but after 30...♖f8! there is no immediate winning plan. One wonders whether there might be a typo, or whatever the term is of a lazy hit on the mouse. It is possible he was intending 30 ♖h5 ♖g6 (29...♕f6? 30 ♖xg5 ♕xh6 31 ♖b8 mate) 31 ♗d3 ♖e6 32 ♗e4, with a bind.

This would be yet another example of the rooks using the a- and h-files to their advantage, then maybe changing ranks and files (♖a4-a2-d2; ♖h5 threatening ♖xg5) to attack various weaknesses in Black's pawn structure. White's dominance of the minor pieces is significant, but something else needs to be added. What is unusual here is that there are no completely open files, and only two closed files (g- and h-files). There are six semi-open files, three on either side. White's a-, c- and f-pawns are safe enough, and cannot be attacked. Black's e5-pawn is also safe, but his a5- and d6-pawns are weak. In addition, White's push with the h-pawn to the sixth leaves White's pawn being slightly weak, but Black's g5-pawn is also slightly weak. It is possible that there might be an exchange of weaknesses. Even here, it is White who is likely to initiate the exchange of pawn weaknesses.

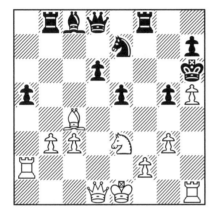

28 0-0

White keeps his flexibility. If Black's king does not move, and does not allow White to push with h6, then the rook is more effective elsewhere, maybe on d1 or a1, again attacking pawns on half-open files.

28 ♖xa5?, intending 28...♕xa5?? 29 ♕xd6+, is careless because 28...♗b7! 29 0-0 d5 gives Black counterplay.

28...♖f6

Black concentrates on trying to defend his d-pawn, rather than immediately trying to extricate his king. If 28...♔g7 29 ♕d3 ♗f5 30 ♘xf5 ♖xf5 31 ♖d1 ♖f6 32 ♕e3 h6 33 ♖ad2, Black is under pressure. White has, by this stage, complete centralization.

29 ♕e2

His first chance to castle on move 28, then his first queen move on move 29. Soon it will be time to bring the rooks together. The completion of the opening phase may have been slow, but the late middlegame phase is quick.

29...♕b6

29...♕e8 30 ♖xa5 ♕xh5 is a pawn exchange that is likely to favour White, allowing him a good passed b-pawn. Leko gives 31 ♖a7 ♗b7 32 ♘g4+ ♔g7 33 ♖xb7 (not 33 ♘xf6?? ♕h1 mate) 33...♖xb7 34 ♕e4 ♖c7 35 ♘xf6 ♔xf6 36 ♖a1 as favouring White; indeed, one would expect, a forced win.

30 ♖fa1

But now there is the danger of taking the a-pawn for nothing.

30...♕c6

Black must find counterplay on the long diagonal.

31 ♖xa5

There is no reason to delay.

31...♗b7

A threat!

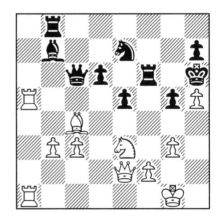

32 ♗d5!

It is the knight that needs to be retained, while the bishop may be exchanged.

32...♘xd5 33 ♖xd5

He wants to keep the knight on its best square, on e3, where it cannot be attacked, and where it is threatening checks and attacks on g4 and f5.

33...♕xc3

33...♔g7 34 ♖a7 ♔h8 35 ♕b5 ♕c7 (35...♕c8? 36 ♖xd6) 36 ♕b4 ♕c6 37 c4 grinds slowly on.

34 ♘g4+

Leko could have set up a trap with 34 ♖a7!? ♗c8 35 ♕f3!, and if 35...♖xf3 36 ♖xd6+ ♔h5 37 ♖xh7 mate. Here 34...♔g7 35 ♘g4 would have transposed into the game, and 34...♕xe3!?, followed by ...♗xd5, may look slightly desperate, but such a sacrifice of queen versus rook and bishop can be difficult to break down.

Leko's immediate check cuts down the opponent's options.

34...♔g7 35 ♖a7

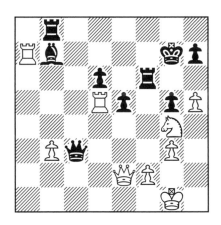

The finish is enlivened by various pins and other tactics, all of which favour White.

35...♖e6

Leko notes the checkmate in midboard after 35...♕c6 36 ♘xf6 ♔xf6 27 ♕f3+ ♔e6 38 ♖xb7 ♕xb7 39 ♕g4+ ♔xd8 40 ♕d4 mate. A battle on the long diagonal. This would have been an attractive finish.

By contrast, White wins slowly, probably on the dark squares, after 35...♕c1+ 36 ♔h2 ♖f7 37 ♖xb7 ♖fxb7 38 ♖xd6. Black's extra exchange does not have much impact when White's queen, rook and knight are drilling away at Black's kingside pawns and exposed king. After 38...♕c3 39 h6+ ♔h8 40 ♘xe5 ♖f8 41 ♘d7, even if there is objectively a win for White, he will have to work hard: 41...♖xd7 42 ♖xd7 ♕f6 43 ♔g1 ♕xh6 44 ♕e4 might at first look long and technical, but again Black's king is exposed, and his pieces cannot do anything other than defend. 44...♖c8 45 ♔g2! is close to zugzwang. If Black does not lose immediately, the b-pawn will decide.

35...♕f3 36 h6+ ♔f8 37 ♕xf3 ♖xf3 38 ♖b5 ♖f7 39 ♘e3 is given by Leko as a win for White, Black being squeezed, but White still has to be careful. After 39...♖c7 40 ♘c4 ♔e7 White does not quite have the luxury of creating an escape square for the king after 41 g4?! ♔d7 42 ♖b6, as Black can jump out of prison with 42...♗c6!. Even if White were to find a winning try in the endgame, this would be long-winded. Once the problem is seen, the solution is easier: 41 ♖b6! g4 42 ♔h2 places Black in zugzwang.

36 ♕c4!

Forcing favourable simplification, or a mating attack.

36...♕e1+

36...♕xc4 37 bxc4 ♔f8 38 ♖b5 ♖e7 39 ♘e3 will win for White.

37 ♔g2

White is not scared of the long diagonal, as he is intending to sacrifice the exchange to eliminate the bishop.

37...♖e7

The only move.

38 ♖xb7

The only move for White, as well. Even if this had not been forced, exchange sacrifices are an important part of the attacking repertoire.

38...♖exb7

38...♖bxb7? 39 h6+ leaves the back row open.

39 ♖xd6

We see a broadly similar set-up to Black's alternative in the notes to Black's 35th with 35...♕c1+. It is not difficult for a player to sacrifice the exchange in such a position.

39...♖f8

Black's best chance is to set up counterplay on the f-file.

40 h6+

Now the king is forced to the back, and is liable to a back-rank checkmate.

40...♔h8 41 ♕d5

White tightens the grip, slowly but surely. His queen and rook are fully centralized, and his knight is excellently placed for both attack and defence. His king is safer than Black's. Indeed, he is heading for a win.

41 ♕e6 ♕e4+ 42 ♔h2 also wins for White, as ♕f6+ is threatened.

41...♖bb8

The only realistic chance. 41...♖bf7? loses immediately after 42 ♕xf7. Naturally there are likely to be some other back-row ideas for White.

42 ♕d3

And also the seventh rank, plus of course a few useful diagonals.

42 ♖d7, with the same idea of attack

on h7, allows Black to try to defend with 42...♕e2. Even here, as Leko notes, White still has a winning attack after 43 ♖b7. If, for example, 43...♖xb7 44 ♕xb7 ♖g8 45 ♘f6!, and the knight joins in for checkmate. One of the biggest sins in chess is the flashy but unsound sacrifice when there is a clear win by normal play. Here 43 ♖xh7+?? ♔xh7 44 ♕d7+ ♔g6 would have been an example. The king escapes to h5.

42...♕b4

Not 42...e4 immediately, as White takes the long diagonal with 43 ♕d4+.

43 ♖d7

Still aiming for h7.

43...e4

The only move.

44 ♕d5

But now White is threatening the long light-squared diagonal.

44...♖b5

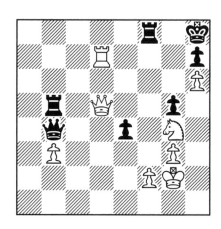

Almost a saving resource.

45 ♘f6! 1-0

Leko has a combination ready. Play would finish with a queen flourish after 45...♖xf6 46 ♖d8+ ♖f8 47 ♕d4+ ♕xd4 48 ♖xf8 mate.

Game 10
V.Ivanchuk-L.Aronian
Russian Team Championship 2006
Ruy Lopez C88

1 e4 e5 2 ♘f3 ♘c6 3 ♗b5 a6

The 3...a6 move is effectively a gain of tempo, and is useful, but it is only a small tempo.

3...♘f6, the Berlin Defence, is discussed in Game 7, Svidler-Topalov.

4 ♗a4

Also there is the Exchange Variation, 4 ♗xc6 dxc6 5 0-0, with various similarities to the Berlin Defence. White has given up his bishop-pair, and Black now has doubled c-pawns. Black has not quite equalized yet, and at top level White has achieved a small plus score. At the moment, the most successful reply at top level seems to be 5...♘e7!?, and a pawn gambit after 6 ♘xe5 ♕d4 7 ♕h5 g6 8 ♕g5 ♗g7 9 ♘d3 f5 10 e5. There are also more traditional lines, such as 5...f6 or 5...♕d6, protecting the e5-pawn.

4...♘f6

The most direct line, perhaps, is 4...b5 5 ♗b3 ♘a5, which Morozevich has tried a few times in blitz events. The sacrifice, 6 ♗xf7+ ♔xf7 7 ♘e5+ ♔e7, is playable, but not wholly convincing. 6 0-0 d6 7 d4 exd4 remains possible, if never particularly fashionable. Black picks up the bishop-pair, and does not have to defend the doubled c-pawns, but is behind in development.

5 0-0

Very much the most common move.

White can instead defend the e4-pawn, but it is not necessary yet.

5...♗e7

5...♘xe4 6 d4 is the Open Variation.

6 ♖e1

Time now to defend the pawn. Other moves are possible, but not so common.

6...b5

Since White is now threatening to win the pawn on e5, after an exchange on c6, it is now time to start counterplay with ...b5.

7 ♗b3

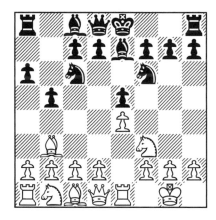

The bishop is now kicked off the a4-e8 diagonal, but is still on a good diagonal, aiming at f7. Compared with the old and very direct Giuoco Piano, with 3 ♗c4, Black has gained two tempi with ...a6 and ...b5, and in many lines he can make use of this, but, as we shall soon see, the black pawns can be a weakness, and White can hit with a4. The Ruy Lopez, the Spanish Game, is much more popular than the Giuoco Piano, the Italian Game, because it has two lines of attack (b5 and f7), rather than just a single line of attack, f7.

7...0-0

A small but highly significant difference in move order. Both 7...0-0 8 c3 d6, and 7...d6 8 c3 0-0 would transpose into the main line, if both players wish. Aronian is a noted advocate of the Marshall Gambit, and so avoids playing 7...d6.

8 a4

And Ivanchuk avoids the Marshall gambit, 8 c3 d5. See further commentary on this popular pawn sacrifice in Game 16, Shirov-Aronian.

There are various other anti-Marshall alternatives with, for example, 8 d3 or 8 d4. Possibly the simplest is 8 h3, when if Black chooses, he could transpose into the main, non-Marshall, line after 8...d6 9 c3. Black has also tried 8...♗b7, but 8...d5?! 9 exd5 ♘xd5 10 ♘xe5 ♘xe5 11 ♖xe5 c6 10 d4 is much easier to defend for White. He would have, in effect, an extra tempo.

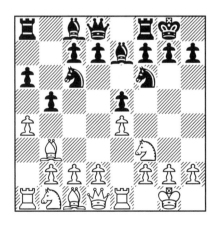

8...b4

The most common reply.

8...♖b8 9 axb5 axb5 10 c3 d6 has tended to favour White slightly. White's control on the a-file is useful.

9 d4

9 d3, with the idea of ♘b1-d2-c4, is a possibility. Here Ivanchuk tries sharper and more open play.

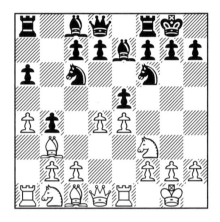

9...d6

Probably rather more stable than 9...♘xd4 10 ♘xd4 exd4 11 e5 ♘e8 12 ♕xd4.

10 dxe5

Strangely, there has been little attention paid on the natural space gain with 10 d5. The first example with this move on the database has been in a game by Aronian, not totally surprising as he has long been a specialist on the Marshall Gambit. This, however, was Aronian with White, and his opponent was trying the Marshall. White demonstrated an edge in L.Aronian-A.Minasian, Yerevan 2001, with 10...♘a5 11 ♗a2 ♖b8 12 ♘bd2 c6 13 dxc6 ♗e6 (a more ambitious attempt at equalizing than the standard recapture) 14 ♗xe6 fxe6 15 ♕e2 ♕b6 16 ♘c4 ♘xc4 17 ♕xc4 d5 18 exd5 exd5 19 ♕b3, although later the game ended up as a draw with equal material in an end-game after complications. Maybe there is the opportunity for other players to explore further? 11...♖b8 might well be slightly irrelevant if he is not going to try ...b3. An alternative perhaps would be 11...♘b7!? followed by ...♘c5.

Earlier, White has also tried various quieter pawn moves, such as 10 c3, 10 h3, or occasionally 10 a5.

10...♘xe5

10...dxe5 has also been tried, but usually Black prefers the knight exchange.

11 ♘xe5

11 ♗f4 ♘g6 has been tried various times, but without making much of an impact on Black's position. White prefers to set up a clear weakness in Black's pawn structure, and attack it.

11...dxe5

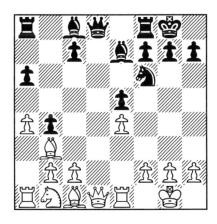

The pawn structure has now been fixed, and White can feel reasonably happy with the outcome. Black has three slight pawn weaknesses, leaving White something to work with. White's bishop on the a2-g8 diagonal is an irritation, putting pressure on the f7-pawn. As a consequence, it is difficult to provide full protection for the e5-

pawn. Black's rook cannot simultaneously provide full cover for both the e-file and the f-file. As a result, he has to make compromises. On the queenside, Black's b-pawn has been encouraged to advance perhaps more quickly than he would have liked, and in consequence, Black's c-file is weakened. White can play, for example, ♘d2-c4 without much opposition.

Having said that, any advantage for White is still slight, provided Black can play actively. Black was careful earlier to exchange knights, giving up his purely defensive c6-knight in return for taking White's active f3-knight. Simplification usually helps the defender, but it cannot solve every problem.

12 ♕f3

White sees his queen as an attacker, his opponent's queen as the defender.

12 ♕e2 or 12 ♗g5 would be less forceful, and 12 ♘d2? would be even careless, in view of 12...♗g4.

12...♗b7

There are some other lines that have been played, but this seems the most direct. *Fritz* gives lines such as 12...c5 or 12...c6 as equal, but what is Black trying to do next?

12...♗e6 covers up White's light-squared diagonal towards f7, but the central tension seems to favour White, for example, after 13 ♘d2 ♗c5 14 h3!?.

13 ♘d2

'Knights before bishops'.

The knight may, though, need some time to manoeuvre itself to the best square, and cannot move instantly from, for example, b1 to g3.

If 13 ♗g5 ♘d7 14 ♗e3 ♗c5, Black is equal. Here 13...h6!? 14 ♖d1 hxg5 15 ♖xd8 ♖axd8 is a provocative queen sacrifice. White will have to work out how to develop his knight and rook; his minor pieces do not work together well.

13...♗c5

In J.Ehlvest-V.Kupreichik, Minsk 1989, Kupreichik provided perhaps a little too direct a hint of a threatened capture on e4 with 13...♔h8. Ehlvest covered the f5-square with 14 g4!? ♗c5 15 ♘c4, but Kupreichik persisted with 15...♘xe4?! (Black was already slightly worse anyway) 16 ♖xe4 f5 17 gxf5 ♖xf5 18 ♕xf5 ♕d1+ 19 ♔g2 ♖f8, but after 20 ♘e3!, Black's attack was over. Could Black play with more finesse?

14 ♘f1

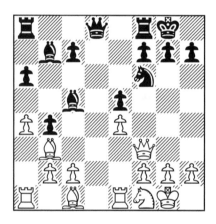

A standard Ruy Lopez manoeuvre, bringing the knight to g3, and then either defending the e4-pawn, or starting a ♘f5 kingside attack. Additionally, White is thinking about ♗g5, and of course White no longer has any back-row problems. One senses that Black has not yet equalized.

14...♕c8

After 14...♕d7 15 h3 White will have a later hit with ♖ad1 (after the bishop move). So the queen shelters to a safer square.

15 h3

One of the less successful games in grandmaster chess continued with 15 ♘g3?! ♕g4 16 ♕d3?! ♖ad8, and White later retreated with 17 ♕f3. Ivanchuk naturally prefers to cover the g4-square.

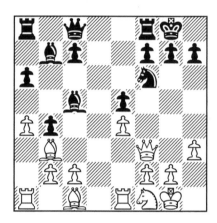

15...♔h8

With ideas of setting up the sacrifice on e4. Ivanchuk suggests, as a possible improvement, 15...a5 16 ♗g5 ♖a6!?, then possibly 17 ♗c4 ♖d6 18 ♘g3 ♕a8.

16 ♘g3

White wishes to consolidate the e4-pawn, or at least partially consolidate. 16 ♗e3? ♗xe4 would, of course, be a mistake.

Ivanchuk gives 16 ♗h6 as inaccurate with good play for Black after 16...♘d7 17 ♗e3 f5. This seems less than clear after 18 ♗d5!, with chances for White for a slight edge. Maybe 16...♘e8 17 ♗e3 ♗xe3 would be more flexible, about equal, after 18 ♕xe3 ♘d6, hitting e4 from another direction.

The ♗h6 move is not a bad idea, but Ivanchuk has analysed something better and more direct. The next few moves are of themselves straightforward enough, but the resulting play is strategically complicated.

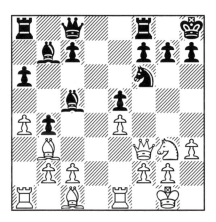

16...♘xe4!?

Clearly the tactic has been in the air for quite a long time.

Ivanchuk gives 16...♕d7 17 ♗g5 ♕c6 18 c3 bxc3 19 bxc3 ♖ab8 20 ♖ab1 as a slight edge for White, but this is hardly surprising given that Black's ...♕d8-c8-d7 has ended up as a loss of tempo.

To try to prove that his previous play was positionally justified, Aronian has to take up the challenge.

17 ♘xe4

17 ♖xe4? f5 loses the exchange.

17...f5

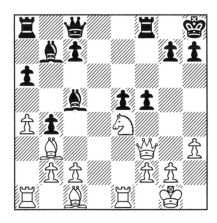

So Black recovers the knight, unless of course White doesn't mind losing the queen for compensation.

18 ♘xc5!

Ivanchuk takes up the challenge. When writing this book, this was one of the first games to select. It is so rare to be able to find positions with queen versus three minor pieces, much rarer than queen versus rook, minor piece and pawn.

I suspect that in home preparation Aronian would have been happy with this position, seeing White's kingside pawn structure as seriously weakened. However, as play goes on, White's pieces start to work together, and Black's play becomes increasingly difficult. Ivanchuk's play is highly original and insightful.

Was dropping the queen forced? Ivanchuk gives as an alternative 18 ♗e6 ♗xe4 (18...♕xe6? 19 ♘xc5 and White wins a piece) 19 ♗xc8 ♗xf3 20 ♖xe5 ♗d4 21 ♖xf5 ♖axc8 22 ♖xf3 ♖xf3 23 gxf3 ♖f8 24 ♔g2 ♖e8 25 ♔f1, and a possible draw by repetition.

Ivanchuk also gives 18 ♗h6, when the simplest reply is 18...fxe4!? 19 ♗xg7+ ♔xg7 20 ♕g3+ ♔h6 (but not 20...♔h8?? 21 ♕xe5+) 21 ♕h4+ ♔g6 with a perpetual. White has no room to manoeuvre for more, as Black is threatening ...♗xf2+. Here 18...♗xe4 19 ♗xg7+ ♔xg7 20 ♕g3+ ♔f6 21 ♕h4+ ♔g6 22 ♕g3+ is also a drawing line, while Ivanchuk also looks at 18...gxh6 19 ♕g3 f4 20 ♕d3, which he gives as unclear.

There are some interesting drawing options, but there is only one real chance of playing for a win.

18...♗xf3 19 gxf3

An unusual material balance. Enjoy it while you can in a game between two top grandmasters.

The material is in theory about equal (9 = 3+3+3), if we assume that Black's e-pawn will drop. If the e-pawn holds, then maybe Black has a slight edge in terms of material, but of course there are many other issues in the position.

Probably White ought to have the better piece structure, if his minor pieces are well guarded, but his bishop on c1 might well be poorly placed. In terms of pawns, Black's queenside pawns are ineffective, but White has weakened kingside pawns, and his king is isolated.

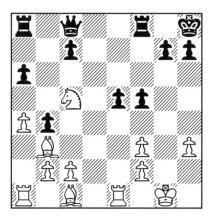

19...f4!?

This is by far the most natural move, with ideas of attacking on h3, and also blocking the bishop on c1. Probably most strong players would want to play this, or at the very least consider it seriously. It may still not be the best. White soon has outposts on e4 and g4, thanks to Black's pawn push.

There are a few alternatives. Ivanchuk gives 19...♖e8 20 f4, and if 20...e4 21 ♗e3 followed by ♔h2 and ♖g1, and White's pieces are rock solid. Black will have to defend weaknesses on the pawn on g7, adding sensitivity to the king, and also along the d-file, and

against threats with either bishop or knight from e6. Similarly, if 20...exf4 21 ♗xf4, and White's minor pieces are excellent.

19...e4!? is an attempt to open up lines for the queen and rooks, although White does not necessarily have to oblige, since 20 f4 closes play down again. Black could of course transpose to Ivanchuk's suggested line with 20...♖e8. There may be improvements, but these are probably not significant. White could also allow the centre to open with 20 fxe4 fxe4 21 ♘e6 ♖f6 22 ♖xe4 ♕b7 23 ♘c5 ♕c6 24 ♗e3. Probably White has the better chances, with complicated play, but there are earlier chances to improve for Black.

Pawns may well have been 'the soul of chess', as Philidor may have suggested a quarter of a millennium ago, but the major pieces, the queen and the rooks, are surely the heart of attack. White's king is open, and one could argue that Black should be concentrating on queen and rook moves, rather than pawn play.

Thus 19...♖e8! looks better, and if 20 ♘e6 ♕h5! 21 ♘xf8 (21 ♗d5 c6 does not help White) 21...♖xf8 22 ♖xe5 ♕xf3. Now it is wisest for White to return the light-squared bishop to the kingside with 23 ♗c4 ♕xh3 24 ♗e2 ♕h4 25 ♖e6 (or maybe 25 ♗f3) 25...a5, and difficult play continues, with Black having a queen and a pawn and a few threats against the white king, and White having rook and two bishops in reply. This is a delicate balance. The computer gives it as equal, but there is no clear perpetual, and the positional balance could easily fall either way after any inaccuracy.

20 ♔h2

White needs to defend the exposed h-pawn, and to tuck his king behind the pawn.

20 ♖xe5? ♕xh3 is much too risky, and after 21 ♗d5? c6 22 ♗xc6 ♖f6 Black is about to mate.

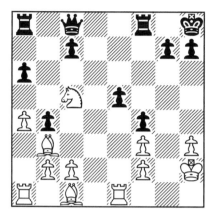

20...♕f5

Black consolidates, and this is indeed natural, stopping White's rook taking control of the e-file, but is it the best? Ivanchuk suggests as an alternative 20...♕d8!?, aiming for counterplay after 21 ♖xe5 ♕h4. Black would there be arguing that the pawn on e5 is not so significant. The other pawns, f4 and b4, are more significant, as if Black can hold on to them, White's dark-squared bishop is out of active play.

Ivanchuk gives as his main line the slightly fragile 22 ♘e4 ♖ae8 23 ♖xe8 ♖xe8, when it is difficult for White to develop his pieces. If, for example, 24 ♗d2?? ♖xe4 25 fxe4 ♕xf2+, and Black wins material. White therefore tries instead 24 ♔g2. There are various ways of handling the position, and certainly 24...♖e5 is natural, and worth considering, but Ivanchuk suggests, with thoughts of safety for both sides,

24...♕h6 25 ♗c4 a5 26 ♗d3 ♕g6+ 27 ♔h2 ♕h5 28 ♔g2 with a repetition after 28...♕g6+. Here 28...♕e5!? could be tried, the queen taking advantage of the vacant square of the pawn, but 29 ♖b2! ♖e6 30 ♗d2 starts a partial unravelling.

Ivanchuk suggests an alternative choice, 22 ♘d3!? (instead of 22 ♘e4), which would seem to be more attractive. The knight puts pressure on the black pawn on f4, and also guards the weak square on f2. Also White keeps his good rook on e5, since if 22...♖ae8? 23 ♖xe8 ♖xe8, White simply has 24 ♗xf4. Ivanchuk gives the position as unclear after the preferable 22...♖ad8 23 ♖e2 ♕h5 24 ♗d2 ♕xf3 25 ♖ae1 a5.

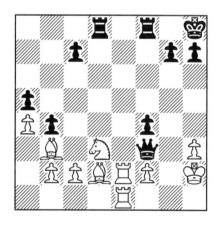

If White were to find a couple of clear tempi, and bring all his extra pieces into play, then he would be better. Unfortunately, just at the moment his pieces lack coordination, with, for example, his two rooks being immobile (26 ♖e7?? ♖xd3). White has to try something quickly, though, as Black's queen is flexible and mobile, and his pawns can try to open White's kingside with ...g5 and ...g4. One senses that there will be tactics:

a) There are, for example, some entreating checks, counterchecks and mate threats after 26 ♗e6?! ♕c6! 27 ♗xf4 ♖xd3 28 exd3 ♖xf4 29 ♗d7. Winning for White? Not quite. Black has 29...♕d6! 30 ♖e8+ ♖f8+, a vital countercheck. White's king moves, and Black covers his mating threats with 31...♖g8!, with a substantial advantage.

b) So let us try a more direct threat, 26 ♘e5. There is only one good queen move, as 27 ♘f7+ is a threat. He must play 26...♕h5 (and if 27 ♘f7+? ♖xf7 28 ♖e8+ ♖f8). Play continues with 27 ♗e6, and if given the chance, White would be happy after ♗g4 and ♗f3. Again one senses tactics, and they soon arise with 27...f3!? 28 ♗g4 fxe2 29 ♗xh5 ♖xd2 30 ♔g2 ♖xc2 31 ♖xe2 b3! (otherwise White is better), and we have reached a much more normal material balance, with rook and pawn against two minor pieces. Probably the position is about equal after, for example, 32 h4 (preventing Black from thinking about ...g5) 32...g6 33 ♗f3 ♔g7 34 ♘d3 ♖d8 35 ♖e3, and the position has stabilized for both sides.

In *Informator*, Ivanchuk gives this line as 'unclear' after White's 25th, and before the tactics come up. In terms of practical over-the-board chess, this seems about right. Neither player can show a clear advantage, while in the alternative line the position is also unclear.

Of course, it would have been beyond the event horizon for Aronian to have been able to decide over the board whether 19...♖e8 would have been better than 19...f4, bearing in mind the additional possibility that he could also have chosen between 20...♕f5 and 20...♕d8.

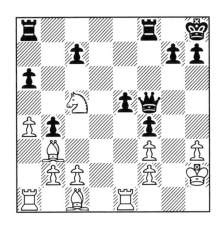

21 ♗d2!

This is an extremely difficult position to interpret, not just in terms of pure chess, but also in terms of chess psychology. Ivanchuk gives this as an exclamation mark, and this is fully understandable in positional terms, developing his queenside pieces, and waiting to see whether the knight should go to d3 or to e4, both good and logical squares, but cannot both be played.

Ivanchuk gives 21 ♘d3 ♖ae8 22 ♗d2 ♕h5, and this could easily transpose into 21 ♗d2 ♕h5 22 ♘d3 ♖ae8 (see the note to Black's 21st), but as we shall soon see, Aronian does not enter the critical line.

Ivanchuk analyses 23 ♖e4! ♖f6! (23...♕xf3 24 ♖ae1 g5 25 ♖xe5 ♖xe5 26 ♖xe5 g4 27 hxg4 ♕xg4 28 ♘xb4 with advantage to White; Black's rook cannot add to the attack) 24 ♖ae1 ♖h6 25 ♘xf4 ♕f5 26 ♔g1 g5 with sharp play, including the possibility of good play by Black. Ivanchuk further gives 27 ♘e2 ♖f6 28 ♖g4! ♕xf3 29 ♖g2 ♕xh3 30 ♘g3, citing this as unclear. One possibility is 30...♕g4 31 ♖xe5 ♕d1+ 32 ♘f1 ♕h5 33

♘g3 with a perpetual.

One cannot help feeling that there are many variations that need to be considered in such an open position, and that Black has started at last to break up White's kingside pawns. There are possible ideas for Black to try to improve, most naturally perhaps 27...♖xh3!?, and if 28 ♘d4? ♕f6 29 ♗xb4 g4!, and White is suddenly in serious trouble, as if 30 ♖xg4 (diverting the rook from the e-file) 30...♕h6 31 ♔f1 ♖h1+ 32 ♔e2 exd4+, and Black is winning. Probably White has to try 28 ♘g3 ♕xf3, but Black is better.

Both 21 ♗d2 and 21 ♘d3 could lead to these lines, which tend to be favourable to Black. There is, however, an important distinction. After 21 ♗d2!, White can avoid all this. See the next note.

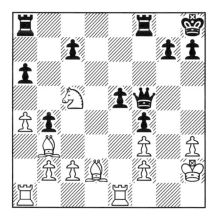

21...♖f6?!

If 21...♖ae8?!, White does not transpose into the above lines with 22 ♘d3, but tries something else: 22 ♖g1!.

After the text move, Ivanchuk again plays the rook to g1 and g4, and Aronian's attacking play looks rather too direct.

21...♕h5 would be another attempt

to enter the lines started with 21 ♘d3, and if 22 ♘d3?! (not 22 ♗d5? ♖ad8) 22...Rae8, with probably a slight edge to Black, as discussed earlier. 22 ♘e4! is better when 22...♕xf3?! 23 ♗e6 is an irrelevant pawn grab, as White is threatening to trap the queen with ♗g4. After 23...♕h5 24 ♗g4, White's position is fully satisfactory. Thus 22...a5! seems best. Then 23 ♗e6 ♖a6 24 ♗g4 follows, with tense play, probably less favourable for White than in the actual game, because ideally White would want the rook rather than the bishop on g4.

22 ♖g1

Safest. White intends to plug the diagonal with ♖g4.

22 ♗xb4? ♖h6 23 ♗e6 leaves Black too much free space after 23...♕xc2!, and if 23 ♖f1 ♖xe6 (among others) 24 ♘xe6 ♕c5.

The computer suggests early on that 22...♖xe6? 24 ♘xe6 ♕xe6 25 ♗c3 ♕c6 is winning, but 26 ♖xe5 ♕xc3 (or 26...♔g8 27 ♖e7) 27 ♖g5 allows White a strong attack with the two rooks and bishop.

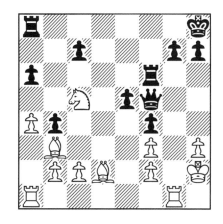

22...♖h6

Black forces the opponent to play what he wants to play anyway.

Ivanchuk gives 22...a5 23 ♖g4 ♖d8 24 ♘e4 ♖h6 25 ♖e1 as unclear. Despite *Fritz*, which suggests that Black is on top, play looks good for White. If, for example, 25...♕h5 26 h4 ♖g6 (or 26...g5 27 ♘xg5 ♕xg4 28 ♘f7+ ♔g7 29 fxg4 ♖xh4+ 30 ♔g2 ♖xd2 31 ♘xe5, and White is doing very well) 27 ♗f7 ♖xg4 28 ♗xh5 ♖xh4+ 29 ♔g2 ♖xh5 30 c3, and the bishop and knight will be more active than the rook and two pawns.

The reader might well wonder why Black is trying to play so sharply. There is a simple reason. If Black does not do something quickly, White's pieces will continue to improve.

23 ♖g4

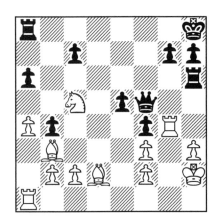

Essential. The rook now blocks everything on the kingside, although it helps that Black cannot attack with any minor pieces. White will at some stage want to open up his position for the bishops with c3.

23...a5

A natural and strong move, not just to save the pawn on b4, but more generally to try to lock the dark-squared bishop into passive play.

24 ♖e1

Some pressure on the pawn on e5 is bound to be useful, cutting down various defensive options for Black, but as we shall soon see, White's plan is not simply a big attack on e5.

24...♖f8

24...♕h5 25 h4 is not fully satisfactory either. Black cannot try ...♖g6 at various stages, in view of ♗f7. Ivanchuk gives 25...♖d6 26 ♘d3 ♖e8 27 ♗c4 as unclear, but White can gradually consolidate his pieces with b3, ♖e4, and maybe manoeuvring his bishop to b2.

25 ♘e4

The one obvious weakness for White at the end of the combinative phase was that his kingside pawns had been broken up into doubled and isolated pawns. Now with fully protected pieces, with the knight on e4 and the rook on g4, the fractured pawn structure is a positive advantage for White.

25 ♘d3 ♖h5 30 h4 ♖f5 is also promising for White, but it seems simpler to aim for complete security on the kingside, before opening up the queenside.

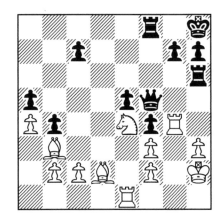

25...♕h5

He might as well force the pawn to advance, but it is not up to much.

25...♖xh3+?? loses material after 26 ♔xh3+ h5 27 ♔g2, and if 27...hxg4? 28

♖h1+, winning.

26 h4

White's rook on g4 is the hero of the defence.

26...♖g6

And this is the only way to get at the white rook.

27 ♖xg6

27 ♖eg1 ♖xg4 28 ♖xg4 is also to be considered, and is good, but with the first set of rooks gone, Black finds it more difficult to attack with the second rook.

27...♕xg6

Again, not 27...♕xh4+?? 28 ♔g2 hxg6 29 ♖h1.

27...hxg6 28 ♔g2 ♕f5 29 c3 gives a clear edge for White. It is difficult for Black to attack any of White's minor pieces.

28 c3

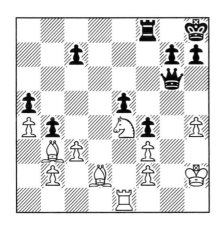

The dark-squared bishop is now back in play, finally completing, in the broadest sense, its full development. Soon White will be able to attack.

28...c5?

Effectively the losing mistake, and probably the result of a misjudgement.

Ivanchuk suggests that White is better after 28...♖f5 29 ♖g1 ♕h6 30 cxb4

♕xh4+ 31 ♔g2 ♖h5 32 ♔f1 axb4 33 ♔e2. The king is safe, and he has an outside passed a-pawn.

28...♕b6 29 cxb4 axb4 30 ♖c1 ♖d8 is better, and Ivanchuk gives it, perhaps generously, as 'unclear'. White cannot lose this, in the absence of a serious error, but he has chances of playing for a win. White's rook and knight are both well placed, and he has the advantage of a passed pawn, but how can he make progress with the other pieces, more particularly the two bishops? The main problem is the dark-squared bishop, which requires some work. A possible idea would be something like 31 ♔g2 g6 32 ♗c4 ♔g7 33 b3 ♔f8 34 ♖c2 ♔e7 35 ♗c1 followed by ♗b2, and the bishop reaches fresh air. Black is certainly not yet safe.

Finally, 28...♕h5 seems almost too elementary for Ivanchuk to mention, even though Black has the chance of winning a kingside pawn. 29 cxb4 axb4 30 ♔g2 gives White a big edge.

29 ♘xc5!

Ivanchuk can quite simply snatch the pawn. Two bishops, a knight and a pawn, in return for the queen, will be enough for White.

29...♖d8

29...♕d6 30 ♘e4 ♕d3 31 ♔g2 is solid for White. He will gradually consolidate. Ivanchuk gives 31...♖d8 32 ♖c1 h6 33 ♗c2 ♕e2 34 ♗d1 ♕d3 35 cxb4 axb4 36 ♗xb4 as winning.

30 ♘e4!

30 ♗c1 ♕b6 31 ♖xe5 bxc3 32 bxc3 is genuinely unclear. White has surrendered most of his pawn support for the minor pieces.

30...♕b6

With threats of ...♖xd2.

It is always hazardous to guess exactly where a player has made a serious miscalculation, but here the likelihood would seem to be that when sacrificing with 28...c5, Aronian had assumed that his queen move to b6 would have been strong. However, Ivanchuk had calculated further.

Ivanchuk gives 30...♕h6 31 cxb4 axb4 32 ♖c1 ♕xh4+ 33 ♔g2 as a big advantage for White. Quite probably the edge is decisive.

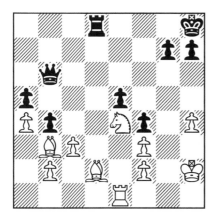

31 ♖d1!

This consolidates everything.

31...♖d3?!

If 31...bxc3 32 ♗xc3!, with a back-rank win after 32...♕xb3?? 33 ♖xd8+. Black loses more slowly after 32...♖xd1 33 ♗xd1 ♕d8 33 ♗e2 ♕xh4+ 34 ♔g2.

Ivanchuk suggests 31...h6 as the best attempt to hold. There are clearly several possibilities for White, maybe starting with 32 cxb4. Ivanchuk himself gives 32 ♔g2 ♖d3 33 ♗c2 ♖d8 34 cxb4 axb4 35 a5! ♕b5 (35...♕xa5 36 ♗xb4!) 36 b3 ♖a8 37 ♘d6 ♕xa5 38 ♘c4 with advantage to White.

32 ♗c4!

Simple and clear. Neither queen nor rook have any good moves.

32...♖xf3?!

32...♖d8 loses a tempo, but at least avoids the quick loss. Ivanchuk gives 33 cxb4 axb4 34 a5 ♕xa5 35 ♗xb4, and White has a substantial edge.

33 ♗e1!

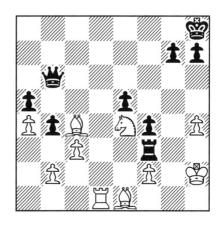

Black's rook is trapped.

33...g5

Black must open up an escape square for the king, otherwise the queen will have no chance of active play.

34 hxg5

Avoiding 34 ♘xg5?? ♖xf2+, when Black may even be better.

34...♔g7

Black's queen cannot try anything. If 34...♕g6 35 ♖d8+ ♔g7 36 ♖g8 mate.

35 ♖d7+

No doubt White can also find ways to win the rook, but in time trouble there are simpler ways. Check, check, squeeze the queen out of the way, then everything is easy.

35...♔f8 36 ♖f7+

Still good, although naturally 36 ♔g2 is also effective.

36...♔e8 37 ♖f6 1-0

It is time for Black to resign.

Game 11
A.Karpov-V.Akopian
Russian Team Championship 2006
Slav Defence D12

1 d4 d5 2 c4 c6 3 ♘f3 ♘f6 4 e3

Karpov avoids the main lines of the Slav (4 ♘c3 dxc4 5 a4 ♗f5), the Meran (4 ♘f3 e6 5 e3 ♘bd7 6 ♗d3 – see Game 1, Kasimdzhanov-Kasparov), and the sharp gambit lines in the Botvinnik Variation (4 ♘c3 e6 5 ♗g5 – see Game 27, Cheparinov-Nepomniachtchi). He is relying instead on simple, natural chess, hoping for a slight technical edge, and to grind away. This has been a successful formula for him over several decades.

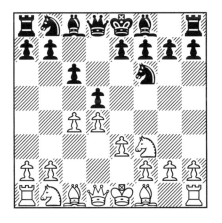

4...♗f5

There are many alternatives, but it is a minor achievement for Black to be able to try ...♗f5 without penalty.

Instead 4...g6 leads to the Schlechter Variation, sometimes reached via the Grünfeld, and 4...e6 5 ♘c3 leads back towards the Meran, although 5 ♘bd2!? is an alternative.

5 ♘c3

5 cxd5!? cxd5 6 ♕b3 ♕c7 7 ♗b5+ is one of the more tempting lines of the exchange systems of the Slav. Maybe Black's bishop is slightly misplaced? Probably though it will gradually fade to equality after 7...♘c6 or 7...♘bd7.

Suppose, though, Black wanted to try to play for more with 5...♘xd5!?. Before the war, many players preferred this as Black, rather than keeping the symmetrical pawn structure. There was, for example, a long and involved draw in the 6th game in the 1935 World Championship Match between Euwe and Alekhine, Euwe playing as White. Definitely worth playing through. Who knows, had Euwe lost this tense game, he might never have become World Champion? He was certainly under great pressure in the endgame.

5...e6

Akopian finds an extra pawn recapture on d5.

6 ♘h4

6 ♗d3 ♗xd3 7 ♕xd3 is of course level, often the prelude for a quick draw offer. The only real chance of an edge is to take the bishop-pair.

6...♗g6

There have been a few attempts to allow the knight to capture on f5, doubling Black's f-pawns and weakening the d5-pawn, but hoping for Black to add extra control over the e4-square.

6...♗g4 has been tried several times, aiming to provoke White's kingside pawns. If 7 f3, then 7...♗h5 should be comfortable for Black. 7 ♕b3 is the attempt for a slight edge for White.

Another bishop escape would be 6...♗e4. White then chooses between 7 f3 and 7 ♕b3.

It is simpler, though, for the bishop to return to g6, and allow White to open Black's h-file. As the game shows, the half-open file becomes useful.

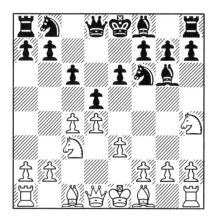

7 ♘xg6

It's simplest to get this exchange out of the way quickly.

7...hxg6

7...fxg6 is just about playable, trying to make use of the f-file, but the centre is slightly weakened.

8 h3

8 g3 has also been tried, not least by Karpov himself, and also Kramnik among others. This blunts the b8-h2 pressure against the h-pawn, and allows White the chance of a kingside fianchetto. White is not, of course, aiming for a big attack, but he would like to think that perhaps he can try for a small edge.

There are, of course, a few other moves: for example, 8 ♗d2 ♗d6 9 h3 ♘bd7, transposing into the main line.

Topalov has tried 8 a3 ♘bd7 9 g3 ♗e7, and then suddenly the more overtly aggressive 10 f4!? in his World Championship match with Kramnik.

Topalov's seemingly quiet a3 move was based on preventing Black from playing ...♗b4, and thereby stopping a ...♗xc3 exchange. Once this precaution has been made, White can play f4 without losing control of the e4-square. Topalov later won after 10...dxc4 11 ♗xc4 0-0 12 e4. His central pawn structure looks impressive but also fragile. Kramnik could not break open White's pawn centre, and after 12...b5 13 ♗e2 b4 14 axb4 ♗xb4 15 ♗f3 ♕b6 (Marin has suggested 15...c5 as an improvement) 16 0-0 e5 17 ♗e3 ♖ad8 18 ♘a4! White kept his central pawn advantage.

From this game, and Game 4, Topalov-Anand, the impression given is that Topalov has closely studied the ways in which he can find a few apparently very quiet pawn moves on the edges, and then set up sudden violent attacking ideas.

8...♘bd7

Knights before bishops – usually. He knows where the knight wants to go, but it is unclear as yet whether the bishop should play to b4, d6, or the quiet e7.

9 ♗d2

A quiet and modest move, but it is better to have the bishop on d2 rather than on c1, obstructing the rook.

If 9 ♗e2 or 9 ♗d3, Black could aim for the gain of tempo, with 9...dxc4, or equally he could ignore it.

9...♗d6

9...♗b4 10 ♕b3 seems to give White a slight edge, so he keeps the bishop more central.

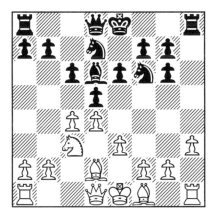

10 ♗d3!?

A slight surprise, perhaps, as White allows the gain of tempo with ...dxc4, but it is certainly not an error. Throughout his career, Karpov has developed a specialty of playing seeming quiet and seemingly uninspiring moves, and then ending up as keeping a slight edge for White, and extending the edge, and quietly winning. As Black, he would try to equalize, and then wait for any slight imperfections in his opponent's play to give himself the opportunity of aiming for a win.

Here the impression might be given that Karpov has done almost nothing with the white pieces, but look closely, and White has achieved a small but important advantage, a safe bishop-pair.

Karpov has also tried 10 ♕c2 ♕e7 11 ♗e2 dxc4 12 ♗xc4 e5 13 dxe5 ♘xe5 14 ♗e2, with a slight edge for White, A.Karpov-R.Felgaer, Buenos Aires (simul) 2003, and duly kept a slight edge and won. He decides, though, that ♕c2 is unnecessary, and that he might as well keep the queen at home.

10...dxc4

Or possibly 10...♕e7. Would Karpov then return to his simultaneous win? Or maybe 11 ♖c1!? instead.

11 ♗xc4 0-0

There are choices here. Castling is perhaps the quietest and safest, adding protection to the f7-square if Black were to try ...e5. Black loses the rook pressure on the h-file, but as the game shows, ...g6-g5-g4 is sometimes an effective attacking play for Black, even without the h8-rook.

12 0-0

Natural development.

12...e5

Recovering space with the pawn structure, but there are now possible weaknesses on the light squares.

13 dxe5

13 ♕c2 exd4 14 exd4 ♘b6 15 ♗b3 is also to be considered. White has weakened his pawns slightly, but has good piece prospects. Karpov prefers to give away nothing.

13...♘xe5

A good square for the knight.

14 ♗e2

Aiming for security, and maintaining the bishop-pair.

14 ♗b3!? is possible, a tactical point being 14...♘d3 15 ♕c2 ♘b4?, and White wins a pawn with 16 ♕xg6, but here 15...♗c7 16 ♖ad1 ♕d6 is about level.

14...g5

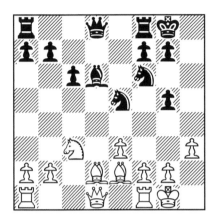

Sometimes the doubled h-pawn is a positive advantage, rather than a slight weakness. The front pawn makes its presence felt against White's kingside, while the rear pawn protects Black's king.

Even so, White is still slightly better. Akopian is setting up counterplay rather than attacking just at the moment.

15 e4

A natural reaction, continuing White's plan of development.

15...♘h7

Protecting the pawn. 15...g4? 16 hxg4 ♘fxg4 17 ♗xg4 ♕h4 18 ♗h3 doesn't work.

16 ♗e3?!

Sadly, Karpov by now was no longer at his extraordinary positional best. This bishop move is natural enough, and maybe still gives White a slight edge, but it lacks coordination with the other pieces. In particular, one thought

is that it is the knight, rather than the bishop, that should reside on e3, covering several important light squares in the centre and on the kingside. Thus 16 ♕c2!? ♕e7 17 ♘d1, then maybe 17...♖fd8 18 ♘e3, and the knight is at least as powerful as Black's. Later White's bishop could emerge on c3, with good play.

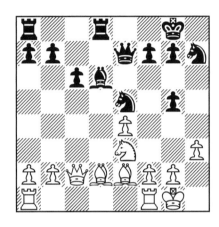

18...g6!? will lead to tactics after, for example, 19 ♘c4 ♘xc4 20 ♗xc4 g4! 21 hxg4 (but not 21 e5? ♕xe5 22 ♕xg6+?? ♔h8, and Black wins material). Then the most direct attack is 21...♕h4?, but White refutes Black's play with 22 e5! ♗xe5 23 ♕xg6+ ♔h8 24 ♕h6 ♕xg4 25 ♗xf7 ♖g8 26 ♗xg8 ♖xg8 27 ♕h1! (an echo of the Adams-Yusupov, Game 3), and Black runs out of attacking ideas.

So we try instead 21...♕e5, and there is an echo from the other side after 22 f4? ♕d4+ 23 ♔h1 ♕h8! 24 ♔h2 g5 25 ♔g3 ♘f6 26 ♖h1 ♕g7 27 ♔f3 ♗xf4 with unclear play. 22 g3 is, of course, better, and after 22...♘g5 23 ♗xg5 ♕xg5 White keeps a slight edge, with an extra doubled pawn in an opposite-coloured bishop middlegame.

Earlier, 16...g4?! is again premature: 17 hxg4 ♕h4 18 ♗f4! blocks Black's critical diagonal. If, for example, 18...♘g5? 19 ♗g3 ♘ef3+ 20 ♗xf3 ♘xf3+ 21 gxf3 ♗xg3 22 fxg3 ♕xg3+ 23 ♕g2, and White pockets the piece.

All this should only be regarded as provisional. There are plenty of ideas to be considered.

16...♕e7

Akopian sets up a plan of bringing his king's rook to d8, then his knight back to f8.

17 ♕c2

A natural move. The computer suggests that there are a dozen ways in which White has an advantage. Quite probably the computer can overstate the bishop-pair. The human player might suggest that it is about equal, that Karpov has not proved any real advantage, and that Akopian has not yet taken control.

17...♖fd8

Continuing his plan.

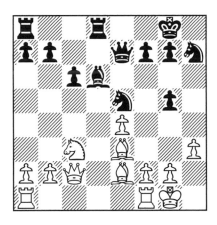

18 ♘a4?!

This is quite simply a strange loss of time. The knight takes three moves to get to a worse square.

18 ♖fd1 ♘f8 19 ♖d2 ♘e6 20 ♖ad1 ♘f4 is about equal.

18...♘f8!

Akopian's knight move is far more relevant. The knight soon returns to e6, then maybe to d4 or f4.

19 ♘c5

It is moving forward, but where to next?

19...b6

Akopian asks the question.

20 ♘b3

20 ♘d3 ♘xd3 21 ♗xd3 ♘d7 is about equal, maybe fractionally better for Black. Again the bishop-pair is of little importance when the opponent has an active bishop and good squares for the knight, preferably with the help of pawns protecting outposts.

Not, of course, 22 ♕xc6?? ♘e5 23 ♕c2 ♘xd3 24 ♕xd3 ♗h2 mate.

20...♘e6

20...c5 looks slightly more accurate, squeezing White's knight into inactive play.

21 ♖fd1

21 ♘d4! ♘xd4 22 ♗xd4 is about equal.

21...c5

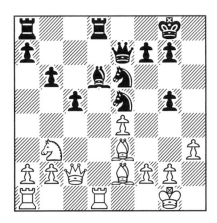

Akopian now has a well-balanced pawn and piece structure in the centre, but he cannot claim yet that Black is better. Karpov still has the bishop-pair, and Black has to be careful to maintain the balance on the light squares.

22 a3?!

An extremely difficult move to annotate. Probably the simplest answer is that Karpov was suffering from fatigue over the last few moves, his play having been discernibly listless. Alas, age drifts in. There are no players aged over 50 in the 2700+ list, and few aged over 40. It is difficult to maintain such intense concentration after the mid-30s.

Quite probably Karpov would have been drifting over the last few moves, not making any gross blunders, but relying a little too much on the assumption that the bishop-pair will keep an edge, and all he has to do is to keep playing steady moves. Akopian is making quite a few constructive moves in reply, and before too long he is able to take the initiative.

22 Rd2 Nc6 23 Rad1 Nb4 24 Qb1 gives White possibly a slight edge, but here 22...Nf4!? is probably equal. If 23 Bxf4 gxf4, the computer suggests that White is better, but after 24 Rad1 there is 24...f3!, a standard pawn sacrifice doubling pawns in front of the king, which cannot even be regarded as controversial. Black should be at least equal.

22...a5!?

Akopian makes active use of the queenside pawn majority. Also, he waits to see whether his knight should end up on d4 rather than on f4. Certainly 22...Nf4 is possible and playable, but by waiting, and advancing a pawn actively, Black is adding to White's tension. It is difficult to find a string of good moves for White to cover both knight moves.

23 Nd2?!

It is as if Karpov senses that he should defend Akopian's attack, and that the resulting position is a draw. Unfortunately, Akopian is not ready for a quick half-half, and finds ways of playing for a win.

But shouldn't White be trying for a slight edge anyway? Sometimes it takes several minor inaccuracies to turn White from having a slight advantage to Black being equal or better. 23 Rac1 is natural, and if 23...a4 24 Nd2. White eventually has to play the knight to d2 anyway, but in comparison with the game, White's Rac1 is far more effective than Black's ...a4. Indeed Black's extra pawn move is a weakness, rather than a strength. If Black were, for example, to play an early ...Rac8, White simply takes the pawn on a4. Here we have:

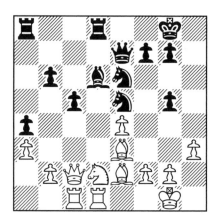

a) After 24...Nd4 25 Bxd4 cxd4 26 Nc4!? Nxc4 27 Bxc4 White would have slightly the better chances.

b) 24...Nc6 is to be considered, but after 25 Nf3 White will have good control of the light squares, with, for example, Bb5 or Bc4.

Of course, it is quite possible that

Black would not want to play 23...a4 immediately. 23...♘g6!? would keep the tension alive.

23...♘d4!

Black is now think of playing for an edge.

23...♘c6 24 ♘f3 ♘cd4 25 ♗xd4 ♘xd4 26 ♘xd4 cxd4 gives White slightly the better chances.

24 ♗xd4

Obviously the only move, but now Karpov loses his bishop-pair.

24...cxd4

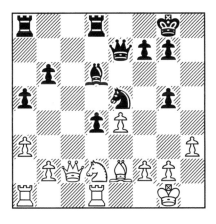

And Black now has a passed, if isolated, pawn. What can he do with the pawn, though?

25 ♘f1

An indication perhaps that Karpov sees that there are now problems with his position. This retreat is not something that one would want to make.

25 ♘c4 allows Black to set up tactics with 25...♖ac8 26 ♕b3 d3 27 ♗xd3 ♕e6 28 ♖ac1 ♗e7. White can just slip out, though, with 29 ♗e2! ♖xd1+ 30 ♕xd1, the point being 30...♘xc4? 31 ♗g4! with a winning skewer. Instead the preferable 30...♖xc4 31 ♗xc4 ♘xc4 32 ♕b3 ♘e5 33 ♕b5!? leads to tense play, ending up about equal in an endgame.

25...♖ac8

Thank you! A gain of tempo starts an attack.

26 ♕b1

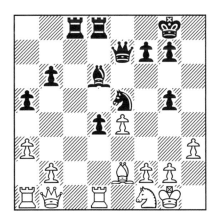

26...d3!?

This pawn sacrifice sets up the win, but on closer examination it is not as convincing as the final result might suggest. Black is by no means worse after his pawn sacrifice, but maybe is not much better.

26...♗c5!? is a secure slight edge, and White forever has to take account of the sword thrust with ...d3. If 27 ♘g3 g6, Black also has the possibility of ...♔g7 followed by ...♖h8, and another thrust, ...g4.

27 ♗xd3

Forced.

27...♗c5

Black's passed pawn has vaporized, but the empty square on d4 allows Black excellent play on the d-pawn and on the b6-g1 diagonal.

A nightmare for the small hours would be 27...♘xd3? 28 ♖xd3 ♕xe4?? 29 ♖xd6 ♕xb1 30 ♖xd8+ ♖xd8 31 ♖xb1, and Black loses a piece.

28 ♗a6

This is more subtle than it looks. The

point is not just that the bishop is attacking the rook, but also, as we shall see later, that the bishop is covering a significant defensive square on c8 for the queen.

It is quite possible that Akopian in his analysis had concentrated more on the more natural defensive move, 28 ♗e2, when Black is doing well after 28...g4 29 hxg4 ♕h4 30 ♘e3 ♗xe3 31 fxe3 ♕g3. White is two pawns up, but with two sets of doubled isolated pawns, a first pawn will go quickly, and most likely soon the second pawn. If White were to try 30 g3, then there is kingside danger after 30...♕h3 31 b4 axb4 32 axb4 ♗d4 33 ♖a2 ♖c3 34 ♖ad2? ♖xg3+. White holds the position better with 34 ♖xd4! ♖xd4 35 ♕a1 ♖dc4. A possible draw is 36 ♖a8+ ♔h7 37 ♖d8 ♘f3+ 38 ♘xf3 ♖xf3 39 ♘d2 ♖fc3! 40 ♘xc4 ♖xg3+ 41 gxf3 ♕xf3+ 42 ♔f1 ♕f3+.

28...♖c6

Aiming for any of the kingside files.

29 ♖xd8+

Simplification is welcome.

29...♕xd8

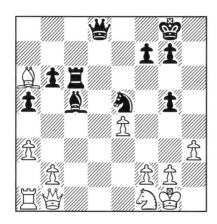

30 ♕d1?!

'If in doubt, centralize.' A useful

principle, but it does not always work.

30 b4!? not just hits the bishop, but allows defence on the kingside after ♖a2. After 30...♗d4 31 ♖a2 g4 32 ♕b3, White's play might still be uncomfortable, but at least he has gained a tempo with ♕b1-b3 instead of ♕b1-d1-b3.

Black can, however, play more aggressively with 30...♗xf2+!? 31 ♔xf2. Then it is not so clear whether Black is genuinely attacking after 31...♕d4+?! 32 ♔e2!?, and if 32...♖f6 33 ♘e3. However, a simpler approach is 31...b5, recovering the bishop, and keeping White's king slightly exposed. White's play is difficult, but he has chances of holding after, for example, 32 ♗xb5 ♕b6+ 33 ♘e3 ♖f6+ 34 ♔g1 ♕xe3+ 35 ♔h1 g4 (or 35...♘g4 36 ♕e1 ♘f2+ 36 ♔h2 ♘g4+, repeating) 36 ♕g1, fizzling out as equality.

30...♖d6

Of course, Black keeps the queens. He wants to play for checkmate.

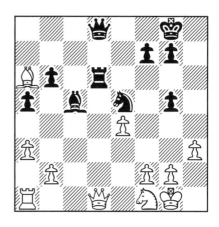

31 ♕b3

Aiming to defend along the third rank.

If 31 ♕e2 g4 32 hxg4 (32 b4 ♗d4 33 ♖c1 ♕h4 is also uncomfortable) 32...♕h4 33 g3 ♕h3 34 g5 ♘g4 35 ♗c8

♖e6!, and White is in trouble.

31...♖f6

31...♕f6 or 31...g4 would both only hold the balance after 32 ♕g3. Black needs to find something spikier on f2.

32 ♕d5

32 ♘e3 ♕d2 33 ♖f1 (33 ♕c2 ♗xe3) 33...♖xf2! 34 ♖xf2 ♗xe3 is a simple sacrificial attack.

32...♕c7

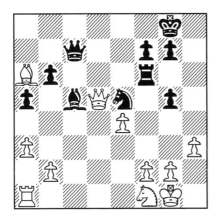

It has become evident that Black is breaking through on the dark squares.

33 b4

Hoping to reduce the damage.

33 ♖d1? ♖xf2 34 ♕d8+ ♕xd8 35 ♖xd8 ♔h7 leaves White facing problems with a discovered check. After 36 b4 ♖d2+ 37 bxc5 ♖xd8 38 cxb6 ♘d7 39 b7 ♘c5, Black is a clear exchange up.

33 ♘e3? ♗xe3 34 fxe3 ♘f3+! 35 ♔f2 (35 gxf3 ♕g3+ leads to quick checkmate) 35...♘h4+ 36 ♔g1 ♕g3, and Black has a winning attack: 37 e5 ♘f3+ 38 ♔f1 ♘xe5+ 39 ♔g1 ♘f3+ 40 ♔f1 ♘e1+ 41 ♔g1 g5 merely lasts a little longer.

33...♗xf2+

If White is not being checkmated yet, then he still has hope.

34 ♔h1 g4

Finally Black has the opportunity of setting up the thematic attack with the front pawn of the doubled g-pawns.

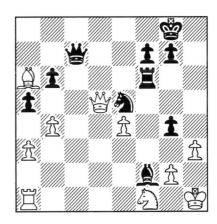

35 ♖d1

35 ♖a2 is possible, and there is no immediate winning attack after 35...gxh3 36 gxh3, but White's lack of pawn structure in front of the king is a concern.

35...♔h7

He doesn't want a queen exchange to occur.

36 ♕d8 ♕c3 37 ♕c8

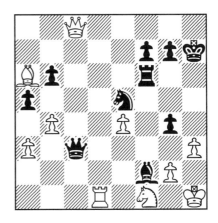

Some chasing after the queen.

37...♖f3!

An attractive way of bringing the other pieces into play.

37...♕xa3? 38 ♖d8 gxh3 39 ♖h8+

♔g6 40 ♖xh3 leaves Black's king in as much danger as White's.

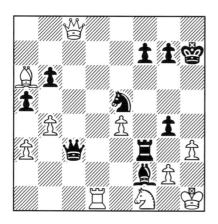

38 ♘h2

Of course, White is checkmated after 38 gxf3?? ♕xf3+ 39 ♔h2 ♕xh3. Similarly, 38 ♖d8?? ♖xh3+ leads to mate.

38 ♕xc3 ♖xc3 39 ♖d2 g3 is uncomfortable. White's king is stuck in the corner, and the other pieces are forced to defend passively.

38...♕xc8 39 ♗xc8 ♖xa3

Both players have been forced to exchange queens, but Black has gained a vital tempo with his ...♖f3 push.

40 bxa5

White would not gain all that much in aiming for a rook and opposite-coloured bishop endgame after 40 ♘xg4 ♘xg4 41 ♗xg4 axb4 42 ♖b1 ♗c5;

White's bishop is totally passive.

40...g3 41 ♘f3

Black will eventually win after 41 axb6 gxh2 42 b7 ♖b3 43 ♔xh2 ♗g3+.

41...♘xf3 42 gxf3 ♖a2!

Black has no need to bother taking the pawn. He is aiming for checkmate.

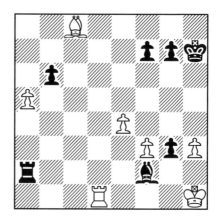

43 ♔g2

If 43 axb6 ♗xb6 followed by checkmate.

43...♗e1+

Again more accurate than taking the pawn.

44 ♔f1 ♗b4

Rather than taking the pawn. Black wants to use the c5-g1 diagonal.

45 ♖d5 g2+ 46 ♔g1 ♗c5+ 0-1

White decides it is not worth giving up the exchange.

Game 12
E.Bareev-Z.Efimenko
Turin Olympiad 2006
Nimzo-Indian Defence E32

1 d4 ♘f6 2 c4 e6 3 ♘c3

For 3 ♘f3, see Game 4, Anand-Topalov, and subsequent games.

3...♗b4

The Nimzo-Indian.

4 ♕c2

Alternatively, for 4 ♘f3, see Game 26, Wang Yue-Movsesian, and for 4 e3, see Game 15, Sokolov-Polgar.

The ♕c2 idea was the original 'classical' variation. White does not want doubled pawns on the c-file, and wants to play a3, while recapturing with the queen after the exchange on c3. It is all very logical, as White gains the bishop-pair, but it also slows down his development. The queen spends two moves, and will quite likely have to move again in view of a possible hit with ...♘e4.

4...0-0

Not the only move, but Black sorts out the kingside quickly.

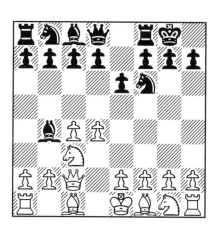

5 a3

Carrying on with the plan.

5 e4 is the most obvious move, and indeed who would not be tempted by this? There is, however, the danger that with his aggressive pawn rush in the centre, White is also creating weaknesses on d4 or e4.

One possibility for Black is the restrained 5...d6, and if 6 a3 ♗xc3+ 7 bxc3 e5 followed by ...♘c6, then perhaps ...b6 and ....♗a6. If White were to try d5, his central pawn structure would now be rigid, and one possibility for Black is to set up a pawn break with ...c6, and with due timing, to open up the half-open c-file. White has to be careful to play actively. In I.Sokolov-V.Bologan, Sarajevo 2006, play continued 8 ♗d3 ♘c6 9 ♘e2 b6 10 0-0 ♗a6 11 f4 ♘d7 12 ♖f3!? ♘a5 13 c5 ♗xd3 14 ♖xd3 with a likely edge for White, who later won.

The alternative for Black is immediate counterplay with 5...d5!?. An indication of the sharpness of play is given by V.Ivanchuk-D.Navara, Antalya 2004: 6 e5 ♘e4 7 a3 ♗xc3+ 8 bxc3 c5 9 ♗d3 cxd4 10 cxd4 ♘c6 11 ♘e2 ♕a5+ 12 ♔f1 ♘b4!? (12...f6 and 12...f5 have also been tried) 13 axb4 ♕xa1 14 f3 f5 15 ♕a1 ♕a4 (15...♕xb1 16 ♗xb1 leaves the knight trapped) 16 ♔e1 a5! 15 fxe4 fxe4 18 ♗c2 ♕xb4+ 19 ♕xb4 axb4, and after 20 cxd5 exd5 21 ♗b3 ♗e6, Ivanchuk eventually had to struggle for a draw.

Golod suggests 20 ♗b3!? dxc4 21 ♗xc4, assessing this as favourable to White. Black has rook and two pawns versus two minor pieces, normally a slight material edge if Black's pawns are well co-ordinated. Unfortunately Black also has two sets of isolated doubled pawns, which require careful guarding. Also, as Golod notes, White can make use of his own advanced pawns with 21...♖a1 22 d5!. This is one of several complicated lines in this opening. Both players will need to be well prepared in the main line after 5 e4 d5.

5...♗xc3+

If you dislike giving away the bishop-pair, you should not play the Nimzo!

6 ♕xc3 b6

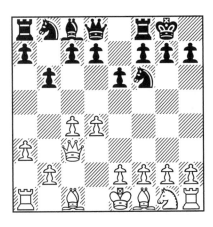

The main line. Black quickly fi-anchettoes on the remaining long diagonal.

6...b5!?, popularized by Adorjan, looks like a complete finger-slip, but if White takes on the extra pawn, Black has annoying compensation with pressure on the light-coloured squares. A recent attempt to hold on to the extra pawn was A.Motylev-A.Naiditsch, German League 2006: 7 cxb5 c6 8 e3 cxb5 9 ♗xb5 ♘e4 10 ♕b3 ♗a6 11 ♕a4 ♕g5 12 ♗f1! ♗xf1 13 ♔xf1 ♘c6 14 f3 ♘d6 15 ♘e2 ♖ab8 16 ♔f2 ♕h4 17 g3 ♕h3 18 ♕d1, and White was able to consolidate, and later won.

6...d6 is fully playable.

7 ♗g5

White in return sets up an awkward pin. One of the drastic ways for Black is to play ...h6 and ...g5, but there is the danger of weakening squares in front of his king.

7 e3 ♗b7 8 ♘f3 is less aggressive. After 8...d5 White has forfeited his pressure with the bishop on the h4-d8 diagonal.

7...♗b7

For the moment he quietly develops.

The drastic 7...♘d5? 8 ♗xd8 ♘xc3 9 ♗xc7 merely wins a pawn for White, but quite often both players need to watch this idea for several moves. If, for example, White plays an early ♖d1, Black can attack the rook after ...♘xc3 in this sequence.

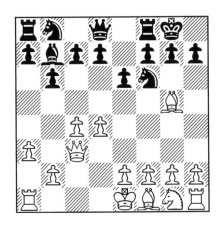

8 e3

For 8 f3, see Game 13, Kramnik-Leko.

8 ♘f3 d6 9 ♘d2 is a possibility, but White has not made much impact with this variation.

8...d6

Black can flick in 8...h6 9 ♗h4, but there is no particular reason to do so. If anything, there is more counterplay for Black if the bishop is on g5, rather than the less exposed square on h4.

9 ♘e2

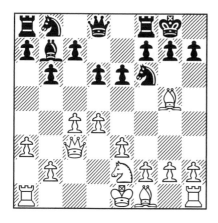

Bareev's favoured line.

9 ♘f3 is more common. The problem is that Black has good control of e4, and may even consider at some stage ...h6; ♗h4 g5; ♗g3 followed by ...♘e4. Sometimes White has played 8 ♘f3 a move earlier, to give the chance of playing ♘d2 quickly.

Bareev's idea is to swing his knight to c3 instead, covering e4. It takes time, not least because the queen has to move yet again, but Bareev could argue that if his pieces can consolidate, without Black being able to create counterplay in time, he will have chances of being better.

9...♘bd7

Completing his piece development. Now he has to decide what to do with the pawns.

10 ♕c2

The less than obvious 10 ♕d3!? has been tried several times, the queen being on a more aggressive square, but

also being more likely to be hit after a pawn exchange in the centre. Bareev played this a couple of times against Karpov, in both cases offering a pawn sacrifice on g2.

E.Bareev-A.Karpov, Wijk aan Zee 2003, continued 10...h6 11 ♗h4 c5 12 ♘c3 ♕e7 13 ♖d1 ♖fd8 14 ♗e2 cxd4 15 ♕xd4 ♘c5 16 ♗xf6 ♕xf6 17 ♕xf6 gxf6 18 ♘b5 d5 19 cxd5 ♗xd5 20 ♘c7 ♗b3 21 ♘xa8 ♗xd1 22 ♗xd1 ♖xa8 23 ♗c2 with a slight edge for White in a rook and minor piece endgame, but Karpov successfully held the draw.

There were a couple of opportunities for Black to snatch the g-pawn, with some degree of risk. For example, 14...♗xg2?! 15 ♖g1 ♗b7 16 e4 allows White definite attacking chances on the kingside. A move later, 15...♗xg2?! (instead of 15...♘c5) 16 ♖g1 ♗b7 allows the previous gambit line with 17 e4, or White could simply recover the pawn with 17 ♕xd6 with a slight edge.

Going back even earlier, in E.Bareev-A.Karpov, Cap d'Agde (rapid) 2002, White omitted ♖d1, pressing on d6, and tried to sacrifice too early with 13 ♗e2?! cxd4 14 ♕xd4 e5! (no ♕xd6 attack for White) 15 ♕d1 ♗xg2 16 ♖g1 ♗c6, and the pawn sacrifice was rather more speculative, although the game again finished as a draw. Quite clearly Bareev will have experimented at home with slightly different sacrifices on the g2-square, aiming for improvements.

10...c5

A natural reaction for Black, exchanging a bishop's pawn against a central pawn with the likelihood of gaining an extra pawn in the centre. Indeed, with Black's c-file being half-open, one can even wonder whether it was wise for White to place his queen on c2. Bareev has, of course, evaluated such positions well in advance, and demonstrates his plan.

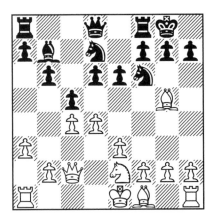

11 ℤd1

Immediately creating pressure on the d-file, a sensible reaction.

In V.Ivanchuk-V.Topalov, Linares 1999, White was in trouble, Black winning the c-pawn, after 11 ♘c3?! dxc4 12 exd4 ♕c7 13 ♗d3 ℤac8 14 0-0 ♗a6. The game was eventually drawn, though, after long rearguard play.

11...ℤc8

Continuing the main plan.

11...♕e7 is probably playable, but it is useful to place pressure on the opponent.

12 ♘c3

A good square for the knight, but of course it is slow. White has gained the bishop-pair, but to set up the knight on c3, he has to make three moves with the queen (♕c2, ♕xc3 and another queen move), an a3 pawn push, and an extra move with the knight (♘g1-e2-c3). Indeed, White has not even found time to castle, and soon has to take drastic measures.

12...cxd4

Not as automatic as it looks. Black has ideas with his queen, and so he disregards such moves as 12...♕e7.

13 ℤxd4

Improving on the older plan with 13 exd4 – compare with the Ivanchuk-Topalov game, above.

13...ℤc5

A hit on the g5-bishop, and finally helping explain why Black did not particularly want to throw in an earlier ...h6; ♗h4 insertion.

14 ♗h4

White keeps his hard-won bishop.

14 ♗xf6 ♘xf6 15 ♘b5 ♕a8 16 ♘xd6 ♗xg2 is possible, but only equal.

14...♕a8

Famed as the 'Réti manoeuvre', startling almost a century ago, but standard now. What is White going to do on the long diagonal?

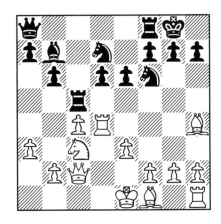

15 ♗e2!

White is prepared to sacrifice a pawn on g2, and will even, as the game shows, allow the pawn to drop after he has castled. White has lost time with his slow and methodical manoeuvring, and he does not want to lose any more.

15 e4, setting up a Hedgehog structure, is the main alternative, but

15...d5! seems to equalize. After 16 b4 ♖c7! (more accurate than 16...♖cc8 17 cxd5 exd5 18 ♗b5) 17 ♗xf6 ♘xf6 18 e5 ♘d7 19 ♘b5 ♖c6 20 f4 (20 ♗d3 ♘xe5!) 20...f6 Black is at least equal. Here 17 ♗g3 e5 18 ♘xd5 ♘xd5 19 exd5 exd4 20 ♗xc7 ♖c8 followed by ...♗xd5 is good for Black. Again, White's lack of development creates problems if the central squares are quickly opened.

15...d5

It is too early to snatch the pawn. After 15...♗xg2?! 16 ♖g1 it is Black's king that is in danger. 16...♗b7 17 ♖xd6 gives White an edge.

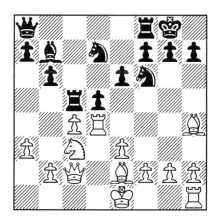

16 b4

Pushing Black's rook to a less effective square, but also weakening the squares on the c-file.

16 0-0 dxc4 is equal, but Dreev looked for an improvement with 16 ♕d1!? e5 17 ♖d2 d4 18 exd4 exd4 19 ♖xd4 ♗xg2 20 ♖g1 ♗h3 21 ♖d6, A.Dreev-D.Jakovenko, Russian Championship, Moscow 2007, and an advantage to White, who has the more active pieces. This may well be an improvement, although Black may also consider 16...♖e8!?.

Naturally Dreev will have played

through this earlier game, seen the original idea as interesting, and looked for slight but significant modifications. This is how chess theory develops.

16...♖cc8

The natural move, but other retreats could be considered.

17 0-0

The only good move, but he has to be prepared to allow his opponent to take the long diagonal.

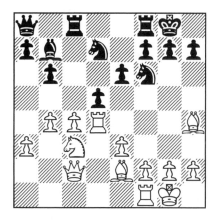

17...e5

17...dxc4 is to be considered, and helps explains why Dreev later chose the 16 ♕d1 idea instead. Dreev would have two major pieces to cover the knight on d7. 18 ♖fd1 attacks the knight, even so, and the position is perhaps best regarded as level, but tense. A quiet way of playing would be 18...♘e5 19 ♗xf6 gxf6. A more aggressive idea for Black is 18...♗xg2 19 e4 ♗h3 20 ♖xd7 ♘xd7 21 ♖xd7 e5, and who plays better, wins. The computer suggests that Black is better, but this is probably usual the point that computers tend to overestimate a slight material advantage.

White instead tried 18 f3!? in R.Kasimdzhanov-A.Grischuk, Moscow

2007, and Grischuk won after 18...♘e5 19 ♗xf6 gxf6 20 ♘b5 ♕b8 21 ♘d6, but this was a blitz game, and one should not make too many conclusions from the result. White was slightly better before he later lost.

18 ♖d2

The only sensible retreat. White needs to have both rooks on the d-file.

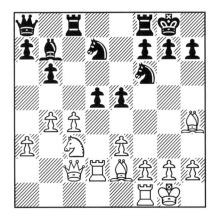

18...d4

Taking the long diagonal by force.

If 18...dxc4 19 ♖fd1?!, Black has gained a useful tempo after 19...♗xg2 20 ♖xd7 ♘xd7 21 ♖xd7 ♗h3, and the rook is already attacked. Black is better after 22 ♖d5 f6. However, 19 f3 would attempt to hold the balance after, for example, 19...a6 20 ♖fd1 ♗c6 21 ♕f5 b5 22 ♗xf6 ♘xf6 23 ♕xe5. Black's passed pawn might look dangerous, but it is difficult to dislodge the knight from c3.

19 exd4

The only move. If 19 ♘b5?, then simply 19...♗xg2.

19...♗xg2

This looks dangerous! Black has now taken the long diagonal, and is threatening to threaten checkmate. But, to adapt a comment by Tarrasch a century ago, if you are worried about a threat of

checkmate, you might just as well give up chess.

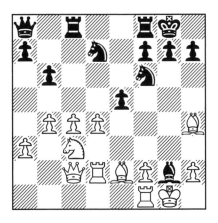

20 ♖fd1

The rooks will now have a dangerous open file.

20...exd4

Otherwise White will block the diagonal with 20...♗h3 21 d5. White would have an advanced protected passed pawn, and Black's minor pieces get in each others' way.

21 ♖xd4

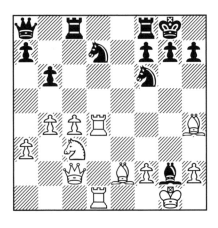

The end of the tactical skirmishes, and the players must work out what is going on, positionally.

The most obvious point is that Black has taken the long diagonal, with queen and bishop, and White's king is exposed through the loss of the g-pawn. Black is not, however, in complete control, and White's pieces are otherwise well placed.

Once it is clear that Black is not about to give checkmate, White has various plus points, which may tip the balance. White has excellent control with the rooks on the d-file, which, with the help of his bishop on h4, places a strain on Black's knights. Indeed, despite the mate threat on g2, White's minor pieces are overall much more imposing than Black's.

And the pawns? We shall see. Imagine several pieces being exchanged, though, and it is easy to work out that White's queenside pawns are much easier to convert for a passed pawn than Black's kingside pawns, despite the pawn isolation of the f- and h-pawns.

White is, in total, slightly better.

21...♗h3

If 21...♗h1, then 22 ♗f1 covers the g2-square, essential but also good. White has one weak square, but the rest of his piece structure is good. Here 22 f3 ♗xf3 23 ♖xd7 ♘xd7 24 ♖xd7 ♗xe2 25 ♕xe2 is far less clear.

21...♘e5 22 ♗xf6 gxf6 23 ♕f5 ♘f3+ 24 ♗xf3 ♗xf3?? is a race for one of the players to check on the g-file, but White wins after 25 ♖1d3. 24...♕xf3 25 ♕xf3 ♗xf3 26 ♖1d3 is better, but White still has a clear advantage, with the better pieces and a better pawn structure.

22 ♘e4

Simple chess. White does not have to worry about complicated lines, such as 22 f3 followed by ♔f2 and ♖g1, when there are straightforward excellent

winning chances by taking control of the centre, and aiming for a good endgame.

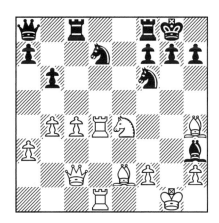

22...♘xe4

Maybe Efimenko is a little too eager to acquiesce for simplification.

22...♔h8!? 23 ♕c3 ♖ce8 24 ♕xh3 ♖xe4 25 ♗f3 ♖xd4 26 ♖xd4 ♕c8 (with possible threats of ...♘e5) is not so good for White as at first appears. If Black can play ...♖e8, with thoughts of protecting his knights on the e-file, he can take advantage of the weaknesses of the isolated pawns on the kingside, with the absence of the g-file making it difficult to cover the f-file. 24 f3!? instead is to be considered. After 24...♘xe4 25 fxe4, the isolated pawn is slightly uncomfortable, given that Black can place the knight on e5, but White's overall piece structure is slightly better, and he has chances of making pressure with the extra queenside pawn.

23 ♕xe4

Endgame coming up.

23...♕xe4

Simplest. 23...♘e5?! is too elaborate, and White gains time after 24 ♕xa8 ♖xa8 25 f4.

24 ♖xe4 ♖fe8

Black does not want to give away control of both central files.

25 ℤxe8+

White may not be worse after various alternatives, but this again is the simplest and most direct. Black keeps the e-file, but White keeps the d-file, and with nurturing the bishop-pair will gradually slightly overrun the bishop and knight.

25...ℤxe8

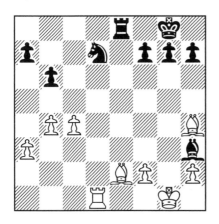

26 ℤd2!

Maybe Efimenko had underestimated this quiet move? White's bishop remains on a good square, and although it is temporarily pinned, Black cannot attack the bishop. After f3, at an appropriate stage, White unravels his pieces with for example ♔f2, and he will have the extra queenside passed pawn, well away from Black's king, and a useful and effective bishop-pair.

28...ℤe4

Black wants to stay active.

27 ♗g3

White is still slightly better. Sooner or later, Black will experience pressure from the fragile queenside pawns.

27...g5

Playable, and indeed probably the best, but on his next move Efimenko seems to change his mind, and loses a tempo as a result.

27...f6 28 a4 ♔f7 29 f3 ℤe3 30 ♔f2 ℤa3 31 ♗d1 ♘e5 saves a tempo for Black, but even here White still has winning chances after, for example, 32 ♗xe5 fxe5 33 c5 bxc5 34 bxc5 ℤc3 35 ℤc2 ℤxc2 36 ♗xc2 ♔e6 37 ♗e4. White's plan of attack would be ♔e3, then ♗b7. If Black were to try ...♗f5, then ♗c8+ would be a win for White. If ...♗f1, then White can push the king away from the critical square on e6 with ♔e4 followed by ♗c8+.

28 a4

If 28 f3 ℤe3, and the rook can attack behind White's queenside pawns.

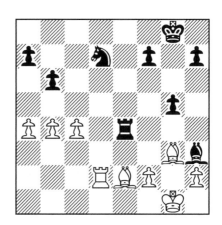

28...f6?

Changing his mind.

28...g4! is better and more consistent. Black can no longer move his bishop again, unless White gives a hand, but White's pieces are equally constrained. In the end, it is going to be more important for White, rather than Black, to unblock the kingside. 29 f3 gxf3 30 ♗d3 ℤe8 31 ♔f2 will probably end up with White having very slightly the better of a draw:

a) 31...♗g4?! 32 c5! bxc5 33 ♗b5 cxb4 34 ♗xd7 ♖d8 35 ♖d5 ♖xd7 36 ♖b5+ leaves Black in trouble though.

b) 31...♘e5 32 ♗xe5 ♖xe5 33 ♔xf3 still requires Black to take care. If the rooks get exchanged, for example, White will probably win. The safest defensive option would seem to be 33...♗e6 34 ♖e2 ♖h5 35 ♔e3 ♖h4, then Black centralizes the king. Play should end up as a draw.

29 ♗c7

Now the bishop is activated.

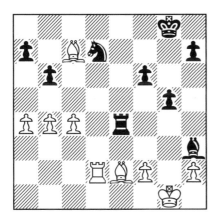

29...♘e5

If Black were thinking of playing 29...g4?!, he has left it too late: 30 f3 gxf3 31 ♗xf3 ♖xc4?? 32 ♗d5+, and White wins a rook.

30 f3

White must deal with the ...♘f3+ threat, but he wanted to play f3 anyway.

30...♖e3

Aiming for a counterattack.

30...♖f4 31 ♔f2 (31 ♗xe5 fxe5 draws) 31...♔f7 32 ♖d8 allows White to break through on the kingside: for example, 32...♘c6 33 ♖a8 ♖d4 34 b5 ♖d7 35 ♗xb6 axb6 36 bxc6 ♖c7 37 ♖a6 ♖xc6 38 a5.

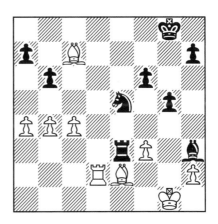

31 ♔f2

King to the centre. If in doubt, this is often not a bad idea in the endgame.

31...♖b3

Black would like to force the b-pawn to advance.

31...♖a3 32 a5 bxa5 33 ♗xa5 ♘c6 34 ♖a6 ♘xa5 35 ♖a6! gives White a substantial edge.

32 b5

The best chance of playing for a win.

32 ♗xe5 fxe5 33 ♖d8+ ♔g7 34 ♖a8 ♖xb4 35 ♖xa7+ ♔f6 36 ♖xh7 ♗e6 37 ♖b7 ♗xc4 ♖xc4 39 ♖xb6+ ♔f5 40 a5 ♖a4 allows Black to hold, even though a pawn down. For example, 41 a6 ♖a2+ 42 ♔g3 ♖a3 43 h3 e4 44 ♖b5+ ♔f6 45 ♔g4 exf3 46 ♖f5+ ♔g6 47 ♖xg5+ ♔h6, draw, or 41 ♖a6 e4 42 fxe4+ ♔xe4 43 ♔g3 ♔f5 44 ♖a8 ♖a3+ 45 ♔f2 ♖a2+ 46 ♔e3 (otherwise, if Black wants to keep the pawn, he has to allow a perpetual) 46...♖xh2 47 a6 ♖a2 48 a7 ♔g4, again with a draw.

32...♖b4

32...♗e6 33 ♖d8+ ♔f7 34 ♗xe5 fxe5 35 ♖a8 should win for White.

33 ♖d8+

A necessary part of White's plan of attack.

33 a5?! ♘xc4 34 ♖d4 ♗e6 35 a6? (35 axb6 draws) 35...♖b2 36 ♗b8 ♘a3! turns out to be good for Black.

33...♔f7

Black prefers to bring the king to the centre. Maybe there is some argument for trying 33...♔g7, to avoid any bishop checks on the a2-g8 diagonal, but this is hardly of any great relevance, as the main checking line will be after a later ♖xa7+.

34 ♖a8

Behind the pawns.

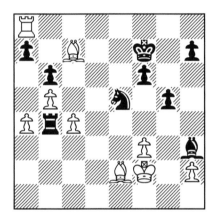

34...♘xc4

This ends up as a win for White.

34...♖xa4!? leads to some interesting play, but does not quite seem to hold. The natural 35 ♗xb6 would lead to a quick win for White after 35...♘xc4? 36 ♖xa7+ ♖xa7 37 ♗xc4+!, picking up a piece after a zwischenzug. However, Black can try for startling cheapo sacrifices with 35...♗e6 36 c5 ♘xf3!? 37 ♗xf3 (37 ♔xf3 ♗d5+) 37...♖a2+, which might occasionally work just before the time control. Then, not immediately obviously, 38 ♔g3! is best, keeping the extra piece. If 38...g4?!, then simply 39 ♗xg4, and the king protects the bishop.

35 ♖xa7

With threats of discovered checks, cutting down Black's defensive options.

35...♔e6

35...♗d7 36 ♗xc4+ ♖xc4 37 ♗xb6 will eventually win for White, maybe with a later b6 advance, ignoring the a4-pawn.

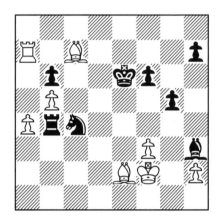

36 ♗xc4+

White is not too bothered about the supposed drawing effects of the bishops of opposite colours when he has a forced win by aiming to queen a pawn. Black's bishop on h3 is out of place when compared with White's a- and b-pawns.

36...♖xc4 37 a5

Aiming for a touchdown.

37 ♗xb6 is possible, but fiddly. Bareev wants to keep the pawn on the board, so he can threaten to attack with axb6.

37...♖c2+

37...bxa5 38 b6 ♖b4 39 b7 queens with the other pawn.

38 ♔e3

Maybe 38 ♔e1 is fractionally more accurate, but both moves win. Usually there is no time to think on move 38. If you see a reasonable move, play it.

38...♗f1

38...f5 39 ♔d3 ♖f2 40 axb6 ♖xf3+ 41 ♔d2 ♗g2 42 b7 ♖f2+ 43 ♔e1 ♖f1+ 44 ♔e2 wins for White.

39 axb6

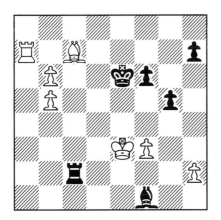

39...f5

A more delicate mating threat is 39...♔d5!? (39...♗xb5 will transpose) 40 b7 ♗xb5 (there are no good discovered checks after 40...♖e2+ 41 ♔d3) 41 f4 (41 b8♕?? ♖e2 mate) 41...g4 42 f5!, and the king escapes and the pawn queens.

40 b7

Winning, but there is one last trick to try.

40...f4+

A last-breath attempt. Naturally, 40...♖c7 41 b8♕ f4+ 42 ♔d2 wins easily for White.

41 ♗xf4

Avoiding 41 ♔e4?? (or 41 ♔d4??) 41...♖c4 mate.

41...gxf4+ 42 ♔xf4 1-0

White queens a pawn.

Game 13
V.Kramnik-P.Leko
Dortmund 2006
Nimzo-Indian Defence E32

1 d4 ♘f6 2 c4 e6 3 ♘c3 ♗b4 4 ♕c2 0-0 5 a3 ♗xc3+ 6 ♕xc3 b6 7 ♗g5 ♗b7 8 f3

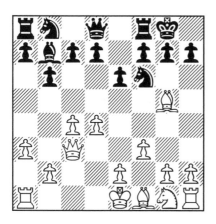

The main line. White is thinking about playing e4, but this is only a subsidiary point. White is more interested in stopping Black from playing ...♘e4, and in blocking the long diagonal.

For 8 e3, see Game 12, Bareev-Efimenko 2006. Readers will note that Bareev had to give up the pawn on g2, both in the game against Efimenko, and against Karpov.

8...h6

Slightly loosening the bishop's grip on the h4-d8 diagonal.

9 ♗h4

He would like to keep the pin, reckoning that a later ...g5 would open up too many kingside pawns.

9...d5

9...d6 is also possible, and if 10 e4 c5 (10...♘xe4? 11 ♗xd5 ♘xc3 12 ♗xc7

makes a break much too early) 11 d5 (11 e5 cxd4 12 ♕xd4 dxe5 is equal), Black must be careful this time to avoid 11...♘xd5? 12 ♗xd8 ♘xc3 13 ♗e7 ♖e8 14 ♗xd6 ♘a4 15 b3 ♘c3 16 e5. The knight has no escape. Instead 11...♘bd7 is about equal, but 11...♘xe4? does not quite work either: 12 ♗xd8 ♘xc3 13 ♗c7 ♘a4 14 b3 ♘c2 15 ♗xd6 exd5 16 ♗xf8 ♔xf8 17 ♔d2 with an edge. It is troublesome for both sides to have to calculate the breakout from the pin every time.

10 e3

10 cxd5!? could be explored further:

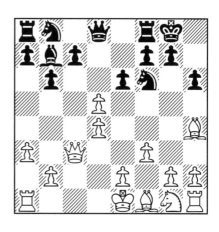

a) The breakthrough this time fails after 10...♘xd5? 11 ♗xd8 ♘xc3 12 ♗xc7 ♘b5 13 ♗xb8 ♖axb8 14 e3, winning a pawn.

b) 10...g5?! 11 ♗f2 ♘xd5 12 ♕c1! leaves Black, unsurprisingly, too weakened.

c) This leaves 10...exd5:

c1) Then 11 ♗xf6 ♕xf6 12 ♕xc7 ♗a6 13 ♕e5 ♕c6 has been tried a few times, although tellingly not at very top level. White is a pawn up, but is a long way behind in development, and Black can create pressure on both the c- and e-files.

c2) There are various untried and slightly exotic ideas, starting, for example, with 11 g4 ♖e8 12 ♘h3 c5 13 ♗f2 followed by g5. In such a line, the idea is to avoid weakening the e-pawn with an early e3, and concentrating on attacking Black on the g-file. Whether this works remains to be proven.

c3) The quieter 11 e3 has been tried several times, with probable equality. After 11...♖e8, if White will need to cover the e3-pawn, with 12 ♗f2, this reduces any possibility of making use of the bishop-pair, but 12 ♗b5 c6 13 ♗a4 allows Black several ways to equalize, not least the thematic 13...♘e4 14 ♗xd5 ♘xc3 15 bxc3 ♖xd8 16 ♘e2 ♗a6 with equality, later drawn, in L.Van Wely-A.Grischuk, Biel 2007.

10...♘bd7

The natural developing move.

11 cxd5

There are, of course, reasonable alternatives, such as 11 ♗d3 or 11 ♘h3, but Kramnik had something he wanted to try.

11...♘xd5

Finally the breakout works! Or at least it is semi-successful, better than any of the alternatives for Black.

What often happens in such lines is that tension builds up, then there is a quick release of pressure, pieces get exchanged and the result is a semi-endgame, without any real middle-

game. Kramnik has been the great specialist of such semi-endgames. It is enough to remember, for example, the way he avoided any loss as Black, and indeed as White, against Kasparov, with the Berlin Defence, and other lines, during his 2000 match in London.

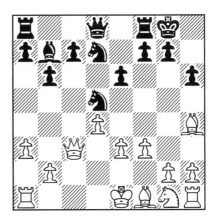

Many writers, more general journalists rather than chessplayers, have commented, on the basis of such a match, that chess is about to dry up, with leading grandmasters being able to equalize at will, with the help of the growth of theory. This is an old theme, dating back until at least the 1920s, but it hardly seems convincing. There must be at least 50 years until chess will dry up because every good player knows everything. One of the central themes in this book is that chess creativity has greatly expanded in recent years, with more and more players reaching super-super-grandmaster level (2700+ level), and correspondingly an increasing number of players reaching higher levels of creativity and of technical accuracy.

11...exd5 12 ♗d3 ♖e8 13 ♘e2 has also been tried, the tactics not quite working for Black after 13...♖xe3? 14

♗xf6! ♕xf6 15 ♗h7+ ♔xh7 16 ♕xe3, leaving White an exchange for a pawn up.

12 ♗xd8 ♘xc3

Naturally the exchanges are forced for both sides.

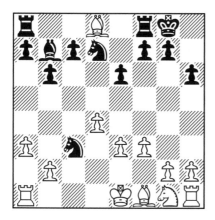

13 ♗h4

But can White grab a pawn? This was tried quite a few times in the late 1980s and early 1990s, with the hope that the far-flung knight might become a weakness after 13 ♗xc7 ♘d5 14 ♗d6 ♘xe3 15 ♔f2 ♘c2 16 ♖d1 ♘f6, but Black equalizes after 17 ♗b5 ♘f6 18 ♘e2 a6 19 ♗d3 ♘d5 20 ♖c1 ♘ce6. The knights are extraordinarily busy.

So White plays the opening quietly, but only the most determined player will try it for a win. Still, in this game, Kramnik shows just how difficult it can be for the defender to hold a minuscule disadvantage against a top technician.

13...♘d5

The only safe move. 13...♘a4?? 14 ♗b5 wins a piece.

14 ♗f2

14 e4 ♘e3 leads to nothing. White will have to relinquish the bishop-pair, in view of the threat of the ...♘c2+ knight fork, and then he has no chances

of playing for an edge.

14...c5

This at the time looked like a safe bet for a steady draw. The current game, however, opens up a couple of doubts.

14...f5 is a good alternative, making it difficult for White to expand in the central squares, but also slightly weakening his own light squares. Play is level after 15 ♗b5 c6 16 ♗d3 e5 17 ♘e2 ♖ae8, most games ending up in draws. Here in a blitz game, Kramnik experimented with 16...c5, but White probably has a slight advantage, helped by the bishop-pair, with 17 ♘e2 ♖ac8 18 0-0 cxd4 19 ♘xd4 ♘e5 20 ♗e2, G.Kasparov-V.Kramnik, Moscow 1998. Presumably the position was level at various stages in a rook and bishop ending with a symmetrical pawn structure, but Kasparov squeezed through.

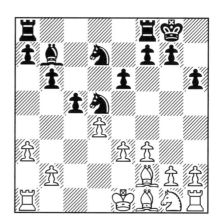

15 e4

After 15 ♗b5, there have been a couple of encounters between Kasparov and Kramnik, the colours reversed second time. Both games ended up as draws. There have, of course, also been encounters between other players. On 15...♖fd8 16 e4, Kasparov aimed to give up a pawn in return for active play with 16...♘c7!? 17 ♗xd7 ♖xd7 18 dxc5 f5! 19 cxb6 axb6, and Kramnik returned the pawn in order to complete his development with 20 ♘e2 fxe4 21 fxe4 ♗xe4, later drawn, V.Kramnik-G.Kasparov, World Championship (Game 8), London 2000.

Entertaining and imaginative defensive play by Kasparov, of course, but the computer suggests that Black might even have a slight edge after 16...♘5f6!?. If then 17 ♘e2 a6, White's bishop move would seem to be premature: 18 ♗xd7 (18 ♗c4 ♖ac8!?) 18...♘xd7 19 ♗xc5 ♘xc5 20 dxc5 bxc5 21 ♖ac1 ♖ac8 forces Black to cover a slight positional weakness, but with a well-timed ...f5, opening up the diagonal, he should stay equal.

And the other Kasparov-Kramnik game? This was again in the aforementioned blitz match, Moscow 1998. Kramnik tried 16...♘e7, then 17 ♘e2 ♗c6. If 18 ♗xc6 ♘xc6 the position is broadly level, but Kasparov played for more with 18 ♗a6. Then 18...b5!?, a useful move for blitz, but not especially accurate. A computer with a couple of seconds would give 19 ♗h4 f6 20 ♗g3 e5 21 a4!, with threats of trapping the bishop, with either d5 or axb5; White is much better. However, even the best humans cannot calculate so quickly at blitz speed, and it was Kramnik as Black who came out ahead after 19 a4 bxa4 20 dxc5. Now 20...♖ab8! is good for Black, and the author naturally recognises the help of the computer in seeing this so quickly. Kramnik played the weaker 20...♘e5?, leaving the knight exposed, and after 21 ♘d4 ♖ab8 22 ♗g3!, so that if 22...♖xd4? (Kramnik tried 22...f6 and later lost) 23 ♗xe5, un-

expectedly there is a bishop fork in the middle of the board.

I am not sure what this proves in terms of technical and theoretical chess over the last few moves, but it seems like gold-dust in terms of the psychology of chess.

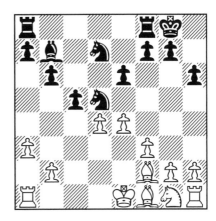

15...♘e7

Black is aiming to deploy his knight to c6, putting pressure on the d4-square.

Naturally other moves may be considered:

a) Postny, writing for ChessBase, suggests that 15...♘f4 16 ♗e3 ♘g6 allows the knight to be misplaced, but this seems ungenerous. Here the point is not that this knight should now be moved to a more active square, but rather that one knight is going to be protecting the other. After 17 ♖d1 cxd4 18 ♗xd4 ♘de5 19 ♘h3 ♖ac8 20 ♗c3 ♖fd8 21 ♗e2 ♖xd1+ 22 ♔xd1 ♘c4! Black threatens ...♘e3+, and so White has no realistic option to keep the bishop-pair. Following 23 ♗xc4 ♖xc4 in V.Kramnik-A.Naiditsch, Dortmund 2003, the game eventually ended up as a draw, Kramnik pressing but not breaking through. There are clear similarities with the Kramnik-Leko game a few years later at Dortmund, with both sides having rook, knight and opposite bishops, and a close resemblance in terms of pawn formations.

We are dealing with microscopic pawn differences. In the Kramnik-Leko game, Leko found his pawn ending up on e5, seemingly not so important if there were bishops of opposite colour, but he lost some degree of flexibility. Naiditsch was able to keep his three pawns united: e6, f6 and g6, and held the game.

16 ♘e2

16 ♗b5, and an exchange of bishops, led to a quick and level draw after 16...♗c6 17 ♗xc6 ♘xc6 18 ♘e2 cxd4 19 ♘xd4 ♘xd4 20 ♗xd4 ♖ac8 21 ♔d2 ♘c5 in V.Topalov-P.Leko, Cannes 2002. Here Leko had done his homework, since a couple of months previously, he had allowed White a slight edge after 18...♖fd8?! 19 0-0-0! cxd4 20 ♘xd4 21 ♔b1, still later ending as a draw, in B.Gelfand-P.Leko, Wijk aan Zee 2002.

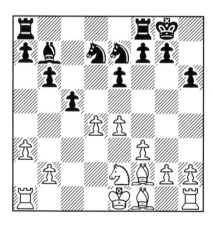

16...♖ac8

The natural reply, avoiding the isolated pawn after, for example, 16...♗a6 17 dxc5 ♘xc5 18 ♗xc5 bxc5 19 ♘c3 with a slight edge for White.

Maybe in view of the result of the game he could have tried to open the position before White could consolidate with 16...f5!?, and if 17 exf5 ♘xf5 18 dxc5 ♘xc5 19 ♗xc5 bxc5, and although Black has conceded three isolated pawns, his pieces are the more active, and should probably hold the balance. Of course, it is only in retrospect that one might consider such a line as necessary. Beforehand, players might well have thought that the position was equal with quiet but direct play.

Here the attempt at refutation with 17 ♘f4?! does not work. After 17...fxe4 18 ♘xe6 ♖f6 19 ♗c4 ♗d5 20 ♘c7 ♗xc4 21 ♘xa8 exf3 22 gxf3 ♖e6+! 23 ♔d1 (the king is forced into a skewer) 23...♗d5 24 ♘c7 ♗xf3+ 25 ♔c1 ♖e2 Black is better. Entertaining tactics, but one cannot be wholly surprised if there are threats if the opponent is spending time with the knight chasing after the far-off rook.

Leko himself later tried 16...f5!, with success. M.Gurevich-P.Leko, 4th match-game, Elista 2007, continued 17 ♘g3 fxe4 18 fxe4 cxd4 19 ♗xd4 ♖ac8 20 ♖d1 ♖fd8 21 ♗c3 ♘g6 22 ♗b5 ♘c5 23 0-0 ♗a6, probably about equal, but a few minor slips by White gave Leko a chance to play for a win.

17 ♘c3

After this, White is ready to complete his development, and make use of the bishop-pair. There is also the niggling threat of ♘b5, which continues to cause problems even into the endgame.

17...cxd4

Black simplifies, at the risk of losing a tempo. Normally he would want to wait until White exchanges with dxc5, when the pawn disappears and Black gains time with the knight after ...♞xc5, but perhaps this is not so practical.

17...♜fd8 completes his development, but 18 ♞b5 is annoying. Black's idea is 18...cxd4 19 ♞d6 ♜c7 20 ♞xb7 ♜xb7 21 ♝xd4 ♞c5 22 ♝e3 when he is better developed, and has no pawn weaknesses, but White has the bishop-pair against two knights. The computer suggests that Black is fully equal, but good humans might well be suspicious of this. Indeed, it's probably a slight edge for White.

18 ♝xd4

The computer is optimistic in suggesting that Black is a touch better. Two of the three suggested moves, 18...a6 and 18...e5, create weaknesses in the pawn structure, which are likely to cause problems later.

18...♞c5

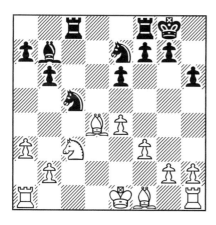

With a threat of ...♞b3, but the rook was planning to develop anyway, so Black does not gain a tempo.

19 ♜d1

White should not allow the bishop for knight exchange. His dark-squared bishop is the best minor piece on the board.

19...♜fd8

Except, of course, that White can think of an exchange with ♝xc5 followed by ♜d7.

20 ♝e3!

White was only level after 20 ♝b5 ♞b3 21 ♝e3 ♜xd1+ 22 ♚xd1 ♞c6 23 ♝xc6 ♝xc6 24 ♚c2 ♞a5, later drawn, in L.Van Wely-P.Leko, Wijk aan Zee 2005, and Leko was presumably happy enough to settle for a draw with Black against Kramnik as well.

There was only a peaceful draw too after 20 ♝xc5 ♜xd1+ 21 ♚xd1 ♜xc5 22 ♚d2 ♞c8, play soon fizzling out in E.Bareev-A.Grischuk, Sochi 2004. Moreover, in another top-level game in 2005, the players agreed a draw before White even got round to playing on move 20.

Kramnik's innovation was not a brilliant move, but rather the view that because he keeps the bishop-pair, as opposed to bishop and knight, he still has a slight edge, and he is justified in seeing whether he can keep his edge, or whether his opponent can hold.

20...♜xd1+

If immediately 20...e5, then White can damage Black's pawn structure with 21 ♜xd8+ ♜xd8 22 ♝xc5 bxc5. Black will have to suffer a long and often uncomfortable defence to try to draw.

21 ♚xd1

There is no point in decentralizing with 21 ♞xd1?!. It is the king that needs to move.

21...e5

Black gains space, but also weakens his light squares.

21...♞g6 is to be considered, avoiding any pawn gaps in the centre, and preparing for ...♞e5, but White is better after 22 b4!. The knight-hopping in the centre favours White after 22...♘d3 23 ♘b5 ♖d8 24 ♔c2 ♘e1+ 25 ♔b3 a6 26 ♗xb6.

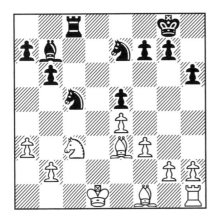

22 b4!

In view of the last comment, the idea of b4 is not quite as unexpected as it looks, but it is still good and imaginative, and typical of Kramnik's extremely high technique.

After 22 ♔c2 ♘a4 23 ♗b5 ♘xc3 24 bxc3 ♗c6 25 a4 f5 26 ♗xc6 ♖xc6 27 ♖d1 fxe4 28 fxe4 ♖c7, Z.Gyimesi-Z.Almasi, Szekesfehervar 2006, White has no serious chances of an edge in view of his isolated pawns, and the game ended as a draw.

In *New in Chess*, Kramnik related that Bareev had tried 22 ♔c2, with another draw against Almasi, in Monaco 2006, and that Bareev afterwards suggested that 22 b4!? might have been an improvement. So big innovations do not automatically arise from deep computer work. A more traditional method can be through going though a postmortem and learning from it.

22...♘e6

After 22...♘b3 23 ♔c2 ♘d4+ 24 ♔b2 White keeps a small edge, one point

being that he can threaten a bishop for knight exchange on d4 at an inconvenient time, while the knight cannot initiate a bishop exchange.

Leko decides that it is the other knight that should move to d4, via c6.

23 ♔c2!

Running into a pin, but Kramnik has worked out, as Bareev previously noted, that he can bring the king to b2, unpinning, and that now he has chances of playing for an edge. The king is only there on c2 for one move, and can run on the next move.

23...♘c6

23...f5 24 ♔b2 threatens little, and leaves the e5-pawn extremely weak.

24 ♔b2

The king moves on.

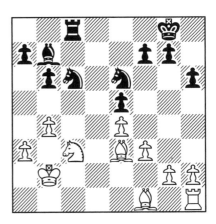

Kramnik has moved straight from the opening into the endgame, bypassing the middlegame. He does this because he feels that he is better. Recent theory may suggest that this should be equal, with a symmetrical pawn structure, and that White's bishop-pair does not achieve that much, given that Black's knights are solid and active, but Kramnik wants to test the waters.

24...♔f8!

Kramnik himself gives this an exclamation mark, centralizing the king for the endgame. He notes that White is slightly better after 24...♘cd4 25 ♗d3 ♘f4 26 ♗xf4 exf4 27 ♖d1, and if at any stage the knight returns to c6, White has ♘d5, attacking the weak pawn, and generally consolidating on an advanced square.

It is far easier to play 'bishop takes knight', rather than 'knight takes bishop', and the player with the two bishops has the leisure to decide whether to exchange one of his bishops for a knight, or whether to ignore it, or wait and keep up the tension. White is not so much aiming for the bishop-pair, but rather playing for the better bishop after a timely trade of bishop for knight.

Postny, writing before he had the chance of seeing Kramnik's own annotations, gave instead 25 ♘b5 (rather than 25 ♗d3). White is no doubt slightly better after, for example, 25...♘xb5 26 ♗xb5 ♘d4 27 ♗xd4 exd4 28 ♖d1 a6 29 ♗f1 ♖d8 30 ♗c4 ♖d7 (avoiding the ♗d5 threat), and again White can play hard for a win.

Leko's king move had a straightforward objective, to bring the king nearer to the centre in an endgame. He can wait to see what White does before deciding where he should move his other pieces.

25 ♗c4

One senses, from Kramnik's exclamation mark, that he had considered as the main line 24...♘cd4, and that he had to readjust his play.

25...♘cd4

Not 25...♘xb4? 26 ♗xe6 ♘d3+ 27 ♔c2, and White wins a piece.

26 ♗xe6!

A good player is always adaptable. The bishop-pair has been useful, but it is now time to give up the bishop-pair in order to break up Black's solid knight pair.

26...♘xe6

Not many players would seriously consider taking the isolated doubled pawns with 26...fxe6?!, even though ♘b5 is prevented. 27 ♖d1 ♗c4 28 f4 is a good line for White.

27 ♘b5

The knight finds itself on a good attacking square, thanks to the removal of Black's knight from d4.

27...♖a8

The only way to cover the pawn. If 27...a6? 28 ♘d6 White wins a pawn.

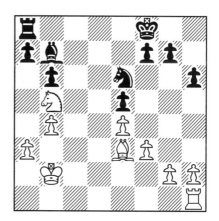

28 a4!

A good example of the principle that if you can't improve your pieces, you have to improve your pawns, here to add protection for the knight on b5. White's queenside pawns also start to put pressure on Black's.

Kramnik would have considered 28 ♖c1 ♗a6 29 ♘c7 ♘xc7 30 ♖xc7 ♗f1, heading for a draw, or, slightly more complicated, 28 ♘d6 ♗a6 29 b5 ♖d8 30

♘xf7 ♔xf7 31 bxa6 ♖d3 32 ♖e1 ♘c7, with a minimal edge for White, which Kramnik regards as level in *Informator*.

28...♗a6

Postny regards this as the source of Black's troubles, preferring 28...♗c6!? 29 ♘c3, and White has been unable to try the ♘b5-a3-c4 manoeuvre. Even so, Black would have to work hard to hold the position after 29...♖d8 30 b5 ♗e8 31 ♖c1! (31 ♘d5? f5 is premature) 31...f6 32 ♘d5 followed by ♘b4, and the knight can find another route to attack.

29 ♘a3

White would like to smother any activity by the bishop.

Kramnik gives 29 ♘c3 ♗c4! as equal, presumably in view of 30 ♖d1 ♖d8, and an exchange of rooks.

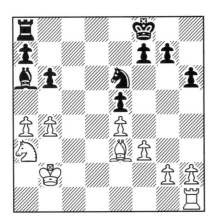

29...♖c8?

This is the move that Kramnik pinpoints as the real weakness. Black needs to keep the bishop in open play. Being stuck with the bishop on b7, behind White's b5- and e4-pawns, is unpleasant.

Kramnik suggests 29...♗d3! 30 ♖d1 ♖d8 31 b5 ♔e7 32 ♔c3 ♗e2 33 ♖xd8 ♘xd8. Black's bishop is now on the far side of the board, attacking pawns on

unprotected squares (a4 and g2), rather than granite-protected squares such as b5 and e4. In addition, there are so many escape squares for the bishop that White cannot round it up.

White is, of course, still better, having gained extra space on the queenside, and setting up an attack on the a7-pawn, or maybe prising open Black's pawns with a5. It is in the nature of such lines that it is almost impossible to establish clearly whether White should win, or whether Black should be able to hold the draw. 'Plus over equals' would be the standard comment when writing up a game.

Kramnik gives here 34 ♘c4 (maybe 34 a5!? could be considered) 34...♗f1 35 g3 f6 36 f4, with a slight edge for White, but 35...♗g2! looks more accurate and more active. If 36 ♘xe5 ♔e6 37 ♔d4 (37 ♘c6? ♘xc6 38 bxc6 ♔d6 favours Black) 37...f6 38 ♘c6 ♘xc6+ 39 bxc6 ♔d6 40 f4 ♔xc6 41 e5, and there are various ways of reaching a level opposite-coloured endgame.

Of course, all this is not forced. It merely happens to be the line that Kramnik suggested in his notes. Leko with his last move indicated that he was worried about White taking up the c-file, which must surely imply that 30 ♖c1!? is well worth considering, avoiding the exchange of rooks. White keeps a slight edge. Whether he has a win with best play is not so clear.

It is often a feature of a well-played technical win that it is far from clear exactly when the loser made the decisive mistake. White was able to keep a slight edge from the opening, but this is still a long way from a clear win. But when did Black make the critical mistake? In most games, even at the highest level, the critical mistake can be isolated, and questioned. Not so in this Kramnik-Leko game. Postny questioned Black's 28th, while Kramnik himself questions Black's 29th instead, but in either case the alternative moves would still leave White with a slight advantage.

A possible thought might be that Kramnik was able to keep the opening edge from early on, and that he played superb chess throughout. Somewhere along the line, possibly in the late opening, Leko made a very slight slip, which Kramnik exploited. The obvious thought would be whether Leko made a mistake later on. We shall see.

30 b5

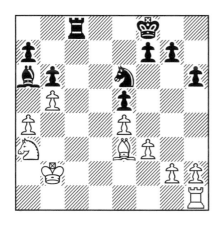

Kramnik now slams the door on Black's bishop.

30...♗b7

And Black has even lost two tempi. Should we say 'tempi', borrowing from the Italian, or 'tempoes', as given by Postny for ChessBase? The pragmatic answer is that it doesn't really matter all that much, so long as the meaning is clear!

31 ♖c1

In chess terms, simplification is often the best way of clarity. The player with the positional advantage would often like to exchange off good defensive pieces.

31...♖xc1

Or 31...♔e7, but Black would not want to surrender the c-file to the rook.

32 ♔xc1

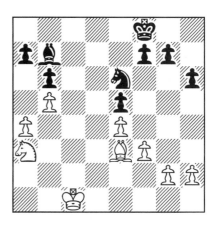

White's bishop is better than Black's bishop, and is capable of picking up pawns.

32...♔e7

Postny notes that 32...f5 33 exf5 ♘f4 34 g3 ♘g2 35 ♗f2 ♗xf3 36 ♘c4 e4 37 ♔d2 gives no counterplay. Black's knight on g2 is stranded.

The immediate 32...♘f4 33 ♗xf4 exf4 34 ♘c4 gives White an advantage too. Black cannot prevent White's king from reaching d4.

33 a5

White prises open a passed pawn.

33...bxa5

33...♘c5?! looks wrong, but proving this might sometimes require more thought. 34 a6 ♗c8 35 ♗xc5 bxc5 36 ♘c4 wins only by a tempo. If the pawn were already on f6 rather then f7, he would draw:

a) If Black were to try to cover the e5-pawn, with 36...f6, White wins after 37 ♘a5! ♚d6 38 b6!, queening on a8, an attractive finish.

b) If instead 36...♗d7 37 b6 axb6 38 ♘xb6 ♗c6 39 a7 ♚d6 40 a8♕ ♗xa8 41 ♘xa8 ♚c6 42 ♚c2 ♚b7 43 ♚c3 ♚xa8 44 ♚c4 ♚b7 45 ♚xc5 ♚c7 46 ♚d5, and if 46...f6?, White creeps in with 47 ♚e6. The best practical chance for Black is to give away a pawn, with 46...♚d7 47 ♚xe5 ♚e7, except that Black would not have much chance of drawing, a pawn down in a king and pawn ending.

34 ♗xa7

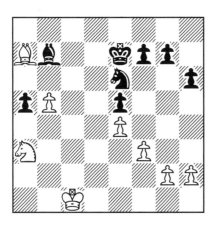

White's passed pawn is much better than Black's. White has extra cover on each square in front of the pawn, whether with the bishop (b6 and b8) or the knight (b7 after White's ♘c4 and ♘a5), whereas Black has no realistic chance of promoting his a-pawn. Also, Black's pieces, notably the king and bishop, are not very flexible. The king cannot reach c5, and the bishop is blocked in by the opposing pawns. Leko decides it is time to sort out this particular problem.

34...f5!

Running for freedom.

Postny gives 34...a4 35 ♘c4 f6 36 ♚b2 ♘f4 37 g3 ♘d3+ 38 ♚a3 f5 39 ♘d2 as winning for White.

35 exf5

Not much choice here, but now Leko has chances of attacking White's king-side pawns.

35...♘f4

Now three of White's kingside pawns are under threat.

36 g3

The doubled pawns are expendable in an emergency, but White needs to keep hold of the g- and h-pawns.

36 ♗b8? ♘xg2 37 ♗xe5 ♘e3 is only a draw.

36...♘h3

Not perhaps the square that the knight would have preferred, but 36...♘d5 blocks his bishop, while 36...♘e2+ 37 ♚d2 ♗xf3 38 ♚e3 ♗h5 39 b6 will queen the pawn.

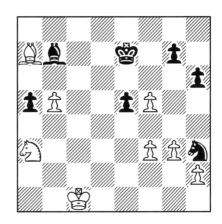

37 ♘c4

Kramnik decides to aim for a direct attack, rather than cutting off the knight with 37 ♗e3. In his notes, he suggests that the bishop retreat is not worse, and hints that it may well have been slightly the more accurate choice:

a) If 37...♘g5 38 ♗xg5 hxg5 39 ♘c4

♗xf3 40 ♘xa5, and White should eventually win with the extra pawn. Black's problem on the queenside is that once White has a pawn on b6 and a knight on a5, it is close to impossible to attack the b-pawn with the king.

b) On other lines, such as 37...♗xf3 38 ♘c4 ♔f6 39 ♘d6 a4 40 b6, Black can struggle on, but his knight on h3 is heavily constrained.

37...♘g5

Leko is alert to the smallest possibility of escape. He needs to bring the knight back into active play.

After 37...♗xf3, Kramnik gives 38 ♘xe5 ♗e4 39 ♘c4, and White should win.

38 ♘xa5

38 f4!? certainly seems well worth considering, especially given that after the alternative it is not totally clear that White is winning. Kramnik gives this as a possibility, without further analysis, while Postny suggests that Black is able to hold.

Postny gives 38...exf4 39 gxf4 ♘f3 40 ♘xa5 ♗d5 41 b6 ♔f6 42 ♘c4! (42 b7 ♗xb7 43 ♘xb7 ♔xf5, equal) 42...♔e7! 43 h3 ♔d7 'with good drawish chances', but 44 ♘e5+! looks highly promising. One of the usual rules of thumb in a bishop of opposite colour and pawn endgame, with two passed pawns, is that three clear files between the pawns will be a clear win, as the king breaks through without difficulty, whereas only two clear files is often insufficient. Here 44...♘xe5? 45 fxe5 followed by f6 is clearly enough to win. When the white king reaches e5, it is effectively all over, Black being unable to cover the b-pawn, the f-pawn, and the king threatening to invade on d6.

Black therefore has to try 44...♔c8, but then 45 ♘g4 h5 (otherwise f6 by White, giving a second passed pawn; 45...♘g1? and 45...♘d4? would each lose a piece after 46 b7+) 46 ♘e3, and White has excellent winning chances. If he has a chance to reach d6 with a knight, he will be winning material.

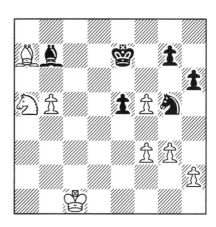

38...♗d5?!

But this time he should take with the bishop, 38...♗xf3!. The immediate tactical point is that after 39 b6 ♔f6 40 b7 ♗xb7 41 ♘xb7 ♔xf5 Black will be safe, White being unable, the king and knight being so far apart, to cover the two remaining pawns.

Kramnik gives 39 ♔d2 ♗d5 as best for both players, but then White's king is not on an especially good square. Black threatens ...♘f3, with check, and also, after 40 b6, there is another check with gain of tempo, with 40...♘e4+ followed by ...♘d6. Kramnik suggests instead 40 ♔e3 ♘e4 41 ♗b8 ♔f6 42 ♘c6 ♔xf5 43 ♘xe5. White is a pawn up, and who knows, he might be winning, or maybe not. There seem to be genuine winning chances though. Black will at some stage need to bring the king to the centre or to the queenside, and that being the case, White will be able to prod the kingside pawns, to set up weaknesses. Play could, for example, continue with 43...♔e6 44 ♘d3 ♗b7 45 ♔d4 ♔d7 (otherwise ♘c5+ is strong) 46 ♗e5, keeping the squeezing options open.

Thus it is possible that Black was losing anyway, even with the best moves.

39 b6

'Passed pawns must be pushed.'

39...♘xf3

And for the defender, pawns must also be taken. Quite often the only hope for the defender is to exchange or capture the final pawns.

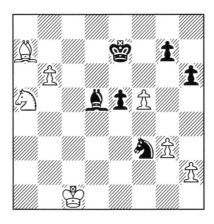

The easy part for White is to win the bishop. How though is he going to keep at least one of his three pawns?

40 h3!

This was played on move 40, at the end of the time control. Normally one cannot analyse in great depth then, and it is a case of positional instinct rather that calculation. Here Kramnik considers that it is better to drop the pawn on h3 rather than on h2. He wants to make it more difficult for Black to return his knight after taking on h3.

It would take a lot of calculation to decide where the pawn will best drop, and in practical terms it would be an irrelevance to analyse what is going on. You could easily lose on time before making a confident decision!

After 40 b7?! ♗xb7 41 ♘xb7 ♘xh2 the knight covers good squares on g4, f3, and f1, holding the balance.

40...♘g5

40...♘g1 is less accurate. After 41 b7 ♗xb7 42 ♗xg1! the win is straightforward. Black's bishop only covers light squares, and so cannot defend on the dark squares.

41 b7

There is no sense in delaying. White will need to bring the bishop into play.

41...♗xb7 42 ♘xb7 ♘xh3

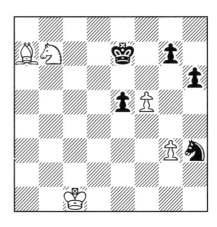

After all the chopping of material, the position still looks unclear. White's king is further away from the critical pawns than Black's king, and there seems to be a significant danger of Black winning the f-pawn, and then exchanging the other pawn. White needs some remarkably delicate play from his bishop.

43 ♗b6!

A quiet but highly effective move. Kramnik plans to manoeuvre his bishop to h4, guarding the g3-pawn, and covering the f6-square, if Black has not already advanced his king. Meanwhile Black cannot move his knight.

We begin to sense that Kramnik has gone beyond just winning a piece, and that he has found a clear winning plan.

43...♔d7?!

This loses a tempo, Black's king no longer being able to play to f6 next move.

Black has a final chance to make mischief with 43...♔f6 44 ♘d6 ♔g5. Then the bishop zigzags with 45 ♗d8+! ♔g4 46 ♗e7! ♔xg3 47 ♗f8 h5 48 ♗xg7 ♘g5 49 ♗xe5+ ♔g2 50 f6 h4 51 ♘f5 h3 52 ♘h4+ ♔g1 53 ♗f4 h2 54 ♗xh2+ ♔xh2 55 ♘f3+ ♘xf3 57 f7, queening the pawn.

44 ♗e3!

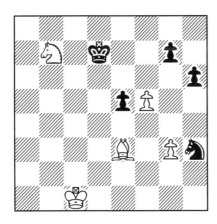

Black's king has now been lured away, and on his next move he has lost a tempo.

44...♔e7

His only hope is to win or exchange White's f5-pawn, and then to win or exchange the g3-pawn. 44...♔c6 45 ♘c5 ♔d5 46 ♔d2 e4 47 ♘e6 g6 48 ♘f4+ ♘xf4+ 49 ♗xf4 covers only the first half of the task, and not the second.

45 ♘c5

With thoughts of stabilizing the centre with ♘e4.

45...g6

The final attempt at keeping the game alive. Kramnik gives as an attempt 45...♔f6 46 g4 e4, but 47 ♘xe4 ♔e5 48 ♘g3 ♘f4 49 ♔d2 wins.

46 fxg6

Obviously.

46...♔f6

Black recovers one pawn, but not the second.

47 ♗xh6 ♔xg6

47...♘f2 48 g7 ♔f7 49 ♘e6 consolidates the extra material.

48 ♗e3 1-0

The knight cannot move, as if 48...♘g5 49 ♗xg5 ♔xg5 50 ♔d2 ♔g4 51 ♘e4 ♔f3 52 ♔e3, and the king gets zugzwanged out. White uses the same idea after 48...♔f5 49 ♔d2 ♔g4 50 ♘e4 ♔f3 51 ♔d3.

Game 14
D.Navara-B.Socko
Polish Team Championship 2006
Ruy Lopez C95

1 e4 e5 2 ♘f3 ♘c6 3 ♗b5 a6 4 ♗a4 ♘f6 5 0-0 ♗e7 6 ♖e1 b5 7 ♗b3 d6

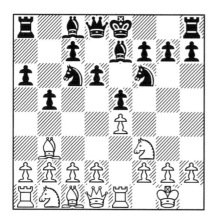

Black is not interested in the Marshall Gambit with 7...0-0 8 c3 d5, see Game 16, Shirov-Aronian, and also the anti-Marshall system with 8 a4, as in Game 10, Ivanchuk-Aronian.

8 c3

The main line.

8 a4 is possible, but perhaps slightly less effective for White than in the Anti-Marshall proper. 8...♗g4 is a reasonable reply.

8...0-0

8...♗g4 is just about playable, but after 9 h3 ♗h5 10 d3! Black's bishop loses cover on the light squares on the queenside. White's basic development plan is to swing the knight from b1 to f1, then maybe gain space with the pawn with g4 and/or play the knight to e3 or g3, setting up a light-squared bind.

9 h3

Whereas here White decides to prevent ...♗g4.

The difference is that after 9 d4 ♗g4, White's central pawns are less solid than in the rock-hard d3 formation, and Black can set up counterplay after 10 d5 ♘a5 11 ♗c2 c6 or 11...♕c8.

9...♘b8!?

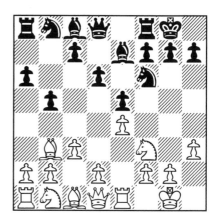

Which was the most sensational new system of the Ruy Lopez in the early 20th century? The Marshall Gambit or this, the Breyer Variation?

If we can demonstrate that the Marshall Gambit is fully and completely equal, then it may be given the top slot. The Breyer Gambit is tough and extremely difficult to beat, but White still has chances of playing for a slight, maybe very slight, edge. There have been times, though, when players with

White, such as Stein have quite simply given up on 1 e4, because of the Breyer. White has found a few ways since then to improve his play.

Breyer's knight retreat intends to re-deploy the knight to d7, keeping the e5-pawn safe, and allowing Black the chance to advance his queenside pawns effectively, with ...c5, so that the pawns become strengths rather than weaknesses.

For 9...♘a5, see Game 33, Karjakin-Inarkiev. There are many other alternatives for Black, not surprisingly when White's last move was a quiet h3. One curiosity is 9...♖e8!? 10 ♘g5!? (10 d4 ♗b7 leads to sharp play) 10...♖f8 11 ♘f3, offering a repetition. If Black wants to play on, he has to try something else, with 11...♘b8, 11...♘a5, 11...♗b7, 11...h6, or a few others.

10 d4

10 a4 ♗b7 gives Black no great problems.

10...♘bd7

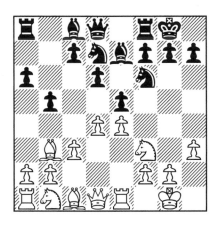

The continuation of the Breyer manoeuvre.

11 ♘bd2

11 ♘h4 used to be popular up to the early 1970s, with the idea that Black's knight blocks the bishop's defence of the f5-square. It soon became appreciated that 11...♘b6 and 11...exd4 12 cxd4 ♘b6 gave Black full equality.

11 d5 ♗b7, followed by ...c6, does not give White much either.

11 c4 c6 sets up Black's barricades well. Black has good chances of equality.

11 ♗g5 ♗b7 12 ♘bd2 h6 13 ♗h4 ♖e8 also seems comfortable for Black.

All of these lines were tried many times in the early 70s, and proved to be extremely solid for Black. Almost by a process of elimination, 11 ♘bd2 survived as the only promising plan.

11...♗b7

Black has to develop.

11...♖e8?? would be careless, as White traps the queen after 12 ♗xf7+ ♔xf7 13 ♘g5+ followed by ♘e6.

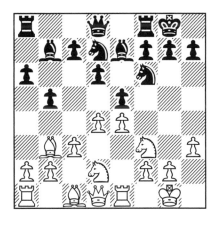

12 ♗c2

White needs to provide extra cover to the e4-pawn, before manoeuvring his knight to the king's file.

If one is getting worried about Black spending three tempi to manoeuvre the knight from b8 to d7, remember that White has spent four tempi manoeuvring the bishop from f1 to c2.

These offset each other.

12...♖e8

Now that White's bishop is off the a2-g8 diagonal, the rook move is much better.

13 ♘f1

A standard Ruy Lopez development plan. White puts pressure with the pawns on the queenside, and sets up possible attacks on the kingside, while keeping his pawns intact in the centre. It is up to Black to set up some counterplay.

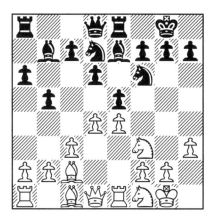

13...♗f8

In 1983 when Spassky was content at being just a highly respected former World Champion, he made some quick draws with 13...d5!?. Tal too was happy with a quick draw against both Spassky and Psakhis. The various pawn exchanges, and also 14 ♘g3, all seemed equal.

Then Kindermann showed, against Spassky in the 1984 Bundesliga, that 14 ♘xe5! ♘xe5 15 dxe5 ♘xe4 16 f3! can still create problems. Spassky tried 16...♘c5 17 b4 ♘d7, but after 18 f4!, White created pressure, and later won. Spassky then tried improving with 16...♘g5 17 ♘g3 f6, but Chandler dem-

onstrated an edge with 18 ♗xg5 fxg5 19 ♕b1, M.Chandler-B.Spassky, German League 1985.

This line soon dropped out of fashion, but maybe Black can improve? Black quietly continues to develop his pieces before setting up the central explosion with ...d5.

14 ♘g3

Carrying on with his main plan.

14 d5 c6 is probably not too dangerous.

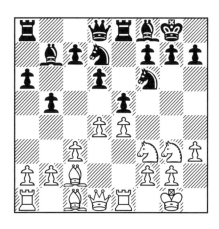

14...g6

This looks like a simple re-fianchetto move, although in fact the bishop does not make it to g7. Black's other idea is more to prevent White from moving his knight to f5.

14...c6 is an alternative. Then 15 ♘f5 ♕c7 (15...g6?! 16 ♘h6+ ♔g7? 17 ♘g5 is unplayable for Black) 16 dxe5 dxe5 17 ♘h2 c4 18 ♕f3 c4 19 ♗g5 has been played a couple of times:

a) Black's play soon collapsed after 19...♕c6?! 20 ♖ad1 h6 21 ♗c1 ♘c5? 22 ♗xh6! in A.Volokitin-E.Bacrot, German League 2007. The point is that if 22...gxh6 23 ♖d6! ♗xd6 24 ♕g3+, checkmate follows, so Bacrot struggled on with 22...♘fxe6 23 ♘g4, but White's minor pieces were swarming alarmingly, and helped to win quickly.

b) Black avoided the immediate danger in Anand-Morozevich, Morelia/Linares 2007, playing instead 19...♖e6! 20 ♖ad1 ♘c5:

b1) Maybe White is slightly better after, for example, 21 ♘g4 ♘xg4 22 hxg4.

b2) Anand tried instead the tempting 21 ♗xf6?! ♖xf6 22 ♘g4 ♖e6, but for much of the time he would have liked to have kept his dark-squared bishop. After 23 ♘ge3 (Marin suggests 23 b4!? as an improvement) 23...♕a5 24 a3 g6 25 ♘d5?! ♖d8!? (ignoring the sacrifice) 26 ♕g3 ♖d7 27 ♘fe3 ♕d8 Morozevich looked to have a good position, but Anand found the better moves, and later won.

14...d5!? is relatively unexplored, although Black usually delays it for the next move. There is no obvious refutation. White could perhaps try 15 ♗g5!? h6 16 ♗h4 g5 17 ♘xg5, the same sacrifice as in the main line, except that White has not played the extra b3 move. Is this relevant for either side? I leave it to the reader.

15 b3

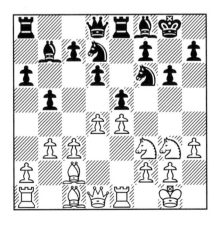

White too aims at a fianchetto, ex-

cept that again neither player completes the development of the long diagonal. Events intervene.

15 a4 is not quite as fashionable at higher levels, but has achieved good results for White, after either 15...c5 16 d5 c4 17 ♗g5 h6 18 ♗e3 or 15...♗g7 16 ♗d3 c6 17 ♗g5 ♘f8 18 ♕d2 ♘e6 19 ♗e3.

In either case, the pawn structure is mainly blocked, quite a contrast with the current main line.

15...d5!?

A central pawn explosion!

Quite often in such positions, and also in such lines with white pawns on c4 and d4, and black pawns on c5 and d5, play can lead to extremely complicated positional calculations, as each player on the new move has to calculate two 'pawn takes pawn' captures, work out whether either of them is good, bad, level or premature, and then has to foresee whether the opponent has the chance of making a good response in reply. Sometimes there is no immediate pawn capture by either side, and the tension increases, no doubt leading to severe time pressure. Play through the next few moves in the game, and there is no central pawn exchange on either side, until Black's 19th, four extra moves on either side. During this time, play has not been quiet, but White has made a violent piece sacrifice.

The aggressive central pawn thrust has only been a relatively recent try, with 15...♗g7 having a much longer history, Tal and more especially Spassky having scored with good wins in this. Also, more recently, Socko has reverted to the more traditional lines, in response to his loss against Navara. For example, M.Carlsen-B.Socko, German League 2006, three months after the loss to Navara, continued 16 d5 ♕e7 17 c4 ♕f8 18 ♗e3 ♗h6 (Black is desperate to exchange the bad bishop) 19 ♗xa6 ♕xa6 20 cxg5 axb5 21 b4, but Black was under pressure, and later lost. There have been many tries for Black after 16 d5, and indeed many defensive attempts by Socko. Black is slightly worse, hence the reason to try 15...d5.

16 ♗g5

He doesn't take anything, but adds to the tension instead. Quite often an extra pin can make all the difference.

Are there any good 'pawn takes pawn' options immediately?

16 exd5 ♘xd5 does not make much pressure against Black, as White's c3-pawn is under threat. Play is level after 17 dxe5 ♘xc3 18 ♕d3 ♘d5. This of course helps explain why Black did not try 14...d5 a move earlier, when White's pawn was still on b2.

16 dxe5 dxe4 gives White nothing, and indeed forces him to play carefully:

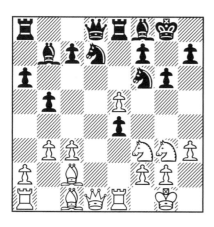

a) If, for example, 17 ♘xe4 ♘xe4 18 ♗xe4 ♗xe4 19 ♖xe4 ♘xe5 20 ♗f4 ♕xd1+ 21 ♖xd1 ♘xf3+ 22 gxf3 c5, and

Black has the better endgame pawn structure.

b) Or 17 exf6 exf3 18 ♗e4 ♗xe4 19 ♘xe4 fxg2 22 ♔xg2 ♘c5 with good play for Black.

c) 17 ♘g5! appears to be the safest option, with a few small tactics ending up in a drawn opposite-coloured bishop endgame after 17...♘xe5 18 ♘5xe4 ♘xe4 19 ♘xe4 ♗xe4 20 ♗xe4 ♘d3 21 ♖e2 ♘xc1 22 ♖d2 ♘e2+ 23 ♖xe2 ♕xd1+ 24 ♖xd1 ♖ad8.

The final central exchange capture looks equal after 16 ♘xe5 ♘xe5 17 dxe5 ♖xe5 18 ♗f4 ♖e8.

16...h6

Now it is Black's turn. Again, he must consider initiating pawn exchanges in the centre. The problem is that the pin on the knight on f6 is so painful for Black that he has to try to break it.

16...exd4?! 17 e5 dxc3 18 exf6 ♖xe1+ 19 ♕xe1 h6 is too wild. Black is sacrificing his minor piece for a few pawns, but his opponent is now attacking, and Black's pawns attack little. A return piece sacrifice with 20 ♗h4! ♘xf6 21 ♕xc3 g5 22 ♘xg5 hxg5 23 ♗xg5 d4! 24 ♕d2! ♕d5 25 f3 keeps the initiative. Black suffers serious gaps in his kingside pawn structure.

16...dxe4?! 17 ♘xe5 puts intense pressure on both black knights. If 17...♘xe5 18 dxe5 ♕xd1 19 ♖axd1 ♘d5 20 ♘xe4, White wins a pawn.

17 ♗h4

Of course, Navara will have prepared this piece sacrifice. Indeed, it has already been tried before, but here he adds a couple of extra details.

In any case, 17 dxe5 Nex5 18 ♘xe5 ♖xe5 19 ♗f4 ♖e6 is only equal, as is 17

♗xf6 ♕xf6 18 exd5 exd4 19 ♕xd4 ♕xd4 20 ♘xd4 ♗xd5.

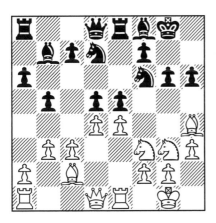

17...g5

Socko takes up the challenge.

Former World Champion, Boris Spassky, played more cautiously with 17...dxe4 18 ♘xe4 (18 ♗xe4 ♗xe4 19 ♘xe4 g5 20 ♗g3 transposes into a later line) 18...g5 in J.Polgar-B.Spassky, 8th matchgame, Budapest 1993:

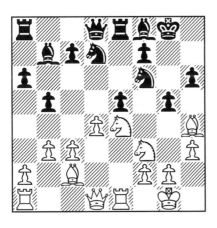

a) Polgar might well have considered 19 ♗g3, and if 19...exd4 20 ♘xf6+ ♕xf6 21 ♕d3 ♗g7 22 ♘xd4 with a positional advantage to White, because of Black's light-squared weaknesses on the king-side. Black improves though with 19...♘xe4 20 ♗xe4 ♗xe4 21 ♖xe4 f5,

with unclear play.

b) Polgar, then only a teenager, showed great flair for setting up a sacrificial attack with 19 dxe5! ♘xe4 20 ♗xe4 ♗xe4 21 ♖xe4 gxh4 22 ♖d4 ♖e7 23 e6! fxe6 24 ♘e5. She had recovered her material, and Spassky's pawn structure proved to be seriously damaged, resulting later in a loss.

On the other central pawn capture, White stands positionally better after 17...exd4 18 e5 g5 19 ♗xg5 hxg5 20 exf6 ♕xf6 21 ♕d3.

18 ♘xg5

He has to sacrifice, and he needs to keep the bishop.

18...hxg5

18...exd4? 19 ♘f3 does not give any material compensation in return for the kingside pawn gash.

19 ♗xg5

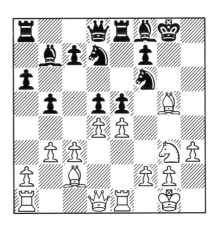

Two pawns for the knight, and good attacking chances against an exposed king. This seems like promising compensation.

19...exd4

19...dxe4 is an attempt at simplification, but White still kept strong king-side pressure after 20 ♗xe4 ♗xe4 21 ♖xe4 ♕c8 22 ♖h4 exd4 23 cxd4 ♗g7 24

♘f5 in A.Sherzer-A.Lesiege, Biel 1993. After 24...♘f8 25 ♕f3 ♖e6 26 d5 ♖e5 27 ♘h6+ ♗xh6 28 ♗xf6 ♗g7 29 ♗xe5 ♗xe5 30 ♖e1 ♘g6 31 ♖g4 White was winning.

20 e5

So that both bishops are on good attacking diagonals, and his other pieces are also in the attack.

20 cxd4? dxe4 21 ♘xe4 ♗e7 is ineffective.

20...♖xe5

Black also faces problems after 20...♘xe5 21 ♘h5 ♗g7 22 exd4 ♘ed7 23 ♕f3. The basic plan of attack is ♘xg7 followed by ♕g3.

21 ♖xe5 ♘xe5

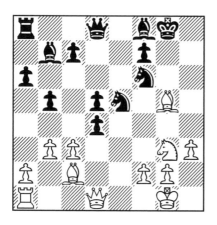

22 cxd4!

A year earlier, Navara had got caught off-guard against the same opponent with 22 ♕xd4?. He soon found out that he had no real compensation for his sacrificed pawn after 22...♕d6 23 ♖e1 ♘e4 24 ♗f4 ♖e8, and a later win for Black in D.Navara-B.Socko, Greek Team Championship 2005.

One can be sure that Navara had prepared this position in detail. White's pawn capture on d4 adds an important centralized pawn, and kicks Black's

knight from another central square, e5. There is no deep tactic, rather just a natural positional attack, taking over some dark squares, and adding pressure on the light squares leading up to h7.

22...♘ed7

A position which has interested the analysts. Where should the knight move? Socko's retreat, helping defend the other knight on f6, seems just about to hold, but requires great accuracy. In other games, Black chose 22...♘c6 instead. This was played by Inarkiev in April 2005, with a later win for Black, given below. This predates the earlier Navara-Socko encounter, which dates from July 2005. Therefore, neither Navara nor Socko covered entirely new ground, and a diligent player could be expected, especially in the days of the Internet, to have had chances of preparing in detail.

22...♘c6 is a more tactical line, putting pressure on the pawn on d4, rather than pure defence:

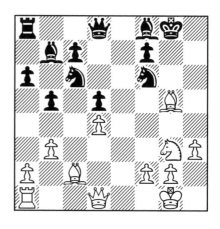

a) White suffered a quick collapse a month after the second Navara-Socko game in J.Polgar-S.Mamedyarov, Essent 2006. After 23 ♘f5?! ('an unfortunate novelty', according to Marin), Black fought back with 23...♗c8! 24 ♖c1 ♗xf5 25 ♗xf5 ♕d6 26 ♗h4 ♘e7 27 ♗g3 ♕b4, Black later consolidating and winning.

b) 23 ♕d3!? ♘b4 24 ♕f3 has also been tried.

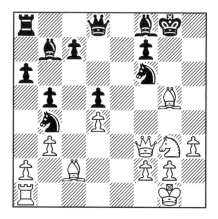

White lures the knight from the centre, but he will soon have to give a tempo with his bishop:

b1) If then 24...♘xc2? 25 ♗xf6 ♕xf6 26 ♕xf6 ♘xa1 27 ♕g5+ ♔h8 28 ♘h5, and White's queen and knight are much more effective than Black's scattered pieces.

b2) 24...♗e7 is far safer, and it could end up as another draw by repetition in a few moves time:

b21) Lukacs and Hazai give 25 ♘f5 ♘xc2 26 ♘xe7+ ♕xe7 27 ♗xf6 ♕e4 28 ♕g5+ ♕g8 28 ♕h4 ♕h7 29 ♕g5+ as a draw.

b22) Instead, A.Grischuk-S.Mamedyarov, Moscow 2006, continued with 25 ♗b1 ♗c8 26 ♕f4 ♘e4 27 ♗xe7 ♕xe7 ♘c6 29 ♗xe4 dxe4 30 ♘h5 ♕d6 31 ♘f6+ ♔f8 32 ♕h6+ ♔e7 33 ♘g8+ ♔e8 34 ♘f6+ ♔e7, draw. Analysis for ChessBase, by Ftacnik and by Lukacs/Hazai, suggests possible improvements for both sides, with 26 ♗f5! looking prom-

ising for White. Black could instead try 25...♘e4! a move earlier: 26 ♗xe7 ♕xe7 27 a3 ♘c6 28 ♘xe4 ♘xd4 29 ♕g4+ ♔f8 30 ♕h5 ♔g7. Clearly there is now an obvious draw. The computer suggests that the unexpected 31 ♘d6! might well be an improvement for White, though. If 31...♘e2+ 32 ♔h1 ♕xd6 33 ♕xe2 ♕f4 34 ♗d3 ♖h8 35 ♔g1 d4 36 ♖e1, White, maybe contrary to initial appearances, is doing well. Black has the passed pawn in the centre, but White controls the other central file with queen and rook, and Black's king is exposed.

There is clearly plenty of play to be analysed in this whole variation, but maybe the quiet positional grind, after the tactics and sacrifices, might be the most effective way of handling things.

c) There is another sharp line, though: 23 ♘h5 ♗e7 24 ♗xf6 ♗xf6 25 ♕d3 ♗xd4 26 ♕h7+ ♔f8 27 ♕h6+ ♔e8 28 ♖e1+.

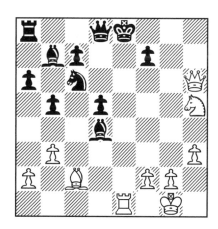

After some natural and logical play, some recent games diverged. Naturally Black must block the diagonal, with either 28...♘e7 or 28...♘e5; 28...♔d7?? 29 ♗f5 mate is not bright:

c1) The earlier game was A.Fedorov-

E.Inarkiev, Sochi 2005, where Black chose 28...♘e7:

c11) Play continued with 29 ♘g7+ ♔d7 (29...♔xg7 30 ♕xg7 ♔d7 31 ♕xf7 ♕e8 32 ♗f5+ ♔d8 33 ♖xe7 ♕xe7 34 ♕g8+ ♕e8 35 ♕g5+ ♕e7 is a perpetual, but Black will want to do more than that) 30 ♘f5 ♘c6 31 ♘xd4 ♘xd4 32 ♕f4 ♘xc2 33 ♕f7+ ♔c6 34 ♕g6+ ♔c5 35 ♕xc2+ ♔b6, and the king was safe, and Black kept an extra bishop.

c12) If White wanted to force a draw, 29 ♗f5!? would sort this out quickly. Black cannot allow the bishop to stay there, so 29...♗c8 and a perpetual after 30 ♕c6+ ♔f8 31 ♕h6+ ♔e8. Therefore there is no realistic prospect of Black refuting White's play in this line.

c13) The most startling line is 29 ♕g5 ♔f8 30 ♗h7 (avoiding the repetition with 30 ♕h6+) 30...♗c3 31 h4 ♕d6 32 ♖xe7 ♖e8! (not 32...♕xe7?? 33 ♕g8+), and a draw was agreed some moves later in K.Landa-V.Kosyrev, Internet 2005.

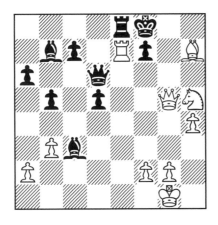

This is a wonderfully strange position. Black is not in fact threatening the rook on e7, since 33...♔xe7 would be illegal, and 33...♕xe7?? and 33...♖xe7?? would allow checkmate with 34 ♕g8.

Black cannot even push the queen away with 33...f6?? in view of 34 ♕g7 mate. So far, this all looks promising for White, except that he cannot make any further advance, with either rook or queen. There are many chances on either side to break though, but if the opponent is alert, the likely result is deadlock.

c2) In a game Mamedyarov-Shirov, Moscow 2006, play continued 28...♘e5 29 ♗f5 ♕d6 30 ♕g5 c5 31 ♘f6+ ♔d8 32 ♘xd5+ ♔e8 34 ♘d5+, and a draw by repetition. There are other possibilities here too: for example, 31 ♗g4 (opening up the f5-square for the knight after ♘g7+) 32...♕e7 32 ♕g8+ ♕f8 33 ♕g5 ♕e7, with another repetition. Instead Lukacs and Hazai suggest 31 ♔f1!? as a possibility, with the idea of f4. Play is complicated, but there are many draws by repetition if White wants. There is a suspicion, though, that with best play, White could try for more. For example, after 31...♔f8 32 ♘f6 ♗c6 33 f4 b4 34 ♗d3, White will capture the knight (as if 34...♘xd3?? 35 ♕h6 mate), with chances of an edge.

We now return to 22...♘ed7:

23 ♕f3

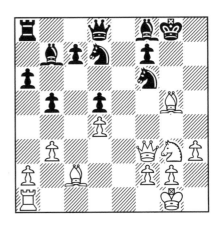

Back to 'normal' chess. We are at the end of the combinational phase, and now it is a case of positional pressure against the black pieces. All White's pieces, apart for the king, are already attacking, or just a move to attacking, while some Black's pieces are quiet defenders. Much depends on whether Black can uncover his pieces.

23...♕e7

Probably the best defensive option.

An initial computer suggestion is 23...♗g7 24 ♘h5 ♗h8, keeping firm control of the pinned knight, but unfortunately Black has little support for the king. 25 ♗h6 ♘e4 26 ♕g4+ ♔h7 27 ♗g7 ♕e7! (27...♕g8?? 28 ♕f5 mate) 28 ♗xh8 f5 29 ♕g7+ ♕xg7 30 ♗xg7 ♔g6 31 g4 keeps Black's alive, although a pawn down. White should eventually win.

If 23...♗e7 24 ♘f5, and Black's position creaks. Playing through the computer options for Black would give 24...♔h8 25 ♖e1 ♗b4 26 ♘h6 ♗g7 27 ♖e3 ♗d2 28 ♘f5+ ♔h8 29 ♘e7 ♔g7 30 ♕g3 ♗xe3 21 ♗h6+ ♔xh6 32 ♘f5+ ♔h5 33 ♗d1+ and mate next move.

If the bishop cannot help, the queen has to take on the burden.

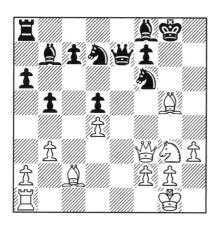

24 ♗f5

White threatens ♗xe7.

The alternative is 24 ♘h5 ♗g7 25 ♘xg7 (25 ♗f5 ♕f8! holds) 25...♔xg7 26 ♕g3 ♕e6!? 27 ♗xf6+ ♔xf6 28 ♕f4+ ♔e7 29 ♗f5 ♕d6 30 ♖e1+ ♔d8 31 ♕h4+ ♕f6 31 ♕h4+ ♕f6 32 ♕g4 ♘f8 33 ♕g8 ♕d6 34 ♕xf7 ♗c6 35 ♖e5, and Black is still under pressure, but not as much as in the game.

24...♕d6

Socko accepts that the best he can do is to allow a repetition. Navara's piece sacrifice has at least held the balance in this game, but can he try for more? One would expect so.

25 ♗f4

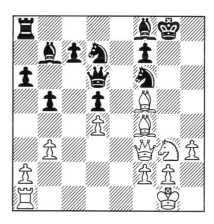

The bishop is able to use another diagonal. Indeed, both white bishops are very strong.

25...♕e7?

Both players would have had the opportunity of analysing their previous encounter some months ago, but it is Socko whose game faltered. He tries to keep the extra minor piece, but his defence crumbles.

A more active way is to make a return sacrifice, with the view of active counterplay. The choice is between 25...♕b6 and 25...♕b4. Either way,

White recovers the knight with 26 ♗xd7 ♘xd7 27 ♕g4+, and then 27...♔h8 28 ♕xd7 (White can, of course, accept a draw with 28 ♕h4+) 28...♕xd4 forks the rook and bishop.

The obvious continuation is 29 ♖c1, giving up bishop rather than rook. After 29...♕xf4 30 ♖xc7 ♖a7 31 ♘f5 it looks at first as though White has a winning attack. But then there is a wonderful tactical resource with 31...♗c6!!, threatening the queen, threatening the rook, and blocking the defence of the queen check on c1. White can just hold out for a draw with 32 ♕d8! ♕c1+ 33 ♔h2 ♕f4+. Some superb tactics, but with the help of computer Navara could well have analysed this line in advance. If I can find it, so could he! Try to imagine how difficult it would be for the over-the-board player finding the draw from move 25. Difficult.

Here White also has a relatively quiet line, with 31 ♖xb7 (instead of 31 ♘f5). After 31...♗c5, there is a perpetual check on 32 ♘h1 ♗xf2+ 33 ♘xf2 ♕c1+ 34 ♔g1 ♕f1+. Play is still equal after 35 ♘d1 ♕xd1+ 36 ♔h2 ♖xb7 37 ♕xb7 ♕h5!. Alternatively here, White has 32 ♕c8+ ♔h7 33 ♕xc5 ♖xb7 34 ♕xd5 ♖c7. After all the wild complications, we reach a relatively stable early endgame with queens, and for White, knight and two pawns versus rook. White is better, and certainly should not lose this, but it would be a long endgame grind to play for a win.

These are the critical main lines, but it remains to be seen whether White can find good alternatives, after either 25...♕b6 or 25...♕b4.

The weaker 25...♕b6?! 26 ♖c1! ♗c6 27 ♘h5 ♘xh5 28 ♕xh5 ♘f6 29 ♕h4

♗g7 30 ♗e5 puts Black under pressure. Therefore he needs to consider the other queen move.

25...♕b4! places the queen on a livelier square.

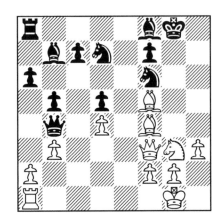

Then White could, as suggested earlier, have tried 26 ♗xd7 ♘xd7 27 ♕g4+, with an edge for him after complicated play.

Or he could try 26 ♖c1 ♗c8 27 ♗e5 ♘xe5 28 dxe5 ♗xf5 29 ♕xf5 ♘e4. Then 30 ♖xc7 ♕e1+ 31 ♘f1 ♕xf2+ 32 ♕xf2 ♘xf2 33 ♔xf2 ♖e8 is level, or perhaps slightly better for Black in an endgame. White also has 30 ♕g4+ ♔h8 31 ♕h5+ ♔g8, and then 32 e6!?, avoiding the repetition. The safest reply is then 32...♕e7!, and then White should take a draw with 33 ♕g4+ ♔g8 34 ♕h5+ ♔g7: 35 ♕xd5? is unwise, as Black has 35...♘xg3!, and if 36 ♕xa8 ♘e2+, forking king and rook.

Complicated, but it seems that 25...♕b4! keeps White down to a slight edge,.

26 ♖c1!

Maybe Socko was hoping for a draw anyway with 26 ♗g5, repeating.

Navara shows that he can add to the pressure.

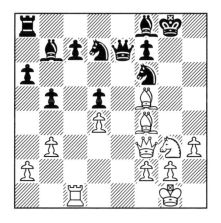

26...c6

Marin gives 26...c5 27 &g5 &d6 as an improvement, but Black's position is unconvincing. After 28 dxc5 &c6 29 &h5 &xh5 30 &xh5 &g7 31 &h7+ &f8 32 &xd7 &xd7 33 &h6 White has a winning attack. Alternatively, 29...&e8 30 &e3 &e5 (30...&xe3 is better, but unsatisfactory) 31 &g3+ &h8 32 &h4 &xh5 33 &xh5+ &g7 34 &h7+ &f6 35 h4! &g6 36 &xg6 fxg6 37 &d4+ leads to a win for White.

Black's mistake was on move 25, not on move 26.

27 &g5

Returning to the pin, and threatening the &xd7 capture.

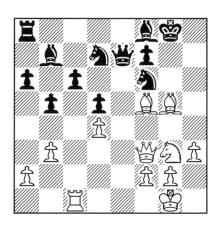

27...&d6

And so the queen returns.

28 &h5

He is not interested in a repetition with 28 &f4.

White has only three minor pieces, but they have much greater impact than Black's four.

28...&g7

The queen breaks through after 28...&xh5 29 &xh5 &g7 30 &h7+ &f8 31 &xd7 &xd7 32 &h6, and if 30...f6 31 &h8+.

White also has a fairly standard attacking win after 28...&e8 29 &f4 &e7 30 &g3+ &h8 31 &h4 &g8 32 &g5+ &h8 33 &xf6 &xf6 34 &e5 &g7 35 &c3.

So many attacking pieces for White, so few defenders for Black.

29 &xg7

Forcing the king into the open.

29...&xg7 30 &f4

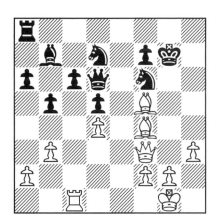

The bishop hits the queen yet again.

30...&e7

Black's queen is stuck on the a3-f8 diagonal, and from White's point of view, it does not really matter where the queen should go. By now, White is winning.

31 &g3+

A strong check.

32...♔h8

If 32...♔f8 33 ♗d6, pins the queen.

32 ♕h4+

Zigzagging through.

32...♔g8

32...♔g7 33 ♗h6+ wins more quickly.

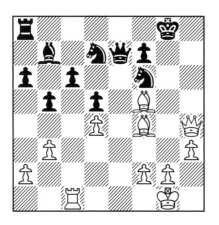

33 ♗xd7

The simplest, even though he is not giving immediate checkmate, or winning the queen.

There is always the possibility of a blunder, even from a winning position, and 33 ♖c3? throws a rook after

33...♕e1+ 34 ♔h2 ♕xc3. White's idea would probably have been 35 ♗h6! ♘e8 36 ♗h7+ ♔h8 37 ♗f5 ♔g8, but it is only a perpetual. Unnecessary sacrifices are not good chess.

33 ♔h2? is over-sophisticated, aiming to play ♖c3 without allowing a queen fork, but allowing a different checking idea. After 33...♘f8 34 ♗g5 ♕d6+! 35 ♗f4 ♕e7 it is time now for a perpetual.

Navara plays it simply, and correctly.

33...♕xd7

Obviously not 33...♘xd7?? 34 ♕xe7.

34 ♕xf6

Now White has recovered his piece, is a pawn ahead, and keeps the more active pieces.

34...♕e6

His one hope is to head for an endgame.

35 ♕g5+ 1-0

Here Black gave up on his position, or possibly lost on time. If 35...♕g6, White does not bother with exchanging the queens, but instead continues the attack with 36 ♕d7.

Game 15
I.Sokolov-J.Polgar
Hoogeveen 2006
Nimzo-Indian Defence E49

1 d4 ♘f6 2 c4 e6 3 ♘c3 ♗b4 4 e3

Simple enough. White wants to bring his kingside pieces into play. There is a slight problem that the dark-squared bishop cannot develop, and this indeed was a significant factor later in this game.

4 ♕c2, keeping open a later ♗g5, is also popular. See Game 12, Bareev-Efimenko, and Game 13, Kramnik-Leko.

Among other possibilities, 4 ♘f3 d5 is seen in Game 26, Wang Yue-Movsesian.

4...0-0

One of many alternatives. 4...c5, and 4...b6 are both main lines, but not covered in this collection. If Black wants to try the Nimzowitsch plan of doubling the c-pawns, and playing against them, the best option would be 4...c5, aiming for 5 ♗d3 ♘c6 6 ♘f3 ♗xc3+ 7 bxc3 d6.

5 ♗d3

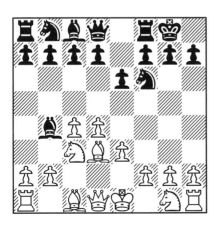

The most common, although 5 ♘ge2 is also popular, planning to recapture with the knight, rather than the pawn, on c3. The knight is slightly misplaced after 5...d5 6 a3 ♗e7, but in compensation Black has lost a tempo with the bishop. White usually tries 7 cxd5, and then either recapture is playable.

5...d5

Aiming for a Queen's Gambit type of position. Black's bishop is more aggressive on b4 than on e7, but he will often be forced to exchange, giving away the bishop-pair. However, White no longer has ♗g5 possibilities.

6 a3

Sokolov's favoured approach, setting up a Sämisch structure.

6 ♘f3, 6 cxd5 and, though less often played, 6 ♘ge2 are also good.

6...♗xc3+

The natural reply.

6...♗e7 is an alternative, and is playable but not very inspiring. Black argues that in comparison with the Queen's Gambit (for example, 1 d4 d5 2 c4 e6 3 ♘f3 ♘f6 4 ♗g5), White does not have the ♗g5 development. Black has, however, lost a 'semi-tempo', and White's a3 is often useful.

6...dxc4 allows extra transpositional possibilities, for example, 7 ♗xc4 ♗d6, but White too has an alternative, with 7 ♗xh7+ followed by axb4, with a slight but secure edge.

7 bxc3

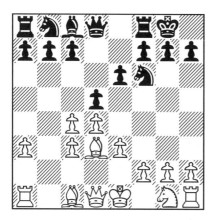

So Black has given up the bishop-pair. This is of course standard in the Nimzo-Indian. Black has free development with his, or her, pieces, and has every opportunity of gaining parity in the centre.

7...dxc4

7...e5!? has been tried a few times:

a) The tactical point is that after 8 dxe5 dxc4 9 ♗xc4? (9 exf6 ♕xd3 10 ♕xd3 cxd3 is about equal) 9...♕xd1+ 10 ♔xd1 ♘g4 Black is doing well, and has recovered the pawn. White's isolated queenside pawn pair will become something of a problem as we get closer to the endgame.

b) White usually prefers 8 ♘e2 e4 9 ♗c2, and after 9...dxc4 there are some similarities to the pawn structure in our main game.

7...c6, as played in I.Sokolov-S.Movsesian, Sarajevo 2007, is a quiet alternative, aiming for gradual equality after 8 ♘f3 b6 9 cxd5 cxd5 10 ♕e2 ♗b7 11 0-0 ♕c8, followed by ...♗a6. The game was later drawn.

8 ♗xc4 c5

8...e5 is again playable, but no longer has the possibility of an ...e4 hit

against the bishop. White could perhaps consider 9 ♘f3 e4 10 ♘e5 ♘bd7 11 f4!? exf3:

a) 12 ♕xf3? is natural, but a serious blunder. Black has a winning attack after 12...♘xe5 13 dxe5 ♗g4! 14 ♕f4 ♕d1+ 15 ♔f2 ♕c2+ 16 ♔g1 ♘e4.

b) 12 ♘xf3! is better, and Black might well have a few problems over the f7-square (0-0, ♘g5 or ♘e5, etc). Perhaps such thoughts help explain why Black does not try an early ...e5.

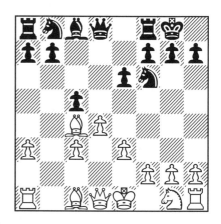

9 ♘e2

9 ♘f3 leads to mainline positions, often reached too via 6 ♘f3.

Sokolov attempts what he hopes will become a more flexible development, covering any problems on the c3-square, and maybe even thinking about gaining pawn space with f3. The trouble is that he no longer keeps control of e5, and Polgar gains a second hit in the centre, with ...e5 as well as ...c5.

9...♕c7

Gaining a minor tempo, with the threatened hit on the bishop after ...cxd4.

'The threat is greater than the execution', as the great chess thinker Aron Nimzowitsch noted. Here 9...cxd4?! 10

cxd4 ♕c7 11 ♗a2 gives nothing for Black. It is better to keep the good pawn in play.

9...♘c6 is a good alternative, keeping the tension. Black will usually play ...♕c7 at some stage, though.

10 ♗a2

Keeping the bishop out of harm's way, and reminding Black that if she tries a quick ...e5, White still has pressure against f7.

10 ♗d3 is the main alternative. Then 10...e5 is well-timed, and should lead to equal play.

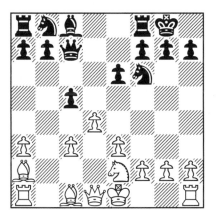

The next stage of the development plan. Black has to decide what to do with the queenside minor pieces.

10...b6

The bishop goes first, either to b7 or a6.

10...e5 has been tried several times. Then the simple 11 d5 might be best. The passed pawn is not a big threat, especially so early in the game, but it demands some respect. Later White may try to bolster the pawn with c4, and possibly f3 followed by e4.

Polgar's move seems more logical, aiming to develop her pieces while giving away nothing.

11 0-0

Or maybe 11 ♗b2, but on the other hand, while we know that White has to castle kingside, we do not quite know whether the bishop is best on b2. It is better to keep flexibility, and to castle immediately.

11...♗a6

Did the reader assume that Black was going to fianchetto immediately on the long diagonal?

Black is not really threatening to attack on g2, not least because White is often quite happy to close the diagonal with f3, if required, and then e4. The a6-f1 diagonal, on the other hand, is more of an irritation. White's doubled c-pawns have gone, but he still has the problem that the c4-square is a slight weakness, making it difficult to play c4, especially if Black's bishop is pressing on this square.

12 ♖e1

To free the knight.

12...♘c6

The natural square. She completes her development, before pushing the pawn with ...e5.

13 ♘g3

13 ♘f4, seemingly more aggressive, has not gained much attention. 13...e5 14 ♘d5 ♘xd5 15 ♗xd5 ♖ad8 16 dxc5 ♘e7! leaves Black comfortable.

13...♖ad8

In such positions, it is often difficult to decide which rook should be placed on the d-file. In previous games, Black had tended to play 13...♖fd8, with the option of placing rooks on the c-file and d-file. Polgar has decided instead that she wants to add extra cover for the f7-square, after she has opened up White's diagonal with ...e5.

14 ♗b2

14 ♘h5 ♘xh5 15 ♕xh5 ♗d3!, followed perhaps by ...♗g6, covers any attack by White on Black's kingside.

White prefers to complete his development, before attacking.

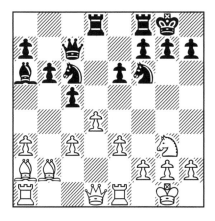

14...e5

She takes over the initiative in the centre, but loosens some light squares.

14...♘a5 15 e4 ♘c4 16 ♗c1 cxd4 17 cxd4 ♕d7 18 ♗xc4 ♗xc4 19 ♗b2 still gives White a slight edge, with the idea of d5 followed by breaking up the pawn structure with ♗xf6.

15 ♕c2

In *Informator*, Polgar suggests as better 15 d5! ♘a5 16 e4 ♗c4. White's connected passed pawn is of course useful, but this is not enough to force an edge of itself. To aim for a realistic plus, White would need to push pieces to the kingside, maybe starting off with 17 ♗b1, taking advantage that Black's knight on a5 is far away from the kingside. Black is not yet equal.

15 ♖c1 ♘a5 16 ♕f3 ♖fe8 17 e4 ♗c4 18 ♗b1 ♘b3 was tried in M.Illescas-F.Vallejo Pons, Spanish Team Championship 2004. It might look as though Black has gained an edge, attacking the

rook, and putting great pressure on the pawn on d4, but White sacrificed the exchange with 19 d5! ♘xc1 20 ♗xc1, keeping a strong pawn centre, and being ready to attack on the kingside. Vallejo opted for safety by returning the exchange, with 20...♖d6 21 ♘f5 ♘d7 22 ♘xd6 ♕xd6, draw agreed.

The computer suggests that White may still be slightly better at the time of the draw agreement, but a strong human player would find it difficult to make any progress. It is difficult to activate the bishop-pair, and it is difficult to open up the pawns. Any exchange of the light-squared bishops will leave Black's knight more effective than White's remaining bishop. Also, Black has an extra queenside pawn, in compensation, obviously, for White's extra central pawn, and Black can try to expand with a later ...c4, or a more general push with ...b5 and ...a5. Probably the position is, as the players agreed, just equal.

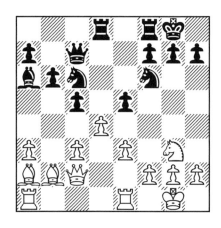

15...♖d7

With great tension on the d-file, most obviously on the d4-pawn, but also an attempt to restrain the pawn from playing to d5.

The immediate liquidation, with 15...cxd4?! 16 cxd4 exd4 17 &xd4, would give White a comfortable slight edge with the help of the bishop-pair.

If 15...♘a5, Polgar suggests 16 dxe5 &d3 17 ♕c1 ♕xe5 18 c4 ♕e6 19 e4 with chances of attack for White.

15...&c8 was suggested by the computer, with the idea that if 16 ♖ad1 &e6!?, Black's isolated pawn structure is no real weakness, and the knight on c6 does not have to reach to a5 to offer a bishop exchange. The simple 17 &b1! leaves White slightly better.

16 ♖ad1

16 ♘e4! ♘xe4 17 ♕xe4 looks like an improvement. White has no pin on the d-file, as opposed to the interpolated 16 ♖ad1 ♖fd8 17 ♘e4 ♘xe4 18 ♕xe4 when Black may safely try 18...♘e7. In the suggested improvement, White might still have a slight edge after 17...♖fd8 18 d5 ♘e7 19 c4.

16...♖fd8

White no longer has an edge on the d-file.

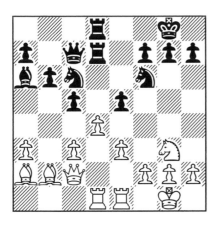

17 h3!?

White's position is fully playable, and remains so for the next few moves. There is no need to criticize Sokolov's quiet move here. Polgar plays dramatic attacking chess later on, and this may easily create the impression that Sokolov's quiet move early on was a mistake of judgement, causing problems much later. Playing through the position move-by-move such an assessment would seem not so clear.

We are in a classic Nimzo-Indian early middlegame, in which both pawns and pieces are finely balanced. There are four possibilities, two on either side, of central pawn exchanges, but neither side would gain from initiating the pawn exchange, and indeed would lose ground. White wants to keep his d-pawn, this being clearly his best and most effective pawn, while Black would not want to exchange with ...cxd4 or ...exd4, when White could recapture with a pawn on d4. The only possibilities of making progress in the centre would either be d5 for White, too early and it would lose a pawn, or ...e4 and/or ...c4 for Black, which would gain space but would release the central pawn tension. Both players will want to keep in mind these ideas.

In the meantime, it is unclear how White should play his next couple of piece moves. 17 ♘e4 is a possibility, but so too is 17 ♘f5. It is unclear as yet which would be the better square for the knight. The bishop would be good on the b1-h7 diagonal, but it is also good on the a2-g8 diagonal, and it is not totally clear that an extra bishop move would be worth a tempo. Other piece moves are also possible, but do not improve their positions.

This leaves off-centre pawn moves. The two main candidates are 17 f3!? or 17 h3!?, as played. The 17 f3 idea is fully playable, preventing Black from trying ...e4 or a possible threat with ...♘g4 after White makes a knight move. White is, however, weakening his dark squares. Sokolov instead pushes his h-pawn, cutting out possible weaknesses on the back rank, and also cutting out ...♘g4.

17...c4!?

Polgar takes the initiative in the centre, not perhaps because of aggression intent, but more from a sense that if play drifts on, Black will have fewer good quiet moves than White.

Polgar suggests 17...♘a5 18 dxe5 ♕xe5 19 c4 ♕e6 20 ♗b1 as a possibility. Here White could continue the theme of trying to play constructive quiet moves with 18 ♗b1 ♘c4 19 ♗c1. It is not fully clear that the knight is better on c4 than on c6. The position is probably about equal, or the usual very slight edge for White.

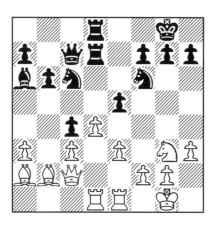

18 a4?!

The first real question mark given by Judit Polgar. It is still more of an indicator that White could have played the line better, rather than any indication that White would be worse. Polgar gives as better 18 ♗b1 g6 (otherwise

♘h5) 19 ♕e2 with much improved centralization.

18...♖e8!

Aiming for ...e4.

19 ♗a3

Sokolov is still presumably aiming for a slight edge, despite his previous two quiet moves, hoping that the bishop-pair will prevail in the long run. Otherwise, there is a simple and natural repetition with 19 ♘e4 ♘d5 20 ♘g5 ♘f6 21 ♘e4 (21 d5 h6 is at least equal for Black). Here Polgar gives 19...♘xe4 20 ♕xe4 g6, but ultimately White should have an edge after, for example, 21 ♕f3 with the bishop-pair starting to become more effective.

19...e4

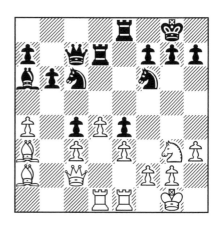

The next stage of the central pawn structure. Both players may presumably be reasonably happy with the pawn structure, White having a secure passed pawn, and Black having set up a couple of tusks with two advanced pawns close to the centre.

20 ♗b1

Sokolov could consider 20 d5!? ♘xd5 21 ♘xe4, but presumably he wants to keep his passed pawn. After 21...♘e5 22 ♖d4 ♘d3 23 ♖d1 play could easily become deadlocked, with any active piece move by either side allowing the opponent to find new squares. The position looks tense but equal, one possibility being 23...h6 24 ♘g3 ♖ed8 25 ♘e4 ♖e8 with a repetition.

Sokolov holds back his passed pawn, but Black's pieces turn out to be the more active.

20...♖d5!?

Very direct. She aims for attack. There will be tactics, but one cannot calculate everything in advance. 20...♘a5 is more solid, and who knows, possibly more accurate, but does not give all that many chances of a win.

21 ♘e2

The knight is the piece that can best improve its position.

21...♖g5

Continuing to attack. This is do-or-die chess, and soon Polgar is obliged to drop a pawn to gain any chance of carrying on the attack against the king.

22 ♘f4

A good square for the knight, assisting both the defence of h3 and g2, and helping a pawn attack with d5.

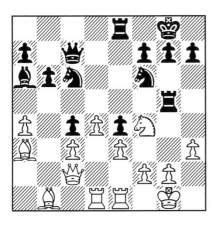

22...♗c8?!

Polgar has played aggressively, but

so far has not been taking risks. She has allowed White to set up a strong passed pawn, but so long as the pawn is not charging forward, that is acceptable, provided she has reasonable counter-play.

Her next move takes risks, though, as no longer is Black's bishop covering the c4-pawn.

22...♕d7!?, suggested by Polgar in her notes, is safer if less ambitious. Black would probably try ...♘e7, and then one of the knights to d5. Black looks at least equal.

My reading of the position is that Polgar's move is a mistake, overpressing, but that she soon recovers well, by aiming for a full-blown attack. See the notes to White's 25th, below.

23 ♕e2

Aiming for the pawn.

Polgar notes the alternative, 23 ♗a2!? ♘a5 24 d5 ♗b7 25 d6 ♕d7 with unclear play. This may well be Black's best line in this line. Indeed, 23...♘d5?! 24 ♗xc4 ♘xf4 25 exf4 ♕xf4 26 ♖e3, also given by Polgar, favours White. After instead 23...♘e7 24 ♗xe7 ♖xe7 25 d5 ♘e8, with the idea of 26 d6 (26 ♖d4 looks equal) 26...♘xd6 27 ♘d5 ♕b7 28 ♘xe7+ ♕xe7 29 ♕d2 ♖g6, Polgar suggests there is compensation for the exchange, but this seems slightly fragile after 30 ♕d5!, and if 30...♗xh3 (30...♕e8 is possible, when maybe the simplest is 31 ♕xd6 ♖xd6 32 ♖xd6 with an edge for White) 31 ♕a8+ ♘e8?! (31...♕e8 32 ♕xe8+ ♘xe8 33 g3 ♗g4 34 ♖d8 ♔f8 35 ♗xc4 with an edge for White) 32 g3 ♕e5 33 ♖d5! ♖xg3+ 34 ♔h1!, and Black's attack fades away after, for example, 34...♗g2+ 35 ♔h2 ♖h3+ 36 ♔xg2 ♕h1+ 37 ♔f1.

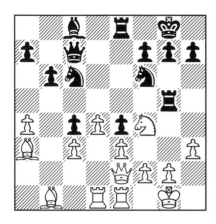

23...♕d7!

She abandons the c4-pawn.

If 23...♘e7 24 ♗a2, and to save the pawn Black would be required to lose two tempi with 24...♗a6. White can try for an edge with 25 ♗xe7 ♖xe7 26 ♖b1.

24 ♕xc4

Naturally.

24...♘a5

Black takes over the light squares, but with pieces rather than pawns.

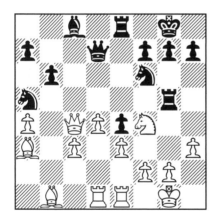

25 ♕b4?

Sokolov is aiming to keep the extra pawn, on a4, but his kingside is too weak.

25 ♕e2! keeps White better centralized. White's isolated a-pawn is not significant enough to try to defend. Polgar gives 25...♕xa4 26 ♗b4 ♘c6 27 ♗c2 ♕a6 as unclear, but the suspicion is that White is better, with the more effective pawn structure, and a dangerous and very safe passed d-pawn. A good starting point might be 28 ♕xa6 ♗xa6 29 ♖a1.

This leaves the question of whether Polgar has overpressed. Indeed, if 25...♘d5, Polgar gives 26 ♗b4! ♘c6 27 ♖c1!, shoring up the defences:

a) The recapture of the pawn is only temporary, since if 27...♘cxb4 28 cxb4 ♘xb4 29 ♕c4 a5, White has 30 ♗xe4!; White's pieces have been carefully set up.

b) There are ways of playing quietly, a pawn down, such as here with 27...♕d8 28 ♗a3 ♕f6, but they are not especially enticing.

c) Finally, the yahoo attack with 27...♘xf4 28 exf4 ♖xg2+? (28...♖g6 29 f5 wins more slowly for White) 29 ♔xg2 ♕xh3+ 30 ♔g1 ♖e6 (30...♗g4 31 ♕f1) 31 ♗xe4 does not work. White quickly shifts the bishop from the queenside to the kingside.

There are various alternatives by Black, but centralization by White seems to keep an edge.

25...♘d5

Something of a reprieve for Black. The exchange of knights now leaves White's pawns on g2 and h3 seriously weak, and behind the pawns there is a frightened king.

26 ♘xd5

26 ♕b5! ♕xb5 27 axb5 ♘xc3 28 ♖c1 ♘xb1 (but not 28...♘xb5? 29 ♗e7! ♖f5 29 ♗xe4) 29 ♖xb1 ♘c4 30 h4 ♖f5 31 ♗c1 a5! 32 bxa6 ♖a5 is still slightly uncomfortable for White, even with the

queens off the board. His bishop on c1 is bad.

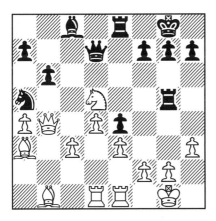

26...♛xd5

On 26...♜xg2+ 27 ♔xg2 ♛xh3+ 28 ♔g1 ♛g4+, the simple 29 ♔h2 gives Black no more than a perpetual. Black has no time for quiet moves, as White's queen bounds around with ♛d6.

Polgar would naturally have analysed the rook sacrifice, and would have wanted to ensure that she had at least a draw, just in case other lines did not work. It would have been in this context that she gave the line, in *Informator*, 29 ♔f1 ♝a6+ 30 ♝d3 exd3 31 ♘c7! ♝c4 32 ♜d2 ♛h3+ 33 ♔g1 ♛g4+, and finally it is a draw after various attempts at refutation.

27 h4

White has no defending pieces supporting his king, and this could easily lead to fatal exposure. If, for example, 27 ♔h2, Polgar gives 27...♝xh3! 28 gxh3 (28 ♛b5 ♛d8!) 28...♛f5 29 f4 ♜h5 with a winning attack.

If instead 27 ♛d6!?, Black could of course simplify, and recover the pawn with 27...♛xd6 28 ♝xd6 ♝xh3 29 ♝g3 with possibly Black keeping a slight edge after 29...♝g4 30 ♜c1 ♘c4, and if

31 ♝a2 ♘b2 32 ♜c2 ♘d3 33 ♜b1 ♝d7. Black has the more active pieces, but she must be careful about White's passed pawn and bishop-pair.

Polgar instead gives 27...♛f5, playing for the attack, with a win after 28 ♔h1 ♘c4 29 ♛c6 ♝d7! 30 ♛xc4 ♜xg2 31 ♔xg2 ♛f3+ 32 ♔h2 ♝xh3 33 ♜g1 ♝e6. The counterattack with 34 ♜xg7+ ♔xg7 35 ♛f1 ♛h5+ 36 ♔g1 ♝h3 does not work. There are possible improvements for White, though, for example with 28 ♛h2 ♛xh3 29 ♝a2 ♛xh2+ 30 ♔xh2 ♝d7 31 d5 ♝xa4 32 ♜d4 ♝b3 33 ♜e2 ♝xa2 34 ♜xa2, although then 34...♘b3! is still advantageous to Black, and if 35 ♜b4 ♘c5.

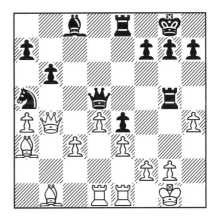

27...♜g4

With an attack on the h4-pawn.

27...♜h5 is a possibility, but then White can force the exchange of queens: 28 ♛b5!? ♛xb5 29 axb5 ♜xb5 with unclear play, but no chances of attack.

28 ♛b5

Naturally Sokolov would still like to swap the queens.

28...♛d8!

An unusual starting point for a vicious kingside attack. All Black's pieces are on the periphery, with only a solitary pawn in the centre. Black's queen and bishop are, however, in the process of regrouping. Polgar is aiming for a direct attack.

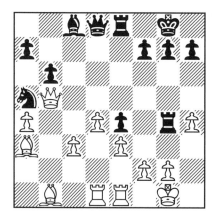

28...♕xb5!? 29 axb5 ♘c4 30 ♗c1 ♗d7 is also good, with a positional edge for Black. But an effective mating attack speeds things up.

29 g3?

This is a weak reply. In a couple of moves time, Black can take the h4-pawn anyway, and White has loosened the pawns in front of his king.

29 ♗d6!? at least brings the bishop to the kingside (29...♕xd6?? 30 ♕xe8+), and keeps the play live. Polgar gives 29...♗d7, without further analysis. After 30 ♕b4 ♕xh4 31 ♗g3 Black has:

a) She could consider sacrificing the exchange with 31...♖xg3 32 fxg3 ♕xg3, maybe about equal, but it seems sensible to wait for the sacrifice until more pieces are developed.

b) So maybe 31...♕g5 32 d5 h5 33 ♔h1 ♘b7 (33...f4?! 34 ♗f4 is premature) 34 ♗c2 (the computer suggests this as best, but it is not so clear that it is better or worse than a few alternatives) 34...♕g6 35 ♖g1 (otherwise ...h4 is

threatened) 35...♘c5 36 a5 ♘d3 37 ♗xd3 exd3 38 ♕b1 ♖xg3 39 fxg3 ♕xg3 40 ♖ge1 ♗a4 41 ♖xd3 ♗c2 42 ♕xc2 ♕xe1+ 43 ♔h2 ♖e4 44 g3 h4 with a winning attack. Not forced, but White would have to find a considerable improvement to hold this.

29...a6!

Forcing the queen from the b5-e8 diagonal.

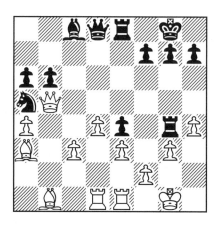

30 ♕b4

What Sokolov had presumably missed was that if 30 ♕h5 ♘c4 31 ♗c1 g6 32 ♕h6 ♘d6, and White's queen is about to be trapped with ...♘f5. It takes four moves by the knight to move from the a-file to the h-file, and sometimes such a manoeuvre may easily be overlooked.

30...♕xh4

Recapturing the pawn, and also re-establishing the rook sacrifice.

31 ♗xe4

If 31 ♕d6 ♘c4 32 ♕c6 ♖xg3+ 33 fxg3 ♕xg3+ 34 ♔h1 ♕h3+ 35 ♔g1 ♗d7! 36 ♕xc4 ♕g3+ 37 ♔h1 ♖e6 (probably the simplest) 38 ♕xe6 ♗xe6, and the queen and bishop still create havoc. White's two rooks and extra bishop, in return for the queen, do not coordinate well, and at the very least White will have to sacrifice a bishop to slow down the attack slightly.

31...罝xg3+!

This rook sacrifice is hardly by now unexpected, but the new feature is no longer the complete demolition of the white pawns, but rather the great pressure on the long diagonal.

32 fxg3 豐xe4

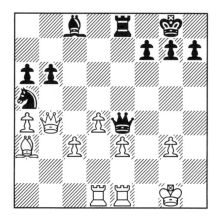

Now the queen is fully centralized, and there are worrying mate threats, with ....奧b7 or ...豐f3 and ...豐xg3+, combined perhaps with ....奧g4 or ...奧h3. This is extremely dangerous, and Black has excellent compensation for the exchange sacrifice.

Is Black winning? Maybe the players might have thought so.

33 罝d2?

White has to find tough and resourceful defensive play, but this isn't it. The alternatives were:

a) Polgar gives 33 d5 ②c4 34 罝d4 豐f3 35 豐xc4 豐xg3+ 36 堂f1 奧h3+ 37 堂e2 罝xe3+ 38 堂d2 豐xe1+ 39 堂c2 罝e2+ with a winning attack. As promised, the queen and bishop work successfully together.

b) 33 豐b2 is a logical defensive plan,

making use of the second rank, but the problem is, of course, the knight fork with 33...②c4. If then 34 豐a2 ②xa3 35 豐xa3 奧b7 36 d5 奧xd5 37 罝xd5 豐xd5, and Black has recovered her material, is a pawn up with active play, and her opponent's pawns are all isolated. It will eventually be a loss, as with various positions where White does not take back the knight after ...②xa3. White slightly prolongs the game, but does not hold it.

c) 33 奧c1!?, cutting out any ...②c4xa3 threats, is a sensible reply:

c1) If, for example, 33...奧b7 34 d5 or 33....奧h3 34 罝d2, White's position is holding.

c2) 33...②c4! is an attractive surprise reply, sacrificing the knight for nothing, and not even attacking anything – a positional sacrifice in the midst of an attack!

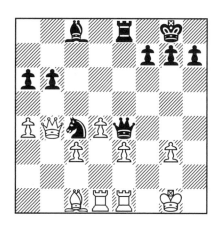

c21) The point is that if 34 豐xc4 奧b7, White cannot play 35 d5??, as the queen is no longer defended. White could still try 35 罝e2 豐h1+ 36 堂f2 豐xd1, but essentially his defence is broken.

c22) A more resilient reply is 34 罝e2!? 奧b7 35 罝f1, aiming to spirit the king to e1 and beyond. 35...♖e6! is the most accurate response, bringing the rook into the attack. If then 36 ♕xc4, Black wins after 36...♕h1+ 37 ♔f2 ♖f6+. If instead 36 ♔f2, White is checkmated after 36...♖f6+ 37 ♔e1 ♖xf1+ 38 ♔xf1 ♕h1+ 39 ♔f2 ♕g2+ 40 ♔e1 ♕g1 mate. It is only a small consolation that the king finally reaches e1.

Is there any further try? It is too early to give up on White just yet.

d) 33 ♕b1! ♕f3 34 ♕a2! seems to give good chances of holding, provided White does not mind returning his extra exchange. After 34...♘c4 35 ♗c1 Black will not be able to force a direct win, but there are two good choices for an endgame edge:

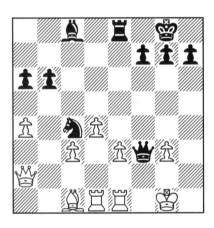

d1) One idea is 35...♗g4 36 ♕f2! ♕xf2+ 37 ♔xf2 ♗xd1 38 ♖xd1 f5 39 ♔e2 (it is too early to hurry with 39 d5) 39...♔f7 40 ♔d3 b5 41 axb5 axb5 42 ♖f1 ♔e6 (42...♔g6 43 ♖f4 holds) 43 e4 fxe4+ 44 ♔xe4 ♗d6+ 45 ♔d3 and White, with care, should draw.

d2) Alternatively, 35...♕xg3+! has the merit of setting up two passed pawns, beneficial in an endgame: 36 ♕g2 ♕xg2+ 37 ♔xg2 ♗g4 38 ♖d3 ♗f5 39 e4 (39 ♖dd1? ♗c2 leaves Black a clear

pawn up) 39...♗xe4+ 40 ♔f2 f6 41 ♖g3 ♔f7 42 ♖g4 f5 43 ♖h4 g6 44 ♖h5. White has defended well so far, but one would expect that Black's three connected passed pawns would eventually break through.

So it seems that Polgar did not have a quick winning attack with best play, but that her opponent had to make concessions.

33...♕f3

With a threatened invasion on g3.

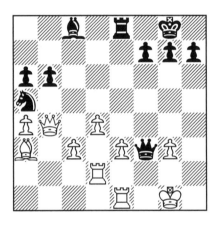

34 ♔h2

34 ♕d6!? sets up a trap. The natural triple knight fork with 34...♘c4 35 ♖f2!, and then 35...♕e4 36 ♕c7 (threatening the check on f7) 36...♗e6 37 ♗c1 ♗d5 38 ♔h2 provides for Black some degree of positional compensation for the exchange, but no dangerous attack. Or 35...♕xf2+ 36 ♔xf2 ♘xd6 37 ♗xd6 ♖e6 38 ♗f4 ♗d7 39 ♖a1 a5 40 ♖b1, and it would be difficult for Black to force a win in the opposite-coloured bishop endgame.

Black would need to play more carefully to force the win: 34...♗b7!, making use of the long diagonal. Then White has to defend against the mating attack, and only then think about ...♘c4.

Play might continue 35 d5 ♘c4 36 ♖f2 ♕g4 37 ♕c7 ♗xd5 38 ♗d6 ♕e4 39 ♖h2 ♘d2, and Black wins.

34...♕h5+

A repetition before the time control.

35 ♔g1 ♕f3

Back to move 33.

36 ♔h2

36 ♕d6!? could again have been tried.

36...♗f5!

Back to normal play. The threat is 37...♗e4, and White has no real resistance.

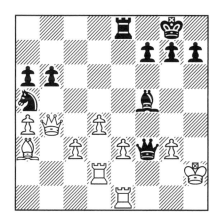

37 e4

White no longer has time to try 37 ♕d6? ♘c4, as Black is simply winning

material, ♖f2 no longer being an option.

On other moves, ...♗e4 is the main threat: for example, 37 ♖ed1 ♗e4 38 d5 ♕h5+ 39 ♔g1 ♕h1+ 40 ♔f2 ♕f3+ 41 ♔e1 ♗c2! with a quick win.

Sokolov tries a desperate exchange sacrifice, but it doesn't work.

37...♗xe4 38 ♖xe4 ♕xe4

Black is now a pawn up, with good centralization and continued chances of an attack on the king.

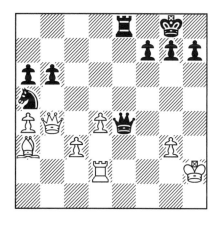

39 d5

White's only hope is his passed pawn.

39...♘c4 0-1

But this squeezes any counterplay.

Game 16
A.Shirov-L.Aronian
Moscow 2006
Ruy Lopez C89

1 e4 e5 2 ♘f3 ♘c6 3 ♗b5 a6 4 ♗a4 ♘f6 5 0-0 ♗e7 6 ♖e1 b5 7 ♗b3 0-0

Varying from the main non-sacrificial line, 7...d6. See the notes to Game 14, Navara-Socko.

8 c3

White knows, of course, that Aronian is happy to offer the Marshall Gambit. In Game 10, Ivanchuk-Aronian 2006, Ivanchuk side-stepped with 8 a4.

Kasparov never allowed the Marshall Attack, in recent years preferring 8 a4 or 8 h3, and earlier, sometimes 8 d4. Shipov, writing in *New in Chess*, commented, tongue in cheek, that it was the Marshall that caused Kasparov to give up chess for politics. Actually, he scored very well in the quieter lines. Maybe it was the Berlin Wall, 3...♘f6, that caused the rift?

8...d5

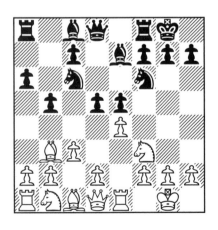

He could still enter the traditional main line with 8...d6, but Black is playing for a more direct attempt at equality, rather than trying to manoeuvre quietly until move 20 and beyond.

9 exd5

9 d3 has been tried several times, but after 9...dxe4 10 dxe4 ♕xd4 11 ♗xd4 it is clear that White is hardly trying for an edge.

9 d4 exd4 10 e5 ♘e4 11 cxd4 ♗g4 12 ♘c3 ♗xf3 13 gxf3 ♘xc3 14 bxc3 f5 15 ♔h1 ♘a5 16 ♗c2 ♔h8 has been tried a couple of times at high level. Both games were drawn, although maybe there are chances for White to try for more. White has the solid passed pawn, but Black can defend against the pawn, and White's doubled f-pawns are blocked.

9...♘xd5 10 ♘xe5

Often the one way to refute a gambit is to accept it. This was what Capablanca tried close to a century ago, and is still the main line.

10 d4!? exd4 11 cxd4 seems to have been under-examined. If one day there is finally an accepted view that the Marshall sacrifice is completely sound, then attention might shift to this. A recent example is L.Nisipeanu-A.Beliavsky, Pune 2004, which continued 11...♗b4 12 ♗d2 ♗b7 12 ♘c3 ♗xc3 14 bxc3 ♘a5 15 ♗c2 ♘c4. Here there are various quiet alternatives for White, the computer suggesting, for example,

16 ♗d3 as a slight edge.

Nisipeanu instead went all-out for a sacrificial attack with 16 ♗g5 f6 17 ♕d3 g6 18 ♗h6 ♖f7 19 ♘g4 ♕d7 20 ♕g3 ♔h8 21 ♗xg6 hxg6 22 ♘xg6+ hxg6 23 ♗f8 ♘de3 24 ♕h4+ ♔xg6 25 ♕h6+ ♔f5 26 ♕h3+ ♔g8 27 ♕h6+ ♔f5, drawn by perpetual.

10 a4 ♗b7 11 axb5 axb5 12 ♖xa8 ♗xa8 13 ♘xe5 ♘xe5 14 ♖xe5 ♘f4 15 d4 ♘xg2 has tended to favour Black. Simple reason – White's king is not safe, while Black's pieces are well developed, and his own king secure.

10...♘xe5 11 ♖xe5 c6

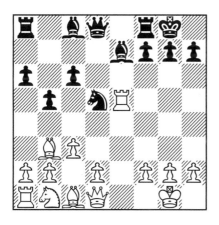

So here we have the Marshall Gambit.

The original Marshall approach was with 11...♘f6 12 ♖e1 ♗d6 13 h3 ♘g4 14 ♕f3, but after a few tactical fireworks with 14...♕h4 15 d4 ♘xf2 16 ♖e2 ♗g4 17 hxg4 ♗h2+ 18 ♔f1 ♗g3, White consolidates with 19 ♖xf2, J.Capablanca-F.Marshall, New York 1918.

In the modern approach, the knight stays on d5. Black is not too worried about the bishop for knight exchange, as the bishop-pair tends to be more important in open attacking play.

12 d4

This is the main line, if White is trying for a win. There are, however, various drawing options. There have been, for example, some painless draws after 12 ♗xd5 cxd5 13 d4 ♗d6 14 ♖e3 ♕h4 15 h3 ♕f4 16 ♖e5 ♕f6 17 ♖e3, and a repetition.

Alternatively, 12 ♖e1 (or 12 g3, soon transposing) 12...♗d6 13 g3 ♗f5 14 d4 ♕d7 15 ♗e3 ♖ae8 16 ♘d2 ♗g4 17 ♕b1 (or 17 ♕c2, soon repeating) 17...♗f5 18 ♕d1 ♗g4, and Black can repeat. This repetition is possible, but is not forced. A recent Aronian win for Black was 18 ♕c1 ♖e6 19 ♘f3 ♗g4 20 ♘g5 ♖g6 21 f3 ♗xf3 22 ♘xf3 ♗xg3 23 hxg3 ♖xg3+ (two minor pieces sacrificed) 24 ♔f2 ♕h3 25 ♔e2 ♕g2+ 26 ♔d3 ♕xf3 (a minor piece down, in return for an attack) 27 ♗xd5 cxd5 28 ♔c2 ♖e8 29 ♗d2 ♕d3+ 30 ♔b3 ♖b8, A.Shabalov-L.Aronian, Calvia Olympiad 2004. If the attack on the king doesn't force a win immediately, the three passed pawns on the kingside will mop things up. White was unable to bring his pieces to good squares.

12...♗d6

12...♗f6?! has been occasionally tried, but not in high-level games. Black needs to attack with the bishop against the weakened kingside, and not against the firmly protected d-pawn.

13 ♖e1

13 ♖e2 has also been tried, with the thought that if 13...♕h4 14 g3 ♕h3, White can flick the queen over to f1, either now (15 ♕f1), or as an alternative possibility, slightly later. White could still, of course, transpose into the main line with 14 ♖e4.

Alternatively, 13...♗g4 14 f3 ♗f5 15 g3 ♕c7 16 ♔f2 ♕d7 17 ♗xd5 cxd5 18

♘d2 ♗d3 19 ♖e3 ♗g6 (Marin notes that Black could force a draw with 19...♕h3 20 ♔g1 ♗xg3) 20 ♘f1 a5 21 a3, agreed drawn in V.Anand-L.Aronian, FIDE World Championship, Mexico City 2007. Naturally there is plenty of play here. Possibly, one suspects, Black could have played on. He is a pawn down, but he has the more active pieces, and White's king is slightly open.

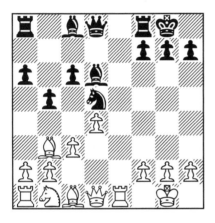

13...♕h4

The only realistic move. If Black does not want to attack, he should avoid gambit play!

14 g3

White has to accept the weakness of the pawns, and this of course adds to the prospects of Black obtaining full compensation for the pawn.

14 f4?! ♗g4 15 g3 ♗xd1 16 hxg4 ♗xb3 17 axb3 f5 gives Black a slight edge. He will soon recover the extra pawn, on f4, and he will have the better queenside pawn structure.

14 h3?! ♗xh3 15 ♗xd5 cxd5 16 gxh3 ♕xh3 17 ♖e5 ♗xe5 18 dxe5 does not provide Black an instant win, but after, for example, 18...♖ae8 19 ♗f4 ♕e6, followed by ...f6, Black has the better prospects.

14...♕h3

Now ...♗g4 is a strong threat.

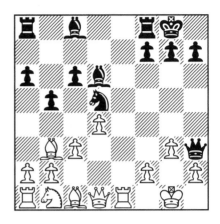

15 ♖e4

A critical choice for White. Here he tries to offer the exchange of queens, in order to soften Black's kingside attack, and he attempts to set up a ♕f1 exchange.

Another try along similar lines would be 15 ♕f3, followed by ♕g2, or alternatively 15 ♗xd5 cxd5 16 ♕f3 followed by ♕g2.

15 ♕e2!? is a more recent idea, with ♕f1 to follow. This perhaps seems less clumsy than the 13 ♖e2 and ♕f1 idea, when the rook is soon hit, but White has in comparison given up a tempo; ♕d1-e2-f1 instead of ♕d1-f1. In the game R.Kasimdzhanov-E.Bacrot, French League 2008, play ended up in a perpetual after 15...♗d7 16 ♕f1 ♕h5 17 ♘d2 ♖ae8 18 f3 ♘f4 19 ♖xe8 ♖xe8 20 ♘e4 ♘h3+ 21 ♔g2 ♘f4+ 22 ♔g1 ♘h3+ 23 ♔g2.

Or quite simply White can try to defend with 15 ♗e3, trying to keep his minor pieces as solid as possible. A recent try, with a win for White, is Wang Hao-A.Grischuk, Russian Team Championship 2008: 15...♗g4 16 ♕d3 ♖ae8

17 ♘d2 ♖e8 18 a4 ♛h5 19 axb5 axb5 20 ♛f1 ♗h3 21 ♗d1!? (there have been a few draws with 21 ♛e2 ♗g4) 21...♛f5 22 ♛e2 c5 23 ♘f3 ♗f4 24 ♛d2 ♘xa3 25 fxe3 ♗h6 26 ♛f2 ♖fe8 27 ♗c2 ♛h5 28 e4! ♖f8 29 ♗d1, and White had finally opened up his position, and won without too much trouble. Here an earlier game, P.Leko-V.Kramnik, Monaco (blindfold) 2007, led to only equality after 27 ♘e5?! ♛xf2+ 28 ♔xf2 f6, though Leko immediately slipped up with 29 ♗g4? (29 ♘g4! is better) 29...♖xe5! 30 ♗xh3 ♗e4+, Black winning a pawn and later the game.

15...g5

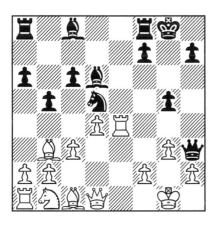

This is standard opening theory, even though Black is opening up lines in front of his king. Black wants to prevent White from pushing the queen away with ♖h4, and he is arguing that if he can keep good control on the kingside, with queen, pawns, bishops and other pieces, White will not get near Black's king.

Various alternatives have been tried, but the pawn push remains by far the most popular.

16 ♛f1

A few players have fallen for 16 ♗xg5?? ♛f5, forking the rook and bishop.

White has occasionally tried an exchange sacrifice with 16 ♛f3 ♗f5 17 ♗c2 ♖xe4 18 ♗xe4, but after 18...♛e6 19 ♗xg5 f5 20 ♗xd5 cxd5 21 ♘d2 f4 22 ♗xf4 ♗xf4 23 gxf4 ♖a7 24 ♔h1 ♖e7 25 ♖g1+ ♔h8, V.Topalov-M.Adams, Sarajevo 2000, Black is clearly better, and later won. While White has three pawns and knight for the rook, neither the pawns nor the knight make much impact against Black's major pieces.

So White instead offers a queen exchange.

16...♛h5

Which Black not too surprisingly declines.

Even so, Black is so far ahead in development that the queen exchange is possible. 16...♛xf1+ 17 ♔xf1 ♗f5 18 ♘d2 h6 (18...♗xe4 19 ♘xe4 allows White to take a second pawn for the exchange, and he will have a lively position) 19 ♖e1 ♖ae8 20 ♘f3 g4 21 ♗xh6 gxf3 22 ♗xf8 ♖xf8 23 ♗d1 ♗g4 is a recent try, unclear, maybe in the end equal. A draw was agreed later on in E.Bacrot-V.Anand, Mainz (rapid) 2007, after 24 a4 ♖d8 25 axb5 axb5 26 ♔g1 ♔g7 27 h3 ♗xh3 28 ♗xf3 ♗e6.

17 ♘d2

A natural developing move.

17...♗f5

And Black too makes a natural developing move, with the intention of gaining a tempo.

17...f5?! 18 ♗d1 ♛h6 19 ♖e1 f4 20 ♘e4 ♗c7 21 ♗d2, as in A.Shirov-V.Akopian, Carlsbad 2007, leaves Black's kingside pawns too loose. Black was unable to keep an attack going, and lost.

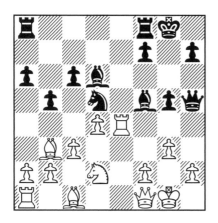

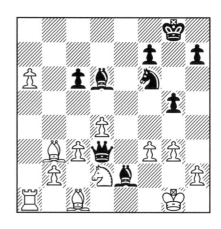

18 f3

White is happy to sacrifice the exchange, if he can keep his extra pawn, he will keep active pieces and the better pawns.

18...♘f6

Taking up the exchange challenge does not seem worth it. 18...♗xe4 19 fxe4 ♘e3 20 ♕f3! ♘g4 21 ♘f1 covers White's kingside weaknesses.

19 a4

One of the deepest opening traps in recent years was exposed in a World Championship game, Kramnik-Leko, 8th matchgame, Brissago 2004. Play continued 19 ♖e1?! ♖ae8 20 ♖xe8 ♖xe8 21 a4 ♕g6 22 axb5 ♗d3 23 ♕f2? (23 ♕d1 ♗e2 24 ♕d1 ♗e2 with a repetition) 23...♖e2!. This obvious and natural move hardly needs comment, except for the point that the computer gives White's position as winning after 24 ♕xe2 ♗xe2 25 bxa6. White is about to queen a pawn, and after the seemingly compulsory sacrifice with 25...♗xa6? 26 ♖xa6, to be followed by ♖xc6, White has a substantial, and winning, material advantage.

Checkmate comes first though, and 25...♕d3!! wins.

The critical line is 26 a7 ♕e3+ 27 ♔g2 ♗xf3+ 28 ♘xf3 ♕e2+ 29 ♔g1 ♘g4 30 a8♕+ ♔g7 31 ♕xc6 ♕f2+ 32 ♔h1 ♕f1+ 33 ♘g1 ♘f2 mate. Kramnik avoided this, but after 26 ♔f2 ♗xf3 27 ♘xf3 ♘e4+ 28 ♔e1 ♘xc3! 29 bxc3 ♕xc3+ 30 ♔f1 ♕xa1 Black had a clear material advantage, and White's a-pawn was by now harmless. Kramnik resigned a few moves later. A superb win for Leko.

This is regarded by some as the greatest win of the decade. At both amateur and professional levels, people talk about it, when relaxing after the game, and talk with great admiration. It is the classic 21st Century win at the highest level. The computer can go far in analysis, but the human analyst, with the help of inspiration, can see things even deeper.

19...♘xe4

19...♗xe4 20 ♘xe4 ♘xe4 21 fxe4 gives White an edge. See further commentary to Black's 20th.

20 ♘xe4

He wants to complete his development, and further to ensure that the knight will become genuinely active.

20 fxe4 ♗e6 21 ♗d1 is about equal.

Pawns without active pieces are not so effective as pieces and pawns together.

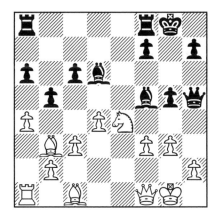

20...♕g6!

We have already seen the position before after 20...♗xe4 21 fxe4. In I.Kurnosov-S.Azarov, Kusadasi 2006, play ended up with a perpetual after 21...♔g7 22 ♗d2 f6 23 ♕f5 ♕e2 24 ♗c2 ♖f7 (24...♕xd2 25 e5 ♕e3+ 26 ♔h1 ♔f7 27 exd6 is winning for White) 25 e5 ♕xd2 26 ♕xh7+ ♔f8 27 ♕h8+? ♔e7 29 ♕xa8 ♕e3+ 30 ♔h1 ♕f3+ 31 ♔g1. White can play for much more than this with 26 exd6!, as Marin notes for Chess-Base. White's king is not in as much danger as it looks, and Black's king, in conjunction with White's excellent passed pawn and dangerous pieces, makes life difficult for Black.

In the game, Aronian is really jettisoning an extra pawn to avoid problems, rather than trying for an edge, although naturally he will be happy to take a chance in the unclear and unbalanced position.

21 ♘xd6

The natural reaction.

21 ♘xg5?! ♖ae8 22 ♘e4 is not worth giving up two tempi for a not very useful pawn. Marin gives 22...♗xe4 23 fxe4 ♖xe4 24 ♗c2 f5 24 ♗xe4 fxe4, and Black has considerable pressure in return for the pawn.

21...♕xd6 22 ♗xg5

22 axb5 axb5 23 ♖xa8 ♖xa8 24 ♗xg5 releases the tension a little too early. At the minimum, White would want to exchange after Black has already moved the king's rook.

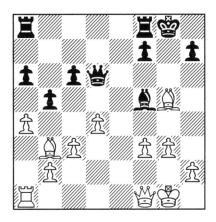

This position had reached before by Shirov, just three days earlier. There was no great excitement in the previous encounter, quickly ending up with perpetual check in A.Shirov-P.Leko, Moscow 2006. Play finished with 22...♖fe8 23 ♖e1 ♕g6 24 ♗e7 ♖a7 25 ♗c5 ♖aa8 26 ♗e7 ♖a7 27 ♗c5, draw agreed.

It is possible, but unlikely, that Shirov would be happy to agree two draws with White in succession. What is more likely is that he would have examined the last few moves, and tried to find an improvement for his game with Aronian, maybe instead of repeating, trying something new like 26 a5!?.

Aronian is a renowned specialist in the Marshall, and while it is possible that he was working hard analysing in the last couple of days in his hotel, it seems more likely that he had seen his novelty a long time before.

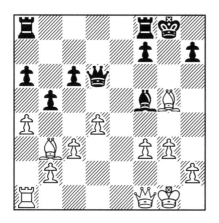

22...♕g6!?

Black is aiming to play actively, to hold the balance, in what could easily have been a poor line.

23 ♕c1

The natural reply, bringing an extra piece into play.

23...♗d3

The bishop circles around. One idea, as in the game, is to play ...♗c4, blocking off the white bishop on the a2-g8 diagonal. Or, as in the Kramnik-Leko game cited above, Black, if given the option, could set up a ...♖e2 attack, supported by the bishop.

24 axb5?!

This may have looked good at the time, but after exchanging the rooks, it turns out that the only remaining rook, Black's, is able to dominate, covering the a- and e-files, and also the opponent's back row. Generally if you are the exchange down, it is best to keep open files closed.

Marin suggests 24 ♕d2!? ♖ae8 25 ♖d1 ♖e2!? 26 ♕xd3 ♖xb2 27 ♕xg6+ hxg6 28 axb5 axb5. This line involves sacrifice and counter-sacrifice, and

Black is about to win a bishop, but before Black can take it, White too has counterplay. Eventually this process could resolve to equality after 29 d5 ♖xb3 30 d6 f6 31 ♗xf6 ♖xf6 32 d7 ♖f8 33 d8♕ ♖xd8 34 ♖xd8+ ♔f7 35 ♖d3 b4. If 36 ♔f2 bxc3, the safest way to defend is to bring the rook behind the opponent's pawn with 37 ♖d6 c5 38 ♖c6 ♖b2+ 39 ♔e3 ♖xh2 40 ♖xc5 c2 41 ♔d2 ♖f2 42 f4.

24...axb5 25 ♖xa8 ♖xa8

Once the exchanges have started, they must continue.

26 ♔f2

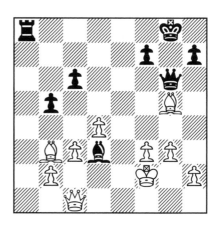

One can in fact see the logic for Shirov's rook exchange, in that now White's pieces appear to have covered any weaknesses on the e-file, while there is no breakthrough on the a-file, and White's two bishops seem to work well together. The next move changes the balance of play, though.

26...♗c4!

An unexpected reply, perhaps, as normally a player would not want to set up doubled isolated pawns. Black's pawns turn out to be easily protected though, and his two isolated pawns clamp White's three connected pawns.

27 ♗xc4

If White meekly withdraws with 27 ♗c2?!, Black can start taking over with rook and bishop, with 27...♕e6 28 ♗e3 ♕h3 29 ♔g1 ♖a2 30 ♗f2 h6!, covering the check on g5. The burden of proof is in Black's favour as he is the exchange up, and clearly has the more active pieces, while White's two extra pawns are ineffective. Krnic gives 31 ♗b1 ♖xb2 32 ♗f5 ♕xf5 33 ♕xb2 ♕xf3 34 ♕d2 ♗d5 35 ♔f1 ♕g2+ 36 ♔e2 ♗c4+ 37 ♔e3 ♕xh2 38 ♕d1 ♕h3 39 ♕f3 ♗d5 40 ♕f4 ♕h1 41 ♕g4+ ♔f8 42 ♕c8+ ♔e7 43 ♕c7+ ♔e6 44 ♕c8+ ♔f6 45 ♕h8+ ♔e7 46 ♕e5+ ♔d7, and Black should eventually win, after some delicate manoeuvring of king versus queen.

27...bxc4

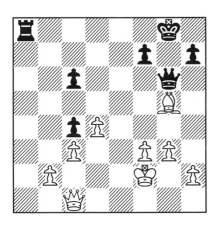

We now have a complicated endgame to evaluate, with of course the added problem that there are clear middlegame features to the position. If either player becomes careless, he is in danger of being checkmated! Black can add pressure to White's b2-pawn, for example, but it is going to be very difficult to attack the pawn with both queen and rook. White in return will find it difficult to attack the doubled isolated c-pawns, which at first glance might have been a problem.

There is the additional problem that we are starting to draw close to the move 40 time control. It is unlikely that there would be serious time trouble as yet, but equally there would probably not be the luxury of either player having a prolonged think, a quarter of an hour or more, to work out strategic problems.

It is unlikely that either player will have been able to play 100% accuracy, and in the case of Shirov's play he must clearly have done something wrong, as he was rather too quickly in a losing position.

28 g4

White wants to add a bolt square for the king. He will not be checked if the king reaches g3. Also, he would be thinking about pressing forward with the pawns on the g-file. At this stage, Shirov might well be thinking of playing for a win.

28 ♗e7 is possible, and if 28...♖e8 29 ♗a3 ♕d3 30 ♕g5+, and then to avoid perpetual check he has to play 30...♕g6, but then White has a draw anyway with 31 ♕c1!?.

White's position is solid, rather more so than it looks. Probably Shirov should have held if he had played ultra-solidly. but Shirov has to take calculated risks in order to try for an edge.

White's g4 push allows Black to think of setting up ...f5 or ...h5 pushes.

28...♖e8

With the queens on the board, the e-file is far more critical for the rook than the a-file. Aronian is planning to attack with the pieces on the light squares, with ...♕d3 and maybe ...♕e2+ or

...♖e2+, following up perhaps with ...f5 or ...h5.

Black could also think of setting up an immediate pawn attack with, for example, 28...h5 when White has to decide whether to hold the position with 29 h3 hxg4 30 hxg4, with only two pawns on the kingside working together, or, more aggressively, 29 gxh5 ♕xh5, and either 30 ♕f4 or 30 ♗f4, and White's pawns have been weakened, but not fatally, and he still keeps a passed h-pawn.

28...f6!? is less direct, and keeps open the possibilities either of pawn attack against g4, or some piece development. After 29 ♗f4, 29...h5? 30 ♕f1!, threatening ♕xc4+. is premature. Therefore 29...♕d3, and if White tries to defend with 30 ♕e3?, Black wins the b-pawn with 30...♕xe3+ 31 ♗xe3 ♖a2 32 ♗c1 ♖a1 33 ♗e3 ♖b1. White is still under long-term pressure in other lines, though. For example, if 30 ♔g3 ♖e8 31 ♕a1 ♕e2 32 ♕b1 ♔h8!?, opening up g8 for the rook, and White will continually have to worry about ...h5.

This line is difficult to assess, but Black seems slightly better. In the end, it is hardly unexpected that the queen and rook have more piece-power than queen and bishop. White's two extra pawns supply compensation, but not quite enough.

29 ♗f4

Into more active play.

29...♕d3?!

Possibly the effects of shortage of time creep in. This move is, of course, highly direct, but Black should probably have covered his defence on the dark squares first, with 29...f6!, much as discussed a move earlier.

It is not wholly clear why Aronian keeps rejecting ...f6, covering the important e5- and g5- defensive squares.

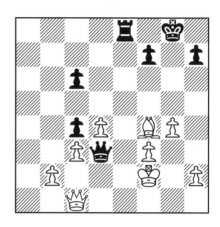

30 ♔g3?

This is a serious missed opportunity. White needs to attack on the dark squares, with 30 ♗e5!.

Krnic in *Informator* suggests the pawn sacrifice 30...f6 31 ♗xf6 ♕e2 32 ♔g3 ♖e3 33 ♕h1 ♕xb2 34 ♗g5 ♖e2 (34...♖xc3? 35 ♕e1! wins) 35 ♕f1. This is a doubtful line for Black, as he has no winning chances, but there are many winning chances for White. Black's rook is pinned, and to unpin with 35...♕a2, White may play 36 h3, followed perhaps with ♗f4 and ♗e5. Black has gone backwards, and his f-pawn has gone. There is a simpler escape for Black, though, as Shipov notes in *New in Chess*. Black has 34...♖xc3! 35 ♗xe3 ♕xe3, and his passed pawn is so strong, White must escape for a perpetual with 36 ♕a1 c3 37 ♕a8+.

Here 30...c5 exchanges one of the isolated pawns, but is likely to veer towards equality. One line is 31 h4 cxd4 32 ♗xd4 ♖e2+ 33 ♔g3 ♕d2 34 ♕a1 ♖g2+ 35 ♔h3 ♖g2+ 36 ♔g3 ♖g2+ with perpetual.

It seems that the best that Black can do, if hoping for a win, is 30...♕g6, repeating. If 31 ♕f1, there is, of course, another draw offer with 31...♕d3 32 ♕c1. Here 31...♕e6 is more ambitious, but 32 g5!? is a promising reply.

Thus with best play, the game should end up as a draw.

30...♕e2?

Again, 30...f6! looks better. It is only when the pawn can stop the bishop arriving on e5 that Black genuinely looks better.

31 ♕b1?

The most serious of these inaccuracies, which allows Black a good endgame. Shirov was presumably not worried about the queen exchange, but after delicate endgame play by Aronian, Black ends up with an advantage.

31 ♗e5! is, yet again, the best and most natural move. Black now has no time to retreat with 31...♕d3? 32 h4! ♕g6 33 h5 ♕e6 34 ♕g5+, winning. We thus return to 31...f6 32 ♗xf6 ♖e3 33 ♕h1 ♕xb2, drawn.

31...♕e1+

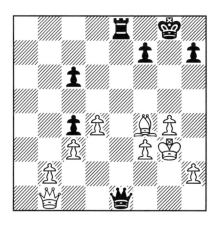

With relief, probably from both sides, that the queens are finally being exchanged. We are still only on move 31, so the players will have to play bristly before the time control. Neither player will be able to adjust completely just yet. The immediate impression is that this ought to end up as a draw, with accurate play. After the queen exchange, White can protect the weak b-pawn with a bishop on a3, but surely White cannot create a kingside passed pawn?

The position proves to be more difficult than it looks, and by move 40, Shirov is already in a losing position, with problems of zugzwang. After all, if the bishop is stuck on a3, that only leaves the king and pawns for White, and sometimes it may be difficult to find good moves.

32 ♕xe1 ♖xe1 33 ♗d6

To lock his queenside pawn structure with the bishop to a3.

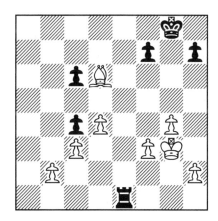

33...♖g1+

Quite often extra random checks in the endgame can prove to be pointless. Here, though, Aronian forces Shirov to decide where the king has to go. Any of the four squares have defects.

34 ♔f2

The king is retreating. If though 34 ♔f4? ♖g2, White loses a pawn. Similarly, 34 ♔h4? ♖g2, and the bishop cannot cover both pawns.

34...♖b1

With a slight but significant gain of tempo.

35 ♗a3

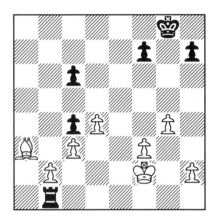

Who is trying for a win here? Or to put it the other way round, which player has the ability just to play quiet moves, and keep the draw without difficulty? Or is it just equal, with either player having the opportunity of holding the position?

The closer one examines, the more apparent it is that White still has difficulties. Black always has the option of moving the rook away, maybe with an attack on the h-pawn, while White's bishop is stuck on a3, for as long as the b2-pawn is threatened. This adds to the possibility of zugzwang. The problem is that pawns can never move backwards, and so once a pawn has moved, there are fewer pawn moves available, and White will eventually have to think about having to play a king move.

35...♔g7

Bringing the king into play, an easy decision to make.

36 ♔g3

Natural enough.

Generally players would not want to make a committal pawn push, such as 36 h4, just before the time control. Such a move might not be a positive improvement, if the pawn push could always be made later. It might, however, create a weakness, and once the pawn has been pushed to h4, it cannot retreat. Here after 36...h5 37 ♔g3 ♔g6 38 ♔g2 Krnic suggests that Black is winning by attacking the g-pawn either with 38...f5 or a preliminary exchange. After 38...hxg4 39 fxg4 f5 40 h5+ ♔g5 41 gxf5 ♔xh5, for example, White's king will be squeezed out by Black's.

36...♔g6

Aronian too makes a quiet move. Soon, however, one of the players is about to open up their pawns.

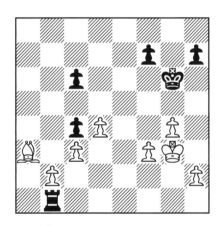

37 h3

Probably no better or no worse than any other reasonable move here. Various writers at the time, such as Marin, Krnic, and Shipov, made no comment on this move, no doubt assuming that White was losing anyway.

37 ♔f4!? is interesting aiming to pick up some queenside pawns, and creating counterplay with his d-pawn:

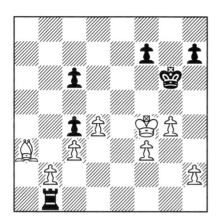

a) Then 37...♖h1? 38 ♔e5! ♖xh2 39 ♔d6 ♖f2 40 ♔xc6 ♖xf3 41 d5, and suddenly Black is in danger, his king being unable to cover White's passed pawn, and his rook cannot cover White's united pawn, king and bishop.

b) Clearly this would be too crude for Black. He needs to cover the e5-square. 37...f6?! is not the best option, though, since if 38 h4 h5 39 gxh5+ ♔xh5 40 ♔f5, and Black's f-pawn drops.

c) This leaves 37...♖e1, and to avoid loss of tempo (after, for example, 38 ♔g3 ♖e2), White tries 38 h4. Then 38...h5, to prevent White playing h5+ himself:

c1) 39 gxh5+ ♔xh5 40 ♔f5 ♖e6! defends Black's pieces with comfort, so White has to try something else.

c2) 39 ♗d6 ♖e2 40 ♗a3 ♖g2?! sets up a zugzwang, but White can play on with 41 ♔e5! hxg4 42 fxg4 ♖xg4 43 ♔d6 f5 44 ♔xc6 f4 45 d5 f3 46 d6 f2 47 d7 f1♕ 48 d8♕. An unexpected result. However, here 40...♖f2! 41 ♔g3 (41 ♔e5 ♖xf3 is too slow for White) 41...♖d2 42 ♔f4 ♖e2 deliberately gives away a tempo, and after 43 ♔g3 hxg4 44 fxg4 f5, we reach positions close to those analysed by Krnic after 38 h4, below,

rather than Shirov's 38 ♔h4.

37...h5

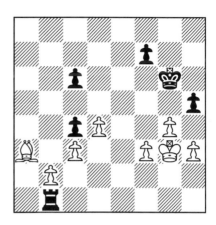

Zugzwang!

Sometimes such zugzwang positions are less than obvious, there being no clear indicator that material is going to be lost. Look closely though, and any move by White is going to be retrograde. If his bishop moves, he is going to lose the b2-pawn. If any pawn moves, his pawn structure will be weakened. Finally his king is on its best square, but that means that any king move will be to a worse square.

38 ♔h4

If 38 ♔f4? h4!, and Black will pick up the h-pawn, and queen his own passed pawn. White therefore no longer has the option of active play. He has to defend passively.

If the king retreats with, for example, 38 ♔g2, Black can use the thematic 38...♖c1 followed by ...♖c2+, and soon a fresh zugzwang arises. The king will not be able to retreat twice to the second row.

If 38 h4 hxg4 39 fxg4 f5, and now if White allows the pawns to split with, for example, 40 h5+ ♔f6 41 gxf5 ♔xf5, Black will eliminate the passed pawn on the kingside, and will gradually squeeze through on the light squares on the queenside, with a win. Here Krnic suggests some counterplay with 40 d5, but he shows that Black is still winning after 40...cxd5 41 h5+ ♔f6 42 ♗c5 fxg4 43 ♔xg4 ♖xb2 44 ♗d4+ ♔f7 45 ♔f5 ♖e2. Play on a few moves, for example, and after 46 h6 ♔g8 47 ♗e5 ♔h7 48 ♔e6 d4 49 cxd4 c3 50 ♔f5 ♖xe5+ 51 dxe5 c2 Black queens a pawn.

38...♖g1!

Krnic gives this as winning in *Informator*, while Marin for ChessBase merely gives it as 'the best chance'. The idea is to set up another zugzwang. With the black rook on g2, White's pieces are immobile. This leaves only the pawns, but zugzwangs are quite often a problem in the endgame, as pawns can never move backwards, and sooner or later they run out of forward moves.

39 ♗c5

For the moment, the bishop may still move, and it being on move 39, he probably moved it quickly after Black attacked the pawn again.

39...♖g2 40 ♗a3

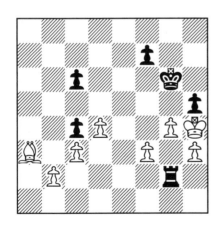

40...f6!

It is always pleasant to play a good constructive move to reach the time control. Black's king and rook are on their best available squares, but he still has a reserve move with the pawn to set up another zugzwang.

41 gxh5+

Forced.

If 41 f4, he will have weakened his g-pawn, and after 41...hxg4 42 hxg4 f5, the win is straightforward. If 43 gxf5+ ♔xf5 44 ♔h3 ♖g8, Black wins the f-pawn, keeps the king out of play on the h-file, and swings his own rook to the queenside.

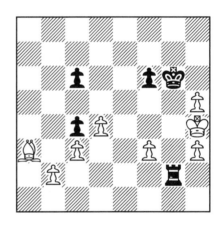

41...♔f5!

This sets up a diabolically crafty trap. It also happens to be the best and most direct move.

41...♔f7 or 41...♔g7 are possible, but more difficult.

The king needs to be active – a basic rule of endgame principle!

42 f4

Shirov's position looks dreadful, but his one saving grace is that if Black's king moves too far forward, White has chances of counterplay with his passed h-pawn.

42...♖g8

And so Black must avoid 42...♔xf4? 43 h6 ♖g8 44 ♔h5, when the only safe reply is a draw with 44...♖g5+ 45 ♔h4 ♖g8.

43 ♗d6

Naturally White must cover the f4-pawn, but now Black gains a tempo, attacking the bishop with the king.

43...♔e6!

Setting up a trap.

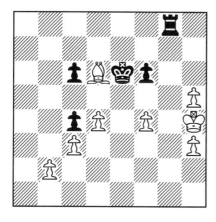

44 h6

And Shirov falls for it. Or rather he is hoping to set up a counter-trap himself, but it doesn't quite work.

44 ♗a3 ♔f7 45 ♗d6 ♖g2 46 ♗a3 ♔g7 leads to a straightforward zugzwang, and Black will win the b-pawn. The next question is, after Black wins the b2-pawn, how Black will be able to pick up another pawn, and eventually win the game?

Marin gives the answer. After 47 ♗b4 ♖xb2 48 ♗a5 ♖b5 49 ♗d8 ♖b8 50 ♗c7 ♖b3 51 ♗a5 ♔h6 52 ♔g4 f5+! 53 ♔h4 (53 ♔xf5?? ♖b6+) 53...♖b2, and here he suggests that with extra pawns still in danger, Black is about to win. There is still some play to follow, however: 54 ♗d8 ♖f2 55 ♗c7 ♖f3 56 ♗e5 ♖xc3 (56...♔h7!?) 57 d5 ♖d3 58 dxc6

♖d5! (rather than the more obvious 58...♖d8?) 59 c7 ♖c5 finally wins for Black.

Therefore it seems that quiet play by White would not have given the draw either.

44...♔xd6!

Setting up a memorable finish.

44...♔f5? 45 ♔h5 ♖h8 46 ♗c7 only draws.

45 ♔h5

Certainly having got this far, White must carry on.

45 f5? ♔e7 46 ♔h5 ♔f7 47 h7 ♖a8 49 ♔h6 ♖h8 ends up losing more quickly.

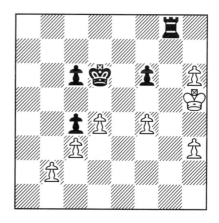

45...f5!

Black has to be very careful. To try to win this, he has to know exactly where the king will have to go, and whether his pawn will be on f6 or f5. Aronian plays the only correct move, and in such pawn endings there is no room for casual thinking.

Fritz, after some thought, gives 45...♔d5 as the clearest and simplest win. If we play on though, the outcome is far less clear. After 46 h7 ♖h8 47 ♔g6 ♔e4 48 ♔g7 ♖a8 49 ♔xf6 (49 h8♕ also draws; as an exercise in calculation, the reader is invited to work out the final line, without using the board or computer – it is notoriously difficult to calculate such king and pawn endgames over the board) 49 ♔xf6 ♔xf4 50 ♔g7 ♖a7+ and the rook returns to a8, holding the draw.

46 h7

Looking good so far. White will win the rook for the passed pawn, and then there is a second passed h-pawn to win.

46...♖h8

Natural enough. The next couple of moves are obvious, but the sting comes later.

47 ♔g6 ♔e7 48 ♔g7 ♔e8!!

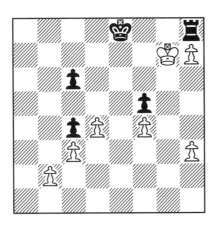

A very big zugzwang. Aronian will have seen this well in advance. White can win the rook, but if he takes it, the h7-pawn will not allow the king to escape.

48...♖xh7+?? 49 ♔xh7 wins for White.

49 ♔g6

There is no chance of a stalemate after 49 ♔xh8 ♔f7 50 h4 ♔f8 51 h5 ♔f7 52 h6 ♔f8. If White were to try 53 b4 cxb3 54 d5 cxd5 55 c4, Black checkmates first and wins with 54...b2.

The alert reader will have noted that if White had no pawn on b2 in the dia-

gram, there would be no win for Black. It would have been stalemate.

In endgame, it is wise for either player to keep in mind possible stalemate ideas. Here Aronian kept everything under control.

Shirov's line kept things going a little longer, but by now he must surely have recognized that he was doomed.

49...♔f8

A necessary triangulation manoeuvre.

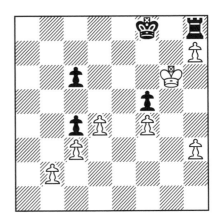

50 h4

The only move. 50 ♔h6 ♔f7 wins quickly for Black.

50...♔e7

And the winning manoeuvre is repeated. Sooner or later, White will run out of pawn moves to push, and then he will lose.

51 ♔g7 ♔e8

An attractive idea, but we have seen this on move 48.

52 ♔g6 ♔f8 53 h5 ♔e7 54 ♔g7 ♔e8

And again.

White's second h-pawn has moved a couple of squares forward since the previous diagram, but this means he is running out of squares, rather than progress.

57...♖xh7 58 ♔g6 ♖f7 0-1

58...♖h8 also wins with the now familiar idea: 59 ♔g7 ♖f8 60 h7 ♖h8 61 ♔g7 ♔e7 62 ♔xh8 ♔f7,

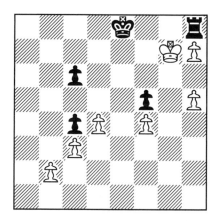

55 ♔g6 ♔f8 56 h6 ♔e8 57 ♔f6

A final try, hoping to make use of his second h-pawn.

57 ♔g7 ♔e7 58 ♔g6 ♔f7 wins easily for Black.

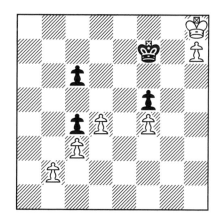

and Black wins after 63 b4 cxb3, en passant.

Game 17
A.Shirov-M.Illescas Cordoba
Pamplona 2006
Sicilian Defence B85

1 e4 c5 2 ♘f3 e6 3 d4 cxd4 4 ♘xd4 ♘c6 5 ♘c3 a6 6 ♗e2

We are heading for a Scheveningen. White makes a quiet developing move with the bishop.

For 6 ♘xc6, see Game 5, Bacrot-Rublevsky.

6...♕c7

Or Black can simply play 6...d6, delaying what to do with the queen, which sometimes stays at home.

7 0-0

Having played ♗e2 quickly, he might just as well castle quickly on the kingside.

7...♘f6

Black aims to catch up his kingside development.

7...b5 is possible, but after 8 ♘xc6 dxc6 (or 8...♕xc6 9 ♗f3) 9 a4!? White keeps a slight edge. If 9...b4 10 ♘b1 followed by ♘d2 and ♘c4, and Black's position is playable, but slightly worse. He has lost his queenside pawn dynamism.

8 ♗e3

For 8 ♔h1, see Game 20, Ni Hua-Jakovenko.

8...d6

This, believe it or not, is a slightly unusual position, even though it seems clearly mainstream. If Black is aiming for a Scheveningen, he generally plays 8...♗e7 first, then later ...d6. There is no real objection to Black's play, it seems just a question of habit. If Black plays

...d6 early on, then quite often what happens is that he usually plays ...♗e7 before ...♕c7.

There was another possibility for Black in trying 8...♗b4. Then 9 ♘a4 ♗e7 (or perhaps 9...♗d6 10 g3 b5; not though 9...♘xe4? 10 ♘xc6 ♕xc6 11 ♕d4 ♗f8 12 c4, with advantage to White) 10 ♘xc6 bxc6 11 ♘b6, and White has the normal slight edge.

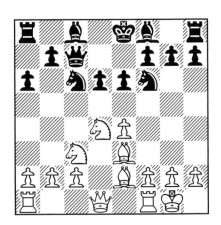

9 f4

The standard attacking plan. White can make a pawn charge with e5, usually as a pawn sacrifice, or f5, or even g4-g5.

9...♗d7

A small piece of originality in the move order, but Shirov, a noted attacking player, has always been confident in finding new ideas in less-explored variations. Illescas is taking something of a risk, and indeed he ultimately loses.

As happens so often in experimental play, the innovator as Black loses, but it is not totally clear that the line is bad. With some extra homework, Black's play could have been improved.

9...♗e7 leads to well established main line theory:

a) 10 ♔h1 transposes into Game 20, Ni Hua-Jakovenko.

b) 10 a4, restraining Black's queenside, is also popular.

c) 10 g4?! is not so effective, though. After 10...♘xd4 11 ♗xd4 e5 12 ♗e3 exf4 13 ♖xf4 ♗e6 Black is equal.

10 g4!

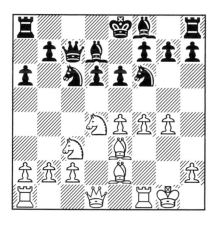

Shirov jumps quickly at any unusual play from his opponent. Probably we shall never find out what Illescas would have been planning after mainline ideas such as 10 a4 or 10 ♔g1.

10...h5

This would have been prepared analysis.

10...♘xd4?! 11 ♗xd4 e5 is less effective than in the ...♗e7 line, since after 12 ♗e3 exf4 13 ♗xf4, Black would have to lose a tempo if he plays 13...♗e6. The computer suggests 12...♕c6 13 ♗f3 h5 as a possibility, but after 14 g5 exf4 15 e5 ♕c8 16 ♗xf4 ♕c5+ (16...dxe5!?) 17 ♔h1 dxe5 18 gxf6 exf4 19 ♕e2+ ♔h8 20 ♖ad1! Black is in trouble with his king.

11 g5

11 gxh5 is possible, but unthematic. If he wants to push forward with the pawns in front of his king, he needs to attack, rather than make unnecessary pawn exchanges. Here 11...♘xd4 12 ♗xd4 e5 is equal.

11...♘g4

With counterattack.

12 ♗xg4

This is positionally forced, Black's two knights being troublesome.

12...hxg4 13 g6!

Not 13 ♕xg4? ♘xd4 15 ♗xd4 e5, and Black wins a piece.

An old game, G.Fiensch-W.Pietzsch, East German Championship, Schkopau 1958, continued instead with 13 ♘xc6 ♗xc6 14 ♕xg4 0-0-0 15 ♘d5 with advantage to White, although after the knight was eventually captured, Black kept some chances. The game was later drawn. A good line for White, one might think, and quite possibly earlier theoretical books might have given Black a question mark at move 9.

One of the most significant influences of modern opening theory is that with the help of a modest computer engine, it is possible to re-establish previously rejected lines. The computer engine suggests that 13...bxc6! is equal, and also that later 13...♕xc6 14 ♕xg4 b5 might give chances of equality. By quietly drinking a coffee, and glancing at the computer, it is easy to find a respectable innovation without effort. The computer then gives, without much effort on my part, 13...bxc6 14 ♕xg4 ♖b8 15 ♖ab1 d5 16 g6 ♗c8. This leads to an interesting and experimental position in which White has an extra pawn, but his kingside pawns are uncomfortably open, and Black has a useful extra passed pawn. Black should probably be reasonably happy with this line, given that the main theoretical problem for Black is to avoid a clear advantage to White.

13...0-0-0

White's pawn stab is dangerous, and Illescas rushes his king to the queenside, in safety, allowing his opponent an extra passed pawn on the seventh, but relying on Black having developed his pieces, and being able to make use of Shirov's advanced and exposed pawns.

13...罩h3!? is to be considered, again with wild open play:

a) The 'positional' approach is 14 gxf7+ 含xf7 15 f5 ⑤xd4! (15...含g8 16 ⑤xe6 急xe6 17 fxe6 ⑤e5 18 ⑤d5 with advantage to White) 16 急xd4 (16 fxe6+ 含g8 17 急xd4 急xe6 18 ⑤d5 急xd5 19 dxe5 g3 20 hxg3 罩xg3+ gives White only a slight edge) 16...exf5 17 豐xg4 含g8 18 exf5, and White has a workable edge.

b) 14 f5 could transpose into the game after 14...0-0-0 15 gxf7. Alterna-

tively, Black could try 14...罩xe3 15 fxg7+ 含d8 16 fxe6 ⑤xe4 17 e7+!, and this must surely deserve a diagram.

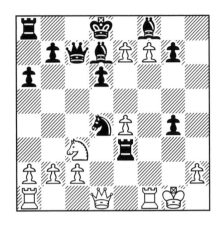

Sometimes diagrams of Shirov's games can, indeed, look like misprints. Here play would continue with 17...急xe7 18 f8豐+ 急xf8 19 罩xf8+ 含e7 20 罩xa8 罩xc3 21 豐xd4, and White is winning.

Black could try to quieten the position down with 13...⑤xd4 14 gxf7+ 含xf7 15 急xd4 含g8, but his position does not look fully secure. 16 罩f2 罩c8 17 罩g2 is good for White.

14 gxf7?!

What else? White snatches a pawn, sets up an annoying pawn on the seventh, and starts to undermine the whole of Black's defensive pawn structure. For an attacking player, this is almost an ideal early scenario. The problem is that Black can also attack on the kingside, against White's exposed king, and Illescas soon sets up counterplay. Black's pawn on g4 can easily create problems, and a simpler way for White is to take the pawn. Not though 14 豐xg4? ⑤xd4 15 急xd4 e5, and Black wins a piece.

Therefore 14 ⑤xc6! 急xc6 15 豐xg4,

and White wins a pawn, and also creates pressure on the light squares with gxf7, f5, or ♘d5. 15...d5 keeps play active, but after 16 exd5 ♗xd5 17 ♘xd5 ♖xd5 18 gxf7 ♕xf7 19 ♖ad1 White retains an edge. Simple play in a complicated line.

14...♖h3

Black now has serious counterplay.

The computer suggests 14...♘xd4 15 ♗xd4 g6 as an alternative, but this soon fizzles out, with advantage to White, after 16 hxg3 ♗c6 17 ♕g4 ♕xf7 18 ♖ad1.

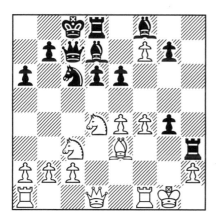

15 f5?

A question mark, even though Shirov's move is imaginative and deeply thought through, and leads to spectacular winning play. This may seem a harsh judgement from the critic, but what other assessment could reasonably have been made? If Illescas Cordoba had played completely accurately, he would have been better. If a player with the white pieces ends up in a worse position, he must have made a mistake.

Shirov is a renowned maximalist, an attacker, although naturally when needed, like all great players, he will switch to steady positional play. Here

he senses it is time for all-out attack. If over the board he cannot find a way for his opponent to find a refutation, then he has every moral right to play for an attack. If he outplays his opponent, he will win. If his opponent outplays him, he will lose. If both players make absolutely the best moves over a long string of moves, then who knows, he might be winning, drawing or losing.

In this particular game, the likelihood would be that Shirov would have assumed that his attack was good. It is only later that doubts may start to be expressed.

Many of us less ambitious players would be more than content to defend and develop quietly with 15 ♕d2!, protecting the bishop on e3, giving away nothing on the b8-h2 diagonal, and waiting to see how Black will deal with the f7-passed pawn:

a) The computer's initial suggestion is 15...♘xd4 16 ♗xd4 g3 17 hxg3 ♖xg3+ 18 ♔f2, but this cannot be good for Black, and indeed the computer revises this as a win for White, who still has the extra pawn on f7, and his pieces are active.

b) Black could also try 15...g3 16 hxg3 ♖xg3+ 17 ♔f2 ♖g4 in which case the simplest for White is to untangle the pieces with 18 ♘b3!?. Again, it would be extremely difficult for Black to demonstrate any chances of equality.

15...d5

Black goes on the basis that that one bishop cannot simultaneously cover both the c7-h2 diagonal and the a7-g1 diagonal.

15...♖xe3? eliminates the bishop, but 16 fxe6 is strong, destroying Black's light squares. As well as the advanced passed pawns, ♘d5 is a threat.

15...♘xd4!? is sensible, if again sharp. After 16 ♕xd4 d5 17 ♗f4 ♗c5 18 ♗xc7 ♗xd4+ 19 ♔g2 ♗xc7 20 fxe6 ♗xe6 21 f8♕ ♖xf8 22 ♖xf8 dxe4 White has an extra exchange, but his knight is not so active, and Black has a good bishop-pair. This would have been an interesting battle after, for example, 23 ♖e8 ♔d7 24 ♖b8 ♗e5 25 ♖d1+ ♔c6 26 ♖e8 ♖xh2+ 27 ♔g1 ♖h6 with White perhaps being slightly better.

Black's move in the game improves on this, provided he plays with great accuracy.

16 ♗f4

At least the bishop is safe, and on a good and active square.

16...♕b6

But now White's knight is pinned, and threatened.

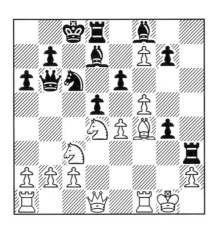

17 fxe6

A radical way of breaking up the opposing pawn structure. Shirov simply captures the opposition pawn chain, and now has White pawns, rather than Black, on f7 and e6.

17 ♘a4? would win quickly if Black were to fall for the trap with 17...♕xd4+?? 18 ♕xd4 ♘xd4 19 ♘b6

mate. The trap is easily avoided, though, with 17...♕a7 18 c3 e5, and advantage to Black.

17...♗xe6

A sensible reply, not least because the knight on d4 is pinned.

17...♘xd4 18 exd7+ ♖xd7 19 ♘d5 ♘f3+ 20 ♔g2 ♕c6 is to be considered, but Black does not quite break open White's kingside, and White can build up his central play. After 21 ♗g3 ♖xf7 22 ♕d3! (centralizing), White keeps an advantage:

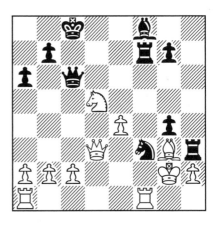

a) For example, if 22...♗d6 (the only realistic chance to attack the h2-square), White has 23 ♘b6+ ♕xb6 24 ♕xd6 with a much better pawn structure for the endgame.

b) 22...♕h6 does not improve on this. White has 23 ♕c3+ ♔d8 24 ♕a5+ ♔e8 25 ♘c7+ ♔d7 26 ♕d5+ ♔c8 27 ♕e6+, and although Black has wriggled well, White still exchanges the queens with an advantage.

c) If 22...♗c5!?, the tactics favour Black after 23 ♖ad1 ♘h4+ 24 ♔h1 ♖xf1+ 25 ♕xf1 ♘f3 26 ♕c4 ♖xg3! 27 ♘b4 (27 ♘e7+ ♗xe7 28 ♕xc6+ bxc6 29 hxg3 with an endgame edge to Black) 27...♕d6 28 ♕g8+ ♕f8 29 ♕xf8+ ♗xf8

30 hxg3, and now Black picks up the knight with 30...♗xb4. However, 23 ♕c4! gives White an advantage, not just with the obvious threats of 24 b4 or 24 ♘b6+, but also with the sideways threat of e5, with thoughts of ♕xg4+.

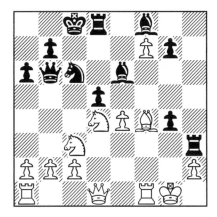

18 ♘a4

18 ♘xd5 is the alternative. Then 18...♖xd5 (18...♕xd4+?? 19 ♕xd4) 19 exd5 ♘xd4 20 dxe6 ♘e2+ 21 ♔g2 results in complications. The trouble is that Black is winning after 21...♕xe6 22 ♖f2 ♕e4+ 23 ♔f1 g3!! (23...♘xf4? 24 ♕xg4+) 24 ♕d2 (what else?) 24...gxh2! (24...gxf2? 25 ♖d1 ♕h1+ 26 ♔e2 ♕f3+ only draws) 25 ♖xh2 ♖f3+ 26 ♖f2 ♘xf4 27 ♖xf3 ♕xf3+, and then a few well-placed checks.

18...♕a7

Not 18...♕xd4+? 19 ♕xd4 ♘xd4 20 ♘b6 mate.

19 c3

Just a quiet defensive pawn push. Not quite such an innocuous move as it looks, though, as the pawn later turns into a queen.

19...dxe4!

This is analytically the best move, even though Illescas later loses. His mistake comes later, and only as a re-

sult of not pushing his passed pawn a second time, a move later. Sometimes the best way of defending is vigorous counterplay.

19...♖d7 is to be considered with the idea of 20 exd5 ♗xd5 21 ♕xg4, and there is no check on the diagonal. Play is unclear, maybe favouring White, after 21...♘xd4 22 cxd4 ♕xd4 23 ♖f2 ♖d3 24 ♖c1+ ♗c6. Moreover, White can continue with 20 ♔g2!, as in Shirov's main line, and if 20...♗xf7 21 ♕xg4 ♖h8 22 e5 White keeps a strong positional edge without complications.

20 ♔g2!

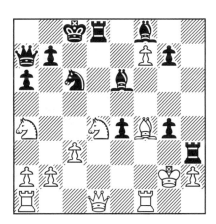

White unpins the d4-knight from the king, but it is still unpinned against the queen. This is, however, very much a minor pin, and in most lines White is more than happy to give up the queen in return for rook and bishop, and so the elimination of two pieces which are covering the pawn on the seventh.

20...♖xd4?

This must surely be one of the most difficult positions in this book for the player to analyse over the board. Almost all of the lines for Black lose quickly. There is just one extremely obscure line for Black which would have given him, unexpectedly, an advantage. We need to strip out the more obvious but less effective tries, to leave, finally, the only good move:

a) Black decides in the game to get rid of the knight as soon as possible. The alternative way of removing the knight immediately, avoiding dropping the bishop on e6, is 20...♘xd4?, but this opens up the c-file too early. Play continues 21 cxd4 ♖xd4 22 ♖c1+ ♔d8:

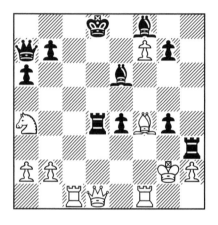

a1) Then 23 ♗b8?! is an attractive tactic, except that Black has a counter-tactic with 23...♖xh2+! 24 ♔xh2 (the only move, but now the queen is no longer attacked) 24...♖xd1 25 ♖cxd1+ ♗d7 26 ♗d6, and Black just has time to set up a perpetual with 26...♕e3! 37 ♗xf6 ♕h3+.

a2) White has an even more attractive, and better idea with 23 ♘c5!, attacking the bishop with the knight and, by breaking up the a7-g1 diagonal, attacking the rook. If 23...♗xc5, then a diversion sacrifice with 24 ♕xd4+ ♗xd4 25 f8♕+ and mate next move Or 23...♖xd1 24 ♖cxd1+ ♖d3 (24...♔e7 25 ♗d6 mate) 25 ♘xe6+ ♔e7 26 ♘xf8 ♖xd1 (or 26...♔xf8 27 ♖xd3 exd3 28 ♗d6 mate) 27 ♗g5+ ♔xf8 28 ♗e7+

♔xe7 29 f8♕+ and checkmate follows. White again makes full use of the passed pawn on the seventh.

b) Black would certainly have considered 20...♖d3, but this allows 21 ♘xe6 ♖xd1 22 ♖ad1. Black's queen is not very effective, whereas White's pieces and passed pawn create dangerous threats. Then 22...b5 23 ♘xf8 ♖xf8 24 ♖d6 is uncomfortable for Black. If, for example, 24...axb4 25 ♖xc6+ ♔b7 26 ♖c7+ ♕xc7 27 ♗xc7 ♔xc7 28 ♔g3, and White will end up with an extra pawn in a rook and pawn endgame.

c) Black could consider developing the back row with 20...♖h8 21 ♘xe6 ♖xd1 22 ♖axd1, but White still keeps a strong attack:

c1) If 22...e3 23 ♗c7 e2 24 ♘b6+ ♕xb6 25 ♗xb6 exf1♕+ 26 ♔xf1, and Black is almost in zugzwang.

c2) Or 22...b5 23 ♘xf8 ♖xf8 24 ♗d6 ♖xf7 25 ♘b6+! ♕xb6 (25...♔d8 26 ♗b8+) 26 ♖xf7, and White's pieces dominate.

d) 20...♖f3 21 ♘xe6 ♖xd1 22 ♖axd1 ends up with a slightly better position for Black than in the previous line, but is not quite adequate:

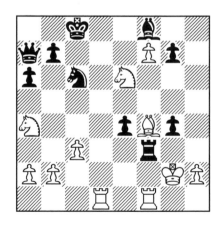

d1) If, for example, 22...♖xf1 23 ♖xf1

b5 24 ♘b6+ ♕xb6 25 ♘xf8, and Black will be unable to defend against queening on f8: 25...♘d8 26 ♘d7 wins.

d2) 22...b5 23 ♘xf8 ♕xf7 24 ♘b6+ ♔b7 25 ♖d7+, and White wins material.

d3) 22...e3 23 ♘xf8 e2 24 ♘d7 exf1♕+ 25 ♖xf1 ♔xd7 26 f8♕ is winning for White. If you lose a queen, setting up a new queen is often more than full compensation.

Finally, there are a few fiddly pawn moves with 20...e3, 20...g3, and 20...g5, which might or might not challenge the balance of play, but which need to be examined.

e) 20...g3 is easy enough to eliminate when considering Black's best move. After 21 hxg3 ♖h8 22 ♘xe6 White is simply a pawn up on variation 'c'.

f) 20...g5 21 ♗xg5 forces White to a different diagonal with the bishop, but it is by no means an inferior one. After 21...♖d5 22 ♘xe6 ♖xd1 23 ♖axd1 White is still winning.

g) Now for the final pawn push, 20...e3!!.

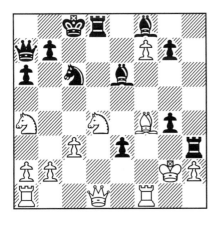

The idea is not so much to try to queen the e-pawn, but rather to open up the long diagonal for the bishop:

g1) Black is a key tempo up after the thematic queen sacrifice with 21 ♘xe6? ♖xd1 22 ♖fxd1 e2 23 ♖e1 b5, and if 24 ♘xf8? ♕xf7.

g2) The critical line is 21 ♕e2 ♘xd4 22 cxd4 ♖xd4.

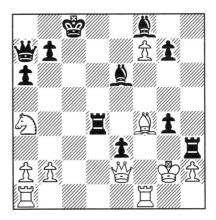

This is about as wild an open position as you can get. In contrast with the previous lines here, Black is attacking sharply, as well as defending. Indeed, Black's attack is at least more dangerous than White's, and therefore play should be at least equal:

g21) 23 ♗xe3? loses quickly after 23...♗d5+ 24 ♔g1 g3!, and if 25 hxg3 (or an inserted check on the c-file) 25...♖h1+ 26 ♔f2 ♖h2+.

g22) That leaves 23 ♖ac1+ ♔d7 and then:

g221) White would suffer the same problem on 24 ♗xe3? ♗d5+ 25 ♔b1 g3.

g222) White might try instead 24 ♖cd1 ♗d5+ 25 ♔g1 when he has set up a useful semi-pin on the d-file. Indeed, after 25...♖d2?! there is an unusual perpetual with 26 ♕xg4+ ♗e6 27 ♕e2 ♗d5! 28 ♕g4+ ♗e6; an attractive finish, but Black can play for more. 25...♖f3! is good for Black. If 26 ♗xe3 ♖xd1 27 ♗xa7 ♖dxf1+ 28 ♕xf1 ♖xf1+ 29 ♔xf1 ♗xf7, reaching a minor piece endgame in which Black is a pawn up and has the bishop-pair against bishop and knight. It is quite likely that Black will win. This cannot be what White would want.

g223) Unfortunately for White, 24 ♖c7+ ♔d8 25 ♘c5 ♗xc5 26 ♖xc5 ♕xc5 is no improvement. After 27 f8♕+ ♕xf8 28 ♗g5+ ♕e7 29 ♗xe7+ ♔xe7 Black has rook, bishop and two pawns for the queen. The queen has no active play, though, and Black should win comfortably. Here even two queens would not hold the position together after 27 ♗g5+ ♕xg5 28 f8♕+ ♔d7. Black should again win.

There is an old question of chess philosophy of whether there is much point for the analyst trying to examine the position so deeply, when neither of the players would have had the chance of calculating any but a few sample lines of a genuinely complicated position. Underlying this point is the recognition that the annotator would also, before the help of the computer, be guessing just as much as the players.

These days, someone wanting to analyse a game in depth would be able to give a reasonable indication of whether in an unbalanced position the attacker is better, equal or worse. I would feel reasonably certain that without the help of computer analysis, I would have been unable to find the critical line, and would have regarded Shirov's attacking play in this game as brilliant and totally sound. Instead Shirov is shown as having overpressed his attack, always of course assuming that I have not made my own errors in interpretation. Indeed, the computer is of considerable help in interpreting what is happening in a game of chess, going

beyond the familiar question of finding innovations in the opening.

We now return to Black's misguided exchange sacrifice:

21 cxd4 ♖d3

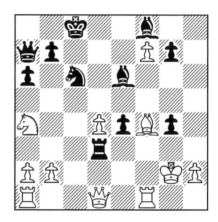

22 d5!

Again, Shirov aims directly for the sharpest line, giving away queen for rook and minor pieces, and relying on his advanced connected passed pawns, and on the difficulties of Black's king.

22 ♕e2 ♕xd4 23 ♖ad1 b5 24 ♘c3 ♔b7 is far from clear. White has the extra exchange, but Black's pieces are becoming coordinated, and it is Black who has the most dangerous passed pawn.

22...♖xd1 23 ♖axd1

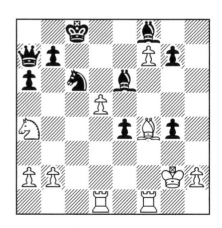

23...e3

23...♗xf7 24 dxc6 bxc6 25 ♗g5 wins for White. Black's king is exposed and his pieces are not well coordinated.

24 ♖fe1

But not the hasty 24 dxe6? e2, and one of White's rooks drops.

24...b5

Hoping for counterplay. 24...♗xf7 28 ♗xe3 soon allows White to win.

25 dxe6

The simplest.

25...bxa4 26 ♖d7

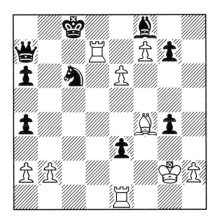

The position is no longer wild. White is slightly down in material, but with two highly advanced passed pawns and a rook on the seventh, supported by the bishop, and also a second rook about to join in, it is clear that White should soon win. In addition to everything, Black's king is exposed, and faces the danger of mate threats.

26...♕b6

Some minor counterplay.

27 ♖xe3

This will do nicely.

27 ♖c7+? ♕xc7 28 ♗xc7 ♔xc7 29 ♖xe3 wins the queen, but gives away some of the advantage.

27...♕xb2+

The queen should neither be overestimated, nor underestimated. Here the queen is still dangerous, but with careful play, White wins.

28 ♔g3

The king is safer here than on the back rank.

28...g5

To stop the winning check on c7.

29 ♗xg5

The trouble is that now the rook has a winning check on d8.

Not 29 ♖c7+?? ♔b8, and White has overextended himself.

29...♘d4

There is still some hope for practical counterplay, especially before the time control.

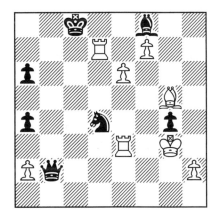

30 ♖d8+!

White needs to play precisely, bringing the king up, before aiming for e7.

30 ♖xd4?! ♕xd4 31 e7 ♗xe7 32 ♖xe7 is far less precise, as the white rook is not giving check. White still wins after 32...♕d6+ 33 ♔xg4 ♕d1+, but he has to negotiate umpteen checks until his final victory.

30...♔b7

30...♔c7 31 ♖xd4 leads to much the same finish.

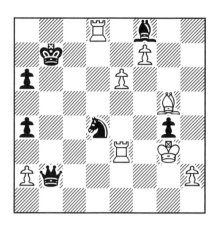

31 ♖xd4

White still needs to be careful of perpetual checks by the queen, and Shirov chooses the safest plan.

31 ♖xf8? leads to one step away from the win, but the final tempo is elusive: 31...♘f5+ 32 ♔f4 (32 ♔xg4? ♘xe3+ 33 ♗xe3 ♕g7+ allows Black to pick up the rook) 32...♕f2+ 33 ♔xg4 ♘xe3+ 34 ♗xe3 ♕e2+! keeps Black alive (but not 34...♕xe3+ 35 ♖b8+ ♔xb8 38 f8♕, with a straightforward win). With careful play on both sides, this will end up in a draw after, for example, 35 ♔f5 ♕d3+ 36 ♔f6 ♕c3+ 37 ♔g6 (37 ♔e7 ♕c7+) 37...♕c2+ 38 ♔g5 ♕g2+ 39 ♔f6 ♕b2+, and the merry-go-round continues.

31...♕xd4 32 e7

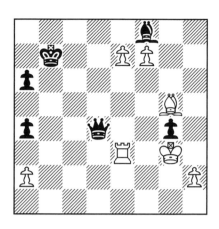

Forced on both sides.

32...♕h8

A last-ditch attempt to give a few checks.

32...♗xe7+ 33 ♖xe7+ loses quickly, as does 32...♕xe3+ 33 ♗xe3 ♗xe7 34 ♗h6.

33 e8♕

Naturally.

33...♕h3+ 34 ♔f4

34 ♔f2 ♕xh2+ still gives Black some hope.

34...♗d6+ 35 ♔f5 1-0

The end. White has too many pieces for Black to be able to set up many more checks. If 35...g3+ 36 ♔g6 or 35...♕h7+ 36 ♔xg4.

Game 18
S.Rublevsky-A.Grischuk
7th matchgame, Elista 2007
Scotch Game C45

1 e4 e5 2 ♘f3 ♘c6 3 d4

The Scotch Opening, which Rublevsky tried out several times in this match. In the end, he lost more games than he won with the white pieces, a serious shortcoming in match-play.

The Scotch is a principled enough opening to be tried, but the general feeling is that opening up the centre so quickly gives rather less long-term pressure than the Ruy Lopez, examined from Game 7, Svidler-Topalov, onwards.

3...exd4

There is probably no need for Black to have to think about other lines.

4 ♘xd4

The nine-times British Champion from the 1950s and 1960s, Jonathan Penrose, was an advocate of the Scotch Gambit, 4 c3. There are certainly many tactical ideas if Black were to accept the challenge, but it is difficult for White to prove any sort of advantage after Capablanca's suggestion, 4...d5!? 5 exd5 ♕xd5 6 dxc4 ♗g4 7 ♗e2 ♗b4+ 8 ♘c3 ♗xf3! 9 ♗xf3 ♕c4!. A peculiarity of the rules of chess is that a player is not allowed to castle with the king over check, so that, for example, 10 0-0 is not allowed, as the queen covers the f1-square, which the king was intending to cross. If castling were allowed in this position, White would be better. Instead it is only equal.

4 ♗c4 has been tried, but isn't White effectively losing a tempo after 4...♘f6 5 e5 d5 6 ♗b5 ♘xe4 7 ♘xd4 ♗d7 with equality?

4...♗c5

In many ways, the simplest and most direct move, developing, and attacking the d4-square.

Black can also try attacking the pawn on e5, the main line being 4...♘f6 5 ♘xc6 bxc6 6 e5 ♕e7 7 ♕e2 ♘d5 8 c4 ♗a6 9 b3 0-0-0. Certainly this breaks the symmetry, with White's pawns in danger of being overextended, and his pieces underdeveloped, while Black's pieces are on strange positions. Rublevsky found an unusual idea after 10 g3 g5!? 11 ♗b2 ♗g7 12 ♘d2 ♘b4 13 ♘f3 ♖he8 14 a3 g4:

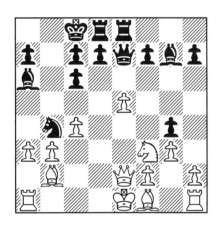

a) Previously White had tried 15 ♘h4 ♗xe5 16 0-0-0 ♘a2+ 17 ♔c2, reaching a strange position where the stray knight on a2 is about to be trapped, and one of

Black's bishops is ineffective, but where everything else is centralized and active. This is maybe equal but complicated.

b) S.Rublevsky-A.Onischuk, Foros 2007, saw instead 15 axb4!? gxf3 16 ♕e3 ♕b4+ 17 ♗c3! ♖xe5! (a good tactic, but not winning) 18 ♗xb4 ♖xe3+ 19 fxe3 ♗xa1 20 ♗h3, and White was two pawns down at the start of the endgame. Black's pieces were unable to cooperate, however, and he soon had to drop pawns. Play continued 20...♗e5 21 0-0 ♗b7 22 ♖d1 c5 23 ♗xc5 ♗c6 24 ♔c2, and White was now clearly at least equal. The game was later drawn, and Black's pawn on f3 was unexpectedly still on the board at the end.

4...♕h4!? is something of an oddity, one possibility being 5 ♘b5 ♕xe4+ 6 ♗e2 ♔d8 7 0-0. Sometimes Black even tries 7...♕e8, exchanging the bed of the king and queen. It is the sort of opening that Steinitz would have enjoyed playing, but he suffered a World Championship loss in M.Chigorin-W.Steinitz, 19th matchgame, Havana 1892, after 6 ♗e3 ♔d8 7 ♘1c3 ♕e5 8 ♘d5 ♘f6 9 ♘bxc7 ♗d6 10 f4 ♕xe4 11 ♗d3 ♕xg2 12 ♖g1 ♕xh2 13 ♕f3 ♘xd5 14 ♘xd5 ♕h6 15 0-0-0. Then, as now, gambit play was difficult to handle for both sides. Players would not be surprised to learn that White won from this position, but the computer gives Black as an edge.

There are few recent games at high level with 4...♕h4, indicating that the pawn grab is regarded with suspicion.

5 ♘xc6

Rublevsky has tried 5 ♗e3 several times, but for this Candidates match, he varies his play. After 5...♕f6 6 c3 ♘ge7 Rublevsky has tried, with some

success, 7 g3!?, with, for example, two wins against Sasikiran in 2005. The general view, though, is that this line tends to give Black good equalizing chances after 7...d5 or 7...h5.

5...♕f6

5...bxc6 6 ♗d3 leaves White slightly better. Doubled pawns are often not serious weaknesses, but the player with the doubled pawns would have liked some compensation in return.

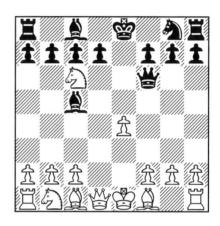

6 ♕f3

Rublevsky had recently dropped trying 6 ♕d2. In S.Rublevsky-V.Akopian, Sochi 2004, play continued 6...dxc6 7 ♘c3 ♗d4!? 8 ♗d3 ♘e7 9 0-0 ♘g6 10 ♘e2 ♗b6 11 ♘g3 ♘e5 12 ♗e2 0-0 13 ♕c3 ♖e8 14 ♗e3 ♘g4 15 ♕xf6 ♘xf6 16 ♗xb6 axb6. Not very exciting if White is trying for a win, and Rublevsky duly overpressed and lost.

6...bxc6

6...♕xf3 7 gxf3 bxc6 is, it has to be said, fairly easy equality, despite much recent interest. After 8 ♗e3 ♗xe3 9 fxe3 ♖b8 10 b3 ♘e7 11 ♘c3 d6 12 f4 f5, Zhang Zhong-V.Akopian, Turin Olympiad 2006, Black was comfortable, and indeed his opponent later overpressed and lost.

7 ♕g3

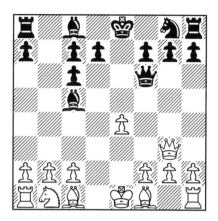

So at least we reach a middlegame. Black's pieces have developed quickly, but his pawn structure is slightly suspect. White has reasonable chances of playing for a slight edge. Moreover, this is one of the few lines where decisive results outnumber draws in the 4...♝c5 variation.

7...h5

7...d5 8 ♝d3 ♝d6 9 f4 gives a slight edge to White. Black prefers to maintain the kingside tension.

8 h4

The usual reply, but White could also ignore the pawn push with 8 ♝d3!? h4 9 ♕f4.

8...♞h6

For so long as this developing move is satisfactory, there is no particular need for alternatives.

8...d5 9 ♞c3 (9 e5 ♕f5 10 ♝d3 ♕g4 is equal) 9...♝d6 10 f4 dxe4 11 ♞xe4 ♕e6 is, at the moment, unclear.

9 f3

Preserving his pawns.

9 e5 ♕f5 10 ♝d3 ♕g4 is comfortable for Black.

9...d5

In a ChessBase annotation, Ftacnik

gives 9...0-0 10 ♞c3 ♖e8 11 ♝e2 as equal. Readers may decide whether 10 ♕g5 ♕d4 11 ♕xh5 is foolhardy, or a refutation of this, or something between.

10 ♞c3

10 e5? ♞f5 11 exf6? (11 ♕f4 ♕g6 bails out to a slight edge for Black) 11...♞xg3 12 fxg7 ♖g8 traps White's rook.

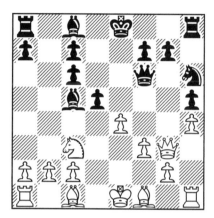

Has White gained anything from his opening? Ftacnik noted at the time that Rublevsky had tested this position five times in Elista, and had won only once, losing twice. Rublevsky really could do with widening his opening range.

10...♝d4

Grischuk varies from their previous encounter.

Shortly before the Grischuk-Rublevsky match, S.Rublevsky-V.Tkachiev, Poikovsky 2007, had gone 10...♝b4 11 ♝d2 dxe4 12 0-0-0 e3 13 ♝xe3 ♝xc3 14 ♝g5!? ♝xb2+ 15 ♔b1 ♝e6 (but not 15...♕c3?? 16 ♖d8 mate nor, more sophisticatedly, 15...♖b8 16 ♝xf6 ♝e5? 17 ♔f1 ♝xg3?? 18 ♖d8 mate) 16 ♝xf6 ♝xf6 17 ♖e1, and sadly Black's enterprising queen sacrifice did not work, and he soon lost.

Who is going to have the bravery to repeat Tkachiev's queen sacrifice? Grischuk was reported as saying that he was prepared to take on Rublevsky in this line, but as we shall see later, Rublevsky was the first to diverge. Indeed, here 15...♖b8! would have sacrificed the queen more effectively, and if 16 ♗xf6 gxf6.

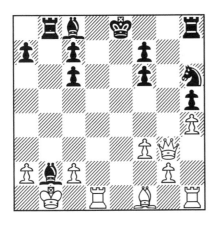

If White wants a quick and easy draw, there is 17 ♕g7!? ♗a3+ 18 ♔a1 ♗b2+ 19 ♔a1 with a perpetual. Can he try for more, though? 17 c3 ♗f5+ 18 ♖d3 is a possible attempt, and if 18...♗a3+? 19 ♔c2 ♖b2+ 20 ♔d1 ♖b1+ 29 ♔e2 and the king escapes, and Black does not have enough for the queen. Better is 18...♗xc3+! 19 ♔c2 ♗e5 20 f4. Ftacnik assesses this as a clear advantage for White, but this seems to overstate White's play. 20...♗d6 looks safest, allowing the pieces and pawns to work together. Two minor pieces and two pawns for the queen would be an uncommon material balance. Black will, though, win the exchange soon, resulting in a more common balance, with Black being roughly half a pawn ahead in terms of material. Much depends on whether White or Black can bring his

pieces working together, and also on whether Black finds he has an overexposed king, or whether some pawns drop. There are so many possible lines to analyse in depth. Quite possibly the position is about equal, and the better player will win.

In one of his other games against Grischuk, Rublevsky decided to avoid the queen sacrifice with 14 bxc3:

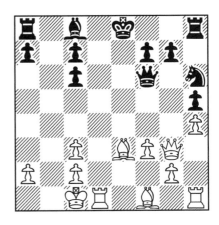

a) This had earlier been tried, with a win for Black, following 14...♘f5?! 15 ♕g5?! ♘xe3 ♕xe3+ ♕e7 16 ♕xe7+ ♔xe7 in Ni Hua-E.Najer, Ergun 2006, and after White mishandled a rook ending.

Marin, annotating for ChessBase, suggests that White has a considerable advantage after 15 ♕c7!, and if 15...♘xe3?! 16 ♖d6 ♗e6 17 ♕xc6+ ♔e7 18 ♕c5! with plenty of nasty discovered checks.

b) Another try is 14...♕xc3, which looks risky, but maybe there are chances of equalizing after 15 ♗d4 ♕a3+ 16 ♗b2 ♕e3+ 17 ♔b1 ♗e6.

c) Finally, we return to S.Rublevsky-A.Grischuk, 4th matchgame, Elista 2007, in which Black tried too hard to avoid tactics, and ended up positionally worse after 14...0-0?! 15 ♕g5 ♘f5 16 ♕xf6 gxf6 17 ♗f4 with a later win for White.

Perhaps we can see why Grischuk changed tack later on.

11 ♗d2

11 ♘d1 seems possible, and complicated, but without any advantage to White.

11...♖b8

Hitting b2. As we shall soon see, Black is reasonably certain of being able to draw, with the help of a perpetual on b2.

What happens, though, if White tries for a win?

12 0-0-0

12 ♘d1 ♕e7 allows Black to take over the initiative.

12...♗e5

Black avoids the temptation of offering a queen exchange:

a) 12...♕e5? 13 ♕xe5 ♗xe5 14 exd5 cxd5 15 ♖e1 pins and wins the bishop.

b) 12...♕d6? 13 ♕xd6 cxd6 14 ♗f4 ♗xc3 15 bxc3 allows White an advantage.

round encounter with 13 ♕g5 ♕d6 14 exd5 0-0 15 ♗c4 cxd5 16 ♗xd5 ♕xd5 17 ♘xd5 ♗xb2+ 18 ♔b1 ♗c3+ 19 ♔c1 ♗b2+ 20 ♔b1 ♗c3+, drawn by perpetual, S.Rublevsky-A.Grischuk, Elista 2007.

13...♗d4

The only move.

14 ♕d3

14 e5 ♘f5 15 ♕f3 ♕g6 16 ♗d3 ♕g4 leaves Black comfortable. In this line, 15 exf6 ♘xg3 traps the rook, as if 16 ♖h2 ♗g1, and 16 fxg7 ♖g8 17 ♖e1+ ♔d8 still does not allow White's rook to escape.

14...♗g4

This might end up as a draw, if White so wants.

14...dxe4 15 ♕xe4+ ♔f8 16 ♗e3 ♗xc3 17 bxc3 ♗g4 18 ♗d4 ♕f5 19 ♖e1 is close to equality, but the small gap between discomfort and safety can be difficult to close. White's two bishops make an impact on both sides of the board, given an open pawn structure, while Black's knight covers only the kingside. After, for example, 19...♖xe4 20 ♖xe4 ♘f5 21 ♗c5+ ♔g8 22 ♖d2 White is better.

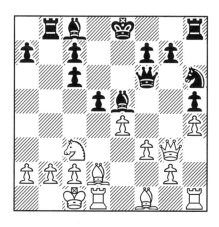

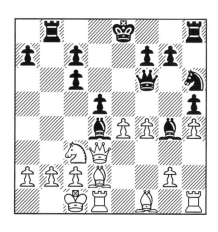

13 f4

In this, the first play-off game, Rublevsky avoids following their sixth-

15 e5

15 ♗e2 is to be considered, but is ultimately not successful:

a) After 15...♗xc3 16 ♗xc3 ♕xf4+ (16...♗xe2 17 ♕xe2 ♕xf4+ 18 ♖d2 also forces Black to work hard, given the threat on g7; maybe 18...0-0, but White has an edge after 19 exd5 cxd5 20 ♕xh5 ♘f5 21 ♕g5) 17 ♕d2 ♕xd2+ 18 ♖xd2 Black's pawn advantage is only temporary, as he is under attack on g7 and e5. Meanwhile, the knight is the least effective of the minor pieces. Playing on, we might have 18...♗xe2 19 ♖xe2 ♔f8 20 dxe5 cxd5 21 ♖e5 c6 22 ♖he1, and White has definite chances of playing for a win, in spite of his pawn minus.

b) So far, so good, for White, but it is unlikely that White should be better. Indeed, further investigation shows that Black has an edge after 15...♗xe2! 16 ♕xe2 0-0!:

b1) After 17 e5 ♕e7 Black is threatening to attack with ...♕b4.

b2) White also has problems with the dark squares after 17 ♕xh5 dxe4, and if 18 ♖de1 e3 19 ♗xc3 ♗xe3 20 bxc3 ♕xc3.

b3) 17 exd5 ♘g4! is a useful zwischenzug. If White deals with the knight fork, then Black recaptures on d5 with advantage. Therefore 18 dxc6 ♘f2 19 ♕xh5 ♘xh1 20 ♖xh1 ♕xc6, but Black's pieces are active, and the extra exchange is more significant than the two pawns.

Rublevsky's move is therefore the best, objectively.

15...♗xc3

The only move.

16 ♕xc3

White can take the queen with 16 exf6 ♗xb2+ 17 ♔b1 ♗xf6+ 18 ♔c1 ♗b2+ 19 ♔b1, but Black has at least a draw. What Rublevsky might have been concerned with is not so much that he is worried about giving away another draw with the white pieces, but rather that White is still in trouble after 19...♗xe1!.

Rublevsky tries to play it safely, and with, he hopes, chances of an edge. Grischuk in reply plays smooth and effective positional chess.

16...♕e6

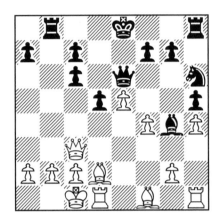

Now the tactical exchanges are out of the way, it is time to assess the positional balance of power.

The immediate thought is that Black has excellent control with his light-square play, with bishop, queen and knight having the opportunity to find useful central and semi-central outposts. White's central pawns are, if anything, in the way. He would like to take advantage of the diagonal from a1 to h8, but the e5-pawn is in the way. Also, White's f4 pawn is in the way. White would have liked to have exchanged bishop for knight on h6, and/or pushed out Black's bishop with f3. Thus White is not better. The practical question is whether White can hold equality, or whether he is worse.

17 ♖e1

It is too early to think about sacrificing the exchange.

17...0-0

Black, of course, castles, bringing both rooks into play. Grischuk waits to see which minor piece should take over on f5. It is best to keep open the option.

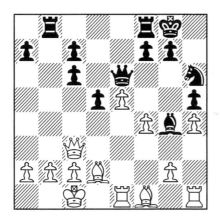

18 ♗e3?!

White wants to use the bishop on the diagonal, but there are too many hits against it, with ...d4, ...♘f5, ...♘g4, or even ...c5, threatening ...d4.

Ftacnik gives instead 18 ♕a5!, which helps tie down Black's queenside pawns, and gives a new lease of attacking chances for the light-squared bishop if he were to try ♗a6 against ...♖b7 or ...♖fc8. Ftacnik gives further 18...d4 19 b3 ♕e7 20 ♗d3 ♘f5 as equal. Playing on a few moves, the computer suggests that White can play for an advantage after 21 e6 fxe6 22 ♖xe6 ♕xe6 23 ♗c4 ♕xc4 24 bxc4 ♘g3 25 ♖e1 ♘e2+ 26 ♖xe2 ♗xe2. The queen and opposite-coloured bishop can easily prove to be highly effective. Imagine, for example, the chances White would have after ♕xd4 and ♗c3. Probably, though, Black should not open up the centre so quickly. 18...♘f5!? is a good pawn sacri-

fice, and if 19 ♕xc7 ♖fc8 20 ♕a5 c5, and Black may feel it is a positive advantage to have given up the backward c-pawn.

18...♖fd8

Preparing a possible ...d4-push. The immediate 18...d4 is already possible, but not yet effective, and after 19 ♗xd4 ♕xa2 20 ♗c4 ♕a4 21 ♗b3 ♕a6 a draw by repetition is likely.

If 18...♘f5, Ftacnik gives 19 ♗xa7 ♖a8 20 ♗c5 ♖fd8 21 a3 d4 22 ♕c4 ♕h6 as equal.

19 ♕c5

Marin notes that 19 ♗a6? would unexpectedly lose to 19...d4 20 ♗xd4 c5!.

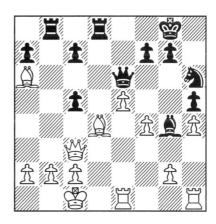

It is sometimes difficult to see why such a move is so strong. Black attacks the bishop on d4, certainly, but surely he won't be able to take it? To make any move in chess, a player moves into a square, but also vacates another square. The square that disappears opens up lines through that square, and here Black is threatening ...♕e6xa6, the queen travels by express through c6.

19...a5!?

Perhaps this is not quite the 'just in time' move that Marin suggests, since

19...♘f5 still gives Black an edge. If 20 ♗a6?!, the hoped for defence, then 20...♖b6 leaves Black happy.

The ...a5 move is useful in helping any attack.

20 ♔b1

And 20 ♕xa5? simply helps Black's attack, with 20...d4 21 ♗f2 ♖a8 22 ♕b4 ♕xa2. White needs to add protection to the a2-square.

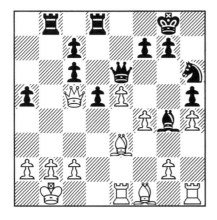

20...a4

Grischuk conspicuously avoids the natural knight move, 20...♘f5, and we shall soon see why. A few moves later, he plays ...♗f5, adding pressure on the h7-b1 diagonal.

21 ♗d3

Rublevsky sees that Black is planning ...♗f5, and so sets up a bishop exchange on d3 with the hope of recapturing with the c-pawn, putting pressure on Black's doubled c-pawns. It doesn't quite work, but maybe it is the next move that is the problem.

Ftacnik gives instead 21 ♕a5 d4 22 ♗d2 ♗f5 23 ♕xa4 ♖a8 24 ♕b3 d3 25 ♕xe6 dxc2+ 26 ♔c1 fxe6 27 ♗c4 ♘g4, which should end up with level play after 28 ♖e2. However, Black can improve with 24...♕xb3! (opening the a-

file) 25 axb3 d3!. Here, with the queens off the board, it is time to start a mating attack: 26 cxd3 ♖xd3 27 ♗xd3 ♗xd3+ 28 ♔c1 ♖a1 mate, or if 26 c4 ♖a6 27 b4 ♖da8 28 b3 ♖a1+ 29 ♔b2 ♖1a2+ 30 ♔c3 ♖c2+, and Black wins a piece.

This is hardly an improvement for White, and 21 ♕a3 is a losing transposition after 21...d4 22 ♗d2 ♗f5 23 ♕a4.

Looking through the other alternatives, 21 ♗d2 looks reasonable, but Black is again better after 21...♘f5 22 ♗d3 ♘g3 23 ♖hg1 ♘e4! 24 ♗xe4 dxe4, and if 25 ♗a5 ♖b5 26 ♕c3 ♖db8 27 ♖xe4 ♖xb2+ 28 ♕xb2 ♖xb2+ 29 ♔xb2 a3+! 30 ♔xa3 ♕d5 31 ♖a4 ♕c5+, spearing the pawn on g1.

21...♗f5

Showing that Grischuk judged well in delaying ...♘f5.

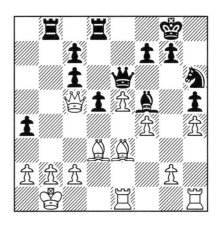

22 ♖c1?!

Both Ftacnik and Marin suggest 22 ♗e2 as giving equality with, of course, a possible repetition after 22...♗g4. However, 22...♗e4! is promising for Black. If then 23 ♗xh5 ♘f5! 24 ♗e2 (to prevent ...♖b5) 24...♘xe3 25 ♕xe3 ♖b6, and as we have seen before, and we shall see again, White is in trouble on the b-file.

Therefore 24 ♗g4, pinning, looks critical, and there are several dead ends, but 24...a3! 25 ♕xa3?! ♗xc2+ 26 ♔xc2 ♘xe3+ 27 ♖xe3 ♕xg4 favours Black. If 28 g3 d4, with attack.

Here White might try 25 b3!? ♖b5, and then take on a3 more accurately with 26 ♕xa3!? ♗xc2+ 27 ♔xc2 ♘xe3+ 28 ♖xe3 ♕g4 29 g3. Then probably Black has a slight edge after 29...c5 30 ♖d1 ♕g6+. Sharper is 29...d4, but it seems that Black has no more than a perpetual after 30 ♖d1 dxe3 31 ♖d8+ ♔h7 32 ♕f8 ♕e2+ 33 ♔b1 ♕e1+ 34 ♔b2.

White may also try, instead of the immediate capture on a3, the intermediate 26 ♗xf5!? ♗xf5 27 ♕xa3, but Black has good attacking chances, and excellent compensation for the two pawns with 27...d4 28 ♖d1 c5 29 ♗f2 ♖db8. There are sacrifices coming up on b3. If, for example, 30 ♔a1 ♗xc2 31 ♖c1 ♗xb3 32 axb3 ♕d5, and the additional threat of ...♖a8 will lead White's position to fold.

In total, the onus is on White to prove he can hold. There is not a simple drawing option available.

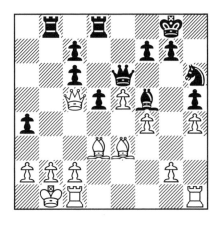

22...♗xd3

Grischuk does not even have to give away any pawns to keep attacking against the king.

23 cxd3 ♘f5

This is a dream square for the knight, provided Black keeps in mind the thought that the knight has the chance of moving to even better squares.

24 ♗f2

24 ♗d2 also ends up in problems. 24...♕g6 25 ♕xc6 ♕xg2 is good for Black, while if White tries to stir things up with 25 ♖hg1 ♘xh4 26 ♕xc6 ♕xd3+ 28 ♖c2, Black has a winning sacrifice with 28...♖xb2+! 29 ♔xb2 ♖b8+ 29 ♔c1 ♕d4.

24...♖b5

Black gains a tempo with his attack on b2. There is no point in defending c6, as White's b-pawn is far more significant than Black's doubled c-pawn.

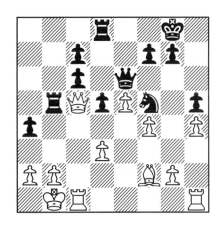

25 ♕xc6

Not satisfactory, but what else is there? Certainly 25 ♕a3 ♖db8 26 ♖c2 ♖b4 27 g3 d4 is miserable.

25...♖db8!

Hitting b2.

26 ♕xe6

The least-resistance option, but it

turns out that Black is winning the endgame. Others:

a) 26 ♖f2?? loses immediately: 26...♖xb2+ 27 ♖xb2 ♖xb2+ 28 ♔xb2 ♕xc6.

b) 26 b3 axb3 27 a4 ♖b4 28 ♕xe6 fxe6 29 ♖xc7 ♖xa4 allows White to keep playing, but obviously he is in serious trouble on the queenside.

c) 26 ♕c2 is a possibility, there being no immediate win after 26...♖xb2?! 27 ♕xb2 ♖xb2+ 28 ♔xb2. Black instead waits until the pieces and pawns are better coordinated, and breaks the tension later with, for example, 26...♕a6!? (with thoughts of threats on d3) 27 ♖cd1 c5 28 ♖hg1 c4 29 dxc4 ♖xb2+ 30 ♕xb2 ♖xb2+ 31 ♔xb2 a3+ 32 ♔b3 ♕xc4+ 22 ♔xa3 ♕c3+ 34 ♔a4 ♕c2+, winning.

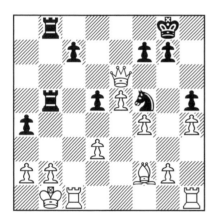

26...♖xb2+

An in-between move, or alternatively a 'zwischenzug'.

27 ♔a1 fxe6

Good knight versus bad bishop, and a rook on the seventh, with no weaknesses in Black's position.

28 ♖b1

The attempt to mix up the position with 28 ♗a7 ♖8b7 29 ♖c6 a3 30 ♗c5

♖c2 31 ♖b1 leads to an attractive mating combination with 31...♘d4!, and if 32 ♖xb7 ♖c1+ 33 ♖b1 ♘c2 mate, or 32 ♗xd4 ♖xb1+ 33 ♔xb1 ♖xc6.

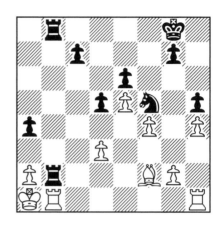

White may still look as though he is able to hold, thanks to the pin, but this is illusory.

28...a3

The only move. After 28...♖xb1+? 29 ♖xb1 ♖xb1+ 30 ♔xb1 d4 31 ♔b2, Black would even have been worse.

29 ♗c5

29 ♖xb2 ♖xb2 30 ♖f1 d4 31 g3 c5 leaves White move-bound.

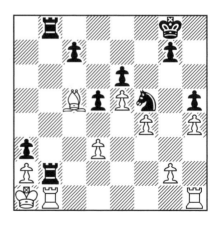

29...♘xh4!

The knight joins the battle.

30 ♖xb2

White's bishop, 'bad' a few moves ago, could set up counterplay with 30 ♗xa3 ♖xb1+ 31 ♖xb1 ♖xb1+ 32 ♔xb1 ♘xg2 33 ♗c1, but one would assume that Black is winning. After all, his passed pawn is the more advanced, and cannot be covered. It is still a close call after 33...h4 34 a4 h3 35 a5 h2 36 a6 h1♕ 37 a7, as analysed by Ftacnik, and unexpectedly White's pawn will be promoted. Black is still a couple of safe pawns up after 37...♘xf4 38 a8♕+ ♔h7, though, and will eventually win. However, Black must be careful not to be over-clever. If 33...♔f7? 34 a4 ♔e8?? (34...h4 still wins) 35 a5 ♔d7 36 a6 ♔c6 37 f5!, and with two passed pawns coming up, it is White who queens and wins.

Perhaps the most entertaining of all the knight tours, ending up with a rook sacrifice, is, as given by Ftacnik, 30 ♖bg1 ♘f5 31 ♖xh5 ♘g3 32 ♗xa3 ♖d2 33 ♖h2 ♘e2! 34 g4 ♖a8 35 ♗b2 ♘c3.

30...axb2+ 31 ♔b1 ♘xg2

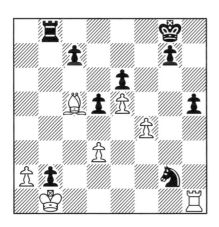

A more straightforward knight tour.

32 f5

This will not change the outcome.

32...♘f4

Or maybe 32...exf5, but Grischuk prefers to keep the knight in play.

33 fxe6

He will not queen the pawn.

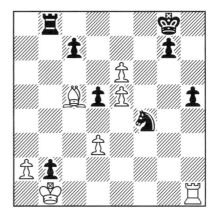

33...♘xd3

As Grischuk appreciates too, and takes another pawn.

34 ♗a3 ♘xe5

And another.

35 ♔c2

If instead 35 ♗xb2 then 35...♘c4 wins the bishop.

35...♘c4 36 ♗c5 ♘d2!

Quickest. Black makes another good knight move to win the rook.

37 a4 b1♕+ 38 ♖xb1 ♘xb1 39 a5 ♖b5
0-1

Game 19
L.Van Wely-T.Radjabov
Biel 2007
King's Indian Defence E97

1 d4 ♘f6 2 c4 g6 3 ♘c3 ♗g7

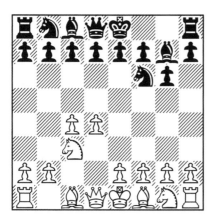

The King's Indian Defence, a favourite opening for Black, especially if he is looking for sharp attacking and counter-attacking chess. It just so happens that the King's Indian is underrepresented in this book, but the two games which are included give a fair indication of quite how complex this opening can be.

3...d5!?, the Grünfeld Defence, is another complicated possibility. After, for example, 4 cxd5 ♘xd5 5 e4 ♘xc3 6 bxc3 White has a big pawn centre just at the moment, but Black can soon counterattack, with 6...c5 or 6...♗g7 followed by a later ...c5.

4 e4

White sets up a big pawn centre. Other moves, for example, 4 g3 or 4 ♘f3, might allow a Grünfeld with 4...d5, or Black might continue with a King's

Indian and ...d6.

4...d6

Sometimes Black may tease the opponent with 4...0-0, and then a move later ...d6, transposing. Older players will remember R.Letelier-R.Fischer, Leipzig 1960, written up in Fischer's *My 60 Memorable Games*. After 5 e5?! ♘e8 6 f4 d6 7 ♗e3 c5 8 dxc5 ♘c6 9 cxd6 exd6 10 ♘e4 ♗f5 11 ♘g3 ♗e6 12 ♘c3 ♕c7, White may have been a pawn ahead, but his development was slow, and his prematurely advanced pawns left several weaknesses in the centre. Fischer won in just 23 moves.

5 ♘f3

For 5 f3, see Game 29, Bu Xiangzhi-Zvjaginsev.

See also comments there on other lines.

5...0-0

With quick development, but what about his pawns?

6 ♗e2

The most popular line. White keeps his bishop on a safe square, and castles quickly.

6...e5

Finally Black recovers some space in the centre. This is very much the main option, although 6...♗g4, 6...♘a6, 6...c5, 6...c6 and 6...♘bd7 are all playable. In the early years of the King's Indian, Black often tried 6...♘c6, with the idea that after 7 d5 ♘b8, White has loosened his dark squares. There is, however, the problem that Black has lost two tempi.

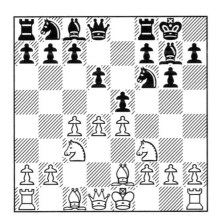

7 0-0

The main line.

7 d5 is an obvious alternative, gaining space immediately, but after 7...a5 followed by ...♘a6, it is difficult for White to gain any more space on the queenside.

7 dxe5 dxe5 8 ♕xd5 ♖xd5 9 ♗g5 (after 9 ♘xe5? ♘xe4 Black is comfortably equal) 9...♖e8!? is probably equal.

7 ♗e3 has been moderately fashionable, with the idea that after 7...♘g4 8 ♗g5 f6 9 ♗h4 (or even 9 ♗c1) Black's kingside has been slightly disrupted.

7...♘c6

This too is the main line, forcing White to decide what to do with his d-pawn. 7...exd4, 7...♘bd7 and 7...♘a6 8 ♗e3 ♘g4 9 ♗g5 are all standard alternatives, and there have been experiments with other moves.

There is so much theory to consider, that all we can do in one game is to give a pointer of some of the alternatives, rather than attempt to try to analyse all of them.

8 d5

The most direct move.

There is the final opportunity of an exchange of pawns on e5. It has been known for a long time that after 8 dxe5 dxe5 9 ♕xd8 ♖xd8 10 ♗g5, the slightly unusual-looking 10...♖d7! leaves Black comfortably equal, so White pushes the pawn ahead instead. Here 9 ♗g5!? is a possibility, and perhaps an irritation to a tactically-inclined opponent.

8...♘e7

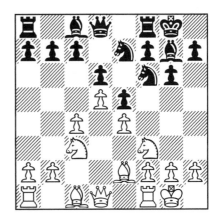

To the uninitiated, this can seem to be extremely passive for Black, but he can usually recoil with great effect with a knight move away from f6, and then ...f5, putting pressure on e4, or maybe advancing with ...f4, and then aiming at a pawn storm with ...g5 and ...g4. There are many examples of this position in Kasparov's play, though only up until a loss against Kramnik in 1997.

9 b4

And this is the move that Kramnik chose.

There are many alternatives, too many theoretical lines to write up in detail here.

9...♘h5

Radjabov goes for the sharpest line, ignoring White's c5 queenside push, and instead ramming through on the kingside with ...f5. As so often, the most direct line leads to complications.

9...a5 10 $\hat{\mathbb{Q}}$a3 axb4 11 $\hat{\mathbb{Q}}$xb4 $\hat{\mathbb{Q}}$d7 12 a4 is a quieter alternative, both sides' attacking chances being slowed down.

10 Ξe1

A waiting move. Black is going to try ...$\hat{\mathbb{Q}}$f4 or ...f5, and White wants to continue his development in such a way that either move by Black is useful in reply.

10 c5 is perhaps slightly premature. Black can hit back on the queenside (and the kingside) with 10...f5 11 $\hat{\mathbb{Q}}$g5 $\hat{\mathbb{Q}}$f6 12 f3 a5!?.

10...f5

Playing for the thematic kingside pawn roller.

The alternative is to try to spike White's queenside pawns with, for example, 10...$\hat{\mathbb{Q}}$f4 11 $\hat{\mathbb{Q}}$f1 a5 12 bxa5 Ξxa5 13 $\hat{\mathbb{Q}}$d2 c5 14 a4 Ξa6 15 Ξa3, but in V.Kramnik-G.Kasparov, Novgorod 1997, White still kept some queenside pressure, and his pieces were unusually well placed to defend on the kingside. Kramnik later won.

After 10...a5 11 bxa5 Ξxa5 12 $\hat{\mathbb{Q}}$d5 $\hat{\mathbb{Q}}$f4 13 $\hat{\mathbb{Q}}$f1 the position transposes into the last line. Black has tried this a few times recently, mostly with depressing results.

Like it or not, Black's strategy is to play sharp tactical lines here. Radjabov usually does not mind attacking chess! Van Wely too is renowned for highly tactical chess, as well as deep theoretical preparation.

11 $\hat{\mathbb{Q}}$g5

Immediately focusing on the weakness on e6. 11 $\hat{\mathbb{Q}}$d2 is possible, but less exciting, for both players.

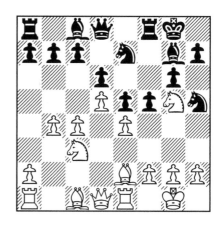

11...$\hat{\mathbb{Q}}$f6

11...$\hat{\mathbb{Q}}$f4 is no longer played at top level. It leads to some unusual pawn structures after 12 $\hat{\mathbb{Q}}$xf4 exf4 13 Ξc1 $\hat{\mathbb{Q}}$f6 14 $\hat{\mathbb{Q}}$e6 $\hat{\mathbb{Q}}$xe6 15 dxe6 $\hat{\mathbb{Q}}$xc3 16 Ξxc3 fxe4. Unfortunately, when White has recaptured his pawn on e4, he has a dangerous passed pawn on e6. In V.Kramnik-A.Shirov, Tilburg 1997, White later won after 17 $\hat{\mathbb{Q}}$f1 e3 18 fxe3 fxe3 19 Ξcxe3 c6 20 $\mathbb{W}$d2 d5 21 cxd5 cxd5 22 $\mathbb{W}$d4.

12 f3

To bolster the e4-pawn.

Radjabov has had to encounter 12 $\hat{\mathbb{Q}}$f3 a few times too. For example, 12...c6 13 b5 (13 $\hat{\mathbb{Q}}$b2!?; 13 $\mathbb{W}$b3!?) 13...h6 14 $\hat{\mathbb{Q}}$e6 $\hat{\mathbb{Q}}$xe6 15 dxe6 fxe4 16 $\hat{\mathbb{Q}}$xe4 $\hat{\mathbb{Q}}$xe4 17 $\hat{\mathbb{Q}}$xe4 d5 18 cxd5 cxd5 19 $\hat{\mathbb{Q}}$a3 dxe4 20 $\mathbb{W}$xd8 Ξfxd8 21 $\hat{\mathbb{Q}}$xe7 Ξxe6 23 Ξxe4 a6, soon agreed drawn in Y.Pelletier-T.Radjabov, Kemer 2007. This was already well known as a standard drawing line, such as in Y.Pelletier-J.Gallagher, German League 2002 (Pelletier played 23 $\hat{\mathbb{Q}}$e3 instead), and a few other games around the same time. What can Black do, though, if both players know their theory, and both players play correctly?

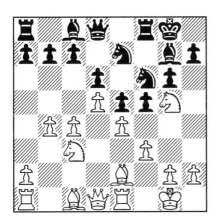

12...♚h8

It is decision time for Black.

After White's f3 move, it has become clear that if the knight is under pressure, it will have to force an exchange with ♘e6. After the resulting pawn is captured on e6, there could be tactics on the a2-g8 diagonal, particularly if White plays c5 at some stage. Therefore the immediate 12...♚h8 has its logic.

A couple of years earlier, Van Wely made excellent use of this semi-long-diagonal after his opponent tried 12...c6 13 ♚h1 h6 14 ♘e6 ♗xe6 15 dxe6 ♘e8 16 ♕b3 ♘c7 17 c5 d5 18 exd5 cxd5 19 ♗b2 ♕e8 20 a4 a6 21 ♖ad1 ♖d8 22 ♘xd5!, L.Van Wely-D.Stellwagen, Dutch Championship, Leeuwarden 2005.

12...♘h5 is worth considering, though, and has been tried a few times. Black's knight is moving backwards and forwards, certainly, but the point is that pawns are not allowed to move backwards, and the h5-square for Black is comfortable. If 13 c5 ♘f4 with complicated play.

13 ♘e6!?

A natural move, certainly, but also, according to Mikhalevski 'a surprising novelty' when reporting a previous Van

Wely-Radjabov game, Khanty-Mansiysk 2005. Thus, there is something of a paradox. The point is that White usually waits for Black to spend an extra tempo with ...h6, before playing ♘e6. If, however, the knight move is good, then quite often there is no need, one would think, to avoid it.

After 13 c5 dxc5! 14 bxc5 h6 15 ♘e6 White has 'gained' a tempo, but with the extra move he has allowed his queenside pawns to deteriorate. 15...♗xe6 16 dxe6 ♕d4+ led to an edge for Black, and later a win in Z.Gyimesi-T.Radjabov, Moscow 2005.

13 ♗e3 has been tried, then maybe 13...♘e8, leaving the danger of a hit with ...f4.

13...♗xe6

Of course. Radjabov has pleasant memories in this position, after previous encounters against Van Wely, although as we shall soon see, there was also a resounding win for White earlier.

14 dxe6 ♘h5!?

14...fxe4 was tried in their first encounter, L.Van Wely-T.Radjabov, Khanty-Mansiysk 2005. Mikhalevski hinted that this might have been inaccurate, 'but right now I can't see anything better'. It was Radjabov himself who first demonstrated the improvement, although Van Wely has, of course, done his own analytical work in reply.

This 2005 encounter continued 15 fxe4 ♘c6 16 ♘d5 ♘xe4 17 ♗f3 ♘f6 18 b5 ♘d5 19 dxc6 ♘b6? (in an extremely complicated game, this is the first serious slip; 19...♘c3! keeps White down to a slight edge) 20 cxb7 ♖b8 21 c5 e4 22 ♖xe4 dxc5 23 ♕xd8 ♖fxd8 24 ♗g5 ♖e8 25 ♖d1 ♗d4+ 26 ♖exd4 cxd4 27 e7 h6

28 ♗f6+ ♔g8 29 ♖xd4 ♔f7

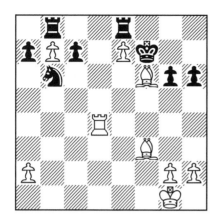

30 ♖d8! ♘d7 (30...♔xf6 31 ♖xe8 ♖xe8 32 ♗c6, and White will queen one of the pawns) 31 ♗h4 g5 32 ♖xd7 ♔e6 33 ♗g4+ and White duly won the game.

Some incredibly complicated tactical chess, with no real mating threats, but move-by-move attack and counterattack throughout. The central theme of the game is, of course, whether White can queen one of the pawns before Black is able to neutralize the pawns, and/or gain material.

I have given the comments without detailed annotation, partly to save space and time, but also as a reminder to the reader of just how complicated top-level chess can be. How many readers could work out what is going on, over-the-board, and without help of computer? Most of us would have fallen by the wayside, whether as White or Black.

We are giving an exceptional win by Radjabov against Van Wely. It is only fair to also mention an exceptional win by Van Wely against Radjabov.

15 c5

In another Van Wely-Radjabov game, Wijk aan Zee 2007 (pre-dating

the Biel game), White tried 15 g3, preventing ...♘f4. Radjabov showed a less obvious way of attacking the advanced but isolated e-pawn with the knight, via 15...♗f6!? 16 c5 f4 17 g4 ♘g7, and after 18 ♗c4 ♘c6 19 cxd6 cxd6 20 ♘e2 ♖c8, it was clear that Black was starting to take over. He later won.

For the next stage of his theoretical battle, Van Wely decided it was better to go for an immediate attack.

15...♘f4

If 15...dxc5 16 ♕xd8 ♖axd8 17 bxc5 ♘f4 18 ♖b1, White is slightly better.

15...fxe4 18 ♘xe4 d5 19 ♘g5 favours White.

16 ♗c4

White's c5-pawn move was not just to play for a queenside pawn attack. He also wanted to open up the c4-square for the bishop, guarding the advanced e-pawn.

16...fxe4

While Black wanted to open up lines on the kingside.

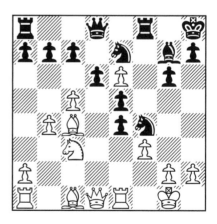

White now has to decide how to recapture the pawn on e4. Which way should he do it? The question is going to be one of tactics, rather than quiet positional play.

17 ♖xe4

Van Wely sacrifices the exchange.

A quieter way of continuing would be 17 fxe4!?, trying to stabilize the pawn centre:

a) The computer suggests 17...dxc5 18 bxc5 ♕d4+ 19 ♕xd4 exd4 20 ♘d5 d3 21 ♖b1 ♘e2+ 22 ♔h1, but it turns out that White's passed pawns are stronger than Black's. White is better.

b) 17...♘c6! shows that while White has good control on the light squares, he is weak on the dark squares with ...♘d4 being a possibility. If 18 cxd6 cxd6 19 ♘b5, Black has 19...♘xe6! 20 ♘xd6 (20 ♗xe6? ♕b6+) 20...♕b6+ 21 ♗e3 ♘cd4 22 ♗xe6 ♕xd6 23 ♗d5, probably about equal.

A plausible line might be 17...d5 18 ♗xf4 dxe4 (18...exf4? 19 ♘xd5, advantage to White) 19 ♕xd8 ♖fxd8 20 ♗g5 ♖d4 21 ♗b3 ♖e8 22 ♘xe4 and White has reasonable compensation with knight (on a good and safe square) and pawn (well guarded) for rook, but without any obvious reason why he should be clearly better:

a) Play might turn out to be around equal after 22...h6 23 ♗xe7 ♖xe7 24 a3 ♔g8 24 ♔f2.

b) Or 22...♘d5 23 b5 ♖xe6 24 ♗e3 ♖d3 25 ♗c4 ♖xe3 26 ♗xd5. Or here 23...♖xb4!? 24 ♖e1!?, with reasonable compensation for the material.

Maybe all this will be examined at some stage over the board.

18 g3!?

The first new move.

L.Van Wely-T.Radjabov, Monaco (blindfold) 2007, continued 18 ♗xf4 exf4 19 ♘d5 ♖e8 20 ♘xf4 c6 21 e7 ♖xe7 22 ♘e5 ♕b8 21 e7 ♖xe7 22 ♘e6 ♕b8 23 ♘xg7 ♖xg7, possibly close to equal, with Black's knight being slightly better that White's bishop, the knight covering squares of both colours. Black gradually took control as play continued.

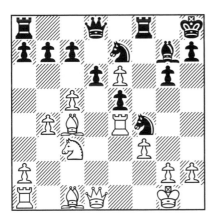

17...♘f5!?

No comment on this move by either Van Wely or Radjabov, but *Fritz* assesses 17...d5 as good for Black. Since Radjabov has already played 17...♘f5 before, and has used this move a second time, we can assume that 17...d5 is probably not quite as good as the computer suggests. Both players have been quiet as to what is actually going on, presumably because the pawn move might be tried on some future occasion.

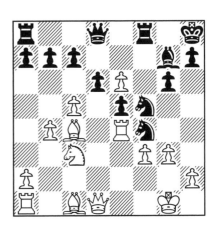

18...♞h3+

'Check!!!' – Radjabov

Obviously the idea is not so much that Black is going to start a big kingside attack. More it is the case that the check gains a tempo, allowing Black to bring his knight to a dangerous if risky square.

Maybe there are some initial indications that White's king might be exposed, but this will happen later, when Black's pieces are more fully developed.

19 ♔g2

He does not want his king on the f-file.

19...♞g5

The knights are dangerous.

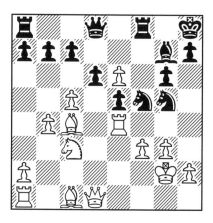

20 ♖g4

This was still within Van Wely's opening preparation, according to Radjabov's notes. The position is certainly complicated, and White has the basic choice either of simplifying or, as Van Wely chooses, making play even more complicated.

Black's g5-knight is threatening, with the danger not just picking up the exchange on e4, but also various tactics with ...♞xf3. Thus we must also examine:

a) The simplification route is 20 ♗xg5 ♕xg5 21 ♞d5 (threatening ...♞e3+):

a1) Radjabov then gives 21...c6!? 22 cxd6 ♞xd6 23 ♖g4 ♕h6 24 e7 cxd5 (24...♖fc8 25 ♞b6!) 25 exf8♕+ ♖xf8 26 ♕xd5 ♞f5 27 ♖e4 ♞e3+ 28 ♖xe3 ♕xe3 29 ♖d1 b6 (or alternatively 29...♕c3) as unclear. White seems better though. Both queens are active, but White's rooks and bishop are far more flexible than Black's.

a2) Quite often it is wisest not to uncover one's full analysis when it is possible that the opening may be repeated at some other event. A computer play-through would suggest that 21...dxc5!? 22 e7 ♖fc8 is highly promising for Black.

b) Another possibility for White would be to gain a tempo, at the attempt of sacrificing the passed pawn with 20 e7!? ♕xe7 21 ♞d5 ♕d8 22 ♗xg5 ♕xg5 23 ♞xc7 ♞e3+ 24 ♖xe3 ♕xe3 25 ♞xa8 e4! 26 f4 ♖xa8 27 cxd6 ♖d8, as noted by Radjabov. All the pieces on both sides, queen, rook and opposite-coloured bishops are active, with also a passed pawn on either side. Neither player has enough to win, and the likelihood is a perpetual after, for example, 28 ♖c1 ♖xd6 29 ♕xd6 ♕f3+ 30 ♔h3 ♕h5+ 31 ♔g2, or 28 ♗f1 g5 29 fxg5 ♕f3+ 30 ♔h3 (not 30 ♕xf3?? exf3+ 31 ♔xf3 ♗xa1) 30...♕f5+ 31 ♔g2 (but not 31 ♔h4?? h6) 31...♕f3+. These lines are given, slightly abbreviated, from Radjabov.

There are many lines on both sides that could be considered, but the general impression is that White at best is aiming only for a draw, with careful play, after an exchange on g5. It is understandable that Van Wely would want to try a more ambitious line.

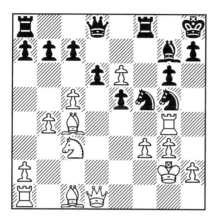

20...♘xf3!

Black ends the knight manoeuvre with a sacrifice, to bring the king into the open.

The computer at first suggests 20...e4?!, with the idea 21 ♗xg5 ♕xg5 22 ♖xg5 ♘e3+ 23 ♔h1 ♘xd1 24 ♖xd1 ♗xc3, but after a few tactics, this is lifeless. After 25 cxd6 cxd6 26 fxe4 Black still has to deal with the passed pawn on e6.

21 ♔xf3

Allowing the scary thought of a discovered check.

Naturally there are too many tactical ideas to allow White to give up the queen for various forces with 21 ♕xf3? ♘h4+ 22 ♖xh4 ♖xf3 23 ♔xf3 e4+. Radjabov gives 24 ♘xe4 d5 25 ♘g5 ♕f6+ 26 ♔g2 dxc4 27 ♘xh7 ♕xh4 28 gxh4 ♗xa1, Black ending up with a winning endgame.

21...e4+!

Black is not so much interested in the discovered attack on the f-file – that will keep – but is more interested in bringing the King's Indian bishop into play, with a violent attack. He would like to recover the material balance.

22 ♘xe4

Black is a clear pawn up, with no particular compensation for White, after 22 ♖xe4 ♗xc3 23 ♗f4 ♕f6 24 e7 ♗xa1 25 exf8♕+ ♖xf8.

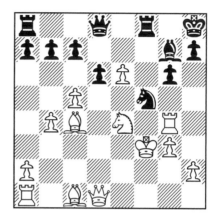

22...♗xa1!

The only move, and play is getting wilder.

Radjabov notes that 22...d5? 23 ♗g5! dxe4+ 24 ♔g2 ♕xg5 25 ♖xg5 ♘e3+ 26 ♔h3 ♘xd1 27 ♖xd1 gives White a clear advantage, not least because White's passed e-pawn is more dangerous than Black's passed e-pawn.

23 ♗g5

The only move, attacking queen and bishop.

23...♘e7+!

Out of all the safe discovered checks, this is in some ways the least expected. The natural reaction is to find something violent, maybe a double check, but Radjabov merely retreats to a safe square where White's passed e-pawn no longer creates an immediate threat.

24 ♔g2

Neither Radjabov nor Van Wely mentioned the obvious 24 ♖f4!? in their notes. If 24...♗e5, White at the very least may transpose into the game with

25 ♔g2!?, with, Radjabov suggests, a complicated draw. Readers might want to experiment in trying for more. Here, though, 24...♖xf4+ 25 ♗xf4 ♗e5 26 cxd6 cxd6 27 ♘xd6 ♕xd6 28 ♕xd6 ♗xd6 29 ♗xd6 ♖e8 30 ♔e4 ♔g7 31 ♗b5 ♘c6 32 ♗xc6 bxc6 33 ♔e5 is comfortable for White.

24...♗e5

To the most dominating square.

Black could consider hibernating with 24...♗g7?!, but the e6-square is worth protecting. After 25 cxd6 cxd6 26 ♘xd6 (26...♕xd6?! ♕c8! favours Black) 26...♕c7 27 ♘f7+ ♔g8 28 ♕d7 White is in control, his passed pawn being troublesome.

25 ♖f4

White is not too bothered about sacrificing the second exchange, so long as he may keep control of the long diagonal.

Van Wely suggests 25 ♖h4 as a possibility, but without closer analysis. Black seems comfortable after 25...♕e8 26 ♕g4 d5! 27 ♕h3 h5 28 ♗xe7 ♕xe7 29 ♗xd5.

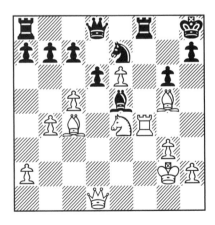

25...♗xf4

So Black is two exchanges ahead, two rooks for two bishops, but those bishops look formidable.

This exchange is so natural, that it could easily not be mentioned. If you can win material, you should take it. Neither Radjabov nor Van Wely give any alternatives here in their notes. This perhaps would be a rather simplified version of events: Radjabov wins after this move, but in later analysis, it becomes clear that the position is only equal after best play. It is possible that this position could be repeated at some stage, and so neither player would want to advertise their analysis prematurely. The computer suggests that there are several good alternatives, with chances of an edge for Black. It only takes one of these lines to be shown as giving a slight edge for Black, for there to be a substantial novelty.

Two promising ideas for Black would be 25...♖xf4!? 26 gxf4 ♗g7, keeping the bishop rather than the knight, and 25...♖c8!?, so that if White exchanges on d6, Black has instant counterplay.

26 gxf4?!

This recapture leaves him significantly worse, whereas 26 ♗xf4! holds. Such a conclusion is the result of pure tactics, playing through several strange lines of attack and defence, and in the end showing that in one critical line the position folds, while in the other critical line the position holds. The position is quite simply far too difficult for the players to analyse with certainty over the board, and while both players make a credible stab in their annotations, written shortly after the game, neither player gives the complete picture.

Radjabov, analysing for ChessBase, suggests that White could and should have taken a draw with 26 ♗xf4!. It turns out that his assessment is correct. This move is instinctively unappealing in that White has released the pin against the knight, but on the other hand White does not face any problems of counter-play along the g-file, as in the game.

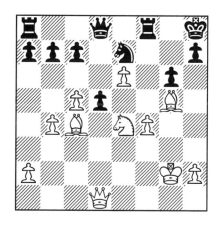

27 f5

This is really just a wild waiting move. Van Wely wants to see what is happening with Black's d-pawn. If Black wants to take on c4 or e4, White has a big check with ♕a1+. If White checks first with 27 ♕a1+, Black covers the diagonal with 27...d4. If, however, White plays a 'quiet' move, and Black plays ...d4, White has saved a vital tempo through not moving the queen to a1.

In a highly charged tactical position, often a quiet move adds to the tension, rather than resolving it. The opponent can't capture everything at once in a crazy game, giving an extra sacrificial course to add to the menu. White's pawn thrust is genuinely dangerous, as he is threatening f6, but there is no good way for Black to take the pawn, or even one of the pieces. Dangerous!

We must explore:

a) 27 ♕d4+ ♔g8 is the obvious start to the attack:

a1) Then 28 ♗h6 ♘f5! is a triple knight fork, covering both of the main attackers, and also the opponent's mating threat. It is difficult to do much more with one defending knight. 29 e7 ♘xd4 30 exf8♕+ ♕xf8 31 ♗xd5+ ♔h8

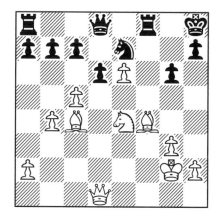

Radjabov gives as the main line 26...d5 27 ♕a1+ (though not 27 ♕d4+?? ♔g8 28 ♗h6 ♘f5) 27...♔g8 28 ♗h6 ♘f5 29 e7 ♕xe7 30 ♗xd5+ ♖f7 31 ♘f6+ ♔h8 32 ♘h5+ with a perpetual.

Or 26...♖xf4!? 27 ♕a1+ ♔g8 28 gxf4 ♕f8 29 ♘f6+, and another perpetual.

Finally, 26...♘f5 27 ♕a1+ ♘g7 28 ♗h6 ♕e7 29 ♗g5 ♕e7 would be another drawing line after 30 ♗h6 ♕e7, but if White wants to play on, 30 e7!? keeps live complications, and a genuine chance of an edge after, for example, 30...♖g8?! 31 ♗f6 32 ♕d4 a6 (avoiding White's b5) 33 ♔g1! and Black is under great pressure. Here 30...♖f7 31 cxd6 cxd6 32 ♘xd6 ♕c6+ might well end up as a draw, although 33 ♔h3!? would force both players to think.

So the bishop recapture on f4 is good and safe.

26...d5

'The position is simply crazy!' – Radjabov.

32 ♗xf8 ♖xf8 gives Black a safe extra exchange.

a2) 28 ♘f6+ ♖xf6 29 ♕xf6 ♕f8 also covers the mating threats, again keeping an extra piece.

b) We return to 27 ♕a1+:

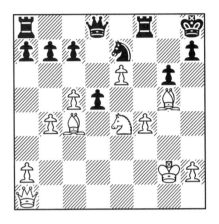

b1) After 27...d4 Van Wely in *Informator* simply stated that 28 ♘d6 was good, but Radjabov showed that he has the same rejoinder as in the main line, 28...h6!. He continues with 29 ♗xh6 ♔h7 30 ♗xf8 ♕xf8 31 ♘f7 ♘f5, claiming a slight plus for Black. The suspicion is that this is slightly optimistic, and that after 32 ♗d3 ♕g7 33 ♘g5+ ♔g8 34 ♗xf5 gxf5 35 ♕b1 White should be about level. White is still the exchange down, not unexpectedly given his earlier sacrifices, but he has an imposing passed pawn, and solid squares for the knight close to the opposing king. Here 35..♖d8!? is an attempt to make use of the extra exchange, but White still draws with 36 e7 (36 ♕xf5 d3 37 e7 also draws, with care) 36...♕xe7 37 ♕b3+ ♔f8 38 ♘e6+ ♔e8 39 ♘xd8, and Black is best advised to take a perpetual with 39...♕e2+.

b2) This leaves 27...♔g8:

b21) Both Radjabov and Van Wely

agree on 28 ♗h6 ♘f5 29 ♗xf8 ♕xf8 (29...dxc4 30 ♗d6 cxd6 31 ♘f6+ ♔h8 is a perpetual) 30 ♘f6+ ♔h8 as leading to an edge for Black after, for example, 31 ♗xd5 c6 or 31 ♘xd5+ ♕g7. The advantage of the exchange persists.

b22) 28 ♘f6+ ♖xf6 29 ♕xf6 ♕f8 is also good for Black, as we noted in variation 'a2'.

b23) 28 f5 gxf5 29 ♗f6 d4 was also analysed as good for Black by Van Wely.

b24) 28 ♗b3!? seems best, but was not given by the players. There is, however, an excellent reason for this omission, in that ♗b3 a move earlier cuts down a couple of options by Black, before the check on the long diagonal.

c) So finally, we reach Van Wely's suggested improvement for White. Go back to the last diagram, and we have 27 ♗b3!?.

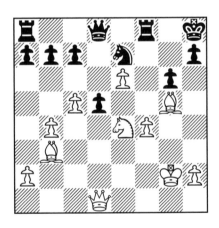

This is a quiet move which means that only one white piece is now attacked. White has more control in his play than after the 'violent quiet move' with f5. If Black takes this piece, 27...dxe4, White has 28 ♕a1+ ♔g8 29 ♗h6 ♕d2+ 30 ♔h1 ♖f6 31 ♕xf6 ♕e1+ with a perpetual.

Quite often in chess, the more that

one tries to analyse, the more that one recognises that hidden resources come alive, and that it takes many attempts to reach any sort of final analysis. Go back a couple of moves, and try 30...♘f5! (not given by Van Wely) 31 ♗xf8! (31 e7+? ♖f7 leads to nothing, Black wins) 31...h5!! (Black cannot take the bishop) 32 e7+ ♚h7 33 ♗f7 (33 ♗e6 ♘d4 34 ♗f7 ♛xf4 wins for Black) 33...♛xf4 34 e8♛ ♖xe8 35 ♗xe8 e3 when White has the extra minor piece, but Black's passed pawn is strong, and will win back a bishop. After 36 ♗b5 ♛f3+ 37 ♚g1 ♛f2+ 38 ♚h1 e2 39 ♗xe2 ♛xe2 Black has an extra pawn, and White's bishop is very badly placed. Black will win.

On the whole, I do not like too many double exclamation marks. A sparingly given single exclamation mark is usually sufficient. If Radjabov's next move, 27...h6!!, is worth giving the double bang, then surely the 31...h5!! in this last variation deserves similar acknowledgement.

Returning to 27 f5:

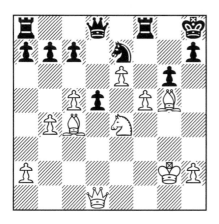

27...h6!!

This extra flight square alters the balance. After some extremely compli-

cated play, Black is now winning.

Radjabov does not give any alternative moves, and from his point of view, why should he? Job done, end of question.

It is nevertheless useful for the reader to consider what alternatives, notably grabbing pieces, should be examined. Only then would we be able to see why Radjabov's move was, indeed, worthy of a double-exclam:

a) The more obvious point is that if 27...dxe4?, Black is shredded on the long diagonal after 28 ♛a1+ ♚g8 29 ♗h6 ♘f5 30 e7+, winning. One of Van Wely's thoughts about his previous f5 move is that he would have wanted, as here, to prevent any queen check on d2.

b) A vastly more subtle approach for Black is 27...♖xf5! 28 ♛d4+ ♚g8 29 ♗h6 (29 ♘f6+ ♖xf6 30 ♛xf6 ♛f6 is also successful for Black) 29...♛f8!, sacrificing the queen. After 30 ♗xf8 ♖axf8 31 ♘g3?! ♖f4 32 ♛e5 dxc4 33 ♛xc7 c3! White is in trouble. Van Wely gives instead 31 ♗d3 as unclear. A first impression might be that the two rooks could outrun the white queen, but Black has problems in doing anything active with the knight. Black is not clearly better.

c) 27...dxc4 28 ♛a1+ ♚g8 29 f6 gives White an extremely dangerous attack, though with only a bishop for two rooks, there is a danger of running out of attacking pieces. The best reply seems to be 29...h6! 30 f7+! (30 fxe7 ♛d5 31 exf8♛+ ♖xf8 32 ♗xh6 ♛xe4+ 33 ♚g1 ♛g4+ 34 ♚h1 ♛f3+ and Black soon wins) 30...♖xf7 31 exf7+ ♚xf7 32 ♛f6+ ♚e8 33 ♛g7 ♚d7 34 c6+ bxc6 35 ♘c5+ ♚c8 36 ♗xe7 ♛d2+, and Black escapes with a perpetual.

Radjabov would presumably have

noted this line up to at least ...h6, and decided that there was at the very least no clear win. The next stage would have been the jump in imagination, in seeing that ...h6! a couple of moves earlier would have been extremely effective, and indeed would probably save a tempo. In the game line Black does not have to play ...♚g8. but can quickly move with the safer ...♚h7.

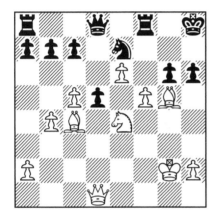

28 ♕d4+

Quite dizzying. White is two exchanges down, and all three of his minor pieces are under attack. White also has chances of attack against Black's king, although opening up the h7-square gives chances of escape by the king. Finally, White has two potential connected passed pawns, allowing chances of recovering some of the sacrificed material.

The verbal commentary might imply that Black should be better, but it is a case of analysing White's chances move by move, just to see whether Black is covering everything:

a) 28 ♕a1+ is a good start. Then after 28...♚h7! (not 28...d4? 29 ♗xe7 ♕xe7 29 ♕xd4+ ♚h7 31 f6 ♕d8 32 ♕e5, and White has a winning attack) 29 f6

(29 ♘f6+ ♖xf6 30 ♕xf6 hxg5!) 29...dxc4! 30 fxe7 ♕d5 31 exf8♘+ ♖xf8 Black wins. There has been much sacrifice and counter-sacrifice in this line, but basically, Black starts off well ahead in material, and keeps staying ahead at every stags. When the position is simplified, he wins.

b) Another attempt to take advantage of the long diagonal is 28 f6. After 28...dxc4! 29 ♕a1 ♘f5, we arrive at the earlier line with 28 ♕a1. As we have seen, Black wins. Here 28...hxg5?! 29 ♕a1 is less clear; Black allows White to move dangerously with the knight to g5.

c) The simple 28 ♗xh6!, which threatens ♕d4+, seems the best line, although White is still only struggling for a draw.

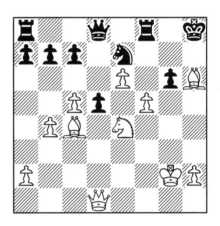

Radjabov gives 28...♘xf5 29 ♕a1+! (his own exclamation mark) 29...d4 30 ♗g5 ♕e8 31 ♚g1 (to avoid checks or pins on the long diagonal) 31...b5 32 ♗b3 ♕c6 33 ♕e1 ♚g7 with a big advantage for Black. With the help of the computer, though, and a little bit of nudging, it seems that 34 e7! is a draw, and more if Black makes even the slightest error:

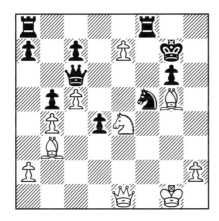

c1) 34...♘xe7?! 35 ♗xe7 ♖f3 36 ♕h4 ♖h8 37 ♕g4 ends up as good for White, not desirable for Black.

c2) 34...♖f7!? is a better try. Then 35 ♘g3! ♘xg3 36 ♕e5+ ♔h7 37 ♕xg3 ♕f3 38 ♗xf7 ♕xf7 39 ♕h4+ ♔g8 40 ♗f6 ♕h7 41 ♕xd4, and White is creating pressure after, for example, 41...♖e8 42 ♕d5+ ♕f7 43 ♕c6.

c3) 34...♖fe8! seems steadier. If 35 ♗f6+ ♕xf6! (35...♔h7? 36 ♘g5+ ♔h6 37 ♗e6, and the three minor pieces are toxic) 36 ♘xf6 ♖xe7! 37 ♘e4 ♖ae8 38 ♗d5 ♘e3 39 ♗c6 ♖xe4 40 ♗xe4 ♖xe4 41 h3 with a likely draw in a queen versus rook, knight and pawn endgame.

Can Black improve on this? Return to move 29, and 29...♔h7! 30 ♗g5 ♘e3+!? (30...dxe4!? 31 ♗xd8 ♖axd8 is given by Van Wely as promising) 31 ♔g1 ♕e8 32 ♗xe3 dxc4 33 ♘f6+ ♖xf6 34 ♕xf6 ♕h8 35 ♕h4+ ♔g8 36 ♕xc4 ♕f6 is analysed by Van Wely. Is Black better? Substantially so. Black's queen and rook will not allow any stability for White's passed pawn, and if the queens get exchanged, Black's king will cover the passed pawn, and the rook will attack White's queenside pawns.

d) Finally, if 28 fxg6, Black must play

28...♕e8!, taking over the g6-square. If 29 ♕d4+ ♔g8 30 g7 ♖f5 31 ♘f6+ ♖xf6 32 ♕xf6 ♕g6 33 ♕xg6 ♘xg6, and with Black's pawns still attacking two different bishops, he wins material. Black has not had the chance of taking either bishop for many moves, which is an indication of the extreme complexity of the game.

We now return to 28 ♕d4+:

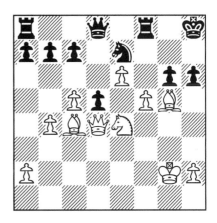

28...♔h7!

Snuggling to the cosiest square. 28...♔g8?? 29 ♗xe7 ♕xe7 30 f6! would even win for White, with the f7+ threat coming up, and if 30...♕xe6 31 ♗xd5, pinning.

29 fxg6+

There is not much coordination in White's remaining attack, although perhaps this is not too unexpected if White has already sacrificed two exchanges, and has three minor pieces under attack.

29 f6? dxe4 does nothing.

29 ♘f6+ ♖xf6 30 ♕xf6 hxg5! 31 ♕f7+ ♔h6 allows the king to slip through. This is difficult to visualize far in advance. Before Black's 27th, the h-pawn was on its starting square, blocking the king. Every time the pawn

moves, it sweeps open a square for the king.

29 ♗xe7 ♕xe7 30 fxg6+ ♚xe6 transposes to the game.

29...♚xg6

Obviously the only sensible move. Black's king is exposed, but that is only for the short term. Black is material up, and his pieces will soon become active.

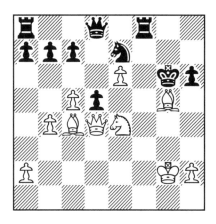

30 ♗xe7

Otherwise White drops another piece.

30...♕xe7 31 ♕xd5

Radjabov gives 31 ♗d3 ♕xe6 32 ♘g3+ ♚f7 33 ♗f5 ♕e8 34 ♕xd5+ ♚g7 35 ♕d4+ ♖f6 36 ♘e4 ♕e7 with a win for Black. Again, winning an exchange for White is not enough when he has already sacrificed two.

31...♖ad8

To win simply, he needs to use all his pieces.

32 ♕e5

32 ♕xb7 ♕h4 starts a mating attack.

32...♖f5

Again, using both rooks.

33 ♕c3

33 ♕g3 ♚h7 wins for Black.

33...♕g7

Setting up a discovered check on the g-file.

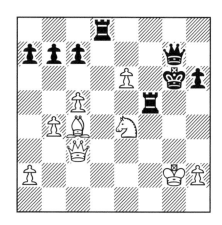

34 ♕g3+?!

A tame finish.

With 34 ♕c2! White could at least have set up a few confusing pins and discoveries to enliven the time scramble. Black cannot escape with the king (34...♚h7+?? 35 ♘g3; 34...♚h5+?? 35 ♘g3+), while if 34...♖d4? 35 e7! and White is turning the pieces around. Thus 34...♖f4! (or maybe 34...♖e5) looks best, allowing the discovered check:

a) If then 35 ♘d6+? ♚h5+, the return discovered check wins, with a quick mate.

b) 35 ♘g3+ ♚f6 36 ♕c3+ ♖dd4 keeps Black's material advantage, and he will escape the pin with ...♚e7.

34...♚h7

Queens gone, no more cheapos.

35 ♕xg7+ ♚xg7 36 ♘g3 ♖d4 0-1

And as a piece falls, it is no longer worth reaching move 40.

Game 20
Ni Hua-D.Jakovenko
Nizhniy Novgorod 2007
Sicilian Defence B85

This is the only game in this collection in which the author knowingly selected a game in which the player eventually later won, but was earlier losing. The impact of the game is outstanding, though. How on earth did Jakovenko win this game? Wasn't he about to get checkmated? The spirit of Emanuel Lasker, the great World Champion of a century ago, survives, even though these days attackers and defenders have immensely greater technique than a century ago, and arguably even a quarter century ago.

1 e4 c5 2 ♘f3 e6 3 d4 cxd4 4 ♘xd4 ♘c6 5 ♘c3 ♛c7 6 ♗e2 a6 7 0-0 ♘f6 8 ♔h1

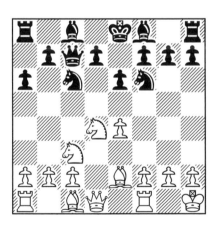

White pushes the king to a safer square, with thoughts of opening up the centre. He will want to keep the king safe.

Not, of course, 8 f4?? ♘xd4 9 ♛xd4 ♗c5, pinning the queen against king, but 8 ♗e3 is possible, and leads to Game 16, Shirov-Illescas.

8...♗e7 9 f4

Clearly aiming for a pawn push with e5, and maybe a later kingside attack.

9...d6

The natural reply, keeping the Scheveningen formation.

9...d5 is also worth considering if Black doesn't mind the isolated d-pawn after 10 exd5 exd5. If 11 ♗f3 0-0, White is only equal if he tries 12 ♘xd5 ♘xd5 13 ♗xd5 ♘xd4 14 ♛xd4 ♛xc2. Instead 10 e5 ♘xd4 11 ♛xd4 ♘d7 leads to something approximating to a French Defence.

10 ♗e3 0-0

Natural development on both sides.

11 ♛e1

The queen wants to attack. This is the most direct plan for White, with the idea of ♛g3 followed by e5.

11 a4 leads to the Scheveningen main line, restraining Black's counterplay on the queenside. Black develops behind the pawns with, for example, 11...♖e8, followed later by ...♗f6, and it is difficult for White to open up the centre with his pawns, while Black is waiting for a good opportunity for ...e5 himself. There is much manoeuvring, often ending up with sharp play. In some lines, Black develops with ...♗e7 and ...♗d7, before re-fianchettoing with ...♗d7-c8-b7 and ...♗e7-f8-g7.

Sometimes White will have played a4 before ♔h1, such as after, earlier, 8 ♗e3 ♗e7 9 f4 d6 10 a4 0-0 11 ♔h1. Ni Hua has been careful to find a slightly less common attacking idea, aiming for an innovation later.

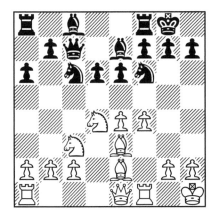

11...♘xd4

Here Black aims to push the b-pawn. The immediate 11...b5?! is premature in view of 12 ♘xc6 ♕xc6 13 e5 ♘d5 14 ♗f3, with pressure on the long diagonal. Black avoids this by exchanging the knights himself.

11...♗d7 is standard, here and in many slightly different positions. It is a developing move, bringing the rooks working together, usually a good start for the middlegame. Also, Black has the idea of playing ...b5, and recapturing with the bishop, rather than the queen, on c6.

11...e5 is possible, but reduces some of Black's flexibility. After 12 fxe5 dxe5 13 ♕g3!?, threatening ♗h6, White has a slight edge.

11...d5 12 e5! resembles a French Defence, except that Black has given a tempo with ...d7-d6-d5, instead of more directly ...d7-d5. White is probably happy.

Various other moves have also been tried.

12 ♗xd4 b5

12...e5? 13 fxe5 dxe5 14 ♕g3 puts Black under pressure in the centre. After 14...♗d6 15 ♖xf6 exd4 16 ♕xd6 ♕xd6 17 ♖xd6 dxc3 18 b3! White will be able to swallow up the advanced pawn on c3 in the fullness of time, and without giving away doubled isolated pawns.

13 a3

He wants to keep his knight on a good square.

13 e5 opens up the position a little too quickly, at least if aiming for an edge. After 13...dxe5 14 fxe5 ♘d7 15 ♘e4 ♗b7 there is:

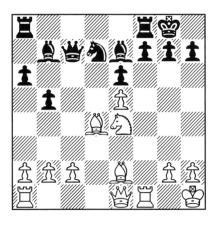

a) White can try a little tactic with 16 ♘f6+, and if 16...gxf6? 17 ♕g3+ ♔h8 18 exf6 ♕xg3 19 fxe7+ e5 20 exf8♕+ ♖xf8 21 hxg3 exd4, and after all the removal of pieces, White is the exchange ahead. However, Black can defend better with 16...♘xf6! 17 exf6 ♗xf6 18 ♗xf6 gxf6 19 ♖xf6 ♕xc2 20 ♕g3+ ♔h8 21 ♕e5 ♕e4 22 ♖xe6+ ♕xe5 23 ♖xe5, ending up as a draw, or maybe as a micro-advantage for Black after 23...♖ae8 24 ♖xe8 ♖xe8 25 ♗f1 ♔g7, and the king is slightly closer to the opponent's king in the endgame.

b) 16 ♗d3 is safer, with probable equality after 16...♖ad8. As one might suspect, there is a string of dangerous pins after 16...♘xe5?. Play continues with 17 ♕g3 f6 18 ♘xf6+ ♗xf6 19 ♖xf6 ♖xf6 20 ♗xe5 ♕f7 21 ♗xf6 ♕xf6 22 ♖f1 ♕e7 (22...♕xb2? 23 ♕c7), and after the tactics, a positional grind follows. White has the more active pieces, and the better pawns, not quite enough to win quickly, but enough to cause pressure. A top-level player would be happy to grind this down. This, however, stems from a mistake by Black. With more accurate play, with 16...♖ad8, followed, if required, by exchanging bishop for knight on e4, play is equal.

13...♗b7

The most accurate move.

The reader will recall that a move earlier, we considered 12...e5, instead of 12...b5 13 a3, and regarded it as unsound. What changes with the extra queenside pawn moves?

Let us try, in comparison with the earlier situation, 13...e5 14 fxe5 dxe5 15 ♕g3 ♗d6 16 ♖xf6 exd4 17 ♕xd6 ♕xd6 18 ♖xd6 dxc3. Black's queenside pawn structure here is more advanced than in the earlier line, and 19 b3?! ♗b7 is now comfortable for Black. White can try instead 19 bxc3 ♗b7 20 c4 ♗xe4 21 cxb5 axb5 22 ♗xb5 ♗xc2, but his outside passed pawn will not force a win after accurate play by Black. For example, 23 a4 ♖fb8 24 ♖d2 ♖xb5 25 ♖xc2 ♔f7 is a drawn rook and pawn endgame.

So is this only equal? Not quite. The tactics do not give an advantage this time, but positional play with 16 ♗e3!

gives White a reasonable chance of a good edge. Black's knight on f6 is under pressure, and his d5-square is weak. White could, of course, have tried this in the corresponding line after 12...e5?, but there would have been less point, as there White's tactical reply was more effective.

14 ♕g3

14 ♗d3 or 14 ♗f3 have been tried, but seem slightly less logical. The queen move is a constructive attacking move, and quiet defending of a pawn is not necessary as yet.

If 14 e5, Black's best attempt at complete equality seems 14...♘d7! 15 exd6 ♗xd6 16 ♕g3 f6, followed by ...e5. White's attack is slightly mistimed.

14...♖ad8

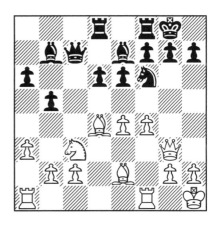

It soon becomes clear that Black is setting up a defensive fortress, rather than aiming for any immediate counterattack. This is, of course, quite common in the Scheveningen. He manoeuvres behind the pawns, taking care that his king will not be in immediate danger, and waits, and waits further. Black also looks for possibilities of counterplay, when given the chance, later on.

The next few moves are all theory.

15 ♖ae1

Obvious enough, although 15 ♖ad1 and 15 ♗d3 are also well worth considering. Black has probably not quite yet equalized in any of these lines, but the edge is slight, just a normal edge. Chess theory holds that White starts off with a small edge, with his extra move, but that this is not a decisive advantage if Black plays accurately.

15...♖d7

This has also been tried after White's previous-move alternatives. For example, 15 ♗d3 ♖d7 16 ♖ae1 would have transposed into the game. Black wants to use the rook on the d-file to defend if White opens up the position with e5. Black also wants to add protection to the knight with ...♕d8. Black is hoping not to have to give way with ...♘e8, with a continued slight edge for White.

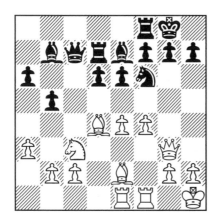

16 ♗d3

The bishops are lining up towards the black king's fortifications.

16...♖e8

A quiet and unobtrusive move, but what else can he play? Look through the position, and imagine Black's moves, piece by piece, and really it is only the rook move that makes sense. The only other constructive move is with the queen, but 16...♕a5?! moves too far away from the kingside defence after, for example, 17 ♕h3, while 16...♕d8?! is too passive.

This leaves the rook moves. 16...♖c8 looks at first slightly more aggressive, but try playing 17 e5 dxe5 18 ♗xe5 ♕d8 (or other queen moves), and there is a problem: 19 f5! is strong. If the rook were on e8, Black could cover this second pawn break.

17 e5

White decides it is time to break open the centre. The only other way of trying to attack on the kingside with quiet moves is 18 ♕h3, but then it is Black's turn to take over the e5-square with 18...e5:

a) If then 19 ♗e3, Black strongpoints the e5-square with 19...♗d8.

b) 18 fxe5?! dxe5 veers to favour Black.

c) The sacrificial line 19 ♘d5 ♗xd5 20 exd5 ♖xd5 21 ♖xf6 ♗xf6 22 ♕xh7+ ♔f8 is quite simply unsound.

17...dxe5

The only good move. 17...♘h5 18 ♕g4 g6 leaves White too much free space after 19 f5.

18 ♗xe5

And this is White's only move.

18 fxe5? drops the bishop after 18...♖xd4, leaving Black a clear pawn up after 19 exf6 ♕xg3 20 hxg3 ♗xf6.

18...♕d8

Black's kingside is under attack. He needs to provide extra cover to the f6-square.

19 ♘e4

Putting pressure on Black's knight.

19 f5 has been tried a few times, but 19...♗d6! equalizes.

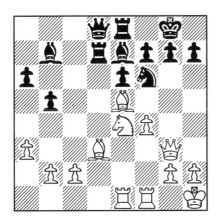

19...♘h5

The knight runs away. Clearly Black will want to protect the knight with ...g6.

19...♗xe4 30 ♖xe4 ♗f8 cuts down any mating attacks, but White keeps the bishop-pair, and reasonable chances of a durable edge.

19...g6!? is well worth considering. Then 20 ♘xf6+ ♗xf6 21 ♗xf6 ♕xf6, and now there is the danger of overpressing with 22 f5?!. Various quieter lines would equalize. The pawn push sets up a few pins and discovered checks, but 22...♕xb2! seems a good response:

a) If then 23 fxe6 fxe6 24 ♗xg6 ♖g7!, and it is not a good idea to win two rooks for queen with 25 ♗f7+?! ♔h8 26 ♗xe8 ♖xg3 27 hxg3 ♗d5. Black's bishop is far stronger than White's, and White's pawns are also weak. Here 25 ♖xe6! is far better, and if 25...♖xe6?? 26 ♕b8+ and a back-rank mate. Thus the position ends up as a draw by perpetual after either 25...♗c8 26 ♖b6 ♖xg6 27 ♖xg6+ hxg6 28 ♕xg6+ ♕g7 29 ♕e6+ ♔h8 30 ♕h3+ or 25...♖a8 26 ♗xh7+ ♔xh7 27 ♖e7! ♖xe7 28 ♕h4+ ♔g8 29 ♕xe7 ♕g7 30 ♕e6+ ♔h8 31 ♕h3+.

b) White has tried instead 23 f6?!,

which is dangerous, with an attempt to throttle on g7, but it is unconvincing. After 23...♕a3 24 ♕h4 ♖ed8! Black can counterattack on the d-file, and defend with ...♕f8. This should cover all attacks: for example, 25 ♖e3 ♖d4 or 25 ♖xe6 ♖xd3 26 cxd3 ♕a2 with a counter-threat on g2.

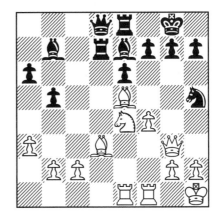

20 ♕e3!?

An innovation. White has tried both 20 ♕h3 g6, and 20 ♕g4 g6, but the apparently promising kingside attacks have proved not to materialize, and in the end White can keep equality, but not much more. We will limit ourselves to exploring the bold 20 ♕g4 g6 21 f5?! exf5 22 ♖xf5:

a) The computer then gives a 'refutation' with 22...♘g7 23 ♗xg7 gxf5, supposedly winning for Black. Look closer, though, and it is in White's favour after 24 ♕xf5 ♔xg7 25 ♘d6! ♗xg2+ 26 ♔g1 ♕b6+ 27 ♔xg2 ♖g8 28 ♕xf7+ ♔h8+ 29 ♔h3.

b) In F.Volkmann-J.Horvath, Budapest 1997, Black won quickly after 22...♖xd3! 23 ♖xh5 ♕d7 24 ♕e2? ♖d5 25 ♕f3 gxh5 26 ♕xh5 f6 27 ♘g5 fxg5, and White resigned. White could, though, have added to the sacrificial complexities with 24 ♖xh7!? ♔xh7 (24...♕xg4?? 25 ♖h8 mate) 25 ♕f4. White is a rook down, but is threatening mate, and attacking the rook, as well as having an extra pawn if the position gets simplified:

b1) 25...♗xe4? 26 ♕xf7+ ♔h6 27 cxd3 ♗f5 28 ♕g7+ ♔h5 29 ♕h7+ ♔g5 30 ♖e3!, threatening h4+ and mate, is a win for White, not surprisingly, given the exposed black king.

b2) 25...f6 26 ♗xf6 ♖d5 27 ♕h4+ ♖h5 28 ♗xe7 with enthralling play. Unfortunately, reality sets in with 28...♖xh4! 29 ♘f6+ ♔h6 30 ♘xd7 ♖g4, and White is in trouble.

Thus if White cannot make progress with his queen on the light squares, then maybe he can try to make progress on the dark squares on the other side of the board?

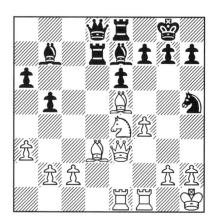

20...♘f6?

Quite often an improvement can have an exaggerated impact. Jakovenko is clearly suspicious of the new move, and offers a repetition with 21 ♕g3 ♘h5, but of course Ni Hua does not have to make yet another queen move. He can play for an edge.

Ftacnik suggests 20...g6, and if 21

♘c5 ♗xc5 22 ♕xc5 ♘f6 23 h3 ♘d5 24 b3 with equality, but White can try to improve with 21 ♖d1!?. If Black wants to exchange bishop for the highly-centralized knight, White should have the opportunity of making Black exchange the light-squared bishop rather than the dark-squared bishop. If 21...♗xe4?! 22 ♕xe4, Black's queenside pawns are weak. 21...♘f6 is another option for an exchange, but again after 22 ♘xf6+ ♗xf6 23 ♗e2!, White is slightly better. He will eventually want to exchange the light-squared bishops.

21 ♗xf6!

By deflecting Black's bishop, White can set up the exchange of Black's light-squared bishop with ♘c5.

21 ♘c5 ♗xc5 22 ♕xc5 ♘g4, as given by Ftacnik, is only equal.

21...♗xf6

21...gxf6 weakens the pawn structure, and so does not help. There are many good tries for White, the most direct being 22 ♖f3!?, pressing on the g- and h-files.

22 ♘c5!

So the bishop goes.

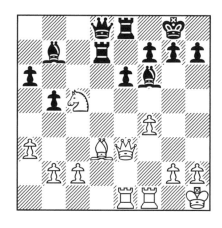

22...♗xg2+!?

Black is in 'another fine mess', borrowing from Laurel and Hardy, based on Ftacnik's comment. How is Black going to escape? There are few examples in this book of tactical escape from a losing or almost losing game, as we are concentrating mostly on classic winning chess, whether through excellent positional chess, or through deep tactical calculation. The art of defence, of changing a losing position into a winning position, is however a vital aspect of chess, even and especially at top level. A century ago, World Champion Emanuel Lasker was the pioneer of aggressive defensive play. Jakovenko continues the great tradition.

It looks as though Black's position is about to collapse very quickly after White's initial attack, but somehow it just about holds, and if there is not a quick win, then there is hope for a draw, maybe even hope for a win. The percentage chances are often more attractive in playing for a win, even in a clearly worse position.

Black's bishop sacrifice, based on the recovery of the piece with ...♗d4, forces White's king out into the open, which provides some hope for Black. His own king looks much weaker, and for a long time he will be faced by a discovered attack. If there is counterplay, though, there is life.

22...♖c7? 23 ♘xb7 ♖xb7 24 ♗xh7+! ♔f8 25 ♗e4 ♖b6 26 c3 (Ftacnik) leaves White a clear extra pawn and active pieces. The percentages are not good. How can Black possibly win this?

Black has another option, 22...♗xb2!? chopping material on the other long diagonal. Then 23 ♘xb7?! ♖xb7 24 ♕e4 ♖c7 25 ♕xh7+ ♔f8 leads only to equality; Black has done some

damage to White's queenside pawns. White can instead grab the exchange with 23 ♘xd7 ♕xd7 24 ♖b1 ♗d4 25 ♕h3 g6 26 c4 bxc4 27 ♗xc4. With bishop and pawn for the rook, there might be hope for a draw if Black's pieces and pawns were watertight. Unfortunately this is not the case, Black's isolated a-pawn is a problem, and also neither bishop is totally secure in the centre.

23 ♔xg2 ♗d4

Forking the queen and knight. White in return sets up play on h7.

24 ♗xh7+

An immediate punch.

24 ♕h3 ♗xc5 25 ♕xh7+ (25 ♗xh7+ ♔f8) 25...♔f8 26 f5 ♕g5+ 27 ♔h1 looks promising, but Black has some intricate bishop play with 27...♗e3 28 ♖f3 ♗f4 29 ♖e4

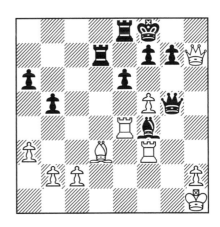

29...♗e5!!, an excellent tactical resource. White equalizes after, for example, 30 ♖fe3 f6 31 fxe6 ♖xe6, but why can't he take the bishop? After 30 ♖xe5, Black has 30...♖xd3!, with queen forks on the second row after either 31 cxd3? ♕c1+ 32 ♔g2 ♕xb2+ or 31 ♖xd3? ♕c1+ 32 ♔g2 ♕xc2+. In each case, a different rook drops. Finally, 31 ♕h8+ ♔e7

32 f6+ ♕xf6 33 ♕xe8+ ♔xe8 34 ♖xf6 ♖d1+ 35 ♔g2 gxf6 ends up with an extra pawn for Black in a rook ending, but it is not going to be easy to win.

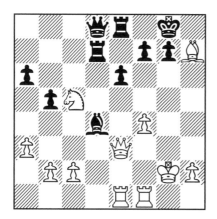

24...♔h8!

A bold decision. Black is now permanently in danger of being under threat of checkmate, and lethal discovered checks. If, though, White is not actually winning, then still there is hope.

Not every player would have tried Jakovenko's move, and many would have decided that it would have been better to take a realistic approach, and concede that Black has gone wrong, and that all Black can do is try to salvage the game with 24...♔xh7 25 ♕d3+ g6 26 ♘xd7 ♕xd7 27 c3 ♕b7+ 28 ♕f3 ♕xf3+ 29 ♖xf3. This would still have been fairly hopeless. White would eventually be able to set up a queenside passed pawn.

In terms of defensive play, sometimes one should not be too worried about leaving the king under severe pressure, so long as the opponent does not have an immediate forced win, especially if the alternative is to end up with a 100% loss.

25 ♕h3

And, one feels, this ought to get to the end.

25...♗xc5

Black recovers the knight, with level material. He doesn't even hold an extra pawn in compensation for the difficulties on his exposed h-file. The one small comfort is that White's king is also exposed, but it is difficult to see how Black can attack it. Black can, of course, slip in an occasional check, if given the opportunity, to gain a tempo, but that is about as much as he can do.

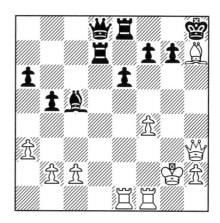

26 ♖e5

'The second truly critical position in a dramatic game', according to Ftacnik. There must be well over half a dozen moves, including four discovered checks from the bishop, that need to be considered, and each of these is likely to be promising, but not quite enough to clinch the issue. One could easily imagine that time trouble was going to be an issue.

There are two broad options to be considered – either to use a discovered check immediately, or to hold the check until later, improving the other pieces first. As we can see, Ni Hua took the second option.

What happens if he gives the check immediately? Thus we have:

a) There is no immediate checkmate, so 26 &g6+?! &g8 27 &h7+ &f8 28 &h8+ 29 &xg7 &d2+ 30 &g3 &f8 seems too crude. If White is not careful, Black can hit hard on the g-file. 31 &f5 (threatening &xg6+) 31...&d6 32 &d1 &c6 holds the balance, but White would have liked to have done more.

b) 26 &f5+ &g8 27 &h7+ &f8 28 &h8+ &e7 29 &xg7 &d6 similarly allows Black to escape.

c) The simple 26 &e4+! &g8 27 &h7+ &f8 28 &c6 is the best of the discovered checks, concentrating on winning the exchange, rather than hoping for checkmate.

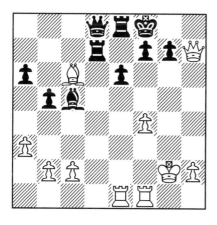

After 28...&d2+ 29 &h1 g6?, hoping for 30 &xe8?? &a8+, White has a winning attack with 30 f5!. If then 30...gxf5 31 &xf5 exf5 32 &h8 mate.

Black therefore tries 29...&e7 30 &xe8 &xe8 31 &h8+ (31 &e4 &xh2+! with a perpetual) 31...&f8 32 &h3. Then 32...&d5+ 33 &f3 &xf3+ 34 &xf3 &xc2 35 f5! still gives White winning chances, but 32...g6! helps consolidate Black's pawn structure, with good chances of holding the draw. So this is

close to a winning try for White, gaining the exchange, but Black's active pieces, and the weakness of White's kingside pawns, and the openness of his king, keep play close to a balance. Ni Hua would have wanted more.

d) Of the other bishop checks, 26 &d3+ &g8 27 &h7+ &f8 28 f5!? &g5+ 29 &h1 &e7, given by Ftacnik, gives White some chances for attack, but is not as good as grabbing the exchange. White can win a pawn after 30 fxe6 fxe6 31 &xe6+ &xe6 32 &e4+ &e5 33 &xe5+ &xe5 34 &e1+ &f4 35 &xe8, but it is unlikely that he would have good winning chances, Black having the more active pieces in a rook and bishops-of-opposite-colour endgame.

e) Of the non-bishop moves, Ni Hua chooses the most aggressive rook move. Also 26 &h1!?, sidestepping checks, is a sensible option, with a possible transposition to variation 'c' after 26...&d2 27 &e4+ &g8 28 &g7+ &f8 29 &c6.

By a process of elimination, Ni Hua's rook move, adding to the pressure on Black's king, would seem the best chance of a large advantage. It is now up to Jakovenko to show whether he can defend.

26...&d4!

Black needs to use the bishop on both diagonals, defending between d4 and h8, and counterattacking towards g1.

26...&d2+? fatally weakens the f7-square. White wins after 27 &h1 &d4 28 &h5 g6 29 &xg6+ &g8 22 &h8+ &xh8 33 &h7+ &f8 34 &xf7 mate.

27 &e4

After 27 &h5 g6 28 &xg6+ &g8, with the rook on d7, there is no immediate checkmate after 29 &h8+?? &xh8.

27 ♗g6+ ♔g8 28 ♕h7+ ♔f8 29 ♕h8+ ♔e7 30 ♕xg7 ♖f8 also runs out of steam after, for example, 31 c3 ♗xe5 32 fxe5 ♔e8.

There is, however, a third option to be considered, the quiet positional move, 27 ♖e2!?. White is arguing that he is not giving checkmate himself, but that he still undoubtedly has an edge, and the best way of handling this is to cut out any awkward counterplay, in particular checks on his second rank. White has several good consolidating ideas, such as c3, ♖d1 and/or a bishop discovered check. It would seem sensible for Black to take the initiative with 27...♗xb2. Play might continue with 28 ♗e4+ ♔g8 29 ♕h7+ ♔f8 30 ♗c6 g6 31 c4. Here there are some complicated options for Black, maybe ending up about equal. The simple line is 31...♖d2!? 32 ♖xd2 ♕xd2 33 ♖f2 ♕d1! 34 ♖xb2 (34 ♗xe8 ♕xg4+ is an immediate draw) 34...♕g4+ 35 ♔f1 (35 ♔h1 ♕d1+ 36 ♔g2 ♕g4+ repeats) 35...♕xf4+ 36 ♖f2 ♕xc4+ 37 ♔g1 ♕c1+ 38 ♖f1 ♕c5+ 36 ♖f2, draw. Except of course that this is 'simple' with the help of computer, but can easily seem very complicated over the board.

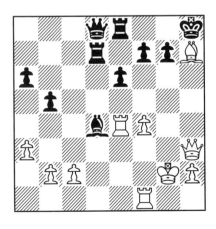

27...♗f6

The bishop has now reached a safe and active square, which is progress for Black.

Even so, Black could consider 27...♗xb2, not so much to grab the pawn, although it is useful, but more to use the queen on the d8-h4 diagonal, while still keeping the bishop on the long diagonal. Ftacnik gives a perpetual check after 28 f5 ♕g5+ 29 ♖g4 ♕h6 30 ♖h4 ♕d2+ 31 ♖f2 ♕g5+ 32 ♖g4 ♕h6, but this is not the whole story.

In this line, White has 29 ♔h1!, and there are no more checks. Black has to give up the queen for rook, bishop and pawn, with 29...♕h6 30 ♖h4 ♔xh7 31 ♖xh6+ gxh6 32 fxe6 fxe6. Material is level, but Black has weaknesses on the light squares, and White's queen, with the help of the rook, will cause considerable problems.

Advantage to White, then? We can go back a move earlier, with the easily overlooked 28...♗c1!?, a startling indication of the mobility of the bishop across the board, but naturally only on the dark squares. Then 29 ♖xc1? overpresses. After 29...♕g5+ 30 ♔f3 ♕xc1 31 ♗g6+ ♔g8 32 ♕h7+ ♔f8 33 ♕h8+ ♔e7 34 ♖xe6+ fxe6 35 ♕xe8+ ♔d6 36 ♕xe6+ ♔c7 Black's king escapes, and White has given up the exchange. It would seem wisest to play safely with 29 fxe6 ♖xe6 30 ♖xe6 fxe6 31 ♗d3+ (or another bishop square), and now the next stage of the bishop excursion continues with 31...♗h6. Black will experience some temporary discomfort after 32 ♕xe6 ♖d6 33 ♕e4 g6, but he should be able to hold.

Jakovenko decides instead not to take the pawn.

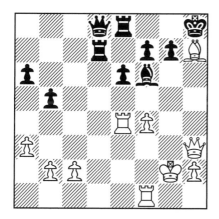

28 ♕h5?!

Ni Hua is still trying to force the win, cutting through the ....♗h4 valve, but with this move, he overbalances. All this can only be seen in retrospect, and Jakovenko in turn makes a mistake in reply.

28 ♖e2 leads to a broadly balanced position after 28...♗h4 29 ♗e4 ♔g8 30 ♗c6 ♖d2 31 ♖xd2 ♕xd2+ 32 ♔h1 ♖c8 33 ♗e4 ♖c4 34 ♕f3. The tactics on both sides finally settle down. Here Black may, of course, also try 28...♗xb2!?, transposing into the line 27 ♖e2!? ♗xb2, probably level.

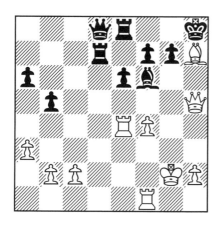

28...g6?

It turns out that Jakovenko did not

quite make a perfect defence after his opening slip up, but how many of us would have seen the hidden defence?

After 28...♖d2+ 29 ♔g3 ♕d5 30 ♕xf7? ♔xh7 31 ♕xe8 ♗h4+!! (31...♕xe4 32 ♕h5+ is a perpetual) 32 ♔xh2 ♖xh2+ 33 ♔g3 ♕d2 White is suddenly in serious danger of being checkmated.

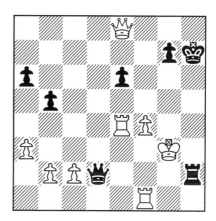

He is a rook up, but his pieces do not coordinate, and he cannot give any saving check. The only way of avoiding an immediate loss is 34 ♖e2 ♕xe2 35 ♕c6, returning the rook, but avoiding checkmate. Black keeps an extra pawn after in the endgame after 35...♕xc2. There may be more ambitious ideas.

White can avoid taking the poisoned bishop, but after 32 ♔f3 ♖xc2 33 ♕xe6 ♕d3+ 34 ♔g4 ♖g2+ 35 ♔xh4 ♕xf1 36 ♕xf5+ ♖g6, Black's win is straightforward, the only slightly difficult point is finding the quiet king move on 37 ♖e3 ♕f2+ 38 ♔h5 ♕xh2+ 39 ♖h3 ♕e2+ 40 ♔h4 ♔h6. If then 41 ♖g3 ♕h2+ 42 ♕h3 ♕f2, zugzwang. A startling resource, analysed by Ftacnik, but one cannot expect that Black should be winning. The run of play has been so much in favour of White that there must surely be drawing resources, or better, for him.

After 30 ♕h3, Ftacnik stops his analysis by suggesting that 30...♕d6 is slightly better for White. Here 30...♖xc2 is more ambitious:

a) If 31 ♖e3?, there is an echo of the bishop check with 31...♗h4+! 32 ♔xh4 (32 ♕xh4 ♕g2 mate) 32...♔xh7, and Black finally gets rid of White's infuriating bishop. Black is then winning.

b) 31 ♖e5! improves. After 31...♖g2+ 32 ♕xg2 ♖xg2+ 33 ♔xg2 ♗xe5 34 fxe5 ♔xh7 35 ♔xh7, and an annihilation of pieces, a level rook and pawn endgame arises.

Going further back, 28...♗xb2!? appears to be another drawing line. Then 29 f5 ♖d2+ 30 ♔h1 ♕f6 31 ♖h4 (but not 31 ♗g6+? ♔g8 32 ♖h4 ♔f8! and the king escapes), leaves Black threatened with a win by ♗g6+, and there are two attempts to hold the position:

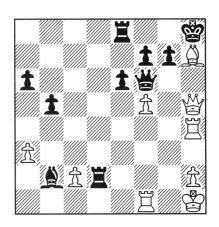

a) 31...♕h6 leads to various sacrifices, but White can eventually make a quiet little move, and Black ends up in trouble. Play continues 32 fxe6 ♖xe6 33 ♕xf7 ♔xh7 34 ♕f5+ ♔h8 35 ♖xh6+ (35 ♕xe6 ♕xh4 36 ♖f8+ ♔h7 37 ♕g8+ ♔g6 37 ♕f7+ is only a draw) 35...♖xh6 36 h3!, and it seems that Black's rooks do not coordinate, nor the bishop. How-

ever, by the time I had started up writing this line, the computer showed a draw after 36...♗xa3! 37 ♕c8+ ♔h7 38 ♕c3 ♗b4!, and now a perpetual after 39 ♕xb4 ♖xh3+. An attractive finish, and yet again the bishop is doing magnificent defensive work.

b) The other try is 31...g5 32 ♗g6+ ♔g8 33 ♗xf7+ ♔f8 (33...♕xf7? 34 ♕xg5+ followed by ♕xd2) 34 ♗xe8 gxh4 35 ♗c6 ♖d8 36 a4 bxa4 37 ♗xa4 with tension still in the position, but after 37...♗d4 it should end up level.

It is, of course, more than understandable why Jakovenko would want to create some fresh air for his king, but he has made a tactical oversight. However, uncomfortable the king might have been, close to suffocation on h8, there was not any direct mating threat, and if Black could set up active play with his other pieces, he still had good chances.

29 ♗xg6+

29 ♕h6? ♗g7 30 ♕h3 ♗xb2 is certainly no improvement for White.

29...♔g7

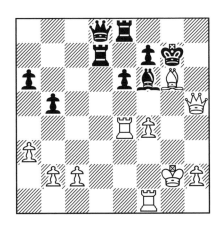

The king slips out.

30 ♕h7+

Effectively forced, but a move one

would want to play anyway.

30...♔f8 31 ♗h5

Likewise.

31...♖d2+

It is too late to take the b-pawn with 31...♗xb2. Ftacnik gives 32 f5 ♖d2+ (or 32...exf5 33 ♖xf5 ♖d2+ 34 ♔h3) 33 ♔h1 ♕f6 34 ♗xf7! ♕xf7 35 ♕h6+, winning the rook.

32 ♔h1

A safe square. Ni Hua should be winning,

32...♗g7

32...♕d7 33 ♖g1 doesn't help Black.

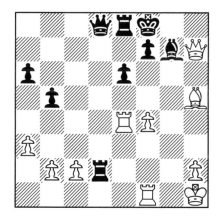

After the complexities of the early middlegame, the last few moves are easy enough to understand, and there have been few chances to deviate from the game. If Black's 28...g6 was wrong, it is now time to refute Black's play.

33 ♗xf7??

A careless transposition turns a well-deserved win into a loss. The move he actually plays allows Black to escape with the king from the back row, and set up counterplay with a later ...♖h8.

33 f5! is better, and wins. Play might continue 33...♕f6 34 ♗xf7! ♔xf7 (34...♕xf7 35 f6 ♗xf6 36 ♕h6+ ♔e7 37 ♕xd2 picks up the rook, keeping extra

material) 35 fxe6+ ♖xe6 36 ♖xf6+ ♖xf6 37 ♕h5+ with a win on material. Or, a move earlier, 33...♕g5 34 ♖g4! (more accurate than 34 ♖g1, given by Ftacnik; White wants to keep a rook on the f-file to support fxe6) 34...♕h6 (34...♕f6 35 ♗xf7! ♕xf7 36 ♖xg7 ♕xg7 37 fxe6+ is winning) 35 ♕xh6 ♗xh6 36 fxe6 with checkmate after 36...♖xe6 37 ♖xf7+ ♔e8 38 ♖g8+.

33...♔xf7

Of course, but now watch the ...♖h8 idea.

34 f5

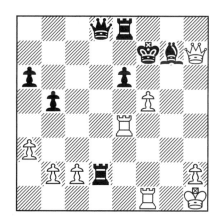

A win? It looks good.

34...♖xh2+!!

Pure serendipity, a marvellous lucky break. Naturally, if a player does not ride his luck, he will deservedly lose.

35 ♕xh2

White could also consider 35 ♔xh2!? ♖h8 36 fxe6+ ♔e8! (but not 36...♔e7? 37 ♖f7+ ♔d6 38 ♖d7+ ♕xd7 39 ♕xh8) 37 ♕xh8+ ♗xh8 38 e7 when the passed pawn on the seventh is a serious annoyance. Ftacnik then gives 38...♕d6+ 39 ♔g2 ♗f6 as winning for Black, but is this so? After 40 c3 ♕c6 41 ♖fe1 ♗xe7 42 ♔h3 Black it seems has no better than perpetual check. Thus Black has to play it more accurately with 38...♕d2+! 39 ♔g3 ♕g5+ 40 ♔h3 ♗e5, and the queen and bishop work together in attack against the king, rather than getting worried about surrounding White's pawn.

35...♖h8

Pinning the queen, but Black had to calculate White's counter-measures.

36 fxe6+

Black's king is exposed and under attack.

36...♔e7!

The only good move. 36...♔g8? 37 ♕xh8+ ♔xh8 38 e7 ♕e8 39 ♖f5 will probably end up level, while 36...♔e8?? 37 ♕xh8+ ♗xh8 38 e7 even wins for White.

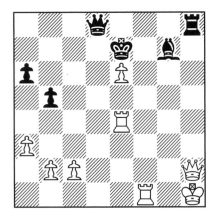

37 ♖f7+

Ni Hua had presumably planned 37 ♖h4, but it turns out that 37...♕d5+! 38 ♔g1 ♗d4+ wins.

If 39 ♖f2 ♗xf2+ 40 ♕xf2 (or 40 ♔xf2 ♕d2+ 41 ♔g3 ♕e3+ 42 ♔g2 ♖g8+ 43 ♔f1 ♖f8+ winning) 40...♕g5+, winning the rook. Or 39 ♖xd4 ♕xd4+ 40 ♕f2 ♖g8+ 41 ♔h1 ♕e4+ 42 ♕f3 ♕h7+ and mate next move.

A remarkable turnaround.

37...♔e8 38 ♕xh8+

38 ♖xg7 ♕d1+ wins, picking up the queen and then an exposed rook.

38...♗xh8 39 ♔g2

There is no hope in trying to hold with 39 ♖f8+ ♔xf8 40 e7+ ♕xe7 41 ♖xe7 ♔xe7 42 b3 ♔d6. If White's king were closer, and Black's king were further away, it might still have been interesting. But they weren't.

39...♕d5

39...♗xb2 40 e7 ♕d2+ 41 ♖f2 ♕g5+ should also win, but it is simpler to stop White playing e7 in advance.

40 ♖ff4

Or 40 ♔f3 ♗xb2.

40...♗xb2

Thank you.

41 c4

If 41 e7, then 41...♗f6 is simplest.

41...bxc4 0-1

It is Black's pawn that queens.

Game 21
E.Alekseev-V.Tkachiev
Spanish Team Championship 2007
Queen's Indian Defence E15

1 d4 ♘f6 2 c4 e6 3 ♘f3 b6 4 g3 ♗a6 5 ♕c2

For 5 b3, see Game 4, Topalov-Anand.

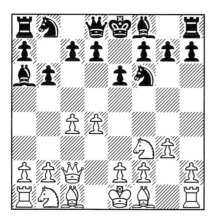

A natural developing move, one might think, covering the c4-square without losing a tempo. Unfortunately, White has released the pressure on the d-file, and according to earlier theory, Black should be able to equalize quickly.

5...♗b7!?

Black even loses a tempo, being unimpressed with White's queen move.

5...c5 has also been tried, but with the likelihood of a transposition after 6 d5 cxd5 7 cxd5 ♗b7 8 ♗g2. With this particular move order 8 e4 has also been tried. Then 8...♕e7 9 ♗d3 ♘xd5 10 a3 ♘c6 11 0-0 ♘c7 12 ♘c3 ♘e6 23 ♗e3 ♕d8 14 ♖ad1 ♗e7 15 ♗c4 with compensation for the pawn, and later a draw, in S.Mamedyarov-B.Gelfand, Wijk

aan Zee 2006. All this is 'unclear', and is attractive for both players, a chance of trying to outplay the opponent, rather than relying on the ever-expanding tentacles of opening theory.

6 ♗g2

White has also tried 6 ♘c3, the most logical reply being 6...c5, with instant pressure on the d-pawn. White then releases the tension with 7 dxc5 ♗xc5. At first sight, there has been a conspicuous loss of a tempo by Black (...♗c8-a6-b7), but look more closely, and White has also lost a tempo with dxc5 ♗xc5 before Black has developed with ....♗e7. The two gains and losses cancel each other out, with perhaps the usual very slight edge for White, or maybe equal.

6...c5

This is what Black is normally aiming for, but even quieter moves such as 6...♗b4+ or 6...♗e4 are not to be rejected out of hand.

7 d5!?

This suddenly became highly fashionable, and led to a renewal of interest in the 5 ♕c2 variation. Mamedyarov kicked this off as White against Gelfand at the start of 2006 (see the note to Black's 5th, above), then Gelfand tried it a few months later as White against Aronian, and then Aronian tried it several times. There were well over thirty games between 2600+ opponents in the next two years. It has become fashionable! It will be interesting to see whether players are going to be equally interested in this line by 2010 and beyond, or whether after later experimenting this gambit will prove to be less interesting for White.

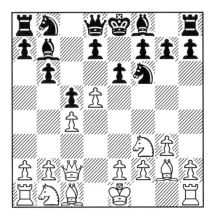

7...exd5

Black might as well take it. There are a few alternatives next move, including either accepting the gambit or declining it.

8 cxd5

8 ♘h4? is pointless: 8...♘c6 9 cxd5 ♘d4 is good for Black.

8...♘xd5

Black is not forced to take the pawn:

a) He could try developing with 8...♘a6!? 9 ♘c3 (9 e4? ♘b4 10 ♕e2 ♗a6, winning material, and making good use of the a6-square) 9...♘b4 10 ♕d2 ♘bxd5 11 ♘e5 ♘xc3 12 ♗xb7 ♖b8 13 ♘c6 ♕c7 14 ♕e3+ ♘ce4 15 ♘xb8 ♕xb7 16 f3 ♕xb7 17 fxe4 ♕b7 18 0-0 ♘xe4, and Black may even have a slight edge, with knight and two solid extra pawns against rook. Here the tactic on c6 is attractive, but probably not the best nor the most thematic. Instead 13 ♗g2!? ♘ce4 14 ♕c2 ♘d6 gives White

an active bishop-pair, and better development in return for the pawn.

b) Another try is 8...♗xd5 9 ♘c3 ♗c6 (9...♗xf3!? 10 ♗xf3 ♘c6 11 ♕a4!? ♖c8 12 ♗f4 ♗e7 13 0-0-0 keeps an initiative, and White later won in L.Nisipeanu-V.Baklan, Romanian Team Championship 2006) 10 e4!?. We are in the realms of gambit play, rather than a clear positional sacrifice. B.Gelfand-L.Aronian, Dortmund 2006, continued 10...♗e7 11 ♗f4 0-0 12 0-0-0 ♗e7 13 ♕e2 (Gelfand suggests 13 a3!?) 13...♘b4 14 a3 ♕c8 15 ♔b1 a5 16 ♘e5, and White was able to roll through on the kingside, later winning. Here Gelfand suggests that 16...b5! would have been an improvement on 16...♖e8?.

9 0-0

9 ♘g5?! ♘e3! 10 ♗xe3 ♗xg2 11 ♖e1 ♗c6 leaves Black comfortable.

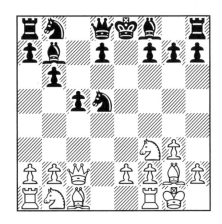

9...♗e7

The position is, of course, complicated, and there are several possible moves for Black to consider, such as 9...♘c6, 9...♘c7 and 9...♘b4. It is quite possible that at least one of these might well be promising. We are at an early stage in this new variation, and it is noteworthy that Black has almost universally chosen the bishop development here, blocking any check on the e-file.

The prevailing assumption would seem to be that Black is a pawn up, that his natural development, aiming for quick castling, cannot possibly be wrong, and that it is up to White to try to prove that his gambit is good or sound.

10 ♖d1

Another piece into play, and adding pressure on the long diagonal. This is overwhelmingly the main line at top level. White has done extraordinarily well in practical terms. It is very difficult for Black to score a win at the higher levels, and White has achieved a substantial plus score.

Probably the ratio will change, as Black finds new resources.

10...♕c8

This is the main line for Black, protecting against any tactics on the bishop. Others:

a) 10...0-0? 11 ♕e4 f5 12 ♕c4 b5 13 ♕b3 c4 14 ♕xb5 is good for White.

b) 10...♘c6 is a natural developing move:

b1) After 11 ♖xd5?? ♘b4 Black wins material.

b2) 11 ♕f5 has been tried a few times, with reasonably good results.

b3) 11 ♕a4!? ♘f6 12 ♘c3 0-0 13 g4! was played in A.Shirov-L.Aronian, 2nd matchgame, Elista 2007. One of Shirov's great trademarks is setting up pawn storms in even the most unexpected of situations, and this is an excellent example. After Black's 10th it would take imagination to find a way of provoking the knight to f6, to allow a pawn push to g5. Play continued 13...♘b4 14 a3

♘bd5 15 ♘xd5 ♗xd5 16 g5 ♗c6 17 ♕h4 ♘e8 18 ♘e5, with a strong attack, although Aronian was later able to squeeze a draw.

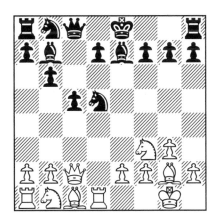

11 ♗g5

There has been no broad consensus to date as to which line might be best for White, several alternatives having been tried. No attempt is made here as to which line is best, not least because some player might well have found a critical innovation in the last couple of weeks:

a) Statistically, the most promising line might seem to be 11 ♕f5, with two wins and two draws between 2600+ opponents from 2007 to April 2008. This sounds good, until one plays through the games, and appreciates that one of the wins by White was in a rapidplay in which Black was a pawn up in the endgame, and would probably have won comfortably in a standard-play game. 11...♘f6 12 ♘c3 ♘c6 13 ♗g5 d5 should, despite the statistics, be comfortable for Black.

b) 11 ♘h4!? ♗xh4 12 ♖xd5 is a 2007 idea. Then 12...♗e7 13 ♘c3 ♘c6 14 ♕e4 0-0 15 ♖h5 g6 16 ♖h3!? looks strange. What is the rook doing on h3? The point is that Black's structure is even more uncomfortable, and it is only due to the white rook adding pressure on the h-file that Black is in danger:

b1) After 16...f5 17 ♕e3 (Krasenkow gives 17 ♕c4+! ♔f8 18 ♘d5 with advantage to White) 17...♖f7 18 ♗d5 both players were evidently feeling uncomfortable with this position, and maybe were also worried about potential time pressure. They agreed a draw in L.Nisipeanu-V.Baklan, German League 2007.

b2) Almasi tried something new with 16...♗f6 17 ♘d5 ♕d8 18 ♗h6 ♗xb2 19 ♖d1 ♖e8 20 ♕g4, and White was starting to break open Black's kingside pawn structure after 20...♖e6 21 ♗g5 h5 22 ♕h4 f6 23 ♗e3 in A.Beliavsky-Z.Almasi, European Team Championship, Crete 2007. Beliavsky won after a sacrificial breakthrough on the kingside. Play is complicated, and Ftacnik has suggested possible alternatives from moves 20 to 25.

In all this, there is an obvious question that has not been asked – why cannot Black grab the exchange? A possible answer is that after 13...♗xd5 14 ♘xd5 ♘c6 15 ♕e4 ♕d8 16 ♗g5 f6 17 ♗h4 ♖c8 18 ♗h3 White has considerable attacking chances in return for the sacrifice.

It is unusual these days for top players to be on unexplored ground so early in the game, and it will take some time for theory to clarify.

11...f6

There are various alternatives here. Indeed, L.Aronian-M.Carlsen, Wijk aan Zee 2007, led to quick equality, and soon a draw, after 11...h6 12 ♗xe7 ♘xe7 13 e4 0-0 14 ♘c3 ♘bc6 15 ♖d2 ♗a6 16 ♗h3 ♘g6 17 ♗xd7 ♕b7 18 ♗h3 ♖ad8 19 ♖ad1 ♕b8 20 ♗g2. Black abandons the backward d-pawn, which allows him to equalize quickly.

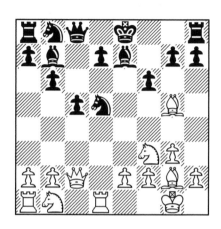

12 ♗c1?!

An unusual, and indeed extravagant, idea. The bishop returns to base immediately, sacrificing a couple of tempi, as well as the pawn, and without any hope of a quick attack on the king. However, pawns cannot move backwards, or indeed sideways, and once the pawn has advanced from f7 to f6, Black cannot cover the a2-g8 diagonal, and he cannot, more specifically, give protection to the e6- or g6-squares. Black will very much want to play ...d5, to cover the central squares, but his light squares will then be seriously compromised.

A few months later, Aronian played the more natural 12 ♗d2 ♘c6 13 ♕a4 ♘c7 14 ♘c3 0-0 15 ♗f4 ♘e6 16 ♗d6 ♖e8 17 ♗xe7 ♘xe7 18 ♕xd7, ending up as a draw in L.Aronian-P.Leko, Wijk aan Zee 2008. Clearly he had looked at Alekseev's game, and was not totally impressed, at least as far as the return to the starting square is concerned. Aronian, Leko and others will presumably have digested Alekseev's strange retreat, and will have found ways to improve Black's play. Tkachiev, in contrast, will have been on his own resources, a difficult situation when it is not clear whether Black is better, equal or worse, and whether he should try to hold on to the extra pawn or to simplify.

12...♘b4

A natural enough move. There are of course alternatives, such as 12...♘c7, 12...♘a6, or even 12...♘c6. The advantage of Tkachiev's choice is quite simple – he hits the queen.

13 ♕b3

The best square, although even that is not so promising. At the moment, it might look as though White has no compensation for the gambit pawn, but maybe this is deceptive?

13...d5

One can imagine that Tkachiev was by now feeling quite confident, and was ready to roll the pawns in the centre, or at least keep the pawns on stable squares on c5 and d5. The problem is that if either of these pawns continues to advance, he will have created weaknesses. Here, for example, White has an excellent outpost on d4 if Black tries ...c4. Further, if the bishop gets stuck on b7, behind the pawn on d5, it is difficult for Black to activate his pieces.

Black could also try 13...♗e4, but the exchange of light-squared bishops with 14 ♘e1 (14 ♘a3 d5 leaves Black in control) 14...♗xg2 15 ♘xg2 accentuates Black's weaknesses on the light squares. If, for example, 15...d5 16 a3 ♕a6 17 ♘f4 with advantage to White.

14 a3

Kicking the knight out of the way.

If 14 ♘c3? c4 16 ♕a3 ♗c6 (but not

16...♘c2?? 17 ♕a4+), and Black wins material.

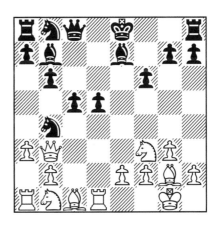

14...c4

A natural move, keeping the extra pawn and holding on to everything. The trouble is that, as Alekseev demonstrates, White can take control of the dark squares. When pawns advance, you gain squares, but you also lose squares, and here the loss is more significant than the gain.

If Black wants to try to refute Alekseev's play, he has to try 14...♘4c6!, which is a good opportunity to return the pawn in exchange for piece activity. For example, 15 ♕xd5 ♘d4 16 ♕h5+ g6 17 ♕h6 ♘xe2+ 18 ♔h1 ♘xc1 19 ♕g7 ♖f8 20 ♖xc1 ♕g4 21 ♖e1 ♘c6 22 ♘c3 (better than 22 ♕xh7 23 ♘xe5 ♗xg2+ 24 ♔xg2 fxe5, and now 25 ♖xe5? ♕f3+ 26 ♔h3 0-0-0! with the winning threat of ...♖h8) 22...♘e5 23 ♖e3 ♖d8 24 ♖ae1. This probably holds the balance, since neither knight wants to initiate the exchange.

This is merely one of several different lines. In practical terms, it would be very difficult to analyse this in depth for Black, knowing that Alekseev would already have considered the variation at home.

15 ♕c3

A slight loss of tempo in that 15 ♕e3?? ♘c2 loses a rook, but White is still happy that he has gained the d4-square.

15...♘4a6

15...a5?! 16 ♗e3! does not help.

16 ♕e3

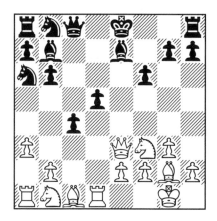

Finally, to the square he wants. It is going to be difficult for Black to castle, either kingside or queenside, and this enables White to develop his blockade.

16...♘c7

Black is curling up in a little corner, with the hope of keeping the extra pawn, and gradually uncurling again.

It is often difficult to decide as an attacker whether a pawn sacrifice is likely to be good or not, and it can be equally difficult to decide whether a player with the extra pawn should keep it, or whether he should jettison the pawn to gain extra play.

After 16...♘c6 17 ♘c3 0-0! Black has very quickly recovered from the problems of his king, and following 18 ♘xd5 ♗c5! even the bishop is on an active square. 19 ♕c3 ♘a5! then covers the c-pawn. Black's knights on the edge might look slightly unusual, but they

cover important squares: the a5-knight defends the pawn on c4, and threatens an exchange on b3; and the a6-knight can offer White's active knight on d5 an exchange via c7. Play is probably about equal, but maybe Tkachiev was hoping for more.

Here a less effective attempt at returning the pawn would have been 17...d4?! 18 ♘xd4 ♘xd4 19 ♗xb7 ♕xb7 20 ♕xd4. The position is simplified, but with White keeping a slight edge.

17 ♘c3

Finally he resumes his queenside development. White's pieces still look uncomfortable, but Black has left some gaps on the dark squares, and White fills in.

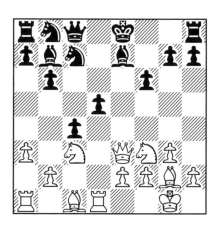

17...♘ba6

Black cannot castle, as his bishop would drop. The only other development idea is to bring the knight into play.

17...♘d7 does not allow any immediate refutation, but it would be understandable if Black felt uncomfortable after, for example, 18 ♗h3 ♕d8 19 ♘d4.

17...♘c6 is an attempt to return the pawn for equality. After 18 ♘xd5 ♘xd5

19 ♖xd5, there is some entertaining knight manoeuvring with 19...♘b4 20 ♖d2 ♘d5 21 ♕e4 ♘c3 22 ♕c2 ♘e4, but the faster-moving pieces sooner or later run away. 23 ♖d4 is good for White.

Tkachiev's move is logical enough, but there is still some unwrapping of the minor pieces to follow.

18 ♘d4

He could try to tempt Black's kingside pawns forward with 18 ♘h4!? g5 (before White can consolidate on f5 with ♕f3) 19 ♘f3 h5!?. It is difficult to decide whether White gains or loses from this interpolation. Black's advanced kingside pawns create a few weaknesses, but one possibility is that after ♕f3, Black can offer a queen exchange with ...♕g4.

18...♕d7

Black keeps open the possibility of castling on either side.

If 18...♘c5, then 19 ♕f3, and Black would soon want to play ...♕d7 anyway.

19 ♕f3

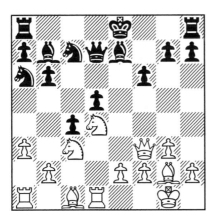

Almost the first indication of what White is trying to do aggressively. Alekseev has shuffled his pieces around, and has provoked a few vaguely weakening pawn moves, but White needs to

do more than this if he has sacrificed a pawn.

Black is now forced to overprotect his d-pawn, since if that pawn drops, then unless there is good positional compensation, his centre will collapse. Naturally White will want to attack this pawn, maybe with pure piece pressure, or maybe with an e4-pawn push. White will be looking for good ways to move the knight from d4, already a good and safe square, to an even more aggressive square. The dark-squared bishop will be able to re-manoeuvre itself to f4, putting pressure on the knight on c7, and in consequence on the other knight on a6.

The one genuine positive thought for Black, apart from his extra pawn, is that if he can hold his defence well, it could well be difficult for White to break through the pawn barriers, and the weakened squares behind them.

19...g6

Black clearly feels uncomfortable about the f5-square.

If 19...0-0 20 ♘f5 ♗c5 21 ♘xd5 ♘xd5 22 e4, Black has not yet equalized: for example, 22...♖ad8 23 exd5 ♘c7 24 ♕g4 g6 25 ♘h6+ ♔g7 26 ♕xc4 ♗xd5 27 ♗xd5 ♘xd5 28 ♘g4 ♖f7 29 ♗h6+ ♔g8 30 ♖ac1. Black has weaknesses on the kingside.

20 ♗f4?!

Before attacking, he needs to develop, but where should the bishop go?

The bishop on f4 is aggressive and active, but Black has several chances of a hit there, with ...g5 being a chance of seizing the initiative for Black, and ...♘e6 being a good and natural move as well.

20 ♗h6! looks more accurate, pre-

venting kingside castling, and keeping the bishop safe. If 20...♘c5, then maybe 21 h4, followed by g4, keeping chances of an initiative.

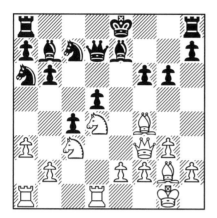

20...0-0

Black has completed development, and is also a pawn up. All this is good news, but Black's three minor pieces on the queenside are only half-developed. Tkachiev's longer-term challenge will to bring these pieces into play.

21 ♘c2

Maybe 21 g4!? immediately. If then 21...♗c5, White could return to the main line with 22 ♘c2. Naturally there are alternatives on either side.

21...♗c5

21...♘c5?! 22 ♗xc7 ♕xc7 23 ♘xd5 favours White.

22 g4

A dual-purpose pawn move. White wants to vacate the g3-square in case he wants to use that square, either for the bishop (after ...g5), or the queen. He also wants to make a pawn prod against the f6-pawn, creating further weaknesses on the dark squares.

Tactically, 22 ♘xd5? ♘xd5 23 e4 would not have been good in view of 23...♕a4.

22...♕f7

Avoiding any pins on the d-file.

23 ♕g3

For the next few moves, both players will need to consider ...g5 by Black. Here 23 h4 g5 25 ♗g3 gxh4 26 ♗xh4 is promising for Black, so White regroups his pieces.

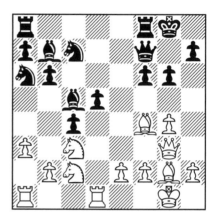

23...♖ad8

We have the classic question of timing during gambit play. Should the defender grimly hold on to the extra pawn? Or should he return the pawn, in return for safety and/or compensation?

Here 23...g5 24 ♗e3 f5 is a chance to escape, but this is probably not the best timing. After 25 gxf5 ♕xf5 26 ♗xc5 ♘xc5 27 ♘e3 ♕f4 28 ♘cxd5 ♘xd5 29 ♗xd5+ ♗xd5 30 ♖xd5 White is clearly better to some extent. Play might continue 30...h6 31 ♖c1 ♘e4 32 ♕xf4 ♖xf4 33 ♖xc4 ♘xf2 34 ♖c7 with White having the more active pieces.

Quite often a useful general approach in gambit play is to return the pawn only if the defender is satisfied that he will have at least clear equality or an edge. If the defender is worried that he will end up in a worse position after returning the pawn, then the likelihood is that the counter-gambit is mistimed.

Tkachiev holds on to the extra pawn, just for now, and this seems correct. The rook is moving to a good square, so this seems fine. The problems of timing will re-emerge later.

24 h4

To gain space for the pawns.

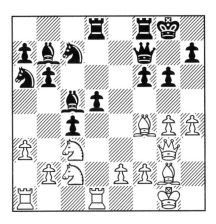

24...♖d7?!

24...g5! seems rather better timing, a move later, not least because there is no return sacrifice:

a) If 25 hxg5?! hxg5 26 ♗xg5?? ♗xf2, winning the queen.

b) 25 ♗e3 ♗d6 26 ♕h3 ♗e5 seems promising for Black, and if 27 ♘d4 ♗xd4 28 ♗xd4 ♘e6.

Alekseev's idea has been extremely original and entertaining, but in the end he has overplayed his hand.

As far as the defender is concerned, his ...♖ad8 idea, rather than ...g5, was good, the rook moving to an active square. The plan of ...♖d7 and ...♖fd8 seems less promising, though, placing pieces on purely passive squares, while ignoring counterplay, and ignoring the possibility of giving up the extra pawn in return for taking over the initiative.

25 ♖d2

Both players are concentrating on attack and defence on the d-file.

25...♖fd8

But again, 25...g5!? seems well worth considering.

26 ♖ad1

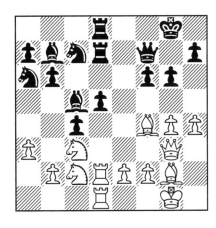

26...♗a8?!

If one were playing through the position quickly, and trying to decide where Black was starting to go wrong, this bishop retreat is an obvious candidate. Is the move really relevant? One would not necessarily expect that Black will go from a good position to a bad position in one move, but it does increase Black's difficulties. However, White will have to play with great vigour to prove that Black faces any problems whatsoever.

This was a good time for Black to give back his extra pawn, and relinquishing the obligation of trying to defend the extra pawn. 26...♘e6! is good for Black, who is able to exchange his quiet knight for an active and aggressive bishop:

a) If now 27 ♘xd5? ♘xf4! and Black wins material: 28 ♘xf4? ♖xd2.

b) 27 ♗xd5?! does not work either:

27...♗xd5 28 ♖xd5 ♘xf4 29 ♖xd7 ♘xe2+ keeps an extra pawn, while gaining active play.

c) White can play quietly, and indeed may well have to, with, for example, 27 e3 or 27 ♗e3, but then the second knight enters active play with ...♘ac7.

This is undoubtedly an improvement for Black.

27 e3

It is important to consolidate d4.

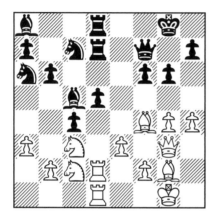

27...b5?!

The psychology is all wrong. In these notes, the author has questioned many of Black's moves, but individually perhaps none are particularly bad. The real question is not identifying any serious blunder, but rather suggesting possible thought processes for the player who started off with an edge, but ended up losing a brilliancy.

The obvious implication is that Tkachiev was coasting. He was a pawn up, with some slight pressure from his opponent, and he was relying on his extra pawn for victory. In particular, it would seem that his main strategy, in terms of chess psychology, was avoiding any complications, avoiding any tactics. The astute opponent will naturally take ad-

vantage of this, and any 2700+ player will have excellent understanding of any weaknesses of his opponent.

27...♘e6 is still possible, although this time he loses the extra pawn. After 28 ♗xd5 ♗xd5 29 ♖xd5 ♖xd5 30 ♖xd5 ♖xd5 31 ♘xd5 ♘xf4 32 ♘xf4 ♘c7 Black keeps a slight edge, his bishop being more active than the opposing knight, and Black having a potentially dangerous extra queenside pawn.

28 g5!

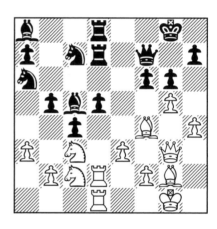

Alekseev obtains a second wind. Suddenly he finds weaknesses to attack. In particular, Black's pawn on f6 will either advance or be exchanged, and this will create weaknesses on the dark squares leading to his king. White now has genuine attacking chances.

28...f5

He prefers to keep his three kingside pawns.

29 ♗e5

White now has genuine compensation for the pawn. At times it has to be admitted that the gambit has looked somewhat speculative, but now White has good control on the dark squares, and is able to consider attacking pawns on the light squares.

29...♗d6

Black decides that it is time to exchange the dominating bishop.

If 29...♖e8, White could consider playing for a kingside push with 30 ♗f3 and later h5.

30 ♗xd6

Or maybe 30 ♘d4, and if 30...♗xe5 31 ♕xe5.

One possible reason for exchanging on d6 immediately is that the queen stays on g3, well covered and unlikely to have to face threats of queen exchanges.

30...♖xd6 31 ♘d4

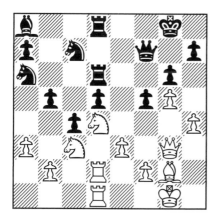

We are reaching the climax of the positional control on the dark squares, but control on half the squares is not necessarily enough to win. Over the next few moves, Alekseev opens up the light squares as well, with the help of the occasional sacrifice.

32...♕e8

Covering the b5-pawn.

32 b4!

He is still finding ways of taking extra control of the dark squares. If Black does not exchange en passant, then it will be very difficult to coordinate his pieces. He will not be able to move a

knight to c5, and it would take considerable time to juggle his queenside pieces to reasonable squares, without dropping the b- or d-pawns. Indeed, how will the bishop find any activity whatsoever?

32...cxb3

Therefore, probably with reluctance, he exchanges his passed pawn.

33 ♘xb3

Now, with four attacking pieces on the isolated pawn on d5, and four defensive pieces, there is obvious tension in the centre. Remember though that Black is a pawn up, and so there is a possibility of relinquishing the isolated pawn in return for the stability of his pieces.

33...b4?!

The simplest defensive plan would be 33...♖b6 34 ♘xd5 ♘xd5 36 ♗xd5+ ♗xd5 36 ♖xd5 ♖xd5 37 ♖xd5 b4 38 axb4 ♘xb4 with probably level play. Visually, it looks as though Black's kingside is weak, but this should not be overstated. As soon as White's queen enters active play, his own king will itself become exposed.

Tkachiev has an understandable desire to hold on to his extra pawn, but Alekseev continues to develop his initiative.

34 axb4 ♘xb4

A fifth piece defending the pawn, but this does not deter White.

35 e4!?

Quite startling, and Tkachiev seems to go off-balance immediately.

White's position was already at least equal, even though he was a pawn down, but it would be difficult to try to force a significant edge through quiet play if he tried, for example, 35 ♘e2 and placing the knights on f4 and/or d4. Somehow, White needs to create just a little extra weakness in Black's pawn structure, and here Alekseev manages this immediately.

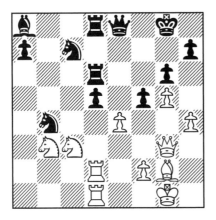

35...f4?

Tkachiev's response is to sacrifice the extra pawn, but this does not help. White will now have level pawns and an aggressive piece formation.

Black cannot take the bold pawn: 35...dxe4?? moves immediately into a pin with 36 ♖xd6, while 35...fxe4 36 ♘xe4 ♖e6 37 ♘f6+ ♖xf6 38 exf6 is not immediately decisive, but is unappealing for Black.

It is better for Black to stand the strain with 35...♕f7! when ...f4 is now a genuine threat. White continues his plan with 36 exf5 when 36...♕xf5?! allows a substantial edge after 37 ♘e4!. Therefore 36...gxf5 is correct, even if Alekseev has achieved his immediate objective of breaking up Black's pawn structure. White seems to have no quick winning plan, but he has plenty of grinding opportunities. It is impossible to analyse this in depth, there being too many possibilities for each position. A line aiming for simplification might

be 37 ♘e2 ♘e6 38 ♘f4 ♘xf4 39 ♕xf4 ♘c6 40 ♘d4 ♘xd4 41 ♖xd4 with a slight edge for White. Black is a pawn up, but he has four isolated pawns, and if one of these pawns were to drop, his remaining pawns will still remain weak. Black has to play carefully.

36 ♕xf4

Thank you.

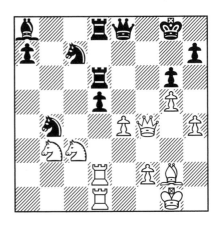

36...♘e6

The first chance for a while to make a threat, but White's pieces are far better coordinated.

37 ♕g4!

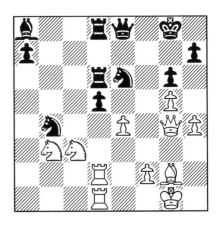

A good move.

There is plenty of chess geometry here. In effect, we have a mirror image of the letter 4, with the tension on the d-file, and White's queen pressing both of Black's knights, on the fourth rank to b4, and the diagonal to e6.

Also, of course, there is tension on the h1-a8 long diagonal: White is threatening exd5, while Black is unable to play 37...dxe4? because of the rook pin.

37...d4

Forced, unless he meekly wants to give up a pawn on d5.

38 e5

Some more chess geometry.

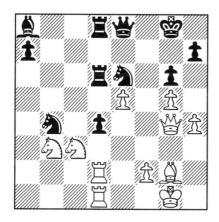

38...♖b6

38...dxc3 is hopeless. White wins after 39 ♖xd6 c2 40 ♕xe6+ (best, and also the most attractive) 40...♕xe6 41 ♖xd8+ ♔f7 42 ♖1d7+.

38...♗xg2 39 ♔xg2 ♖6d7 40 ♘xd4 ♘xd4 41 ♖xd4 ♖xd4 42 ♖xd4 ♖xd4 43 ♕xd4 leaves White with a comfortable extra pawn in the endgame.

39 ♗xa8

Diverting the rook from the d-file.

39...♖xa8

39...dxc3 40 ♖xd8 ♘xd8 41 ♕c8 wins for White.

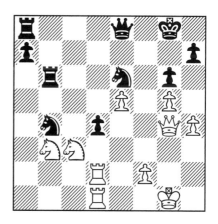

40 ♘e4

40 ♘xd4 is also good.

40...♘d5

40...♕e7 41 ♘f6+ ♔h8 42 ♘xd4 leaves White with a safe extra pawn.

41 ♘xd4

As does this.

41...h5

Just hoping for something. It is possible that the players would still have been thinking that the time control had not yet been reached.

42 ♕f3

Simplest, adding pressure on the long diagonal.

42...♘ef4

Maybe there is a chance to grab the pawn on e5?

43 ♘f6+

Not really.

43...♖xf6

Can he keep the knights together?

44 exf6 1-0

It's not worth Black carrying on.

Game 22
D.Stellwagen-P.Eljanov
German League 2007
Ruy Lopez C67

1 e4 e5 2 ♘f3 ♘c6 3 ♗b5 ♘f6 4 0-0 ♘xe4 5 d4 ♘d6 6 ♗xc6 dxc6 7 dxe5 ♘f5 8 ♕xd8+ ♔xd8 9 ♘c3 ♗d7

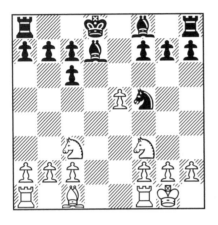

For 9...♘e7, see Game 7, Svidler-Topalov, with Black trying for ...♘g6. Eljanov here tries an earlier Kramnik plan.

The emphasis in the Berlin Variation is for complete solidity by Black, and in this game it is not too surprising that we end up in a minor piece endgame. Trying to squeeze this is difficult with either colour, even more so with Black, who is suffering slightly from the doubled pawns, making his queenside pawns less dynamic than White's kingside pawns. However, play must continue.

10 b3

This apparently modest move has gradually become the most popular since the 9...♗d7 line was tried from the late 1990s. There is no ideal development square for the c1-bishop, and the pawn on e5 will block the fianchetto, but at least White defends the pawn on e5, which might otherwise have been a weakness. If White can somehow roll through with his kingside pawns, the bishop may yet become powerful.

This is not the sort of opening line where bishops are likely to outplay rooks. There are few chances of long diagonals for either side, but neither can the knights find any unrestricted outposts.

10...♔c8

10...h6 11 ♗b2 ♔c8 was tried twice by Kramnik against Kasparov in the 2000 World Championship. He drew comfortably on each occasion, and in fact Kasparov did not score a single win in the match. This naturally made other players interested in the Berlin. To squash Kasparov's attacking play as White is quite an achievement.

There are, of course, alternatives for both sides, but the 'Berlin Wall' has proved extremely difficult to break through.

11 ♗b2

Continuing his plan. There was no need to develop the rook to d1, since Black's plan was to play ...♔c8 anyway. White can try to find a more active line with the move he saves.

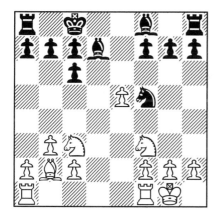

11...♗e7!?

Aiming to consolidate even more thoroughly than Kramnik tried in the first and third games of the 'Berlin Defence match'. First time round against Kasparov, Kramnik played 11...h6, by transposition (the games actually went 10...h6 11 ♗b2 ♔f8), with play continuing 12 h3 (maybe too quiet?) 12...b6 13 ♖ad1 ♘e7 14 ♘e2 ♘g6 15 ♘e1. Kramnik then tried 15...h5!?, despite the loss of tempo. After 16 ♘d3 c5 17 c4 a5 18 a4 h4, and a later ...♖h5, the game was blocked, soon agreed drawn.

Second time around, in Game 3, Kasparov played more directly: 12 ♖ad1 b6 13 ♘e2 c5 14 c4 ♗c6 15 ♘f4 ♔b7 with perhaps a small edge for White, but Kramnik was able to hold for a draw. Kramnik prevented his opponent from finding any improvement in this match, with slightly different set-ups.

Eljanov would have noted Kramnik's ...h5 idea, and would doubtless have wondered whether ...h6 is necessary. We see his plan unfolding over the next few moves. The first step is to develop his bishop, and to cover the g5-square, while avoiding having to play ...h6.

12 ♘e4

Stellwagen naturally wants to being a second knight to cover g5.

12 ♖ad1 a5 13 a4 ♖d8 14 h4 h5 ended up as equal in Z.Almasi-A.Aleksandrov, Moscow 2007; two great Berlin connoisseurs in opposition here.

12...h5!

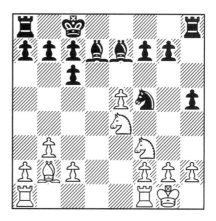

With a revised version of the Kramnik idea. Eljanov wants to keep the knight safe, preventing g4.

13 ♘fg5

Looking promising so far.

13...♗xg5!

The usual assumption is that the pair of bishops is worth retaining, and that quite often even a single bishop against a knight is useful. Flexible thinking in chess is necessary, though, and here Eljanov is quite prepared to give up bishop for knight – twice! The resulting outcome leaves Black more comfortable than he would have been otherwise.

14 ♘xg5 ♗e6!

He is not too concerned about the possible isolated pawn on e6. White's e5-pawn stops any attacks along the e-file, and of course there are no light-square attacking pieces, bishop or knight, to attack e6.

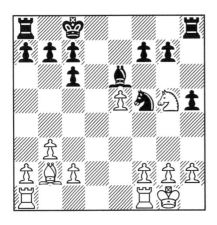

15 h3?!

Not so bad in itself – it is a quiet move which does no great damage in a closed position – but part of a misplaced strategy. After the pawn roller on the kingside, with f4 and g4, it turns out that it is Black who takes control with the rooks on the h-file.

The more straightforward 15 ♖ad1 seems better. Then, for illustrative purposes, 15...♖d8?! 16 ♖xd8+ ♔xd8 17 ♘xe6+ fxe6 18 ♗c1 ♔e8 19 ♖d1 ♖d8 20 ♖xd8+ ♔xd8 21 c3, followed by centralizing the king, gives White the better chances in the endgame. White will be able to improve his pieces, and then think about what to do with the pawns.

Black would not want to exchange pieces so quickly. Maybe 15...a5, then perhaps ...b6, ...♗b7, ...c5, and keeping both pairs of rooks on board. White would find it difficult to claim any sort of edge.

15...c5

Black wants to give the option of playing ...♘d4. Also, more generally, he might want to consider a queenside structure with pawns on c5, c7, b6 and a5.

16 g4?!

Still overplaying his kingside attack.

16 ♖ad1 or 16 ♘xe6 fxe6 17 ♖ad1 allows White a minimal edge, or, Black might argue, equality.

16...♘e7!

16...♘d4 17 ♗xd4 cxd4 18 ♘xe6 fxe6 19 ♖fd1 c5 is drawish, but Eljanov sees the opportunity to play for a slight edge.

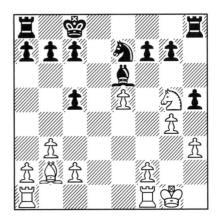

17 f3

Stellwagen holds the pawn on g4.

The computer suggests that the knight for bishop exchange, with 17 ♘xe6 fxe6, favours White, but it is difficult to agree with this. Black's bishop was doing nothing much, while White's knight was mobile. After the exchange, Black's knight would be better than White's bishop. Knights are often better than bishops in semi-closed pawn structures. In positions such as this, the bishops can be blocked by pawns and are ineffective, whereas the knights have good outposts, guarded by pawns. Often, as here, it is only of secondary importance whether the pawns are damaged by being isolated or doubled, provided they cannot be attacked. It is useful, though, to have a good aggressive minor piece on the board if the pawn structure is damaged. Play might continue 18 ♖ad1 ♘d5 19 ♔g2 b5 20 ♔g3 ♔b7 21 ♖d2 hxg4 22 hxg4 g5 23 ♖fd1 ♖h7, followed by doubling on the h-file, and Black is slightly better, maybe even more than that.

17...♔d7

There is nothing to be done on the kingside yet, so Eljanov straightens up his queenside, and develops his rook.

18 ♔f2

Stellwagen holds similar thoughts on the kingside.

18...♔c6

Ditto.

19 ♔g3

Ditto.

19...a5

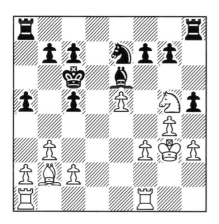

At no stage does either player try to make use of the rooks on the open file. There are no breakthrough points. Black is concentrating here on opening files on the outside, the a- and h-lines.

20 f4

While White is trying to push through his pawns on the kingside with f5.

20...g6

Black must prevent this.

21 a4

Not quite so necessary, but it is useful to stop Black from playing ...a4.

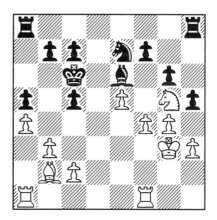

21...♖h6!

The 'mysterious rook move', as Nimzowitsch used to say. The rook plunges into its own pawns, and Black is planning to bring the other rook to h8, with no escape square. What is his idea? It is not difficult to see now. He will exchange pawns on g4, and then Black will take control, or at least create pressure on the h-file.

22 ♖f2

To cover the h2-square, and to give the chance of doubling up his own rooks on the f-file.

Black's position is comfortable after 22 ♘xe6 fxe6 23 g5 ♘f5+ 24 ♔f3 ♖hh8 25 ♖ad1 ♖ad8. White blocks the h-file, but Black has an excellent blockading square for the knight on f5.

22...hxg4

22...♖ah8 23 ♖af1 hxg4 24 hxg4 transposes.

23 hxg4

23 ♘xe6?! ♘f5+ 24 ♔xg4 fxe6 does not help White's position.

23...♖ah8

The mysterious rook move now makes clear sense.

24 罝af1

White too is doubling up rooks, not taking an open file, but rather pressing behind his kingside pawn majority. If White can push with f5 successfully, then all Black's ingenuity will still leave him worse.

24...罝h1

Therefore Black must try to exchange rooks. 24...罝h4?!, for example, leaves White better after 25 f5 gxf5 26 gxf5 罝4h5 27 ♗c1.

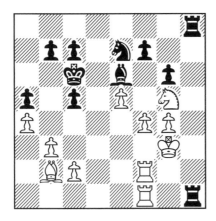

25 c4

In endgames, players need to push their pawns carefully. White is undoubtedly weakening his queenside pawn structure, but he also has to take account of the possibility of placing the knight or bishop on d5, or the possibility of Black opening up his queenside pawn majority with ...c4 at some stage. Stellwagen decides to consolidate.

25 罝xh1 罝xh1 26 ♘xe6 fxe6 is to be considered, but even here it seems wisest to close up the queenside with 27 c4. If instead 27 ♔f3, for example, then 27...♘d5, and Black's rook and knight start to become annoying. A careless 28 ♔e4?! 罝h3 would even allow a mate threat.

25...b6

Eljanov is happy to wait, and consolidates his queenside pawn chain.

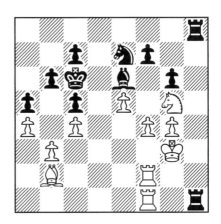

26 罝xh1

Stellwagen is in a minor zugzwang, and this must have been disconcerting for him later on. There was no need for him to crumble so quickly, though.

White has no pawn moves, and neither has he got any progressive rook move. The immediate minor piece exchange, 26 ♘xe6?, even drops a pawn after 26...罝1h3+ 27 ♔g2 fxe6. The quiet king move, 26 ♔f3?!, also leads to trouble after the exchange sacrifice 26...罝1h3+ 27 ♘xh3 罝xh3+ 28 ♔g2 罝xb3 when White's pawns start to drop.

If White makes a quiet move with the bishop, for example 26 ♗c3, Black could try 26...罝8h4 27 罝xh1 罝xh1, much as in the game. The slight change in the position of White's bishop is of no great significance.

White might just as well exchange immediately.

26...罝xh1 27 ♘xe6

A second piece exchange in succession.

27 ♘f3 is not particularly safe, as after

27...♖b1 28 ♖d2 ♘g8! Black can hit on the g4-pawn with ...♘h6. After 29 ♘g5 ♖g1+ 30 ♖g2 ♖xg2+ 31 ♔xg2 ♗xg4 32 ♘xf7 ♗d1 Black's bishop escapes, and wins all the queenside pawns. Such a prospect persuades White to get rid of the bishop.

27...fxe6 28 ♖h2

A third exchange in succession. Black's rook is potentially far more active than White's, and so White will probably have to offer the exchange anyway, for example with 28 ♔g2 ♖d1 29 ♗c3 ♖b1 30 ♖b2.

28...♖xh2

Eljanov is happy to exchange.

29 ♔xh2

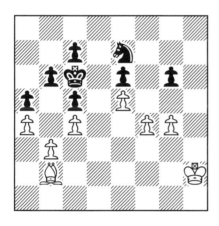

Heading for a draw? White pushes his king to g5, Black defends with the king to h7, and then there seems to be no progress.

29...g5!

Black has been saving this idea for a long time. Strategically, he is making a minority attack on the kingside, aiming for two pawns to outplay three pawns, maybe with simplification of the pawns, and hoping to reduce the opponent's kingside either to an ineffective isolated pawn, or preferably nothing at all. Black is a pawn up on the queenside, and hopes to eventually take advantage of this.

Black is, however, sacrificing a pawn. What is the compensation? At the very least, after 30 fxg5, Black can blockade White's kingside with 30...♘g6, and the king cannot break through. This will be a comfortable draw. Maybe though the black king can reach g6, trying to hoover up the kingside pawns.

29...♔d7?! 30 g5 is only a draw: for example, 30...♘f5 31 ♔g2 ♘d4 32 ♗xd4 cxd4 33 ♔f3 c5 with complete blockage. Here 33...♔c6?! 34 ♔e2 ♔c5? 35 ♔d3 ♔b4? would be wildly ambitious: 36 f5! allows White a pawn breakthrough.

30 ♔g3

White could, of course, take the pawn with 30 fxg5. The idea is not so much for Black to blockade with the knight on g6, which would give equality, but rather to take the trek with the king to g6. Most of the lines are broadly similar to the main line. One alternative would be 30...♔d7 31 ♔g3 ♔e8 32 ♔h4 ♔f7 33 ♔h5 ♔g7 34 ♗c3 ♘g6 35 ♗a1 ♘f4+ 36 ♔h4 ♔g6, and we are about to rejoin the main game.

30...♔d7

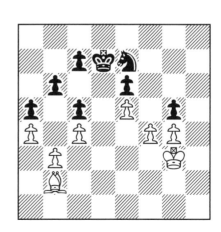

The king returns to the kingside.

What Black must not do is to exchange with 30...gxf4+? 31 ♔xf4, and the king invades via g5, and it is White who is heading for an edge. Black must blockade the pawn on g5.

31 ♔f3

Waiting.

31...♔e8

Black continues his main plan.

32 fxg5

He could continue waiting with 32 ♔g3 ♔f7 33 ♔f3. Then it is time for 33...gxf4 and ...♔g6. Once Black's king is on g6, the extra white pawn on g5 is almost an irrelevance. White's king will have to move at some stage, and Black's king will move on g5, either recapturing the pawn or quite simply just moving into space.

32 ♔e4 gxf4 33 ♔xf4 ♔f7 34 ♔xg5 ♔g7! at first sight might look effective for White, as he has a passed pawn and a king helping to advance the pawn. In fact White is in trouble, as Black has ...♘c6 and ...♘d4, and if the bishop exchanges, the king and pawn endgame is winning for Black, as in the game.

32...♔f7

Naturally it is the king that wants to move to g6. White will not be able to advance his doubled pawns.

33 ♔e4

Centralizing.

33...♘c6

33...♔g6 is, of course, also possible.

34 ♗c3

A quiet move.

34...♔g6

Then a constructive move.

35 ♔f4

35 ♗d2 ♘d4 36 b4? axb4 37 ♗xb4 cxb4 38 ♔xd4 c5+ wins for Black.

35...♘d4

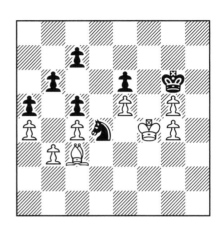

Superb strategy by Black, who has achieved his ideal position. Even at this late stage, analysis shows that he is not yet winning, though.

36 ♗xd4??

Unfortunately, White immediately collapses just before the time control.

His only chance is to accept that his b3-pawn will fall, but that he can make it difficult for Black to make any further progress. White has two isolated queenside pawns, indeed five isolated pawns altogether, but it is difficult to see how Black can make progress. In particular, it is difficult for Black to convert his four queenside pawns to overcome White's two opposing pawns.

After 36 ♗d2! ♘xb3 37 ♗e3! Black can win the b-pawn, but it is very difficult to attack either the a-pawn or the c-pawn, and Black's king is tied down to defending White's passed pawn. To try to break through with the extra pawn, Black would have to try ...a6 and ...b5, with either the help of the king or the knight, and the other piece defending on the kingside. Black redevelops with 37...♘d4 38 ♗d2, and then makes his choice:

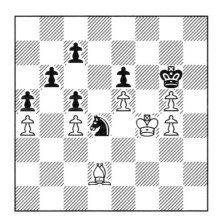

a) The quicker and more direct approach would be 38...c6 39 ♔e4 b5 40 axb5 cxb5 41 cxb5 ♘xb5 42 ♗xa5 ♔xg5 43 ♗g6 c4 44 ♔f3, but White holds.

b) Therefore Black needs to try the long way round. White's defensive plan is to give up a second pawn, on g5, at the necessary time, in order for the bishop to take advantage of the h4-d8 diagonal, with hopes of chewing up a few of Black's queenside pawns. Play might continue 38...♘c6 39 ♗c3 ♘d8 40 ♗e1 ♘f7 41 ♗h4 c6 42 ♔e4, and if Black is too ambitious, with

42...♘xg5+?, he would even turn out to be worse after 43 ♔f4 ♘f7 44 ♗e7. Perhaps Black's most dangerous idea is 39...♘b4 (instead of 39...♘d8), trying to set up a few zugzwangs in a battle between knight and bishop, and then 40 ♗a1 ♘a2! 41 ♗b2 c6 42 ♗a1 ♘c1!. Black has made good use of minor zugzwangs, and now it is time for White to cut his losses with 43 ♔g3 ♔xg5 44 ♗b2. Black cannot quite seem to make progress.

Sometimes the Sherlock Holmes principle needs to be applied in chess, that if all other lines fail, the one that does not fail needs to be played. If White is a pawn up, it does not necessarily mean that the loss of two pawns will lead to a loss. It may still be possible to recover from being a pawn down.

36...cxd4

The king and pawn ending is simple. A sad finish.

37 ♔e4 c5 38 ♔f4 d3 0-1

If 39 ♔e3 ♔xg5 40 ♔xd3 ♔g4 41 ♔e4 ♔g5 42 ♔e3 ♔f5, winning the pawn and the game.

Game 23
M.Carlsen-S.Tiviakov
European Team Championship, Crete 2007
Queen's Indian Defence E17

1 d4 ♘f6 2 c4 e6 3 ♘f3 b6 4 g3 ♗b7

The most natural move, placing the bishop on the long diagonal, and challenging the white bishop on g2. This move is, of course, sound, logical and solid, but the general impression is that at top level there have been many draws, a few wins for White, and not many wins for Black.

For 4...♗a6, see Game 4, Topalov-Anand. This tends to lead to much livelier play.

5 ♗g2 ♗e7

Also possible, and transposing into the Bogo-Indian is 5...♗b4+, but Black's results have not been very successful recently. 6 ♗d2, in this particular line of the Bogo, is the most popular.

6 ♘c3

6 0-0 0-0 7 ♘c3 could transpose to the main line in this game after 7...♘a6. Quite often, though, White does not castle immediately.

6...c5 7 d5 exd5 8 ♘h4 keeps an edge for White.

6...♘a6

The old main line, 6...♘e4, and then 7 ♘xe4 ♗xe4 8 0-0 0-0 9 ♘e1 (or 9 ♘h4, soon transposing) is generally regarded as boring and drawish. 7 ♗d2 f5 is the current main line. White is not too worried about the knight versus bishop exchange, with 7...♘xd2 8 ♕xd2, as he has more control in the centre.

6...0-0 is also standard main-line play if White castles immediately, but 7 d5!? attempts to play more aggressively. Tiviakov has played 7...♗b4 a few times, giving up a tempo, but arguing that White too has made concessions with his early pawn advance. He has also played 7...♘a6.

7 0-0 0-0

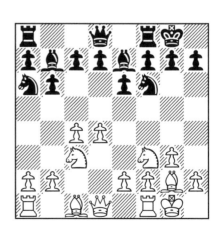

Standard castling by both sides, but

where will White develop his pieces? Or, indeed, should he move a pawn?

Tiviakov's favourite knight move in this opening looks slightly unnatural, perhaps. The knight is on the edge, and it will take some time for it to get back into play, maybe with a timely ...c5. Even so, all his minor pieces are off the back rank, he has castled, and he is not under immediate attack. In other words, he has completed his development. Soon he will have to sort out his central pawns.

8 ♗f4

This too is just a developing move to get the minor pieces out of the back rank. It does not really attack anything, but at least the bishop is active if the centre opens up. Carlsen is aiming for a quiet edge, trying nothing spectacular.

8 d5 is more combative, pushing the pawn to the other side of the board, but one senses that this is slightly anti-positional. White is allowing the knight to escape to c5, which can create pressure on the e4-pawn. Maybe Black can try 8...exd5 9 cxd5 ♖e8 with equality.

8...♘e4

A standard defensive idea of this opening, but usually played without ...♘a6 and ♗f4. Going through Tiviakov's games on the database, it is clear that he is careful to have tried different moves, here and earlier, just to create a little bit of variety. It is useful not to allow his opponent to know exactly what he is going to try in the opening. Tiviakov has, for example, tried 8...c5 and 8...d6, with different ways of playing on.

Here he tries possibly the steadiest and safest plan. Black wants to exchange White's knight on c3, making it difficult for White to create pawn pressure with d5 and/or e4. If 9 ♘xe4 ♗xe4, it is difficult to activate White's kingside pieces for attack.

9 ♖e1

Maybe White can still claim a micro-advantage, even so, after 9 ♘xe4 ♗xe4 10 a3!?, trying to prove the knight is misplaced. If 10...c5 11 dxc5 ♘xc5, for example, White is doing well after 12 b4. Here 10...c6!? provides a different escape route for the knight.

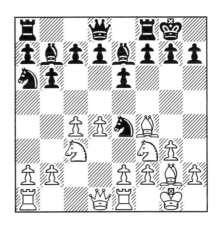

9...d5

9...♘xc3 10 bxc3 looks fully playable, doubling the c-pawns, and then maybe 10...f5 or 10...♗e4.

Tiviakov's move is also good. Whatever else Carlsen achieves in this game, he has not managed to dent Tiviakov's pet opening.

10 cxd5

If 10 ♘d2 ♘xc3 11 bxc3, the computer suggests a stonewall-type defence with 11...g5 12 ♗e3 f5, and maybe 13 ♘f3 f4 14 ♗c1. The experienced human player would tend to be suspicious of this, seeing the e5-square as a serious weakness for Black, not helped by the knight being on the edge on a6. Also, are Black's forward pawns starting a genuine attack, or are they merely creating weaknesses for his own king?

11...c5 12 cxd5 exd5 is a standard-enough idea for both sides.

10...exd5

There is no need to offer the knight exchange first. The knight is still strong on e4.

11 ♖c1

11 ♘e5 c5 12 ♘xe4 dxe4 13 dxc5 ♘xc5 14 ♕c2 is probably also about equal.

11...c5

Black could have tried blocking White's c-pawn with 11...♘xc3, since if 12 ♖xc3?? ♗b4 Black wins the exchange.

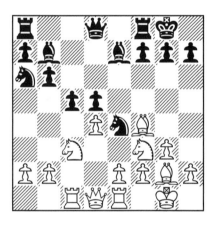

Now we have reached the characteristic Tarrasch pawn structure in the centre. Black will probably have to endure an isolated d-pawn, which is a weakness in the pawn structure, but so long as his pieces remain active, as here, the pawn can survive. It follows that Black would want to allow the isolated pawn quickly, if at all, rather than trying to attempt any slow manoeuvring.

12 dxc5

It is difficult for White to develop his

pieces further, and still maintain tension in the centre, and so Carlsen decides it is time to exchange pawns, and force Tiviakov to declare his intentions.

After 12 ♕a4, the computer suggests another Stonewall with 12...g5 13 ♗e3 f5. Right or wrong, it is certainly different, and there is far less likelihood of a quiet draw.

12...♗xc5

The one recapture that may be considered and rejected quickly is 12...bxc5?! 13 ♘xe4 dxe4 14 ♘e5. White has active pieces, and Black has two uncomfortable isolated pawns, while the e4-pawn is also a problem. If Black needs to play ...f5 to defend the pawn, then he is wholly open on the a2-g8 diagonal.

12...♘exc5?! should barely even be considered too. Black's pieces are moving backwards, and getting in the way.

Of the other moves, 12...♗xc5 at least attacks something, and gains a tempo, although the knight on a6 is still a slight problem, and 12...♘axc5 gets in the way of the bishop, and it is the bishop that needs priority at the moment.

13 e3

Carlsen cuts off the diagonal immediately. After 13 ♘d4, White will probably have to play e3 anyway, so he might as well do it now, without loss of time.

13 ♘xe4 dxe4 14 ♘e5?! (14 ♘g5 ♕e7 might give Black a fractional edge) 14...g5! runs into tactical problems: 15 ♗d2 ♗xf2+ 16 ♔xf2 ♕d4+ wins a pawn, while 15 ♗e3 ♗xe3 17 fxe3, with doubled isolated pawns, is not inspiring.

13...♘xc3

Simplest, relieving the tension on e4 and d5.

14 bxc3

14 ♖xc3? ♗b4 wins the exchange.

14...♕e7

The computer suggests 14...♕f6, but Tiviakov would have wanted to avoid a ♗g5 fork after ...♖ad8.

15 ♘d4

Still trying to squeeze an edge. Other moves are equal.

15...♖ad8

It would be unwise to trap the bishop with 15...g5?. After 16 ♕g4 h6 17 ♘f5 ♕f6 18 h4 ♗c8 19 e4 dxe4 20 ♗xe4 it is Black's attacking pawn that falls, not White's defender.

16 h4

But now it is useful for White to secure the g5-square.

16...♖fe8

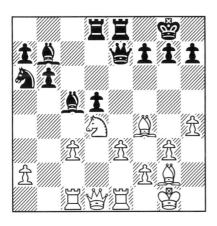

Standard development by Black, bringing both rooks into play. It is unclear as yet whether the other underdeveloped piece, the knight on a6, should play to c7 or, after a bishop move, to c5. He therefore waits.

17 ♗f1

Carlsen gains some slight pressure on the f1-a6 diagonal, but loses pressure on the long diagonal. Does he gain anything overall with this? Who knows?

The important point is that White's play remains solid both before and after his move, while Tiviakov's play remains equally solid. A level position. It is only when one player falters, and either plays indecisively, or overpresses, leaving behind weaknesses, that the other can start to take advantage.

17...♗a3

Black decides he must bring the knight into play before being pressed on a6.

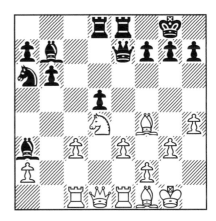

18 ♖c2

At first it seems there is no real difference between this move and 18 ♖b1, both looking about equal. Keeping the protection of the pawn on c3 is useful though in case play speeds up.

18...♘c5

The knight finally emerges, either to e6 or to e4.

19 ♘b5

White attacks something, but play is still equal. Once White's knight moves, Black's knight can move to e6, a safe square.

19...♘e6

And so it proves.

20 ♗e5

If 20 ♘xa3 ♕xa3 21 ♗e5, Black may

transpose into the main line with 21...♗c6, or there may be other more active choices. However, here 20...♘xf4?! would be a case of over-pressing. After 21 ♘b5 White has a better bishop, and has an edge. The pawn sacrifice with 21...d4?! 22 cxd4 ♕e4 23 f3 ♕g6 24 ♔f2 is unconvincing.

20...♗c6

Asking the knight to make a decision.

Maybe 20...♘f8!? could be slightly more accurate. If 21 ♘xa3?! ♕xa3, Black is even slightly better, while if 21 ♗d4 ♗a6, Black is holding satisfactorily.

21 ♘xa3?!

An obvious move, gaining the bishop-pair, but a slight inaccuracy.

21 ♕g4! is better, with pressure against the king.

21...♕xa3 22 ♕g4

The right idea but mistimed.

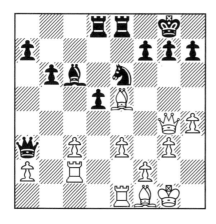

22...♕a4!

Equalizing.

23 ♕xa4

He cannot avoid the queen exchange, as the rook was under attack.

23 ♕f5?! ♘c5 is promising for Black.

23...♗xa4

After the exchange White has achieved nothing in terms of an edge. If anything, Tiviakov as Black should have slightly the easier position.

What is interesting about this game is not so much any in-depth strategy, from opening through to endgame, but rather the way in which quite suddenly Carlsen was able to overrun his 2600+ opponent from an apparently easily equal endgame. A few slight slips, and Carlsen is on the way.

Quite often it is the younger player who succeeds. He will have the energy to keep playing, and carry on keep playing, hour upon hour, waiting for the slightest slip-up by the opponent. The older player is more likely to relax, seeing the opportunity of aiming for a clear draw and a half-point without extra effort. Then slight mistakes start to slip in, and suddenly the older player has to work hard to hold the position, and then maybe he will make further slight mistakes, and increasingly there is a danger of losing.

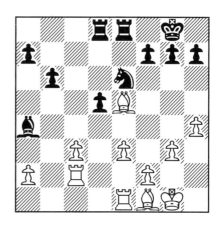

24 ♖d2

The rook has to move, and he might as well keep some pressure on the isolated pawn.

24...♘c5

Black can force an exchange of knight for a bishop, if required. To maintain complete security, he would like to exchange the knight for a light-squared bishop, keeping the excellent drawing prospects of bishops of opposite colour.

Black could also exchange the other bishop with 24...♘g5!? 25 hxg5 ♖xe5. Then 26 c4 d4! 27 ♖b1 d3, and perhaps 28 ♗xd3 ♖d7 (White threatened ♗xh7+) 29 ♖bb2 ♖xg5 30 ♗e2 gives Black even slightly the better pawn structure. Instead 26 f4 ♖ee8 27 ♔f2 might well end up as equal, although it is possible that White can create pressure with his kingside pawn mass. Who knows?

Tiviakov plays it cautiously.

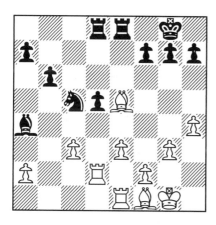

25 ♗d4

Centralizing, and keeping the bishop-pair.

White has slightly more chance of drifting into a worse position, but with reasonably strong play on both sides, one would normally expect a draw.

25...♖c8

Putting pressure on the c3-pawn.

26 ♖b2

Now Black no longer has a chance to hit d2 with tempo after ...♘e4.

White could also have added extra defence to the pawn with 26 ♖c1.

26...♖c7

All good moves are presumably equal here. Tiviakov creates the option of doubling on the c-file.

27 ♖b4

27 ♗b5 ♗xb5 28 ♖xb5 ♘e4 29 ♖xd5 ♘xc3 ends up as a drawn rook and pawn ending.

27...♗c2

Black's bishop is now on a better diagonal.

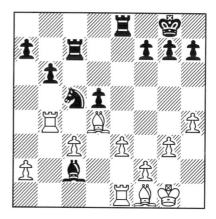

28 c4

Leading to an 'obviously drawn' opposite-coloured bishop endgame. To play for a win, sometimes one has to exploit the most micro of micro-advantages.

28 ♖a1!? avoids the opposite-coloured bishops, and maybe this too can lead to microscopic pressure. White's hope would be to play c4 at some stage, while still keeping the bishop-pair.

28...♘d3

The natural move, though other replies are not necessarily bad.

29 ♗xd3 ♗xd3 30 cxd5

The pawn gain is only temporary.

30...♖d7

And Black wins it back.

31 ♖c1

A slight sense of an initiative. White controls the open c-file, and Black's d-pawn is blocked because the bishop on d4 is securely guarded by the e3-pawn.

31...♖xd5 32 ♖a4!?

Many players, and *Fritz*, might prefer 32 ♖c7 ♖a5 33 a4, but Carlsen prefers to avoid spending a tempo with a4. To be able to do something effectively with his tiny edge, he needs to move quickly.

32...♖d7

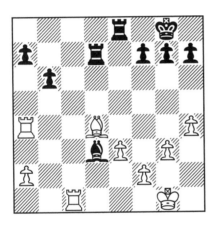

Time for a general assessment, and in particular to answer why the players did not simply agree a draw.

We start with the bishops. White's bishop is slightly more active than Black's because his bishop on d4, already strong by itself, is supported by a solid potential passed pawn on e3. Black cannot attack this bishop with any of his pawns. Black's bishop is not quite so secure, though. Naturally it can run quickly when attacked, but Black cannot rely on the security of counterplay with the bishop on a central square.

The bishops by themselves would not give White any chances of playing for an edge, were it not for White having the more active rooks. White has control of the open c-file, and he creates pressure on the a7-pawn. Black, in contrast, keeps rooks on the d-file and the e-file, but cannot attack any pawns.

His rooks and his bishop then slightly outweigh his opponents', so there is no particular reason for White to agree a draw. What about his pawns, though? We shall soon see.

33 g4!

Carlsen is pressing forward, and if Tiviakov plays quietly, perhaps lulled by the seeming dullness of the position, then Carlsen can start to take the initiative.

White wants to stop Black from playing ...h5, which would allow his opponent to create, if not exactly counterplay, then at least some solid squares for the bishop on the light squares.

33...h6?!

Probably this was intended as a quiet and natural move, played quickly to help reach the time control. Tiviakov creates an escape square for the king, and prevents for the moment a g5-advance. He needs, though, to defend more actively.

33...♗e2! is equal. If, for example, 34 g5 h6 35 gxh6 gxh6 and Black has broken up White's kingside pawn phalanx. The isolated pawns for Black are of no great weakness. White can try instead 34 ♔h2 ♗xg4 35 ♗xg7 (35 ♖g1? f5) 35...♔xg7 36 ♖xg4+ ♔f8 37 ♔g3 ♖e6, but Black should have no trouble in holding the rook endgame.

34 f3

Now White is gaining ground. A 4-3

pawn initiative often creates many more problems for the defender than a 3-2 initiative. Even more importantly, Black's 2-1 queenside initiative provides less punch.

34...♔h7?!

Black is just stalling. Clearly the king is going in the wrong direction, but any other piece move could have possibly worse consequences.

It is often a difficult judgement to decide whether to defend passively a slightly inferior position, or whether to change the balance of the position. Here 34...f5!? looks tempting. After 35 gxf5 ♗xf5 White has a passed e-pawn, but the opposite-coloured bishops help to defend the weaker player; White will not have much opportunity to advance the pawn beyond e5. Meanwhile, Black's pieces have rather more freedom of action than in the actual game.

It is quite likely, especially given time shortage, that Black would have been worried about 35 ♖a3 ♗e2 36 ♔f2?!, but he has a tactical resource, 36...fxg4! 37 ♔xe2 ♖xd4. White should still hold with 38 ♖xa7, but this is not really what he wanted.

35 ♔f2

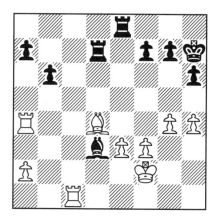

This king move, closer to the centre and the advancing pawns, makes more genuine progress.

35...♖ee7

Allowing Black to advance with ...b5, without losing the pawn.

It is unexpectedly difficult for Black to coordinate his pieces now. His bishop has few squares, while his rook on d7 is tied down to his pawn, and his other rook does not coordinate well. Also, his king is tied down to the pawn on g7.

Maybe it is time for Black to play 35...f6 immediately, rather than shuffling around with the rooks. White still has some slight pressure after 36 h5 ♔g8 37 ♖a3 ♗h7 38 ♖ac3 ♔f7 39 ♔g3 f5, but Black should be able to hold. He is not fully equal though.

36 ♖a3

Forcing the bishop to a worse square.

36...♗b5

36...♗g6? 37 h5 loses the bishop.

37 ♖ac3

White has taken control of the c-file, whereas Black's rooks do not press against anything. White's bishop is again more secure than Black's. White is better.

37...♖d8

Understandable in that he does not want his opponent to control the back rank.

38 ♔g3

The king needs to advance, but only when the pawns have started to push. It is all a question of proportion – kings and pawns need to work together. White's bishop will soon work well with the king and pawns.

38...f6

Belatedly, but Black will not want to

have to keep the king guarding the g7-pawn.

39 f4

More pressure from the pawns.

39...h5

Black seeks counterplay, breaking open the connected pawns on the fourth rank, and giving some chance of making use of the light-squared pawns, but in the end, he is just moving closer to a possible zugzwang. Black is not losing yet, but any small error will lead to trouble.

39...♔g6 is an alternative, with a slight edge for White.

40 g5

40 gxh5 ♗e2 holds.

40...♔g6

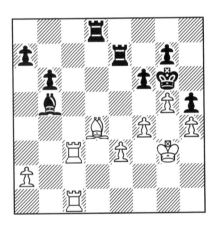

The time control. Carlsen has worked hard for his edge, but he has not broken through, and the position still looks close to equal.

41 ♖b1!

This apparently simple move adds pressure on Black's bishop.

41...♖d5

Alternatively:

a) If 41...♗d7?, aiming to prevent f5+, the unfortunate bishop runs into a pin with 42 ♖c7, probably winning.

b) If 41...♗a4 42 f5+ ♔xf5 43 ♖f1+ ♔e6 44 gxf6 gxf6 45 ♖xf6+ ♔d7 46 ♖a3, and the driftwood of Black's pieces ends up facing a strong ocean current. Black can survive, just about, with 46...♔c8 47 ♗xb6 ♖g7+ (but not 47...axb6? 48 ♖a8+ ♔c7 49 ♖a7+, winning the exchange) 48 ♔f3 ♖d1 49 ♖c3+ ♔b7 50 ♗d4. He is a pawn down though.

c) 41...♗a6 covers any rook ideas on the f-file (42 f5+? ♔xf5 43 ♖f1+?? ♗xf1), and it is difficult to find anything for White by direct means. For example, after 42 gxf6 gxf6 43 ♖c6 ♖f7 44 ♖g1 ♗b7 45 ♔h3+ ♔f5 46 ♗xf6 ♗xc6 47 ♗xd8 ♖d7 Black should be able to hold. Perhaps the best plan for White would be to drill away on the queenside with 42 a4!?: for example, 42...♖d6 43 a5 bxa5 44 ♖a1 fxg5 45 hxg5 ♗b5 46 ♖xa5 a6 47 ♖c5 ♖f7 48 ♔f3, and the pressure continues. If 48...♗d7 49 e4, and if then 49...♖xd4? 50 ♖xa6+, winning.

One cannot imagine that Tiviakov had an easy choice to make, but here he probably chose correctly.

42 ♖c8

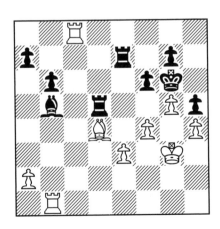

Into the back rank.

42...♗e8

Trying to seal things off. With this and the next few moves, at first sight Tiviakov's plan looks absurd, moving into passivity. In fact, though, it takes only a good move for Black to hold the position together.

43 ♖bc1

43 gxf6 gxf6 does not help White.

43...f5

Black continues to close the drawbridge.

44 ♖b8

White doubles up on the end rank.

44...♖d6

And Black doubles on the e-file.

45 ♖cc8 ♖de6

Both players continue their plans.

46 ♗e5

It looks close to zugzwang, but fortunately Black's position is not so desperate.

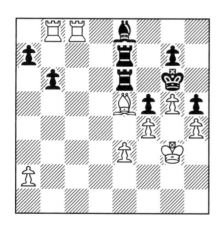

46...♔f7?!

Tiviakov seems so fascinated about setting up a barricade, keeping the rooks and bishop unmoved, that he forgets about the need for activity.

The simple 46...♗c6! holds the balance comfortably. Carlsen has done as much as he can to try to play for a win, and undoubtedly he has handled his play more creatively than the opponent in the endgame, but one of the basic rules of chess strategy is that one cannot force a win in chess from a level position, unless the opponent makes a mistake. Often there will be a large margin of error in a level endgame, but here the margin is about to slip.

47 ♖d8

Waiting for something to happen.

47...♔g6

Tiviakov sees himself as safe. Dangerous!

After 47...♗c6 there are a couple of attempts by White to aim for an edge, but Black holds: 48 ♖h8 ♔g6 49 ♖bg8 ♖xe5 50 fxe5 ♖xe5 51 ♖h6+ ♔f7 52 ♖xg7+ ♔xg7 53 ♖xc6 ♖xe3+ 54 ♔f4 ♖e2 55 ♔xf5 ♖f2+ 56 ♔e5 ♖xa2 57 ♖c7+ ends up as a draw, and, similarly, 58 e4 ♗xe4 (58...fxe4?? 59 ♖f8 wins immediately) 59 ♗d6 ♖b7 50 ♖xb7+ ♗xb7 51 ♖d7+ ♔e8 52 ♖xb7 ♖xd6 53 ♖xa7 leads to another level rook endgame.

48 ♔f2

Carlsen continues his quiet manoeuvring.

48...♔f7?

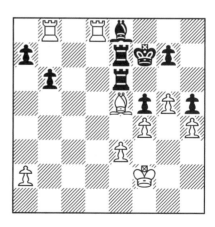

And Tiviakov loses his sense of danger.

48...♗c6 was still playable.

49 e4!

Time for a breakthrough. The pieces are now on their optimum squares for both sides, either attacking or defending, and White's king has quietly centralized but can do no more, so the only way to make progress is with the pawns.

49...♔g6

If 49...fxe4, White now has a pawn break with f5. Play continues with 50 ♗d6 e3+ 51 ♔e1 ♖d7 53 ♖xd7+ ♗xd7 53 ♖f8+ ♔g6 54 f5+, winning the rook.

The exchange sacrifice with 49...♖xe5 50 fxe5 ♖xe5 should ultimately be unsuccessful: 51 g6+ ♔f8 pins the pieces down, and after 52 exf5 ♖xf5+ 52 ♔e3 ♖e5+ 54 ♔f4, one idea for White is 54...♖e6 55 a4 ♖e1 56 ♖b7 ♖e7 57 ♖xe7 ♔xe7 58 ♖a8 a5 59 ♔g5 ♗xa4 60 ♖g8, and while Black has two connected passed pawns with the bishop, White's passed pawns, with the help of the rook, will be quicker.

49...g6 looks extremely unappealing, taking away the g6-square from the king, and weakening the dark squares. After 50 ♗d6 ♖d7 51 e5! (more accurate than 51 ♖xd7+ ♗xd7 52 e5 ♖e8 when Black will be able to activate some of his pieces) 51...♖xd8 52 ♖xd8 ♗c6 53 ♖f8+ ♔g7 54 ♖c8 ♗e4 51 ♖c7+ White has a comfortable extra pawn.

50 ♗d6

The only sensible move. 50 exf5+? ♔xf5 activates Black's pieces.

50...♖d7

Now Black has broken up his defensive e-file structure, and White has made further progress.

51 ♖xd7

There is still the chance of a blunder.

After 51 ♖xe8? ♖exd6, Black has at the very least perpetual check on the d-file.

51...♗xd7 52 e5

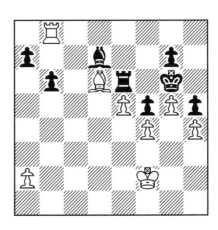

Through sheer stamina, and of course excellent chess understanding, Carlsen has somehow performed some magic in a 'completely drawn' opposite-coloured bishop endgame.

52...♗c6

52...♖e8 53 ♖b7 ♗c6 54 ♖xa7 wins a pawn, much as in the game.

53 ♖c8

Into the seventh rank.

53...♗e8

Back to passive defence.

53...♗e4 54 ♖c7 ♖e8 55 e6 ♖xe6 56 ♗e5 threatens mate, and after 56...♖xe5 57 fxe5 White has a second advanced e-pawn, which with care should lead to a win.

54 ♖a8

The pawn goes.

54...♗f7

To cover the g7-pawn.

55 ♖xa7

Further progress.

55...♖e8

At last the rook can move somewhere.

56 a3

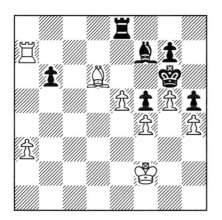

Securing the pawn, so he can move his rook.

56...♗d5

Black can do nothing constructive.

57 ♔e3

While White gradually improves his position.

57...b5

Maybe the pawn is a little safer?

58 ♔d4

But what about Black's bishop?

58...♗g2

After 58...♗c4 59 a4 White has a clear run with the pawn.

59 e6

We have seen this idea before. See the note to Black's 53rd.

59...♖xe6

Not much choice.

60 ♗e5

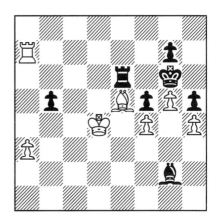

With a collapse on g7.

60...♔h7

60...♖xe5 61 ♔xe5 also wins quickly.

61 ♖xg7+ ♔h8 62 ♖e7+ 1-0

Game 25
G.Kamsky-M.Carlsen
Khanty-Mansiysk 2007
Petroff Defence C43

1 e4 e5 2 ♘f3 ♘f6

For lines starting with 2...♘c6, see Game 7, Svidler-Topalov, and the many later games.

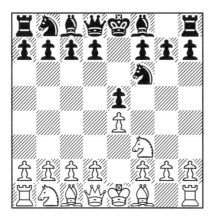

We are now in the Petroff Defence, or the Russian Defence.

Black's opening is solid, aiming for a symmetrical pawn structure, with quick and steady development for both sides. If White is happy with a steady draw, quite common if he is lower-rated, it is difficult for Black to enliven the game. If, however, White is trying to play for an edge, then chances arise for both sides, and tense games may result. Top grandmasters do not like having quick equality as White.

Kamsky was out of chess during the late 1990s and early 2000s, and Carlsen will no doubt have reckoned that his opponent would be slightly out of practice in certain openings, and could be vulnerable. His strategy worked – to some extent!

3 d4

3 ♘xe5 is the normal line. Then all juniors at some stage will have been taught that if Black tries to take the symmetry too far with 3...♘xe4? 4 ♕e2 ♘f6?, White wins the queen with a discovered check, with 5 ♘c6+.

Black's main line is 3...d6 4 ♘f3 ♘xe4. If White is happy with ultra-symmetry, with 5 d3 ♘f6, or even 5 ♕e2 ♕e7 6 d3, it is difficult for Black to make play interesting. Sometimes, though, there may be catastrophic results if one of the players suddenly breaks the balance, overpressing and overbalancing. A recent example is N.Short-P.Harikrishna, Montreal 2007: 5 d3 ♘f6 6 d4 d5 7 ♗d3 ♗d6 8 0-0 0-0 9 h3 h6 10 ♘c3 c6 11 ♖e1 ♖e8 12 ♖xe8+ ♘xe8. At this stage, it would not be unexpected if the game finished after 19 moves with a draw, but Short went for the jugular with 13 ♘e5 ♘d7 14 ♗f4 ♘f8 15 ♕h5 ♗e6 16 ♖b1? (planning to defend against ...♕b6; he can still back out to equality with 16 ♘e2) 16...f6 17 ♘g6 ♗f7! 18 ♗xd6 (as if 18 ♗xh6 f5!, and White will lose one of the pawns, without compensation) 18...♘xd6 19 g4? (19 ♕g4 ♘xg6 20 ♗xg6 ♗xg6 21 ♕xg6 ♕e7 leaves Black slightly better developed, but without great advantage) 19...♘e4, and Harikrishna won a pawn.

In symmetrical positions, it is best, when trying to attack, to ensure that the attackers are more powerful than the defenders.

3...♘xe4

3...exd4 has tended to be unfashionable at top levels. White keeps a very small edge after 4 e5 ♘e4 5 ♕d4 d5 6 exd6 ♘xd6 7 ♘c3 ♘c6 8 ♕f4.

4 ♗d3

If 4 dxe5, there is sharp play after 4...♗c5 5 ♕d5 ♗xf2+, but Black has usually avoided the challenge with 4...d5.

4...d5

4...♘c6!? – no misprint, Black is dropping the knight – is one of the most remarkable opening innovations in the last quarter century, at least in terms of paradox. If 5 ♗xe4 d5 6 ♗d3 e4, and Black is equal, albeit with play tending to be drawish. Here 5 d5 ♘c5 6 dxc6 e4 7 ♗e2 exf3 8 cxb7 ♗xb7 9 ♗xf3 is an attempt at a microscopic edge for White, but it should only be equal. Thus, mostly, White usually ignores the pseudo-sacrifice with 5 dxe5.

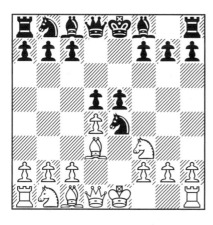

5 dxe5

This worked on the day, but it may well be inferior. White's pawn on e5

ought to have been slightly overloaded.

There is some history here. In the sixth game of the match between Karpov and Kamsky in 1996, Kamsky as White tried the standard 5 ♘xe5, play continuing 5...♘d7 6 ♘xd7 ♗xd7 7 0-0 ♗d6 8 ♘c3 ♕h4 9 g3 ♘xc3 10 bxc3 ♕g4 11 ♖e1+ ♔d8. Probably play is around equal after the exchange of queens, but Kamsky played ambitiously with 12 ♗e2 ♕f5 13 ♖b1 b6 14 c4 dxc4 15 ♗xc4 ♖e8 16 ♗e3 ♗c6 17 d5 ♗d7, and Black started to take over the attack. Kamsky had not reached this line again at high level, and might well have felt nervous.

5...♗e7

Carlsen is being careful not to play 5...♘c6 too quickly. He knows where his bishops want to go, and he would like to keep open the option of castling as soon as possible.

6 0-0

Maybe 6 ♘bd2, but Black should be reasonably happy with either 6...♘xd2 or 6...♘c5.

6...♗g4

Black should have excellent chances of equalizing. The pin allows him to create pressure on White's e5-pawn.

7 h3

A useful move to slip in. He cannot be checkmated on the back row.

7 ♗xe4!? dxe4 8 ♕xd8+ ♗xd8 9 ♘d4 might well be best, though. This was tried a few months earlier in A.Shirov-M.Adams, 6th matchgame, Elista 2007, Shirov later winning. Play continued 9...0-0 10 ♘c3 ♘d7 11 h3 ♗h5 12 e6!? fxe6 13 ♘xe6 ♖e8 14 ♘xd8 ♖axd8 15 ♗g5 with a slight advantage to White, Black having to deal with an isolated pawn. Ftacnik suggests instead 12...♘c5 13 exf7+ ♗xf7, and then 14 ♘b3 ♘xb3

15 axb3 ♗g6 with equality. Sometimes such lines never quite equalize fully, and here 14 ♗e3 ♗f6 15 ♖fb1!?, a computer suggestion, causes some difficulty. If White's minor pieces can become firmly entrenched in the centre, he does not have to be too afraid of the bishop-pair, hampered by Black's slightly weakened pawn structure.

7...♗h5

It is a little to early to exchange with 7...♗xf3 8 ♕xf3. Black wants to create some more pressure with the pin.

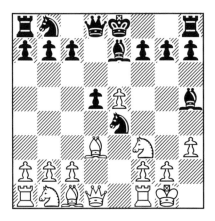

8 ♖e1

8 c4 ♘c6 9 cxd5 ♕xd5 10 ♗c2 ♕xd1 11 ♖xd1 ♘c5 ends up with a slight edge for Black. The c-pawn push takes up two tempi, while Black makes two developing moves. In some lines, however, the c4 and cxd5 idea could be good.

It is too late to attempt to emulate Shirov's idea with 8 ♗xe4 dxe4 9 ♕xd8+ ♗xd8 10 ♘d4, as Black may now comfortably play 10...♗g6 with equality.

8...♘c6

8...♘c5 also looks fine.

9 ♘c3

White cannot grab the pawn. 9 ♗xe4? dxe4 10 ♕xd8+ ♖xd8 11 ♖xe4?

♖d1+ 12 ♖e1 ♗xf3 wins a piece for Black.

9 ♘bd2 ♘xe5 11 ♘xe4 ♘xf3+ 11 gxf3 dxe4 12 ♗xe4 ♕xd1 13 ♖xd1 c6 gives Black a fractional edge. He has the better pawn structure.

Kamsky dropped chess for several years, and he has occasionally since not been fully focussed in terms of modern opening theory. Once he gets into the middlegame or endgame, though, he can still play superb top-level chess, as we shall soon see.

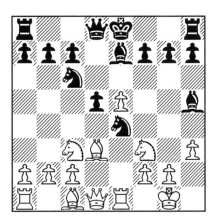

9...♗g6?

One senses that Carlsen is suspicious of preparation, and plays quietly. Black has good reasons, though, for playing for an edge:

a) Even the straightforward 9...♘xc3 10 bxc3 is more than equal for Black.

b) 9...♗xf3!? is more ambitious. If 10 ♕xf3 ♘xe5, Black takes the pawn: for example, 11 ♕f5 ♘xd3 12 cxd3 ♘xc3 12 bxc3 0-0, and he grinds on. The alternative 10 gxf3 ♘xc3 11 bxc3 allows a massive gash in White's kingside pawn structure. The queenside pawn gash is less significant, as the king is not being exposed. After 11...♗c5 (threatening ...♕h4) 12 f4 ♕h4 13 ♕f3 there are several choices for Black, and at least one of these could prove promising. The most straightforward is 13...0-0-0 14 ♕g4+ ♕xg4 15 hxg4 h5 with good chances for Black.

10 ♗d2!

White is not worried about losing his bishop for knight. He consolidates his central piece and pawn structure.

10 ♘xd5 ♕xd5 11 c4 ♕e6 12 ♗xe4 ♕xc4 13 ♗d5 is promising too, but after 13...♕b5 Black is close to equality.

10...♘xd2

After 10...♘xc3 11 ♗xc3 Black is yet to prove that he is fully equal. If then 11...d4? 12 ♘xd4 ♘xd4 13 ♗xd4 ♕xd4?? 14 ♗b5+, Black loses his queen. On more sensible alternatives, White keeps the positional threat of e6: for example, 11...♕d7 12 e6 fxe6 13 ♗xg7 ♖g8 14 ♗xg6+ hxg6 15 ♗c3, and Black's pawns have been weakened.

11 ♕xd2

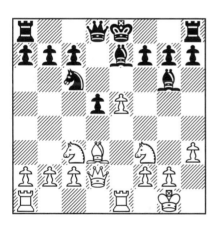

After the unfortunate 9...♗g6, Black has quickly moved from a slight edge to a nagging disadvantage.

The bishop-pair is not always an advantage, and here the extra knight is more useful after the bishop exchange. The central point is not so much the pawn structure, but rather the development of the pieces. White is ahead, and can gain space with the minor pieces in the centre. Black has lost time with his ...♗c8-g4-h5-g6 manoeuvre, and will take time to catch up with castling and centralizing the rooks. White meanwhile can move on.

11...d4

Carlsen decides that if the pawn is weak on d5, he might just as well push towards d4. This is not an aggressive pawn push. He is merely trying to stabilize the centre.

11...♗h5 12 g4! ♗g6 loses more time for Black, and White should consequently be able to avoid serious weaknesses on the kingside: 13 ♗b5 a6 14 ♗xc6+ bxc6 15 ♘d4 ♕d7 16 e6 fxe6 17 ♘xe6 is good for White. The knights and rooks work well together, whereas Black's bishop-pair is passive and ineffective. White is attacking.

12 ♘e4

12 ♗xg6? dxc3 loses material.

12...0-0

Carlsen would not have enjoyed keeping the king in the centre, but now Kamsky stabilizes his centre, and keeps a better pawn structure.

Alternatively:

a) 12...♕d5? leaves the king stuck in the centre after 13 ♘f6+! gxf6 14 exf6. White has a clear advantage.

b) 12...♗b4!? 13 c3 dxc3 14 bxc3 damages White's pawn structure, but Black has also lost time. Then:

b1) 14...♗e7 15 ♖ad1 0-0 16 ♕e3 gives White piece pressure in the centre, with ♘eg5 to follow. If 16...♕d5 17 ♘f6+ gxf6 18 ♗xg6 ♕xa2 19 ♗e4, White has a strong attack. The pawn-grabbing is not worth it.

b2) 14...♗a5 gives livelier play for Black, but also weakens his kingside. There are unclear possibilities after 15 e6 fxe6 16 ♘c5 0-0. However, 16 ♖ad1 0-0 17 ♕f4 is a simpler and more effective plan, White thinking either of ♘c5 or more probably of ♘eg5.

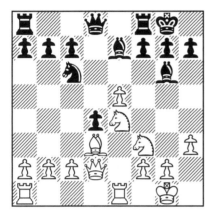

13 a3!

This little quiet move with the pawn, cutting out the opponent's attack, is often so important in helping a smooth attack.

If 13 ♕f4 immediately, Black is at least equal after 13...♘b4.

13...♕d5

13...♗h5 14 g4 ♗g6 15 ♗b5! allows White to win a pawn. After 15...♕d5 16 ♗xc6 ♕xc6 17 ♘xd4 ♕b6 18 ♕c3, followed by ♘f5, White has covered the kingside weaknesses.

14 ♕f4

Building up on the kingside, and in particular making sure that the e5-pawn is heavily protected, indeed 'overprotected', as Nimzowitsch (or, of course, his translator) used to say.

14...♖fe8

Black wants to keep some pressure on the e5-pawn, otherwise White's guardians of the overprotected pawn will be able to switch to dangerous attacking squares.

15 ♖e2

More overprotection.

15...♗f8

The bishop gets out of the way.

16 ♘g3

The knight starts to join in the attack.

16...♗xd3

Black exchanges, before White exchanges on g6, doubling the pawns.

17 cxd3

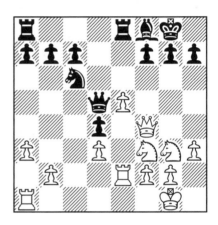

A glance of the pawn structure may at first look about equal, but in fact Black has considerable difficulties. White's e5-pawn is attacked, but it can be defended without difficulty, and Black's queen, two rooks and knight are all being defended with corresponding force. The remaining minor pieces, the white knight on g3 and the black bishop on f8, strongly favour White, though. White is going to be able to improve his pieces, while Black soon faces his limitations.

17...♖e6?

Black has to be careful, but Carlsen seems to have missed Kamsky's positional manoeuvre.

Black should overprotect his advanced but potentially weak pawn on d4. With the rook and knight both covering, Black has the chance to swing the queen around, probably to b3, making it difficult for White to set up an unimpeded attack. Black's position is well balanced, and so is White's. Play might continue something like 17...♖ad8 18 ♖ae1 (18 ♘h5 ♘e7! holds) 18...♕b3 19 ♖d2 g6! 20 ♘e4 ♗g7 (at last, the bishop does something, even if it is only plugging a pawn weakness) 21 ♘f6+ (21 ♘c5?! ♕d5 22 ♘xb6? ♖b8 naturally leaves the knight in trouble) 21...♗xf6 22 ♕xf6 (22 exf6? ♖xe1+ 23 ♘xe1 ♕e6, and Black is better) 22...♕d5 with good chances for Black of holding.

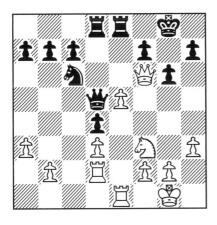

This is an unexpected result, but it all has sound positional logic. Black's bishop has been a weakness, and he would very much like to exchange the bishop for knight, to equalize the number of attackers and defenders of e5. To do this, Black would need to play ...g6 and ...♗g7, to add to the number of attackers of e5. This creates an additional weakness on the dark squares in front of the king, but provided Black keeps attacking on e5, it is difficult to divert the attack against Black's king.

Play might continue with 23 ♕h4 h5 (another weakness, but necessary) 24 ♖de2 ♖e6 25 ♘g5 (otherwise ...♖de8 and a positional deadlock) 25...♖xe5 26 ♘e4, and then probably a perpetual after 26...♔g7 27 ♕f6+ ♔g8 28 ♕h4.

Having established that ...g6 is a promising idea, could Black have tried it earlier? The problem would be that White would recapture with the pawn on f6. For example, 17...g6 18 ♘e4 ♗g7 19 ♘f6+ ♗xf6 20 exf6!, and White is better, Black facing problems on g7. Or, more drastically, 17...♖ad8 18 ♖ae1 g6?? (instead of the preparatory 18...♕b3 19 ♖d2 g6) 19 ♘e4 ♗g7 20 ♘f6+ ♗xf6 21 exf6! ♖xe2 21 ♕h6, and White gives checkmate.

18 ♘h5!

Black no longer has the chance to play ...g6.

18...♖ae8

The natural move, but White's e-pawn remains stubbornly well protected. Maybe 18...♕b3 19 ♕e4 ♖d8 as an alternative.

19 ♖ae1

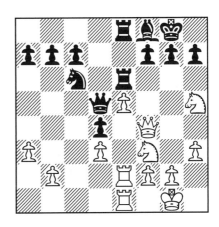

Four pieces attacking the e5-square, four defending. If White can hold on to this square, he will be better, but can he do this?

19...a5

Black is unexpectedly now in serious trouble, as the alternatives also reveal:

a) 19...f6? 20 ♕g4! (with threats on f6) 20...fxe5 (or 20...♘xe5 21 ♘xe5 fxe5 22 ♘f4!, with the same tactical theme) 21 ♘f4!, winning the exchange through a combination of knight fork and pin.

b) 19...♖g6 20 ♘h4 ♖ge6 offers a draw by repetition with 21 ♘f3?!, but White can do better with 21 ♕g4! with knight threats on f4 and f6. After 21...♘xe5 22 ♖xe5 ♖xe5 23 ♘f6+ ♔h8 24 ♘xd5 ♖xe1+ 25 ♔h2 White is ahead on the material count, and should win. There are also various ways that Black can sacrifice the exchange for a pawn, not least in this line 21...♕d8 22 ♘f6+ ♖xf6 23 exf6 ♖xe2 24 ♖xe2 ♕xf6, but such lines should in general be winning for White.

c) So how can Black hold this position? One answer is pure Steinitzian grit, with 19...♖6e7!? 20 ♕g4 ♔h8, avoiding pawn moves for as long as possible, defending pawns as far as possible, and getting away from the knight check on f6. The computer suggests good prospects to hold for Black, but the human player would sense that there ought to be something for White. The answer is to ram the e-pawn with 21 ♘f4 followed by e6, breaking open Black's kingside pawns. So 21...♕d7 (or most other queen moves) 22 e6! fxe6 23 ♘g6+ hxg6 24 ♘g5, entombing Black's king with the threat of ♕h4+.

It becomes understandable that Carlsen in effect does nothing, but Kamsky, of course, can do something.

20 ♕g4!

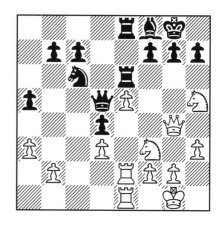

Vacating the f4-square for a knight fork, and pinning Black's g-pawn with another fork on f6. The queen and knight are working smoothly. White is gaining material by force, which must have been an unexpected surprise for Carlsen.

20...♖g6

20...♘xe5? 21 ♖xe5 wins.

21 ♘f4!

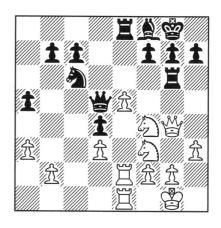

Sometimes there is no need to move the queen when it is attacked. There is generally an almost automatic response to look for checks when the queen is attacked, but on occasion a player might be slow in seeing that it may be possible to counterattack against the opposition queen.

21...♖xg4

The best chance of holding.

22 ♘xd5 ♖g6

The rook is short of squares, and Kamsky now decides he wants to take advantage of this.

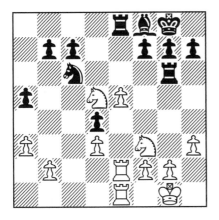

23 g4

Threatening ♘f4, and if ...♖h6, then g5 trapping the rook, with the help of the pawns and two knights.

23 ♘xc7 ♖c8 is, of course, also good, but often it is more effective to win with an extra exchange rather than an extra pawn.

23...♖d8

If 23...♖h6, then 24 g5 ♖xh3 25 ♔g2 ♖h5 26 ♘f4 again snares the rook.

If 23...h5, White must of course avoid 24 ♘f4?? hxg4 25 ♘xg6 gxf3, and Black is winning, but 24 g5 ♗e7 26 h4 is better. If Black makes an escape square with his rook, by moving his knight, then White will win both the c7- and d4-pawns.

24 ♘f4

Yes, the rook will fall.

24...♖h6

A tiny hope. He tries to provoke the pawn to g5, allowing the knight to cre-

ate a none too effective outpost on f5.

25 g5

Of course, winning the exchange is more important than allowing Black the extra square.

25...♖e6

Blocking White's e-pawn.

26 ♘xe6 fxe6

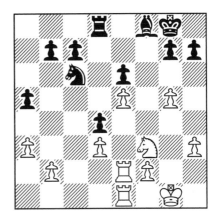

White is the exchange up. Black's position is not quite resignable just yet, so in an important knockout game he plays on. The rest of the game is not all that exciting, and Kamsky does not loosen his grip. Only brief notes for the remaining moves, therefore.

27 ♖c1 ♖d5 28 ♖c4

Adding pressure to Black's d4-pawn.

28...♗c5

Defending. The trouble is, of course, that the bishop is only defending, it can attack nothing.

29 h4

Over the next few moves, Kamsky brings forward his kingside pawns to add pressure on his opponent's kingside. He also starts to centralize his king. Carlsen attempts to find better moves for his pieces, but he cannot make much impact on his opponent.

29...♗b6 30 ♔g2 ♘e7 31 h5 ♖d8

Black can do nothing on the e5-pawn by now, but maybe he can add pressure to the f-file?

32 ♖e4

White resumes the squeeze on the pawn on d4.

32...♘f5

If 32...c5, White breaks open with 33 b4.

33 ♘h4

Aiming to exchange Black's most active piece.

33...♘e7

33...♘xh4 34 ♖xh4 ♖f8 35 f4 should not cause much technical difficulty. If 35...c5, White has 36 b4 cxb4 37 axb4 a4 38 ♔f3 a3 39 ♖h2 ♖a8 40 ♖a2, etc.

34 ♔g3 g6 35 ♔g4

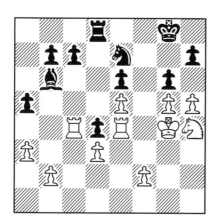

Two more king moves to add to the pressure.

35...♖d5 36 hxg6 hxg6

36...♘xg6 37 ♘xg6 hxg6 38 a4 is no better, no worse.

37 a4

Avoiding having to think about ...♖b5.

37...♔f7

Extra cover, to give the knight the chance to move.

38 ♖c1 ♖d8 39 ♖h1

Without this plan, making use of the open h-file, it could still have been difficult for White to break through.

39...♔g7

Black cannot afford the exchange of rooks after 39...♖h8 40 ♖ee1 followed by ♘g2 and ♘f4.

40 ♘g2 ♘f5

Covering the h6 option, but of course White has several alternatives here.

41 ♘f4

White's knight is even better than Black's.

41...♖e8 42 ♖ee1

To double on the h-file.

42...c5 43 ♖h3 1-0

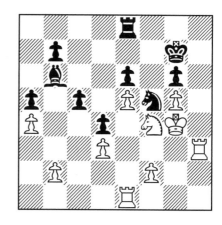

The end. ♖eh1 crashes through.

Game 25
A.Morozevich-K.Sakaev
Russian Championship, Moscow 2007
Slav Defence D10

1 d4 d5 2 c4 c6 3 ♘c3 ♘f6

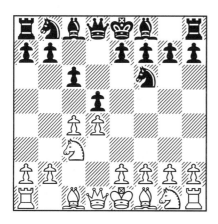

4 cxd5

For 4 e3, see Game 1, Kasimdzhanov-Kasparov, and many other games. Here 4...a6!? 5 ♘f3 b5 6 c5, as in Game 32, Inarkiev-Ni Hua, gives the closest structural similarities with the Morozevich game, in that the pawns in the centre are blocked, and cannot be further attacked by the c-pawns. In both cases, the players have to work hard to make the position interesting.

On 4 ♘f3, the traditional main line of the Slav is 4...dxc4 5 a4, but these days Black tends to prefer at top levels the Semi-Slav with 4...e6.

In this game, though, we reach the Exchange Variation of the Slav. Strong players, and of course Morozevich is an extremely strong player, may use this as part of a 'plus over equals' philosophy. As the game develops, White is unlikely to lose, but if he finds that he has even the slightest chance of an edge, he can grind away indefinitely.

A lower-graded player might get anxious about the strength of his opponent, and use the Exchange Variation as an excellent chance to keep the play dull, equal, and, all being well, as a good drawing option. Among stronger players, the player with the white pieces might simply want to take the percentages. The Slav is difficult to play for an attack with White, and it will take a lot of effort to try to find an edge against good opposition, and this would in any case lead to some degree of risk. Why not play a simple and symmetrical line, with little chances of a loss, aiming for a standard 55% score with White without taking up much effort? Morozevich, as we shall soon see, tends to score rather more than 55% in this line.

4...cxd5

Black cannot avoid the symmetry: 4...♘xd5?! 5 e4 keeps White ahead in development.

Quite often, Black players may want to avoid the Exchange Variation, either avoiding the Slav completely, or, if aiming for a Semi-Slav, kicking off with 1 d4 d5 2 c4 e6 3 ♘c3 ♘f6 4 ♘f3 c6. The danger for this approach is that the Orthodox Exchange Variation, with 4 cxd5 exd5, is if anything more pleasant for White than the Slav Exchange.

5 ♗f4

A useful developing square. Morozevich is being careful not to commit the knight with 5 ♘f3, although that move is, of course, possible.

5 ♗g5 is worth considering, though less popular than ♗f4. White is aiming for a slight edge.

5...♘c6

Natural development.

6 e3

6 ♘b5? ♕a5+ is a waste of time. Now, though, the knight threat at least forces the opponent to consider this possibility.

6...a6

A few days later, Grischuk tried 6...♗f5, again against Morozevich. After 7 ♗b5 e6 8 ♕a4 ♕b6 9 ♘f3 ♗e7 10 ♘e5 0-0 11 ♗xc6 ♖fc8 12 0-0 bxc6 13 ♖fc1 c5 14 dxc5 ♖xc5 15 b4 ♖cc8 16 a3, Black should probably be equal. In A.Morozevich-A.Grischuk, Russian Championship, Moscow 2007, Grischuk seriously overplayed his position with 16...d4? 17 exd4 ♕xd4 18 ♘c6 ♕d7 19 b5, and Morozevich quickly won. However, other lines, such as 16...♘g4!? 17 ♕d7 ♘xe5 18 ♕xe7 ♘d3, would have led to comfortable play for Black.

The quiet pawn push, with 6...a6, is aiming for great solidity, and perhaps later some pawn counterplay with ...b5. First of all, White cannot start an attack with either ♘b5 or ♗b5.

7 ♖c1

A favourite with Morozevich.

7 ♘f3 has been tried several times in recent years, although often only as a prelude to a quick draw. Black can squash out any thoughts of his opponent of setting up pressure with ♘e5 by playing 7...♗g4, and exchanging on f3. With such a fixed and stable pawn structure, there is not much chance of taking any real advantage of the bishop-pair.

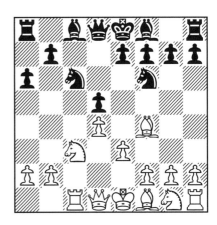

7...♗g4

Black wants to keep play interesting.

7...♗f5 is possible, with no realistic chances of an advantage for Black, but every chance of holding the draw with careful play. For example, 8 ♘f3 ♖c8 9 ♗e2 e6 10 0-0 ♗d6 11 ♗xd6 ♕xd6 12 ♘a4 0-0 13 ♘c5 ♖c7 14 0-0, draw agreed, A.Morozevich-V.Malakhov, Sochi 2005.

8 f3

Morozevich gives his first indication that he is not going to accept a quick draw. Indeed, soon play gets lively.

8 ♕b3 ♘a5 9 ♕c2 e6 gives good chances of equality.

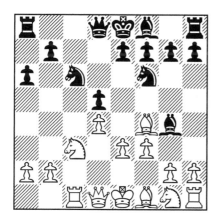

8...♗d7

The bishop retreats to a good defensive square, happy that White has no chance of creating pressure with ♘g1-f3-e5.

9 g4

Are those kingside pawns going to become strong or weak? Naturally there are arguments for both sides.

Morozevich some time earlier had tried 9 ♘ge2 e6 10 ♗g3 ♖c8 11 ♘f4 ♘a5 12 ♗e2 ♘c4 13 ♗xc4 ♖xc4 14 ♘d3 ♗e7 15 ♘d3 ♗e7 15 ♕b3 b5 16 0-0 0-0 17 ♘e5 ♖c8 in A.Morozevich-P.Leko, Wijk aan Zee 2005, but was unable to demonstrate a lasting edge. The game was eventually drawn. Morozevich tried 18 ♘e2 ♗b6 19 ♗h4 ♕b6 (and if 20 ♗g3 ♕b6, repeating), but possibly 18 ♗h4!? immediately might improve.

9...e6

9...♖c8 is possible, but Black would probably want, after 10 h4, to play 10...e6 anyway.

10 h4

There is no real point in playing 10 g5 just yet, in view of 10...♘h5. To jus-

tify White's kingside pawn push, he needs to keep going with h4 and h5 first, giving Black no time to respond with ...♘h5 after g5.

10...♗e7

To complete his development.

11 ♗d3

11 ♕b3 is possible, but after 11...b5 White's queen is arguably on the wrong side of the board.

11...0-0?!

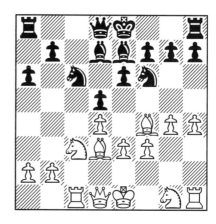

Could this be premature castling? Morozevich would like to argue so. Sometimes it is best to think about castling, but only to make the final decision later. Here if 11...♖c8 12 h5 h6!, Black has defended successfully, keeping the rook on the h-file and making it difficult for White to play g5.

White can instead try quiet development with 12 a3 ♕b6 13 ♖h2, keeping the guesswork open on both sides as to whether White is ready to play h5, or whether Black has decided it is now time to castle, with no other constructive moves being available:

a) Black could try a tactical break with 13...e5!? 14 dxe5 ♘xe5 15 ♖hc2 ♘c4, leading to likely equality.

b) Black can try 13...♘a5?!, but this

seems less effective. White sets up some knight galloping with 14 ♘a4 ♖xc1 15 ♘xb6 ♖xd1+ 16 ♔xd1 ♗b5 17 ♗xb5+ axb5 18 ♘c8! ♘c4 19 ♖c2 ♔d7 (otherwise 19...♗f8 20 ♘a7! is unpleasant) 20 ♘xe7 ♔xe7 21 ♘e2, leading to an edge.

12 ♗b1

With obvious intentions of setting up a queen and bishop battery on the b1-h7 diagonal.

White's g1-knight is undeveloped, but with the help of a couple of moves to bring it into play, it could become effective in a kingside attack. Indeed, 12 ♘ge2! looks more accurate, with thoughts of helping a later kingside pawn push with ♘g3. If 12...♘e8 13 ♗g3 ♖c8 14 a3, White does not have a drastic edge, given that the pawn structure is symmetrical, and Black's pieces are developed, but he should still have some chances of a nibble. White's ♗d3 move could have been delayed until later.

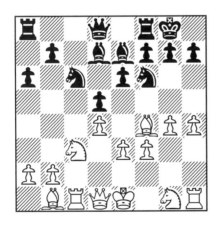

12...♕b6

In a later game, I.Khenkin-E.Postny, Maalot-Tarshiha 2008, Black was tempted to force the White king to move with 12...♘e8 13 h5 ♗h4+?! 14

♔f1, but this was totally unnecessary. The king is as safe on f1 as on e1. After 14...♗g5 15 ♗xg5 ♕xg5 16 f4 ♕e7 17 ♕c2 White had a strong attack, and later won.

Sakaev's move seems better.

13 ♖h2

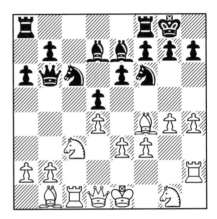

Defending on the rank, while attacking on the file, a useful combination.

13...♖fc8

Black is still holding the balance, but he is defending, not attacking. If White cannot force a kingside breakthrough, then in the longer term Black will have useful chances on the queenside.

In other words, Black is close to equal, and White must be careful not to drift.

14 h5

There are many sensible but quiet moves, none of which creates an edge. If, for example, 14 ♕d3, with thoughts of g5, Black can simply push the queen away with 14...♘b4, nothing gained, nothing lost, for either side.

White could consider covering the b4-square with 14 a3, but this weakens the light squares, and 14...♘a5 allows Black to keep the balance.

14 g5 ♘h5 15 ♕d3 g6 is again possi-

ble for White, but does not create any real initiative.

14...♗e8

14...h6!? is possible. The tactical point is that White cannot break through on the kingside with 15 g5? hxg5 16 ♗xg5 in view of 16...♘g4!:

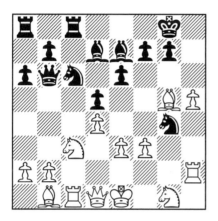

a) If now 17 ♗xe7 ♘xh2 18 ♗d6 ♘xd4! 19 ♗xh2 ♕xb2 20 ♕d2 ♕xd2+ 21 ♔xd2 ♘b5, and Black is ahead on material.

b) Black also keeps a slight positional edge after 17 fxg4 ♗xg5, with pressure on the e3- and d4-pawns. If, for example, 18 ♖e2 ♘xd4 19 exd4 ♗xc1 20 ♕xc1 ♕xd4, and Black is better. Thus 18 ♕d3 ♘xd4! is critical (White could also transpose with 17 ♕d3 ♗xg5 18 fxg5 ♘xd4!):

b1) Then 19 ♕h7+ ♔f8 20 h6 (there are no other effective attacking moves) 20...♘f3+! wins by force for Black.

b2) Therefore he has to play 19 h6 immediately, but Black still wins after 19...♗xe3 20 ♕xh7+ (20 hxg7 f5!) 20...♔f8 21 hxg7+ ♔e7, the king escaping and White's passed pawn being ineffective.

b3) If White tries to side-track, avoiding checks by 19 ♔d1, then 19...♘b5! is

good for Black.

White must not play so hastily. Indeed, 15 ♘h3! keeps reasonable attacking chances. If 15...♗f8 16 ♖g2 ♔h8, then maybe 17 a3!?, aiming to play ♕d3 or ♕c2 without any threats of ...♘b4.

Perhaps it is this quiet plan that Sakaev would have been concerned about. Pushing a pawn in front of the king opens up potential weaknesses, and the pawn push is ideally to be avoided for as long as possible.

15 ♕d3

The computer's initial suggestion is 15 g5 ♘d7 16 h6 g6, but then the only way to attack would be to try to give mate on g7, and unfortunately the bishop can easily cover with ...♗f8. Often it is better in defence to allow one weak square in front of the king, but without a pawn exchange, rather than try to defend against open lines, such as the h-file or the b1-h7 diagonal. This theme recurs throughout the rest of the game.

The text move is natural enough, but 15 a3 would probably have been more accurate.

15...♘b4

To gain time for the defence with ...♘d7 and ...♘f8.

16 ♕d2

He is not yet ready to repeat with 16 ♕d1 ♘c6.

16...♘d7

Black continues his plan. A knight on f8, next to the king, is extremely difficult to dislodge, and with knight and a couple of bishops to defend the king and pawns, he can cover White's queen attack. The only ways of trying to attack the king would be a piece sacrifice or putting pressure on the g7-square.

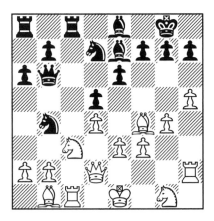

17 ♘h3?!

Morozevich seems stumped by Sakaev's accurate defence, and for the time being he drifts around. It is easy enough to demonstrate, in retrospect, that this knight move must have been a positional error, since before too long Morozevich switched around the attack with ♘g1 and ♘f3 (after f4 with the pawn), but without gaining any positional advantage.

17 g5!?, gaining space with the kingside pawns, looks better. Then after 17...♘f8 18 ♘ge2 White has improved his coordination. White could start to coordinate his rooks with the help of

♔f2, and maybe think either of a central pawn push with e4 or put pressure on the g- and h-files.

17...♘f8

With extra cover on the h7-square. White will have to do more than simply attack on the b1-h7 diagonal.

18 ♗g5

18 h6 is again to be considered, but again 18...g6, followed later by ...f6, blocks out most attacks.

By contrast, an exchange of dark-squared bishops will be of more concern to Black, though it is still not so clear that White is then better.

18...♕d8

18...♗d6 19 f4 f6 20 ♗h4 ♗f7 gives White more space on the kingside. Whether this is likely to convert into any real initiative is open to question.

19 ♗xe7

The exchange of the dark-squared bishop will happen sooner or later. White has additional freedom with his kingside pawns, but this will not lead to any significant advantage.

19...♕xe7

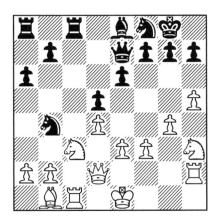

Black has defended carefully, and is close to equal. All White has is some extra space with his pawns on the kingside, while Black can set up some pressure on the queenside when the rooks have been doubled on the c-file.

20 f4!?

The pawn push starts.

20...f6

And Sakaev sets up his kingside barriers.

20...♕h4+?! looks tempting, but after 21 ♕f2 ♕xg4 22 ♘g5! White threatens to trap the queen with ♖h4. Black can survive with 22...e5 23 ♖h4 ♕d7 25 fxe5, but this is not what he really wants. Here Black could instead exchange queens with 21...♕xf2+ 22 ♘xf2, but White keeps a slight edge. With the possibilities of g5 and ♘g4, followed with h6, White if anything has better chances of kingside pressure without the queens.

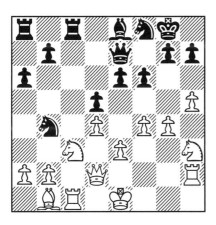

21 ♔f2

It is very difficult to play with complete accuracy a string of strategic moves, without making an unnecessary move with loss of tempo. A perfectionist might well be wondering whether this king move was necessary, especially with the king getting in the way of the second rank (queen to f2 or g2).

21 ♘g1!? might be better, and after

quiet play by Black, White has avoided the king move. White played this knight move next time round, so the question is one of timing.

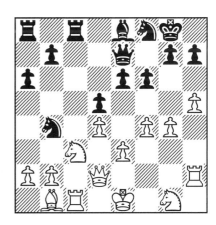

If Black wanted to try to open up the game, before White has the chance of playing ♘f3, then he could try 21...e5 22 dxe5 fxe5 23 fxe5 (23 ♘ge2 is to be considered) 23...♕xe5 24 ♘f3 ♕g3+ 25 ♕f2, and Black's isolated d-pawn is under pressure, whether the queens are on the board or off. If, for example, 25...♕d6, White has 26 a3 ♘c6 27 ♗a2 with an edge.

Psychologically, it is of course difficult for White to retreat to his earlier knight move, ♘g1-h3, and return with ♘h3-g1 and ♘g1-f3. Very few players would want to consider it, and fewer would actually play this line. Here too it is doubtful whether White would have been more than level after 21...♖c7 22 ♘f3 ♕ac8 anyway.

21...♕d6

Possibly Sakaev felt he wanted to prevent f5.

21...♖c7 is again about equal. See too the note to Black's 26th, below.

22 ♘g1

Redeveloping.

22 e4?! is visually aggressive, but leaves far too many weaknesses on the kingside and in the centre after 22...dxe4 23 ♘xe4 ♕b6.

22...♖c7 23 ♘f3 ♖ac8

Natural moves by both sides.

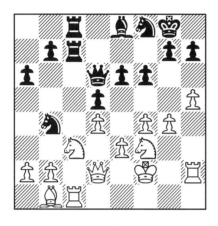

24 h6

White wants to weaken Black's dark-squared pawns on g7, f6 and e5. He is quite probably not expecting that Black would allow the opening of the h-file, but the ...g6 reply will weaken the f6-pawn.

24 g5 f5 is at best equal for White, since if he were to try to take advantage of the e5-square with 25 ♘e5, Black can offer the exchange of knights with 25...♘d7 or 25...♘c6. White would need to be careful about Black's pressure on the c-file, helped perhaps by ...b5.

24...g6

Of course, Black wants to keep the files closed.

25 a3

If 25 e4?! dxe4 26 ♘xe4 ♕e7 27 ♖xc7 ♖xc7 28 g5 ♘d5, and Black's knight gains a critical defensive square. After 29 gxf6 ♘xf6 30 ♘xf6+ ♕xf6, Black has if anything slightly the better of equality, White's three pawns in the centre

and on the kingside each being isolated.

25...♘c6

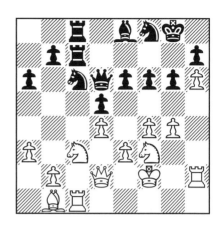

26 e4

He plays to continue the attack, necessarily so.

26 g5?! f5 might look at first to be equal, but Black now even has a slight edge, White's a-pawn push having weakened his queenside. Black could consider at various stages ...♘a5, or possibly ...b5-b4.

26...♕d8

Bringing the queen back to a safer square, in case of e5, or, after ...dxe4 then ♘xe4. Maybe there is a slight question mark over Black's 21...♕d6. Was this the most accurate?

26...dxe4 27 ♘xe4 ♕d8 28 g5 makes some progress for White on the dark squares.

27 ♗a2

White adds a little pressure first before pushing with e5: 27 e5 b5 is premature.

27...♘e7

Black decides to be suspicious of opening up the centre with 27...dxe4 28 ♘xe4 ♔h8 29 g5 f5 30 ♘f6. There are too many dangerous open lines after, for example, 30...♘d7 31 ♘xd7 ♕xd7 d5!. Here the computer gives an interesting tactical idea with 29...♘e5?! 30 ♖xc7 ♘g4+ 31 ♔g3 ♖xc7 (or 31...♕xc7 32 ♖e2) 32 ♖e2, but Black's knight is exposed and does not attack effectively. The strong human player will always be careful about such desperado tactics, and sometimes they work, but not here.

28 e5

White decides it is time to close up the kingside pawns, and hopes that he can make some advantage of his extra squares.

28 exd5?! ♘xd5 29 ♗xd5 exd5 would not be so appropriate. This would be fine if he had castled, and his kingside pawns had not pressed forward, but just here, there are too many hits on the kingside pawns: for example, ...♕d6, ...♗d7, ...♘e6, and Black can, of course, use his rooks on the e-file.

28...f5

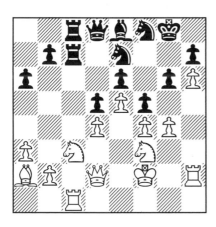

Black is happy to block the kingside. Indeed, he might even have been thinking of trying to play for a queenside edge, French-style.

The pawn structure is no longer symmetrical in the centre, once White has played e4 and e5, as White's d4-

pawn cannot be protected by any pawns, while the corresponding black pawn on d5 is protected by the e6-pawn. Thus White has to be careful.

29 ♖g1

29 g5? would be a positional blunder. White would have no chance of an advantage on either side, while Black could gradually make a few useful pin-pricks on the queenside.

Morozevich instead wants to open up lines with gxf5.

29...♖c6?!

It is difficult to work out what Black is planning with this move. Maybe he is just deciding that it is equal, and that all he needs to do is to hold the balance for a draw.

A more constructive approach, perhaps, would be to advance his queenside pawns with 29...b5, followed by ...a5 and even ...♖b7, by now a better square for the rook than c6.

30 ♗b1

Morozevich by contrast is playing rather more directly, putting pressure on f5. Even so, any possible edge for White would seem microscopic.

30...♔h8

Moving away from the g-file.

31 ♖hg2

A bit more pressure on f5. 31 gxf5 ♘xf5 32 ♗xf5 exf5 would have been ineffective in terms of winning. Black can plug the gap with ...♘e6, with comfortable play.

31...fxg4

Do not forget that Sakaev has his own ideas of active play. This is a convenient time to exchange pawns, then cement his kingside, and gradually switch the focus to the queenside.

32 ♖xg4 ♗f7

The bishop is now going to be a 'big pawn' on f7 or g8. If this is required to hold up the defensive pawn structure, then so be it. The bishop plays an important role.

33 ♘e2

The knight gradually shifts over to the kingside attack.

33...♘d7

While Black thinks of starting counter-pressure on the queenside. It is only because the bishop can defend h7 that Black can release the knight from f8.

34 ♘g5

More pressure, but Black is holding.

34...♗g8

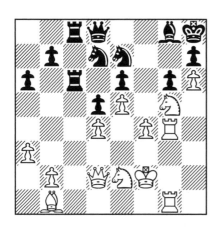

Sakaev has built up a strong fortress, and it is extremely difficult to see a clear breakthrough. Indeed, if anything, Black could even be better. If, for example, Black has the chance of playing ...♘b6, the initiative could start to swing round to him.

35 ♖4g3

The rook needs to cover both sides of the board.

35...♘b6

The counterplay starts.

36 b3

So White covers both squares, but loses control of the a3-square.

36...♕f8

With pressure on the a3, f4 and h6 pawns. It is easy enough to cover two pawns, but three starts to create problems.

37 a4

A slightly reluctant pawn push.

37...♘d7

The knight manoeuvre to b6 has done its job, provoking White into playing b3 and a4, and now Sakaev finds a fresh manoeuvre, bringing the knight eventually to b4, via d7, b8 and c6.

He is not interested as yet in taking the h6-pawn, which is dangerous, opening up the h-file.

38 a5

Morozevich would like to play b4, but ...♘b6 would be a good reply. Hence an extra pawn move, although in structural terms it is not particularly desirable. The run of play is in favour of Sakaev.

38...♖6c7

Preparing his alternative knight manoeuvre.

39 ♖f3

He decides he needs to overprotect the f4-pawn. The h6-pawn is not too great a concern.

39...♘b8

Continuing his plan.

40 b4

Probably more to keep the pawns guarded, rather than to try to take the initiative.

40...♘bc6?!

The last move before the time control, and not the most accurate. Another knight move, 40...♘f5!, keeps White under pressure, with the rook-pair making it difficult for White to cover weaknesses on the b- and c-files.

41 ♖c1!

With the chance of ♖c5, blocking most of Black's queenside play.

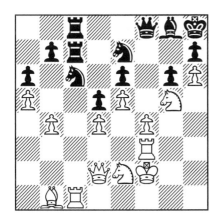

41...♕xh6?!

This is very committal, almost surprisingly so just after the time control. It is often difficult to establish what is going on psychologically when a player suddenly does something unusual or controversial. Black has disdained the pawn grab for so many moves, but now he plays it, giving his opponent the first chance he has had of a genuine attack.

Probably Sakaev is making something of a reflex reaction after his previous slight error, allowing White to bring his rook to the c-file. If he can do nothing more on the queenside, the only possible chance he has of winning is on the kingside, and so he takes his risks.

41...♘f5 42 ♖c5 is safe for Black, but he is not necessarily playing for a win here.

42 ♖h3

He must use the h-file, and not 42 f5? ♕h2+.

42...♕f8

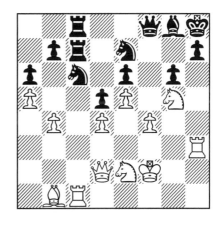

Back to the f-file.

43 f5!

A second sacrifice to vaporize a second pawn. White needs to advance the knight to f4 in order to keep the momentum of his attack, but he cannot do this if the pawn is blocked there.

43 ♖ch1 ♘f5 leaves Black ahead.

43...♘xf5

If 43...exf5, there will be more sacrifices coming up. The pawn sacrifices so far by White have been to open up lines for his pieces, so that he can start to think of a piece attack. The second phase would be to destroy Black's pawn defences, with piece sacrifices, and then aim for checkmate:

a) 44 ♘xh7?! is enterprising, but there is no need to hurry. If Black's pawn can be forced to reach h5, there will be even better sacrifices there.

b) After 44 ♖ch1 h5 45 ♘f4 ♕e8 46 ♖xh5+! gxh5 47 ♘xh5, White will win either king or queen. Or 45...♘d8 46 ♘xh5 gxh5 47 ♖xh5+ ♔g7 48 ♘h7 with another breakthrough.

It is more natural for Black to keep open the f-file for pieces. After all, White's king is still vulnerable on the f-file.

44 ♘f4

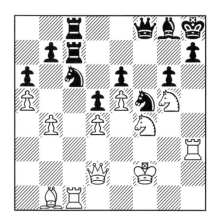

From a blocked pawn structure, and following a few clearance sacrifices, all of White's pieces are attacking. All except for the king, which would rather be well hidden.

This position is now critical. If there is any weakness in Morozevich's sacrificial play, either Sakaev will find a refutation, or at least hold the balance, or alternatively his position will fold.

44...♕e8

Black crawls back to passive defence once he has grabbed the pawn, but could he have played more actively?

a) After 44...♕xb4 45 ♕xb4 ♘xb4 46 ♘xg6+ ♔g7 47 ♖xc7+ ♖xc7 48 ♘f4 Black is two pawns up in the early endgame, but it is clear that White's pieces are far the more active, and that Black's bishop on g8 is by now highly ineffective:

a1) If now 48...♘xd4, White can win a rook with a few tactics after 49 ♘gxe6+ ♗xe6 50 ♘xe6+ ♗xe6 51 ♖xh7+.

a2) To cover the knight check on e6, Black can try 48...♗e7, but White still plays 49 ♘fxe6+ when Black has a choice of recapture:

a21) 49...♗xe6 50 ♖xh7+ ♔g8 51 ♗xf5 ♖xh7 52 ♗xh7+ ♔h8 53 ♘xe6 ♔xh7 54 ♘d8 ♔g8 (but not 54...♘c6? 55 ♘xc6 bxc6 56 ♔e3, and White will win the king and pawn ending) 55 ♔e3! (55 ♘xb7? ♘c6!, and Black eventually draws) 55...♔f8 56 ♘xb7 ♔e7, and White is now a safe pawn up.

a22) 49...♖xe6 50 ♗xf5 ♖h6 51 ♖b3, and again White is better, although as before it is not absolutely clear that Black will lose.

In practical terms, 44...♕xb4 is unsatisfactory, except only for use in emergency.

b) 44...♘fxd4! is far more combative, grabbing a second pawn again, but also attacking, and breaking open White's central pawn structure. White still has heavy attacking forces, and Black is relying on the pin on f4:

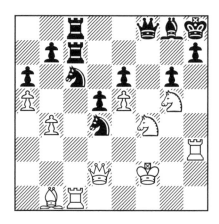

b1) 45 ♘f3 is a way of breaking the pin, with great complications after 45...♔g7, a computer suggestion. The human player might well feel more at ease as Black after 45...♖g7!? 46 ♘xd4 g5, breaking White's attack quickly, and giving Black an advantage.

b2) 45 ♔g2! is more secure, ending up as a probable draw after 45...♕xb4

46 ♘xg6+ ♔g7 47 ♕f4 ♘f5 48 ♗xf5. If then 48...♕xf4 48 ♘xf4 exf5 50 ♘ge6+ ♗xe6 51 ♘xe6+ ♔g6 52 ♖ch1, and White holds with reasonable care. Naturally he cannot force a win in this endgame after so many pawn sacrifices. Alternatively, 48...exf5 49 ♕xf5, and it ends up in a perpetual check after the continuation 49...♕d2+ 50 ♔g3 ♔e3+ 51 ♕d2+.

One gets the feeling through many of Morozevich's games that while he is in his element over the board in such complicated tactical play, few others can stand the pace.

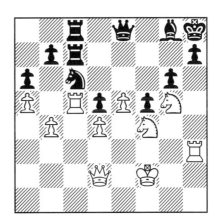

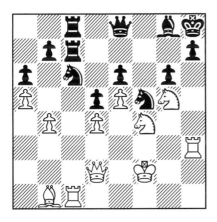

45 ♗xf5

White is more than happy to block the f-file.

45...exf5

Black elects to keep as many pawns as possible on the kingside.

45...gxf5 weakens the g-file and the h5-square.

46 ♖c5

White has in compensation the strong passed e-pawn, and later in the game this decides the result. First he consolidates his c-file.

46 e6? ♘e5! 47 ♖xc7 ♘g4+ is premature, though.

46...♖d8?!

A more active try is 46...♘e7 with difficult play. Black's idea is to open the valve with the knight, allowing an exchange of rooks, and then counterplay with ...♕a4. Later, Black will be able to close the valve with ...♘c6. The critical line is 47 ♘fe6! ♖xc5 48 bxc5:

a) There are then various sacrificial threats on h7. If Black tries 48...h5, White keeps the initiative flowing with 49 ♘e4! f4 50 ♘f6 (50 ♕xf4? ♘f5 favours Black, while 50 ♘d6 ♕d7 is less clear than the main line) 50...♕f7 (or 50...♗xe6 51 ♘xe8 ♗xh3 52 ♘f6 with advantage to White) 51 ♘g5 ♕f8 52 ♕f4, and White is pressing hard.

b) 48...♘c6 49 ♘xh7 ♗xh7 50 ♕h6 regains the piece with advantage after, for example, 50...♕g8 51 ♕h4 ♕f7 52 ♘g5 ♕e7 53 ♕f4.

c) A potentially more dangerous try would be 48...♗xe6, and if 49 ♘xh7?, Black has 49...f4! 50 ♘f6+ ♗xh3 51 ♘xe8 ♖xe8 52 ♕xf4 ♔g8!, and White would have overplayed his sacrifices. However, with 49 ♖xh7+ ♔g8 50 ♔g1 (there may be other good moves) 50...♕d7 (50...♕a4 51 ♖xe7 wins for White by positional means) 51 ♕h2 ♔f8

52 ♖h8+ ♗g8 53 ♕h7 ♔e8 53 ♕f7+ ♔d8 55 ♘e6+ ♕xe6 59 ♕xe6 White wins.

So Black's play seems not quite satisfactory in this line.

47 ♕e3

The queen adds her force behind the passed pawn.

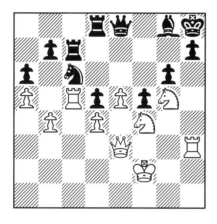

47...h5

Such a move must be an encouragement for the attacker. There is a clear danger of a knight sacrifice on h5, and the g6-pawn is also weakened. White in the game does not sacrifice on these squares, but Black's pieces are forced to take extra cover of these squares, adding to the defensive problems.

Black can still set up a tight ship with 47...♖g7 48 e6 ♖d6! (48...♘xb4?! 49 ♕e5 ♘c6 50 ♕f6 is too greedy; if 50...♕e7?? 51 ♘g6 mate, an attractive double pin), and White has no obvious breakthrough. However, the exchange sacrifice, 49 ♖xc6!, maintains the pressure, opening up the e5-square for White's queen. Then 49...bxc6 50 ♕e5 ♖d8 51 e7 is reminiscent of the game, and just as difficult for Black, and 49...♕xc6 50 ♕e5 threatens the ♘xg6 mating idea, and gives Black nothing to

try, other than to aim for a perpetual: 50...♕c2+ 51 ♔g3 ♕b3+ 52 ♔h4! ♕d1 53 ♘xg6+ hxg6 54 ♔g3+ wins for White.

48 e6

Progress! As well as advancing the passed pawn, White is planning to play ♕e5+, obviously with preparation by an exchange sacrifice on c6.

48...♖e7

If, for example, 48...♖g7, White has 49 ♖xc6 bxc6 50 ♕e5. Black is in fact a tempo ahead on the game, but this is of no great significance. The computer gives only quiet moves with the other rook, with 50...♖a8, 50...♖b8, or 50...♖c8, and White could then continue his plan of constriction. Black is moving close to zugzwang.

49 ♖xc6!

This simplest, and the most efficient.

White also has a tactical win after 49 ♘f7+!?, with complicated twists and turns. There is a hidden and spectacular queen sacrifice after 49...♗xf7 50 ♘xh5 ♗xe6 51 ♕h6+ ♖g7 52 ♕g7+!! ♖xg7 53 ♘f6+ ♖h7 54 ♖xh7 mate. White still needs to subdue Black's play after 49...♖xf7! 50 ♘xg6+ ♔g7 51 ♕g5 ♖f6, though, but he has a winning attack after 52 ♘f4+ ♖g6 53 ♕xh5 ♖xe6 54 ♖g3+ ♔f8 55 ♕g5 ♗f7 56 ♕g7+ ♔f7 57 ♘xe6.

It is better, though, when given the choice, to play simple wins rather than complicated wins.

49...bxc6

Or 49...♕xc6? 50 ♕xe5+ ♖g7 51 ♘xg6 mate.

50 ♕e5+

The critical check. Note how White has complete control over the dark squares.

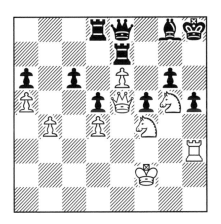

50...♖g7

Forced.

51 ♕f6

The queen finds an even better dark-coloured square.

52...♖b8

Black is only a toehold away from a catastrophic piece loss. If the queen moves into 'safety', White has ♘xg6 mate. If the bishop moves, with 52...♗h7, White wins with 53 ♘f7+. Only the other rook may move.

52 e7

The pawn pushes harder.

52...♗h7

Again, 52...♕xe7? 53 ♘xg6 mate.

52...♖xb4 allows White to queen the pawn after 53 ♘xg6+ ♕xg6 54 ♕xg6 ♖xg6 55 ♖xh5+ ♔g7 56 e8♕.

53 ♖e3

Another thump on the e-file.

53...♔g8

If 53...♖xb4, then 54 ♕f8+.

54 ♕e6+

Forcing the king back.

54...♔h8

What now? The computer even sug-

gests that the position is drawn, but with a little finesse White still has a win.

55 ♕f6

White repeats, mainly one suspects to gain time on the clock.

55...♔g8 56 ♕e6+ ♔h8 57 ♕d6!

Second time round, Morozevich uses the zugzwang.

57...♖a8 58 ♕c7

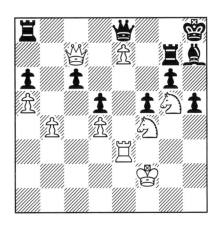

A throat-choker. White no doubt has other winning lines, but planning to exchange the knight for the light-squared bishop, and then promoting the pawn, is quickest.

58...♖g8

Black could last longer with 58...♗g8 59 ♖e5 ♗f7 60 ♘xf7+ ♖xf7 61 ♕b7 ♔h7 62 ♕xa8 ♖xa8 63 e8♕ ♖xe8 64 ♖xe8, but White, a knight up in return for a few ineffective pawns, will win. If 64...♖b7, then simply 65 ♘d3.

59 ♘fe6 1-0

If now 59...♕b8, White has 60 ♘f7 mate, and after 59...♖g7 60 ♘xg7 ♔xg7 White several ways to win, maybe the simplest being 61 ♖e6 followed by ♖c6.

Game 26
Wang Yue-S.Movsesian
Pamplona 2007
Queen's Gambit Declined D38

1 d4 ♘f6 2 c4 e6 3 ♘c3 ♗b4 4 ♘f3

For alternative lines against the Nimzo-Indian, see 4 ♕c2 in Game 12, Bareev-Efimenko, and 4 e3 in Game 15, Sokolov-Polgar.

4...d5

The Ragozin Variation. It can be reached via either a Queen's Gambit or, as here, the Nimzo-Indian. Naturally there is a mixture of both sets of ideas.

More standard Nimzo-Indian plans would include 4...c5, 4...0-0, or perhaps 4...♘e4.

5 cxd5

White treats it as a version of the Queen's Gambit Exchange Variation, normally played with ...♗e7 rather than ...♗b4. The Nimzo bishop pins the White knight on c3, but also allows Black's knight to be pinned on f6 by ♗g5. This allows sharper play for Black, but in return is less solid.

5...exd5

5...♘xd5 and 5...♕xd5 would be playable, but slightly less trustworthy.

6 ♗g5

Continuing the main line.

6 ♕a4+ ♘c6 7 ♘e5 may be a temptation, but after 7...♗d7 Black is comfortably equal. If 8 ♘xd7 ♕xd7, Black is ahead in development, making White's bishop-pair of little significance. If instead 8 ♘xc6 ♗xc3+ 9 bxc3 ♗xc6 10 ♕a3 ♘e4, Black is equal.

6...0-0

Black wants to play ...c5 without the preparatory ...♘bd7.

The standard main line is 6...♘bd7 7 e3 c5 8 ♗d3 ♕a5 9 ♕c2 c4 10 ♗f5 0-0 11 0-0, maybe slightly favouring White. The bishops often drop back to h4 and g3.

6...h6 7 ♗h4 (7 ♗xf6 is level) 7...g5 8 ♗g3 ♘e4 is the most uncompromising line for Black, quickly gaining space with his pieces, though before the remaining pieces have developed, and leaving the king open.

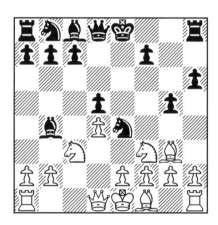

After 9 ♘d2 ♘xc3 10 ♗xc3 ♗xc3 11 ♖c1 ♗b2 12 ♗xc7 ♕e7 13 ♗d6 ♕e6 14 ♖b1 ♗c3, the general impression might well be that White keeps an edge, but it has been difficult for him to prove this.

The endgame seems better for White after 15 ♗a3 ♘c6 16 e3 ♗xd4 17 ♗b5 ♗e5 18 0-0 ♗d6 19 ♗xd6 ♕xd6 20 ♘e4 ♕e5 21 ♕xd5 ♕xd5 22 ♘f6+ ♔f8

23 ♘xd5 ♘e7 24 ♘c7 ♖b8. Following 25 f4 ♗f5 26 e4 ♗xe4 27 ♖be1 ♘d5 28 ♖xe4 ♘xc7 29 ♗c4 ♘e5, I.Sokolov-A.Onischuk, Poikovsky 2006, White kept a very slight endgame edge, but Onischuk carefully held the draw. Less than a fortnight later, Sargissian demonstrated a much clearer endgame advantage with 25 e4 ♔g7 26 ♖fd1 a6 27 ♗f1 ♗g4 28 f3 ♖hc8 29 ♖bc1 ♗h5 30 ♔f2, and duly won in G.Sargissian-K.Landa, German League 2006. White's advantage in this was to create an attacking force with the kingside pawns, rather than, as in the Sokolov game, concentrating on his pieces.

7 e3

White develops his second bishop.

7 ♕b3!? looks promising, but seems almost unexplored.

7...c5

Movsesian aims for immediate central counterplay.

Mimicking the Queen's Gambit Exchange with, for example 7...c6 8 ♗d3 ♘bd7 9 0-0, seems promising for White. The bishop on b4 is not adding to the defence, when compared with the bishop on e7 in the QGD.

8 dxc5

White forces Black to decide how to recover the pawn. Other moves allow Black to equalize.

8...♘bd7

8...♗xc5? 9 ♗xf6 ♕xf6 10 ♕xd5 allows White to win a pawn for inadequate compensation.

9 ♖c1

White has tried 9 ♗e2 ♗xc3+ 10 bxc3 ♘xc5 11 ♗h4 ♘ce4 12 ♕d4 ♕a5 13 ♕b4 ♕c7, drawn in V.Loginov-G.Kuzmin, Tashkent 1987, without much progress. Wang Yue plays some-

thing far more ambitious, and this, indeed, is the current main line.

9...♕a5

Black needs to keep up pressure on the diagonal, otherwise he is worse. 9...♘xc5 10 ♕d4 ♗xc3+ 11 ♕xc3 leaves White happy.

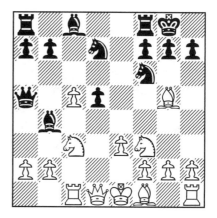

10 a3!?

This is not the only try, but it is certainly the most enterprising. White sacrifices the exchange, but keeps the extra pawn, and sets up a dangerous queenside pawn majority.

Alternatively:

a) 10 ♗xf6 ♘xf6 11 ♕d4 ♗xc5 12 ♕d2 ♗e6 is about equal. White can gain a pawn with 13 ♘xd5 ♕xd2+ 14 ♘xd2 ♗xd5 15 ♖xc5 ♖fc8, but it is unlikely that he will keep it permanently.

b) 10 ♘d2 leads to a few minor tactics after 10...♘e4 11 ♘cxe4 dxe4 12 a3 ♗xc5 13 b4 (White can perhaps try something else here) 13...♗xb4 14 axb4 ♕xg5 15 ♘xe4 ♕e7 16 ♕d4, but once Black has brought the knight into play with, for example, 16...♘b6, he is equal.

10...b6, tried a couple of times, is inventive. Play continued with 11 c6 d4 12 cxd7 dxc3 13 bxc3 ♗xc3 14 ♗xf6 gxf6 15 ♖xc3 ♕xc3 16 dxc8♕ ♖axc8, which is the end of Black's attack. After 17 ♗a6 ♖cd8 18 ♔e2, A.Moiseenko-G.Giorgadze, Spanish Team Championship 2005, Black should not have convincing compensation for rook versus two bishops, but White's play later crumbled, possibly the result of time pressure.

10...♗xc3+ 11 ♖xc3

11 bxc3 is possible, and will give reasonable compensation for a pawn sacrifice, but Wang Yue is aiming for much more with an exchange sacrifice. He is following a line devised by Topalov, quite often a guarantee of sharp and intricate play.

11...♘e4

The only sensible move.

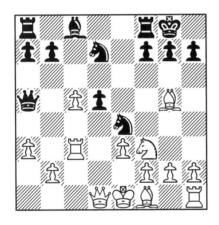

12 b4

12 ♕a1 ♘xc3 13 b4 transposes, but Black may have additional possibilities with 12...f6!? 13 b4 ♕d8 14 ♗f4 ♘xc3 15 ♕xc3 ♖e8!?, giving chances of equality. It is often best to cut down the additional possibilities.

12...♘xc3

A queen move is absurd here. He must accept the sacrifice, otherwise he is a pawn down.

13 ♕a1

Or 13 ♕b3, transposing.

13...♕a4

Black is aiming for counterplay. 13...♕c7 14 ♗f4 ♕c6 15 ♕xc3 allows White easy play.

14 ♕xc3

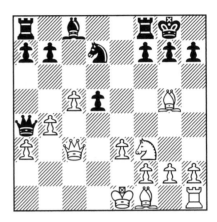

14...a5!?

Movsesian is aiming for a quick sacrificial counterattack before White has developed his kingside. It is an interesting idea, but not totally convincing.

Another possibility is 14...f6 15 ♗f4 ♖e8:

a) If 16 ♘d4 a6, White has to avoid 17 ♗b5? axb4!. 17 b5 is possible, but after 17...♘e5 18 ♗e2 ♗g4 White cannot trap the queen, and Black probably keeps a slight edge.

b) 16 ♗d3 seems to give White a slight edge after 16...♘f8 (16...a5? 17 ♗c2 axb4 18 ♕d3) 17 ♘d4 ♗d7 18 ♗c2 ♕a6 19 ♗b3 (or, of course, 19 ♗d3, repeating) 19...♗c6 20 a4 ♗xa4 21 ♗xd5+ ♔h8 22 ♗c4 b5. Black is the exchange for a pawn up, but White has the more impressive minor pieces, and a strong passed pawn. Moreover, Black's bishop on a4 is just about on the worst possible square.

Movsesian has every reason to avoid this line. The problem is on his next move.

15 b5

He wants to keep his pawns strong and active.

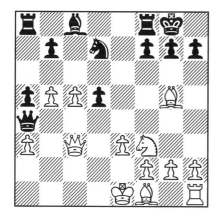

15...♞xc5?!

This had been played many months earlier by Carlsen (see the notes to Black's 16th). Movsesian clearly overestimated the improvement he had analysed.

It is always difficult for the defender whether to make a return sacrifice after a gambit, or whether to try to defend. Here it seems that defence would have been the better option.

Black would probably have done better in the style of Steinitz, keeping the extra material, and manoeuvring with pieces rather than pawns, giving nothing away. 15...♖e8, followed by ...♞f8, and if required ...♞e6, puts the onus on White:

a) After, for example, 16 ♞d4 ♞f8 17 ♗d3 ♞e6 18 ♗c2 ♛c4 19 ♛xc4 dxc4 20 ♞xe6 ♗xe6 21 ♔d2 ♖ac8 Black seems to be slightly better.

b) Or 16 ♗d3 ♞f8 17 0-0 ♗d7 18 ♞e5 ♖ac8 19 ♖b1 ♖xe5 20 ♛xe5 ♛xa3

with advantage to Black.

16 ♛xc5 ♗d7

It is essential for Black to develop with the bishop, taking control of the d-file with the rook. It is also useful to try to attack the b5 pawn. Black needs to set up a queenside pawn majority as soon as possible in case of any piece simplification.

16...♗e6? 17 ♛c1 ♖fc8 18 ♛a1 ♛c2 19 ♗e2 ♛c1+ 20 ♛xc1 ♖xc1+ 21 ♗d1 ♖a1 22 a4 was a quick win for White in V.Topalov-M.Carlsen, Wijk aan Zee 2007. Movsesian demonstrates an improvement, but Wang Yue still shows that Black's play is inadequate.

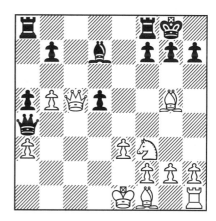

17 ♗e2

White must develop quickly, before his king is in trouble.

The computer suggests grabbing another pawn, with a likely winning advantage after 17 ♛xd5, but the experienced player will be likely to regard this as much too greedy. 17...♗e6 18 ♛d3 ♖ac8 19 e4 is White's defensive idea, but after 19...h6! the bishop cannot cover both the d8- and c1-squares. If 20 ♗d2 ♖fd8 21 ♛b1 ♛xa3, even the computer admits Black is now winning.

17...♖fc8

Black has a choice of moving rooks to c8. He is being careful, though, to keep the queen's rook on a8 to help the pawn being pushed through.

18 ♕xd5 ♖c1+

18...♗xb5 19 ♗d1 ♖c1 transposes to the notes to Black's 19th move. Here 19...♕c4 20 ♕xc4 ♗xc4 leaves Black's rook less active than in the main line.

19 ♗d1

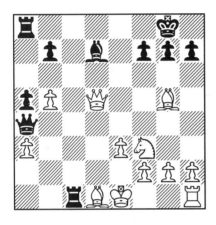

The only move.

19...♕xb5

Hoping to salvage something in the endgame. Black has a rook and pawn for two minor pieces, which would mean that Black is about half a pawn-point down in terms of material balance. If, though, Black is able to exchange queens, and start his queenside pawns moving, the play might become unclear.

19...♗xb5 20 ♔d2 ♕xa3 21 ♕xb5 ♕a2+ 22 ♔d3 (22 ♔xc1?? ♖c8+ leads to checkmate) 22...♖ac8 continues with wild and sacrificial play, but in the end Black runs out of attack. A rook versus three minor pieces is a large deficit. Here 23 ♘d4 ♖1c5 24 ♕xb7 ♕c4+ 25 ♔e4 ♖xg5 26 ♗b3 ♕c5 27 f4! allows Black to recover a piece, but leaves

White firmly in control.

20 ♕xb5

The simplest and most direct way of playing.

Lines such as 20 e4 ♖a1 21 ♗e3 are possible, but do not necessarily gain ground.

20...♗xb5 21 ♘d4

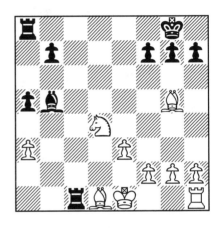

The dream centralization of the knight, which ensures that White's position is, at the very least, secure, and now White can play for a win.

Is it absolutely certain that he is indeed winning by force? It is difficult to say. Black will have chances of creating counterplay with his extra queenside pawn, and this could easily create problems if he is accurate. White has done the best he can so far, and if it can be shown that he is not winning, then so be it. The onus is on Black to play extremely precisely. The fact that he has to resign on move 32 would appear to indicate that he is not defending so well.

21...♗d7

A choice to be made here.

The inaccurate way of playing the defence would be 21...♗a4? 22 ♔d2 ♖xd1+ 23 ♖xd1 ♗xd1 24 ♔xd1, and after simplification, Black has no counterplay. White's overall plan is to centralize the king, maybe to d3, and put pressure on Black's queenside pawns. White has two minor pieces versus only one rook, and if a black pawn is under attack from both sides, it is difficult to set up a good defence.

21...♗a6 is more sensible. A computer suggestion is 22 ♔d2 ♖ac8 23 ♗g4 ♖xh1 24 ♗xc8 ♖xh2 25 ♗h3, but on the whole human players do not want to sacrifice a pawn just for simplification unless, of course, there is a clear win. They would prefer 22 a4 ♖ac8 23 ♗e7 ♖b1 24 ♔d2 b5 25 axb5 ♗xb5 26 ♘xb5 ♖xb5 27 ♗c2. This position is difficult to assess, although clearly Black is not better. Can White win? Or can Black hold?

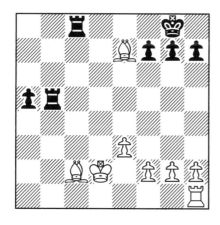

The extra pawn on the kingside would be a win for White if Black's a-pawn drops. Black's defensive hopes are to keep the a-pawn alive, and preferably dangerous. White will then find it difficult to bring the king to the a-or b-files. Also, while the bishops would help defend any push with the a-pawn, it is hard to attack the pawn directly.

Ultimately, though, it would be

unlikely for Black to defend. Try, for example, 27...♖d5+ 28 ♗d3 ♖d7 29 ♗h4 f6 30 ♖a1 ♖cd8 32 ♖a3 ♖d5 when Black will be unable to improve his pieces, not least because if the king centralizes with, for example 31...♔f8, White's bishops can start to attack the kingside pawns, such as after 32 ♔c2. White meanwhile will be able at some stage to bring the dark-squared bishop into play, and maybe start pushing some kingside pawns.

Movsesian prefers to keep control with the bishop on the e8-a4 diagonal.

22 0-0

This is played not so much to bring the king to safety, but rather to allow the bishop to move, without using up any more time.

After 22 ♔d2 ♖a1, the bishop is still pinned. 23 ♗e7 ♗a4, followed perhaps by ...♖a2+ or ...♖c8, gives chances to defend for Black.

22...♖ac8

The rooks need to help.

22...b5 23 ♗c2 ♖xf1+ 24 ♔xf1 b4 25 axb4 axb4 26 ♔e2 ♖a2 27 ♔d3 would allow White to swallow up Black's passed pawn with little difficulty.

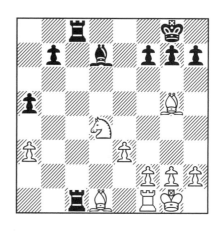

23 ♗f3?!

He would like to bring his pieces into play, naturally, but this provides weaknesses, in particular making it easier for Black to set up a queenside passed pawn.

23 ♗e7! is tighter, covering the a3-pawn. There is no easy way for Black to push the bishop off the diagonal. If 23...b5? 24 ♘b3, White gains a pawn with a knight fork.

23...♚f8!

Movsesian keeps the bishop away from e7, and does not mind so much giving up a pawn on b7. Naturally, he will want to take White's a-pawn.

23...b5 24 ♗e7 is a critical alternative. Black cannot safely breakthrough with 24...b4 25 axb4 a4 26 b5, as now the bishop covers a3, and White also keeps his passed pawn. Here 24...♖1c3 looks complicated at first, but 25 ♗e2! successfully attacks Black's queenside pawns.

24 ♗xb7

A pawn gone, but this is not the whole story.

24...♖8c3

White's pawn will drop too.

Much will depend on Black's remaining a-pawn. If this pawn can be held indefinitely, then he has good chances of holding. If not, then with two extra minor pieces and an extra pawn in return for the rook, White will win.

25 a4!?

A clever response? Or a good bluff?

If the a-pawns are exchanged, White should still have a winning material advantage. If, however, White has to give up the a-pawn, and Black still keeps his own a-pawn, the position could quite likely end up as a draw. To put this the other way round, it doesn't really matter whether White keeps his a-pawn or not. All that is important is getting rid of Black's pawn.

This helps explain why White strangely gives up his a-pawn. White wants to stop Black playing ...a4 himself, when the bishop protects the pawn.

25...♗xa4

Naturally, but now the bishop is blocking the a-pawn.

26 ♗d8

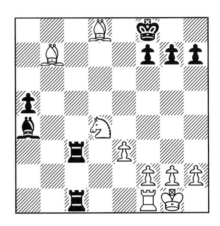

All part of his plan.

26...♗b3

One gets the impression that Movsesian changes his mind halfway through, and decides next move that he feels forced to make a piece sacrifice in desperation.

26...♖c5 27 ♗b6 ♖xf1+ 28 ♚xf1 ♖c1+ 29 ♚e2 ♖b1 30 ♗c5+ ♚e8 31 ♗d5 ♗d7 gives much better chances for Black to hold. Even so, the likelihood is that White should win with careful play.

27 ♘xb3

Or was Movsesian merely setting a desperate trap? 27 ♗xa5?? ♗c4 wins a rook, as if 28 ♗xc3? ♖xf1 mate.

Taking the bishop by White is more natural anyway.

27...♖xf1+ 28 ♔xf1

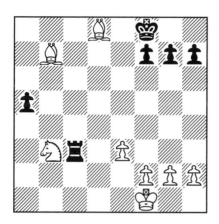

And when Black has taken the knight, a few tactics mean that his a-pawn will not be lost, and so the struggle remains.

28...a4??

A strangely panicky response.

Black could still force White to work hard with 28...♖xb3 29 ♗c6, and then 29...♖c3. Compared with positions discussed on Black's 21st, White's pieces are much more fluid. Play would still be delicate, though, after 30 ♗e4 a4 31 ♗a5!, making use of checks and pins on b4:

a) If then 31...♖b3 32 ♗c2! ♖b2 (32...♖a3?? 33 ♗b4+) 33 ♗xa4 ♖a2 34 ♗b4+, and the bishops escape when White wins.

b) Black lasts longer with 31...♖c1+ 32 ♔e2 ♔g8 (32...a3 33 ♗b4+) 33 ♗d2 ♖h1!, and it is still a genuine fight. After 34 h3 a3 35 ♗d5 Black's advanced passed pawn looks dangerous, but White's king and two bishops will pester Black's rook, and cover the advance of the a-pawn: for example, 35...♖a1 36 ♗c3 ♖c1 37 ♔d3 ♖d1+ 38 ♗d2 ♖a1 39 f4 a2 40 g4 h6 41 ♗b3 ♖h1 41 ♗xa2 ♖xh3, and while the pawns are level, and on the same side of the board, the two bishops will eventually outplay the rook.

It is always difficult to interpret the psychology of a player making obvious mistakes. A possible interpretation might well have been that Movsesian had appreciated that his opening preparation was seriously flawed, and that he felt depressed at his play, and so tried a wild stab.

29 ♘d4

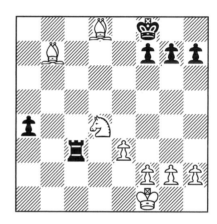

This will do nicely. The three pieces should be able to block Black's outside passed pawn. Even if by some chance the pawn will advance and force the sacrifice of a minor piece in return, the other two pieces will win.

29...♖c5

If 29...a3, then simply 30 ♗d5.

30 ♗b6

All three minor pieces are working together.

30...♖e5

30...♖c1+ 31 ♔e2 a3 32 ♗d5 is also simple enough for White.

31 ♗a6 a3

As far as it gets. Black's bishop sacrifice was nowhere close to working.

32 ♗c4 1-0

The end.

Game 27
I.Cheparinov-I.Nepomniachtchi
Wijk aan Zee 2008
Semi-Slav Defence D43

1 d4 d5 2 c4 c6 3 ♘f3 e6

This is still part of the Semi-Slav family. 3...♘f6 is usual, but there is nothing wrong with the text.

4 ♘c3

If 4 e3, Black can keep the Stonewall option with 4...f5. The argument is that White no longer has the option of trying for an advantage with g3 (in comparison with lines in the Dutch starting with 1 d4 f5 2 c4 e6 and ...d5). Here 5 g4!? is an attempt to try to break up the wall: 5...fxg4 6 ♘e5 ♘f6 7 ♘xg4 ♗e7 8 ♗d3 0-0 .♖g1 ♕e8 1 ♘c3 ♘xg4 11 ♕xg4 ♗f6 12 ♕g2 looked promising for White, and ended up as a win in S.Volkov-M.Kobalija, Russian Team Championship 2005.

4...♘f6

Black keeps to the established main lines.

4...dxc4 is another sharp Semi-Slav pawn grab on c4. After 5 e3 b5 6 a4 ♗b4 7 ♗d2 ♗b7 8 b3 a5, play is already tense on 9 bxc4 ♗xc3 10 ♗xc3 b4 or 9 axb5 ♗xc3 10 ♗xc3 cxb5 11 bxc4 b4 12 ♗b2. Black has his queenside pawn advances, and has created either a single passed pawn or two of them, but he has lost influence on the kingside.

Morozevich has found something even sharper with 9 ♘e4!? f5 10 ♘c5!. The tactics were already on full blast in A.Morozevich-K.Miton, Sochi 2007, with 10...c3 11 ♘xc7 ♕e7 12 ♘c5 e5! (there is no hurry to take the knight) 13 ♗e2 e4 14 0-0 (14 ♗xc3? exf3 favours Black) 14...exf3 15 ♗xf3 cxd2 16 axb5 ♘f6 17 bxc6. This would be an extremely difficult position to evaluate and find the best move for Black, untutored and over the board. Ftacnik suggests 17...♘e4 or 17...♘a6 as possibilities. Instead Miton played quietly, not bringing the knights into play, and after 17...♖a7?! 18 ♘d3 0-0 19 ♘xb4 ♕xb4 20 ♕c2 White was better, with bishop and two powerful passed pawns against the two ineffective knights. Morozevich later won.

In retrospect, this might have been a better game to give as a representative win for Morozevich than his game against Sakaev. In both cases, Morozevich showed his exceptional imagination, but it has to be admitted that against Sakaev he overpressed badly before winning.

5 ♗g5

With highly complicated gambit play, advocated by Botvinnik over half a century ago, and by many other top grandmasters since.

5 e3 reaches the other main lines of the Semi-Slav. For the latest example in this book, see Game 31, Mamedyarov-Nepomniachtchi.

5 cxd5 exd5!? avoids, for Black, the dullness of the symmetrical Slav Exchange (5...cxd5). The Orthodox Exchange after 5...exd5 tends to be slightly less effective than when the ♘f3 move has been delayed after, for example, 1 d4 d5 2 c4 e6 3 ♘c3 ♘f6 4 cxd5 exd5. It is a question of timing. White would like to play ♗g5, e3, ♕c2, and ♗d3 quickly, but the extra knight move slows him down.

5...h6

Avoiding the 5...dxc4 6 e4 b5 7 e5 h6 8 ♗h4 g5 9 ♘xg5 hxg5 10 ♗xg5 ♘bd7 Botvinnik main line. Forgive the author if we do not add several pages to the discussion of this extraordinarily complicated variation. We merely note that 5...h6 is currently far more fashionable.

5...♘bd7 6 e3 leads back to a Queen's Gambit Declined.

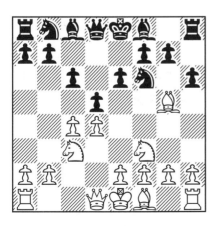

6 ♗h4

For 6 ♗xf6, see the notes in Game 30, Gelfand-Alekseev.

6...dxc4

So it is still a gambit.

This is by far the most popular, although the Orthodox lines such as 6...♘bd7 and 6...♗e7 are also to be considered.

7 e4

The main line.

7 a4, to prevent ...b5, has been tried a few times, but is not especially dangerous after 7...♗b4.

7...g5

7...b5 8 e5 h6 9 ♗h4 g5 transposes into the Botvinnik system. Again, as at move 5, the players dodge this.

8 ♗g3 b5

Holding the c4-pawn. Black is a pawn up, and he has a dangerous queenside pawn majority. This is all good news so far, but Black has made seven pawn moves out of his first eight, which means that first his pieces development has been slowed down, and second that the quick advance of the pawns leaves behind several weaknesses, which White would like to take advantage of.

9 ♘e5!?

A recent experiment. This looks like the natural move, starting the attack on the king, and making it easier to play h4 without allowing a ...g4 counterattack, but it has not often been played. One problem is that White's king gets stuck in the centre for a long time, and the general feeling has been that it is difficult for White to start an attack when he is also being forced to watch his own king.

As a result, White has usually tried 9

♗e2, developing and keeping the king safe. Quite often it is a case of one quiet move, and then wild tactical play. Just before Kasparov's retirement, Dreev surprised him by sacrificing a rook after 9 ♗e2 ♗b7 10 h4 g4 11 ♘e5 h5 12 f3 ♘bd7 13 fxg4 hxg4 14 0-0 ♘xe5 15 ♗xe5, and now 15...♘d7!, G.Kasparov-A.Dreev, Russian Championship, Moscow 2004. Quite a shock, but Kasparov kept his composure. After 16 ♗xh8 ♕xh4 17 ♗xg4 ♕xh8 18 e5 Dreev made one sacrifice too many, and after 18...♘xe5? 19 dxe5 ♗c5+ 20 ♖f2 ♕xe5 21 ♕e2 White was material ahead, but Dreev took his opponent to a long hard struggle. Apparently Dreev had forgotten his home analysis, which would have gone 18...0-0-0 19 ♕e2 c5 20 ♘xb5 a6 with complicated play. This is one of many, many complicated lines in this sharp opening, and it is only human for even the top professionals to lose track of their analysis.

9...♗b4

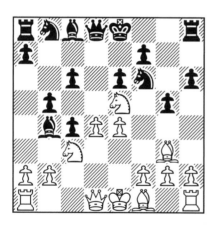

This is unusual, but surely must be a critical idea. Black is pressing on both the d- and e-pawns, with ...♘xe4 being a threat. As so often in chess, if both players try totally logical moves, sharp

tactical play soon results. Black is attacking in the centre, certainly, but he is also moving the bishop well away from his kingside, and White is soon able to start an attack. It is too early to say with confidence whether Nepomniachtchi's move, presumably looked at but rejected by other analysts, is good, bad, or merely one of a few alternatives. The line cannot be rejected on the basis of just one game when there are several alternatives for Black later on.

A few months after this game, Alekseev tried 9...♗b7, and lost. See Game 30.

10 ♗e2?!

Dangerous, but probably not fully correct.

Cheparinov ignores his opponent's central pawn attack, and concentrates first on developing his pieces, and then pressing hard on his opponent's weaknesses. He has eyes on Black's king. White has already gambited a pawn, and now he gives up a second pawn, and soon a third pawn. This is quite a responsibility for White, trying to ensure that he will keep his piece activity for as long as it takes, but at least he is giving away only pawns, and not pieces.

Most players would probably be content with 10 f3, shoring up the pawn centre, and starting to attack Black's kingside pawns with h4. There seems to be good compensation for the gambit pawn.

Another idea is 10 ♕f3. Then P.Eljanov-V.Potkin, St Petersburg 2002, continued 10...♗b7 11 ♖d1 ♘bd7 12 ♗e2 ♕e7 13 0-0 0-0-0 14 d5, and later was agreed drawn in an unclear position after multiple exchanges in the centre. Here 10...♕xd4? is an attempt to force a quick draw by perpetual, but after 11 ♕xf6 ♗xc3+ 12 bxc3 ♕xc3+ 13 ♔e2 White's king can escape, even in some lines via ♔e2-f3-g4-h5. After 13...0-0 14 ♖d1!, White is safe with an extra pawn: for instance, 14...♕c2+ 15 ♔e1 ♕c3+ 16 ♖d2, and Black has been forced out of position with the queen checks. In time, White will win with the extra piece.

Accepting gambit pawns is often fully playable, if requiring good nerves. The extra pawn is useful, but the opponent will keep good chances with the pieces. When taking a second or a third gambit pawn, there are two basic possibilities. Either the extra sacrifice is completely unsound, and will lose, or the defender has swallowed too many pawns, and the attacker's pieces are far too strong, and will overrun the defender. Grabbing pawns is often an extreme way of playing, but sacrificing a string of pawns too casually is not good either.

Sometimes the position may be finely divided. It is feasible that the attack may be sound, but will not be decisive if the opponent has made no mistake. Then the natural result would be a sharp perpetual check. Cheparinov's game is close to the edge throughout. He won, but was his gambit idea as powerful as it looks? Or is it ultimately unsound? Or are we heading for the knife-edge of a draw? This remains to be seen.

10...♘xe4

Consistent with his last move.

11 0-0

White must bring his king out of checks as soon as possible. There is no point in giving away several pawns for an attack, when the opponent has the chance of a counterattack against the king.

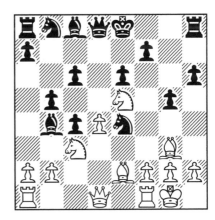

Now Black has three main captures. Also perhaps 11...♘f6, but then White still has good gambit chances after 12 f4.

11...♗xc3

This seems the safest.

11...♘xc3 12 bxc3 ♗xc3 is thoroughly natural, but White can add a piece sacrifice to all the pawn sacrifices with 13 ♘xf7. This is scary, but White's attack does not necessarily win. After 13...♔xf7 14 ♗h5+ ♔g8 15 ♕f3 ♕e7 16 ♕xc3, there is no immediate mating threat, and Black has time to manoeuvre his knight into play with 16...♘d7 followed by ...♘f6-d5.

The computer suggestion is not always the best, and instead of the immediate sacrifice on f7, White can improve with 13 ♗h5!:

a) Probably White's position is to be favoured after 13...0-0 14 ♗xf7+ (14 ♘xf7? ♕d4!) 14...♖xf7 15 ♘xf7, and now, for example, 15...♕xd4 (15...♕f6 16 ♖c1!?) 16 ♗e5 ♕xd1 17 ♖axd1 ♗xe5 18 ♘xe5. Further exploration may well be needed. White's rooks and knight are useful, but if Black can activate his minor pieces and pawns, he might have useful chances.

b) Another try is 13...♕d5 14 ♘xf7 ♖f8, but now, instead of the obvious discovered check (and a possible exchange sacrifice after 15 ♘xh6+ ♔d8 17 ♘f7+ ♖xf7), White has 15 ♖c1 ♗xd4 16 ♗f3! ♕c5 17 ♗d6 with advantage.

It can be so difficult for an unprepared player to try to outplay an opponent who is well prepared, and with the help of computer preparation. Nepomniachtchi opts for something slightly less sharp, and correctly so, it would seem.

11...♘xg3 12 fxg3 ♗xc3 13 bxc3 0-0 leads to unclear play, but Black again has to be careful with his king.

12 bxc3 ♘xc3

Or, as just noted, 12...♘xg3 13 fxg3 0-0 with unclear play.

There seems no good reason, though, to avoid picking up the third extra pawn.

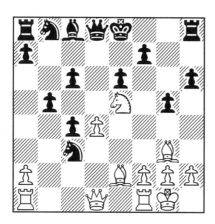

13 ♕c2

He must cover e2, and this seems the best of the alternatives if Black were to decide not to take the bishop.

13...♘xe2+

13...♕xd4? 14 ♖ad1 ♘xd1 15 ♖xd1 would be far too greedy. White soon hits back after 15...♕c5 16 ♘xf7 ♔xf7 17 ♗h5+ ♔e7 18 ♕g6 with a mating attack. Here 14...♘xe2+ 15 ♕xe2 is also good for White; see the notes to Black's 14th, below.

14 ♕xe2

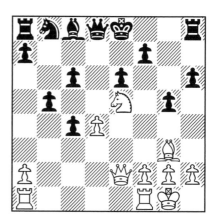

A strange position and, one might assume, critical. If Black does not handle the next few moves well, he could easily lose quickly. If White can find a few good moves, he might have reasonable attacking chances. Maybe though Black can win with perfect play, or maybe, perhaps most frighteningly, Black is already in serious trouble.

14...h5!

This is risky, in that he now has to play with complete accuracy. It is not an error, as on move 16, as Black could still have steered the position to at least a perpetual check, and indeed even an advantage.

There are alternatives in which Black can go seriously wrong. For example, 14...♕xd4? 15 ♖ad1 ♕b6 16 ♕h5 is foolhardy. Giving up the open file for White's d-pawn is too much. After

16...♖f8 17 ♕xh6 ♘d7 18 ♕g7 Black's defences crack.

14...♕d5!? makes far more sense, keeping the file closed, and placing the queen on a good central square which is not easily attacked. Then 15 ♕h5 (15 ♘g4 ♘d7 is a possibility, but perhaps too indirect for White, who has given up some pawns) 15...♖f8 16 ♕xh6 c5, and the battle continues. An interesting position to analyse, but in terms of finding the best play for both sides we should concentrate on the main line, where Black has a later improvement.

15 f4

White has to open up the f-file, otherwise his attack soon folds, and he would be a few pawns down.

15...f5

Black tries to keep the f-file closed, or at least semi-closed. Black succeeds to some extent, but it is clear that he now has serious weaknesses on the dark squares, with e5 being the stepping point for possible invasions on the black side of the board. That is, of course, not the whole story, and later it becomes clear that Nepomniachtchi has done nothing wrong, so far.

The alternatives are:

a) 15...♕xd4+? 16 ♗f2 ♕xf4? 17 ♗c5 ♕h4 18 ♖xf7 would be no improvement for Black. He might have gained five extra pawns (now down to four), but his pieces are close to collapse, and his extra pawns in any case attack nothing.

b) Other lines also lead to difficulties. For example, 15...h4 16 ♘xf7 ♔xf7 17 fxg5+ ♔g8 18 ♗e5, and only a computer might think, if only for a moment, that Black is doing well. In fact, Black's king is far too exposed, and his material advantage of little signifi-

cance. Play might continue 18...♕e8 19 ♗xh8 ♔xh8 20 g6 ♕xg6 21 ♖f8+ ♔g7 22 ♖xc8 with a winning position.

c) Or 15...f6 16 fxg5 fxe5 17 ♗xe5 ♖h8 18 g6 ♖e7 19 g7 ♔d7 20 ♖f8, and White wins.

d) 15...g4 makes it difficult for White to open the f-file, but with 16 f5 he can still persist:

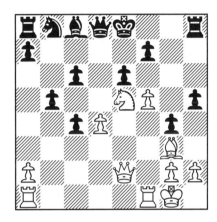

d1) 16...f6 17 ♘g6 ♖h7 18 fxe6 ♕xd4+ 19 ♔h1 only temporarily blocks the f-file, since after, for example, 19...♖g7 20 ♖ad1 ♕c3 21 ♗e1 the queen relinquishes the long diagonal, and ♖xf6 should win.

d2) 16...♕xd4+ 17 ♔h1 gives another four-pawn plus, but it is unclear how Black is going to defend:

d21) The initial computer suggestion is 17...0-0 18 ♖ad1 ♕c3, but after 19 f6! Black's kingside soon collapses, with either a sacrifice on g4 or White kicks Black's queen out with ♗e1, and gives his own queen a check on g5, via e3 or d2.

d22) 17...h4 allows White to continue his pawn push with 18 fxe6. If then 18...♗xe6 19 ♘xf7, and Black's final pawn in the centre collapses, and so too will the king, and 18...fxe6 19 ♖ad1

♕xd1+ 20 ♖xd1 hxg3 21 ♕d2 also leads to the king folding. Black's pieces are completely undeveloped, once he has given up the queen, but White's pieces are still in play. Finally, 18...hxg3 19 exf7+ ♚d8 20 f8♕+ ♖xf8 21 ♖xf8+ ♚c7 22 ♖d1 ♕c5 23 ♖dd8 ♗e6 24 hxg3 keeps Black alive, but it is not very promising.

16 fxg5

White absolutely has to open up lines on the kingside. If Black has the chance to play ...h4 followed by ...g4, then he will be solid on the kingside and on the queenside, and with a couple of extra pawns. It is not enough for White just to sit on a few weaknesses on the e-file.

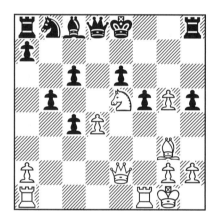

16...♕xg5?

Nepomniachtchi is naturally anxious about the possibility of keeping White's advanced g-pawn on the board, but his queen is now decentralized, and this allows White to regroup with his pieces.

An immediate 16...h4! keeps White on his toes:

a) The immediate attempts at quick tactics do not work for White. If 17 ♘g6? fxg3 18 ♘xh8 ♕d4+ 19 ♚h1 ♕xh8, and Black wins. Or, even worse,

17 g6?? hxg3 18 g7 ♕d4+ 19 ♚h1 ♖xh2 mate. Both lines indicate very good reasons why Black should retain his options with the queen on d8.

b) White must move his bishop, but if 17 ♗f2?! ♕xg5, he has clearly lost some time in comparison with the main line.

c) Therefore 17 ♗f4, keeping his passed pawn. Play is complicated, with any slight deviations from both sides often ending up as quick losses. A finish with honour on both sides would be 17...♕xd4+ 18 ♚h1 ♕e4 19 ♕xe4 fxe4 20 g6 ♘d7 21 ♘xd7 ♗xd7 22 g7 ♖g8 23 ♗d6 0-0-0 24 ♖f7 ♗e8 25 ♖c7+ ♚g8 26 ♖d7+ ♚c8 27 ♖c7+ with a perpetual.

This is by no means the end of the story. On move 24, White has a passed pawn on the seventh, and an attacking rook and bishop, and it would be understandable for Black to settle for a draw. Black though has four passed pawns, two on each of the c- and d-files, and even if White can remove the front two pawns, at the cost perhaps of some simplification, there are two more passed pawns in reserve for the endgame. The onus is on White to prove the draw after 24...e3!?.

There are too many alternatives for either side to prove whether Black wins, or, probably more likely, that it's an ultimate draw. In practical terms, if strong players were to analyse this whole game in depth, it would be highly unlikely that such a player would want to try this position in depth against one of his peers. Therefore, one might expect, Cheparinov's imaginative gambit idea will disappear fairly quickly, although perhaps a mainstream player might find it interesting.

Without pretending that this is anything like a full analysis, one possibility is 25 ♖e1 c3 26 ♖xe3 b4 27 ♗xb4 (two pawns down, but Black still has three more passers) 27...♗e8 (now that White no longer has ♖c7+) 28 ♖f1 c2 29 ♖c3 ♖d1 30 ♖g1 ♗g6, and now it is clear that Black's passed pawn on the seventh is far stronger than the White's.

17 ♖ae1

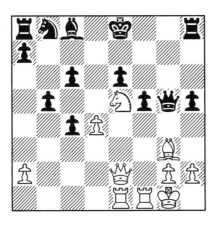

With no immediate counterattacks against him, White completes his development, setting up forceful attacking play after a quick interlude of manoeuvring his minor pieces.

17...h4

Now this is a move too late.

Black could bring another defensive piece into play with 17...♖h7, but even here White keeps pressure with 18 ♖f4 followed by ♘f3.

18 ♘f3

The knight has done its job on e5. Now it is the turn of other pieces to land there, or to pass through the diagonals and files.

18...♕g4

If 18...♕d8? 19 ♗xb8 ♖xb8 20 ♕e5, and White forks both rooks.

18...♕h5 19 ♗xh4 ♕g4 is to be con-

sidered. Black loses a tempo, but White's bishop is on a less dangerous diagonal. 20 ♕e5 still gives White excellent chances on the dark squares. If 20...♖xh4 21 ♕c7 ♗d7 22 ♕b7, and quite unexpectedly White switches his attention from the kingside to the queenside.

19 ♕e5

There is no gain of material after 19 ♗xb8? ♖xb8 20 ♕e5, and the skewer of the two rooks, as Black comfortably sidesteps with 19...♖g8.

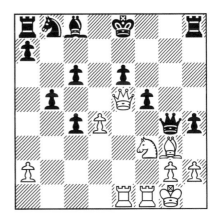

19...0-0

The king is out of the centre, but neither on the kingside is it satisfactory.

If 19...♖h5 20 ♘xh4 ♖xh4 21 ♖f4, and White has a winning attack. There are a couple of ways for Black to keep the position alive for a few moves, but with White's queen and attacks with other pieces, the game will still not last for long. Or here 20...f4 21 ♕c7 e5 22 ♗xf4 ♗e6 23 ♗xe5, and now with Black's e- and f-pawns gone, and his king still attacked by all the major pieces, he will not last for long.

20 ♘xh4

Now White is only two pawns down.

20...♖f7

If 20...♕g7, then White simply keeps the queen with 21 ♕e3, with a continuing attack. If 21...♕f6 22 ♘xf5 exf5 23 ♗xb8, and Black is down to only one extra pawn, while White's pieces remain strong in attack. The drop of the pawn on the e-file leads to extra weaknesses. Here Black could perhaps consider 22...♖xb8 23 ♕g3+ ♕g7 24 ♕xb8 ♕xd4+ 25 ♔h1, getting rid of the mighty bishop, but White's queen and rooks continue to create dangerous threats.

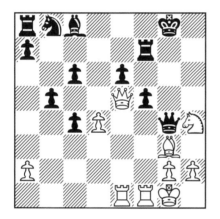

21 ♕d6

The invasion of the dark squares pushes into far-flung territory.

21...♘d7

Black feels obliged to give up his e-pawn in return for the chance to develop his pieces. It seems a little too late. Apart from anything else, White will have full control of the e-file with his rook.

21...♔h7 does not help. White wins after 22 ♖f4 ♕g7 23 ♘xf5 exf5 24 ♖h4+ ♔g8 25 ♖e8+ ♖f8 26 ♖xf8+ ♕xf8 27 ♖h8+.

22 ♖xe6

Simple and good.

22...♘f8

The knight plugs any back-rank checks, so that there is no quick checkmate, but White's rook is still almighty, even without checks.

23 ♖e8

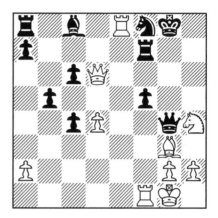

Black is now pinned to extinction.

23...c3

Can Black queen the pawn? Probably not, but Black can do little else, and if White were to play slackly, there might be a slight chance of jumping back into the game.

24 ♘g6

White plays vigorously.

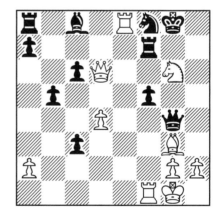

24...♗e6

24...♗b7 25 ♖xa8 ♗xa8 26 ♘e5 does not help.

25 ♘e7+

Possibly 25 ♖xa8 ♕xg6 26 ♕xc6 is more accurate. The black queen cannot take the pawn on d4.

25...♖xe7 26 ♖xa8

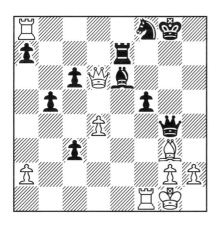

26...♕g5?

This loses quickly. After 26...♔f7, White still has to work:

a) If White were to concentrate on grabbing Black's advanced c-pawn with 27 ♕c3? ♗d5 28 ♕xc3, Black is better after 28...♖e2.

b) 27 h3 ♕g7 28 ♕c5 is a more accurate way of implementing this, the point being that if 28...♕xg3 29 ♖xf5+ White is winning. If 29...♔g6 30 ♕xe7, Black soon runs out of checks. Otherwise, 29...♗xf5+ 30 ♕xf5+ is soon checkmate. There is a similar, if slightly more complicated, theme, after 28...♘d7 29 ♕xc3 ♘b6 30 ♖d8 ♘d5 31 ♕xc6 ♕xg3 32 ♖xd5 ♕e3+ 33 ♔h1 ♕e2 34 ♖fxf5+ ♗xf5 35 ♖xf5+ ♔g8 36 ♖g5+ ♖g7 37 ♕d5+, and White soon wins.

White should win, even after best play, but there are chances of an error short of time in a complicated position.

27 ♕d8

With mate threats, and gaining a tempo.

27...♕g7

A sad retreat.

28 ♗e5

Kicking the queen to a less effective square.

28...♕f7 29 ♗d6 1-0

Winning further material.

Game 28
P.Eljanov-R.Ponomariov
Kharkiv 2008
London System D00

1 d4 d5 2 ♗f4

One of those reasonable but obscure openings that has not been given a clearly recognized name. How about the Mason Variation after the American (formerly Irish) player from the 19th Century? And then there is the Steinitz Counter-Gambit, 2...c5. These were the names given by the late Hooper and Whyld, co-authors of *The Oxford Companion to Chess*. Presumably in other countries, other names have been allocated, but 2 ♗f4 is often regarded under the 'London' umbrella: 2 ♘f3 ♘f6 3 ♗f4 is the London System proper.

There is nothing wrong with this move, if we take the slightly negative sense that White cannot be worse yet. Whether White can be better remains to be seen. The bishop move is a developing move, and does not get in the way of anything, but it creates no pressure against the opponent. Even 2 ♗g5 at least pins the e-file, and obtains pressure when at some stage Black develops with ...♘f6.

The psychology of such an unusual move is not too difficult to appreciate, at least in broad terms. Eljanov naturally has knowledge and good grasp of the opening, but Ponomariov is, of course, also extremely well prepared. Does Eljanov feel it is a good time to try something new for his opponent?

2...c5

And so we reach the Steinitz Counter-Gambit. This is, of course, the only direct way to try to punish White's centre, but other moves are, of course, reasonable.

2...e6 3 e3 ♗d6 4 ♗g3 is a steady line briefly explored a century ago, and in a much more recent top-level blitz game, V.Kramnik-S.Rublevsky, Moscow 2007. Did the players make a mistake, as early as move 3? It seems not. The computer gives 4 ♕g4 as an advantage for White, but playing though the moves, it becomes clear that after 4...♘f6 5 ♕xg7 ♖g8 6 ♕h6 ♖g6 7 ♕h4 ♖g4 8 ♕h6 ♖g6 the position is heading for a perpetual.

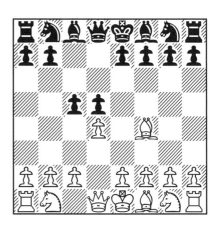

3 e4

This could conceptually be regarded as an 'Albin Counter-Counter-Gambit', in recognition of Albin's idea of the late 19th Century, 1 d4 d5 2 c4 e5!? (or perhaps '?!') 3 dxe5 d4. Presumably both players were trying to work out the implications of the additional ♗f4 in the main line. On the whole, the extra bishop move seems useful, but we shall see...

The J.Mason-W.Steinitz, London 1883, game continued with 3 dxc5 ♘c6 4 ♘f3 f6 followed by ...e5, and Black recovered his pawn with good chances for an edge.

3 ♗xb8!? ♖xb8 4 dxc5 ♕a5+ 5 ♘c3 e6 6 e4! ♗xc5 7 exd5 ♘f6 8 ♗b5+ ♔e7 has been tried a few times about a century ago. Mason scored one of his greatest scalps, admittedly after a blunder by his opponent, with 9 ♘f3 ♘xd5 10 ♕d2 ♘xc3?? 11 ♕g5+ f6 12 ♕xc5+ ♔f7 13 ♗e8+, and Black resigned in J.Mason-M.Chigorin, New York 1889. Chigorin later played a World Championship match against Steinitz in 1892. Here 10...♗b4! gives Black a small plus after 11 ♘xd5+ exd5 12 c3 ♕xb5 13 cxb4 ♖e8, while 11 ♕g5+ ♔f8 14 0-0 is unclear. There are no recent examples in this line. Explorers might also wish to consider 9 ♕d2 ♗b4 10 ♘ge2, aiming for a slight edge.

Or White could quietly play 3 c3 or 3 e3.

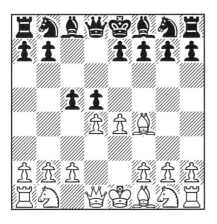

3...dxe4

3...♕b6 4 ♘c3 e6 is reasonable and also unexplored, but grabbing the 'poisoned pawn' with 4...♕xb2? 5 ♘xd5 takes too many risks.

4 d5

4 dxc5 ♕xd1+ 5 ♔xd1 is deeply uninspiring, but should be about equal. Naturally there are many lines in which a player can press through for an edge with even the smallest of opportunities, but this does not seem to be one.

4...♘f6

4...e6 leads to a memorable trap, known from the Albin Counter-Gambit. After 5 ♗b5+ ♗d7 6 dxe6 ♗xb5?? (6...fxe6 seems playable) 7 exf7+ ♔e7 White wins with an under-promotion – 8 fxg8♘+!!.

5 ♘c3

There is no time to set up pawn barricades with 5 c4.

5...a6

To cover any threats on b5.

Rudolf Spielmann, an exponent and theorist on the art of sacrifice in chess, found himself on the wrong end of an attack after 5...g6 6 ♘b5 ♘a6 7 d6 ♗g4 8 f3 exf3 9 gxf3 ♗f5 10 ♕d2 ♕b6 11 a4. White won quickly in B.Toupalik-R.Spielmann, Prague 1912. This was a simultaneous game, and Spielmann would presumably have been able to find improvements in proper tournament time limits.

6 ♕e2

6 f3 exf3 7 ♘xf3 b5 is pure gambit play, with the hope for White of being able to develop quickly and start an attack in return for giving up a pawn. Black's ...b5 and ...b4 sets up good countermeasures.

The text move, advocated by the Belgian Grandmaster, Luc Winants, forces Black to work harder for the extra pawn.

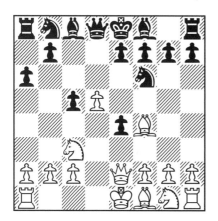

6...g6

Black returns the pawn, in the hope of a quick and safe equality with the possibility of playing for more.

6...e6 or 6...♗f5 may tend to be more speculative.

7 ♘xe4

Material is level, and White may even entertain hopes of playing for an advantage after quick play.

7 0-0-0 is also possible, and led to a transposition after 7...♗g7 8 ♘xe4 ♘xe4 9 ♕xe4 0-0 in the McShane-Illescas game cited later.

7...♘xe4

Avoiding the beginners' traps, 7...♕xd5?? 8 ♘xf6+ and 7...♘xd5?? 8 ♘d6+, in either case with a winning pin on the e-file.

8 ♕xe4 ♗g7

Or 8...♗f5, but there is no need to hurry with this. Ponomariov prefers to threaten the queen with ...♘d7 and ...♘f6.

9 0-0-0

If one were to take the view that this aggressive queenside castling creates too many chances of counterplay for Black, then 9 c3!? is worth considering.

9...0-0

It would be unwise for the king to stay for too long in the centre.

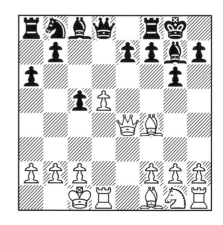

10 ♘e2

10 ♘f3 or 10 ♗e5 are other possibilities, maybe equal, maybe with a slight edge for White. One cannot assume just from the quick win for Black in the game that White is automatically worse.

10 ♗c4!? provokes Black into attacking the bishop:

a) However, after 10...b5 11 d6 ♖a7 12 ♗g5 ♗f6 13 ♗xf6 exf6 14 ♗d5 ♖d7 15 ♕f4 ♔g7 16 ♗f3 White is better.

b) 10...♘d7!?, suggested by Wells, seems a good response for Black.

c) Instead, L.McShane-M.Illescas Cordoba, European Team Championship, Gothenburg 2005, continued 10...♗f5 11 ♕f3 b5, and now the strange and interesting 12 ♗f1!?. White gives up two tempi with his bishop, but he has lured Black's bishop to f5, and will soon hit back with g4. After 12...♕a5 13 g4 ♕xa2!? 14 gxf5 ♕xb2+ 15 ♔d2, Black could have drawn by perpetual after 15...♕b4+ 16 ♔e2 ♕c4+, but Illescas played for more with 15...♘d7 16 ♘e2 ♘b6, and later lost after unclear and complicated play. Wells suggested 13...♗c8!, as Black too gives up two tempi with the bishop. Black's idea is to follow up with 14 a3 ♗b7, and White has problems on the long diagonal.

10...♘d7

10...♗f5 is also possible, again with complicated play.

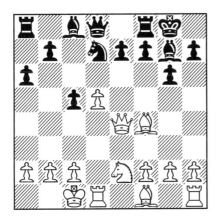

11 ♕e3

White is going to be hit with ...♘f6 anyway, and so he decides to move the queen out of the way first. The hope is that White can hit the c5-pawn.

Again, there are choices here. This line is still unexplored in what is an unclear position. Two other possibilities, to cut out counterplay from Black's light-squared bishop, might be 11 h3!? and 11 ♘g3!?.

11...♘f6

11...♘b6?! sets up the trap, 12 ♕xc5? ♘a4, but this is hardly difficult for White to avoid. After 12 ♘c3 ♗d4 13 ♕f3 Black's knight is misplaced.

Ponomariov decides it is time to gambit a pawn.

12 ♘c3

12 ♕xc5 ♗f5 provides good attack-

ing lines against White's king. Eljanov decides not to take the bait.

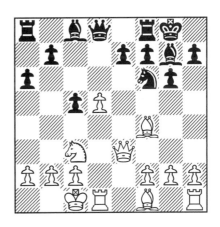

12...b5!?

With some sharp gambit play. It is not necessarily the best move, but it is playable, and offers the chance of surprise. Maybe Eljanov reached the previous position, and tried to analyse it, but probably he had not seriously considered Ponomariov's gambit idea. If White grabs the pawn, Black can take control of the c-file, and this is far from negligible.

There is a strong element of psychological pressure. Eljanov must clearly have decided beforehand that he wanted to mix the position up in the opening, trying to find unusual plans and sacrifices, and all that happens is that Ponomariov himself decided to take over the initiative through sharp counterplay.

The result of Ponomariov's enterprising play is that Eljanov soon looks disorientated, misses a not too difficult sacrifice, and loses in 22 moves. Ponomariov is generally a solid grinder in terms of chess, but like other top grandmasters, he can attack on occasion like the late Mikhail Tal.

What were the alternatives for Black? It would have been tempting to have tried 12...♗f5?!, with the idea that if 13 ♕xc5?! ♖c8 Black can sacrifice the c-pawn without the unnecessary ...b5. White sidesteps, though, this with the simple 13 h3!, aiming to push the bishop out with g4. Here 12...b6 is dull, allowing White a slight edge after 13 ♗e2, but 12...♘g4!? deserves serious consideration. If then 13 ♕xc5? b6, and the queen is pushed away, and the knight will make a fork on f2: 14 ♕c6 ♗d7 does not help. Maybe best is 13 ♕e1!? ♗xc3 14 bxc3 with unclear play. This seems the best of the alternatives.

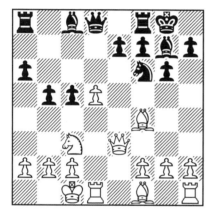

13 ♕xc5

'Prove it!'

13 d6 is the main alternative, with play possibly fizzling out to equality after 13...♖e8 14 dxe7 ♕xe7 15 ♕xe7 ♖xe7 16 ♖d8+ ♖e8 17 ♖xe8+ ♘xe8. White can pick up a pawn instead with 14 ♕xc5 exd6 15 ♗xd6 (or 15 ♖xc5 ♕a5 16 ♗d3 ♗e6) 15...♗e6, but Black has clearly the more active piece play, and it is difficult for White to force any simplification with exchanges. Neither is White likely to be able to push forward with his pawns: 16 ♗c7 ♕c8 17 ♗b6

♕b7 18 ♕c7 ♕xc7 19 ♗xc7 b4 would be too simplistic an option. Black has by far the superior development, and stands better after 19...b4.

Earlier, Black could also consider 13...e5?!, but White can avoid complications after 14 ♕xe5, instead trying 14 ♗g5!, cutting down Black's diagonals, and keeping White's advanced pawn.

13...♗f5

The natural reply. Once Black has played ...♖c8, the bishops will create pressure with the rook, with attacks on c2 and c3.

14 ♕b4?!

Eljanov is hesitating, both on this move and the next. There are probably a dozen reasonable moves for White to consider, and it would be difficult to have the chance of considering more than a few of these to analyse over the board. Indeed, it would be difficult enough to find the best move at home with the computer. The wider the choice, the more difficult it is to find a convincing choice.

There are many ways in which White can shuffle around with the pieces, and Eljanov chooses one of them. A pawn push, to open up his own pieces, is another idea; 14 d6!? is at the very least worth considering:

a) 14...♖c8 15 dxe7 ♕xd1+ 16 ♔xd1 ♖xc5 17 exf8♕+ ♗xf8 18 ♗e3 followed by ♗e3 gives Black some slight compensation for the sacrificed pawn, but not as much as he would like.

b) 14...♘d7!? attempts to improve:

b1) 15 dxe7 ♘xc5 16 exd8♕ ♖fxd8 17 ♘d5 ♗e4 gives Black compensation for the pawn, but more to hold the balance of play, rather than to try for an edge.

b2) White could try instead 15 ♕a3!? exd6 16 ♗xd6 (16 ♗d3 is about equal) 16...♖c6 17 ♗xf8 ♗xf8 18 ♕xa6 b4, but after the exchange sacrifice Black's position looks promising. One line is 19 g4 ♗xg4 20 ♖g1 ♗xd1 21 ♘xd1 b3!! 22 axb3 ♖a8 23 ♕d3 ♗h6+ 24 ♘e3 (24 ♔b1 ♕a5 gives checkmate) 24...♗xe3 25 fxe3 ♕f6!, and this turns out to be a winning attack for Black with threats of ...♕f2 or ...♖a1+.

This is of course only scratching the surface, and if any strong grandmasters would be interested in testing this line, new ideas would undoubtedly emerge.

14...♖c8

An important half-open file.

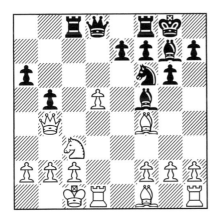

15 ♖d2?

Overly-defensive, although it is not easy to find good alternatives:

a) White might want to try to kick out Black's light-squared diagonal, but if 15 ♗e2 ♘e8 16 g4?, Black has 16...♗xg4 17 ♗xg4 ♖c4.

b) 15 h3 seems logical, but Black now has attacking chances after 15...♗xc2! 16 ♔xc2 ♘xd5 17 ♕b3 e6. If then 18 a3 ♕f6 19 ♗d2 ♕xf2 20 ♔b1 ♘xc3+ 21 ♗xc3 ♗xc3 22 bxc3 ♖fd8, and Black has ample compensation for the sacrificed piece. Here 18 ♗d2 is even better for Black after 18...b4 19 ♗xa6 ♖c5 20 ♗e3 ♘xe3+ 21 fxe3 ♕a5.

c) White needs to improve on this. 15 ♗e5! is best, blocking Black on the long dark squares, rather than trying to cover the light squares. If 15...♗h6+ 16 ♔b1 ♘d7 17 ♗d4, and White is comfortable, but 15...♕b6! is the most dangerous reply. Then there are a few tactics to beware:

c1) If, for example, 16 ♗d4? ♘xd5! 17 ♘xd5 ♖xc2+ 18 ♔b1 ♖c4+ 19 ♗d3 ♖xd4, and Black is winning.

c2) Or 16 ♕xe7? ♕xf2 17 ♗d3 ♘xd5 18 ♘xd5 ♖xc2+ 19 ♔b1 ♖xb2+ 20 ♗xb2 ♕xb2 mate.

c3) 16 ♕d4 is natural, but after the queen exchange Black keeps a slight advantage: 16...♕xd4 17 ♖xd4 (17 ♗xd4? b4 18 ♗xa6 ♖a8!) 17...♗h6+ 18 ♔b1 ♘d7 19 ♗f4 ♗g7 20 ♖d2 ♗xc3 21 bxc3 ♖xc3 allows level material, while White's pawns have been damaged.

c4) Perhaps the best try for White, but not easy to visualize, is 16 ♖d2! ♗h6 17 f4 ♕e3 18 ♔d1 ♘d7 (18...♘g4? looks threatening, but 19 ♖e2! holds everything together) 19 ♕d4 ♕xd4 20 ♗xd4 ♗xf4 21 ♖f2 with equality.

The mistake, it seems, is not so much the ♖d1 move itself, but rather in playing it a move too early.

15...♘e8!

This is vicious, and very easy to underestimate. One expects players when attacking to move pieces forward, rather than backward. The knight is moving towards a significant defensive square on d6, but the more significant point is that Black's two bishops now have clear and effective diagonals, and work very well with the rook. The queen and knight are also ready to enter the attack, and there could be some dangerous prods with the queenside pawns. Black is better.

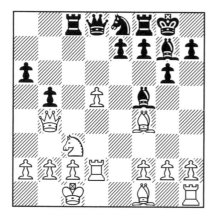

16 ♗d3?

A blunder, but Eljanov was under pressure. Two slips in consecutive moves can turn a position from being comfortable to being in danger, but the third slip can often be quickly decisive.

16 ♘d1?, which may have been his intended move, would allow Black to saw through the queenside after 16...♛xd5! 17 ♖xd5 ♖xc2+ 18 ♔b1 ♖xb2+ 19 ♔c1 (19 ♔a1 ♖b1 mate) 19...♖c2+ 20 ♔b1 ♖c4+.

White's best would be 16 ♗e2, and then hope for the best. The computer might suggest that White is comfortable after, for example, 16...a5 17 ♛xb5 ♘d6 18 ♗xd6 ♛xd6 19 ♘d1 ♖c5 20 ♛a4 ♖b8, but a good human player would find White's position extremely uncomfortable. Black can attack, while it is difficult for White to coordinate. For example, if 21 ♗f3 ♗h6 22 ♘e3 ♛e5 23 ♛a3 ♛c7, and Black is pushing.

16...♗xd3

As simple as that. Black is now

clearly winning.

17 cxd3

If 17 ♖xd3 ♖c4, winning the bishop.

17...♛xd5

Pawns are now level, and the queen is forking the pawns on a2 and g2. If that is not enough, Black also has the more active pieces.

18 ♔b1

18 f3 ♛xa2 is horrible.

18...♛xg2 19 ♛e4

This speeds things up. A decent rook move keeps the position just about alive, although Black should win.

19...♛xe4 20 dxe4

If 20 ♘e4, then Black rolls through with 20...e5 followed by ...f5.

20...♘f6

Completing his development!

20...♗xc3 21 bxc3 ♖xc3 22 ♖d7 makes life more difficult.

21 ♖hd1?

Dispirited, Eljanov falls for another trap. 21 f3 ♘h5 22 ♗g5 ♗xc3 23 bxc3 f6 24 ♗h6 ♖fd8 might allow White to struggle to the time control.

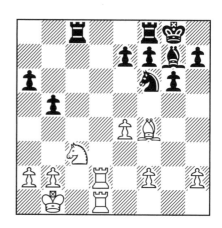

21...♖xc3! 22 bxc3 ♘xe4 0-1

Winning a second pawn in a simplified endgame.

Game 29
Bu Xiangzhi-V.Zvjaginsev
Russian Team Championship 2008
King's Indian Defence E83

1 d4 ♘f6 2 c4 g6 3 ♘c3 ♗g7 4 e4 d6 5 f3

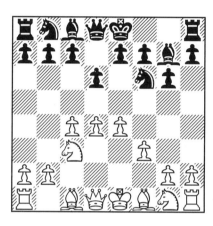

The Sämisch variation. There is also another Sämisch system in the Nimzo-Indian, after 1 d4 ♘f6 2 c4 e6 3 ♘c3 ♗b4 4 a3!? ♗xc3+ 5 bxc3, often with the idea of setting up a big pawn centre with f3 and, if given the chance, e4.

Clearly 5 f3 here has the same general idea, but playing against a different defensive opening. In the 'hypermodern' days, advocated by Nimzowitsch, Tartakower, Réti and others, leading players often experimented with Black on concentrating on quick piece development, but delaying pawn advances in the centre. Sämisch tended in his younger years to defend as Black with the hypermodern ...♘f6 and ...e6 after White's initial 1 d4. He most certainly was not the sort of dogmatist to have argued that the big pawn push in the centre would have refuted the

modern systems. Rather, he was trying out new ideas.

These days, White usually prefers to develop his pieces in the King's Indian, such as with 5 ♗e2 and ♘f3, as in Game 19, Van Wely-Radjabov. As Bu Xiangzhi demonstrates, however, there are still advocates for Sämisch's ideas.

5...0-0

Black develops. He knows he is going to have to castle sooner or later, and decides to do it now. He is waiting to see what White is going to do, and will then decide what to do himself. Is it, for example, going to be ...c5 or ...e5? Or even ...a6, ...c6 and ...b5?

6 ♘ge2

The obvious 6 ♗d3 tends to be less popular, the bishop getting in the way. 6...c5!? 7 d5 ♘bd7, with a quick ...♘e5, should be equal.

6 ♗e3 could easily transpose into the main line. 6...c5!? is possible, and White usually offers a Dragon structure with 7 ♘ge2. White can, of course, win a pawn with 7 dxc5 dxc5 8 ♕xd8 ♖xd8 9 ♗xc5 ♘c6. He has weakened his dark squares considerably though, and experience has suggested that this is only an equalizing line after 10 ♘d5 ♘d7 11 ♘xe7+ ♘xe7 12 ♗xe7 ♗xb2 13 ♖b1 ♗c3+ 14 ♔f2 ♗d4+ 15 ♔g3 ♖e8 16 ♗g5 ♘f6. This position has, indeed, occasionally been agreed drawn around here, but in A.Graf-E.Inarkiev, Spanish

Team Championship 2007, Graf tried to squeeze on with 17 ♗xf6 ♗xf6 18 ♗e2 ♖e5 19 ♖b5 ♖xb5 20 cxb5 ♗e6 21 f4 ♗c3 22 ♘f3 ♗xa2 23 e5. In this book, we have seen several examples of White trying to play for an edge in a 'drawn' endgame. White had chances of trying for an edge, but eventually the game was drawn.

6...a6

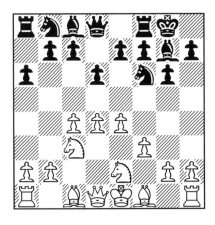

This strange looking move, seemingly developing nothing and attacking nothing, is based on the original idea of Oscar Panno in the mid-1950s. He wanted to try some new lines against the g3 fianchetto line of the King's Indian, and developed the idea of attacking White's c-pawn, no longer defended by the bishop, with moves such as ...a6, ...♘c6, ...♗d7, ...♖b8, and later ...b5. If White were to exchange on b5, then maybe ...♘a5 or ...♘e5 followed by ...c5.

The Panno system may be applicable against the Sämisch as well. White has a big central pawn structure, and the pawn to attack is often the c-pawn, preferably from the flank.

6...c5 is perhaps the most straightforward option. Dreev has tried 7 d5 e6 8 ♘g3 a few times, without great success, and has since reverted to the main line pseudo-Dragon with 7 ♗e3.

7 ♗e3

7 ♗g5 is also possible, and Black has a choice between continuing with a Panno, with 7...♘c6, or pushing a pawn forward with 7...c5 or 7...c6.

7...♘c6

More aggressive than 7...♘bd7.

8 ♕d2

8 d5 ♘e5 is a more direct attempt for an edge in the centre, but the trouble is that the knight in the centre is secure, as if at some stage White plays f4, Black has ...♘eg4 with counterplay. Several years earlier, Bu Xiangzhi tried 9 ♘d4 c5 10 ♘c2 e6 11 a4 exd5 12 cxd5 ♘h5 13 ♗e2, but Black started to take over the initiative in Bu Xiangzhi-Ye Jiangchuan, Yangon 1999. Play continued 13...f5 14 exf5 gxf5 15 0-0 f4 16 ♗f2 ♕g5 17 ♔h1 ♗f5 18 ♘a3 ♖f6 19 ♘e4 ♗xe4 20 fxe4 ♖g6, and Black later won.

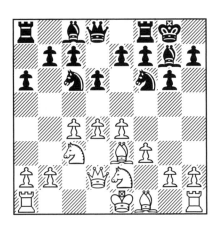

Bu Xiangzhi now uses a much more aggressive way of handling the game. He starts by developing. Before too long, he will castle queenside, and start a pawn rush on the kingside with ideas of h4 and g4, if given the opportunity.

8...♗d7

Sticking to the Panno theme. Black has also tried 8...♖b8, with a similar idea, and this is the most common move at top level. Then 9 ♖b1 e6 10 b4 ♘d7 11 g3 (abandoning the pawn rush; he now just wants to castle) 11...♘b6 12 ♕d3 f5 13 ♗g2 fxe4 14 fxe4 d5 15 c5 dxe4 16 ♘xe4 ♘d5 17 ♗d2 e5 was agreed drawn in Bu Xiangzhi-P.Svidler, Internet 2004. Here 9 ♖c1 ♗d7 10 ♘d1 is an attempt at side-stepping the Panno plan. After 10...b5?! 11 c5!, White keeps an edge, and does too after 10...e5 11 d5 ♘e7.

If 9 h4, Black could, as in the main game, try 9...h5. Instead 9...b5 10 h5 e5 11 d5 ♘a5 12 ♘g3 bxc4 13 0-0-0 leads to sharp play with castling on opposite sides, and attacks on the files against either king. The latest try is 13...♗d7 14 ♗h6 ♗xh6 15 ♕xh6 ♕e7 16 ♗e2 ♖b4 17 ♖d2 c6 18 ♘f2, J.Lautier-P.Svidler, Internet 2004, and now Hazai suggests 18...♖fb8 as promising. Svidler tried 18...♔h8 19 hxg6 fxg6 20 ♕xg6 cxd5?, but 21 ♘e3!, with an attack on d5 and pressure on f5, proved good for White, who later won.

The alternative approach is 8...♖e8. The problem for White is that it is difficult to develop his kingside minor pieces, so that, for example, after 9 ♘c1 e5 10 d5 ♘d4 11 ♘b3 ♘xb3 12 axb3 White has given away enough tempi with the knight to allow Black reasonable chances of equality.

9 h4

Does this look as though White is about to punch the Dragon? Be assured that this is no illusion. White is aiming for a quick and direct mating attack, with plenty of sacrifices. Enjoy it!

The Dragon Variation in the Sicilian has always been popular, with sharp tactical play, and the chance of quick demolition after a slight mistake by either side. Such attacking ideas are also possible in the Sämisch King's Indian. White has to be aware, though, of the differences in the pawn structure between the Sämisch and the Dragon. Had White tried 9 ♗h6?!, for example, Black would have had comfortable counterplay with 9...e5.

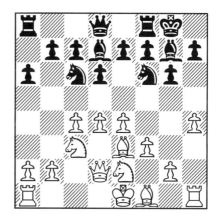

9...h5

It is not pleasant to make a pawn push in front of the king, but allowing White to push further with h5 is even more uncomfortable.

9...e5 10 d5 ♘e7 11 g4 gives White excellent chances of rolling through. In this particular line, Black's ...a6 proves to have been a waste of time, and White plays extremely vigorously.

9...b5 10 axb5 axb5 11 ♘xb5 ♘a5 (threatening ...♘b3) 12 ♘a3 at least diverts attention from the kingside, but Black probably does not quite have sufficient compensation for the pawn.

Finally, 9...♖b8 is slower than the line given with 8...♖b8 (instead of 8...♗d7).

10 ♗h6

10 0-0-0 is just as aggressive as in the game. In A.Miles-M.Jadoul, Brussels 1986, play continued 10...b5 11 ♗h6 ♚h7, and now White side-stepped the bishop exchange with 12 ♗g5!?. The idea is, of course, to lure the king to the h-file, to open up a scorching attack with g4, and if ...hxg4, then h5. Few players would be happy to defend such a position, and Jadoul attempted to pacify the h-file with a piece sacrifice with 12...bxc4 13 g4 ♘xg4 14 fxg4 ♗xg4 15 ♗h3 ♗xh3 16 ♖xh3. Black had three pawns for the piece, but it was White's extra piece that won the day. I leave it as an open-ended exercise for the reader to decide what is going on, presumably with computer assistance, after 13...hxg4 14 h5 ♘xh5.

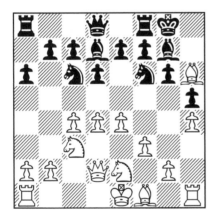

10...e5

Following the lead of the Miles-Jadoul game, 10...♚h7!? would perhaps be a safer option. 11 ♗xg7 ♚xg7 loses a tempo for Black, but he would be happy with his kingside defensive structure, with ...♖h8 after g4. Here 11 ♗g5 ♘a5!? 12 ♘g3 ♘c6 13 ♘ge2 is a possible draw. There is no clear advantage for White after 13 d5 ♘e5 14 f4 ♘eg4.

11 0-0-0

11 d5 ♘a5 12 ♗xg7 ♚xg7 13 ♘c1 b6 leaves Black comfortable.

11...b5

Both players are aiming for a sharp battle.

11...♘xd4 12 ♘xd4 exd4 13 ♗xg7 ♚xg7 14 ♕xd4 ♖e8 is a steadier approach, White trying to make use of the pinned knight. However, 15 g4?! hxg4 16 ♗e2 gxf3 17 ♗xf3 ♖e5 18 ♖dg1, following a computer suggestion, turns out not to be good. 18...♕h8! 19 h5 ♕h6+ 20 ♚b1 g5 keeps Black's extra pawn. There are, of course, quieter lines on move 15, generally ending up about equal.

12 ♘d5

Like it or not, White has to take the initiative. 12 ♗xg7?! ♚xg7 is already better for Black, White's central pawns being under pressure, leaving his king slightly too open.

12...♖e8

12...bxc4? loses material after 13 ♘xf6+ ♕xf6 14 ♗g5 ♕e6 15 d5.

12...♘xd5 13 ♗xg7 ♚xg7 14 cxd5 ♘d4 15 ♘xd4 exd4 16 ♕xd4+ gives White a slight positional edge. Black will have to work out what to do with his backward c-pawn. If ...c5 at some stage, White will have dxc6, and Black's pawn on d6 is isolated.

Zvjaginsev continues to play for his own attack.

13 g4

Now it is definite that tactics, attacks and sacrifices are going to take place, and that there will not be a quiet, close-to-equal middlegame. The last chance for placid play would have been 13 ♘xf6+ ♗xf6 14 d5 ♘e7 15 ♘c3, roughly equal.

13 ♗g5?! is a sensible idea, except that after 13...♘xd4 14 ♘xd4 exd4 15 ♕xd4 Black can jump out of the pin with 15...♘xd5!, and is slightly better.

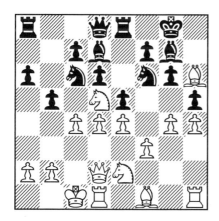

We are now reaching as close to pure tactics as anyone is likely to find. All the pieces are on the board, there are three 'pawn-takes-pawn' captures on either side, which will suddenly change the pawn structure, maybe in unpredictable ways. Also there are knight-takes-knight and bishop-takes-bishop captures, which might help simplify the position, or alternatively might set up further tactics. Once minor pieces go, there are more chances, on either side, for attack against the king.

There is no time for delicate calculation as to whether there is a weakness in the pawn structure. All that a player can realistically do is to capture something, look for checks, get out of the opponent's checks, and if the player has the chance of a breather, find the occasional quiet developing move for a piece, which is then brought into the attack.

13...hxg4!?

If White is pushing all his pawns for-ward, a natural reply by Black is to start taking them.

13...bxc4 14 ♗xg7 ♔xg7 15 gxh5 ♘xh5 16 ♕c3 is playable but unclear. However, Black is probably far more likely to be concerned about 14 ♗g5!?. With the help of the computer, it is easy enough to be able so show a few entertaining wins for White:

a) For example, 14...hxg4 15 h5 gxf3 16 ♘g3 ♘xd4 17 h6 c3 18 bxc3 ♘e6 19 hxg7 ♘xg5 20 ♕xg5 ♘g4 21 ♘f6+! ♕xf6 (21...♘xf6? 22 ♖h8+ ♔xg7 23 ♕h6 mate) 22 ♖h8+ ♔xg7 23 ♘h5+ ♔xh8 24 ♘xf6, and White wins.

b) Or 14...♘xd4 15 ♘xd4 exd4 16 gxh5 c3 17 bxc3 dxc3 18 ♕g2 ♗a4 19 hxg6 ♗xd1 20 ♗c4!, and Black is in great trouble on the kingside.

c) In either case the ...c3 pin-prick is useful, but does not quite work. Black can get his retaliation in first, though, with 14...c3!?, and any capture with the queen (15 ♕xc3 exd4 16 ♘xd4 ♘xd4 17 ♕xd4 ♘xd5!), or knight (15 ♘exc3 ♘xd4) is inconveniently timed. The straightforward 15 bxc3! seems best, covering the d4-square. White's king is now opened up, but it is difficult for Black to start an attack there:

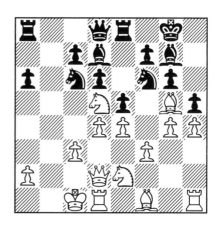

c1) 15...exd4 16 gxh5 dxc3 17 ♘exc3 is promising for White.

c2) 15...hxg4 16 h5 gxf3 17 ♘g3 exd4 18 cxd4 leads to tense play, and with quiet moves, White will create some pressure, and Black will defend. Black can try for a tactical escape with 18...♘xd4 19 ♕xd4 ♘xd5!?. If now 20 ♕xd5? ♕b8!, and Black is clearly better, White's king now being fully exposed with Black's queen and two bishops threatening to attack. Thus White needs to simplify. A possible finish might be 20 ♗xd8 ♗xd4 21 ♖xd4, and Black cannot quite equalize: for example, 21...♘c3 22 ♗f6 ♘xa2+ 23 ♔d2 ♖e6 24 e4 dxe5 25 ♖xd7 ♖xf6 26 ♗c4 with a substantial edge.

Maybe Zvjaginsev's move is best, but he still has to play extremely accurately afterwards.

14 h5

Having gone this far, he must continue with all-out attack.

14...gxf3

White will quickly chew up the kingside after 14...♘xd5 15 cxd5 gxf3 16 hxg6 fxe2 17 gxf7+ ♔xf7 18 ♗xe2 ♘xd4 19 ♗h5+ ♔g8 20 ♗xg7.

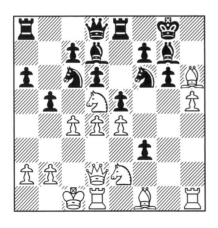

15 hxg6

A useful practical technique of attack is to force the opponent to have to make the critical and difficult decisions. Here the most direct method of play would be 15 ♗xg7 ♔xg7 16 hxg6, but then there is 16...♘g4!? with complicated play not necessarily in favour of White. This knight move is not difficult to see, and creates problems. Bu Xiangzhi transposed the moves slightly, and after 15 hxg6 Black has several options to make, of which 15...♘g4 is but one.

15...fxg6?!

Watch out now for some heavy sacrifices.

If 15...fxe2, then White does not bother taking back the pawn with 16 ♗xe2?!, sound but not advantageous after, for example, 16...♘xd4 17 ♗xg7 ♘xe2+ 18 ♕xe2 ♔xg7 19 ♖df1. There is some complicated play to follow, and Black could easily make a wrong turn, but with care Black has chances of holding the balance with 19...♖h8 20 ♖xh8 ♕xh8 21 ♘xf6 ♕h6+ 22 ♔b1 ♗e6. Indeed, there could be a repetition after 23 gxf7 ♗xf7 24 ♕g4+ ♕g6 25 ♕d7 ♖f8 26 ♕xc7 ♕g2 27 ♘h5+ ♔g8 28 ♘f6+ ♔g7.

Instead White can continue sacrificing with 16 ♗xg7!! exd1♕+ 17 ♔xd1.

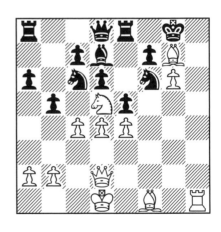

It is highly unusual for a player to make four pawn captures with the same pawn on four successive moves, and the natural inclination is that White cannot give away so many pieces, or indeed pawns. White is only a rook down, though, and material may quickly be recovered. More importantly, can Black escape from mate?

a) 17...♘h5 18 ♕h6 fxg6 19 ♖xh5 ♗g4+ 20 ♔c1 ♗xh5 21 ♗xf6 ♕xf6 (the only move) 22 ♘xf6+ ♔f7 23 ♘xe8 ♖xe8 24 ♕h7+ ♔f8 25 ♕xc7 ♘xd4 26 ♕xd6+ forces Black to lose too much material to avoid checkmate.

b) 17...♗g4+ 18 ♔c1 ♘h5 19 ♕h6 soon transposes.

c) This leaves 17...♘g4, irritatingly covering the h6- and h2-squares from the queen, and also the f6- and f2-squares. There is another sacrifice coming up: 18 ♗f6! ♘xf6 (18...♕xf6 19 ♘xf6+ ♘xf6 20 ♕h6 does not slow White down) 19 ♕h6 and White wins on the h-file. If 19...♗g4+ 20 ♔c1 ♗h5 21 ♖xh5 ♘xh5 22 ♕h7+ and mates.

A stunning finish, but there is more to follow. We have not seen a queen sacrifice just yet, and on cue there is 15...♘xe4 16 ♗xg7 ♘xd2 17 ♗f6.

Naturally Black must soon give the queen back, and after 17...♕xf6 18 ♘xf6+ ♔g7 19 ♘xe8+ ♖xe8 20 gxf7 ♔xf7 21 ♔xd2 fxe2 22 ♗xe2 White remains a safe exchange ahead.

If instead 17...fxg6, White has, of course, the guarantee of a perpetual check after 18 ♖h8+ ♔f7 19 ♖h7+, since if 19...♔e6?? 20 ♗h3 mate. There are two other king retreats: 19...♔g8! forces a perpetual in 20 ♖h8+; 19...♔f8 is also a likely draw by perpetual, but White has for now 20 ♖xd2!.

However wild and aggressive the attack becomes, the number one rule of chess is that if no mistake is made on either side, the end result is a draw. In wild games, as here, it is likely to end up as a perpetual check, while in quieter games it is more likely that the defender will gradually equalize in an endgame.

But the game is not yet finished. Bu Xiangzhi won quickly, and Zvjaginsev therefore lost quickly, but maybe the mistake came later on? We shall see.

16 ♘ec3

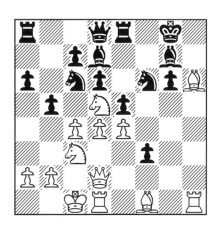

The right way, even though the knight is going away from the kingside. The d5-square is an excellent square for

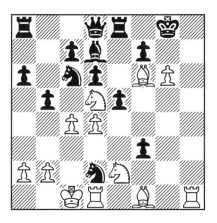

the knight, and if White exchanges the first knight for a good defender, then the second knight will jump in.

White has a more bloodthirsty alternative with 16 ♗xg7 ♘xe4 17 ♖h8+ ♔f7 18 ♖h7 ♘xd2 19 ♗xe5+ ♔f8 (19...♔e6?? 20 ♗h3 mate) 20 ♖h8+ ♔f7, but this is only a perpetual. Moreover, Black does not have to comply with a draw: 16...♔xg7!? 17 ♕h6+ ♔f7 18 ♘fc3 would transpose into the main line after 18...♘xd4, but Black has alternatives, the simplest being 18...♖h8!? with advantage to Black.

16...♘xd4

Black's problem is that he cannot make any serious threat so as to slow down White's attack. Take a pawn? Attack a knight? That is nothing, when compared with serious mating threats against an exposed king. If, for example, 16...b4?! 17 ♗xg7 bxc3 18 ♕h6 cxb2+ 19 ♔b1, and Black has run out of ideas, while White has one big idea. There is a similar idea after 16...exd4 17 ♗xg7, while various other possibilities end up with a quick win for White.

16...♘h5! is the toughest defence, adding an extra barrier on the h-file. If White were to sacrifice the exchange on h5 at some stage, an annoyance would be for Black to play ...♗g4 after ♖g1. The pawn on h5, apparently feeble, helps block up the kingside highly effectively. The other black kingside pawn, on f3, makes all the difference between White winning easily, and White having problems.

The verdict of 'unclear' is never fully satisfactory, and it is better for both the analyst and the reader to be able to say that either White is better, or Black is better, or the position is equal or very close to equal. In practical terms, over the board, an 'unclear' assessment is often the best that a player can achieve. A player will try to make good moves, and wait to see whether the opponent will make a mistake.

Here 17 cxb5!? is sensible, there being no obvious kingside winning plans for White. He recovers a pawn, and possibly more importantly, he brings the light-squared bishop into play, most probably with ♗c4. Then:

a) 17...♘xd4 18 ♗c4 seems good for White. If 18...♗e6 19 ♖xh5 gxh5 20 ♖g1 axb5 21 ♖xg7+ ♔h8 22 ♖xc7 ♗xd5 23 ♗xg7+ ♔g8 24 ♘xd5 bxc4 25 ♘f6+ and White wins.

b) 17...axb5! sets up counterattacks. After 18 ♗xb5 ♘xd4 19 ♖xh5 we have:

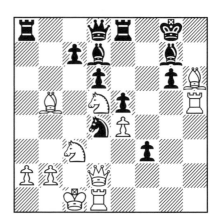

b1) After 19...♖xa2!? 20 ♗c4 (20 ♘xa2? ♘b3+) 20...♖a1+ 21 ♘b1 White is ahead on material at the moment, and this makes the position easier for him. If 21...♗e6 22 ♗xg7 ♖a4 23 b4 gxh5 24 ♗f6, and White wins. Or 21...♘e2+ 22 ♘xe2 fxe2 23 ♖g1 gxh5 24 ♖xg7+ ♔h8 25 ♕xe2, and White is clearly better, such as after 25...♗g4 26 ♖xg4 hxg4 27 ♕h2.

b2) Sometimes when defending, it is

best to grab material first, and then return the extra material later. Therefore 19...gxh5! is indicated: 20 ♗xd7 ♕xd7 21 ♖g1 ♗f8! 22 ♖xg7+ (22 ♗xg7 f2!) 22...♕xg7 23 ♗xg7 f2 24 ♘e3 f1♕+ 25 ♘xf1 ♖xf1+ 26 ♘d1 ♖xa2, and after complicated play, with sacrifice and counter-sacrifice, Black is winning. So White has to reinforce, or at least speed up, his attacking ideas with 20 ♖g1:

b21) One idea for Black is to pick up the bishop on b5, but this seems slow: 20...♘xb5 21 ♖xg7+ ♔h8 22 ♗g5! wins for White: for example, 22...♘xc3 23 ♗xd8 ♘xa2+ 24 ♔b1 ♔xg7 25 ♕g5+, soon giving checkmate, or 22...f2 23 ♕xf2 ♖f8 24 ♕g2!.

b22) 20...♗xb5 21 ♗xg7 ♘e2+!? 22 ♘xe2 f2!? 23 ♗f6 fxg1+ 24 ♘xg1 ♕d7 is a cleverly thought-out defensive plan by Black. Visually, one would expect that White would be winning comfortably, but Black is two exchanges ahead. The help of the computer suggests that there is still a win after 25 ♕g5+ ♔f7 26 ♕xh5+ ♔g8 27 ♕g6+ ♔f8 28 ♘f3!.

b23) The next, and most secure, option is to set up a pawn-and-bishop defensive chain with 20...♗g4!:

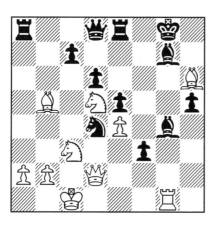

b231) If then 21 ♗xe8? ♖xa2!, and Black has successfully set up winning counterplay.

b232) 21 ♗g5 ♗h6! sees excellent use by both sides of the two bishop-pairs, combining attack and defence of various sets of pins. After White accepts the bishop sacrifice with 22 ♗xh6, it is time for Black to show what can be done with rook and knight with 22...♖xa2!. Then the tactics continue after 23 ♗c4 (23 ♘xa2 ♘b3+ or 23 ♔b1 ♖a1+ 24 ♔xa1 ♘b3+ would both pick up queens with knight forks) 23...♖a1+ 24 ♘b1 ♔h7. If now 25 ♗g5?!, there is a win for Black after 25...f2!: 26 ♖xg4 ♘b3+ 27 ♗xb3 f1♕+, and Black should win as the two queens are powerful, or 26 ♖f1 ♘f3 27 ♗xd8 ♖xb1+ 28 ♔xb1 ♘xd2+ followed by ...♘xf1, and Black wins on material.

White needs to sacrifice the exchange a move earlier, with 25 ♖xg4! hxg4 26 ♗g5 f2 27 ♗xd8 ♘b3+ 28 ♗xb3 f1♕+ 29 ♕d1 ♕xd1+ 30 ♗xd1 ♖xd8 31 ♗xg4. After plenty of tactics, we reach an unusual endgame of two rooks, plus an extra pawn, versus three minor pieces. Black must be better, as he can create a passed pawn, while White cannot, and Black is more able to create pressure with his pieces than White. Whether Black can win is open to question.

But this is just one complicated line of a complicated variation. There are several more ideas to be considered. Instead of the capture on b5, White could simply try 17 ♗g5!?.

Then 17...♕c8 releases the tension somewhat, and 18 cxb5!? axb5 19 ♘xb5 ♖xa2 20 ♗c4!?, for example, gives White reasonable attacking chances. It is possible that there might still be an improvement on this.

More critical, with chances of death or glory, would be 17...♕b8!? when White must do something quickly. Indeed, 18 ♖xh5 gxh5 19 ♘f6+ ♗xf6 20 ♗xf6 ♔f7 21 ♕h6 ♖g8 is critical:

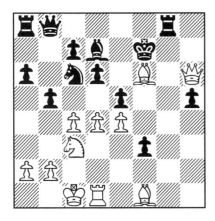

a) 22 ♕h7+ ♔xf6 23 ♘d5+ ♔g5 24 ♕xd7 ♘xd4 25 ♘xc7 ♖a7 26 ♕e7+ ♔g4 27 ♗h3+ ♔g3 28 ♖g1+ ♔h2 is too wild. Black's king hides between White's pieces.

b) 22 ♘d5 ♕f8 23 ♕xh5+ ♖g6 24 ♕h7+ ♖g7 25 ♕h5+ ♖g6 ends up as a repetition.

c) 22 dxe5! seems at first a little too straightforward and obvious, when one would normally expect some heavy sacrifices, but the pawn bolsters the bishop on f6, and can also take other pawns. There is, of course, a pin on the d-file.

22...♕e8!? offers a quick repetition, but White can play for more with 23 ♕h7+ ♔f8 24 exd6! ♖c8 (this seems the best) 25 ♗e7+ ♘xe7 26 dxe7+ ♕xe7 27 ♖xd7 ♕xh7 28 ♖xh7 ♖e8!. The first impression might well be that Black even has the more promising play, as he has kept his passed f-pawn, and White

could easily have to sacrifice his extra material. 29 ♖xh5!? ♖g1 30 ♖f5+ ♔g7 31 ♖xf3 ♖f8 32 ♖xf8 ♔xf8 will soon end up as a drawn endgame, though, and White can improve: 29 ♔d2! ♖g1 30 ♔e1! (30 ♗d3?! f2 31 cxb5 axb5 32 ♖xh5 f1♕ 33 ♗xf1 ♖xf1 only draws), and White, with bishop and knight against rook, remains in control, possibly also winning.

Maybe Black is already in trouble by now. We now return to the game and 16...♘xd4:

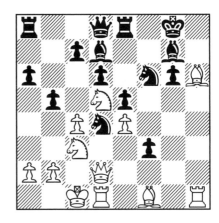

17 ♗xg7

Black's kingside fortress is now knocked down into the open. A result, even if three pawns have fallen.

17...♔xg7 18 ♘xf6

18 ♕h6+? allows too many chances of offering a queen exchange after 18...♔f7 19 ♘xf6 ♕xf6 20 ♘d5 ♕g7.

18...♕xf6 19 ♘d5

After the complications of the previous gambit play, it is within range to calculate that White is clearly better. He has not sacrificed any pieces, as opposed to pawns, and has by far the more active pieces, with Black's king being seriously open to attack.

19...♕f8

The only move. 19...♕f7? 20 ♕h6+ is hopeless.

20 ♕h6+

20 ♘xc7 ♖ac8 21 ♘xe8+ ♗xe8 is about equal, but White can do better.

20...♔f7 21 ♕g5

In this extremely fierce attack, this is the first time that White has retreated one of his pieces. Even this is only to get away from the rook, which wants to run through to h7 with a winning check.

21...♕g7

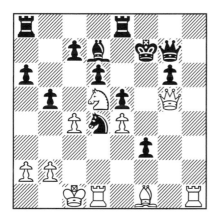

Black has covered the threat. It even looks as though he might have guarded against the attack.

22 ♖xd4!

White sacrifices, just in time.

22...exd4

22...c6 would by now be a desperate try. 23 ♖d3 cxd5 24 ♖xf3+ ♔g8 24 ♖h6 ♖e6 25 cxd5 wins.

23 ♕f4+

Now there is no doubt that White is winning.

23...♗f5

23...♔g8 24 ♘f6+ ♔f8 25 ♖h7 ♕xh7 26 ♘xh7+ ♔g7 27 ♘g5 ♖f8 28 ♕h2 should end up as a win for White, queen and piece outweighing two

rooks and a few pawns, especially if the pawns have no clear promoting prospects.

Of course, 23...♔e6? 24 ♗h3 mate wins immediately.

24 exf5

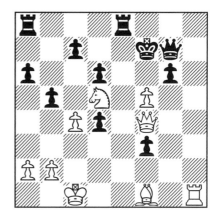

Now White has an extra piece – bishop and knight versus rook – and he has every reason to think that he has won the battle.

24...g5

Black cannot allow the f-file to be opened.

25 ♕g4

25 ♕xf3? g4! allows Black counterplay.

25...♖e1+

The computer suggests that various alternatives might be equal, but these turn out to be nothing. For example, 25...♕e5 26 ♕h5+ ♔f8 27 ♗d3 f2 28 f6 ♕e1+ 29 ♔c2, and White is winning.

25...♖h8 might last longer, but do not expect a second time control after 26 f6 ♖xh1 27 ♕d7+ ♔g6 28 ♕xg7+ ♔f5 29 f7.

26 ♔d2

26 ♔c2? d3+ 27 ♔xd3 ♖h8 leaves Black better. It is a standard principle of attacking chess not to allow the oppo-

nent to make unnecessary checks.

26...♖ae8

26...f2 27 f6 wins for White.

27 ♕h5+ 1-0

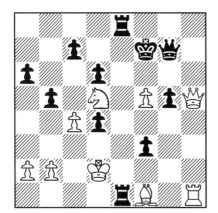

And Black resigns. Obvious maybe, with White having strong attacking chances, and he still has two minor pieces versus the rook. Even so, Black's resignation must surely have been premature, as White, despite initial appearances, is not giving checkmate.

The likelihood is that Zvjaginsev was so shattered by the ferocity of Bu Xiang-zhi's vigour of attack, and so short of time, if indeed he had not already lost on time, that he had quite simply surrendered. After 27... ♔f8 28 f6 ♕g8 the simplest line would seem to be 29 ♕xf3!? g4 (29...♖ef3 30 f7!? wins) 30 ♕f4 bxc4 31 ♕h6+ ♔f7 32 ♗xc4.

Game 30
B.Gelfand-E.Alekseev
Russian Team Championship 2008
Semi-Slav Defence D43

1 d4 d5 2 c4 c6 3 ♘f3 ♘f6 4 ♘c3 e6 5 ♗g5 h6

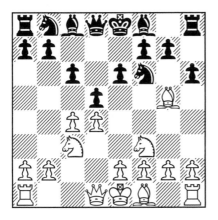

6 ♗h4

Only to be played if you are ready for sharp and complicated play.

6 ♗xf6 ♕xf6 is quieter. There were a couple of quiet and steady draws, with Gelfand as Black, in this very event. Also, a few months earlier, a game E.Alekseev-B.Gelfand, Moscow 2007, in which Alekseev tried 7 ♕c2 dxc4 8 e3 b5 9 a4 ♗b7 10 axb5 cxb5 11 ♘xb5 ♗b4+ 12 ♘c3, and play was level, drawn at move 24. Yes, the colours were reversed!

7 e3 ♘d7 8 ♗d3 dxc4 9 ♗xc4 g6 10 0-0 ♗g7 is the main line after the bishop-for-knight exchange. White is ahead in development, and has extra space with his pawns, but it is not so easy to break open the centre. If the pawn structure is opened, Black's

pieces soon become active.

6...dxc4 7 e4 g5 8 ♗g3 b5 9 ♘e5!? ♗b7

There is a wide choice here.

For 9...♗b4, see Game 27, Cheparinov-Nepomniachtchi.

9...h5!? 10 h4 g4 11 ♗e2 ♗g7 12 0-0 ♘bd7 leads to a popular line at top level, and one which can also come about via a 9 ♗e2 move order.

The statistics show that over a large number of 2600+ games, White keeps an insignificant plus score, over the relevant time period, and more than half the games have been decisive. This clearly is attractive for Black if he wants to play for a win, but White too has excellent chances.

10 h4

Naturally he wants to prod the pawns.

10...g4

In a couple of games in Georgia in

the late 1990s, Jobava showed a significant innovation for White, with a piece sacrifice, after 10...♗g7 11 a4 a6 12 hxg5 hxg6 13 ♖xh8+ ♗xh8 14 ♗xc4!. The bishop is too dangerous to touch. After 14...bxc4? 15 ♘xc4 there is a big knight threat on d6, and if 15...♗c8 16 e5 ♘d5 17 ♕h5 ♔e7 18 ♕xg5+ f6 19 ♕g6, Black's king is in serious trouble.

Black can, however, decline the piece sacrifice, giving back his extra pawn. It is by no means obvious why giving up the extra doubled c-pawn should be any worse than Alekseev's return of the g-pawn in the illustrative game. Black was not yet fully equal, even so, after either 14...b4 15 ♘a2 a5 16 ♕d3 ♕e7 17 0-0-0, B.Jobava-S.Nikoladze, Tbilisi 1999, or 14...♘bd7 15 ♕b3 ♕e7 16 ♗e2 ♘xe5 17 ♗xe5, B.Jobava-V.Raceanu, Artek 1999. Jobava won both games.

Let us get up to date. Gelfand-Alekseev was played on the 5th of April 2008. A fortnight or so later, on the 22nd, Karjakin tried something new with 10...♖g8!? 11 hxg5 hxg5.

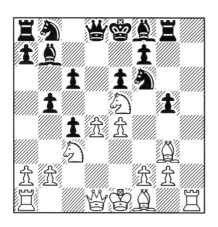

Now Black was a pawn up, so White had to do something quickly. A.Grischuk-S.Karjakin, Baku 2008, finished up as a perpetual after 12 ♘xf7

♔xf7 13 e5 ♘d5 14 ♖h7+ ♔g7 15 ♕h5+ ♔f8 16 ♕f3+ ♔e8 17 ♕h5+ ♔f8 18 ♕f3+ ♔e8 19 ♕h5+. Quite possibly both players had worked out in advance that this could end up as a draw, but that 10...g4 would have been discouraging for Black.

11 ♘xg4

The obvious move, but 11 ♗e2 h5 transposes into well-known main lines.

11...♘bd7

11...♘xg4 12 ♕xg4 ♕xd4 13 ♖d1 ♕g7 14 ♕xg7 ♗xg7 15 e5 ♗f8 16 ♘e4 ♗b4+ 17 ♔e2 ♘d7 18 h5! gives good compensation for the pawn. Instead Black had an edge, and later won, in P.Eljanov-A.Dreev, Sochi 2005, after 14 ♕f4?! ♘a6 15 ♗e2 ♗e7 16 e5 (Lutz has suggested 16 0-0!?) 16...♘b4 17 ♘e4 ♘d5.

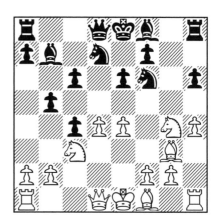

12 ♘xf6+

There are various alternatives, but none seem to keep an edge. Gelfand forces his opponent to decide which way he will recapture.

12...♘xf6

12...♕xf6 is also possible: for example, 13 ♕d2 0-0-0 14 h5 ♗g7 15 0-0-0 (15 ♗h4?! ♕xd4 favours Black) 15...♕e7 16 ♕e3 with maybe a slight edge for

White, and later drawn in B.Gelfand-E.Najer, Odessa (rapid) 2008.

13 ♕f3

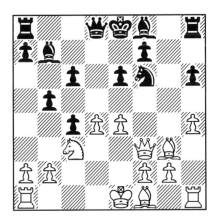

White has good reason to be happy with his position. He has kept his central pawn structure, and his pieces are well developed. He has not even needed to worry about the sacrificed pawn.

13...♖g8

Black must avoid 13...♕xd4?? 14 ♖d1, winning a piece.

13...b4 loosens up the queenside pawns. After 14 ♘e2 c5 15 ♗e5 ♗g7 16 ♘g3 cxd4 17 ♗xc4 White keeps an edge. It seems too early to open up the queenside.

13...♗g7 does not quite seem satisfactory either. After 14 ♗e5 it is White who takes control of the long diagonal, and the knight is awkwardly pinned.

14 ♗e2?!

Quiet development, indeed too quiet. Gelfand aims to castle kingside, keeping the king safe, and once this has been done, he will aim, perhaps, to attack in the centre.

Unfortunately this seems mistimed. 14 ♖d1! is better, keeping the d4-pawn safe, and more generally bringing another piece in play. If 14...b4?! 15 ♘a4,

and there is no clear follow-up, as if 15...c5? 16 ♘xc5 ♗xc5 17 dxc5, and it is White who is attacking. Or 15...c3 16 bxc3 bxc3 17 ♗d3, and if 17...♕xd4?? 17 ♗c2, winning a piece.

14...a6?

A waste of a tempo, and from now on, Gelfand plays superbly.

After 14...b4! 15 ♘a4 c5 16 ♗e5? there is no pin on the e5-h8 diagonal, and Black simply plays 16...♘xe4.

16 ♗xc4 would in effect admit that White has lost a tempo with his previous ♗e2. After 16...♘xe4 17 ♗b5+ ♔e7 18 dxc5 ♗xf3 19 ♗d6+ ♕xd6 20 cxd6+ ♔xd6 21 gxf3 ♖c8 Black has the much better pawn structure.

White can play for equality with 16 ♘xc5 ♗xc5 17 dxc5 ♘xe4, but Black still keeps an edge after 18 ♕e3 ♘xg3 19 fxg3 ♕c7 or 18 ♕f4 ♕d4!.

15 ♖d1

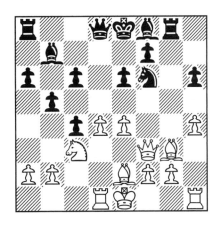

Now White is again in control. White's 14 ♗e2 and Black's 14...a6 are both inaccurate, but the end result of the slips on either side has been to gain an extra tempo for development.

15...♘d7

It is also unfortunate that he has to retreat after playing ...♘d7xf6 earlier.

One can sense that it will soon be time for White to start a direct attack.

16 0-0

But first he must complete his development.

16 ♗f4!? is also worth considering.

16...♛f6

Some more backtracking when one compares with Black's 12th-move alternative. A reminder that in the Gelfand-Najer game, Black played ...♛d8xf6 in one move.

16...♗g7 is a possible alternative.

17 ♛e3

Naturally he does not want to exchange queens. He is looking for an attack.

17...0-0-0

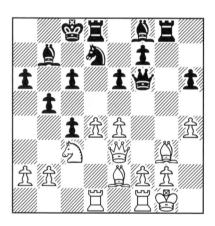

And Black has castled his king into some sort of safety, in draughts formation on the light squares. There might be a few question marks on the dark squares, particularly on the h2-b8 and g1-a7 diagonals, but so long as Black is safe on the light squares, he should be able to hold the dark squares.

18 b3!

So Gelfand quickly sets up pawn clashes on the light squares. Black's c4-pawn looks impressive, but as soon as it is exchanged, White can open lines on the c-file and the f1-a6 diagonal. Suddenly Black is on a breezy fortress.

18...cxb3

This is unpleasant for Black, but after 18...b4? 19 ♘a4 c3 20 a3 a5 21 axb4 axb4 22 d5! White has standard mating ideas:

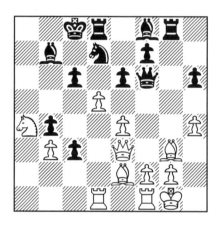

a) If then 22...cxd5 23 ♛a7 (threatening ♛b8+) 23...e5 24 ♖xd5! with a winning attack. The most precise line after 24...♗xd5 is 25 exd5 (avoiding the queen sacrifice after 25 ♗a6+ ♛xa6) 25...♖g6 26 h5!, and Black can do nothing.

b) 22...exd5 23 ♛a7 ♗d6 24 ♗a6 ♗xa6 25 ♛xa6+ ♚c7 provides more resistance, but after 26 exd5 ♗xg3 27 fxg3 ♛d6 28 ♛a7+ ♚c8 29 dxc6 ♛xc6 30 ♖xd7! White wins. Black's position folds on 30...♖xd7 31 ♘b6+ ♚d8 32 ♛b8+ ♚e7 33 ♖e1+!.

Black's best chance is an immediate counterattack with 18...c5!. He needs to keep the bishops in full play. White too has an excellent diagonal, on the h2-b8. Tactics will come thick and fast, e.g. 19 bxc4 cxd4 20 ♖xd4 (20 ♛xd4? ♛xd4 21 ♖xd4 ♖xg3! 22 fxg3 ♗c5 favours Black) 20...♗c5 21 ♖xd7 ♗xe3 22 ♖c7+ ♚b8.

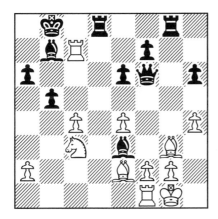

This would have been a nightmare position to analyse over the board. After 23 ♖xf7+ ♖xg3 24 ♖xf6 Black's rook and bishop have somehow been forked by an unmoved pawn. After further tactics with 24...♗d4! 25 ♖xe6 ♖xc3 26 cxb5 axb5 27 ♗xb5 ♖c2 28 ♖xh6 ♗xe4 Black has an extra bishop in return for a few pawns. Black has no pawns, but his two rooks and two bishops are active. The computer gives this as equal, but White's pawns do not do not work very well. White could try 29 ♖e6 ♗d5 30 ♖e2 ♖g8 31 ♖e8+ ♖xe8 32 ♗xe8 ♖xa2, which is entertaining, but White is clearly not better, and so it is necessary to find an improvement.

So we return to considering White's options earlier. 19 e5! cxd4 20 ♖xd4 ♘xe5 21 ♖xd8+ ♔xd8 22 ♖d1+ ♔c8 23 ♗xe5 ♖xg2+ 24 ♔f1 ♕h4 25 ♗f3! is almost disappointingly quiet after the previous tactics, but the point is that White has kept his extra piece, is defending and can attack himself.

The elaborate line is interesting, but sometimes the simplest and more direct line is to be preferred.

19 axb3

Black has two extra pawns on the queenside, covering the a-, b- and c-files, but what can they do that is active? If the pawns advance, the king will be opened up. Meanwhile, White has an extra pawn in the centre, the d-pawn, and this constricts Black's hopes for ...c5 or ...e5.

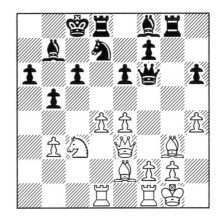

Black's pieces, and in particular the light-squared bishop, will find themselves constrained in trying to defend the weak pawns in front of the king, and this in the end makes it difficult for him to stay in the game.

19...♗e7

19...e5!?, opening up the dark squares for both sides, is close to the edge. After 20 dxe5 ♘xe5 21 ♖xd8+ ♔xd8 22 ♕a7 ♔c8 23 ♘d5 ♕e6 24 ♘b6+ ♔c7 25 ♘d7! ♕e7 (25...♗d6 26 ♗xe5 ♕xd7 transposes) 26 ♗xe5+ ♗d6 27 ♖d1 ♖g6, it looks at first as though it is all over with an attractive double pin with 28 h5 ♖e6 29 ♗g4. Black can, however, swiftly equalize with 29...♖xe5! 30 ♗xd7 ♗c5, trapping the queen.

With care White would still have an edge through gradual positional play with, for example, 28 ♕c5 ♕e7 29 ♖xd6 ♖xd6 30 b4 f6 31 ♗g3 ♗c8 32 h5, and

White slowly improves his position, fixing perhaps on the h6 weakness, and eventually breaking through. There are too many zugzwangs to allow Black to survive.

20 ♖c1

Eyeballing the c-file.

20...♕h8

If 20...e5?!, White has the advantage, and can even win a pawn with 21 ♘d5 ♕e6 22 ♘xe7+ ♕xe7 23 d5 c5 24 ♕xh6. Black thus decides to move the queen out of the way before playing ...e5.

20...♕g7 at first seems more natural, but Alekseev wants to keep open the possible exchange sacrifice with ...♖xg3. Here 21 ♗f3 e5 22 ♘d5 ♗d6 23 ♖fd1 keeps an edge for White.

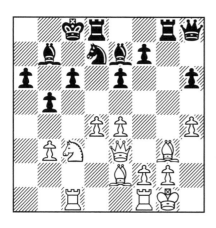

21 ♗h2!

Gelfand decides he does not want to allow the ...♖xg3 sacrifice.

21 ♗f3 is to be considered, although 21...e5 22 dxe5! (22 ♘d5 ♗d6 23 ♖fd1 ♔b8 is equal) 22...♖xg3! (22...♘xe5 23 ♘d5 ♗a3 24 ♕a7, and White has some advantage) 23 ♘d5! (23 fxg3?? ♗c5) 23...♗a3 24 fxg3 ♗xc1 25 ♖xc1 ♕xe5 26 ♕xh6 ♔b8 27 ♘e3 ♕xg3 28 ♘f5 ♕c7 winds up as about equal after fast-moving play.

22...♕g7

And Alekseev decides he might as well take the extra tempo, with the threat of mate on g2.

22 ♗f3

22 ♕g3!?, forcing an exchange of queens, gives an edge, but he can try for more. White intends to keep the queen on the board, within the view of mate threats.

22...e5

The b8-h2 diagonal just has to be covered.

23 ♘d5

Naturally, Black's c-pawn is pinned. Also his pawn on e5 is under enormous pressure.

23...♗d6

23...♗xh4 is to be considered. Then 24 ♕c3 ♖de8 25 ♕a5 ♗d8 26 ♖xc6+! ♗xc6? 27 ♕xa6+ soon wins for White, the other rook joining the attack. 26...♔b8! provides a better defence, when Black is attacking queen and rook, but after 27 ♕c3 ♖e6 (27...♗a7 28 ♘c7 keeps the attack going) 28 ♖xe6 fxe6 29 ♘b4 ♗b6 30 ♘c6+ ♗xc6 31 ♕xc6 ♔a7 32 ♖a1 Black is still under great pressure.

24 ♕c3

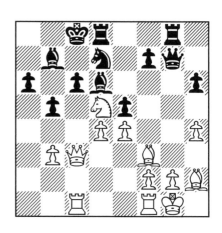

The creaking pressure continues.

24 ♖fd1 also adds to the pressure, and if 24...exd4?? 25 ♗xd6 dxe3 26 ♘e7 mate.

24...♖de8?

Allowing a clean and attractive sacrificial attack.

Black needs to open his defences on the second rank with 24...f5!. After 25 exf5 exd4! 26 ♗xd6 dxc3 there is no checkmate. Of course, White continues with 27 ♘e7+ (if 27 f6 ♕xf6!) 27...♕xe7 28 ♗xe7 ♘e5 29 ♖xc3 ♘xf3+ 30 ♖xf3 c5 31 ♖g3 ♖xg3 32 fxg3 ♖d2 33 ♖f2 ♖d1+ 34 ♔h2 (he is not interested in a draw) 34...♗d5 35 ♗xc5 ♗xb3. After a breather to work out what is going on once the tactics have subsided, it soon becomes clear that there is no draw with the opposite-coloured bishops, and that White's kingside pawns are more numerous and better placed than Black's queenside pawns.

There may be other possibilities for White, but this seems the clearest. 25 ♕a5, for example, gives an edge for White, but probably not a decisive one after 25...fxe4 26 ♗xe4 ♔b8 27 ♖xc6 ♗xc6 28 ♕xa6 ♘f6! 29 ♕b6+ ♕b7 30 ♕xb7+ ♗xb7 31 ♘xf6.

25 ♕a5

Again with ideas of a rook sacrifice on c6.

25...♖e6

Black wants to add an extra defence to the bishop on d6 and the pawn on c6. This is sensible, but it doesn't quite work.

White still has the same winning idea after 25...♕g6 26 ♖xc6+ ♗xc6 27 ♖c1! (not 27 ♕xa6+? ♗b7, and both bishops are defended) 27...♘b8 28 ♖xc6+!, etc, with a winning attack.

25...♔b8 26 ♖xc6 ♗xc6 27 ♕xb6 ♖c8 28 ♖c1 should win for White comfortably, even though he is currently a rook down. Black is about to drop a minor piece, and White still has good attackers and a few extra pawns. If, for example, 28...♕g6 29 ♖xc6 ♖xc6 30 ♕xc6 ♖c8 31 ♕xb5+ ♔a8 32 ♘b6+ ♘xb6 33 ♕a4+ ♔b8 34 ♕xb6+ ♔a8 35 ♕a5+ ♔b7 36 ♗xe5, and White will eventually win.

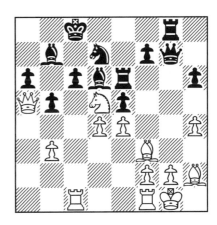

It is now time for Gelfand to think about a sacrificial attack, pushing away Black's remaining queenside pawns.

26 ♖xc6+

It works!

The computer shows interest in 26 dxe5 ♘xe5 27 ♘b6+ ♔b8 28 ♗xe5 ♗xe5 29 ♘d7+, but at best it is only a slow technical grind. If tactics work, use them.

26...♗xc6 27 ♖c1

Clearly Gelfand was not interested in 27 ♕xa6+? ♗b7.

27...♘b8

The most consistent reply. He might as well force White to make a second sacrifice.

27...♔b7 28 ♖xc6 ♔xc6 29 ♕xa6+ ♘b6 30 ♕xb6+ ♔d7 31 ♕b7+ ♔d8 32 ♘b6 wins for White.

28 ℤxc6+

Of course, White must carry on the demolition.

28...♘xc6

After this Black has two rooks for a bishop, yet his position is hopeless. His queen is out of action, while White's queen and knight chew up Black's king and a few random pawns or pieces.

29 ♕xa6+

Now Black cannot protect his b5-square.

29...♔d8

If 29...♔b8 30 ♕xb5+ ♔a7 31 ♕b6+ ♔a8 32 ♕xc6+ ♔b8 33 ♕b5+ ♔a8 34 ♘b6+ ♔a7 35 ♘d7, and White wins.

30 ♕b6+

Not 30 ♕xc6?!, as with a preliminary check he can aim to take the knight with check.

39...♔d7 31 ♕b7+ ♔d8

With his last two moves, though, Black has avoided the fatal capture with check. What now?

32 ♘b6!

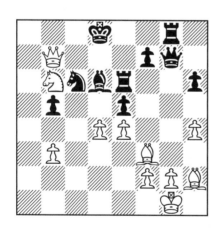

With mating threats.

32...f5

32...♘b8 33 ♕c8+ ♔e7 34 ♘d5 mate would have been an attractive finish.

Or 32...ℤe7 33 ♕c8 mate.

33 ♕c8+

It is time for hoovering up.

33...♔e7 34 ♕d7+

34 ♘d5+ ♔f7 35 ♗h5+ is also good, indeed slightly more accurate.

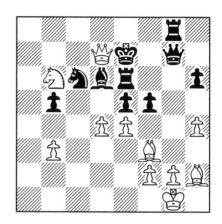

34...♔f8

34...♔f6!? might well have caused a flutter in time scramble. After 35 ♘d5+ ♔g6 36 ♕xe6+ ♔h7 37 ♘f6+ ♔h8 38 ♘xg8 ♘xd4 39 ♕xd6 ♘xf3+ 40 ♔h1 ♘xh2 41 ♘f6 White would have safely achieved the time control, keeping a material advantage.

35 ♕xe6

He has recovered the rook, and still has a big attack.

35...♕e7

If 35...♕g6 36 ♘d7+ ♔g7 37 ♕xg6+ ♔xg6 38 exf5+ ♔xf5 39 ♗xc6, and a win on material.

36 ♕xh6+

36 ♕xf5+?! ♔g7 37 ♘d5 ♕f7 allows complications.

36...ℤg7

Similarly, 36...♔e8 37 ♘c8 wins.

37 ♘c8 1-0

Now the bishop goes, and other pieces will soon fall.

Game 31
S.Mamedyarov-I.Nepomniachtchi
Russian Team Championship 2008
Semi-Slav Defence D47

1 d4 d5 2 c4 c6 3 ♘c3 ♘f6 4 ♘f3 e6 5 e3 ♘bd7 6 ♗d3 dxc4 7 ♗xc4 b5 8 ♗d3 ♗b7 9 e4

For 9 0-0, see Game 1, Kasimdzhanov-Kasparov. We are still very much in main-line play, which makes it all the more noteworthy that Mamedyarov was able to find a whole unexplored variation just a few moves later.

9...b4

Black kicks the white knight away from the centre, which is good, but he is also weakening his queenside pawn structure.

The computer shows some initial interest in 9...c5!?, but there are too many pins after 10 ♗xb5 ♘xe4 11 ♘e5 ♘ef8 12 ♗g5 ♗c8 with advantage to White.

10 ♘a4

10 e5? bxc3 11 exf6 bxc2 12 fxg7 ♗xg7 13 ♗xb2 c5 leads to an edge for Black.

10...c5

Black is now attacking both central pawns, but White's pawns can run. White often needs to attack with the pawns before Black is fully developed.

11 e5

He has to attack with the e-pawn.

11 d5? exd5 is mistimed here. In comparison with the Kasimdzhanov-Kasparov encounter, White no longer has a knight on c3.

11...♘d5

Clearly the best move. 11...♗xf3 12 ♕xf3 ♘d5 is just about playable, but White has the advantage of the bishop-pair in an open position.

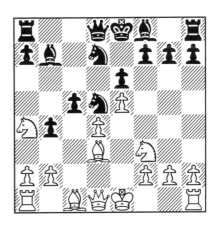

12 0-0

The early stages of a new idea.

Mamedyarov had already tried 12 ♘xc5 ♘xc5 13 dxc5 ♗xc5, which gave a win against Topalov, a big result, but Black can improve, and Mamedyarov has moved on from this line.

Here 14 &b5+?! does not gain much. The king has to move to a slightly worse square, but White's bishop has given up a tempo to go to a weaker square. Black is equal.

14 0-0 is best, and if 14...0-0? 15 &xh7+ &xh7 16 ♕c2+ White wins a pawn. Therefore 14...h6 is necessary, and after 15 ♘d2!? we have:

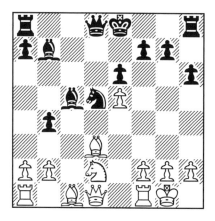

a) If 15...0-0, the standard line, White had a slight edge, and later a win, with 16 ♘e4 &d4 17 ♘d6 &c6 18 &h7+ &xh7 19 ♕xd4 in S.Mamedyarov-V.Topalov, Essent 2006.

b) A success, but the next month Gelfand showed he was able to equalize after 15...♘c3!? 16 ♕c2 ♕d5 17 ♘f3 ♖d8 18 ♘e1 &d4 19 &d2 ♘b5 in S.Mamedyarov-B.Gelfand, Moscow 2006:

b1) 20 &xb4 &xe5 has been tried a few times, but with Black having equalized.

b2) Mamedyarov tried 20 ♘f3, Gelfand continuing with 20...&b6 21 &c4 ♕c5 22 &e3 ♕c6 23 ♕e2 ♘c7. White's position looks slightly more promising just at the moment, but it could easily fade to equality. The game finished

with 24 ♖ac1 &xe3, and a draw was soon agreed after 25 fxe3 0-0 26 &d3 ♕b6 27 ♘d2 &a6 28 &xa6. Here Krasenkow gives 25 ♕xe3 ♕b6 26 ♕xb6 axb6 27 &b3 ♘d5 as equal, but one cannot help thinking that White has a micro-edge after 28 ♖fd1.

There are plenty of alternatives at earlier stages, and Mamedyarov no doubt wanted to try something new against a well booked-up opponent.

12...cxd4

Black opens up White's pawn centre, but White also has his pieces. This position is still known.

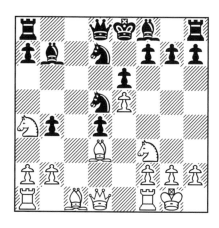

13 ♘xd4

But this is less common, and Mamedyarov was clearly thinking in terms of a follow-up. White gambits a pawn. 13 ♖e1 is the normal move, but White has given up a tempo to secure the e5-pawn. 13 ♖e1 g6 14 &g5 ♕a5 is about equal. Some months earlier, a draw was agreed in S.Mamedyarov-B.Gelfand, Moscow 2007, after 15 ♘d2 ♖c8 (15...&a6 was the older way, but the exchange sacrifice is promising) 16 ♘c4 ♖xc4 17 &xc4 &g7 18 ♖c1 ♘xe5 19 &f1 ♘d7 20 a3 0-0 21 &d2 ♖b8 22 ♕b3 &a8 23 ♖c4 ♘e5 24 ♖c5 ♕d8 25 axb4 d3 26

♕d1 ♘d7 27 ♖c4 ♘e5 28 ♖c5 ♘d7 29 ♖c4 ♘e5. White has the exchange for a pawn, but Black's minor pieces, plus passed pawn, are difficult to dislodge.

If Mamedyarov is going to search for a win, he has to try something new.

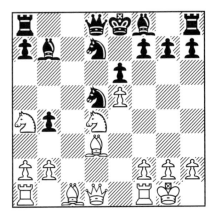

13...g6

But can't Black just take the pawn? After 13...♘xe5 14 ♗b5+ ♘d7 White has played many times the slightly unconvincing line 15 ♖e1 ♖c8 16 ♕h5 g6, with some degree of compensation for a pawn, but not really giving a plus.

Then a high-level quickplay game showed that White could dispense with ♖e1, thereby not giving the extra defensive resource ...♖c8. J.Piket-A.Shirov, Monaco (rapid) 2002, continued 15 ♕h5 ♘5f6 16 ♘xe6! ♘xh5 17 ♘xd8 ♖xd8 18 ♖e1+ ♗e7 19 ♘c5 ♗c8 20 ♗g5 ♘hf6 21 ♗xf6 gxf6 22 ♖ad1, and although Black was a piece up, the multiple pins meant that he could not escape, and sooner or later would have to move the king, giving away the extra piece, and settling to aim for an uncomfortable but playable rook and minor piece endgame. Indeed, Shirov chose 22...♖g8 23 f4 ♔f8 24 ♘xd7+ ♗xd7 25 ♖xd7 ♗c5+ 26 ♔f1 ♖xd7 27

♗xd7 ♔g7, and the game was later drawn.

White, with more time for reflection, realized that the bishop for knight exchange on f6 was unnecessary. So 21 ♖ad1 was tried, although after 21...a6 22 ♗a4 h6 23 ♗xf6 gxf6 24 ♘xd7 ♗xd7 25 ♖xd7 ♖xd7 26 ♖d1 0-0 27 ♖xd7 ♖c8 29 g3 Black was eventually able to draw in Radjabov-Shirov, Wijk aan Zee 2003. Some entertaining tactics, followed by long endgame grinding, that is the modern way.

After 15 ♕h5, Black can also try 15...g6 16 ♕e5 ♕f6 17 ♘f3. However, Black still has some pin problems, one idea being 17...♖c8 18 ♗g5 ♕g7 19 ♖ac1, and if 19...♖xc1 20 ♕b8+, with mate to follow. Black can, of course, improve.

Finally, there is a possible queen sacrifice with 15 ♘c6?! ♕c7 16 ♕xd5 exd5 17 ♖e1+ ♗e7 18 ♘xe7 ♔f8, but White has only two minor pieces for the queen, and it is not enough.

14 f4

Strangely this is a new line, yet what could be more natural than protecting the advanced pawn?

The main continuation has been 14 ♕g4, with the not too deep idea that if 14...♘xe5? 15 ♗b5+ ♘d7, White can regain the piece, with a winning attack, after 16 ♘xe6 fxe6 17 ♕xe6+.

There have, of course, been tactics after, for example, 14...♗g7 15 ♗g5, and if 15...♘xe5 16 ♘xe6 ♘xg4 17 ♘xd8:

a) If 17...♖xd8 18 ♗b5+ ♖d7 19 ♖ae1+ ♘e5 20 ♘c5 ♗c8 21 ♗h6! 0-0 22 ♗xg7 ♔xg7 23 ♖xe5 ♖d6, and after various tactics, White keeps a slight positional edge.

b) Or 17...h6 18 ♗h4 g5 19 ♘xb7 gxh4 20 ♗c4 ♘b6 21 ♘xb6 axb6 22 ♘d6+ ♚e7 23 ♘xf7 ♖he8, V.Razuvaev-A.Bagirov, Jurmala 1987, and although White is probably better, the opposite-coloured bishops helped lead to a draw.

Entertaining, but has Black ever tried 14...♕a5, the computer recommendation? 15 ♘xe6 ♕xa4 makes White's attack look silly, while if 15 ♗b5 ♗a6 Black is doing well. If White abandons his queen for the kingside, quite often a good response is for Black to take over on the queenside.

14...a6

It is understandable for Black to want to prevent ♗b5, or even ♘b5 after an early ...♗g7, but it is also slow, and Mamedyarov unleashes an aggressive pawn sacrifice.

We are still on the cutting edge of modern opening theory, and between the time that the game was played in 2008, and my annotation a few months later, and the book being published in 2009, developments will have been found. It is difficult to believe that Mamedyarov's line will prove to have been a truly decisive opening innovation, but for the time being, it works.

Watch this space.

14...♖c8 and 14...♕h4 are to be considered.

15 f5!!

The double exclamation mark is for shock value. Although this pawn sacrifice is hardly unexpected, dating back to the ideas of Pillsbury and others, it is a position which has not been seen before. So we have a position which Mamedyarov has seen before, but Nepomniachtchi hasn't. This can be extremely difficult for the defender, who has to

play with 100% accuracy over the board, while the opponent is able to use his home analysis.

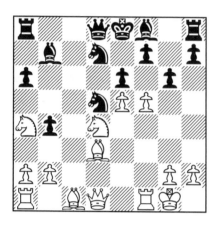

Nepomniachtchi is comfortably a 2600+ player, aiming for more, but he loses in 23 moves. Given a second chance, he would have been able to find an improvement.

15...♕h4?

A big miscalculation, which leaves him on the way to a quick loss.

There are three ways of taking the pawn, and we must consider the three captures:

a) 15...gxf5 would be instinctively be rejected by a top player, and indeed by many others. After 16 ♘xe6 fxe6 17 ♕h5+ ♚e7 18 ♗g5+ ♘7f6 White has several ways of playing for a winning advantage. Probably the most clear-cut is 19 ♗xf5 exf5 20 exf6+, and Black is fatally exposed to White's queen and two rooks. Even here, though, Black's play is not wholly to be discounted. After 16...♕e7! 17 ♘xf8 ♖xf8 18 ♗xf5 ♘xe5 19 ♕d4 Black equalizes with 19...♖g8!, hitting g2. There are plenty of alternatives, and maybe someone will try it.

b) 15...exf5 is another possibility,

again with wide open central play. After 16 e6 fxe6 17 ♘xe6 ♕f6 18 ♖e1 ♘e5 19 ♘ac5 ♗xc5 20 ♘xc5 0-0-0! Black has escaped the problems with the king on the e- and d-files, and is a pawn up.

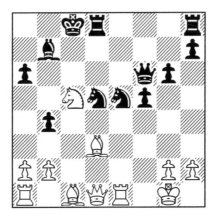

White opens Black's king on the queenside with 21 ♗xa6 ♗xa6 22 ♘xa6 ♕b6+! 23 ♔h1 ♘c7 (much clearer than 23...♘g4?! 24 ♕c2+ ♘c3 25 h3! with no perpetual check) 24 ♕e2 ♘d3 25 ♘xc7, and now Black can force a repetition with 25...♘f2+ 26 ♔g2 ♘h3+, but 25...♘xe1? 26 ♗e3 would be unwise. A draw, unless of course Mamedyarov has found something even deeper for White.

c) Finally, there is 15...♘xe5 16 fxe6 fxe6 17 ♘xe6 ♕d6. The computer gives this as equal, through several possible lines, but the human player might well slightly prefer the two bishops after 18 ♘xf8 ♖xf8 19 ♖xf8+ ♕xf8, and maybe something like 20 ♗e4 ♖d8 21 ♕e1 ♕e7 22 ♗d2 ♗c6 23 ♗c2.

We can suggest, for the sake of argument, that there were four reasonable moves, two of which were equal, one a very slight advantage for White, and one was close to losing. How often it happens that when a player is suddenly under severe pressure, he plays the very worst move!

16 fxe6!

Much better than the presumably anticipated 16 ♘f3 ♕h5, although even here White is slightly better after 17 fxe6 fxe6 18 ♘g5.

16...♕xd4+

He takes a knight with check!

16...fxe6 17 ♘xe6 ♕e7 is an attempt to repair the damage, but Black is effectively a tempo down.

17 ♔h1

We are only four moves away from well-known theory, but Black is already in a desperately poor position, and we can be reasonably certain that Mamedyarov has analysed this in advance, and seen it through to the end.

17...0-0-0?!

Avoiding the critical line.

Unfortunately, if 17...fxe6, or indeed any knight escape, White wins the queen with 18 ♗xg6+ (or 18 ♗b5+ after a knight move).

The computer suggests 17...♕xe5 18 exd7+ ♔xd7 as the best chance, but Black's pieces are fragile, with the king out in the open, and plenty of pins, and there must be significant danger. 19

♗f4 seems sharpest, speeding up his development, and more or less forcing Black to open up the d-file with 19...♘xf4:

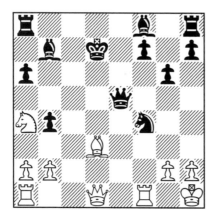

a) If then White uses a double-check, with either 20 ♗b5+ or 20 ♗f5+, the king can scurry away with 20...♔e7, and then on to f6, with likely equality.

b) 20 ♗e4+! is more accurate. If then 20...♘d5 21 ♗xd5 ♗xd5 22 ♘b6+ ♔d8 23 ♖e1 ♕d6 24 ♘xd5, and White is much better, Black's king still being under pressure, and his development is slow. Thus 20...♗d6 21 ♗xb7 seems critical:

b1) If 21...♖ad8, White can coordinate with 22 ♘b6+ ♔c7 23 ♘c4 ♕e7 25 ♕f3 with a positional edge.

b2) 21...♘e2 (21...♘h5 transposes) 22 g3 ♘xg3+ 23 hxg3 ♕xg3 leads to a mating threat and possible perpetuals. The position is incredibly open, and White has chances of countering the counter-attack: 24 ♘c5+! ♔d8 (the only safe king move) 25 ♖f2! overturns Black's counterplay after, for example, 25...♕h4+ 26 ♔g1 ♕g5+ 27 ♗g2 ♗xc5 28 ♗xa8 with a win for White.

So it seems that Black is in trouble, anyway.

18 exd7+

But this is clearly winning.

18...♔b8

18...♖xd7 19 ♗f5 ♕xd1 20 ♗xd7+ wins the exchange for White.

19 ♗xa6

Here he grabs a pawn, while keeping his own advanced pawn for as long as possible.

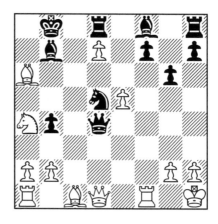

19...♕xe5?

Black can still keep the position alive, just about, with 19...♕xd1 20 ♖xd1 ♖xd7. The computer may suggest that White is effectively positionally two pawns ahead, but it can sometimes be difficult to convert this into a win. White is in fact only one pawn up, and it is going to be a long time before he will be thinking about a quick promotion. Black's pieces, slightly uncoordinated at the moment, can soon work together.

The computer's main line is 21 ♗xb7 ♔xb7 22 a3 ♗e7, and then if 23 ♗g5 (23 axb4 ♗xb4 24 ♗d2 ♗e7 25 ♗g5 is slightly less effective) 23...♖hd8 24 ♗xe7 ♖xe7 25 axb4 ♖xe5, and White's doubled extra pawn is only a slender plus in the equation. More important, perhaps, is that even in the endgame

Black's king is isolated and under attack from two rooks and a knight.

There are many possible ideas for innovation here, perhaps starting with 22 ♗h6 or 22 ♗e3. For the author, this has been a long and hard exercise to write such a complicated book, and the temptation is to give an end-of-term exercise to ask the reader to find the best line for White. This is, after all, the type of exercise that top players are increasingly having to work on.

At the very least, Black's position is not collapsing yet. Instead, after Nepomniachtchi's possibly dazed reply, Mamedyarov finishes quickly.

20 ♖e1

Gaining time by attacking the queen.

20...♕d6

Most other moves lose to the same reply.

Of others, White has 20...♕h5 21 ♗xb7 ♔xb7 22 g4, winning the knight.

21 ♖e8!

All sorts of pins and small tactics now come up, based on the use of the rook on the back rank. Perhaps there is nothing particularly deep at this stage, but the point is that White was able to take advantage of the isolated pawn on d7 before it drops.

This is very much in the style of Kasparov. Not even Tal would have been able to play a game like this, since he never had the technology available of extremely deep computer-based theoretical analysis. As we have seen from this collection, there are more and more players who have been able to combine both ultra-deep theoretical knowledge, and the clarity of thought

over the board. The challenge of the newer super-super-grandmasters is whether they can emulate Kasparov's achievements, and whether anyone can go beyond, even if only slightly. Chess carries on, chess continues, and chess evolves.

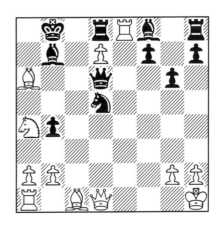

21...♕xd7

Or 21...♗g7 22 ♖xh8 ♗xh8 23 ♗xb7 ♔xb7 24 ♗f4! ♕xf4 25 ♕xd5+ and Black's king will soon drop.

22 ♗f4+!

The first bishop move, and it wins. For such a situation to have worked, all the other developed pieces must have coordinated with maximum effectiveness.

22...♗d6

If 22...♔xa7 23 ♗xb7 ♕xe8 (23...♔xb7 24 ♖xf8! and ♘c5+) 24 ♗xd5, and the poor king has no cover.

23 ♖xh8 1-0

Black has had enough. 23...♖xh8 24 ♘c5 ♕e7 25 ♗xd6+ ♕xd6 26 ♗xb7 ♕xc5 27 ♕xd5 wins a piece, or 23...♘xf4 24 ♖xd8+ ♕xd8 25 ♗xb7 ♔xb7 26 ♘c5+ ♔c8 21 ♖c1 with an easy win.

Mind-blowing attacking chess.

Game 32
E.Inarkiev-Ni Hua
Russian Team Championship 2008
Slav Defence D10

My apologies to Grandmaster Inarkiev for introducing two losses of his from within a fortnight. What happened is that I had already decided that Karjakin's win (Game 33) was well worth publishing, and much later on there were only three wins for Ni Hua to be selected from (players over 2700 beating someone over 2600). The other two wins were regarded as not fully publishable by the standards of games of the highest level. This one is, I hope, far more enjoyable for the reader.

1 d4 d5 2 c4 c6 3 ♘c3 ♘f6 4 e3

For the Exchange Variation, 4 cxd5 cxd5, see Game 25, Morozevich-Sakaev. Over the next few moves, White keeps the option of setting up a symmetrical exchange on d5. Usually, though, he avoids it in this line, as the pawn on e3 prevents the bishop developing on f4.

4 ♘f3 dxc4 5 a4 (preventing b5) is the standard main line of the Slav Defence. White regains the pawn, and keeps slightly more activity with his pieces, but Black's position is very solid. Black usually plays ...♗b4, taking advantage that White cannot attack that square with the a-pawn.

There are also, of course, many examples of the Semi-Slav with 4...e6. The reader can track through the games beginning with Kasimdzhanov-Kasparov, Game 1.

With 4 e3, Inarkiev cuts out any further gambit options.

4...a6

Black's ...a6 move is not really a waste of time. In the Morozevich-Sakaev game, Black quickly played ...a6 voluntarily anyway. Black cuts out any ♗b5 or ♘b5 ideas, and can later make ground himself with ...b5.

5 ♘f3

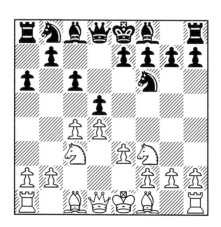

Straightforward development.

5...b5

The obvious continuation, but Black can still move into a Schlechter Variation with 5...g6, as tried by Kamsky a few times.

6 c5

The main line in recent years, by a small majority. White gains space on the queenside, but cannot make any useful open lines there. Meanwhile, Black has if anything slightly the better structure in the centre and on the kingside, his pawn on c6 giving extra protection to d5, while White's pawn on c5 has shot through any protection of d4. The problem for White in trying to take an edge is whether he can make advantage of a queenside push with b4 and a4. This does not happen in the game, as Black sets up a counter-initiative in the centre, with ...e5, based on the point that if White takes with dxe5, his pawn on c5 drops.

6 b3 is also popular, though again it has proven difficult for White to claim an edge.

Then, of course, there is another Exchange Variation, with 6 cxd5 cxd5, and the likelihood of equality.

6...g6

Black develops his pieces and castles, before deciding what to do with the pawns in the centre and on the queenside. A bishop on g7 will, of course, help a pawn advance to e5 later on. Also the g6-pawn blocks any pressure against h7 after ♗d3. 6...♘bd7 and 6...♗g4 are other possibilities.

7 ♘e5

7 ♗d3 has been tried a few times, then maybe 7...♗g7 8 h3 0-0 9 0-0 ♘bd7. It is not clear that White

achieves much of an edge. Black can try to equalize with a later ...e5, and if White tries e4 himself, then it is again not clear that he can try for an edge.

So Inarkiev tries a Stonewall set-up, with f4 to follow, to prevent Black from playing ...e5, and maybe to set up a later attack on the kingside.

7...♗g7

The obvious continuation, although 7...♘fd7 might even be more accurate:

a) If 8 ♘f3, then who would blink first to avoid the quick repetition? The answer to this conundrum is that Black, if he wants to be ambitious, might try 8...e5!?.

b) Similarly, 8 ♗d3 e5!?.

c) 8 f4?! ♘xe5 9 fxe5 f6 10 exf6 exf6 11 ♗d3 f5 allows Black to start taking control of the centre, so is not satisfactory.

d) 8 ♘xd7 ♘xd7 9 e4 dxe4 10 ♘xe4 ♗g7 is equal.

8 f4

Building up the Stonewall.

In most other recent games, White has started off with 8 ♗e2, maybe deciding later whether to push with f4 or with h4. This tends to give Black time to respond with ...f5 after White's f4. For example, 8 ♗e2 0-0 9 0-0 ♘fd7 10 f4 f5 11 ♘d3 a5 12 ♗d2 ♘f6, and Black was able to equalize in A.Moiseenko-Ni Hua, Beersheba 2005. Later on, Ni Hua was able to take control of the f-file, and eventually won after White opened up the g-file with g4, and Black then created counter-pressure with ...g5.

8...♘fd7

To eliminate the strong white knight.

9 ♘d3

This is better centralized than 9 ♘f3.

9...a5

If 9...f5, then White has gained time on the queenside, by quickly playing the knight manoeuvre to d3, and by delaying any bishop move, and 10 a4 gives a slight but clear edge on the queenside.

10 g4

Premature? It certainly provokes his opponent to go for the attack quickly himself.

10 ♗e2, then castling, is quietly equal.

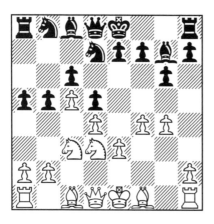

10...e5!?

The spirit of the gambit still continues. Otherwise, there must be half a dozen ways to equality, or at least something very close to it.

11 fxe5

White should take it, and with the f-pawn, not the d-pawn: 11 dxe5 ♘a6 would allow Black to at least equalize.

11 ♘xe5 ♘xe5 12 fxe5 ♕h4+ 13 ♔d2 ♗xg4 again allows Black comfortable equality, or more, without loss of a pawn. The problem is not so much that White's king is going to be directly attacked, but rather that the king is seriously in the way of the queenside pieces.

White has the same sort of problem in the main game, but at least he does not need to give back the extra pawn. In the game, it is a considerable irritation for Black that White keeps the pawn on g4, cutting out for quite a while any attacks with the bishop on f5.

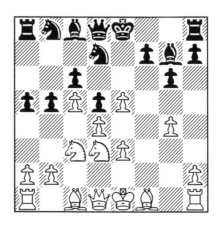

11...f6

This is the point of the previous sacrifice. Black opens up the e- and f-pawns with the hope of pressure in the centre, and later an outright attack.

The basic idea is, of course, well known, and such gambits were often popular in the 19th Century. The Blackmar Gambit, 1 d4 d5 2 e4 dxe4 3 ♘c3 ♘f6 4 f3, has had sporadic popularity at amateur levels, but is not really sound after good professional play by Black. Here, though, White has free play with his pieces. What is remarkable in Ni Hua's idea is that he gives away the pawn without being able to activate his queenside pieces quickly. Should it work? White's pieces are also constrained, but one cannot help sensing that White should be able to overcome the gambit.

12 exf6

White might just as well take the extra pawn. A quick flick through the computer gives 12 e6 ♘f8 13 e4 ♘xe6 14 exd5 ♘xd4 15 ♘f2 f5 16 ♗e3 ♕e7 17 ♘ce4 fxe4 18 ♗xd4 e3 19 ♘e4 ♕xe4 20 ♗xg7 ♖g8 21 ♕d4 ♕f3, and Black is on top.

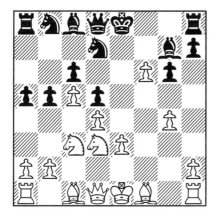

12...♗xf6?!

A difficult choice among the three recaptures, and even, one might suspect, his second-choice reply after a change of mind. It does not quite seem fully worthwhile to set up a bishop check on h4 in return for giving up a pawn, when White's king can run to safety on the queenside. There were easier ways to equalize:

a) 12...♕xf6 13 h4 seems comfortable for White.

b) 12...♘f6!? is more natural, and might well have been Ni Hua's earlier choice, but 13 g5 forces Black's knight to move onwards before Black can kick White's knight with ...b4. Then:

b1) 13...♘g8 looks appealing, with the idea of setting up a blockade on f5 with ...♘e7, but Black is a tempo short of realizing his plan. After 14 h4 h6 (14...♘e7 15 h5, with an edge to White) 15 ♘f4 hxg5 (or 15...♗f5 16 ♗d3, breaking Black's blockade on the diagonal) 16

♘xg6 ♖g6 17 h5 ♗f5 18 ♗d3 White safely keeps the extra pawn.

b2) 13...♘h5! seems an improvement, then 14 ♖g1 0-0. After 15 ♗e2 ♕e8, for the moment Black does not have to develop with the bishop and knight on the queenside. Instead he can give priority to the rook with ...♖a7, and then either ...♖e7 or ...♖af7.

Black seems fully equal, and with chances of playing for more if White does not find a good way of developing his queenside. After the text move, the suspicion is that White remains slightly better, despite the final result in favour of Black.

13 ♗g2

He cannot keep both bishops at home, and he must keep an open square on d2 for the king.

13...♗h4+

A useful little stab, but while giving check on h4, the bishop has no influence on the queenside.

14 ♔d2

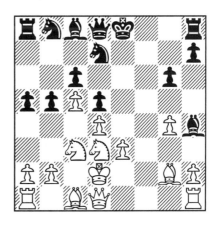

Uncomfortable, but with the central pawn structure closed White will have reasonable chances to bring the king to safety, quite likely on b1.

14...0-0

Over the next few moves Black has to decide whether to poke the knight with ...b4. He does not want to allow the white knight to remain on c3, but on the other hand after ...b4; ♘a4 Black will be concerned about the hole on b6.

Here 14...b4 looks reasonably well timed. Then 15 ♘a4 0-0 could later transpose into the main line, or there might be minor improvements on either side. If 16 ♖f1, to prevent Black from castling, then 16...♘f6 17 h3 (17 ♘b6? ♗xg4 18 ♕b3 ♘e4+ 19 ♗xe4 ♖xf1 20 ♘xa8 ♗d4 favours Black) 17...♘bd7, and at least Black would be reasonably comfortable with his development, but it not so clear that he has full compensation for the sacrificed pawn. White could instead give up the knight for three pawns, with 15 ♘xd5 cxd5 16 ♗xd5 ♖a6 17 ♕a4, but 17...♕g5 is only unclear. It is too early to give back the extra material.

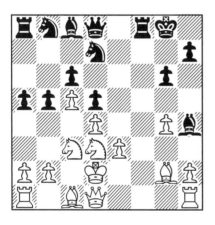

15 ♔c2

Has he missed an opportunity? The computer suggests that 15 ♘xd5!? ♘xc5 16 dxc5 cxd5 17 ♕b3 is good for White. He has broken up Black's pawn centre, and he will win a second pawn, if he wants. The only problem is that

White's king is stuck in the centre, potentially exposed, and his bishop and rook are thereby undeveloped.

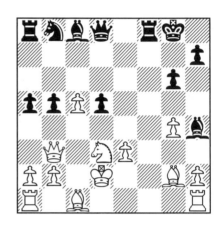

After 17...♗e6 18 ♘f4 ♕d7 there are pins for both sides if White were to take the central pawn:

a) If 19 ♗xd5?, Black is winning after 19...♖xf4!.

b) 19 ♖f1 is natural, but after 19...♘a6, White cannot chew up the d5-pawn to advantage. If, for example, 20 ♘xe6 ♕xe6 21 ♗xd5 ♖fd8 22 e4 ♘b4, and White is in trouble with the exposure of his king.

c) This suggests that it is time to escape a move earlier with 19 ♔c2 ♘a6 20 ♗xd5+ ♗xd5 21 ♘xd5 (21 ♕xd5+ ♕xd5 22 ♘xd5 ♖ad8 gives White no realistic winning chances, Black's pieces being so active) 21...♖f7, and then after 22 ♘b6 ♕c6 Black is better.

In these comments, the temptation is to knock out the bishop on e6, and to win the d-pawn. Maybe, though, that pawn should be left. It is the b-pawn that should be taken, not opening lines in front of the king. 18 ♕xb5! gives Black some piece compensation for the two pawns, but there is no obvious breakthrough, and White should be able to keep an edge.

Even after quiet play, as in the game, White should be able to stay ahead.

15...♞a6

Starting to bring the knight into play.

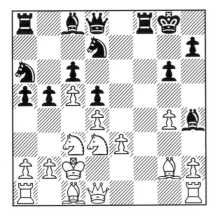

16 a3

A difficult choice to make, or even maybe a relatively easy but lazy move. It is difficult to decide, without actually watching the players. White is, of course, worried about ...♞b4+, and if the knights are exchanged, then Black has options of attack with ...♖f2+, or maybe on the h7-b1 diagonal. Thus Inarkiev cuts out the b4-square with a defensive pawn. The trouble is that while he is eliminating the knight move, he is positively encouraging the pawn push, ...b4, opening up the b-file. Inarkiev has, of course, seen this possibility, and has noticed that ...b4 by Black would allow White to reply with ♞a4, and possibly later ♞b6 with counterplay.

The old principles of Steinitz would suggest that the defender should not advance pawns in front of the king. Pawns cannot retreat, and any pawn advance, however slight, creates a broader weakening in the pawn structure. These days, the Steinitz idea cannot be regarded as a dogma, or even as a majority opinion, as it is recognized that there are so many opposing ideas to be considered in a complicated game, and that sometimes it is best to cover an immediate weakness, not being too worried about giving up a theoretical longer-term weakness. Nevertheless, it is often a starting point for examination. Thus we should consider alternatives at this point:

a) 16 ♔b1!? is a possibility:

a1) Then if 16...♞b4 17 ♞xb4 axb4 18 ♞xd5 ♖f2 19 ♞f4, White's position looks dodgy at first, but Black has no immediate attack on the king, and after 19...g5 20 ♗xc6 Black's centre collapses, and it will be easy for White to defend.

a2) Black would do better to think about using both sides of the board with 16...♞f6 17 h3 g5, followed by ...♕e8 and ...♕g6+. The position remains unclear. After, for example, 18 ♖f1 ♕e8 19 ♗d2, it is perhaps time for Black to abandon any ideas of ...♖b8, and play to centralize with 19...♖a7, followed by ...♖af7 or ...♖e7. That said, 20 ♞e2 seems to keep a slight edge for White, as Black's bishop on h4 is now out of play.

b) The opposite approach for the defender is to play for tactics himself, here to try to break up the attacker's central pawns, to try to stop the attacker's pieces from working together. The idea would be 16 ♞xd5 ♞dxc5 17 ♞5f4 ♞xd3 18 ♞xd3 ♞b4+ 19 ♔b1, but White's pieces look uncomfortable, with problems on the light-squared diagonal. Therefore 19...♞xd3 20 ♕xd3 ♗xg4, and while the computer might be impressed by White, human players will tend to favour Black's chances:

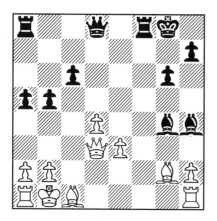

b1) 21 ♗xc6 would be too greedy. White is heavily reliant on the queen and bishop on two diagonals, and if one falls, the whole position is likely to collapse. Black plays 21...♖c8, and if 22 ♕xb5 ♖xc6 23 ♕xc6 ♗f3 24 ♕e6+ ♔h8 25 ♖f1 ♖e8, and White has to relinquish the queen. Likewise, 22 ♗xb5 ♗f3 makes use of a different diagonal. If 23 ♖f1 ♕d5 24 ♖xf3 ♕xf3, and White is under pressure.

b2) Maybe White can improve earlier with, for example, 21 ♗e4, but his position is still uncomfortable.

c) 16 ♗d2 is another option, and usually in over-the-board chess it is difficult to analyse confidently three unclear positions, let alone four. White's idea, apart from development, is to create an extra escape square for the king on b1:

c1) If now 16...♘b4+ 17 ♘xb4 axb4 18 ♘xd5, and White is on top, his king now being safe, even after 18...b3+ 19 ♔xb3.

c2) 16...♘f6 is better, and after 17 ♘e5 ♕e8 the position is finely balanced.

The purpose of using computer analysis, for the player or writer, is not so much to try to analyse with certainty the next twenty moves through thickets of lines and sidelines. What is generally of more interest is to examine a few critical lines, and give an indication of which of the candidate moves is most promising. Then the analyst may have the chance of comparing his or her first impressions with comparison to computer-assisted analysis. In a position where the opponent has gambited a pawn, when should a player immediately counterattack? Or when should he develop? Or when should he quietly push a pawn to cover an attack? Or when should the king try to run to safety? None of these questions can be answered with confidence without analysis of the critical positions, and trying to analyse such positions is useful for the player to understand different types of position. This is what is known as experience.

In conclusion, Inarkiev's 16 a3 seems good, and also 16 ♔b1. The quiet developing move, 16 ♗d2, is playable, but not as promising. The tactics with 16 ♘xd5?! are, though, best avoided.

16...♘f6?!

Black wants to catch up with his development. His light-squared bishop is seen as important. This seems slightly mistimed, though.

Another angle of approach is an immediate 16...b4, instead of delaying it a couple of moves. The point is that after 17 ♘a4 White will be unable to try ♘b6, Black's knight being able to cover that square. After, for example, 17...♖b8 18 ♖f1 ♖xf1 19 ♕xf1 bxa3 20 bxa3 ♘c7 21 ♖b1 ♗a6 Black has reasonable compensation for the pawn. It is possible that Ni Hua might have been slightly worried about 17 ♘xd5 ♘dxc5 18 dxc5 cxd5 19 ♘f4. After 19...♗b7 20 ♗xd5+ ♗xd5 21 ♕xd5+ ♕xd5 22 ♘xd5 ♖ad8 23 e4 ♘xc5 24 axb4 axb4 25 ♘xb4 ♖f2+ 26 ♔b1 ♘xe4 White is a pawn up as we start reaching the endgame, but it is an isolated pawn on its initial square, and Black's pieces are more active. The likelihood is a draw.

17 h3

Building up the pawn defences.

17 ♘e5 ♕e8 18 ♖f1 b4 is a possibility, but White with his knight advance has weakened his grip on b4.

17...♗e6

Again 17...b4 is a possibility, but after 18 ♘a4 the b6-square is an annoyance. 18...bxa3 19 bxa3 ♖b8 20 ♖f1 gives White an edge. He still keeps the option of blocking the b-file with ♘b6.

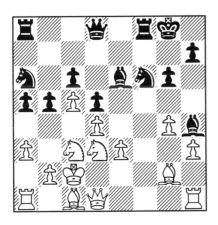

18 ♔b1

Inarkiev clearly feels more comfortable behind the unadvanced pawns than out in the open. We have already seen a possible danger, though. There have been lines in which Black plays ...b4 and exchanges the pawn, opening up at least part of the danger file.

18 ♗d2!?, developing, would seem to be a possible improvement, then maybe ♖c1 before ♔b1, castling by hand.

18...b4

Ni Hua breaks the tension. He will, of course, be well aware that White's knight can end up on b6, which is an irritation, but he is ready to give up the exchange, rook versus pawn and knight, to take much greater control with his own queenside forces.

This game would have been very difficult to handle over the board, with both players having to undertake complicated defensive manoeuvres, while continually having to bear in mind that tactics may arrive at any stage. Probably Black should play quietly with 18...♕e8!?, defending the pawn on c6 in case White were to try ♘e5, and aiming to use the queen on the h7-b1 diagonal after Black tries ...g5. It also helps that the queen is in position on the half-open e-file. Then if 19 ♖f1, a natural choice for White, Black opens the diagonal with 19...g5, keeping ...b4 as an option, but keeping White waiting.

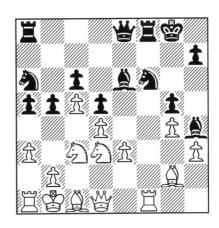

There are many quiet moves, but 20 e4 is the most direct, and forcing. Then after 20...b4 (20...dxe4 21 ♘xe4 favours White) White can create a passed pawn, either on the e-file or on the c-file, but it is not totally clear that he can create a serious advantage, provided Black stays in touch with the h7-b1 diagonal. If, for example, 21 e5 ♘d7 22 ♖xf8+ ♘xf8 23 ♘e2 ♗f7, and Black now has the plan of ....♗g6 and a pawn exchange on a3. If the rook recaptures there, Black has ...♘g4. If the pawn recaptures, Black has the open file leading to the king.

The position remains complicated, and one cannot cover all lines. A reasonable attempt for White, and the computer's suggestion, is 24 ♘g1!?, attacking with ♘f3, and defending with ♗f1. Then 24...♗g6!? 25 ♘f3 ♗f2, with a sneak attack on the d4-pawn. If 26 ♔a2 ♕b8!, and White's knight on d3 is still pinned by tactics, as if 27 ♘xf4? ♘b4+ 28 axb4 axb4+, with a quick checkmate. Instead 27 ♗xg5 is the further computer suggestion. After 27...♘e6 28 ♖f1 ♗xd4 29 ♘xd4 ♘xd4, Black's position is still very much alive: 30 ♗e3 b3+ 31 ♔a1 ♘c2+ 32 ♖xc2 bxc2 33 ♕xc2 is probably level.

19 ♘a4

The thematic response over the last few moves, although 19 axb4 is also promising. If 19...axb4 20 ♘e2, and White will be thinking about pressing forwards with the knights with ♘ef4 and/or ♘e5.

19...♘e4

The point of Black's last, although it is remarkable that White does not at any stage give a bishop for knight exchange on e4, eliminating the strong knight and cutting out any open diagonals leading to b1. Moreover, White's

bishop-pair is nothing special. In semi-blocked positions, with good outposts for knights, the bishop-pair is often useful, but sometimes its main use is to exchange a bishop for a good knight.

20 ♘b6

A natural response, but later he will have to take care of exchange sacrifices on b6.

20 ♗xe4 dxe4 21 ♘e5 ♕c7 is to be regarded as unclear, and hence no genuine improvement for White, who still has genuine aspirations for an edge.

20...♖b8

Ni Hua is relying on the possibility of sacrificing the exchange to break open his opponent's queenside advanced defences.

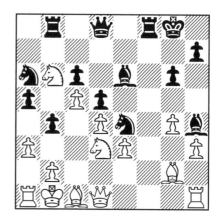

21 ♖f1?!

Despite the final result, and despite Ni Hua's creative attacking play, Inarkiev's position is better. He could have played more vigorously himself with 21 ♕a4!, attacking all his opponent's pawns and knight on the queenside:

a) After 21...♖xb6 22 cxb6 ♕xb6 23 axb4 ♘xb4, White is effectively a tempo up on his queenside defensive manoeuvres in the main game. The computer suggests that 24 ♘f4 ♖xf4 25 exf4 ♕xd4 is winning for White, but many players would be sceptical. White's two extra rooks do not work together, and Black has two strong extra minor pieces, plus a protected passed pawn. This could be difficult. Instead the simple plan would be 24 ♘xb4 axb4 26 ♗xe4 dxe4 26 ♗d2 ♗e7 27 ♕a7 ♕b5 28 ♕a6, and White squeezes through with his one extra exchange.

b) 21...♘f2 does not help Black: 22 ♕xc6 ♘c7 23 ♘xf2 (23 ♘f4 ♖f6! holds the balance for Black) 23...♖xf2 24 ♖g1 gives White excellent chances of a win. His pawns are by now very solid, and defend excellently, while Black's depleted pawns are crumbling.

21...♕c7

The first real chance to develop the queen.

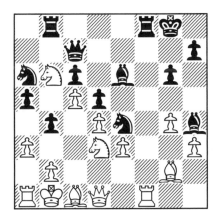

22 axb4

The immediate 22 ♘f4 ♗f7 23 ♗xe4 dxe4 24 ♕e2 is certainly not worse. After 24...♖xb6 25 cxb6 ♕xb6 26 a4 ♗b3 White is better, but not decisively so.

22...♘xb4

22...♕h2 is reckless. After 23 ♖xf8+

♖xf8 24 ♗xe4 dxe4 25 ♘f4 ♘xb4 26 ♘xe6 ♖f1 27 ♕b3 ♖xc1+ 28 ♔xc1 ♕g1+ 29 ♕d1 White has covered all his weaknesses.

23 ♘f4

23 ♗xe4 fxe4 24 ♘f4 is also good.

23...♗f7

The bishop is important.

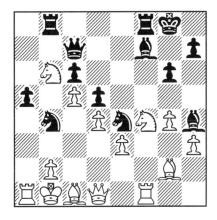

24 g5?

Probably the sort of strange move that can be played only with time on the clock for reflection. Few players would hit on this idea quickly. The point is that Black is threatening ...g5, and if the knight moves, then ...♗g6. Inarkiev temporarily stops Black's pawn advancing to g5 by advancing his own pawn instead, hoping to gain a useful tempo. Unfortunately a few moves later, Ni Hua again creates threats on the diagonal leading to White's king, and with greater impact.

The alternatives were:

a) 24 ♖xa5 g5 25 ♕a4 gxf4 26 ♕xb4 ♗g6 27 ♔a1 fxe3 28 ♖xf8+ ♖xf8 29 ♗xe3 ♕g3 30 ♗xe4 ♗xe4 causes some problems for White, with attacks on the back rank.

b) 24 ♗xe4! fxe4 25 ♗d2 gives White a clear positional edge.

24...♗xg5

Of course.

25 ♖xa5

If 25 ♕g4 ♗xf4 26 exf4, Black takes over the initiative with an exchange sacrifice with 26...♖xb6 27 cxb6 ♕xb6.

25...♗xf4

An important white piece to exchange. Now the knight can no longer cover good squares against the light-squared bishop, and Black's attack speeds up.

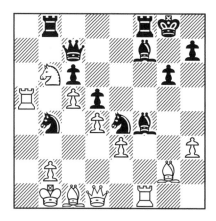

26 exf4

Visually the least impressive of the three recaptures; White has broken up his pawn structure. The problem is that after the more natural 26 ♖xf4, Black quickly sets up an open diagonal against the king with 26...g5. However, White then has good counterplay with 27 ♖xe4! dxe4 28 ♕g4 ♕d8 29 ♗xe4. It is he who covers the critical b1-h7 diagonal. After, for example, 29...h5 30 ♕g2 ♘d5 31 ♗d2 White is starting to make good use of the bishop-pair.

Indeed, even at this late stage of the game, White still has good chances of being better. Perhaps this is not all that surprising. White starts off with a slight advantage, and it is not all that fre-

quent for Black to be able to obtain an edge early on, especially if White is a strong grandmaster.

Instead 26 ♗xe4 fxe4 27 ♖xf4 ♘d5 28 ♖xe4 ♘xb6 29 cxb6 ♕xb6 probably ends up about equal. White has an extra pawn, but Black can create pressure with bishops of opposite colour, plus queens and rooks. It is doubtful whether White can play for a serious edge.

26...♗e6

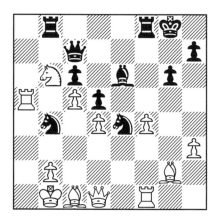

The bishop is about to move to the winning diagonal on f5.

27 ♕b3?

A serious miscalculation. Did he think he was winning material, without redress?

It is probable, though, that the position has already swung towards Black:

a) 27 ♗xe4?! dxe4 is by now an irrelevance, as Black can set up checks with ...e3 and ...♗f5.

b) 27 ♖a4 ♘xc5 28 dxc5 ♗f5+ 29 ♔a1 ♗c2 30 ♕d4 ♗xa4 31 ♕xb4 ♗c2 leads to obvious problems for White's king on the a-file. After 32 ♕a3 ♕b7 33 ♗d2 ♖a8 34 ♘xa8 ♖xa8 35 ♗a5 ♕b5 36 b4 ♗e4! 37 ♗xe4 (37 ♕g3? ♕xb4) 37...♕xf1+ 38 ♗b1 ♕xf4 the position tends to favour Black. Usually White's bishop-pair would be expected to be more impressive than rook and pawn, but here the rook is superior. White's bishops cannot move far away from covering the ranks and diagonals leading to his king on a1, while there is no prospect for White in setting up an attack against Black's king.

c) 27 ♔a1 would quickly transpose to our last variation after 27...♗f5 28 ♖a4 ♘xc5.

d) 27 ♕a4!? is a more accurate way of moving the queen when compared with the game; the rook on a5 does not get attacked. Moreover, there is a highly unexpected defensive idea by White, involving a perpetual. Play might continue 27...♖xb6 28 cxb6 ♕xb6 29 ♗xe4 dxe4 30 ♖c5 ♖f7!? 31 ♕a8+ ♔g7 (31...♖f8 32 ♕a4 is a tame repetition) 32 f5! ♗a2+ 33 ♔a1 ♖a7 34 ♗h6+ ♔xh6 35 ♕f8+ ♔h5. Now at first White's play would seem to be hopeless. However 36 fxg6+! leads to a perpetual check, very easily missed by mere humans:

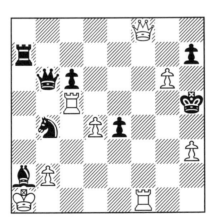

d1) If 36...♘d5, White should give perpetual with 37 ♕f5+ ♔h6 38 ♕f8+ ♔h5. Not, though, 37 ♖f5+? ♔xg6, and White unexpectedly runs out of win-

ning checks, or indeed any other playable checks.

d2) 36...♗d5+ is in many ways a more obvious reply, a discovered check in reply to the opposing discovered check. Black has to be careful not to be too ambitious, though, after 37 ♔b1 ♖a1+ 38 ♔xa1 ♕a6+ 39 ♔b1 when he can repeat with 39...♕d3+ 40 ♔a1 (40 ♔c1?? ♘a2 mate) 40...♕a6+, but 39...♕a2+? 40 ♔c1 ♕a1+ 41 ♔d2 ♕xb2+ 42 ♔e3 allows White to escape and win.

27...♖xb6

He is more than pleased to offer the exchange sacrifice.

28 cxb6 ♕xb6

All of Black's minor pieces are on attacking squares, while White's minor pieces are purely defensive. Black has better pawns than White's, and White's four isolated pawns in some cases get in the way of the pieces.

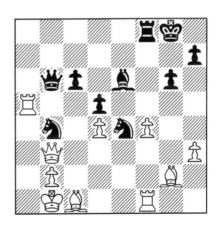

29 ♖a4

White loses a tempo because his rook is under attack.

There may well be a case for returning the exchange with 29 ♗xe4 ♕xa5 30 f5 ♕b5 (30...♖a8 31 ♕a3 holds) 31 ♖f3 gxf5 32 ♗c2, and while Black is better, it will be difficult to prove strong winning chances. This is a reasonable alternative for White, but his decisive mistake is not on this move, but rather a move later.

29...♗f5

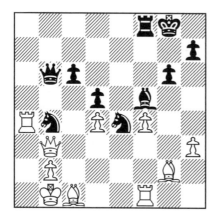

30 ♕xb4?

Presumably short of time, he falls for a quick checkmate.

30 ♔a1 allows White to resist for longer, but after 30...♕xd4, Black's three minor pieces, plus of course the open lines for queen and rook, make it impossible for White to defend:

a) If 31 ♕xb4 ♕xb4 32 ♖xb4 ♖a8+ 33 ♔b1 ♘c3 mate, much as in the game.

b) If 31 ♖d1 ♘c5 32 ♖xd4 ♘b3 mate, the three minor pieces mating.

c) If 31 ♗e3 ♘c5 32 ♕a3 ♘c2+ 33 ♔a2 ♕xa4, winning material for Black.

d) 31 ♕a3 ♖b8 gives no immediate checkmate, but White is completely tied up by threats of ...♘c2+ followed by ...♕b6.

e) 31 ♖f3! forces Black to have to work hard. The point is that after 31...♘d2 32 ♗xd2 ♕e4, apparently mating, White has 33 ♖d3! ♕xd3 34 ♕xd3 ♘xd3 35 ♗f1, surviving to an endgame, though a pawn down. Probably it is best not to allow the opposite-coloured bishops in the endgame, so therefore 35...♘c5 36 ♖a3 ♘e4, followed by ...c5, and Black should win.

An earlier try for Black, involving an exchange sacrifice, is 32...♕xd2 33 ♕xb4 ♕xg2 34 ♖e3. This is tempting, but does not seem conclusive. If, for example, 34...c5 35 ♕e1, and if Black decides to block the e-file with 35...♗e4, White returns the exchange with 36 ♖exe4 dxe4 37 ♕xe4 ♕xe4 38 ♖xe4 with a drawn rook and pawn ending. Or 34...♕c2 35 ♖e1 c5 36 ♕b5 ♕d2 37 ♕a5 (37 ♕e2? ♕xf4!) 37...♕f2 38 ♕c3, which gives White chances of holding, after either 38...d4 39 ♕c4+ ♔h8 40 ♕c1 or 38...c4 39 ♕e5 ♖d8 40 ♕e7.

30...♕xb4 31 ♖xb4 ♘c3+ 0-1

Not every one of the eight discovered checks win, as if Black is careless, the king can escape via a2 and b3, but 31...♘d2+ or 31...♘c5+ also give mate with ...♖a8 next move.

Game 33
S.Karjakin-E.Inarkiev
Baku 2008
Ruy Lopez C99

1 e4 e5 2 ♘f3 ♘c6 3 ♗b5 a6 4 ♗a4 ♘f6 5 0-0 ♗e7 6 ♖e1 b5 7 ♗b3 d6 8 c3 0-0 9 h3 ♘a5

For 9...♘b8, see Game 14, Navara-Socko.

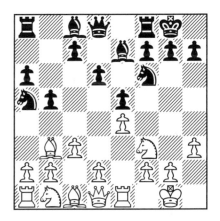

Inarkiev plays the natural move, the Chigorin Defence, attacking the bishop, with a likely gain of tempo. This is the most popular, but once White's bishop has moved, the knight often finds itself out of play. Usually it will retreat to c6.

10 ♗c2

The bishop-pair should be kept, unless there is a specific reason otherwise. 10 d4?! ♘xb3 11 ♕xb3 has been almost completely ignored in the last century or more, Black being easily equal.

10...c5

This in turn is the natural reply for Black.

The American Grandmaster William Lombardy tried 10...c6 several times back in the 1950s and 1960s, and if 11 d4 ♕c7 12 ♘bd2 ♖e8. White still keeps a slight edge, but the same can be said of the ...c5 line.

A fashionable, very recent modern gambit is Gajewski's 10...d5!?.

11 d4

Again, the main line. White tries to take over the pawn initiative in the centre.

11 d3 is a more modest approach, but seems reasonable enough.

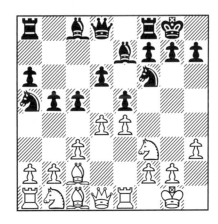

11...♕c7

This avoids any unwanted queen exchanges, when Black's pawns would become weak. With queens on or off the board, Black needs to be careful with his e5-pawn. That said, after 11...♗b7 12 dxe5 dxe5 13 ♖xd8 ♖axd8 14 ♘xe5 ♘xe4! 15 ♗xe4?! ♗xe4 17 ♖xe4? ♖d1+ Black is doing well.

In an old game, Leonid Stein showed that classic queen and knight Lopez play could cause pressure after 13 ♘bd2 ♕c7 14 ♘h2 ♖ad8 15 ♕f3 ♗c8 16 ♖df1 ♘c4 17 ♘g3, L.Stein-A.Bannik, USSR Championship, Moscow 1961, and Black's position eventually crumbled. Black's problem was that his bishop on b7 was found to be misplaced.

Oleg Romanishin has experimented a few times with 11...♘c6!?, the obvious reply being 12 d5 ♘a5. After 13 ♘bd2 Romanishin's idea was 13...g6!? followed by ...♘h5. Normally placing both knight moves on opposite edges would not be recommended, but either knight would have the chance of jumping into central play with ...♘c4 or ...♘f4. The alternative 14 b4 ♘b7 15 a4 ♗d7 has given reasonable chances of equalizing for Black.

11...♘d7 was recommended by Paul Keres, as readers of Bobby Fisher's *My 60 Memorable Games* will recall. It still remains popular in top-level play, but the results tend to favour White. Without analysing this variation in depth, we note that the next few moves may run in parallel with the Karjakin-Inarkiev game (starting with 11...♕c7). Play could, indeed, continue 12 ♘bd2 cxd4 13 cxd4 ♘c6 14 ♘b3 a5 15 ♗e3 a4 16 ♘bd2. Black is more flexible with 11...♘d7, than in the corresponding variation with 11...♕c7. and play is equal after 16...exd4 17 ♘xd4 ♘xd4 18 ♗xd4 ♘e5. This line is for illustration, and for comparison with the Karjakin-Inarkiev game. In practice these days, White, after 11...♘d7, regularly exchanges with 12 dxc5 dxc5 13 ♘bd2, then quite often ♕e2 followed by ♘f1 and ♘e3 or ♘g3.

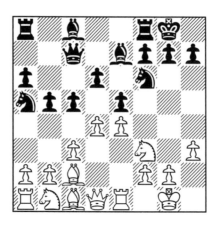

12 ♘bd2

White follows the very well established main line.

12 d5 looks tempting, gaining some space in the centre, and making it difficult for Black to bring his knight from a4 back into play. Kasparov tried this a few times in his teenage years, and even pre-teenage years, but some of the tension has been broken, giving Black reasonable chances of equality. Karjakin has also tried this move a few times, mainly with draws against top-level opponents. An example is 12...♗d7 13 ♘bd2 g6 14 ♘f1 ♘h5 16 ♗h6 ♘g7 17 ♕d2 f6 18 g4 ♘d7 19 ♘g3 ♘f7 20 ♗e3 a5 21 a4 bxa4 22 bxa4, S.Karjakin-P.Harikrishna, Dos Hermanas 2005, with a blocked pawn structure, and later a draw.

Perhaps the best argument that this line is essentially harmless is by making a comparison with Romanishin's line, given earlier, with 11...♘c6!? 12 d5 ♘a5. If Romanishin is happy with this, and has scored good results against grandmaster opposition despite losing a couple of tempi, then 11...♕c7 12 d5 should not be dangerous. There is a counter-argument though that

11...♕c7 12 d5 seems to give White a plus score in recent years. Make of this what you want!

12...cxd4

It is difficult to say whether this is statistically the best line or not, but it is certainly attractive in terms of setting up open play. Black quickly opens up the c-file, setting up some attacking hits before White has completed his queenside development.

12...♗d7 13 ♘f1 ♖fe8 14 ♘e3 g6 15 dxe5 dxe5 16 ♘h2 ♖ad8 17 ♕f3 ♗e6 18 ♘hg4 ♘xg4 19 hxg4 was well-established theory from the 1950s and 1960s. White is behind in piece development, but this is not all that important. After all, the bishops will quickly bounce back. What is more significant is that Black has slight but annoying pawn weaknesses in the centre, notably on d5, and even on f5, with the possible help of a knight attack. This helps explain why Black generally tries to exchange with ...cxd4, rather than waiting for White to exchange with dxc5 or dxe5.

13 cxd4

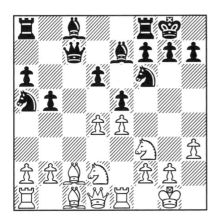

13...♘c6

Another branching point. The knight

return adds pressure on White's d-pawn, and also, as we shall soon see, creates space for Black's queenside pawns to push through.

The developing moves, 13...♗d7 (met mainly by 14 ♘f1), and, less popularly, 13...♗b7 (met usually by either 14 d5 or 14 ♘f1) are the chief alternatives.

14 ♘b3

Karjakin is being careful not to press on with 14 d5, although it is of course playable, and has reasonable chances of an edge after 14...♘b4 15 ♗b1 a5. The point is that Karjakin wants to retain his options in the centre. A pawn advance with d5 is useful, but so too is the exchange on e5, with the possibility of an attack on Black's e5-pawn. It is not absolutely certain that White will want to exchange the pawns, but it is in White's interest to maintain the tension.

14...a5

The usual choice. Keres experimented with 14...♖d8 a couple of times, many years ago, but White has an edge with 15 d5!.

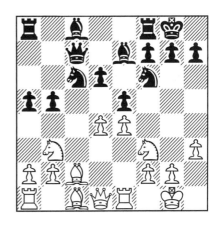

15 ♗e3

Developing, and overprotecting the d4-pawn. Once that pawn is fully covered, he does not have to be scared of ...a4.

15 a4 bxa4 16 ♖xa4 ♘b4 is equal.

15...a4

15...♘b4 16 ♗b1 a4 17 ♘bd2 a3 18 bxa3 ♖xa3 19 ♘b3 gives White a slight edge.

16 ♘bd2

The knight is going backwards and forwards, while Black's a-pawn advances. Black is not gaining any advantage, however, and White can now put pressure on Black's b5-pawn.

16...♗d7

If in doubt, develop. The bishop no longer obstructs the rooks, and on d7 the bishop is helping support the b5-pawn, and also keeping an eye on the kingside. 16...♗b7 gives neither of these defensive options.

17 ♖c1

Very natural. The rook plays itself on the long c-file, with an almost certain gain of tempo, given the pressure on Black's c7-pawn.

17 a3 is also a reasonable try.

17...♕b7

We are still in main line opening play. There have been gradual divergences for both sides from most of the previous positions, and soon the number of games thin down further, and before long there will be unique innovations.

17...♖ac8 has been tried a few times, usually with the idea of retreating to the queen on b8, and sometimes following up with ...♖c7 and ...♖fc8. In P.Leko-M.Adams, 6th matchgame, Miskolc (rapid) 2005, play continued 18 ♘f1 ♕b8 19 ♗b1!? (maybe 19 ♕d2!?) 19...♖c7 (19...♘a5!? 20 ♖e2 ♖xc1 22 ♗xc1 ♖c8 22 ♘e3 g6, draw agreed,

E.Vladimirov-E.Magerramov, Abu Dhabi 2003) 20 ♕d2!, preventing ...♘a5, and Adams could find nothing more, given the quick time limit, than 20...exd4 21 ♘xd4 with a structural edge for White, Leko later winning.

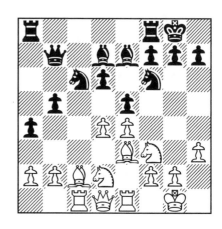

18 ♘f1

The most straightforward, although 18 ♕e2, a developing move, also gets played. A comparison may be made with an earlier game, A.Shirov-V.Akopian, Wijk aan Zee 2004, where play continued 18...♖fe8 19 ♗d3 ♖ab8 20 dxe5 ♘xe5 21 ♘xe5 dxe5 22 ♘f3 ♗b4 23 ♗d2 ♗d6 24 b4 axb3 25 axb3 h6, and Black had equalized. A week later, Shirov aimed to improve with 23 ♖ed1 ♗c6 24 ♗c5 ♗xc5 25 ♖xc5 ♘d7 26 ♖c3 ♘f6 27 ♖e1 b4 28 ♖c5 ♘d7 29 ♖c4 ♘f6 30 a3 bxa3 31 bxa3, and Black was unable to equalize the position in A.Shirov-I.Dorfman, French League 2004.

There has also been a game, V.Kramnik-M.Adams, Sofia 2005, in which Kramnik slightly varied with 22 ♗c5 ♗c6 23 ♗xe7 ♖xe7 24 ♘f3 h6 (to prevent a later ♘g5 after ...♖e6) 25 ♖c5 ♘d7 26 ♖c3 ♖e6 27 ♖ec1 ♖d8 28 ♕c2 ♘f6, and Adams was able to hold the endgame after 29 ♘xe5 ♗xe4 30 ♗xe4 ♕xe4 31 ♕xe4 ♘xe4 32 ♖c8 ♖ee8 33 ♖xd8 ♖xd8.

Quite clearly Karjakin had studied these games and learnt from them. He also has thought about the opening, and the attempt to find the most accurate way of reaching this type of endgame. These days, it is ever more the case that to study the opening, the top player needs to study the resulting endgame with depth and precision.

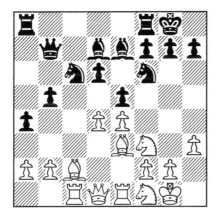

18...♖fe8

Black is still trying to shore up his defences.

Another possibility is 18...h6 19 ♘g3 ♖fc8 20 ♗b1 ♗d8. Then White kept up a slight edge after 21 dxe5 dxe5 22 ♘h4 ♘e7 23 ♕f3 in V.Akopian-M.Kobalija, Moscow 2005, although the game ended up as a draw.

Here 21 ♕e2 ♗b6 22 dxe5 ♘xe5!? seems close to being equal, Black being more active than in the analogous game in Karjakin-Inarkiev. Ivanchuk instead went for a sharp sacrificial attack after Black tried 22...♗xe3 in V.Ivanchuk-L.Bruzon Bautista, Skanderborg 2005. Play continued 23 ♖xc6!? ♕xc6 24 exf6 ♗f4 25 ♘h5 ♗e5 26 fxg7

♖a6. So far, so good, for White, and he has genuine long-term positional pressure after, for example, 27 ♘xe5 dxe5 28 ♖d1. Ivanchuk appears to have missed a tactic after 27 ♘h4?, and following 27...♕c1! 28 ♘f5 ♗xf5 29 exf5 ♕xe1+! 30 ♕xe1 ♖ac6 White was powerless to keep the extra queen. Black later won.

19 ♘g3

White could also have tried 19 d5 here and at many other stages, and maybe after 19...♘b4 20 ♗b1 he has chances of keeping a slight edge, in view of his extra pawn space.

The reason he delays is in order to keep his opponent guessing whether he will push with d5, exchange on e5, or keep the central pawn tension. These are three different possibilities that Black has to defend against, while White can decide what to do in his own time.

19...♗d8

All Black can do is wait.

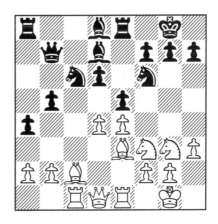

20 ♕e2!

An innovation. White has usually preferred 20 ♗b1, another quiet waiting move, but Karjakin is thinking about the positional pressure after the exchange on e5, and pressure on Black's b5-pawn after ♕e2 and ♗d3.

When compared with the 18 ♕e2 alternative (instead of 18 ♘f1), Black has added ...♖fe8 and ...♗d8, against White's ♘f1 and ♘g3. White has gained from these extra moves, and it is up to Karjakin to try to show that he has an edge.

20...h6

Continuing with quiet waiting moves.

20...exd4 21 ♘xd4 ♘xd4 22 ♗xd4 leaves White's pieces better developed. If 22...d5 23 ♕f3 dxe4 24 ♘xe4 ♔h8 25 ♘xf6 ♖xe1+ 26 ♖xe1 ♕xf3 27 ♘xd7! ♗a5 28 gxf3 ♗xe1, Black's bishop attacks nothing of importance, and the rook does not cooperate well, whereas White's three minor pieces work well together.

20...♗a5 21 ♖ed1 and 20...♘b4 21 ♗b1 would keep slight edges for White, there being no really effective follow-up for Black.

21 ♗d3

Again 21 d5!? is a possibility, but White has in mind a more interesting alternative.

21...♖b8?!

21...♘b4 22 ♗b1 does not gain much for Black, and indeed may lose time if the knight retreats.

Maybe it is time for Black to force White to make a decision in the centre, with 21...♗b6!?:

a) If then 22 ♗xb5 exd4 23 ♗f4 d5 24 ♗xc6 ♗xc6 25 e5 ♘e4, and Black is equal.

b) 22 d5 ♘b4 23 ♗xb6 ♕xb6 24 a3 ♘xd3 25 ♕xd3 ♖ac8 26 b4 axb3 27 ♕xb3 is also only about equal.

c) White can try 22 dxe5 ♘xe5 23 ♘xe5 dxe5 when in comparison with the main line, Black now has ...♗b6 instead of ...♖ab8. This seems an improvement for Black. If, for example, 24 b4 axb3 25 ♗xb6 ♕xb6 26 axb3, Black's rook is on a better file, and 26...♖a3, among others, seems close to holding the balance.

In slow manoeuvring positions, there is always a danger of moving a piece from a better square to a worse square, and this seems to be what is happening to Inarkiev.

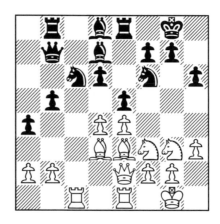

22 dxe5!

Karjakin has kept the tension for a long time, but now he must make a decision. His pieces are on their optimal squares, and he cannot make good piece manoeuvres, so he must do something with the pawns.

22 d5, gaining space, looks natural, but after 22...♘b4 23 ♗b1 ♘a6, followed by ...♗b6, Black exchanges the 'bad bishop', and is very solid. White can cut across the bishop exchange with 24 ♗d3, but then, of course, Black can repeat with 24...♘b4.

Karjakin instead exchanges pawns, with a symmetrical pawn structure, and demonstrates that he can play for a clear edge.

22...♘xe5?!

This helps the attacker. Inarkiev might be worried about the knight getting in the way of the bishop on d7, but Black's knight is stronger than White's knight on f3. Black should keep open the possibility of playing ...♘d4, and if there is an exchange and Black recaptures with a pawn, he has the chance of pressing against White's e4-pawn. A possible line would be 22...dxe5 23 ♖ed1 ♗b6:

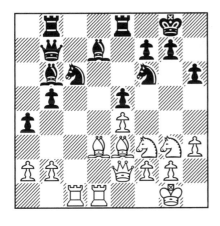

a) If now 24 ♗c5 (24 ♗xb5? ♗xe3 26 ♗xc6 ♗xf2+ with advantage for Black) 24...♘d4 25 ♗xd4 exd4 26 ♗xb5 ♘xe4 27 ♘xd4 ♖xd4 28 ♕d3 with equality.

b) White still has chances of an edge, but maybe only slight after 24 b3 ♗xe3 25 ♕xe3 axb3 26 axb3. This resembles the pawn structure of the main line, except that because of the knights remaining on the board, White has less pressure on the dark squares. 26...♖a8!? 27 ♖c5 b4 28 ♗b5 ♘d4 29 ♗xd7 ♘xd7 30 ♖d5 ♘f6 is a draw. Possibly better is 28 ♗c4!? with a slight advantage. It is never easy in such positions to equalize completely as Black when White plays accurately.

Going back several moves, to the notes on 18 ♕e2 (instead of 18 ♘f1),

there is the interesting question as to whether after 18...♖fe8 19 ♗d3 ♖ad8 20 dxe5 dxe5, Black would have been safer after 20...dxe5 (rather than 20...♘xe5). One possible answer is that in the Shirov line, White's knight is still on d2, so that after 21 b3 White would create considerable pressure with the help of the knight on the queenside. In the Karjakin line the knight is on the kingside, and is far less supportive to the queenside.

One suspects that Inarkiev falls for a common positional slip, remembering a particular recapture known in a specified position, but using the same recapture in a less appropriate position.

23 ♘xe5

23 ♗b1!? also looks good: for example, 23...♘c4 24 ♗d4 d5 25 b3 axb3 26 axb3 with an edge. Karjakin prefers playing for a symmetrical pawn structure with the more active pieces. This tends to make the game much easier to play for the attacker.

23...dxe5

23...♖xe5 24 ♗f4 ♖e6 25 ♘f5 is uncomfortable for Black.

24 b4

Gaining space with the pawns.

24...axb3

Taking en passant. Black exchanges the pawns while he can. Black's pawns are more advanced on a4 and b5 than White's b4- and a3- (or a2-) pawns. Black's pawns are, however, weaker than White's, since it is much easier for White to attack the backward pawn on b5 than for Black to attack a2. Black's b-pawn is exposed, and could easily drop. If one black pawn falls, the other is likely to drop. Better just to have the danger of losing one pawn, if necessary.

25 axb3 25 ♗b6

Exchanging, or offering to exchange, Black's weaker dark-squared pawn, but Black also has a weaker light-squared pawn.

26 b4

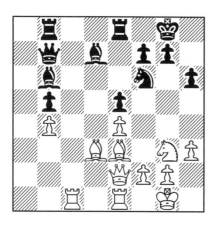

With a symmetrical pawn structure, and apparently level pieces, but quite often even the slightest edge in such a position can end up with a big plus, as the player with the better pieces allows no chance for the opponent to create any counterplay.

Here the dark-squared bishops are going to be exchanged. What about the light-squared bishops, though? White's bishop is active, and puts pressure on Black's b5-pawn. Black's bishop is passive, and can do little other than protect the same pawn. If White can add pressure to this weak pawn, he has excellent chances of gaining material. This essentially is the story behind the rest of the game.

26...♖ec8

Challenging the c-file.

27 ♔h2

Not 27 ♖xc8+ ♖xc8 28 ♗xb5? ♗xe3 29 ♗xd7 ♗xf2+, and Black is even slightly better.

Karjakin's quiet move sets up the continued attack on b5, if appropriate. Also he cuts out any checks on the back row.

27...♗e6

The bishop starts to show some life.

27...♖xc1 28 ♖xc1 does not quite allow Black to equalize.

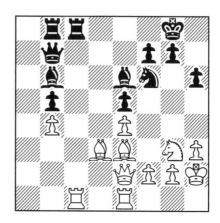

28 ♖xc8+

One of Black's recaptures will be a weakening move. White is not simply giving away this c-file.

28...♕xc8

If 28...♖xc8 29 ♗xb5 ♗xe3 30 ♗a6! (as Black has no check on f2) 30...♕xb4 31 ♗xc8 ♗xf2 32 ♕xf2 ♗xc8 33 ♖d1, White has a rook against bishop and pawn, but his e-pawn is isolated. It is not totally clear that White is winning by force, but few as Black would want to take on this position. The danger here is not so much of trying to set up a passed pawn for White, as this is unlikely in the short term. Rather, White would try to force the other pieces to cover the attack on the king, thereby weakening the pawns on e5 and f7.

Inarkiev elects to carry on the defence with level material.

29 ♖c1

White regains the c-file.

29 ♗xb5 ♗xe3 30 fxe3 is only a draw.

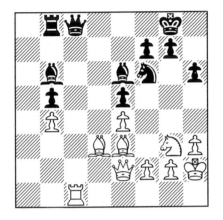

The critical position. If Black can manage a way of keeping some piece activity, then maybe he still has chances of holding for a draw. If not, then 'the rest is a matter of technique', as the older generation used to say. These days, we have a plus over minus symbol.

29...♕d8?

Black needs active counterplay, and in particular making use of the occasional threat. Indeed, 29...♕f8! is more accurate, hitting White's b-pawn. Pawns do not run away, especially if blocked by opposing pawns, while pieces can quickly sprint off. Attacking a bishop, here on d3, can often have little impact, as the bishop can run, as well as being guarded.

If 30 ♗xb6 ♖xb6 31 ♖c5 ♘d7 32 ♖xb5 ♖xb5 33 ♗xb5 ♕xb4, Black is now fully equal. Similarly, after the bishop exchange, 31 ♕b2 ♖d6 33 ♗xb5 ♖d4 eliminates the queenside pawns, holding the draw. Here 31 ♕e3 ♘d7 32 ♖c7 ♕d6 also equalizes.

This leaves 30 ♗c5 as the only likely chance of an edge, Black exchanging with 30...♗xc5. Then 31 ♖xc5 ♘d7 leads to a standard draw. So White could try 31 bxc5!?, with passed pawns on both sides. Both pawns are dangerous, but both can be blocked after, for example, 31...b4 32 ♕b2 ♖c8 33 ♕xb4 (or 33 c6 ♕d6, equal) 33...♘d7, regaining the pawn, and drawing. Or 32 c6 ♕e7 33 ♗a6 ♕c7 34 ♖b2 b3, and while both queens would be slightly uncomfortable in having to defend the advanced passed pawn, it is not so clear how either of the queens may be dislodged.

30 ♗xb6

Now Black is slightly weak on the dark squares.

30...♖xb6

Somehow Black's pawns do not fall immediately after 30...♕xb6 31 ♖c5 ♗b7 32 ♘f5 (32 ♖xe5? ♕d4) 32...♕e6 33 ♕b2 ♖e8, but there is a clear sense that Black would not hold indefinitely after, for example, 34 f3.

31 ♕e3

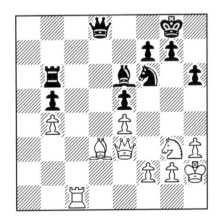

The next stage of the battle. White has exchanged the first set of bishops and can now think about trying to win the weak isolated b5-pawn. He can attack it three times, with the queen, rook and bishop, while Black can defend it three times. This is an unstable equality, though, as White can put pressure on other squares. The attack of two weaknesses can overbalance Black's defence.

White's last move puts pressure on the rook, and after ♕c5 he can also put pressure on the e5- and b5-pawns.

31...♕b8

31...♘d7 32 ♗e2 ♖b8 33 ♕a7 piles on the pressure.

32 ♕c5

White is making inroads. It is in the nature of such positions, relatively stable but with one of the sides being clearly better, that there is often no quick attacking win against a single specified major weakness. It is more a case that the stronger player battles square by square, and the weaker player finds it difficult to hold these squares. One square may hold, but it is often not so clear which weakness will decide the position.

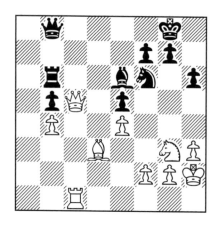

32...♗d7

Black is defending the two weak pawns, but what next?

33 ♖a1

White takes over the a-file, again with no immediate win, but making Black feel uncomfortable.

33...♖c6

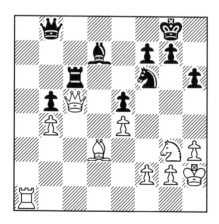

Black wants the c-file.

34 ♕e3

White stays centralized. His control of the a-file, and the pressure on the diagonals with the bishop and queen have more impact than the c-pawn, which is well protected.

34 ♕xb5?! ♖b6 31 ♕c5 ♖xb4 would be a mistake. White wants to keep the pawns on the board. It is far more likely that White can win the b-pawn for nothing than Black can. If the pawns are exchanged, Black would not have to worry about defending them.

34...♖d6

If 34...♖c3 35 ♕d2 ♕c7 36 ♖a5, Black has problems on b5 and c3. Inarkiev therefore retreats.

35 ♘e2

Continuing to centralize. The knight has not been doing much over the last few moves, and by the time that it can be activated, the danger will be that Black's defensive pieces will be overloaded.

35...♗c6

At last, some slight counterplay.

36 f3

White adds an extra pawn defence on e4. This is not immediately necessary, but sooner or later he will want to do it.

36...♞d7

Covering the c5-square.

37 ♖a5

White still has the c5-square if Black's knight is moved again.

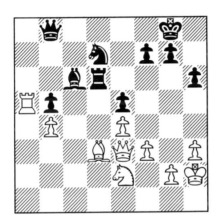

37...♖d4

Almost the height of Black's counterplay, but it is nothing.

38 ♕d2

Not 38 ♘xd4?? exd4+, giving away a queen.

The simple retreat covers the b4-pawn, and again threatens the rook.

38...♖d6

All Black can do is retreat.

39 ♘g3

Black's pieces are so tied up with the defence of the b5- and f5-squares that White can suddenly change the attack to the kingside, and in particular f5. The problem is that Black's knight is obstructing the bishop on d7.

39...♘f8

Black too tries to activate his knight,

but White is a move quicker.

40 ♕c3

Or 40 ♘f5, which is probably slightly more accurate, forcing Black to decide immediately whether he should play 40...♖e6 (defending) or 40...♖d7 (pinning). If 40...♖e6, White would almost certainly not want to try 41 ♕c3?!, transposing into a line given in the next note, but could consider 41 ♕e2!?, winning the b-pawn. If 40...♖d7 instead, White can revert to the 41 ♕c3 plan.

At move 40, one must find a good and solid move quickly, rather than find the very best move. Here White should win in either case.

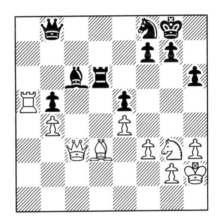

40...♕b6?

A more serious slip, again on move 40. The queen move is ineffective.

The choice here is difficult to make at speed, but 40...♖e6! 41 ♘f5 ♚h7 keeps the balance for the time being. There will be a lot of grinding manoeuvring to follow, with one defensive idea for Black being 42 ♕c5 ♘d7 43 ♕e3 ♘f6 44 ♗c2 ♕f8 45 ♗b3 ♖e8 46 ♕c5 ♕xc5 47 bxc5 ♖a8 48 ♖xa8 ♗xa8 49 ♗xf7 ♘d7 50 ♗e8 ♘xc5 51 ♗xb5 ♚g6, and at the minimum White will have to demonstrate he can win, a pawn up but with all the pawns being on the king-side.

41 ♘f5

The natural move.

41...♖d7?!

Missing a tactic. 41...♖e6 42 ♕c5 is, though, a merciless grind. If 42...♕xc5 43 bxc5 b4 44 ♗c4 ♖e8 45 ♖a6 ♗d7 46 ♘d6 ♖e7 47 ♖a7, and Black's pieces fall apart.

42 ♗xb5

42 ♕xe5 f6 43 ♕g3 ♔h7 wins a pawn for White, but takes more time to subdue the opponent.

42...♖d1

If 42...♗xb5, then 43 ♕xe5, forking the bishop and the mating square on g7. White wins two pawns.

43 ♘e3 1-0

Avoiding a trap: 43 ♕xc6? ♕g1+ 44 ♔g3 ♕e1+ 45 ♔g4 ♕d2!, with a draw. There are several other ways for White to win. All that he needs is to avoid being greedy.

It is now time to finish. We have shown that the more that players study chess, the more that new ideas continue to be found. We have clearly not reached the point that there is nothing new in chess, and no competent player will ever lose a game. There are always surprises, and the inventive player, with the help of the computer, will find many new ideas.

The reader will have noticed that we did not consider games from after spring 2008. At some stage, there needs to be a cut-off point, but no doubt brilliant new games have been produced in great numbers. Several more players have passed 2700 since then, but for the moment, there is neither space in the book nor time to give analysis to the further top players. There is, though, always the prospect of a sequel.

It is much easier to write up a game at leisure, rather than trying to analyse up-to-date in a magazine. I have had the chance to examine positions several times over, finding new ideas, and possibly correcting misconceptions. If I have done my job well, the book format should have a more measured approach than magazines or journals or an online approach. This is for the reader to decide.

Index of Openings

Figures refer to ECO codes and page numbers

Semi-Slav Defence

Sicilian Defence

Slav Defence

Index of Games